FROM THE REALM OF A DYING SUN

Volume II: The *IV. SS-Panzerkorps* in the
Budapest Relief Efforts,
December 1944–February 1945

DOUGLAS E. NASH SR.

CASEMATE

Philadelphia & Oxford

Published in the United States of America and Great Britain in 2020 by
CASEMATE PUBLISHERS
1950 Lawrence Road, Havertown, PA 19083, USA
and
The Old Music Hall, 106–108 Cowley Road, Oxford OX4 1JE, UK

Hardback Edition: ISBN 978-1-61200-8738
Digital Edition: ISBN 978-1-61200-8745

A CIP record for this book is available from the British Library

Maps by Thomas Houlihan and Phillip Schwartzberg

Printed and bound in the United States of America by Sheridan

Typeset by Versatile PreMedia Service (P) Ltd

For a complete list of Casemate titles, please contact:

CASEMATE PUBLISHERS (US)
Telephone (610) 853-9131
Fax (610) 853-9146
Email: casemate@casematepublishers.com
www.casematepublishers.com

CASEMATE PUBLISHERS (UK)
Telephone (01865) 241249
Email: casemate-uk@casematepublishers.co.uk
www.casematepublishers.co.uk

Contents

SS-Obergruppenführer Herbert Gille (left) with *SS-Obersturmbannführer* Manfred Schönfelder standing in Gille's command vehicle, a *Horch mittlerer Einheits-Personenkraftwagen* (medium-size standard passenger car) *Kraftfahrzeug (Kfz.) 21 "Cabriolet,"* as they observe the fighting around Modlin in late November or early December 1944. On the left front fender, the corps symbol can barely be seen under a layer of mud. Gille's command pennant is also displayed on both the bumper and front fender. (Lange)

Introduction

This is the second of three volumes, which together trace the history of the *IV. SS-Panzerkorps* (*IV. SS-Pz.Korps*) from its inception until end of the war. The first volume focused on the activation of the corps, its structure and organization, leadership, and the history of its two core divisions—the *3. SS-Panzerdivision Totenkopf* and the *5. SS-Panzerdivision Wiking*. It then traced the history of the corps after its introduction to battle on 28 July 1944, its participation in the massive tank battle of Praga, its role in the three defensive battles of Warsaw, and ended on 26 November 1944 with the siege of Modlin and the transfer of the corps to *2. Armee*. The first volume described some of the heaviest fighting ever witnessed on the Eastern Front, which forged the *IV. SS-Pz.Korps* into a responsive and lethal instrument of war. This phase of the corps' history, which began with its participation in a highly mobile, fluid battle, ended with its troops engaged in static trench warfare reminiscent of World War I.

This second volume picks up at the end of November 1944, where the first left off, with the corps still engaged in defending the so-called "Wet Triangle," that tactically significant chunk of terrain situated between the Narew and Vistula Rivers. Seemingly relegated to a secondary front, the corps was jolted out of its holiday preparations when the *Oberkommando der Wehrmacht* (*OKW*) ordered it to begin moving by rail to another theater of operations on Christmas Eve. Thus would begin the final phase of the war in the East, with the corps once again called upon to carry out one of the most audacious attacks of World War II—the relief of an encircled city. During the see-saw fighting that ensued, the *IV.SS-Pz. Korps*, along with a large number of other German Army divisions, sought in vain to relieve the embattled garrison of Budapest and to re-establish the old front line along the lower Danube. The final volume in this trilogy will focus on the last three months of the war, which witnessed not only the Third Reich's last large-scale offensive of the war, Operation *Frühlingserwachen* (*Spring Awakening*), but the Red Army's Vienna Operation, which drove German and Hungarian forces out of Hungary and deep into southeastern Austria, as well as the fall of Vienna.

Volume 3 will conclude with the last-minute surrender by the *IV. SS-Pz.Korps* to U.S. forces along the Enns River on 9 May 1945 and the postwar fate of some of its members. In the first volume, the author had access to the nearly complete war diaries of *Heeresgruppe Mitte* (*H.Gr. Mitte*) and the *2.* and *9. Armee* for July until the end of November 1944, as well as those of *SS-Pz.Rgt. 5* and *I. Abt./SS-Pz.Rgt. 5*. In drafting the second volume, he encountered a paucity of primary sources from units of the *IV. SS-Pz.Korps* due to the destruction of official records at the field-army level and below for the period encompassing December 1944 until the end of the war. Ironically, the *Kriegsarchiv* (wartime archive) of the *Waffen-SS* in Sesmuk had reprimanded the corps' *IIa* (its adjutant, or chief personnel officer) on 16 January 1945 for his failure to submit the corps' annual historical report and all of the related material, such as its war diaries, records of tank assaults, etc. for archiving.

Involved as he and the rest of the *Korpsstab* were at that time in the relief of Budapest, it is understandable that *Stubaf.* Karl-Willy Schulze failed to meet the deadline, but one wonders what happened to all of the corps' historical material, or whether it was delivered to the *Kriegsarchiv der Waffen-SS* at all. Consequently, with a few exceptions, the author has had to rely on a number of secondary sources, some of which are unit histories written after the war by participants in the campaign, while others, such as Krisztián Ungváry's *The Siege of Budapest: 100 Days in World War II*, were composed by military historians using such records that survived the war.

The primary sources consulted for this work include an electronic copy of the war diary, or *Kriegstagebuch* (*KTB*), of *Heeresgruppe Süd* (*H.Gr. Süd*, or Army Group South) *Führungsabteilung* (Operations Section), the headquarters responsible for planning and coordinating German operations in Hungary, which covers the period from 1 February to the end of March 1945. *Heeresgruppe Süd* was the higher headquarters two levels above the *IV. SS-Pz.Korps*, so it primarily concerns the actions and activities of the three to four German and one Hungarian field armies under its command, and not individual corps. Therefore, events happening at the lowest tactical level of the division, regiment, and battalion have been "filtered" somewhat by the need to simplify and reduce the amount of information being sent from front-line units up the chain of command. The *KTB* used includes three separate sections: the summarized daily *KTB*, the *Meldungen* (daily reports) of the subordinate armies and other major subordinate units, as well as various command-related *Befehle* (orders), other reports, troop strength, armor strength, proclamations, and so forth, totaling thousands of pages of documents.

Another source recently uncovered in the German records cache in Moscow and published online by the German-Russian consortium, *Deutsch-Russisches Projekt zur Digitalisierung Deutscher Dokumente in Archiven der Russischen Föderation*, also known as the "German Documents in Russia" website, includes several hundred pages of captured reports, situation maps, and messages from *Armeegruppe Balck*

(*A. Gr. Balck*)/*6. Armee* for the entire months of December 1944 and January 1945, leading into the first week of February 1945. Unfortunately, this hoard of documents does not include its *KTB*, but instead incorporates what was usually included in a separate annex to the *KTB* in a folder normally titled *Meldungen und Befehle* (Reports and Orders). Still, it is an extremely valuable resource because it includes weekly personnel readiness reports stating each unit's *Kampfstärke* as well as armored vehicle and antitank gun availability with *A. Gr. Balck/6. Armee*, including Hungarian units.

This cache of captured documents also includes the complete daily intelligence reports compiled by the *6. Armee Ic* staff officer for the entire month of January 1945, which provides a detailed, day-by-day description of the operations carried out by each corps under its command, including the *IV. SS-Pz. Korps*, as well as the air situation and assessments of Soviet plans and activities. In this manner, it is similar to the *Ia KTB*, though not as detailed or as comprehensive. Another equally valuable resource contained within this archive are the full-color daily situation maps in either 1:200,000 or 1:300,000 scale maintained by the *A. Gr. Balck/6. Armee Ia* from 28 November 1944 until 31 January 1945 that depict the location of all the units under its command, including Hungarian units, as well as the position of the German front line on any given day. Some maps also depict suspected locations of Soviet units and the directions of their attacks. While this proved to be an invaluable source, it is unfortunate that information for December 1944 and January 1945 was all that survived intact. In *toto*, this records grouping proved to be an invaluable source that contains many documents submitted by or pertaining to the *IV. SS-Pz. Korps* for the month of January 1945 that would have been destroyed had the Red Army not overtaken a portion of the *A. Gr. Balck/6. Armee*'s staff caravan transporting them before the war ended.

Another long-overlooked primary German source has recently become available, thanks to the efforts of Mr Perry Pierik, who referenced the *IV. SS-Pz. Korps* in his own book published 24 years ago, *Hungary 1944–1945: The Forgotten Tragedy* (Aspekt Books, 1996). Written in December 1981 by the former chief of staff of the *IV. SS-Pz. Korps*, Manfred Schönfelder, this account, *Einsatz der Verbände der Waffen-SS auf dem Kriegsschauplatz in Ungarn in der Zeit vom 1.1.–31.3.1945* (Actions of the Units of the *Waffen-SS* in the Hungarian Theater of War from 1 January to 31 March 1945), is a 22-page manuscript based on his postwar notes that was written as a point-by-point rebuttal against accusations leveled by Hermann Balck, the former commander of *A. Gr. Balck/6. Armee*. In his memoirs, *Order in Chaos*, Balck makes the case that the *IV. SS-Pz. Korps* and its commander were responsible for the failure to relieve Budapest, and not Balck's own defective leadership. In addition to setting the historical record straight, Schönfelder also provides an excellent daily account of the corps' activities during this same timeframe, shedding additional light upon a period of the war not generally understood in the West.

In addition to Mr Pierik's work, several other works stand out in their thoroughness of the coverage of this phase of the war, with particular attention being paid to the role played by the *IV. SS-Pz.Korps*. The first is an eyewitness account written by the late Georg Maier, *Drama Between Budapest and Vienna: the Final Battles of the 6. Panzer Armee in the East–1945*. This excellent work of military history covers the campaign in great detail, focusing on the period from the end of December 1944 until the end of the war. Maier, a *Kriegsakademie*-trained general staff officer and the former *Ia*, or operations officer, of *SS-Oberstgruppenführer* Sepp Dietrich's *6. Pz.Armee*, was a friend of fellow *Kriegsakademie* graduate Manfred Schönfelder. As such, Maier was in a good position as a general staff officer to observe the events as they unfolded from an operational perspective. Consequently, his work is primarily concerned with the actions of *6. Pz.Armee* and neighboring units during this final phase of the war, but the *IV. SS-Pz.Korps* receives its fair share of attention, especially concerning the controversy between Generals Balck and Gille during the three relief attempts of Budapest, *Unternehmen Konrad I–III*. Buttressed by no fewer than 130 appendices, most of which consist of reproduced contemporary documents as well as 30 original maps, this immense study—appearing first in German in 1984 and translated into English by J. J. Fedorowicz Publishing in 2005—is absolutely essential for anyone desiring to study the war in Hungary in general and the role played by Hitler's elite SS divisions in particular.

Another extremely useful primary source is the contemporary personal diary kept by the *O1* (assistant operations officer) of the *Wiking* Division, *Ostuf.* Günther Jahnke. As an aspiring general staff officer himself, Jahnke was being groomed to become a division *Ia* some day after he had attended the *Kriegsakademie*. Possessing a sharp memory and the self-discipline to continue making entries in his diary until the end of the war, Jahnke's account is extremely invaluable in helping the historian understand what was going on behind the scenes in the division's leadership circles, adding details that often escape the drafting of official reports submitted up the chain of command.

Another important primary source is the personal notes kept by *Ogruf.* Gille himself, although his name is found nowhere on the document. For years, it resided in the *Wiking* Division's *Truppenkameradschaft* (Veterans Association) archives, which were donated to the *Bundesarchiv-Militärarchiv* in Freiburg several years ago. Based on the formal style of writing, the old world, early 20th-century military terminology used, and the perspective that could only have been held by a senior officer in command (including referring to himself in the third person), a number of *Waffen-SS* historians consulted for this volume agreed that the only person in a senior-level position that could have written this document was Herbert Gille himself. Although only four pages long, it covers in shorthand form the events experienced by the *IV. SS-Pz.Korps* from 24 December 1944 to 30 March 1945, with a large gap appearing between that and the last entry of 8 May 1945. Especially valuable are the personal insights he provides about contemporary events and details of operational matters.

A companion to Gille, Maier, and Jahnke's accounts is the final volume of Wolfgang Vopersal's *Soldaten, Kämpfer, Kameraden*, the magisterial six-volume history of the *3. SS-Pz.Div. Totenkopf*, an eight-year project that began in 1983. Like Maier, Vopersal frequently references the *H.Gr. Süd* war diary, Soviet sources, and existing records of the *Totenkopf* and *Wiking* Divisions, as well as hundreds of individual accounts by surviving members of the division. Volume Vb, which the author consulted extensively for this book, traces the history of the division from the fall of 1944 until the end of war, when it was handed over *en masse* by the U.S. Army to the Red Army as prisoners of war, an ordeal from which many of its men did not return until the release of all former German POWs in 1955. Vopersal's account remains to date the most detailed and factual description of this controversial division, which outgrew it concentration camp origins and developed into one of the most lethally effective divisions in the *Waffen-SS*.

Another groundbreaking work frequently referenced in this manuscript, written from the American military perspective, is the transcript of proceedings from the 1986 Art of War Symposium conducted by the U.S. Army War College's Center for Land Warfare, *From the Vistula to the Oder: Soviet Offensive Operations—October 1944 to March 1945*. Consisting of a series of presentations and lectures delivered over five days during July 1986 to the faculty and student body of the War College, it featured guest speakers from the former Soviet Union, Great Britain, the United States, and no fewer than 10 former officers of the *Wehrmacht* and the *Waffen-SS* then serving in or recently retired from the *Bundeswehr*, who had been participants in the fighting in and around Budapest and Vienna.

This work, the third volume in a series studying the War in the East from 1941 to 1945, covers in detail the fighting in Hungary, Poland, East Prussia, and Berlin, comprising the final phase of the war in Europe. Brilliantly directed and edited by noted Sovietologist Colonel (retired) David M. Glantz, the proceedings from this seminar incorporated into an 803-page masterpiece contain 416 maps, charts, and organizational diagrams that make it invaluable for the study of the final phase of the Red Army's operations against Nazi Germany. The copies of actual Red Army daily situation maps depicting the actions and unit locations of the divisions, corps, and armies of the Second and Third Ukrainian Fronts, as well as German units, from October 1944 until the end of the war are definitive and allowed the author to verify the accuracy of contemporary German operational maps.

The other work frequently cited in this work is Norbert Számvéber's *The Sword Behind the Shield: A Combat History of the German Efforts to Relieve Budapest 1945— Operation 'Konrad' I, II, and III*, the English language edition that was published in 2015 by Helion & Company after first appearing in Hungary two years before. A thoroughly researched and documented study, the author brilliantly illuminates the heavy fighting that ensued when *IV. SS-Pz.Korps* carried out its three relief attempts of Budapest, followed by the initial February 1945 Soviet counteroffensive that occurred in the wake of the Germans' failure to relieve the city.

As much a study in tactics, technology, and command & control as it is a history of the fighting, Számvéber displays his extensive knowledge of German, Soviet, and Hungarian source material, which he puts to good use in telling his story. Though not a unit history of the *IV. SS-Pz.Korps per se*, Számvéber's work is a must-have for anyone seriously attempting to study in detail the operations that unfolded during the first five weeks of 1945. In this work, he has provided a wealth of information and analysis about the *IV. SS-Pz.Korps*, which is unavailable anywhere else. The works by Pierik, Maier, Glantz, and Számvéber have been frequently consulted during the drafting of this book, and the author is indebted to all four in crafting this history of the *IV. SS-Pz.Korps*.

Another recently published study that devotes considerable attention to the Budapest Operation, which the Red Army designated the battle's official title, is Aleksei Isaev and Maksim Kolomiets's *Tomb of the Panzerwaffe: The Defeat of the Sixth SS Panzer Army in Hungary 1945*, translated and published in 2014 by Helion. A product by two Russian military historians, the book's primary focus is the defeat of Sepp Dietrich's *6. SS-Pz.Armee* after the failure of his *Frühlingserwachen* Offensive in March 1945. However, in Part I of the book, the authors set the stage for Germany's last offensive on the Eastern Front by describing over the course of the first seven chapters how the relief attempt of Budapest by the *IV. SS-Pz.Korps* and the Red Army's strong reaction to it created the necessary conditions for the much larger battles that were to follow in its wake.

Drawing upon numerous contemporary Red Army accounts, including the war diaries of the Third Ukrainian Front and that of its artillery commander, the war diary of the 4th Guards Army and those of three other field armies (the 26th, 27th, and 57th), and finally the war diaries of three separate mechanized corps (XVIII and XXIII Tanks Corps and the I Guards Mechanized Corps), all of which played key roles in defeating *Unternehmen Konrad I–III*, this should be a mandatory reference work for anyone attempting to understand the battle. Though it is written from the perspective of the Red Army, it is even-handed and free of Communist-era jargon and is noteworthy for its cold-blooded evaluation of the results of the various engagements between January and March 1945, as well as lessons learned to be applied during future conflicts.

Lastly, the translation of the Red Army's general staff study written during the final phase of the war in Hungary is included in *The Budapest Operation 1945: An Operational–Strategic Study* (published in 2017 by Helion & Company), now available in English. This 1945-dated study, Number 21 in the Red Army's *Sbornik Materialov po Izucheniyu Opyta Voiny* series (Collection of Materials on the Study of

War Experience), is a critical, relatively unvarnished account that is often at odds with the official story presented by the propaganda organs of the former Soviet Union.

It also includes a 1957 internal publication issued by the Red Army's General Staff Academy, *The Third Ukrainian Front's Operation in the Budapest Operation*, written by Major General S. P. Tarasov, which details the efforts by that army group to block the three German relief attempts of Budapest, especially the fighting to stop Gille's *IV. SS-Pz.Korps*. While the *Sbornik* describing the operations to liberate Warsaw between July and November 1944 has yet to be published, this recently published translation of the Red Army's account of its Budapest Operation proved to be a boon to the author, providing an insider's view of the internal workings of large-scale Soviet formations, whose armies, corps, and divisions proved to be the *IV. SS-Pz.Korps'* last major and most formidable adversaries.

Taken together, these sources provide sufficient details and information to reconstruct the operations of Gille's corps during the last months of the war, beginning with the relatively inactive month of December 1944, then its rapid transfer to Hungary, its participation in the relief attempts of Budapest, positional warfare east of Lake Balaton, its role in the last major German offensive of the war—*Unternehmen Frühlingserwachen*—and the various delaying actions it fought during the last two months of the war as the *IV. SS-Pz.Korps* and other German formations fruitlessly attempted to block the Red Army's entry into Vienna and beyond.

In this volume, Hungarian names of towns, villages, and terrain features are used as much as possible, though German names for major Hungarian cities are used unless otherwise noted, such as Raab (Győr), Gran (Hron), and Komorn (Komarom). English names for major lakes and rivers are also used as appropriate, such as the Danube and Gran Rivers and Lakes Balaton and Velencze. The reasoning behind this decision is that German armed forces during World War II almost exclusively referred to locations using updated versions of Austro-Hungarian maps, which used German-language place names, except for instances when the German and Hungarian place names were identical. In some cases, after each initial use of the German place name, the modern Hungarian equivalent immediately follow, so that anyone using current maps to trace the course of the fighting should have no difficulty in locating the same locations today using online tools, such as Google Maps.

While many of those who provided assistance in the drafting of the first volume have already been mentioned, several additional historians who have helped exclusively with this volume also deserve to be recognized. First, I would like to thank Perry Pierek of the Netherlands, who generously shared a copy of Manfred Schönfelder's detailed monograph about the *IV. SS-Pz.Korps'* role in the relief of Budapest. The original document, which at one point was in the *Wiking* Division's *Truppenkameradschaft* (veterans association) archives, has since been lost. I would also like to thank Norbert Számvéber of Hungary for his help, as well as that provided by U.S. Army Colonel (retired) French MacLean and Lieutenant Colonel (retired) Mark Reardon. I would also like to thank Charles Trang of France and Mirko Bayerl of Norway for their generous help in providing photographs depicting the combat operations of Gille's corps during the closing days of the war.

Mr Bayerl, probably the world's most knowledgeable expert on the course of the three Budapest relief operations, was especially helpful in freely sharing additional material he has collected during his research into the operations of the *Wiking* Division in Hungary over the past 30 years. Among other items he has shared with the author, including the personal dairies of participants such as Manfred Schönfelder, Günther Jahnke, Willi Hein, and Manfred Renz, he also shared additional maps and original documents. He has also walked the ground several times where many of the key actions occurred while leading "staff rides" of the battlefield for foreign military historians. Through Mr Bayerl, the author was introduced to Viktor Ukhov, a resident of Rostov, Russia, who translated a number of captured German documents, including operations orders and communications of the *IV. SS-Pz.Korps* that have never before been translated into English.

I would like to once again thank *Oberstleutnant der Bundeswehr* (retired) Günther Lange, former *Begleitoffizier* (aide-de-camp) of General Gille, for his continuing advice and encouragement. He has also been extremely gracious in sharing the contents of his considerable archive with me, without which there would have been many gaps in my narrative. Throughout this process, he has been extremely kind and patient with my many requests for information and clarification in regards to original documents as well as photographs. Along with the help of his son Wolfgang Lange, who conducted all of the translation and served as a go-between for his father and I, his assistance has been simply invaluable.

I also want to express my thanks once again to those stalwarts who have been behind me all the way in this process, including the crew from Casemate Publishers, especially David Farnsworth, Ruth Sheppard, Daniela Lipscombe, Isobel Fulton, Tony Walton, and Felicity Goldsack. In addition, I would like to mention the continuing assistance of Herbert Ackermans, Tom Albright, Christian Ankerstjerne, Christoph Awender, Predrag Blanusa, Martin Block, Geir Brenden, Prit Buttar, Carol Byrne, Andrew Found, Tim Haasler, Justin Horgan, my map maker Tom Houlihan, Petter Kjellander, John Moore, Tommy Natedal, Kamen Nevenkin, Roland Pfeiffer, Marc Rikmenspoel, Remy Spezzano of RZM Publishing, Bram van Straalen, Viktor Ukhov, Jan-Hendrik Vermeulen, Hans Weber, Lennart Westberg, Lars Westerlund, Ian Michael Wood, David O'Keefe, and Jess T. Lukens. My thanks to you all.

Lastly, I would like to thank my wife Jill for her support and encouragement throughout this five-year process. The many days and hours spent downstairs in my "bunker" while working on this manuscript meant that we both had to forego several vacations, weekend getaways, and other activities that we normally pursued, all sacrificed in the course of this project. Throughout the past several years, including recent months of isolation while the Coronavirus raged unabated, she has been my rock and guiding star, always there for me and with a ready cup of coffee or a glass of wine when I needed it. I would never have finished this without her. I owe you big-time, Jilly!

Douglas E. Nash Sr.
Washington, D.C., June 2020

List of Maps

List of Figures

1. The 4th Edition of the *Kämpfer des Führers* (Warriors of the Führer), the troop newspaper of the *IV. SS-Pz.Korps*, dated 8 December 1944. Produced by the corps' National Socialists Welfare Officer (VI Staff Officer, or *NSFO*) and the staff *SS-Kriegsberichter* (war correspondent), it featured news stories from around the world written and edited by SS war correspondents, as well as standard articles produced by Reich Minister of Propaganda Joseph Goebbels's office and the SS Main Leadership Office. (Courtesy of Günther Lange)
2. A hand-drawn sketch of the Hegyk Castle Estate east of Bicske, which was seized by the *Panzergruppe* of the *5. SS-Pz.Div. Wiking* on 5 January 1945. Between 5 and 12 January 1945, it was defended by 20 tanks of *SS-Pz.Rgt. 5* led by *SS-Ostubaf.* Fritz Darges, *I. Btl./SS-Pz.Gren.Rgt. 23 Norge* led by *SS-Stubaf.* Fritz Vogt, and several smaller units, including elements of the division's engineer and armored reconnaissance battalions. Despite numerous attacks by Soviet armored units, air attacks, and constant shelling, the *Panzergruppe* defended this isolated position until ordered to withdraw. Known as the "Fort of the Unbreakables," it was completely destroyed during the fighting. (Courtesy of Mirko Bayerl)
3. The monthly *Zustandbericht* (status report) of the *3. SS-Pz.Div. Totenkopf* for the month of December 1944, compiled on 1 January 1945. These reports were submitted to the German Army's Inspectorate of *Panzer* Troops in Berlin, which was responsible for the doctrine, organization, training, manpower procurement, infrastructure, and leadership development of all *panzer* troops, regardless of whether they were from the *Heer*, *Waffen-SS*, or *Luftwaffe*. (Courtesy of Martin Block)
4. The monthly *Zustandbericht* (status report) of the *5. SS-Pz.Div. Wiking* for December 1944, compiled on 1 January 1945. The monthly report provided information on both personnel and material readiness, including the number of casualties suffered, replacements assigned, actual unit strength, and amount of armored fighting vehicles and other vehicles needed to enable a *panzer* division to operate as intended. The reverse side was used by commanders to express certain issues that influenced their combat readiness. (Courtesy of Martin Block)

5. The periodic *Erfolgseite* (Success Page) of the *3. SS-Pz.Div. Totenkopf*, published in the division's troop newspaper, the *Totenkopfmelder* (the *Death's Head Messenger*). This example lists the results of the division's combat action between 1 January and 28 February 1945, which portrays the amount of Red Army tanks, guns, and other weapons destroyed or captured by the division during that period. (Vopersal, Vol. Vb, 687)

6. Missing in Action photo of *SS-Stubaf.* Fritz Rentrop from the album of the missing compiled by the *Deutsches Rotes Kreuz* (German Red Cross), depicting the date and the location where he was declared to be missing in action (the actual date he was captured was 2 February 1945). Rentrop's body has never been recovered.

7. Missing in Action photo of *SS-Sturmmann* Gottfried Hofmann, Rentrop's driver, from the album of the missing compiled by the *Deutsches Rotes Kreuz*. His body has not been found either, although his unidentified remains, like Rentrop's, might lie in the German War Graves cemetery in Budaörs or Szekesfehervar, Hungary.

CHAPTER I

The Lost Month
27 November–27 December 1944

Despite their numerous and occasionally heated disagreements over tactics and Soviet intentions, *Gen.d.Pz.Tr.* von Lüttwitz and *Ogruf.* Gille parted on good terms. The *9. Armee* commander greatly appreciated the contribution that *IV. SS-Pz.Korps* had made to the successful defense of Warsaw and was genuinely sorry to see Gille and his men leave. In recognition of their accomplishments and sacrifices, von Lüttwitz issued the following proclamation upon their departure:

> To the *IV. SS-Pz.Korps*: As of 26 November 1944, after nearly four months of service, [you] will no longer be under the command authority of the *9. Armee*. With pride and satisfaction, the *9. Armee* looks back upon this period, in which the *IV. SS-Pz.Korps*, under the tried and true leadership of your commanding general, *Obergruppenführer und General der Waffen-SS* Gille, has once again attached immortal glory to your banners. In an exemplary display of comradeship, the SS divisions under his command, along with the divisions of the German and Hungarian armies, repeatedly broke the onslaught of a greatly superior enemy force in three bloody defensive battles east and north of Warsaw. The *3. SS-Pz.Div. Totenkopf* and the *5. SS-Pz.Div. Wiking* both contributed significantly to these considerable successes. I would like to express my appreciation and thanks for their magnificent feats of arms and extend to the *IV. SS-Pz.Korps* heartfelt wishes for the future. Our fight goes on until the final victory! Long live the *Führer*![1]

By the end of November 1944, the *IV. SS-Pz.Korps* had been fighting along the Vistula *Hauptkampflinie* (main line of battle, or front line) for four months. Although it had lost much ground during that period and its divisions had suffered the loss of thousands of their men, the corps had prevented a major breakthrough by the First Belorussian Front and had inflicted an enormous number of casualties upon the Soviet and Polish forces, as well as destroying hundreds of tanks. Having withdrawn to the *Fuchsstellung* (Fox Defensive Position) in the wedge of land formed by the Narew River in the north and the Vistula River to the southwest, in the area nicknamed the "Wet Triangle" by the troops, the corps had been engaged in siege warfare since 28 October 1944. There are few records remaining from this "lost" period in the corps' history, but using a variety of sources, an outline is presented here for the first time.

Though no major actions had taken place throughout November and December, the troops of *Ogruf.* Gille's corps had endured daily bombardment by Soviet artillery and air attacks by the Red Air Force's 16th Air Army. Daily patrolling, sniper duels, repair of fighting positions, and enduring night raids by the opposing force had filled the days and nights of the men from the *Totenkopf* and *Wiking* Divisions. Fortunately, the width of the front lines in this sector was so narrow that it could be held by just two regiments abreast, allowing each division to frequently rotate troops in and out of the line and grant them some rest as well as to dedicate time towards training the thousands of new replacements each division had received during the past month. By early December, only one regiment with three battalions was sufficient to hold this portion of the front, a testimony to the strength of the fortifications constructed during October and November.

North of the Narew, the corps defended a narrow strip of land less than 20 kilometers wide with one tank battalion from *SS-Pz.Rgt. 5* and the *Germania* Regiment with several attached *Heeres* battalions (see Map 9 of Volume 1). Positioned on its left flank was the *542. Gren.Div.* (officially renamed as a *Volks-Grenadier Division*, or *V.G.D.*, on 9 October 1944), of the neighboring *XX Armee-Korps*. Until 26 November, *IV. SS-Pz.Korps* had been serving under *Gen.d.Pz.Tr.* von Lüttwitz's *9. Armee*, but when that army was detached and transferred to the control of *H.Gr. A* on that date, *Ogruf.* Gille's corps remained in place but came under the command of *Gen.O.* Weiss's *2. Armee* of *H.Gr. Mitte.* However, which field army Gille's corps was subordinated to made little difference in the overall scheme of things until the situation in Hungary began to deteriorate markedly in mid-December.

By this point, most of the decisive fighting had shifted elsewhere, leaving the *IV. SS-Pz.Korps* serving in a tactical backwater until the end of the month. Casualties within the corps' two divisions were correspondingly low, while those suffered by *Korpstruppen* were practically nil.[2] By the end of December 1944, the *Totenkopf* had suffered the loss of only 10 soldiers wounded in action and no deaths; the *Wiking* had lost six men killed, 35 wounded, and two missing, a total of 53 men in all for both divisions, a far cry from the astronomical losses both suffered between August and October 1944.[3] In December, the number of men reported as sick (120 and 194, respectively) for the first time outnumbered the killed, wounded, and missing. In comparison, during the same period, the *542. V.G.D.*, which joined the corps on 28 November, suffered 518 casualties in December, an indication of the width of its sector and the aggressiveness of enemy troops opposing it.[4] The only officer killed in action throughout December was *Ustuf.* Karl Östvig, a Norwegian platoon leader in the newly arrived *I. Btl./Norge*, who was killed in a Soviet night raid east of Modlin on 25 December.

The troops themselves seemingly did not mind the "quiet" front, since they had fought without a break for nearly four months and both divisions had passed the point of exhaustion. Not only had each division suffered thousands of casualties and had to absorb an equal number of new replacements into their ranks, but their weapons, vehicles, and equipment were worn out and needed replacement or significant servicing in order to become fully combat-ready again. There were shortages of some weapons, especially light machine guns and machine pistols, but in the main, the troops had nearly a full complement of infantry weapons.[5] Though new troops (most only recently transferred from the *Luftwaffe*), guns, and vehicles had begun flowing into their shattered regiments, one item was not being replaced—the primary symbol of the *Panzer* division, their tanks.

Due to the higher priority assigned to re-equipping the *panzer* divisions on the Western Front scheduled to take part in the upcoming *Wacht am Rhein* (Operation *Watch on the Rhine*) counteroffensive in the Ardennes, the Eastern Front received only half the number of replacement armored vehicles that the Western Front did, despite the looming threat posed by the resurgent Red Army. There were also nearly three times as many divisions fighting in the East as there were in the West, so the number of tanks that the *Ostheer* did receive were far less than what was required to replace those that had been lost in fighting that summer.[6] Hitler, as he was wont to do, had assumed that once he had finished with the Western Allies in the Ardennes, he could simply redirect his forces to the Eastern Front, where they would quickly finish off Stalin's forces; a gross and irresponsible miscalculation, to say the least.

What this meant for the *panzer* regiments of the *Totenkopf* and *Wiking* Divisions was that they would have to make the best of the few tanks they had left. The *Totenkopf* Division's *SS-Pz.Rgt. 3* had received its last four *Panzer (Pz.) V* Panthers on 27 July 1944 and its last 17 *Pz. IV*s on 9 August 1944; the division would have to wait until 3 May 1945, less than a week before the war ended, before it would receive any more. The case was similar with the *Wiking* Division's *SS-Pz.Rgt. 5*. It had received its last eight Panthers on 23 April 1944 and its last 17 *Pz. IV*s on 26 September, of which nearly half were lost in a single day less than three weeks later in the fighting at Nieporet during the third defensive battle of Warsaw. Each of its remaining Panthers had amassed well over 1,000 kilometers on their odometers since their first operation during the relief of Kovel at the end of March 1944 and were displaying their hard usage in the form of worn-out tracks, engines, transmissions, and final drives. The *Wiking* Division would also receive no more replacement tanks until 8 April 1945, when seven *Jagdpanzer V*s and one *Pz. V Bergepanther* recovery vehicle were issued to *Kampfgruppe Wiking* fighting near Hannover on the Western Front, far from the rest of the division.[7]

The net effect of this policy, of course, was to ensure that two of the *Waffen-SS's* most experienced *panzer* divisions soon became armored divisions in name only, with the *Totenkopf* and *Wiking* Divisions having 68 and 40 tanks, respectively—only a battalion's equivalent, or less than a battalion in the case of *SS-Pz.Rgt. 5*. The situation was only slightly better regarding assault guns and tank destroyers, with the *Totenkopf* Division having 52 and the *Wiking* Division just 18. At their authorized strength, the corps' two divisions would normally have had a combined total of 475 tanks, assault guns, and tank destroyers, but by the end of November 1944, they had only 178 on hand (roughly 37 percent), and not all of these were operational.

Since neither division would receive any replacement vehicles in significant numbers before the war ended, the role of each *panzer* regiment's maintenance company became even more important. At least in regards to their authorized number of *Schützenpanzerwagen* (*SPW*) to ferry their *Panzergrenadiers* to battle, the *Wiking* Division was relatively well off, with 227 of the *Sd.Kfz. 250* and 251 *SPW*s on hand (out of 308 authorized), while the *Totenkopf* was not, having only 88 on hand, not all being operational.[8] Thus, while the *Wiking* Division had more tactical mobility, the *Totenkopf* had more armored fighting vehicles, a factor that would later influence how each division was employed in future operations.

With no new tank deliveries to count on, each of the remaining vehicles had to be kept at the highest state of readiness possible by their crews and maintenance personnel in order to provide the commanders with the greatest number of tanks for battle at any given time. Even recovery of badly damaged tanks assumed greater importance, for these, even if destroyed, could provide a wealth of spare parts to keep the remaining ones running. In a situation like this, the few *Bergepanzer* each regiment possessed assumed an importance out of all proportion to their number. The number of operational tanks during December would not noticeably increase, which meant that the corps' two *panzer* divisions would go into battle with the same low number of tanks they had a month earlier, despite the best efforts of everyone involved at the corps headquarters level and below.[9]

Ironically, the crews to operate a full issue of new vehicles were available, but when new tanks did not arrive, both divisions were forced to form their own ad-hoc units to prevent them from being used as infantry replacements. The *Wiking* Division established a two-company *Lehrabteilung* (training battalion) of approximately 200 men in late November 1944 with these men and had them transferred from the front lines to the SS training area in Schieratz before being finally shipped to the Sennelager tank training area in February 1945.[10] The *Totenkopf* collected its excess tank crews—some 210 men—in a *Sammelkommando* (collection unit) on 31 January 1945 at Veszprém, Hungary, and shipped them on 15 February 1945 to Sennelager too.[11]

Here, both units waited in vain until the war's end for the tanks which they so eagerly sought. When these men were used to form the *SS-Panzerverband Westfalen* on 29 March or *SS-Kampfgruppe Wiking* four days later, the war was practically over. Their experiences were typical. With tank production already failing to keep pace with tank losses on all fronts as early as July 1944, resupplying the *IV. SS-Pz. Korps* with replacement *panzers* after September 1944 simply was not a priority. This situation prevailed until the end of the war, but in all fairness, by early 1944, Adolf Hitler personally set the monthly priorities for tank production and allocation based on his own unrealistic strategy for winning the war, not the priorities of the *OKW* or the *OKH*, which normally would have fulfilled that role.

Though the situation concerning the number of armored fighting vehicles was worsening, as far as unit *Iststärke* (actual unit strength) was concerned, the situation was improving. However, incorporating the thousands of *Luftwaffe* replacements into the ranks of the *Panzergrenadier* regiments had been problematic, for a number of reasons, all of which were recounted in the previous volume. The greatest personnel challenge that remained was preparing the former *Luftwaffe* NCOs who had been assigned to fulfill their new roles as leaders at the infantry squad and platoon level. These men, though well-intentioned, simply lacked the experience and tactical savvy needed to lead troops in ground combat, and two or three weeks of classroom instruction at the divisions' *Feld-Ersatz Bataillone* could not compensate for this. Nevertheless, on paper at least, all four SS *Panzergrenadier* regiments looked healthy and were gaining in strength with each passing day.

The corps commander knew the true situation, of course, as did his two division commanders. How these replacement junior leaders would perform in a major battle had yet to be seen, but Gille, Helmuth Becker (commander of the *Totenkopf* Division), and Karl Ullrich (*Wiking* Division commander) were not optimistic. The junior *Luftwaffe* enlisted men had performed well during the past month, though they had suffered very high casualties when introduced to battle due to their inexperience, but at least they were more amenable to life as an infantryman compared to their NCOs. They were also more motivated and imbued with a National Socialist *Weltanschauung* (political world view), having been raised since children in an atmosphere where loyalty to the *Führer* was all they had ever known.

An unexpected improvement in the overall combat strength of the *Wiking* Division occurred on 17 November 1944, when the *I. Btl./SS-Pz.Gren.Rgt. 23 Norge*, commanded by *Stubaf.* Fritz Vogt, and *I. Btl./SS-Pz.Gren.Rgt. 24 Danmark*, commanded by *Stubaf.* Hermann im Masche, were assigned. Both arrived via rail at the division's reception point at Modlin train station that same day and were immediately sent to the front lines that evening. Both were nominally part of the *11. SS-Pz.Gren.Div. Nordland* and had been undergoing reconstitution at the Hammerstein SS training area in Pomerania (modern-day Czarne) since September 1944 after being nearly destroyed during the battle of Narwa the previous January.

Due to Gille's urgent request for more troops at the end of the third defensive battle of Warsaw, *Ogruf.* Ernst Jüttner at the *SS-FHA* (main SS leadership office) in Berlin belatedly decided to do what he could to alleviate the problem and on 16 November directed that both of these battalions be temporarily attached to the *Wiking* Division instead of being sent back to their parent division, which in any case was cut off and isolated in the Kurland peninsula by this point. Rather than being assigned to either the *Germania* or *Westland* Regiments, they would instead operate either independently under division control or by temporary attachment to either regiment.[12] Though neither of them were manned at their authorized full strength, both still had approximately 600 men assigned, serving under the command of experienced SS officers and NCOs. Most of their rank and file were young German conscripts from Austria or *Volksdeutsche* from southeastern Europe, while approximately 40 Norwegian officers and NCOs were still with Vogt's battalion.[13]

Few if any *Luftwaffe* transferees were counted among the ranks of either battalion, which still had a number of veteran *Waffen-SS* officers and NCOs, which might explain the high fighting efficiency that both battalions would later display. Upon arrival at the front, both *Stubaf.* Vogt and *Stubaf.* im Masche's battalions were placed under the tactical control of *Ostubaf.* Franz Hack's *Westland* Regiment, which allowed him to move his *II.* and *III. Bataillone* into a reserve position behind the lines for a well-earned rest. *Sturmbannführer* Vogt's *I. Btl./Norge* went into the line adjacent to *III. Btl./Totenkopf*'s sector in the Wet Triangle, with *Stubaf.* im Masche's *I. Btl./Danmark* arrayed in the center. Holding the *Westland*'s left flank along the Narew adjacent to the *542. V.G.D.* was the regiment's *I. Bataillon* under *Stubaf.* Nedderhof. The arrival of the two new battalions was not officially reported to *2. Armee* until 27 November, when the *IV. SS-Pz.Korps' Quartiermeister* had to report both of them separately as part of its personnel strength in order to draw their allotment of rations.[14]

Many of the troops from the two battalions of the *Nordland* Division who arrived during this period found life in the trenches hard, especially compared to the relative comfort of the troop training areas they had just left. One soldier from *I. Btl./Norge*, Norwegian SS-Volunteer Jan Barstein, wrote after the war that in November 1944 a few days after their battalion arrived in the Modlin area,

> ... we were [assigned] to rifle pits, located in a flat, sandy area. A few holes in the ground served as our living quarters, which were hardly worthy of being called a bunker. A narrow ditch led from the front line trench to our shelter. In each of these holes lived five of us, which would accommodate us if we all lay down on the same side at the same time ... It was about 80–100 meters away from the Russian [*sic*] trenches. No-man's land was mostly potato fields with a little barbed wire and land mines. We had no oven and every second evening we received a so-called Hindenburg candle that would give us light for about three-quarters of an hour. It was a black, cold winter. There was little to eat, and what we got we had to eat in the dark, and [the food] was usually frozen and full of sand when it arrived ... it was two kilometers from our trenches to where rations had to be picked up. The worse thing about it was that we never got enough water and what we received along with our rations we drank right away; we were always thirsty.[15]

Though combat activity throughout December 1944 continued at a relatively low level, this did not mean that the troops of *IV. SS-Pz.Korps* remained idle. Far from it, in fact. Several units developed inventive schemes designed to keep their opponents occupied and to deceive them as to their actual strength and real location. For example, *I. Abt./SS-Pz.Rgt. 5* had been engaged in constructing dummy tanks of wood and scrap metal since 13 November to attract Soviet artillery fire along their security line north of the Narew River. Periodically, they would take them apart and erect them elsewhere, where they would soon attract the attention of their opponents' forward observers. To enhance their realism, on at least one occasion troops from the battalion engaged in this effort erected their dummy tanks near gun positions of one of the *Germania* Regiment's antitank platoons. Whenever the guns fired, the Soviets, mistaking them for actual *panzers*, would respond by placing a mortar barrage on their location. On another occasion, one of these dummy tanks was destroyed by artillery fire, thus "accomplishing their purpose."[16]

The weather during this last period of relative inactivity continued to worsen and it became bitingly cold. The wind whipped the heavy snowfall into knee-high drifts, which obscured minefields and other obstacles in no-man's land. Commanders scaled back infantry patrols due to the danger of them being detected against the white background, whether they were carried out in the day or night. Rainwater seeped into fighting positions and froze. It was everything that troops in exposed forward positions could do to keep themselves from freezing to death, necessitating the frequent rotation of men in observation posts in front of the main defense line.

Life continued underground, as the men took advantage of the well-constructed fighting positions erected by German, Polish, and Hungarian labor battalions during October. Small stoves provided some warmth and tiny Hindenburg lamps provided sufficient light to write letters by once the sun set. Quiet moments were occasionally interrupted by a stray enemy shell or machine-gun fire. While it was a miserable existence, the few remaining Eastern Front veterans from *Totenkopf* and *Wiking* Divisions had seen far worse. To everyone, it must have seemed that this phase of the war would last forever.

Thoughout this period, the normal arrival and departure of units from the corps' order of battle continued. On 26 November, *schw.Heeres-Art.Abt. 154* returned to *9. Armee* control, followed the next day by the departure of *Stellungs-Werfer Rgt. 103*, with its eighteen 15cm *Nebelwerfer 41* (*Nb.W. 41*) and fifteen 30cm *Nb.W. 42* rocket launchers, whose firepower would be sorely missed. On 28 November, the *542. V.G.D.*, along with *Fest.Inf.Btl. 1405*, joined the corps when *Ogruf.* Gille's northern boundary was extended farther to the north, taking over another portion of the front formerly held by *Gen.Lt.* von Roman's *XX. Armee-Korps*.[17] At some point after 1 December, von Roman's corps headquarters had been "castled," or transferred to the northernmost sector of the *2. Armee* front, with its former portion of the front line divided between the *IV. SS-Pz.Korps* and the *XXVII. Armee-Korps*.

Also on 1 December, the sector defended by the *Germania* Regiment north of the Narew was taken over by *Gren.Rgt. 1077* of the *542. V.G.D.*, thereby allowing *Ostubaf.* Hans Dorr's regiment to go into corps reserve. The only exception was *Hstuf.* Pleiner's *II. Bataillon*, whose four companies remained behind. It was ordered to remain in its current position, where it was responsible for defending the northern bank of the Narew from the eastern outskirts of Debe as far west as the village of Orzechowo, until it was finally relieved on the night of 5–6 December by *Füsilier-Bataillon 542*.[18] At the same time, *Lds.-Schtz.Btl. 998*, which had been attached to the *Germania* Regiment, was relieved and sent back to the *9. Armee*. This shift finally meant that the only *Waffen-SS* troops actually fighting in the Wet Triangle were from the *Westland* Regiment of the *Wiking* Division, with three battalions engaged, including *Stubaf.* Vogt's in the arc stretching from the Narew southwest to the Vistula. The *Germania* Regiment, except for one battalion (the *II. Btl.*), was finally granted the opportunity to reform its ranks in the remaining time available when it was pulled out of the line and designated as part of the *IV. SS-Pz.Korps* reserve.[19]

A major development occurred the following day, when the *Totenkopf* Division was designated as the *2. Armee* armored reserve, which would mark the first time since June 1944 that *Brig.Fhr.* Becker's division had not been in combat. Pursuant to this order, its companies, battalions, and regiments began pulling out of the front lines on 3 December and started moving into their new positions encompassing the area straddling the large towns of Nasielsk and Plöhnen (modern-day Płońsk). The only element of the division still positioned in the Wet Triangle, *III. Btl./SS-Pz. Gren.Rgt. 5 Totenkopf*, was relieved in the lines by *Stubaf.* Vogt's newly arrived *I. Btl./Norge*, which extended its lines to the south. The only other unit of the division exempt from this order was *I. Abt./SS-Pz.Rgt. 3*, which was ordered to stay behind in Modlin as the *IV. SS-Pz.Korps* armored reserve with its 26 remaining *Pz. V* Panthers.

The *Totenkopf* Division's new *Gefechtstand* (command post) was located in the town of Wolka, northeast of Nowy Miasto, while its *Ib/Adjutantur* moved into its new location at Kuchary-Zydowski. Although the division was now directly subordinate to headquarters, *2. Armee*, it would remain under the administrative jurisdiction of the *IV. SS-Pz.Korps*. Despite the fact that *Ogruf.* Gille had temporarily lost control of one of his *panzer* divisions, he still commanded the over-strength *Wiking* Division as well as the *542. V.G.D.*, should the Soviets show any inclination towards resuming their offensive. In addition, Becker and his troops were not far away in case of an emergency, being located on average merely 30 kilometers away from Modlin.

At first, the *Totenköpfler* (the nickname the troops called themselves) were disappointed in their new living areas, which in many cases were simply empty buildings or private homes whose Polish inhabitants had been forcefully evacuated. According to the commander of *11. Kompanie* of the *Totenkopf* Regiment, whose troops were billeted in the rural village of Katne, "Our [new] quarters were rather primitive: a cottage and two barns for the entire company ..."[20] Most of these structures were without electricity, heat, or fuel, but troops soon got to work to improve them any way that they could to make them as habitable as possible for what promised to be a long, cold winter.

The *Totenkopf* Division's leaders would not let this precious reprieve go to waste. Besides the important need to service and maintain equipment, the division finally had an unfettered opportunity to institute a rigorous training program, aimed at instilling in its thousands of new recruits the motivation and dedication for which its "SS spirit" had become famous. Training, weather permitting, would be conducted at the individual and collective level, ranging from squad to platoon, then from company to battalion, and finally from regimental to division level. When they were not training, its men would be engaged in conducting rear area security duties, ever alert against the significant threat posed by Polish partisans.

Whenever possible, soldiers who had not had the opportunity for a two-week *Heimaturlaub* (home leave) would be given a chance to go home and visit loved ones while there was still time. Awards were bestowed upon deserving soldiers, such as *Stubaf.* Gerhard Pellin of *SS-Pz.Aufkl.Abt. 3*, awarded the German Cross in Gold on 7 December, *Uscha.* Alfred Tischkus of the same battalion, who received the Knight's Cross on 11 December, and *Hascha.* Helmut Büch, who was presented with that most rare of awards, the *Nahkampfspange im Gold* (Close Combat Badge in Gold) on 12 December. The latter decoration was only awarded to those who had engaged in 50 days of hand-to-hand or close-in combat with the enemy. Few lived long enough to receive this official recognition of their skill (and luck) as a front-line soldier, and those who wore it were afforded tremendous respect from their peers. Once he recovered from the wound he received during his most recent action, Büch would be granted a special 21-day home leave.[21]

The rotation of units in and out of the *IV. SS-Pz.Korps* continued apace. On the same day that the *Totenkopf* Division began moving to its reserve position, the *II. (azerbaijani) Bataillon* of *Sonderverband Bergmann*, one of the several "foreign legions" responsible for rear area security in the *2. Armee Korück*, departed. Two days later, in relation to the shift of the *XX. Armee-Korps*, *Ogruf.* Gille assumed responsibility for most of its entire former defensive sector on 5 December. With this development, his corps now assumed command and control of both the *35.* and *252. Inf.Div*, adding to his own 20-kilometer-long defensive line another 30 kilometers, extending it from the area west of Serock as far north as Pułtusk. On that same date, *Luftwaffe Flak-Rgt. 77* and *Werfer Brig. 1* were added to *IV. SS-Pz. Korps'* lineup. For the first time in the *IV. SS-Pz.Korps'* history, soldiers from the *Wehrmacht* outnumbered those of the *Waffen-SS* within its ranks.

On 6 December, the lack of corps heavy artillery assets was partially made up by the attachment of *II.Abt./schw.Heeres-Art.Rgt. 69 (mot.)* by *2. Armee*. The corps' designated heavy artillery battalion, *schw.SS-Art.Abt. 504*, was still undergoing its necessary instruction period at the Beneschau training area in Bohemia and Moravia, and would not be ready for another two months. Until then, *Wehrmacht* artillery units would have to fulfill that role. As an indication of the overall low level of combat activity along the Vistula and Narew defense lines in December, ammunition expenditures were minimal throughout this period, with only 15–20 tons of artillery, mortar, and small-arms munitions being fired on an average day. Incidentally, the *Stab* and *II.Abt./schw.Heeres-Art.Rgt. 69 (mot.)* was the last unit of any significance to join the corps' order of battle during December, so that by Christmas Eve, the *IV. SS-Pz.Korps* consisted of the *Wiking* Division, the *35.* and *252. Inf.Div.*, and the *542. V.G.D.*, as well as the aforementioned corps troops, roughly 65,000 men in all. On 7 December, *Fest.Inf.Btl. 1405* departed the corps' order of battle for the third and final time, being pulled out to serve as part of the army group's reserve.

Besides witnessing the coming and going of units within the framework of *Ogruf.* Gille's corps, a number of other incidents filled the calendar from the end of November and throughout December 1944. For instance, on 28 November, Hitler issued a directive that granted authority to subordinate leaders to take command should their leaders not display the proper willingness to fight. It stated:

> I therefore command: If a troop leader, who on his own, believes that he must give up the fight, he must first ask his officers, then NCOs, then the troops, if one of them wants to fulfill the mission and continue the fight. If this is the case, he must hand over the command—regardless of the rank—and subordinate himself to his junior. The new leader takes over the command with all decision-making authority and duties.[22]

This order was promulgated by the *OKW* to address Hitler's belief that *Wehrmacht* leaders at all levels were displaying insufficient enthusiasm for continuing the war—even defeatism—as well as the lack of dedicated leadership needed to continue fighting at the tactical level. *Der Führer* felt that this tendency manifested itself in a lack of aggressiveness and indecisiveness that often resulted in the enemy seizing the advantage and turning the tables on German troops. As of yet, this was not a problem within the ranks of the *Waffen-SS*, its leaders having been inculcated in the "proper" National-Socialist outlook since the earliest days of its founding.

On 1 December 1944, in recognition of its conduct during the battle of Modlin, Himmler issued an order praising the *IV. SS-Pz.Korps* and its subordinate units: "The [performance] of the *IV. SS-Pz.Korps* under the leadership of *SS-Obergruppenführer* Gille with subordinate *3. SS-Panzer Division Totenkopf* and *5. SS- Panzer Division Wiking* during the fighting northeast of Warsaw in the month of November 1944 was characterized by special bravery and steadfastness."[23] While such praise was appreciated by the corps' members, what they really needed was more tanks to replace those they had lost since the end of July, not empty though well-meaning phrases.

On 3 December, because of the near-daily loss through capture of German front-line soldiers in their fighting positions by Soviet night patrols, *Ogruf.* Gille issued a corps order that threatened severe punishment to any officers or NCOs, who, through their own negligence or lack of fighting spirit, made their particular sector of the front line vulnerable to nightly forays by the enemy. This order was issued due to two night raids carried out in the sector defended by the *542. V.G.D.* during the past two days, resulting in the loss of several men taken prisoner. In both cases, neither infantry company involved had a response force readily available to conduct a counterattack to regain the prisoners, prompting investigations by the division's commander, *Gen.Lt.* Karl Löwrick. The *IV. SS-Pz.Korps'* commander required that all individuals involved in each incident be interrogated to determine the cause and to apportion blame. Gille directed his ire towards one of his own SS units, since one of the cases involved the capture of a soldier from 6. *Kompanie* of the *Germania* Regiment, commanded by *Ustuf.* Hans-Jürgen Koch.[24]

These cases were not isolated incidents. As an antidote to what *Gen.O.* Weiss saw as an increasingly lax attitude developing among the front-line troops of 2. *Armee*, on 5 December he ordered that a series of *Alarm* exercises be planned and carried out by all of his army's corps. Consequently, that same day, *Ogruf.* Gille ordered both the *Wiking* and *542. Volks-Grenadier* Divisions to plan and carry out these readiness drills in their respective rear areas, set to commence three days later. The order specified that units were to regularly train their men to carry out counterattacks by night as well as by day, to rehearse movement to alternate defensive positions, and to coordinate their actions on a regular basis with adjacent units in order to improve cross-boundary communications. In addition, all units concerned were ordered to improve their local communications network that had been set up to warn of tank attacks and to prepare demolition charges for bridges, antitank ditches, and key fortifications in their defensive sectors. *Obergruppenführer* Gille himself or his chief of staff would personally observe these readiness drills.[25]

On 7 December, the *IV. SS-Pz.Korps Ib (Qu.)* and *Adjutantur* relocated from the Smoszewo Palace to Plöhnen, though Gille and his *Gefechtstand* remained in Modlin. The following day, the *Totenkopf* Division's *Ib* and *IVa* (the personnel and administrative offices) relocated to Sechocin, 5 kilometers northeast of the corps' *Quartiermeister*. In regards to personnel, during this period men who had been wounded returned from convalescent leave to rejoin their old companies, but not all of them. Some were permanently disabled, fit only for light duties back in the homeland such as guarding concentration camps or working as a clerk in an office at the *SS-FHA*. Not all recovered from their wounds. On 13 December, *Ostuf.* Wilhelm Warnke, commander of *11.Kp.* of *III.(gep.)/Germania*, died at a *Reserve Lazarett* (hospital) in Sagan from a lingering infection after being severely wounded in action by artillery fragments on 13 August while leading his company in a counterattack to regain ground lost near Grabow during *Unternehmen Brückenschlag*. He had taken command of the company the previous May and had led his *SPW*-mounted company with skill and bravery during the bloody summer east of Warsaw.

Another noteworthy event was the rotation of the entire artillery regiment of the *Wiking* Division with that of the *Totenkopf* in mid-December. Battery by battery, the incoming guns and gun crews from *SS-Pz.Art.Rgt. 3* replaced those of their sister division, while those of *SS-Pz.Art.Rgt. 5* crossed over the Vistula or Narew and occupied the same winter quarters that the *Totenkopf's* gunners had just given up. According to one artillery battalion commander of the *Wiking* Division, "The new positions were well constructed and lay in a forest ... Sufficient bunkers were available to suit our needs. For our planned Christmas celebrations, the *2. Batterie* even constructed a large common bunker, big enough to hold everyone. In general, the time passed quietly …"[26]

Another development worthy of note during this period was the reinforcement of the old Czarist fort at Debe, deemed the most critical terrain in the *IV. SS-Pz. Korps* sector. This fort, located adjacent to the town of the same name along the northern bank of the Narew and defended by *Füs.Btl. 542*, offered commanding views both to the north as well as within the Wet Triangle to the south. *Gen.Lt.* Löwrick, commander of the *542. V.G.D.*, rightly pointed out that should it fall, the Soviets would have excellent observation into the rear area positions of the *Wiking* Division as far as the Vistula, as well as that of his own division. Consequently, he offered a plan to *Ogruf.* Gille on 18 December describing what he intended to do to fortify this position and a laundry list of the construction materiel, barbed wire, and mines (3,100) needed to accomplish this. In addition, 8,400 meters of trenches needed to be constructed or improved to make the position more defensible. To perform this task, since he did not have enough troops of his own, Löwrick requested the assignment of a *Bau-Pionier* company of 150 men or the temporary loan of a company from the corps' attached *Feldstrafgefangenen Abteilung 1* (field punishment prisoner battalion). Work was still underway on *Fort Debe* at the end of the month when the *IV. SS-Pz.Korps* was transferred.[27]

To recognize the achievements, both on and off the battlefield of corps troops as well as attached *Heerestruppen*, a host of awards were distributed by *IV. SS-Pz. Korps'* headquarters under Gille's signature during the latter half of December. While the corps' divisions administered their separate programs to recognize their own troops as previously mentioned, unit commanders working directly under the supervision of the corps headquarters routinely submitted the names of their own men for approval through the *Korps IIa, Stubaf.* Schulze. Taking advantage of the lull in the fighting to catch up on its paperwork, throughout December Schulze's office processed 260 awards, including eight Iron Crosses First Class (*EK I*) and 83 Iron Crosses Second Class (*EK II*) for valorous conduct in battle, and 170 War Service Crosses Second Class with Swords (*KvK 2. Kl.m.Schw.*) for exceptional performance of duty not involving direct combat. Of course, Gille did not present each decoration in person, which would have been impractical except for the eight *EK I*s, but he did sign the remaining awards.

Of these, officers assigned to the headquarters of *IV. SS-Pz.Korps* garnered two of the *EK I*s. One of these was awarded to *Stubaf.* Herbert Jankuhn, the corps' *Ic*, while the other went to *Hstuf.* Heinrich Fockenbreck, who succeeded *Hstuf.* Werner Westphal as the *O1*. Fockenbreck had died in the SS hospital in Hohenlychen on 21 November from wounds received the previous month, so his award was posthumous. In addition to these high awards, 22 *EK II*s and 145 *KvK 2. Kl.m.Schw.* were presented to SS troops. Not surprisingly, *SS-Werf.Abt. 504* received the lion's share of the Iron Crosses (17) for the bravery its men displayed during the third defensive battle of Warsaw, where the rocket launcher battalion suffered nearly 20 percent casualties. The remainder of the awards were distributed evenly throughout the rest of the corps troops, including five *EK IIs* for members of *SS-Nachr.Abt. 104.*[28] Perhaps the oddest one awarded was an *EK II* presented to an aviator, *Feldwebel* Friedrich Schulze, a Fieseler 156 *Storch* (Stork) pilot assigned to the *Luftwaffe* squadron dedicated to supporting the SS and Police, *7. Staffel/ Flieger-Geschwader z.b.V. 7.* Although the details are not available, he was most likely engaged in flying the corps commander and other key leaders to meetings at higher headquarters locations as well as performing other aerial liaison duties, including flying reconnaissance missions against the Polish partisans during *Unternehmen Sternschnuppe* the previous October.

On a cloudy 21 December 1944, the *Wiking* Division conducted a ceremony within the Modlin fortress for hundreds of its veteran *Führer* and *Unterführer* assembled therein to commemorate the fourth anniversary of the division's founding, featuring rousing speeches by the commander of *IV. SS-Pz.Korps* and the division's incumbent commander, Karl Ullrich. Both Gille and Ullrich verbally traced the division's history from its establishment on 21 December 1940 to its introduction to battle in June 1941, the victorious advances into the Ukraine and the Caucasus Mountains during 1941 and 1942, the freezing winters, the massive battles during the summer of 1943, the withdrawal to the Dnieper, the encirclement and breakout from the Cherkassy Pocket, and its epic relief and defense of Kovel.

With strains of Wagner and Beethoven blaring from loudspeakers set up for the occasion, the two men held forth for nearly an hour, as the participants shivered in the icy wind that howled through the ancient fortress. Special recognition was afforded to the few remaining "Nordic" volunteers in the ranks— men from Denmark, Norway, Sweden and Finland, whose families back home were hated and being persecuted by their fellow countrymen for the actions of the sons, brothers, and fathers who had embarked on the "great crusade" that began on 22 June 1941. According to one eyewitness, Gille and Ullrich recounted that the division was:

> The first in the attack against the enemy and the last during the retreat—that's how the [*Wiking*] division etched its deeds in the bloody history of the campaign in the East. It was a captivating picture: The gloomy Polish fortress, the volunteers assembled in it from practically all European countries ... men, scoffed and scorned, who left everything behind for four years, placed their young lives on the line, buoyed by a belief in a better future ...[29]

Had they only known what their immediate future held, these veterans most likely would have concluded differently. But on 21 December 1944, with Hitler's promise of wonder weapons that would end the war in Germany's favor already rolling off the assembly lines, there was still room for hope, despite the gloom hovering over the embattled fortress.

Figure 1. The 4th Edition of the *Kämpfer des Führers* (Warriors of the Führer), the troop newspaper of the *IV. SS-Pz.Korps*, dated 8 December 1944. Produced by the corps' National Socialists Welfare Officer (VI Staff Officer, or *NSFO*) and the staff *SS-Kriegsberichter* (war correspondent), it featured news stories from around the world written and edited by SS war correspondents, as well as standard articles produced by Reich Minister of Propaganda Joseph Goebbels's office and the SS Main Leadership Office. (Courtesy of Günther Lange)

The following day, *Ogruf.* Gille issued a Christmas message to the men of *IV. SS-Pz.Korps*—both *Wehrmacht* and *Waffen-SS*—which appeared in the sixth issue of the corps' newsletter, *Kämpfer des Führers* (see Figure 1). In addition to offering the usual holiday greeting and acknowledging this "most German of all holidays," he closed by invoking the seriousness of Germany's situation and the important role being performed by their corps:

> The defense of our homeland and thus the defense of Europe is an important mission that has been assigned to us. By defending our wives and children here in the East, at the same time we are safeguarding the life of generations to come, and thus the eternal existence of Europe. The guarantors of our victory [in this struggle] are our strength, the steadfastness of our hearts and the invincibility of our weapons. Under the leadership of Adolf Hitler, final victory will be ours![30]

At this point it was evident that no one, not even Gille, anticipated that the corps would be celebrating Christmas in anything other than relative peace. True, daily artillery exchanges with the enemy, patrolling, repelling Soviet raiding parties, and improving defenses would continue as they had for the past two months, but no one was expecting anything out of the ordinary.

Many men took advantage of the opportunity to visit their families in Germany, such as *Ogruf.* Gille's *Begleitoffizier, Ustuf.* Günther Lange, who had stood by his commander's side since May 1944 until being seconded to *SS-Pz.Rgt. 5* for a three-month assignment as its *O1* on 18 December. He had not seen his fiancée or his family in Hamburg-Altona for nearly two years, so he leapt at the chance for a two-week *Kriegsurlaubschein* (home leave pass).[31] Commanders at all levels encouraged their men who had not taken home leave to apply for it; however, the backlog was so great that a method of prioritization had to be developed. For example, men who had earned the *Panzervernichtungsabzeichen* (Tank Destruction Badge) were automatically given home leave, as were those who had earned other prestigious awards. For men not yet eligible for leave, the commander of the *Totenkopf* Division came up with an innovative idea for rewarding and boosting the morale of soldiers whose wives had given birth in their absence by allowing the division's *VI* Staff Officer (acting as its *NSFO*) to award them a savings account of 3,000 *Reichmarks* out of division funds for every newborn child.[32]

On 23 December, the *IV. SS-Pz.Korps* headquarters issued an order that echoed an identical one sent by *2. Armee* earlier that day that directed all of its front-line units to increase their level of security on 24 and 25 December. Fearing a Soviet surprise attack designed to take advantage of the relaxation attendant to the Christmas holiday, the order directed all divisions of the corps be prepared to deal with local attacks by having units pre-designated to carry out counterattacks standing by in prepared positions. To ensure there were enough troops available for such a contingency, as well as to enable front-line infantrymen to be rotated back to second- or third-line defensive positions to briefly enjoy a Christmas meal that evening, up to 25 percent of each division's artillerymen and all of their antitank battalions were ordered to organize strong *Stossreserven* (assault troop reserves). These units were to report that they were formed up and ready for possible employment by 2 p.m. on 24 December.[33]

As the Christmas holiday approached, the troops made every effort to make their bunkers, living areas, and dugouts resemble their *Julfest* (Yule festival) at home as much as they could. Wreaths were crafted and hung on doors and bunker entrances. *Weihnachtsbäume* (Christmas trees) were cut down and brought forward from the rear area, installed in troop bunkers and living areas, and decorated by the men with bright paper, hand-made wooden decorations, and candles for illumination. If a company was lucky enough to have a *Spiess* (first sergeant) who had good "organizing" skills, perhaps there would be cakes, cookies, and other delicacies, or maybe a roast piglet or at least a duck for the traditional Christmas Eve feast.[34] Some lucky few received gift parcels from home, which might contain sausage, cheese, and perhaps *Oma's* (grandmother's) *Käsekuchen* (cheese cake), despite severe food rationing at home. Wine and other alcoholic beverages such as homemade schnapps or slivovitz to enliven the festivities were shipped from Germany or procured from local farmers, eager to sell some of their precious liquor to earn enough money to feed their families.

For this Christmas—the war's sixth—much of Europe's material and agricultural wealth had been exhausted and shortages of certain foodstuffs, such as beef or pork, were commonplace. Still, the soldiers of the *IV. SS-Pz.Korps* would try their utmost to create a sense of normalcy and enjoy the holiday, if only for a short time. Perhaps someone would have a radio to listen to the *Soldatensender* (German armed forces radio) or, if they had a gramophone, the latest hit songs from home, such as *Es geht Alles vorüber, es geht Alles vorbei* (There's an end to it all), sung by German songbird Lale Andersen. The lyrics were emblematic of the prevailing melancholic mood of the German people, as exemplified by the refrain:

> Everything passes,
> There's an end to it all;
> Every December
> Is followed by May.
> Everything passes,
> There's an end to it all;
> But two who love one another,
> Always remain faithful.

As the holiday approached, *Ogruf.* Gille planned a reception and simple dinner to celebrate Christmas Eve at the fortress in Modlin, inviting all of the corps staff, division, and regimental commanders from the five divisions of the corps, including the *Totenkopf,* still enjoying its status as the *H.Gr. Mitte* reserve. Though each of Gille's subordinate leaders would have made every effort to visit their own men throughout the holiday period, they would have taken pains to observe the normal peacetime courtesies regarding their corps commander's invitation.

As Christmas Eve dawned, no major Soviet attack developed, despite the intelligence report's warning. During the early morning hours, however, enemy assault troops made several small-scale attempts to penetrate the front lines of the *Wiking* Division and the *542. V.G.D.* to gather information and take prisoners. Since the Germans had been alerted the day before, none of the Soviet incursions met with success and their patrols were chased off with artillery or small-arms fire. The sounds of tank tracks and engines were also reported by forward outposts, but when nothing happened, the defenders assumed (correctly, in this case) that the Soviets were playing recordings of tank noises through loudspeakers as a tactical deception crafted to unnerve the Germans, as they had done before. A heavy ground mist began to form during the late afternoon, obscuring the area beyond the front lines, making observation difficult.[35] Other than this slight disruption, preparations for the *Heiligabend* (Christmas Eve) celebrations continued apace.

As darkness began to fall, troops began to rotate in shifts between the front lines and rear areas to eat dinner. Troops located further to the rear in reserve positions or in safer *Tross* areas and the various headquarters locations in Modlin or Nowy Dwór made their way to whatever shed, barn, or building had been converted—for one night at least—into a makeshift banquet hall. Mess sergeants and troops designated to serve as dining room orderlies began to shuttle food from the *Gulaschkanone* (mobile field kitchen) to the tables. In the fortress at Modlin, the corps commander's Christmas Eve reception was about to begin. Troops, especially front-line infantrymen and combat engineers who had been living off cold food in the trenches for much of the past month, looked forward to a tasty hot meal with as many of the trimmings that the company *Spiess* and *Feldkoch* (cook) could improvise.

Many of the younger soldiers could be forgiven for thinking that perhaps this war was not going so badly. After all, were not German forces in the Ardennes gaining victory after victory over the Anglo-Americans? Had not the Soviet forces in Hungary been smashed by strong German and Hungarian armored counterattacks? Though the *Wehrmachtbericht* (the daily *Wehrmacht* communiqué) and the broadcast by the *Soldatensender* made it seem as if the tide was finally turning in Germany's favor, the few surviving veterans taking part in the festivities knew how to read between the lines of the news reports and had learned to separate propaganda from truth.

As final preparations for the evening were underway, the telephone rang in the corps command post's *Führungsabteilung* shortly after 5:05 p.m. It was a call from the *2. Armee* watch officer at *Gen.O.* Weiss's headquarters. After writing down the details, the *IV. SS-Pz.Korps* tactical group officer on duty that evening (most likely *Hauptsturmführer.* Velde or *Oberscharführer* Schlemmer) quickly relayed the contents of the message to *Ogruf.* Gille and his chief of staff. After briefly mulling over its import and probably verifying its authenticity through a telephone conversation with his army commander, or perhaps the *SS-FHA* in Berlin, Gille ordered that the *Totenkopf* and *Wiking* Divisions be immediately notified. Gille would inform the commanders of his two SS divisions himself. Less than an hour later, at 6 p.m., the *Hellschreiber* machines in the corps command post's *Führungsabteilung* began to hum with activity. A decoded message from Hitler's *Führerhauptquartier* (*Führer* headquarters) in Ziegenberg confirming the warning order and detailing the new mission began to spool out to be collected and pasted onto message forms, then carried to the corps commander for his immediate attention.[36] His own Christmas Eve social gathering in the Modlin fortress would most likely have been cancelled forthwith.

Each SS division received the news in a similar fashion. At approximately 9 p.m. on 24 December, the telephone rang in the *Gefechtstand* of the *Wiking* Division. The *O1, Ostuf.* Günter Jahnke, acting as the watch officer, was handed the phone by the *Unteroffizier vom Dienst* (NCO on duty). On the other line was the corps chief of staff, *Ostubaf.* Schönfelder, who asked for the division commander. After informing

Schönfelder that *Oberf.* Ullrich had gone forward to visit the troops in the front lines, Jahnke was curtly told to stand by. The next moment, Jahnke was speaking to *Ogruf.* Gille himself. "I hear that 'Isegrim' [codename for Ullrich] isn't there, so listen carefully," said his corps commander, who now had the young lieutenant's full attention. "*Wir dorpmüllern zur Julischka* ... have you got that?" Jahnke, screwing up his courage to the sticking point, then responded, "When, *Obergruppenführer?*" The answer came right away: "Immediately! [*Kampfgruppe*] *Dorr* this evening, you [i.e., division headquarters] tomorrow morning!" Then he hung up.[37]

As the notification worked its way down through each division's chain of command, units began to become aware that something out of the ordinary was in the air. For instance, just as *Stubaf.* Messerle, battalion commander of *IV. Abt./ SS-Pz.Art.Rgt. 3*, was about to give his Christmas speech to the assembled men of his *10. Batterie* that evening, the battalion's runner burst into the barn, which had been converted into a banquet hall for the occasion. Proceeding immediately to his commander, the young soldier handed him a message from regimental headquarters. Upon opening it, Messerle read the word "*Ilmensee*" (Lake Ilmen) written on the top line. This was the division's standing code for the highest state of alert, meaning that its units were to make themselves ready to march immediately. Every other unit in the division received the same message at roughly the same time.

Shortly thereafter, Messerle received another message, also an appropriately coded deployment order. Just like the one the *Wiking* Division had received, it too emphatically read "*Wir dorpmüllern zur Julischka!*" Accordingly, Messerle gave the appropriate order. The Christmas Eve celebration was quickly forgotten, as the men scrambled to get everything in order, colliding with one another as each hustled about to perform their prearranged task. No one knew where or when they were going, or even if they were going. Messerle later recalled, "After thinking about it for a moment, then I understood. *Dorpmüller* is the State Minister for Transport, whose main role was to operate the railways.[38] Yes, and the *Julischka?* Then it dawned on me! Railway movement to Hungary! Yet another fire brigade mission!"[39]

CHAPTER 2

The Hungarian Theater of Operations
September–25 December 1944

After receiving the dramatic alert message on Christmas Eve, the troops of *IV. SS-Pz. Korps* quickly began preparing for rail movement to Hungary. While a few fortunate companies and battalions were able to enjoy a curtailed Christmas holiday celebration that had been painstakingly prepared by their unit leadership, most of the corps' troops were deeply involved in preparing for their new assignment. Over the next several days, thousands of SS men loaded their vehicles and equipment and began boarding troop trains that would transport them to their new area of operations by New Year's Eve.[1] Some of the units had to board trains in the Modlin–Nowy Dwór area, still within range of the enemy's guns, and were given a deadly farewell by artillery fire that fell near the rail yards as they departed. According to one member of the *Wiking, Ostuf.* Günther Jahnke, the division's *O1*, the Wet Triangle would not be missed. After the war, he wrote, "We were glad to be leaving the 'Modlin Fortress' … everyone there feared being surrounded because it was unlikely that we would have ever escaped."[2]

Despite the fact that *Gen.O.* Georg-Hans Reinhardt, the commander of *H.Gr. Mitte,* had declared Gille's corps as being essential for the defense of the Vistula Front in light of the Soviet winter offensive expected to occur on or about 12 January 1945—a point of view also echoed by the *OKH* chief of staff, *Gen.O.* Heinz Guderian—the corps was still sent to what many perceived as being a secondary front. This left many to ask, why Hungary, and why now? In order to understand how this seemingly ill-advised transfer came to pass, and how *Ogruf.* Gille's veteran corps found itself almost immediately involved in heavy sustained combat upon arrival in Hungary, a brief review of the events of the past three months is in order.

While the several battles for Warsaw fought between 27 July and the end of October 1944 were important events in their own right, they were only part of the vast struggle that raged along the entire Eastern Front in the wake of Operation *Bagration*. In addition to the tribulations inflicted upon *H.Gr. Nord* and *Mitte* by the Red Army during this period, between August and October 1944 a series of cataclysms befell the German forces and their allies arrayed in southeastern Europe.

Beginning on 25 August with the destruction of *Gen.d.Inf.* Johannes Friessner's *H.Gr. Südukrain* with its *6.* and *8. Armee* in Romania at the hands of the Second and Third Ukrainian Fronts—aided and abetted by the treachery of the Romanian government—the rest of Germany's southeastern front collapsed like a house of cards. Invaded by Colonel General F. I. Tolbukhin's Third Ukrainian Front on 8 September, Bulgaria immediately switched sides, thereby opening the door to the Balkans, where 900,000 German occupation troops were fighting various resistance movements at the end of a long and vulnerable supply line, including 300,000 men in Greece alone.[3]

While *Generalfeldmarschall* (*G.F.M.*) Maximilian von Weichs, serving as both *Oberbefehlshaber Südost* (commander in chief, Southeast) and commander of *H.Gr.F*, attempted to simultaneously reconstruct a coherent front line in the wake of Bulgaria's defection and evacuate as many German troops from Greece and Yugoslavia as possible, the main Soviet effort, spearheaded by General of the Army Rodion I. Malinovsky's Second Ukrainian Front, quickly closed up on the eastern slopes of the Carpathian mountain range by 5 September, the last natural barrier to the *Puszta*—the wide-open plains of eastern Hungary.

At the same time as Tolbukhin's front was busily engaged in chasing von Weich's forces out of southern Romania, Bulgaria and northeastern Yugoslavia after several weeks of fighting for the critically important mountain passes in the Carpathians, Malinovsky's forces were able to force their way through and enter the Hungarian plain between Oradea and Arad by 5 October. By this point, Friessner's *H.Gr. Südukrain* (renamed *H.Gr. Süd* on 23 September), cobbled together from the remnants of *6.* and *8. Armee* and bolstered by a mishmash of German and Hungarian units of varying quality, was able to reassemble a coherent front, of sorts. While on paper it looked like his new line could be successfully defended, Friessner feared that it would splinter when struck hard by Malinovsky's forces.[4]

The Hungarian Regent, Admiral Miklós Horthy, and his supporters were also under no illusions as to which direction the wind was blowing, sensing that unless peace was made with the Soviet Union as soon as possible, their country would be destroyed in the fighting that would soon follow. While Friessner was frantically attempting to reconstruct the front line and marshal as many German and Hungarian divisions as possible to defend it, Horthy—through his representatives—was just as frantically trying to negotiate terms with one of Stalin's intermediaries. Although Horthy made every effort to keep these negotiations secret, these developments did not escape unnoticed in Berlin; Hitler made it clear to his subordinates that he would not tolerate Hungary changing sides, like Romania and Bulgaria had the previous August. Hitler, the supreme commander of Germany's armed forces, felt that at this stage of the war that if Hungary—with its strategic oil fields, natural resources, and large population—fell into enemy hands or joined with the Soviet Union, the war was as good as over.

Notified by Friessner and other contacts of Horthy and his cabinet's conspiracy, Hitler, in his capacity as head of the *OKW,* ordered a preemptive strike in Budapest to be conducted on 15 October 1944 by two of his SS "specialists," *Ogruf.* Erich von dem Bach and *Ostubaf.* Otto Skorzeny. Codenamed *Unternehmen Panzerfaust,* this SS-led task force initiated a coup that began with the kidnapping of Horthy's youngest son, Miklós Jr. This deed compelled the Regent to resign his office and be taken to Germany as a "guest" when the SS threatened to kill his son unless Horthy gave in. The political vacuum that immediately ensued allowed *Ogruf.* von dem Bach, nicknamed the "Butcher of Warsaw" by the Poles, to quickly seize Budapest with a minimal amount of bloodshed.

German troops rapidly took over all the key points in the city—including the telephone exchange, radio station, key bridges and road intersections—and confined the Hungarian Army to its installations in the city.[5] Before he was bundled away to Germany, Admiral Horthy, at Hitler's expressed order, dissolved his cabinet and installed a pro-German government, led by the notorious Arrow Cross Party's leader, Ferenc Szalási, a fascist who professed his guarantee to Hitler that Hungary would remain loyal until the bitter end, but who was little more than a puppet. To ensure that Szalási's loyalty did not waver, actual control of the Hungarian government was entrusted to *Brig.Fhr.* Edmund Veesenmeyer, whom Hitler appointed Reich plenipotentiary in Hungary after the German occupation.

With his political flank now protected, Friessner's *H.Gr. Süd* could direct its attention to the heavy fighting that awaited. His army group's situation had begun to improve by 15 October, after several *panzer* divisions under the control of the commander of *8. Armee, Gen.d.Art.* Maximilian Fretter-Pico, encircled and nearly destroyed three Soviet corps during the tank battle of Debrecen. Sensing an opportunity, Malinovsky had sought to take advantage of the Hungarian government's disarray by incautiously splitting his forces and launching a daring drive towards Budapest on 6 October, though he did not have the accustomed overwhelming superiority that his front normally enjoyed. During the heavy fighting that took place from 10–15 October 1944, German and Hungarian forces managed to inflict significant damage to the 6th Guards Tank Army, which suffered the loss of over 200 tanks on 12 October alone.[6]

Although this counterattack stabilized the Hungarian front, it proved to be only a temporary reprieve, albeit one that gave the *OKH* and *H.Gr. Süd* time to evaluate the situation. Using this breathing space, Guderian—with Hitler's permission—ordered Friessner to pull his forces back to the Tisza River, a more defensible line than the one *H.Gr. Süd* had previously tried to hold. Viewing his defeat at Debrecen as only a temporary setback, Malinovsky ordered the 6th Tank Army and Cavalry-Mechanized Group Plieyev to closely pursue the withdrawing Axis divisions in hopes of encircling and destroying the bulk of their forces before they could cross the Danube. Too closely, as it proved. Taking advantage of the headlong Soviet advance, Fretter-Pico's forces turned about on 23 October and conducted a pincer attack of their own led by *Gen.d.Pz.Tr.* Hermann Breith's *III. Pz.Korps*, cutting off and destroying three more Soviet corps by 26 October.

This German–Hungarian victory brought major operations by both sides in Hungary to a halt until 28 October, the first time since mid-August that Friessner's army group had enjoyed a cohesive, though thinly occupied, front line.[7] Taking advantage of this brief pause in operations, Friessner did everything he could to strengthen the new front along the Tisza, especially the reorganization of the Hungarian forces, which were in complete disarray by this point in the wake of the resignation or defection of many of its senior officers after Horthy's failed attempt to make a separate peace with Stalin. Additional German units, deemed more capable and reliable, were inserted into the line between Hungarian units, to serve as *Korsettenstange* (corset stays) to buttress the defense and deter their defection, as well as to ensure that their allies carried out their share of the burden in defending their own country.

Malinovsky resumed his offensive towards Budapest on 29 October (codenamed the Budapest Operation), having had time to concentrate his forces and replace the tanks he had lost the week before. The German front along the Tisza was soon pierced at several points by the 46th Army after the Hungarian *3. Armee* disintegrated under its hammer blows. With little to slow his army down, Lt.Gen. Ivan Shlemin's spearheads, with their left flank demarcated by the line of the Danube, had pushed west and north to a point only 10 kilometers away from the southeast suburbs of Budapest by 2 November. The following day, his tanks had broken through the city's outer defense line on the eastern side of the Danube, but a series of counterattacks from 4–5 November by the *8.* and *22. SS-Kav.Div.*, as well as the *13. Pz.Div.*, soon joined by two other *panzer* divisions, forced the 46th Army back.

During this tank battle, fighting could clearly be heard in the distance by the city's population, who began to display signs of panic despite assurances from Arrow Cross members that the Red Army would never enter the city. Matters were made more complicated when a German engineer inadvertently ignited demolition charges emplaced on the Margarethe Bridge over the Danube that linked the two sides of the city (Buda and Pest). The explosion heavily damaged the bridge and caused a portion of it to fall into the river, at a time when the German and Hungarian defenders needed this bridge more than ever. Neither did this engender much trust between the city's population and their German overseers, who believed that the Germans would sacrifice their beloved city to delay the Soviet advance, though the bridge's destruction was purely accidental.

Despite the nearness of the Soviet vanguards, very little had been done by this point to fortify the city or prepare it to withstand a long siege, especially against an attack from the western bank of the Danube, should the Red Army seize a crossing site and attempt an envelopment. According to Friessner in his postwar account, during one of his visits to Budapest during this period, the city still seemed to have a peacetime atmosphere. He later wrote, "While in Budapest, I realized that the population had no clue about how serious the situation at the front was. Everywhere I was still seeing scenes of the deepest peace and, unfortunately, this poured some bitters drops into the festive cup for the victories at Debrecen."[8]

Between 11 and 22 November, Malinovsky, using four of his armies (the 7th Guards, 27th, 40th, and 53rd), fought and maneuvered against determined German resistance, advancing along a broad front from the Tisza to the Danube before finally closing up along the Danube south of Budapest by 25 November. On his right flank north of Budapest, the Fourth Ukrainian Front struggled against a determined German defense staged by *Gen.d.Inf.* Otto Wöhler's *8. Armee* in the eastern Matra Mountains of Slovakia, barely managing to push the Germans back as far as Miskolc after suffering heavy losses. On Malinovsky's left flank to the south of Budapest near Baja, Tolbukhin's Third Ukrainian Front initiated its own attack on 22 November, breaking out of the bridgeheads his troops had established over the Drava River at Apatin and Batina.

Blasting through the thin German defenses arrayed in the Drava–Danube triangle, Tolbukhin's 4th Guards and 57th Armies had seized the key city of Mohacs by 26 November, ripping open the flank of *H.Gr. Süd's* neighbor to the south, *H.Gr. F*, thereby opening the way to the Lake Balaton region, home of Germany's last substantial oil reserves. By 29 November, the historic city of Pecs fell to Tolbukhin's spearheads, and two days later his 4th Guards Army arrived along the Danube, linking up with the 46th Army of Malinovsky's Second Ukrainian Front on 1 December, thus creating a continuous front along the Danube from Mohacs to just a few kilometers short of Budapest.[9] Neither *H.Gr. Süd* nor *H.Gr. F* had been able to do much to stop it, with their few reserves being switched from one crisis point to the next before another one broke out somewhere else, much like the fabled Dutch boy frantically trying to plug holes in a dyke.

The next round of fighting would happen along the southern and northern approaches to the city. As Tolbukhin's forces inexorably approached the area southwest of Lake Balaton, Malinovsky's attention focused on Budapest. While the 46th Army crossed the Danube and struck out towards the northern end of Lake Balaton, the 7th Guards Army and 6th Guards Tank Army attacked north of Budapest, taking the key city of Hatvan by 5 December. By 8 December, these two armies had taken the town of Vac on the Danube, less than 30 kilometers north of the capital, while at the same time Tolbukhin's forces had completely closed up along the *Margarethestellung* (the Margaret Position). This was to be the German and Hungarians' new main defensive position that ran along the line Lake Balaton–Stuhlweissenburg (Székesfehérvár)–Lake Velencze and was a natural defensive position southwest of Budapest. It was manned by the troops and tanks of *6. Armee/A.Gr. Fretter-Pico*, a mixture of German and Hungarian units.[10] Although they had originally intended to incorporate Budapest into its *Hauptkampflinie*, the defenders' lack of sufficient infantry to hold the portion of the *Margarethestellung* that stretched between the northeastern corner of Lake Velencze and the southwestern corner of Budapest would have fateful consequences 12 days later.

With Malinovsky's and Tolbukhin's armies concentrated north and south of the city and hence unable to quickly come to the aid of one another, *Gen. O.* Guderian sensed another opportunity to strike at least one of the two Soviet spearheads in the flank and destroy it. As the *OKH* chief of the general staff, on 11 December he ordered Friessner to concentrate three of his *panzer* divisions (the *3.*, *6.*, and *8. Pz. Div.*) and three heavy tank battalions under the operational control of Breith's *III. Pz. Korps* as quickly as possible and launch this counteroffensive, codenamed *Unternehmen Spätlese* (Operation *Late Harvest*), within two or three days at the latest. However, Guderian and Friessner disagreed as to which Soviet concentration to attack; that in the north or in the south of the city? With the generals at loggerheads, Hitler intervened and chose the course of action favored by Friessner, who wished to launch the *Spätlese* counteroffensive towards the south between Lakes Balaton and Velencze, beginning on 17 December 1945.

While Friessner was assembling his forces, the weather intervened and delayed preparations. Heavy rain and thawing conditions turned the Hungarian roads into ribbons of mud, making any kind of movement by armored vehicles—not to mention trucks and cars—extremely difficult. On Friessner's directive, the offensive was put off for several days until the temperature dropped and the roads hopefully froze solid again. By 17 December, it was still raining and the roads had not improved, although the *panzer* divisions had been assembled and—except for the weather—everything was ready for the offensive to begin. In justification of his decision to delay the attack, Friessner wrote afterwards that "sending the designated armored formations into an immediate attack in the mud could not be justified; it was crucial to wait for the frost in order to be able to operate away from only paved roads."[11]

While this was occurring, the 6th Guards Tank Army, operating north of the Danube despite the inclement weather, took the town of Sahy east of the Gran (Hron) River on 14 December when its vanguards easily pushed through the ineffective defense offered by the *SS-Dirlewanger Brigade*, which had been shipped south from Slovakia to hold the line recently vacated by most of the *24. Pz. Div.*, which had left behind only a small *Kampfgruppe*. For the next three days, Guderian and Friessner argued back and forth about the urgency of launching *Spätlese*. Friessner was cautious, not wishing to sacrifice his carefully husbanded tanks, while Guderian—mindful of the big picture—urged his subordinate onwards as he watched the possibility of a quick victory begin to slip away.

When Malinovsky's tanks from the 6th Guards Tank Army broke through the Berzsenyi Mountains south of Sahy and north of the Danube on 20 December, it created an existential threat to the survival of *H. Gr. Süd*, for on that same day,

Tolbukhin's forces struck on either side of Lake Velencze. Hitler, for his part, was growing impatient and demanded action. With a crisis plainly unfolding before his eyes, Guderian—prodded by a *Führerbefehl* issued by Hitler the previous day—was forced to act. Ordering Friessner to leave the tanks behind with *III. Pz.Korps* of Fretter-Pico's *6. Armee* to carry on with *Spätlese*, Guderian moved the division staffs and infantry components of the *panzer* divisions to the mountainous region south of Sahy along the Gran River. Here, they could at least stop the advance of the Soviet tanks before they broke out into the Danubian plains northwest of Budapest that led to the gates of Vienna.[12]

Meanwhile, the *panzer* regiments and heavy tank battalions (nearly 400 *panzers* in all), operating under Breith's *III. Pz.Korps*, attempted to follow the *Spätlese* plan against Tolbukhin's forces, but their attacks met with little success.[13] Churning through the mud, the German *panzers* used up massive amount of scarce fuel as they attempted to maneuver against their more nimble opponent. The employment of these tank regiments and separate battalions proved to be a difficult challenge for Breith to command or control, since their accustomed division headquarters had been sent north of the Danube along with most of their signal battalions. The last-minute creation of *Divisionsgruppe* (*Div.Gr.*) *Pape* on 21 December, an attempt to use the division commander and staff of the *Pz.Gren.Div. Feldherrenhalle* (*FHH*) for this purpose, came too late to make much difference. Without adequate infantry support, these 10 tank battalions were easy prey for the Soviet infantry and antitank guns and were finally forced to withdraw behind the safety of the *Margarethestellung*, and *Unternhemen Spätlese* came to an inglorious end the following day, 22 December.

Although Fretter-Pico's armored assault had achieved none of its goals, *III. Pz.Korps'* aborted offensive had at least limited the scope of the Second Ukrainian Front's advance due to excessive caution on the part of the Soviet commander. Providentially for the Germans and Hungarians, Malinovsky had evidently decided not to risk converting his Front's penetration into a deep attack with so many *panzers* lurking about, but instead to conduct a shallow envelopment of Budapest from the west, which would seal the fate of the city's defenders. That same day, Friessner took the opportunity to request permission to withdraw the troops of the *IX. SS-Gebirgskorps* (*SS-Geb.Korps*) from Fretter-Pico's *6. Armee* defending Budapest on the eastern bank of the Danube, a move that he believed would free up a badly needed infantry division but would also result in the abandonment of Pest. This Hitler categorically refused to consider, believing it important to hold the eastern side of the city for political reasons. Budapest would continue to be held at all costs.[14]

By this point, both Hitler and Guderian had lost patience with Friessner and Fretter-Pico, leaders whom they judged to be too cautious and lacking in the kind of fighting spirit that the extreme situation required. Consequently, on the night of 22 December, Friessner and Fretter-Pico were notified by the Operations Branch of *OKH* that they would both be relieved of their commands within the next 24 hours. The new commander of *H.Gr. Süd* would henceforth be *Gen.d.Inf.* Wöhler, formerly commander of *8. Armee*, while Fretter-Pico, commander of *6. Armee*, would be replaced on 24 December by *Gen.d.Pz. Tr.* Hermann Balck, who would be brought over from the Western Front, where he had been commanding *H.Gr. G.* At least Wöhler was familiar with the situation, having commanded the *8. Armee* since August 1943, so his elevation to command of the army group would be relatively seamless. Balck, on the other hand, had been fighting on the Western Front for the past three months, and although he was an Eastern Front veteran, would need to quickly orient himself in regards to his new duties and responsibilities.[15]

While the Germans dithered, Malinovsky and Tolbukhin relentlessly pushed forward. Though neither of these commanders possessed the strategic or operational talents of other more gifted Soviet commanders such as Zhukov, Konev, or Rokossovsky, they were good at following orders from the *STAVKA* and were certainly up to the challenge of commanding army groups in a region of limited operational scope such as Hungary. Wherever the Germans displayed weakness, they exploited it; where their enemy showed strength, they went around it or crushed him with overwhelming firepower. On 23 December, 4th Guards Army took the city of Bicske against negligible resistance, thus severing all ground communications with Budapest (see Map 1).

The following day, Wöhler, echoing his predecessor in command, telephoned Guderian at *OKH* and briefed him on the deteriorating situation. Wöhler requested that he be given the authority to order the city's garrison to evacuate the eastern bank of the Danube and move into the inner defensive ring on the west bank of the Danube, which comprised the Buda portion of the city. This was ironically the same position that Friessner had also advocated and was one of the factors that had led to his abrupt dismissal.[16] Surprisingly, Guderian did not reject his plea outright, but informed him that he would pass his request on to Hitler, who upon being notified of the *H.Gr. Süd* commander's request, characteristically refused to consider any mention of a withdrawal.[17] Hitler had previously designated Budapest a *Festung* (fortress) on 1 December, and as such it would be defended to the last man and the last round of ammunition.[18]

Soviet tanks reached the city of Gran (Esztergom) on 26 December. Budapest was now completely encircled. Although on paper the defending German–Hungarian force appeared strong, it lacked sufficient food, fuel, and ammunition for the 70,000-man garrison led by *SS-Ogruf.* Karl Pfeffer-Wildenbruch, commander of the *IX. SS-Geb.Korps*, and was hardly in any shape to withstand a long siege. As for the city's population of nearly 800,000 men, women, and children, no food or fuel had been stockpiled for them at all, other than what they had managed to hoard on their own initiative. To rescue the city and its garrison, a relief operation would have to be launched immediately. The only consolation, if there was one, was that a *panzer* corps was being hurriedly brought down from Poland at that very moment

Map 1: The Eastern Front
25-31 December 1944

to lead the relief effort, and that corps was none other than Gille's *IV. SS-Pz.Korps*. *Dorpmüllern* to the *Julischka*, indeed!

At this point, members of Gille's corps can be forgiven for wondering why they were being shipped so hastily to Hungary. After all, they might have asked, was not the *Führer* always right? Were things not going according to plan, and was the tide not finally turning back to favor Germany? According to all official communiques, the mighty *Wehrmacht* was had stopped the Allies at the Gothic Line in Italy, the Red Army was being held at bay in Poland, Courland, and East Prussia, and various "wonder weapons"—such as the V-1 and V-2—were already pounding the British Isles. According to the same reports, the *Kriegsmarine* was sinking record numbers of enemy ships, the *Luftwaffe's* new jet aircraft were systematically shooting down the enemy's air fleets of Flying Fortresses and Liberators, and Germany's enemies were suffering crippling losses everywhere. New tanks, aircraft, and U-boats were rolling off the assembly lines in numbers never before imagined, and new units, such as *Volks-Grenadier* divisions, were being activated by the dozens.

Most of all, Nazi media outlets were reporting that the *Wacht am Rhein* offensive in the Ardennes seemed to be going according to plan, with American and British armies routed and thousands of prisoners taken. Antwerp was almost in the bag, though there was a bit of fighting at some place called Bastogne. Even in Hungary, the Red Army had reportedly suffered severe reversals, while hundreds of thousands of German troops had been successfully evacuated from Greece and Yugoslavia. At least, that is the impression a naïve young soldier would take away from viewing the latest newsreel of *die deutsche Wochenschau* in the cinema, scanning the newest *Signal* magazine, or reading *Das Schwartze Korps* newspaper.

So why was it necessary to send the *IV. SS-Pz.Korps* to Hungary? While no doubt glad to be leaving the Wet Triangle in Poland, even veteran SS officers and enlisted men must have believed that when the time came, their divisions would be fighting on Germany's eastern borders to prevent Stalin's so-called "Bolshevik hordes" from entering their homeland, not serving in a backwater of a front in southeastern Europe. If *Ogruf.* Gille had felt any such doubts, he did not express them, but instead seems to have been focused exclusively on the mission ahead of him and the important role his corps would play in the upcoming relief operation, as he always did.

Though seemingly illogical, there was method in Hitler's madness. While most of his military advisors, including Guderian, thought the emphasis should be on preparing to repel the impending Soviet winter offensive against eastern Germany expected after 12 January 1945, Hitler had decided that the Hungarian theater of operations was where the war would be won or lost. After being forced to abandon the vast Romanian oil fields at Ploesti four months before, Hungary's rather modest oil fields at Nagykanizsa were soon producing more oil than any other source within Hitler's shrinking empire, including the synthetic oil production facilities in Germany that had been badly damaged by the American Eighth Air Force.

Although paltry by contemporary American industry standards, the 600,000 tons of oil pumped out of the Nagykanizsa fields that year, combined with a much smaller amount from Austria's Zisterdorf wells, provided nearly 80 percent of Germany's remaining oil production by late 1944. Without oil to refine into petroleum and associated by-products, there would be no fuel for the new tanks, aircraft, and submarines rolling off the assembly lines. Without these powerful weapons, Germany's war was as good as lost.[19] So there was some logic to Hitler's single-minded focus on Hungary. To Hitler, not only was it vital to relieve Budapest, the capital city of his last significant ally and an important political objective itself, but the oil fields at Nagykanizsa had to be protected at all costs.

There was also the 730,000 tons of steel that Hungary shipped to Germany every year, a not insignificant amount, considering Albert Speer's drive to increase armaments production. To Hitler's way of thinking, holding on to Hungary was just as important towards winning the war as was the Ardennes or Alsace offensives. Consequently, what few mobile reserves Germany could still spare on the Eastern Front at that particular moment would be sent to *H. Gr. Süd*, including Gille's corps. As soon as the *Wacht am Rhein* offensive was successfully concluded and the Allied armies in the west destroyed, the SS *panzer* army operating under the command of *SS-Oberstgruf.* Sepp Dietrich would then be shipped to the east to play its part in the next act of the drama unfolding between Budapest and Vienna.

To buttress the case that Hitler made, his viewpoint was backed up by the Chief of Staff of the *OKW*, *G.F.M.* Wilhelm Keitel, and the chief of his *OKW* Operations Staff, *Gen.O.* Alfred Jodl, two men who usually agreed on everything that *der Führer* said. Against this coalition, Guderian was able to make little headway. In the end, two of the *Ostfront*'s 14½ *panzer* or *Panzergrenadier* divisions remaining on the Eastern Front were shipped to Hungary at the end of December 1944, leaving only 12½ mechanized divisions as the reserve to reinforce an enormous front line stretching over 800 kilometers from the Carpathian Mountains in the south to the Baltic Sea coast in the north.[20] In comparison, the much smaller Hungarian Front had seven of these powerful formations and would soon gain four more when the *6. Pz.Armee* was transferred from the Western Front at the end of February 1945, which would by that point amount to nearly 18 percent of all of the armored formations in the entire *Wehrmacht* and *Waffen-SS* order of battle.[21]

This leads to the final question, which was why was it deemed necessary to transfer the *IV. SS-Pz.Korps* to carry out the relief operation, when other similar reserves were available that were not already committed at the front, unlike Gille's corps? To understand why, one must first examine a number of factors that were in play between 20 and 25 December 1944. The idea of relieving Budapest was first discussed at a meeting held at the *Adlerhorst*, Hitler's supreme headquarters in Ziegenberg, on Christmas Eve 1944, the day Bicske fell. As early as 20 December, it was already apparent to everyone in attendance, including Hitler,

Keitel, Jodl, and Guderian, as well as Heinrich Himmler, that Budapest would soon be surrounded.

At the meeting on 24 December, Guderian aired his opinion that Budapest should be given up, with the forces holding the city allowed to break out and used instead to form a new defense line west of the city. The reasons why he advocated this course of action were clear to him, at least, for he favored reinforcing the Eastern Front at the expense of every other front, including withdrawing forces from the Ardennes, which by 23 December already appeared to have little chance of succeeding. He also wanted to withdraw as many divisions from the *Brückenkopf Kurland* (Courland bridgehead) as possible, where *H. Gr. Nord* had been completely bottled up in the Lithuanian peninsula since 9 October 1944. Guderian's driving motivation, above all, was to prepare his theater of operations to resist the massive Soviet offensive expected in early January and to prevent the Red Army from penetrating Germany's eastern heartland. This, he believed, is where the war would be won or lost, not in Hungary.[22]

For the reasons stated above, Hitler overruled his chief of the *OKH*, and ordered *Festung Budapest* to hold out until relieved, much to Guderian's disappointment. Despite his protests, the meeting concluded when Hitler told Guderian that the *OKH* theater of operations—the Eastern Front (consisting of *H. Gr. Süd, A, Mitte*, and *Nord*)—would have to "take care of itself" for the foreseeable future.[23] Since *H. Gr. Süd*'s three armies (the *3. ung, 6.*, and *8. Armee*) lacked sufficient mobile forces of their own to both hold their current positions (including protecting the vital Nagykanizsa oil fields) and fight their way through the Second or Third Ukrainian Fronts to relieve Budapest, Wöhler's army group would obviously have to be reinforced with an additional *panzer* corps, but not one from the Western Front.

That corps was to be Gille's; the choice was Hitler's, and Hitler's alone. One of the reasons why he picked it was due to its proximity on the map. It was in the *H. Gr. Mitte* area of operations, and could be moved by rail relatively quickly. This choice may have been supported by the fact that the Narew–Vistula sector had been relatively static for the past two months, so Hitler might have felt that he was incurring little risk, despite Guderian's arguments to the contrary. Additionally, the *Totenkopf* Division was in a position behind the front lines acting as the *2. Armee* armored reserve, so it was available for immediate movement.

Perhaps the deciding factor was that Hitler knew that Gille had successfully commanded troops during the breakout from the Cherkassy Pocket a year earlier and had done the same during the battle of Kowel, where he took command of a demoralized and disorganized garrison and led the defense of the city until it was relieved three weeks later. Hitler had personally bestowed the Swords to Gille's Knight's Cross with Oakleaves for his deeds at Cherkassy on 20 February 1944, and the Diamonds for his performance of duty at Kowel two months later, so the

Commanders and Staff, 1945

General der Infanterie Otto Wöhler, Commander, *Heeresgruppe Süd*. (Author)

General der Panzertruppe Hermann Balck, Commander, *Armeegruppe Balck/6. Armee*. (Author)

SS-Oberstgruppenführer Sepp Dietrich (shown here with Gille), Commander, *6. Pz.Armee*, taken outside of Gille's *Hauptquartier* in Inota during early March 1945 shortly before the beginning of the *Frühlingserwachen* Offensive. (Lange)

Generalmajor Heinz Gaedke, Chief of Staff, *Armeegruppe Balck/6. Armee.* (Author)

SS-Oberstgruppenführer Gille, Commander, *IV. SS-Panzer-Korps*, with *SS-Obersturmbannführer* Schönfelder and *SS-Untersturmführer* Günther Lange in Modlin, December 1944. (Lange)

General der Panzertruppe Hermann Breith, Commander, *III. Panzer-Korps/Korpsgruppe Breith.* (Author)

General der Kavallerie Gustav Harteneck, Commander, *I. Kavallerie-Korps.* (Veterans Association of the 72. *Infanterie-Division*)

SS-Brigadeführer Helmut Becker, Commander, *3. SS-Pz.Div. Totenkopf,* in January 1945 during *Unternehmen Konrad III.* (Photo by *SS-KB* Hermann Grönert, courtesy of Mirko Bayerl)

SS-Oberführer Karl Ullrich, Commander, *5. SS-Pz.Div. Wiking,* shown here presenting awards at Dobogókő in the Pilis Mountains, January 1945, during *Konrad II.* To his immediate left stands the commander of *SS-Pz.Gren.Rgt. 10 Westland, SS-Obersturmbannführer* Franz Hack. (Photo by *SS-KB* Alfons Jarolim, courtesy of Mirko Bayerl)

Generalmajor Hermann Harrendorf, Commander, *96. Inf.Div.*, shown here as an *Oberst*. (Author)

Generalleutnant Josef Reichert, Commander, *711. Inf.Div.*, shown here as a *Major* before the war. (Author)

Generalmajor Eberhard Thünert, Commander, *1. Pz.Div.*, stands on the right, while his corps commander Gille stands on the left. In the middle, the commander of *SS-Nachr.Abt. 104, SS-Obersturmbannführer* Herbert Hüppe, can be seen. Photo taken during the retreat from Stuhlweissenburg, late March 1945. (Lange)

Generalmajor Wilhelm Söth, Commander *3. Pz.Div.*, shown here as an *Oberst*. (U.S. National Archives and Records Administration)

SS-Sturmbannführer Adolf Pitschellis, Commander, *SS-Pz.Rgt. 3* of the *Totenkopf* Division. (Courtesy of Lennart Westberg and Geir Brendan)

SS-Sturmbannführer Fritz Eckert, Commander, *SS-Pz.Gren.Rgt. 5 Totenkopf*, shown here in a pre-war photograph as an *SS-Mann*. (Courtesy of John P. Moore)

SS-Obersturmbannführer Franz Kleffner, Commander, *SS-Pz.Gren.Rgt. 6 Eicke*. (Moore)

SS-Obersturmbannführer Fritz Darges, Commander, *SS-Pz.Rgt. 5*, outside of Stuhlweissenburg, early March 1945. (Erich Kern)

SS-Obersturmbannführer Hans Dorr, Commander, *SS-Pz.Gren.Rgt. 9 Germania.* (From the *Truppenkameradschaft Wiking* Archive, courtesy of Lars Westerlund)

SS-Sturmbannführer Fritz Vogt, Commander, *I. Bataillon/SS-Pz.Rgt. 23 Norge* and *SS-Panzeraufklärungs-Abteilung 5 Wiking,* shown here as an *SS-Hauptsturmführer.* (Moore)

SS-Obersturmbannführer Franz Hack, Commander, *SS-Pz.Gren.Rgt. 10 Westland,* shown here in the center in April 1945 with (from left to right) *SS-Sturmbannführer* Karl-Heinz Bühler, Acting Commander *SS-Pz.Gren.Rgt. 9 Germania,* Hack, *SS-Sturmbannführer* Wilhelm Klose (Division *Ia*), and Gille with back to camera. (Lange)

Generalmajor Rudolf Holste, Commander, *4. Kavallerie-Brigade*. (Author)

Generalmajor Claus Kühl, Commander, *356. Infanterie-Division*, seen here as an *Oberst*. (Author)

SS-Obersturmbannführer Karoly Ney, Commander, *SS-Regiment Ney*, seen here presenting some of his Hungarian volunteers with the Iron Cross. (Bayerl)

SS-Obergruppenführer und General der Polizei Karl von Pfeffer-Wildenbruch, Commander, *IX. SS-Gebirgs-Armeekorps* and the Budapest garrison. (Petersen)

Marshal of the Soviet Union Rodion Malinovskiy, Commander, Second Ukrainian Front. (Ministry of Defense of the Russian Federation, www.Mil.ru)

Marshal of the Soviet Union Fyodor Tolbukhin, Commander, Third Ukrainian Front. (Ministry of Defense of the Russian Federation, www.Mil.ru)

dictator knew Gille both by reputation and by sight—important factors in Hitler's way of assessing leadership.

Gille, Hitler thought, would know the mentality of encircled troops better than anyone. The mere mention of his name in connection with a relief force, the thinking went, would be enough to bolster the morale of the troops holding *Festung Budapest* and would encourage them to hold out until relieved.[24] According to Georg Maier, former *Ia* of the *6. Pz.Armee*:

> The garrison [of Budapest] was informed by radio that Gille and the *IV. SS-Panzerkorps* was being brought in. From that point on, the name Gille brought new hope to the besieged, from the senior commander to the lowest grenadier. This knowledge and their faith in their approaching comrades, who would relieve them, allowed those surrounded by the enemy to endure, even in the most apparently hopeless of circumstances. It also gave them the courage and strength to patiently bear the heaviest physical and spiritual burdens as they bravely defended Budapest, fighting to the last round.[25]

Although Hitler's judgment in this matter can be questioned, his reasoning was shared by *Ogruf.* Felix Steiner, who wrote afterwards that it had been said of the commanding general of the *IV. SS-Pz.Korps* that "he had already been in a pocket once and he would know better than anyone else the mood of his surrounded comrades. For this reason, he and his forces were especially well suited for the relief of Budapest."[26]

As if to remove all doubt, Heinrich Himmler himself sent a telegram to Gille on 24 December, within hours of receipt of the original alert order, that stated, "The *Führer* has directed you to carry out the relief of Budapest with your corps. The justification of this decision is based on the fact that you have already proven that you and your corps can successfully relieve encircled units." The head of the dreaded SS Empire then closed with the ominous line, "The *Führer* expects you and your corps to relieve Budapest and I personally expect that you will not disappoint me."[27]

Once they had detected the movement of Gille's corps several days later, the Anglo-American intelligence staff, bolstered with "special intelligence" provided by ULTRA, were mystified as to why the Germans had switched their last remaining armored reserve on the Eastern Front from Poland to Hungary, especially when the Germans themselves acknowledged that the Soviet winter offensive in Poland was only weeks if not days away: "Not content with holding the Russians [*sic*] west of the city [of Budapest], the Germans made frantic efforts to batter their way through to relieve it. In order to do so, they not only fatally denuded other fronts, but also uselessly shattered a powerful armored force which would have been very helpful in the Hungarian Offensive of March 1945."[28] Regardless of the logic of the decision, the die was cast and until the end of the war, the *IV. SS-Pz.Korps* would fight with *H.Gr. Süd*.

CHAPTER 3

Arrival in Hungary
25–28 December 1944

As related in the previous chapter, formal orders from *OKH* in Zossen transferring the *IV. SS-Pz.Korps* and all of its sub-units to Hungary were received via *Hellschreiber* at Gille's headquarters in Modlin at 6 p.m. on 24 December 1944.[1] The corps' units, including the *Totenkopf* and *Wiking panzer* divisions, which were in the midst of preparations for celebrating the Christmas holidays, had to cancel their plans and immediately begin preparing for their imminent transfer by rail to the Hungarian theater of operations, codenamed *Julischka*.

Combat activity on Christmas Eve had been relatively minimal, allowing most of *IV. SS-Pz.Korps'* units to continue their preparations for their rail movement to Hungary undisturbed. However, during the early hours of Christmas Day, the Soviet 186th and 250th Rifle Divisions of the 47th Army each launched a battalion-sized probing attack in the *Westland* Regiment's sector at Chotomów and Kałuszyn. Both attempts to penetrate the *Westland* Regiment's defenses were driven off by artillery and small-arms fire without any German ground being lost or suffering any casualties worth mentioning. However, it was more than a minor affair; the scale of the German response can be adjudged by the *IV. SS-Pz.Korps'* expenditure of artillery ammunition that day, which amounted to 37 tons, nearly twice the corps' average for that particular period of the war.[2]

After the failure of their reconnaissance in force attempt, neither Soviet division made any further effort that day. Today, after 75 years have gone by, it is unclear whether the First Belorussian Front had become aware of the impending transfer of Gille's corps; perhaps both attacks were thinly veiled efforts to tie up and prevent the *Westland* Regiment from pulling out, or just another example of the well-established record of Soviet commanders determined to seize prisoners for interrogation, especially along a static front. According to ULTRA intercepts, the Anglo-American Special Intelligence Branch was unaware of anything out of the ordinary taking place and would not notice the transfer of the *IV. SS-Pz.Korps* for another week.

Despite the convoluted manner of Hitler's decision-making process in prioritizing which front would receive reinforcements and selecting which corps would be sent to assist in the relief of Budapest, this was a simple matter compared to the physical process of moving a corps of nearly 40,000 men, 421 armored vehicles (including inoperable ones), and at least 4,544 soft-skinned wheeled and tracked vehicles of all types by rail in less than a week. In addition to their vehicles and other equipment, Gille's troops also had to load over 250 individual heavy weapons, including artillery pieces, antiaircraft and antitank guns, and rocket projectors, as well as hundreds of trailers.[3]

Since there would be no food, fuel, or ammunition immediately available upon arrival in Hungary until *IV. SS-Pz.Korps* could connect with the logistics and administrative apparatus of *6. Armee*, the corps and its affiliated units had to bring along everything they had, including at least three days' worth of bulk rations (not counting emergency iron rations), 94,761 gallons of fuel (both gasoline and diesel, not counting what was already in each vehicle's fuel tanks), and 4,544 tons of all types of munitions, ranging from 9mm pistol rounds to 15cm artillery ammunition.[4] To complicate matters, loading all of these combat vehicles and other pieces of heavy equipment would all have to be done manually, in freezing weather, and with inadequate lighting at night. Still, it would be done in record time, though how many men were accidentally killed or injured during the loading process is not recorded.

Evidence indicates that ULTRA finally did detect the movement of *IV. SS-Pz. Korps* to relieve Budapest on 2 January 1945, the day after the operation began, when it intercepted and decoded the following radio message from Himmler's liaison officer with Hitler, *Gruf.* Hermann Fegelein, described by the officer writing the ULTRA history of the war on the Eastern Front as a "colorful racketeer." On that day, Fegelein had wired *Ogruf.* Pfeffer-Wildenbruch, "Heartiest good wishes for the New Year! The *Führer* appreciates your exemplary behavior. Gille comes on apace!" As the ULTRA report on the message stated, "This was rather startling ... That the Germans, knowing that a Soviet offensive was imminent in Central Poland, were yet prepared to switch to the Budapest front their only effective armored reserve for meeting that offensive was a measure of the importance they attached to the southern fighting."[5]

With the corps' departure from the Warsaw front proceeding at a rapid pace, the sector held by *Wiking* Division would have to be completely turned over to the *73. Inf.Div.* as quickly as possible. As for the *Totenkopf* Division, its role of serving as the *2. Armee* armored reserve would be fulfilled by the understrength *7. Pz.Div.*, which was also undergoing a rest and reconstitution period behind the lines.[6] Because *Ogruf.* Gille's corps headquarters, the *Totenkopf* Division, and *K.Gr. Dorr* were deemed as being "immediately available" for movement, these units began loading for rail transport as early as 25 December, with the first train departing late that evening. With *Ogruf.* Gille's corps headquarters and its signal battalion departing, this meant that the *Wiking* Division would have to be temporarily placed under the tactical control of *XXXVI. Pz.Korps* of the *9. Armee*, until it could be relieved east of

Modlin and join the rest of the corps in Hungary.[7] The commander of the *73. Inf. Div.*, *Gen.Maj.* Schlieper, was notified as early as the evening of 25 December by *9. Armee* that his troops would have to relieve the *Wiking* Division, which meant that he would have to move his division battalion by battalion across the Vistula using the bridges at Modlin and Nowy Dwór to carry out this new mission.[8] His division's former sector north of Warsaw would be taken over by *Sperr-Brigade 1* on the night of 27–28 December.

This brigade, which had been attached to the *VIII. Armee-Korps* until 26 December, was not an infantry unit at all, but consisted primarily of various combat engineer units culled from the entire *9. Armee* area of operations, with a sprinkling of artillery, antiaircraft, and antitank units in support. Since it was defending a portion of the west bank of the wide Vistula south of Warsaw, it had to be quickly pulled out of the line and shipped to the area north of the ruined city, while a neighboring division was forced to stretch its own front lines to compensate for the brigade's departure, thus weakening that portion of the front even further.

The *9. Armee* commander, *Gen.d.Pz.Tr.* Smilo Freiherr von Lüttwitz, was caught completely off guard by the sudden transfer of Gille's corps from the neighboring *2. Armee*. Even more surprising was the accompanying directive to take over the defense of the Narew–Vistula triangle, which he must have thought his army was finally rid of on 26 November 1944. In his commander's report that evening, he complained bitterly to the commander of *H.Gr. A*, *Gen.O.* Josef Harpe, telling him that he simply did not have enough forces to carry out this added responsibility. In particular, he brought to his commander's attention the enormous disparity in combat power between the departing *Wiking* and the *73. Inf.Div.*, which had only recently been rebuilt following its total collapse on 12 September 1944 during the second defensive battle of Warsaw.[9]

In the same evening report, *Gen.d.Pz.Tr.* von Lüttwitz informed his army group commander that it was imperative to reinforce the weak *73. Inf.Div.* to the point where it would be able to successfully hold the new sector being vacated by the *Wiking* Division on its own, should the Soviet 47th Army launch a major attack, but that at the present time, his army had no assets of its own to spare. To do this, he felt, *H.Gr. A* would need to provide additional assets so von Lüttwitz could reinforce Schlieper's division with at least one *Heeres-Artillerie Abteilung*, a *Pionier* battalion, and an assault guns brigade with at least two batteries to compensate for the loss of the *Wiking* Division's *panzer* regiment.[10] Despite von Lüttwitz's pleas for additional forces, they fell on deaf ears, for Harpe had other defensive priorities that ranked higher than holding the Vistula–Narew triangle that demanded what few reserves his army group did possess. Ironically, less than a month later, Harpe was proven correct when the great Soviet winter offensive began, sweeping the forces of *H.Gr. Mitte* and the *9. Armee* from *H.Gr. A* before them and forcing the hasty abandonment of the Vistula–Narew triangle almost without a fight.

While the commander of *9. Armee* haggled with his army group commander for more forces, the transfer of *IV. SS-Pz.Korps* in the *2. Armee* area of operations continued apace. To enable the movement of the *IV. SS-Pz.Korps, Heeresgruppe Mitte* tasked *2. Armee* to arrange transportation using railheads in its own area of operations, which occupied the efforts of the staff officers responsible for arranging transportation for nearly a week. Hundreds of special rail cars for tanks, other armored vehicles, trucks, and troops had to be marshaled from all over eastern and southeastern Europe, involving nearly a hundred locomotives, but all were brought together in a remarkably short amount of time.

Within less than 30 hours of receipt of the initial order on the evening of 24 December 1944, the first trains carrying troops from the *Totenkopf* Division were already rolling towards Hungary; an amazing feat in itself.[11] Between 26 and 31 December, the corps' *Hauptquartier, SS-Nachr.Abt. 104*, other corps troops, and most of its two divisions entrained for Hungary. They used over 164 trains from as many as 50 different rail-loading sites in the *2. Armee Rückwärtiges Armeegebiet* (rear area).[12] To do this, they used nearly every possible rail yard or loading ramp in the cities of Modlin, Zichenau, Nasielsk, Plöhnen, Mielau, and Schröttersburg, as well as from many tiny rail sidings in numerous villages and towns located along the rail line.[13]

The new assignment came so suddenly and so unexpectedly that many members of the corps and its two divisions were left behind, or nearly so. *Hstuf.* Hans Flügel, who was at home in Germany on holiday leave, received a surreptitious telephone call—a gross violation of operational security considering the secrecy surrounding the transfer—informing him about the new mission. He hurriedly packed, said goodbye to his family, and departed the same day on a civilian passenger train to catch up with his battalion, *II. Abt./SS-Pz.Rgt. 5*, part of *K.Gr. Dorr*, before it departed for Hungary on the evening of 26 December.[14]

Late in the evening on 25 December, the first element of the *Totenkopf* Division, *SS-Pz.Aufkl.Abt. 3*, departed on its *Blitztransport* (express) journey to Hungary. The 700-kilometer roundabout trip took them through Bromberg, Posen, Breslau, and Vienna before finally arriving at the end of the line between Raab and Komorn (Komárom) on 28 December. Most of the troops traveled in unheated passenger cars, if they were lucky, or in freight cars, if they were not. At various whistle stops along the way, commanders would allow their troops to disembark, stretch their legs, and be served a hot meal by *Betreuungs* (troop welfare) units. If any of the passengers brought along tobacco or alcoholic beverages, both would be passed around to help relieve the cold and monotony of the nearly 48-hour journey. With the corps headquarters' departure, on that same day the *XLVI. Pz.Korps* assumed tactical control of the *Wiking* Division, as well as the responsibility for defending the Wet Triangle, at 8 a.m.[15] For three days at least, Ullrich's division would be once again under the command of von Lüttwitz's *9. Armee*.

Wednesday, 27 December was the last date that the *IV. SS-Pz.Korps* reported to the headquarters of *2. Armee.*[16] It was a cold and cloudy day, with temperatures hovering slightly below freezing, making life miserable for the men stationed at the various railheads loading vehicles and equipment. The corps *Führungsabteilung* hastily tied up loose ends and prepared to vacate the old fortress at Modlin. The corps communications link remained active until *Ogruf.* Gille was informed by *Gen.O.* Weiss that at one minute after midnight on 28 December, his corps would initially fall under the command authority of *H.Gr. Süd* until it reached its final destination.

The signalers then reeled in their cables, packed up their equipment, and headed for the rail station to join the rest of the *Hauptquartier*, where *Hstuf.* Zachmann, the headquarters commandant, was ensuring everyone was accounted for. *Kampfgruppe Dorr* from the *Wiking* Division, which had been serving as the corps reserve a few kilometers northwest of Modlin, began its own rail movement to Komorn that day. *Obersturmbannführer* Dorr's battlegroup consisted of his regimental headquarters and regimental companies of his *Germania* Regiment as well as its *I., II.,* and *III. Bataillone* and all operational *panzers* of SS-Pz.Rgt. 5. *Kampfgruppe Dorr* would be the first element of the *Wiking* Division committed to battle less than a week later.

The movement of corps troops was no small matter either. In addition to the *Hauptquartier* in Modlin, its supporting corps signals battalion, *SS-Korps-Nachr. Abt. 104*, its corps artillery headquarters, *SS-ARKO 104*, and antiaircraft battery, *SS-Flak Abt. 104*, as well as the corps' other *Korpstruppen*—SS-Werf.Abt. 504, SS-San. Abt. 504, SS-Feld-Laz. 504, and its supply and transport column, *SS-Kraftfahr-Kp. 104*—also had to pack up all of their vehicles and equipment and head to their designated railheads. Since the corps' *Quartiermeister* and *Adjutantur* staff sections were located in Plöhnen and not in Modlin, they would have to travel separately. All told, nearly 2,500 corps troops, with the *Führungsabteilung* (the operations and intelligence staffs) in the lead, made the same journey as the corps' two divisions, reaching the town of Acs, 10 kilometers southwest of Komorn, by 1 January 1945, where they unloaded.[17]

Upon arriving in Acs, the corps' signal battalion would immediately begin laying wire and locating the best locations in the town to position its array of radio antennae, while the corps adjutant, *Stubaf.* Schulze, worked alongside with the headquarters commandant, seeking out suitable living quarters, work areas for the staff and corps troops, and parking areas for their array of motor vehicles. Gille himself and his chief of staff, including several other officers and a small security detail in a second staff car, drove from Modlin to the headquarters of Balck's *6. Armee* at Martinsburg (modern-day Pannonhalma) on Christmas Day to be apprised on his corps' new mission, as well as to get a sense of the overall military situation.[18]

That same day, to mark the corps' departure, *Gen.O.* Reinhardt of *H.Gr. Mitte* issued a *Tagesbefehl* praising *Ogruf.* Gille and his two divisions for their performance while under his command:

Today, the *IV. SS-Pz.Korps* with the SS *Panzer* Divisions *Totenkopf* and *Wiking* depart from the sphere of command of Army Group Center. The two SS *Panzer* Divisions first came to the Army Group during the desperate hours marking the beginning of the summer of 1944 and through their exemplary bravery, displayed first on the battlefields at Grodno and Brest-Litowsk, and in early August—under the command of the glorious defender of Kowel … threw the Soviet summer offensive back from the gates of Warsaw in a victorious tank battle and erected an impenetrable wall to prevent the Red flood from breaking through … in the heavy defensive battles that followed between the Vistula and Bug [Rivers] the SS Corps displayed exemplary steadfastness and combat readiness and successfully threw back repeated assaults by an overwhelmingly superior enemy force, which then set the proper conditions for the establishment of a solid German defensive front on the southern flank of East Prussia. Since I must bid farewell to the *IV. SS-Pz.Korps* and its two brave SS *Panzer* Divisions today, I want to extend to them my personal gratitude and let them know of my genuine recognition of their magnificent feats of arms. May my best wishes accompany your leaders and troops towards their new and difficult assignment.

Signed, Reinhardt

Commander, Army Group Center
27 December 1944.[19]

That day also marked the moment when, at 10 p.m., the headquarters of the *XXVII. Armee-Korps* took over the sector north of the Narew previously held by *IV. SS-Pz. Korps*, when Gille's *Gefechtstand* began moving to Hungary (see Map 2).

Command and control of the *Heeres* divisions under its banner—the *35.* and *252. Inf.Div.* and the *542. V.G.D.*—now became the responsibility of this neighboring corps, which had to extend its own span of control significantly.[20] All of the *Heerestruppen* supporting Gille's corps remained behind with the *2. Armee*, including the heavy artillery battalions, rocket launcher brigade, engineer battalions and units responsible for rear area security. The *IV. SS-Pz.Korps* would be allotted new ones once it arrived in the *6. Armee* area of operations.

In addition to the changes already mentioned above, the regimental headquarters of *Gren.Rgt. 70* from the *73. Inf.Div.* arrived in Modlin that same day and assumed responsibility for commanding the forces deployed in the Wet Triangle, taking over from the regimental headquarters of the *Westland*, freeing up *Ostubaf.* Franz Hack and his staff to begin moving to the nearest railyard.[21] The *I. Btl./Westland, I. Btl./ SS-Pz.Gren.Rgt. Norge*, and *I. Btl./SS-Pz.Gren.Rgt. Danmark* had to temporarily remain in place, while they took direction from the commander of *Gren.Rgt. 70*. They would not have to wait long. At the same time, *I. Abt./SS-Pz.Art.Rgt. Wiking* was relieved by *II.Abt./Art.Rgt. 173, SS-Pz.Pi.Btl. 5* by *Pi.Btl. 173*, and *SS-Pz.Jg.Abt. 5* by *Pz.Jg.Abt. 173*. All of these units began moving according to plan to the nearest local railheads to start loading for movement to Hungary.

On 28 December, the first elements of the *IV. SS-Pz.Korps, Stubaf.* Pellin's *SS-Pz. Aufkl.Abt. 3*, begin arriving at the rail station in Raab (Györ), Hungary, where his men immediately started unloading their vehicles and equipment. This also marked the day when the main body of the *Hauptquartier* of the *IV. SS-Pz.Korps* arrived at the railroad yard in Acs, a town southwest of Komorn. On the same day in Poland,

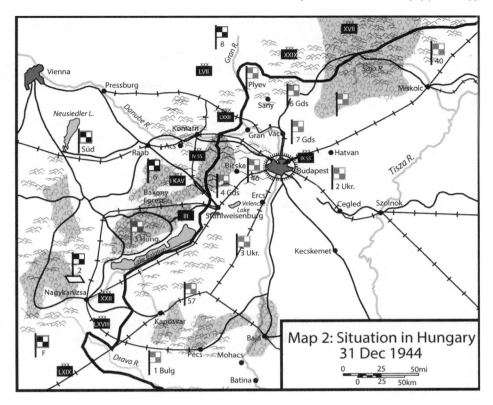

Map 2: Situation in Hungary
31 Dec 1944

the *73. Inf.Div.* formally took control of the sector formerly held by the *Wiking* Division. In the Wet Triangle, the *I. Btl./SS-Pz.Gren.Rgt. Danmark* was relieved in the front lines by *I.Btl./Gren.Rgt. 186* of the *73. Inf.Div.*[22] By this point, all but two battalions of the *Wiking* Division had handed over their positions to the incoming units from the *73. Inf.Div.*, thereby allowing these battalions to join the main body of the division in the rail movement over the next several days.

On 29 December, *Stubaf.* Vogt's *I. Btl./SS-Pz.Gren.Rgt. Norge* was finally relieved in the line by *II. Btl./Gren.Rgt. 186* and began marching to Modlin to board its awaiting train. His troops had been occupying defensive positions for over a month by this point, but had seen little combat except for intermittent shelling, sniper fire, and small-scale night raids by their opponents. *Füsilier Bataillon 173* began its relief of *Stubaf.* Nedderhof's *I. Btl./Westland* after midnight. By the following day, 30 December, the relief in place of *I. Btl./Westland* was complete, marking the point when the last of the *Wiking* Division's constituent elements were disengaged and loaded on trains for movement to Hungary.[23]

At the same time that *Ogruf.* Gille's *IV. SS-Pz.Korps* and his two divisions were moving towards their new area of operations, two other divisions from the *Heer* designated to join up with the corps were notified that they would also be shipped to Hungary. Each would depart from separate theaters of operation—the *96. Inf. Div.* from *H.Gr. A* near Tarnow in the Beskids Mountains and the *711. Inf.Div.* from *H.Gr. B* reserve in Holland, where it had recently undergone reconstitution to bring it back up to its authorized strength. The *96. Inf.Div.* would unload at Komorn, west of the confluence of the Gran (Hron) and Danube Rivers, and move into a forward assembly area encompassing the towns of Búc, Karva, and Mužla. The *711. Inf.Div.* would do the same at various railroad stations in the Raab and Komorn area before moving to its forward assembly area near Tokod. Neither division had ever worked before under Gille's command, but both formations would enjoy good working relationships with the corps and were a welcome addition to the *IV. SS-Pz.Korps* order of battle, bringing badly needed foot soldiers to the upcoming operation.

When Gille's headquarters received the unexpected news of the transfer of *IV. SS-Pz.Korps* to Hungary, an equally important development was unfolding that would also have a decisive impact on the corps' future. Since *Gen.Oberst* Fretter-Pico, the hapless commander of *6. Armee*, had been sacked on 22 December for his alleged bungling of Operation *Spätlese*, he would have to be replaced immediately by someone Hitler trusted who could lead the Budapest relief operation, which was to be primarily a *6. Armee* mission. That someone was the aforementioned *Gen.d.Pz. Tr.* Hermann Balck. For the next four months, the fates of Gille, his corps, and that of Balck would be intertwined, for better or worse. Before proceeding though, a brief background on the career of the brilliant and controversial Balck is in order.

Born on 7 December 1893 in Danzig, Balck came from a distinguished military family, his father being *Gen.Lt.* William Balck, a noted tactician of the *Kaiserheer*. After attending the military academy in Hannover, he served as an infantry officer in World War I, fighting on the Eastern, Western, Italian and Balkan fronts. Highly decorated, he was wounded in action six times and by the war's end had been promoted to *Leutnant*. One of the few officers selected to form the new *Reichswehr* in 1920, Balck served primarily in cavalry and mountain infantry units, rising from platoon leader to battalion commander. By 1933 a member of Hitler's new *Wehrmacht*, Balck had risen to the rank of *Oberstleutnant* by 1938, based on his outstanding performance in helping to develop *panzer* troop doctrine and tactics.

From that point on, his career progressed rapidly. While commanding a motorized infantry regiment of the *1. Pz.Div.*, he led it with distinction throughout the Battle of France in 1940 and was promoted to *Oberst* later that year. From 1941–44, he commanded in succession *Pz.Brig. 2, 11. Pz.Div., Pz.Gren.Div. Grossdeutschland, XIV. Pz.Korps, XLVIII. Pz.Korps,* and *4. Pz.Armee* during fighting in Greece, the Soviet Union, Italy and Poland. During this same period, he progressed in rank from *Oberst* to *General der Panzertruppe*, earning a reputation as a highly talented tactician and a strict taskmaster who insisted that his orders be carried out swiftly and faithfully.

Frequently hailed as a bold and decisive leader, he had an ego to match his larger-than-life reputation among his fellow officers. In many ways similar to *G.F.M.* Walter Model, Balck was a blunt and outspoken personality, and like Model was someone not to be trifled with, though he did have a sense of humor that manifested itself in crisis situations. According to one of his biographers, by late 1944 he had become one of the very few generals whom Hitler could trust, and was rewarded accordingly, being one of only 27 German soldiers awarded the prestigious Knight's Cross with Oak Leaves, Swords and Diamonds by the *Führer* himself on 31 August 1944.[24]

On 20 September 1944, he was transferred from the Eastern Front to command *H.Gr. G*, responsible for defending Alsace-Lorraine against the approaching Franco-American forces. When he relieved *Gen.O.* Johannes Blaskowitz of command, he found a front line in disarray and its divisions, corps, and armies reeling from defeat. Arriving at the front after the *5. Pz.Armee's* poorly planned and hastily assembled counteroffensive in Lorraine was already well underway, his forces were able to achieve little against well-led American troops and were compelled to retreat after the forces of *Gen.d.Pz.Tr.* Hasso von Manteuffel's *panzer* brigades were defeated at Arracourt by the U.S. 4th Armored Division.

Cobbling together an effective defense using odds and ends of various shattered German units, he was able to slow down and then stop the American advance at Metz by mid-November 1944, just as preparations for *H.Gr. B's* Ardennes offensive unfolded on his army group's right flank. By mid-December, although he had been forced to give up Strasbourg, he was satisfied that his troops had done everything possible to stop the Allies, though his reputation was tarnished somewhat when he ordered the summary execution of an artillery officer for being drunk and absent from his unit in the midst of a decisive battle. He also had bitter disagreements with *G.F.M.* Gerd von Rundstedt, the *Oberbefehlshaber West* (Commander in Chief, Western Front), whom Balck thought to be "militarily still stuck in World War I," having not "developed in his thinking" about operational matters since the previous conflict.[25] Improvidently, Balck had mentioned this as well as other matters concerning the leadership on the Western Front in a rather critical 10 October 1944 letter to *Gen.O.* Jodl, which later came to Hitler's attention.[26]

The manner in which Balck was chosen to take command of *6. Armee* is even today still a matter of some controversy. According to his former chief of staff, *Gen.Maj.* Friedrich W. von Mellenthin, Balck had been outmaneuvered by Heinrich Himmler, who had been conducting a series of behind-the-scenes palace intrigues against the *H.Gr. G* commander in a gambit to take control of the army group himself.[27] Mellenthin further speculated that abandoning Strasbourg without permission may also have had something to do with Balck's relief of command, though there is no evidence to support this claim. However, Balck had previously ignored Hitler's explicit orders to defend the city, the *Führer* admonishing him afterwards in a letter that stated. "I thank you for [your] excellent leadership. I expect, however, that you will continue to do everything possible to hold the current line." Guderian is mute in his own memoirs on the topic, although he and Balck had served together once before as lieutenants in the same regiment at Goslar and knew each other well.[28]

Balck himself wrote that he was completely surprised when he received the message from *OKH* relieving him of command on the evening of 23 December 1944, when he had just sat down for dinner. In addition to the unwelcome news, the message also ordered him to report immediately to *OKH* headquarters in Zossen for a new assignment. Like Mellenthin, Balck believed that Himmler held an animus towards him, allegedly due to him being "too tough on his SS divisions," but felt that this was not sufficient reason for his removal.[29] Upon reflection years later, Balck wrote that Hitler "wanted someone from the [Western Front] who would follow his orders, and he preferred to use me again in the East," where there was ample opportunity to once more apply his skills as a tactician.[30] Balck was replaced as commander of *H.Gr. G* a few days later by *Obst.Gruf.* Paul Hausser, one of the Himmler's most capable SS generals. Although Balck does not mention this in his memoirs, it must have rankled when he learned a few days later of Hausser's appointment.

Although he initially viewed this transfer from command of a *Heeresgruppe* to that of an *Armeegruppe* (*A.Gr.*, an army group-sized task force, composed of German and Hungarian field armies, but led by a German officer) as a demotion, this was not the case; by December 1944, Hitler was beginning to run out of general officers qualified for high-level positions who were both politically reliable and able to get things done. Balck, who like Gille was no Nazi, met both requirements. He certainly possessed the skills needed to master the crisis unfolding in Hungary, and would follow orders to the utmost of his ability; not because he was an adherent of National Socialism, but because he was a professional soldier. If anyone could relieve Budapest and reestablish the old front line, it was Balck.

After a nighttime flight across Germany, Balck was ushered in at 3 a.m. on 24 December to see Guderian at *OKH* headquarters in Zossen, south of Berlin. There, Guderian told Balck that he would take over command of *6. Armee* from Fretter-Pico that same day and would lead the effort to relieve Budapest with his new command, now renamed *A.Gr. Balck/6. Armee*.[31] Incidentally, on the same morning that Balck learned that he would assume command of *A.Gr. Fretter-Pico/6. Armee*, Fretter-Pico himself was notified that he was to be relieved of command by Balck the following day, and sent out a message to his staff and troops accordingly, urging them to support their incoming commander as much as they had supported him.[32]

Guderian then briefed him on the overall situation in Hungary, and what Balck heard did not sound promising, especially when he learned that the *Panzergrenadier* regiments and division staffs from three of the *panzer* divisions in *III. Pz.Korps* (the *3., 6.,* and *8. Pz.Div.*) had been separated from their armored elements on 19 December and sent to assist *LVII. Pz.Korps* north of the Danube.[33] The elements remaining under *III. Pz.Korps* control that participated in *Spätlese* included each division's *panzer* regiment, their *SPW*-mounted *Panzergrenadier* battalion, self-propelled artillery battalion, and an *SPW*-mounted *Panzerpionier Kompanie.* "This must have been done by some real armor expert," he sarcastically remarked to Guderian, not suspecting that it was the chief of the general staff of the *OKH* himself who had issued the order.[34]

Balck later wrote that it was no mystery why Operation *Spätlese* had failed; to him, modern warfare was always an all-arms proposition, with success demanding the integration of the capabilities of each branch of service (infantry, armor, artillery, engineers, etc.) into a seamless whole. Balck immediately recognized that the failure of *Spätlese* was primarily due to the lack of supporting infantry. German armor doctrine, which Balck helped write, recognized that *panzers* needed to work in close cooperation with *Panzergrenadier* regiments, which habitually protected tanks against close-in enemy infantry and antitank weapons. This truth had been borne out in countless instances in all of the Third Reich's major combat operations involving mechanized forces. After informing Balck that he would be getting the *IV. SS-Pz. Korps* within the next few days as a reinforcement, the situation briefing by Guderian concluded and Balck was then flown that same day to his new headquarters, located in the Hungarian town of Martinsberg (*Győrszentmárton*, now called Pannonhalma), 20 kilometers southeast of the city of Raab and approximately 50 kilometers from the nearest front line.

Upon arrival in Martinsberg during the afternoon of Sunday, 24 December, Balck discovered that his headquarters complex was located aboard a train that sat on a siding on the edge of the town's *Bahnhof* (railway station), on the town's western outskirts. Situated within 12 railcars, including both office and sleeping cars, most of his army's key staff elements were crammed together inside since the town itself offered little in the way of suitable buildings in which to operate. An old locomotive came by twice each day to provide steam heat, which either proved to be too hot or not hot enough to keep the staff warm during what was becoming a bitterly cold winter. On temporary loan from *H.Gr. Süd*, the train would prove to be a very convenient field headquarters throughout January 1945 until Balck was forced to send it back to Vienna to have it serviced, whereupon it was destroyed a few days later in an Allied air attack.[35]

One of the first staff officers he met from his new command was his chief of staff, *Gen.Maj.* Heinz Gaedke. Gaedke, a 39-year-old general staff officer from Guben, East Prussia, had been appointed to the position on 15 August 1944, arriving only several days prior to the destruction of the *6. Armee* during the Red Army's invasion of Rumania. Surviving this catastrophe, Gaedke was instrumental in rebuilding the army and managing its retreat and subsequent defense of eastern Hungary during the fall and early winter of 1944. As he stood before *Gen.d.Pz.Tr.* Balck, Gaedke's new commander gave him a looking over and later remarked in his memoirs, "The Knight's Cross that [Gaedke] had earned for the breakout from the Korsun–Cherkassy Pocket told me much about the man and his well-rounded, strong personality."[36]

The pair quickly formed a close bond, and Balck soon learned to trust his new chief of staff implicitly. For his part, Gaedke later remarked that their relationship evolved into like that of a father and son, in which the older Balck passed on his knowledge and experience to the younger officer in the limited amount of time they spent together.[37] As Gaedke later described it, a better commander and chief of staff arrangement could not be hoped for, a relationship that would stand the test of time until the war's end and afterwards.

One of Gaedke's first tasks was to brief Balck on the overall situation of *6. Armee*, as well as that of the neighboring *8. Armee* on its left flank and *2. Pz.Armee* on its right. As of 24 December, Budapest had yet to be completely surrounded, but it was evident that it would be within the next several days, and there was little that *6. Armee* could do to prevent this from happening. Additionally, the offensives by the Second and Third Ukrainian Fronts had not yet run their course, having only been delayed—at least *Unternehmen Spätlese* had done that.

One of the first orders Balck issued was to reassemble the *panzer* divisions that had been split up between their armored elements taking part in *Spätlese* and the motorized elements fighting north of the Danube under the command of *Gen.d.Pz.Tr.* Friedrich Kirschner's *LVII. Pz.Korps*. When Gaedke told him that this had been done on express orders of the *OKH* headquarters, Balck characteristically replied that he wanted it done anyway, and would suffer the consequences later if it did not work out. The order was immediately issued and the subject was not brought up again, though it took over a week for it to be carried out since the departing *panzer* divisions had to cross the Danube and be replaced by other units.[38]

As the situation briefing continued, the new army commander quickly realized that it was pointless to leave the *IX. SS-Geb.Korps* and its German and Hungarian garrison in Budapest—the city would be impossible to defend and its troops would soon be lost if they tried to hold out. Gaedke also informed him that Balck's new command lacked sufficient troops to hold its current line, let alone relieve Budapest, and that its partner Hungarian *3. Armee*—now subordinated to his command—could not be relied upon; for his part, Balck felt it was too weak and its men unmotivated to even defend their own country (this was not strictly true).

When Balck gave his chief of staff the news that *6. Armee* would soon be reinforced by Gille's *IV. SS-Pz.Korps*, he later wrote that Gaedke turned pale. When queried by his surprised commander, Gaedke, after regaining his composure, replied that he knew Gille from the time of the Cherkassy encirclement the year before, where he had been serving as the chief of staff with the rank of *Oberst* in *Gen.d.Art.* Wilhelm Stemmermann's *XI. Armee-Korps*, while Gille was commanding the *Wiking* Division. He warned Balck that he should exercise caution when dealing with Gille.[39]

When asked to explain, Gaedke described Gille as being a headstrong individual who often ignored orders, most specifically when he defied a direct order from Stemmermann on one occasion. This concerned the latter's directive to Gille to take several hundred men from his division's *Trosseinheiten* (supply troops), burn their excess vehicles, and convert them into infantry in order to bolster the strength of his two *Panzergrenadier* regiments immediately prior to the breakout from the pocket on 16 February 1944. Gille refused, stating that he wanted to preserve as many of his vehicles as possible for future operations.

Rebuffed, Stemmermann verbally threatened Gille on the spot with a *Standgericht* (summary court-martial) and would have him shot for disobedience. Gaedke, by his account, immediately took him aside and talked Stemmermann out of this idea, telling him that it would make no sense to have a commander shot on the eve of the breakout, especially one who had his soldiers' utter loyalty.[40] It was better to let him die leading his troops in combat during the breakout, Gaedke advised. As it turned out, most of the *Wiking* Division's vehicles had to be left behind or destroyed anyway, since most of them became mired in the rough terrain in the escape corridor between Shanderovka and Hill 239 and had to be blown up by their drivers, who then fled on foot.[41] Ironically, Stemmermann himself was killed while riding in an SS vehicle that he had commandeered after losing his horse while the breakout was still in progress.

Of course, Gille's adherents had their own recollection of Gaedke's conduct from that operation, as did other member of the *Wiking*'s staff. Allegedly, Stemmermann and Gaedke had seriously considered the Soviet commander's 8 February offer of surrender of all German forces trapped in the *Kessel* (pocket), an idea that Gille strongly remonstrated against. According to the *Wiking* Division's postwar history, "This intention of General Stemmermann was frustrated by the resolute attitude of *Gruppenführer* Gille and his commanders."[42] Another count against Gaedke was levied by Gille's *O5* at the time, *Ostuf.* Günther Jahnke, who spotted Gaedke riding on horseback on the opposite bank of the Gniloy Tikich creek in relative safety while the breakout was still in progress on 17 February. Supposedly tasked with helping Stemmermann lead the *Nachhut* (rear guard) during the breakout, Jahnke and other officers from the division staff sarcastically asked Gaedke why he was there ahead of the *Wiking* Division, instead of leading the troops from the *Nachhut* along with Stemmermann. This encounter immediately developed into an argument, and according to Jahnke, Gaedke could not answer their questions satisfactorily, leading them to believe that he had deserted his men.[43]

In his own autobiography, Gaedke does not mention this incident at all, only his joy at having escaped, nor did he include any mention of Stemmermann having entertained the thought of capitulation. Gaedke did recall the demoralized state of the commander of *Gruppe Stemmermann* on the eve of the breakout, though. He wrote that Stemmermann, towards the end of the encirclement—probably due to the physical stress and mental strain of the great responsibility he had to bear—had become a bitter complainer and pessimist, not at all like his previous professional, even-tempered persona.[44] Given the dire straits of the German forces trapped in the ever-shrinking pocket, such human behavior would have been altogether understandable in any commander; although Stemmermann had a reputation as a calm and collected leader in the days leading up to his death, he was not superhuman.

Gaedke's recollection of this experience, including Gille's behavior at Cherkassy, combined with Balck's existing mistrust and dislike of the SS, helped cement in the mind of the new *6. Armee* commander an impression that would negatively color all of his future relations with Gille and *IV. SS-Pz.Korps*, which would later have adverse implications during the Budapest relief operation.[45] As proof, in his memoir Balck regarded Gille, upon meeting him for the first time, as "a strong egocentric type who had no understanding of operational context and possibilities ... He was the type of *Waffen-SS* commander who as a matter of principle always resisted orders from any *Heer* officer," evidence that he and Gille did not hit if off very well when they first met.[46] As one historian has argued, perhaps the two men were too much alike to be compatible, since both had strong egos and were hard-driving, blunt-spoken commanders who were bound to clash at some point.[47]

After listening to Gaedke's summary, later that day Balck telephoned *Gen.Lt.* Walter Wenck, the head of the *Heeresführungsstab* (leadership staff) and Guderian's right-hand man at *OKH*. He described the situation he found in his army's area of operations, including that of Budapest, as "a mess."[48] Balck, echoing Wöhler, suggested two courses of action and urged Wenck to approve them immediately. The first was the recommendation that the 70,000 men about to be trapped inside the city be allowed to break out at once and link up with the rest of *6. Armee* west of Budapest, which would abandon the city to its fate but at least save its garrison. Once reincorporated into his army's order of battle, these men would then be used for a counteroffensive that would throw the Soviet forces back across the Danube. The other course of action was simply to abandon Pest, the half of the city that lies on the eastern bank of the Danube, and bring the troops there—who comprised the majority of Pfeffer-Wildenbruch's *IX. SS-Geb.Korps*—over the river to the Buda side of the city, where they would have a better chance of withstanding a siege.

That evening, as the forward elements of the Second Ukrainian Front began to complete their envelopment of Budapest from the north, Balck wrote in his journal the following assessment of the situation as of 24 December and his intentions for the next few days:

> The situation is hellish. Within the next 24 hours it will unfold as follows: The *III. Pz.Korps* will hold [its present position]. To the north in the Bakony Forest the enemy will infiltrate with strong infantry forces. With only *panzers* and no infantry, we will not be able to stop them. The enemy will encircle Budapest from the west, and that will threaten us with a new Stalingrad. It is very questionable if we can hold Budapest as a fortress, because we do not have enough

infantry there. The Russians [*sic*] can infiltrate into the sea of houses. The city of 800,000 is hungry and is getting restless. A *Putsch* by communist elements is possible at any time. North of the Danube [note: where his *LXII. Pz.Korps* was fighting] the correlation of forces will balance itself out. My decision: *IV. SS-Pz.Korps* with the *Wiking* and *Totenkopf* Divisions will advance to Budapest and hold the outer ring of the city. Meanwhile, one division in Budapest will be detached and sent toward the west.[49]

However, a plan was already being developed between the *OKH Führungsstab* and *H.Gr. Süd*, and it did not include any mention of giving up Budapest. Driven by Hitler's intention of retaining the capital of Hungary for political purposes, the plan was also influenced by his well-known predilection for never wanting to give up an inch of ground to the enemy and his already remarked-upon desire to protect the Hungarian oil fields. How this plan was developed and the ultimate role that the *IV. SS-Pz.Korps* would play in it would soon have fateful consequences.

Preparations for the Relief of Budapest—*Unternehmen Konrad* 28 December 1944–1 January 1945

The general outline of the plan to relieve Budapest began to take concrete form by 27 December 1944. It was finally issued to the three armies comprising *H. Gr. Süd* the following day, after *Gen.d. Pz. Tr.* Balck paid his first visit to *Gen.d.Inf.* Wöhler's headquarters. Located in the lavish Habsburg Esterháza palace near the town of Fertőd, a few dozen kilometers south of the Austrian border on the southern shore of the Neusiedlersee, the army group's headquarters was over 150 kilometers away from the front lines.[1] Here, Balck and his new chief of staff had learned that his *Armeegruppe* would be tasked with two separate but equally important missions. The first was the relief of Budapest, using the *IV. SS-Pz.Korps* as his main effort, a task which he already anticipated. The second was to reestablish the front along the Danube between Komorn and Budapest, including the portion of the *Margarethestellung* between Budapest and Stuhlweissenburg (Székesfehérvár) that had been overrun by Tolbukhin's Third Ukrainian Front since 20 December. This second task came somewhat as a surprise to Balck, who considered the forces insufficient to achieve this ambitious goal.

It is important to note that at no point was this operation ever considered by *H. Gr. Süd* and Guderian at *OKH* to be purely a rescue operation, *a la* the Cherkassy Pocket. No breakout and abandonment of Budapest was envisioned, and none were planned or authorized until the very end when it was far too late. Budapest would be merely relieved and its garrison reincorporated into a restored *Margarethestellung* main defense line between the Danube and Lake Velencze, a situation similar to what had occurred after the relief of Kovel on 5 April 1944. How this intent would soon be misinterpreted or misunderstood by the corps actually tasked with carrying out the operation a week later, depending on each commander's point of view, would soon cause a great deal of controversy and contribute to Balck's already established mistrust of Gille, as will be seen.

General der Infanterie Wöhler then tasked Balck that same day to develop a plan that would accomplish both objectives and to be prepared to initiate the attack on 31 December. Nor was *Festung* Budapest left out in the plan. *Gruppenführer* Pfeffer-Wildenbruch was ordered to hold the city with his *IX. SS-Geb.Korps* until relieved, using four German divisions (the *8.* and *22. SS-Kav.Div.*, *13. Pz.Div.*, and *Pz.Gren.Div. FHH*) and two Hungarian divisions (the 10th and 12th Infantry, plus remnants of two others), and to defend both banks of the Danube at all costs in conformance with the previously ordered *Führerbefehl.* The order made it clear that he was not to evacuate the eastern bank, including Pest, unless Wöhler himself gave him permission to do so.

Balck's two neighboring armies from *H.Gr. Süd—Gen.d.Pz.Tr.* Hans Kreysing's *8. Armee* located north of the Danube, where it was defending a line along the Gran River and Carpathian Mountains, and *Gen.d.Art.* Maximilian de Angelis's *2. Pz.Armee* located southwest of the *Plattensee* (Lake Balaton)—were both ordered to continue improving their current defensive positions and to be prepared to assist Balck at short notice if the situation warranted with a division-sized *Eingreifreserve* (reaction force).[2] The only details of the plan that the order did not yet specify were the origin and direction that Balck's relief attack would actually take. Normally, this was left up to the discretion of the actual commander on the ground, but since Hitler was personally overseeing this operation from the *Führerhauptquartier* in Ziegenberg, it would have to be written by Balck's staff, submitted to *H.Gr. Süd* and then approved by the supreme commander of the *OKW* and *OKH* (i.e. Hitler) himself.

In the final operational analysis carried out by the staffs concerned before their commanders could decide upon the actual direction of attack, four key factors predominated: terrain, distance, time, and fuel, along with, to a lesser extent, the enemy. It would take three days of back and forth between Balck, Wöhler, and Guderian's staffs before a decision regarding the attack's direction was finally reached. Because these factors would play such a key role in the upcoming operation, it is important at this point to examine each of them in turn.

For the *IV. SS-Pz.Korps* to get to Budapest, there were essentially two ground avenues of approach that amounted to separate courses of action, with the terrain posing advantages and disadvantages for the attacking force in either case. The route that offered the most promise was the southern approach, originating from the general area of Stuhlweissenburg between Lakes Balaton and Velencze. The attacking force would first strike southeast between the lakes and then conduct a wheeling movement to the left or northeast in the direction of Budapest, where the terrain was much more favorable for the employment of armor.

Here, the landscape was mostly flat, with few forested areas and a well-developed road network. It was also the longest route to the objective, approximately 110 kilometers by road, and there were numerous canals and streams running perpendicular to the direction of advance, so the seizure of bridges was a matter of concern. The attacking force would also have to punch through an area where the enemy was assessed to be the strongest (approximately three rifle corps and at least one mechanized corps), which would require more time to overcome initially, but once through, there were few Soviet reserves standing in the way until they got to the objective.

This course of action was dubbed the *Südlösung*, or southern solution, and was subsequently designated *Unternehmen Paula* (the letter "P" in the German phonetic alphabet signified the "P" in *Plattensee*). However, the disadvantages of this plan was that the *A. Gr. Balck* staff planners estimated that it would take more time to cover the distance to Budapest (up to five days) and would demand three times as much fuel as the other course of action, approximately 237,755 gallons or 900 cubic meters, to get the tanks and other vehicles to the objective. On 28 December, *H. Gr. Süd* only had half that amount available in its own stocks of gasoline, but expected to get more as it wrung out the last amount of fuel from the Hungarian reserves.[3]

Another disadvantage to consider was that the *IV. SS-Pz. Korps* and its two divisions were already being directed to the railheads in Komorn, Acs, and Raab, over 70 kilometers north of Stuhlweissenburg. Thus, it would take at least a day's march to move all of Gille's troops to the designated assembly areas for *Unternehmen Paula*, as well as several more days before both of his divisions could be completely formed up. This would also require more fuel. Although the lead elements of Gille's corps had already begun arriving as early as 28 December, its entire movement would not be complete until the first week of January 1945. Given that the situation in Budapest was already deteriorating more quickly than anticipated, this course of action might take too long, though both Wöhler and Balck believed it was a gamble worth taking. Based on these calculations, the earliest date that *Paula* could realistically be attempted was 3 January.

The other course of action, dubbed the *Nordlösung* (northern solution)— soon renamed *Unternehmen Konrad* ("K" for Komorn, its point of origin)—would be launched from the area between the city of Komorn and Tata. The attacking force, with its left flank anchored on the southern bank of the Danube offering some protection against attacks from the north, would advance towards Budapest in a southeasterly direction. This plan had advantages too. In addition to being the shorter route to the outer ring of the German defenses at Budapest, approximately 65 kilometers by road, the staffs estimated that it would require less than half of the fuel that the *Südlösung* would require. Since the troops participating in the relief effort would begin their attack directly from the existing front lines defended by *III. Pz. Korps*, *Konrad* could begin two or three days earlier than *Paula*, and if all went according to plan, the northern option would reach Budapest earlier than the most optimistic estimates for the southern option.[4]

Another advantage of this plan was that the *H. Gr. Süd Ic* staff had determined that the area east of Komorn, recently seized by the Red Army, was lightly defended by three weakened rifle divisions of Maj.Gen. Alexander Utvenko's XXXI Guards Rifle Corps of Gen. G. F. Zakharov's 4th Guards Army (the 80th, 34th, and 4th

Guards Rifle Divisions), backed up by a depleted armored brigade (the 170th) of Maj.Gen. P. D. Govorunenko's XVIII Tank Corps, estimated at only 27 tanks, and 15 SU-85 self-propelled guns from the 1438th Artillery Regiment.[5] German intelligence reports indicated that Utvenko's corps had not yet had enough time to build up a solid defense line, establish *Pakfronts* (integrated antitank defenses), or bring up all of its artillery. Soviet reserves were located south and east of the Lake Velencze, where the Third Ukrainian Front commander anticipated any German relief attack would originate.

There were significant disadvantages to this option though, which caused *A.Gr. Balck's* staff to favor the *Südlösung* initially. The first was that the attacking force in the north would have to penetrate Soviet defenses arrayed in the Vértes and Gerecse Mountains, terrain that was not favorable for the employment of tanks and would require more infantry to protect them. Steep defiles and inclines, mountain peaks (some as high as 700–800 meters above sea level), narrow roads, and extensive forests posed additional challenges. The rugged terrain would also complicate use of radio communications. The road network was not as developed as it was in the south, with many of the routes consisting of only dirt or graveled roads.[6] A determined enemy force could easily delay the advance if not overcome quickly.

Once Gille's force had broken through this natural barrier, it would still have to negotiate a portion of the Pilis Mountains west and northwest of Budapest, but German intelligence assessments indicated that the Third Ukrainian Front would have few forces left to stop any determined attack, unless the city's outer encirclement ring held by the 46th Army of the Second Ukrainian Front was redirected to block Gille. One saving grace offered by the terrain was the paved highway that ran parallel to the southern bank of the Danube. If the Germans could secure this roadway, it would greatly speed up the main attack.[7]

Based on this mission analysis, on 29 December Balck's chief of staff recommended the approval of the *Südlösung* (*Unternehmen Paula*) to his counterpart at *H.Gr. Süd*, *Gen.Lt.* Helmuth von Grolman. Though it would take a few days longer to assemble the forces, more fuel to cover the extra distance, and take more time to accomplish, both Gaedke and his commander felt that it still offered the greatest chances of success. *Gen.d.Inf.* Wöhler agreed, and von Grolman submitted the conceptual plan to *OKH* for approval.[8] That evening, von Grolman spoke personally with Guderian, who himself was of a mixed mind about there being any significant differences between either plan. For his part, von Grolman recommended the northern attack, despite Wöhler and Balck having preferred the southern attack. After a lengthy discussion, Guderian concluded that the odds were slightly better if the attack from the south was selected, and called von Grolman back at 10:40 p.m. that night to tell him to proceed with *Paula*.[9]

Surprisingly enough, that did not settle the issue. *Generalleutnant* Wenck of the *OKH Führungsstab*, Guderian's chief of operations, also preferred the northern attack route. Truly, *OKH* faced a dilemma—"If we attack from the south, a greater success could be achieved, but it is more secure if we attack from the north."[10] But before making a final decision, which would require Hitler's final approval, Wenck flew to *H.Gr. Süd* headquarters the following day, 30 December, to meet with Wöhler, von Grolman, Balck, and Gaedke and to hear their arguments for either course of action. After listening to the advantages and disadvantages of *Paula* and *Konrad* offered by von Grolman, Wenck gave his preliminary approval to the *Konrad* plan, and directed it to begin no later than 7:30 p.m. on 1 January 1945.

His reasoning was persuasive, for three reasons—"time was of the essence; the defensive forces in Budapest were nearing the end of their capabilities to resist; and the shorter distance to the operational objective had to be the determining factor."[11] *Heeresgruppe Süd* confirmed this decision and communicated it to *A.Gr. Balck/6. Armee* that evening.[12] *Generaloberst* Guderian's ambivalence has already been noted—he was far more concerned about the impending Soviet offensive in Poland than what he regarded as a sideshow in Hungary.

The commanders tasked with carrying out the mission still harbored doubts. Wöhler himself was skeptical and worried that all of Gille's corps would not arrive in time, that the necessary fuel and ammunition would be equally as late, and that the Soviet commanders would move first, especially against his old *8. Armee* arrayed north of the Danube.[13] He was not alone. In his own memoirs, Guderian later wrote, "Hitler expected much from this attack. I was skeptical since very little time had been allowed for its preparation and neither the troops nor their commanders possessed the same [aggressiveness] as in the old days."[14] After the war, Balck wrote that although he preferred the *Südlösung*, he thought neither course of action stood much chance of success because the correlation of forces—i.e., the force ratios—were decidedly not in his army's favor.[15] At the time, however, he did not express such doubts.

For the operation, Balck's *Armeegruppe* would have six *panzer* divisions (including the two divisions of the *IV. SS-Pz.Korps*), one *Panzergrenadier* division-equivalent (*Div.Gr. Pape*), one division-sized cavalry brigade (the *4. Kav.Brig.*), and four infantry divisions (including two from the Hungarian Army). Although he also had four other Hungarian divisions under his control, he entirely discounted their capabilities, except for *Gen.Maj.* Zoltán Szügyi's *Szent László* Division, a recently formed infantry division that Balck rated as excellent. To relieve Budapest, his troops would have to fight their way through an estimated 38 Soviet rifle divisions, nine tank or mechanized corps, one fortified area (a division-sized static defense organization unique to the Red Army), and associated supporting arms, including artillery, antitank, antiaircraft, and rocket launcher units (see Map 3).[16]

This estimate included the troops from the 46th Army manning the inner and outer encirclement rings around Budapest. Of course, most of these units were probably at half-strength themselves since they had been fighting at the end of a

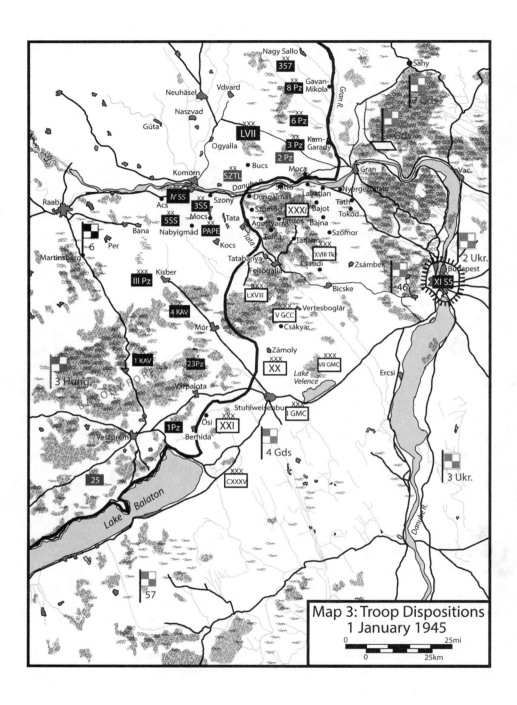

Map 3: Troop Dispositions 1 January 1945

long supply line since August 1944, and were just as exhausted as the Germans. Still, they outnumbered Balck's forces by a factor of three to one. In addition, the 4th Guards Army still had portions of one mechanized corps and one rifle division in reserve.[17] As for the four German and two Hungarian divisions trapped in Budapest, Balck did not factor them into his calculations at all, since they had been ordered to defend the *Festung* and were only useful for tying down Soviet forces that could have been employed elsewhere. Should the relief force get close enough to the outer defensive ring, *IX. SS-Geb.Korps* might be able to launch a supporting attack from the inside, but that would be the most it was capable of doing. The longer the relief operation took, the weaker the encircled forces would become, so it was increasingly doubtful that they could do even that.

Throughout the planning process, the staff planners recognized that logistics would determine the success or failure of the operation, just as it had for the Ardennes offensive, which by that time was floundering around Bastogne. Originally, the start date had been set as 31 December, but late delivery of fuel and ammunition needed by the attacking forces had forced the planners to move it to the following day. Of the 403,655 gallons (1,528 cubic meters) of fuel required, only enough had been delivered (211,338 gallons, or 800 cubic meters) by 30 December to enable the main effort (Gille's corps) to be able to advance approximately 60 kilometers. That would be sufficient for the initial phase, and subsequent delivery of the remaining fuel would provide enough to carry it all the way to Budapest, if everything worked out as planned.[18]

The critical decision of where the attack to relieve Budapest would originate and what direction it would follow having been made, the staffs of the attacking corps then had one day to write their own final version of the plan, which would have to be submitted to Balck for his approval the following day, 31 December. Once the plan had his approval, the subordinate divisions would then have less than a day to put the final touches to their own plans.

The general outline of the *A.Gr. Balck/6. Armee* concept of operations came as no surprise to the corps and divisions commanders and their own staffs, since they had been conducting concurrent planning of their own since 28 December after receiving the original warning order from *H.Gr. Süd*. The broad outline of the plan, as issued by *H.Gr. Süd* on 31 December, read as follows:

> It is important to cross the Vértes Mountains at the quickest pace possible, on a wide front line and as unexpectedly as could be; the Vértes Mountains will be a great hindrance to the armored fighting vehicles, so it is necessary to advance forward to the south and south-east in order cut off as much of the enemy forces from their supplies and destroy them as soon as possible. With the deployment of the *96. Infanterie-Division*, the later arriving units that are to be brought forward by motor-vehicle transport and with other infantry forces they will aid the quick crossing of the mountains by the *SS-Panzer* divisions in order to exploit the moment of surprise and retain the combat power of the *SS-Panzergrenadiers* without weakening them before the *panzer* divisions are deployed.[19]

In general, the *A. Gr. Balck/6. Armee* individual corps tasks as described in the army's operations plan were as follows. In the center, the main effort, involving Gille's *IV. SS-Pz.Korps*, would attack in an easterly direction from the Komorn area, initially with two divisions (the *3.* and *5. SS-Pz.Div.*). The attack would be supported on the left by a river crossing operation conducted by the *96. Inf.Div.*, which would establish three bridgeheads across the Danube behind Soviet lines. In addition to encircling enemy forces directly in front of the *Totenkopf* Division, this attack would also free up the paved highway running southeast along the bank of the Danube for exploitation by the armor. Upon arrival, the *711. Inf.Div.* would pass through the *96. Inf.Div.* and conduct its own attack to seize the city of Gran on the southern bank of the Danube.

Once both *panzer* divisions had penetrated the enemy's front line in the Gerecse and Vértes Mountains, they would be joined on the right flank by *Div. Gr. Pape* from *Korpsgruppe Breith* and all three divisions would execute a turning movement *en echelon* to the right, changing their direction of march from the east to the southeast, and strike towards Budapest as rapidly as possible through the Pilis Mountains, not halting until they reached the western outskirts of the city's main defense line.[20]

To the right of *IV. SS-Pz.Korps*, *Korpsgruppe Breith* (*Gen.d.Pz.Tr.* Hermann Breith's *III. Pz.Korps*, *I. Kav.Korps*, and the *II. ung.Armee-Korps*) would support Gille's attack using *Div. Gr. Pape*, which would be tactically subordinated for a limited time to the *IV. SS-Pz.Korps*. This division-sized formation, which had no fixed organization structure, would initially carry out a supporting attack along the line Tatabanya–Felsőgalla using *K.Gr. Philipp* (from *6. Pz.Div.*) and *K.Gr. Knoop* (from *8. Pz.Div.*).[21] Strong in armor, this force lacked sufficient infantry of its own to provide adequate support for its tanks. This attack, designed to protect the right flank of *IV. SS-Pz.Korps*, would be joined after 5 January by the rest of the *6. Pz.Div.*

Positioned to the south of *IV. SS-Pz.Korps* was the rest of Breith's *Korpsgruppe*, which included *Gen.d.Kav.* Gustav Hartenek's *I. Kav.Korps* with two *panzer* divisions (*3.* and *23. Pz.Div.*) and the *4. Kav.Brig.*, sandwiched between Breith's *1. Pz.Div.* and *Gruppe Pape*. This cavalry corps, subordinated to Breith's *Korpsgruppe* for the operation, would continue its defense of the area between Sárkeresztes and Mór, while operating in conjunction with the *1. Pz.Div.* The latter division would carry out a large-scale diversionary attack towards Ösi between Lakes Balaton and Velencze to draw the attention of the commander of the 4th Guards Army.

The *1. Pz.Div.*, commanded by *Gen.Maj.* Eberhard Thünert, had been involved in heavy fighting on the far right flank of *III. Pz.Korps* and to the right of *I. Kav. Korps* for the past 11 days. It was tasked with carrying out *Unternehmen Konrad's* secondary effort, a diversionary attack towards the town of Ösi, generally orienting towards the tactically and operationally significant city of Stuhlweissenburg. This movement was designed to make it appear to the Soviet chain of command that the relief of Budapest would be coming from the southwest.[22] Slated to occur on

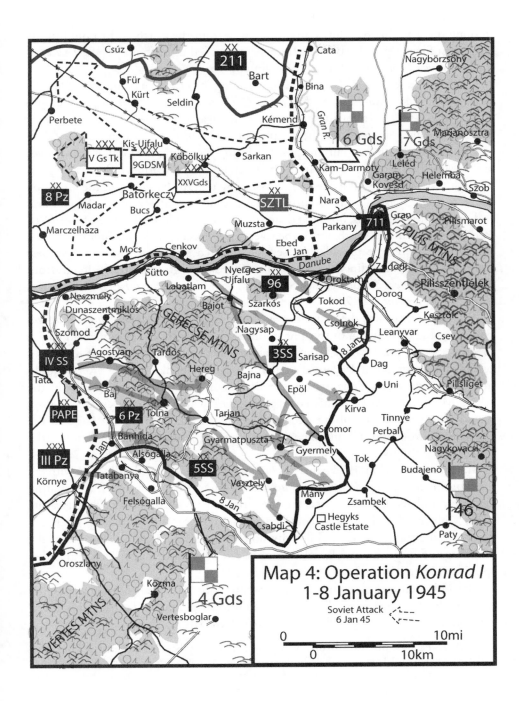

Map 4: Operation *Konrad I*
1-8 January 1945

Soviet Attack
6 Jan 45

0   10mi
0   10km

the evening of 31 December, the diversionary attack by *1. Pz.Div.* was intended to draw the 4th Guards Army's attention away from the north and to bind up its reserves sufficiently to keep them from being moved against the *IV. SS-Pz.Korps*, the offensive's *Schwerpunkt* (point of main effort).

On the left of *IV. SS-Pz.Korps*, positioned along the northern bank of the Danube in Czechoslovakia, *Korpsgruppe Kirschner* (*LVII. Pz.Korps*)—consisting of the bulk of *6.* and *8. Pz.Div.* (minus their armor, which was with *Div.Gr. Pape*), the *211. V.G.D.*, a *Kampfgruppe* from the decimated *357. Inf.Div.*, and the *Szent László* Division—would hold its current position facing east along the Gran (Hron) River and the northern bank of the Danube between Gran and Kormorn. It was assigned the task of supporting both the river crossing by the *96. Inf.Div.* and the attack by the *Totenkopf* Division with its corps artillery. Once the attack by *IV. SS-Pz.Korps* had made initial progress, both the *6.* and *8. Pz.Div.* would be detached from *LVII. Pz.Korps* and brought south across the river to reinforce Gille's and Breith's attacks. Air support would be provided by several hundred aircraft of the *I. Fliegerkorps* from *Luftflotte 4*, including *Focke-Wulf Fw-190 F* and *G* ground-attack aircraft from *Schlachtgeschwader* (Ground Attack Squadron) *4* and *Henschel Hs-129 B* tank-busters from *Schlachtgeschwader 9.*[23]

This, in general, was the plan of operations for Phase I of *Unternehmen Konrad*. Following the completion of this phase, once the attack by Gille's corps had begun to draw Soviet forces away from the approaches to Budapest, Phase II would commence on or about 14 January, in which the left flank of *III. Pz.Korps* would initiate its own attack designed to clear the enemy from the southern area of the Vértes Mountains between this corps and Gille's, while Harteneck's *I. Kav.Korps* would retake Stuhlweissenburg and advance in tandem with *III. Pz.Korps* to the Danube, destroying or forcing the withdrawal of the Third Ukrainian Front to the other side of the river.

The operation, echoing elements of *Unternehmen Paula*, would culminate with the reestablishment of the *Margarethestellung*, including a solid front line incorporating Budapest and its garrison.[24] Because the situation in Budapest was deteriorating daily, Wöhler ordered Balck to commence his attack on the evening of 1 January before all the trains carrying Gille's divisions had arrived, acknowledging that the advantage of surprise outweighed that of attacking with complete units, and that speed was better than overwhelming numbers.

On 30 December, as the units of the various corps prepared for their upcoming mission, Balck's chief of staff gave Gille additional guidance regarding his corps' mission in a telex message delivered via *Hellschreiber*:

> *IV. SS-Pz.Korps* will attack to destroy the enemy in the area between Budapest and the Vértes Mountains on 1 January 1945. In furtherance of this, at 5:30 p.m. the *96. Inf.Div.* will conduct a preliminary attack that will consist of a surprise river crossing of the Danube between Duna Mocs and Nyerges Ujfalu. A special assault group [from this division] will then pass through

Nyerges Ujfalu as rapidly as possible to the reach the road intersection at Tat [Táth] in order to block enemy forces approaching to the west from the direction of Gran.[25]

This last-minute clarification had become necessary because Balck had initially directed Gille to use a regiment from the *Totenkopf* Division to conduct the river-crossing operation, but had been overruled by Wöhler himself, who insisted upon keeping Gille's two *panzer* divisions focused on the primary objective. As events were soon to prove, this was a fortuitous decision.

As previously discussed, Gille had the aforementioned four divisions assigned or attached to carry out this operation. Before delving into the mission of each individual division in his corps, a brief overview of the condition of each of them is in order. It must first be noted that *IV. SS-Pz.Korps* had been occupying a static defensive position in Poland since the end of October 1944, and with the exception of the *Totenkopf* Division, which had been pulled out and sent into a reserve position behind the lines at the end of the first week of December, the rest of the corps' units had been employed continuously in the front lines of *Festung Modlin*. There had been little opportunity for units to train or conduct any large-scale maneuvers, unlike most *panzer* corps of the *Heer* on the Eastern Front that had been designated as a reserve. The corps and its two constituent divisions had also arrived with approximately only half of their normal establishment of rations, fuel, and ammunition, which would have to be made good as soon as possible by *A.Gr. Balck*.

The composition of the corps headquarters and corps troops had changed little since their establishment during the late spring of 1944, with the exception of the addition of *SS-Werf.Abt. 504* in September. The corps' newly established heavy artillery battalion, *s.SS-Art.Abt. 504*, was still undergoing the final stages of instruction at the SS training area in Bohemia and Moravia, and would not arrive until 8 February 1945 at the earliest. Also missing was the corps' dedicated artillery observation battalion, *SS-Beob.Abt. 504*, which also would not finally join the *IV. SS-Pz.Korps* until early February.

The lack of these two critical assets meant that *A.Gr. Balck/6. Armee* would have to provide them from its own pool of *Heerestruppen* per the existing doctrinal practice, just as the *9.* and *2. Armee* had been required to do during the defense of Warsaw. To address this shortfall, Balck's chief of staff approved the attachment of *III.* and *V. Abt./Volks-Art.Korps 403*, *Volks-Werf.Brig. 17*, and *lei.Beob.Abt. 32*, giving the *SS-ARKO 504* two heavy artillery battalions, an observation battalion, and two additional rocket-launcher regiments, not including the artillery regiments in each of its divisions. This impressive amount of firepower was further increased by the attachment of *Sturmpanzer Abteilung (Stu.Pz.Abt.) 219*, equipped with up to 42 *Sd.Kfz. 166 Sturmpanzer IV Brummbär* ("Grizzly Bears"), a heavily armored assault vehicle mounting a 15cm howitzer in its turretless chassis. The corps was also augmented by the attachment of *Heeres-Pi.Btl. 751*, which could clear obstacles and minefields as well as carry out temporary repairs of roads and bridges.

In regards to both the *Totenkopf* and *Wiking* Divisions, their leadership, material readiness, and personnel status had changed little since departing the Modlin area, as described in the previous chapter. At nearly full strength in personnel, their greatest limiting factor was the already mentioned shortage of *panzers*, trucks, and machine guns. However, the amount of combat power they could initially bring to bear depended on the *Reichsbahn*, which had still not managed to transport all of either divisions' troops or equipment to the Komorn–Raab area by the time their role in *Konrad* was scheduled to begin at 7:30 p.m. on 1 January.

On the eve of the attack, only 66 percent of the *Totenkopf* Division had arrived, while just 32 percent of the *Wiking* Division had.[26] Fortunately, the armored elements had been loaded first, ensuring that they would be the first units to arrive in Hungary. This meant that the *Totenkopf*'s SS-Pz.Rgt. 3 would launch its attack with all of its 101 operational tanks, tank destroyers, and assault guns, while the *Wiking*'s SS-Pz.Rgt. 5 would have to begin its own with only 51.[27] To compensate for the absence of the bulk of the *Wiking* Division's artillery regiment to support the first day of the attack, *I. Abt./Pz.Art.Rgt. 80* from *8. Pz.Div.* and *II. Abt./Heeres-Art. Brig. 959* would be temporarily attached to Ullrich's division until all of *Ostubaf.* Hans Bünning's SS-Pz.Art.Rgt. 5 had arrived. With these last-minute attachments, the attack would go forward as scheduled and the units that followed would be fed into the battle upon arrival. It would not be until 7 January that all of Becker's division arrived, while on the same date only 70 percent of the *Wiking* Division had; thus, not every unit of Ullrich's division participated in what became known as *Konrad I*.

Another division in the offensive's starting lineup was the aforementioned *Div. Gr. Pape*, which was really not a division at all, but a temporary organization of division size that was created on 21 December to control all of the *panzer* regiments taking part in *Unternehmen Spätlese* when their parent divisions were sent north of the Danube to fight with LVII. Pz.Korps. Led by *Gen.Maj.* Günther Pape, who up to that point had been the commander of *Pz.Gren.Div. FHH*, he had been forced to relinquish command when he was ordered out of Budapest while leaving the rest of his division in the hands of his most senior subordinate, *Oberstlt.* Joachim Wolff. While not officially a part of the *IV. SS-Pz.Korps* for the initial stages of *Konrad*, Gille would have tactical control of Pape's unit to ensure close cooperation with the neighboring *Wiking* Division.

While *Div.Gr. Pape* was strong in armor (on 31 December it had 119 operational tanks, assault guns, and tank destroyers), it was weak in infantry and artillery, as well as the normal allocation of division-separate battalions and logistics troops.[28] On the second or third day of the offensive (2 or 3 January), *Div.Gr. Pape* would be *vorübergehend unterstellt* (placed under the temporary tactical control) of *IV. SS-Pz. Korps* for the first week of *Konrad*, but after 10 January it was scheduled to revert to the full control of *Korpsgruppe Breith*, where it would thereafter be dissolved and its various *Kampfgruppen* returned to their original divisions. *Generalmajor* Pape himself would then be released to begin the complete reconstitution of his *Pz. Gren. Div. FHH*, which in the meantime had been effectively written off as part of the Budapest garrison.

Meanwhile, north of the Danube, only 43 percent of the *96. Inf. Div.* had arrived by the time the operation was scheduled to commence, but since it had far fewer vehicles to transport, all of it had arrived by 4 January 1945. This division, activated on 21 September 1939 as part of the fifth mobilization wave, began its service as a triangular division, consisting of three infantry regiments of three battalions each. Following service on the Western Front between December 1939 and July 1941, it fought thereafter in the East, participating in battles fought at Staraya Russa, Leningrad, Volkhov, Shepetovka, the *Hube Kessel*, Tarnopol, and in the Carpathian and Beskids Mountains in Czechoslovakia.[29]

By 1 January 1945, it had many campaigns behind it and had developed into a veteran organization, led by competent officers who knew how to get the most out of its men and weapons. Led by 48-year-old *Oberst* (soon to be promoted to *Generalmajor*) Hermann Harrendorf, it still fielded all three of its original regiments (though now with only two, not three battalions, in accordance with the *Kriegsetat 1944* structure), *Füsilier* and *Pionier* battalions, 10 assault guns, 17 antitank guns, and 12 batteries of horse-drawn artillery organized into four battalions with a total of 41 guns. Numbering over 2,600 men in its *Kampfstärke*, it was still a relatively strong division for the standards of the time and would acquit itself well in the days to come.[30]

The *711. Inf. Div.* was a different case entirely. Originally established on 1 May 1941 as a static division designed specifically for the defense of the English Channel coast, it initially fielded two three-battalion regiments, three artillery batteries, no antitank weapons to speak of, and no vehicles. Composed of overage personnel, it had been smashed by the Allies during the latter stages of the Normandy campaign and its remnants retreated into Holland by early September 1944. It underwent a complete reconstitution in the vicinity of Rotterdam in December 1944, a process that converted it into a three-regiment division along the lines of the *Kriegsetat 1944* standard structure, with a full three-battalion artillery regiment, *Füsilier* and *Pionier* battalions, and a *Panzerjäger Abteilung*.[31]

Thousands of involuntary transfers from the *Kriegsmarine* and *Luftwaffe* filled out its ranks, many of whom still wore their former service's blue uniforms when they went into battle in Hungary several weeks later.[32] Their commander was 53-year-old *Gen. Lt.* Josef Reichert, who had led the division since March 1943. When it finally arrived at the railyard in Raab by 6 January 1945 after a lengthy trip of over 2,000 kilometers across war-torn Europe, the division reported a *Kampfstärke* of 2,564 men and 28 artillery pieces. Its antitank battalion, with 12 7.5cm guns, would be augmented by the attachment of a company of 14 *Jg. Pz. IV*s from *Pz. Abt. 208* before its attack. Deemed by nearly everyone a second-rate unit composed mostly of new, inexperienced personnel, it would still perform creditably well during *Konrad*.

It was these four divisions and corps troops—totaling approximately 70,000 men, 262 tanks, tank destroyers, and assault guns, and over 250 artillery tubes (not including mortars)—that Gille had at his disposal to carry out his mission. Each division would play a specific role and be tasked with achieving certain objectives. They were not given an adequate amount of time to conduct their own planning processes, and none of them went into battle at full strength on account of the delayed rail shipments. Some units were sent directly into battle from their trains, with no time at all to plan anything, other than to receive brief orders that read to the effect that they were to "advance to this location, and there you'll be given the rest of your instructions."

But time was of the essence, and the longer the attack was delayed, the stronger the Soviet defenses would become, and the weaker the encircled garrison of Budapest, not to mention the fate of 800,000 Hungarian civilians trapped with them. Fortunately, as of the morning of 1 January 1945, there were no indications that the Third Ukrainian Front and its 4th Guards Army expected an attack from the Komorn area, nor did they yet seem to know about the arrival of *IV. SS-Pz. Korps*, though the *STAVKA* knew that it had departed the Modlin area and was in transit somewhere.[33]

There would be no lengthy artillery preparation or *Luftwaffe* attacks upon Soviet positions, in order to increase the likelihood of surprising the defenders. The corps' attack would be initiated shortly after sundown on 1 January, when *Oberst* Harrendorf's *96. Inf.Div.* would begin its river crossing operation under the cover of darkness. In order to ferry the division's assault battalions across to their individual objectives, over 100 small boats and rubber assault rafts had been assembled and hidden on the northern bank of the Danube. The division's initial objectives were the towns of Sütto, Labatlan, and Nyerges Ujfalu located along a 15-kilometer-wide stretch of the southern bank of the Danube.[34] This portion of the Soviet defenses was held by less than 1,000 men from the 11th Guards Rifle Regiment of Colonel Parfenov's 4th Guards Rifle Division, which on 29 December 1944 reported only 5,351 men present for duty, slightly more than half of its authorized strength of 9,373.[35]

Once Harrendorf's regiments had seized their assigned beachheads, they would then fan out to the east and west and secure the paved highway running parallel to the Danube as far east as the crossroads at Táth, destroying any Soviet formations encountered along the way. This action would then clear this high-speed avenue of approach for the *Totenkopf* Division, which would then link up with Harrendorf's troops using a *Panzergrenadier* battalion and begin the exploitation phase of their breakthrough. Once this had been achieved, the *96. Inf.Div.* would cover the left flank of the main body of Becker's division, which would pass through Harrendorf's positions at Táth to begin its wheeling movement to towards the southeast. Once it had arrived, *Gen.Lt.* Reichert's *711. Inf.Div.* would then pass through the lines of the *96. Inf.Div.* and advance towards its own objective of Gran, 10 kilometers to the northeast. Harrendorf's division would also continue its wheeling movement to the southeast and continue covering the *Totenkopf* Division's left flank.

To the west of the *96. Inf.Div.* river crossing operation, the *Totenkopf* Division would commence its own attack, beginning at 7:30 p.m. with an armored battlegroup. After conducting a forward passage of lines with the leftmost unit of *Gruppe Pape* (*K.Gr. Bieber*, formed around the remnants of the *271. V.G.D.* along with *Marsch-Btl. Feldherrenhalle* and *Pz.Abt. 208*), the division's lead infantry elements would ford the shallow Tatai River north of Naszály and push eastwards along the road parallel to the riverbank towards Dunaalmas, the first objective of Becker's division. At some point during its advance, *Brig.Fhr.* Becker expected to encounter tanks from the 170th Tank Brigade of the XVIII Tank Corps. His division would then continue its advance until it linked up with elements of the *96. Inf.Div.* that were to have taken Süttö as part of their amphibious assault. Once the assault had begun, the division would move its headquarters forward to the town of Mocsa to be closer to the fighting.

Upon reaching the town of Nyerges Ujfalu on the northern bank of the Danube and relieving the regiment from the *96. Inf.Div.*, a portion of the *Totenkopf* Division's spearhead would peel off to the south and push onwards through the Gerecse Mountains towards the town of Bajót, in order to cover the right flank of the main effort and retain contact with the left flank of the neighboring *Wiking* Division on its right. During the course of this movement, it would turn the right flank of the 80th Guards Rifle Division, forcing it to either withdraw or be encircled and destroyed. Continuing onwards, the main body of the *Totenkopf* Division, traveling in column, would relieve Harrendorf's easternmost regiment at the critical crossroads at Táth, where it would then fan out and begin its southeastwards wheeling movement oriented along the main highway leading to Budapest. Once it had taken the important town of Zsámbék, it would link up with the *Wiking* Division on its right flank and continue the attack towards Budapest.

To the south of the *Totenkopf*, the *Wiking* Division would pass through the lines held by *K.Gr. Bieber* and attack at the same time towards the east from its forward assembly area located between Naszály and Tata, orienting on its initial objectives of Szomód, Agostyán, and Baj. Using its armored group, *K.Gr. Dorr* (all that had arrived by 1 January)—consisting of the *Germania* Regiment and most of Darges' *SS-Pz.Rgt. 5*—would have to initially overcome resistance by two regiments from the understrength 80th Guards Rifle Division before pushing onwards towards its intermediate objective of Tardos.

During this phase, *K.Gr. Dorr* would be entering the Vértes Mountains and beginning its own wheeling movement to the southeast, the most critical phase of its operation. Fortunately, there were few Soviet forces located in this area to slow it down, but Dorr's force would have to move quickly. Gaedke, Balck's chief of staff, anticipated that either the 4th Guards or the 46th Army would begin moving reserves into the area to counter the German advance once they realized what was happening. How long it would take for either the Second or Third Ukrainian Fronts to react was unknown; but given the Red Army's known ability to rapidly improvise, the movement and employment of reinforcements might take only a few days, if not hours.

Having fought its way through this natural obstacle, *K.Gr. Dorr*, which by this point would be joined by the *Westland* Regiment, would then debouche upon the relatively flat valley encompassing the town of Tarján. Once Dorr's troops took this town, his *Kampfgruppe* would proceed directly to its next objective, the critically important crossroads town of Bicske, only 37 kilometers away from the Castle District in Budapest. From Bicske to Budapest, the ground is relatively level and suitable for the employment of armor, and from this point onwards, the *Wiking* and *Totenkopf* Divisions—operating abreast—would carry out the final phase of *Konrad* and link up with the encircled garrison by day three of the offensive, at the earliest. Once the assault had begun, the *Wiking* Division's headquarters would move forward to the town of Kocs, but given that it only arrived at 9 a.m. on 1 January, it most likely would have moved there directly after unloading from its trains.[36]

Meanwhile, after the initial wave of *IV. SS-Pz.Korps'* attack had passed through its front-line positions, *Div.Gr. Pape*—with most of its tanks and assault guns (119 operational as of 31 December) and four battalions of infantry—would come under the tactical control of the *IV. SS-Pz.Korps*, when Pape's various *Kampfgruppen* would shift to the south in order to cover the right flank of the *Wiking* Division by attacking the position of the 34th Guards Rifle Division blocking the paved highway leading to Tata. After securing that town, *Div.Gr. Pape*, reinforced after 5 January by the *6. Pz.Div.*, would continue its attack towards its intermediate objective of the industrial district encompassing Felsőgalla. Once Gille's corps had pushed into the mountains, it would be augmented on or about 7 January by the Hungarian *23. Res.Div.*, which would be sent forward in the wake of the *Totenkopf* and *Wiking* Divisions' advance to mop up any bypassed elements of the Soviet XXXI Guards Rifle Corps.

While the plan for *Unternehmen Konrad* was developed and continually adjusted from 28–31 December by the various commanding generals and their staffs, the leader and troops of the *IV. SS-Pz.Korps* did not remain idle. Upon arrival in their new area of operations, troops unloaded their vehicles and equipment from their trains, formed up in march serials, and moved out along the roads to their designated locations with quiet efficiency, as noted by one Hungarian observer.[37] The first element to arrive on 28 December from the *Totenkopf* Division, *SS-Pz.Aufkl.Abt. 3*, was soon followed by *Pz.Gren.Rgt. Eicke* and a portion of the division's *panzer* regiment. After unloading their vehicles from the Komorn railhead, the SS men quickly formed up and moved to occupy the numerous assembly areas designated for their division, stretching from the region south of Raab in the west, to Komorn in the east, and to Tarkany in the south. Temperatures hovered around freezing and it had started snowing earlier that day, covering the landscape with a white carpet. The new arrivals found the local Hungarian inhabitants friendly and welcoming.[38] The division headquarters was at first located in Komorn, only a few kilometers away from the corps main headquarters in Acs.

By 29 December, only 18 trains from *Totenkopf* Division had arrived, and only 10 from the *Wiking*. The traffic jams at each offloading site were considerable, as dozens of vehicles jockeyed into position as they prepared to depart the railyard while new trains loaded with troops, tanks, and equipment constantly arrived. Fortunately, the bad flying weather prevented the Red Air Force from detecting this frenzied activity, thus preventing the premature disclosure of the operation. The division headquarters of the *Wiking* Division did not arrive until 9 a.m. on 1 January, but was quickly sent on its way by the *Streifendienst* (traffic regulating units) to the link-up with *Kampfgruppe Dorr* at its own assembly area in the vicinity of Raab.[39] Ullrich himself and several of his staff officers from the *Wiking* Division arrived that same day after driving down from Modlin, as Gille had done on Christmas Day. Some troops were quartered in civilian homes, while others were assigned to large public buildings. In most cases, they did not stay there long, and their reacquaintance with civilization—with all of its comforts such as running water, flushing toilets, and soft beds—proved to be fleeting.

During the brief period between the first arrivals of the corps and its units on 28 December and the launching of the attack less than five days later, myriad tasks had to be accomplished by everyone ranging from the lowliest *SS-Mann* to general staff officers. In addition to finding their way to their designated assembly areas, the leaders of companies, battalions, and regiments had to find their own commanders' headquarters to receive instructions concerning where to draw supplies, where to find maintenance units to repair broken-down vehicles, the locations of field dressing stations for men who had become ill during the long train ride, and so on. Communications wire had to be laid, radio installations set up, ammunition depots established, and many mundane, yet equally important, tasks had to be performed.[40] Leaders sought copies of Hungarian military maps to familiarize themselves with their new mission, and soldiers who had somehow become lost along the way from Modlin struggled to find their companies. Yet despite this seeming chaos, order reigned. The commanders and their NCOs had done this many, many times before, for some going as far back as September 1939. This was, as some of their American contemporaries might be wont to say, "not their first rodeo."

The official records generally do not document this kind of activity or what goes on behind the lines in preparation for battle, but occasionally some useful bits of information emerge. For example, the *Ic* of the *Totenkopf* Division, *Ostuf.* Roland

Willer, met with *Oberstlt.* Hans-Werner Wüstenberg, the *Ic* of *A. Gr. Balck/6. Armee*, at his office in Martinsberg on 28 December to receive an intelligence briefing on Soviet troop positions, the status of local anti-espionage efforts, and the activities of any partisans behind the lines. The following day, the *Ic* of *IV. SS-Pz.Korps, Stubaf.* Herbert Jankuhn, who had just arrived, met with Wüstenberg for the same briefing.[41] *Obergruppenführer* Gille's *Quartiermeister, Ostubaf.* Hans Scharf, would have sought his *Oberquartiermeister* counterpart at Balck's headquarters, *Oberstlt.* Otto Mitlacher, to notify him of his logistics requirements and to arrange for the beginning of deliveries of all categories of supply to the three—soon to be four—divisions arrayed under the *IV. SS-Pz.Korps'* banners.

The *Adjutant* and *Quartiermeister* of Gille's corps and all of their various administrative staff assistants and specialists would also have sought their counterparts in the *A. Gr. Balck/6. Armee* staff. Physical connections would have to be made with the various logistics installations located within *Korück 593* too, the rear area command of the *6. Armee*, including fuel and ammunition dumps, hospitals, ration issue points, and prisoner of war collection centers. A great deal of coordination would have to be made in a very compressed period of time in order to ensure that *IV. SS-Pz.Korps* had as much support as possible before it began its assault.

The evening before *Gen.d.Inf.* Wöhler's first visit to Gille's corps headquarters on the morning of 1 January, he issued a *Tagesbefehl* to the troops of *H.Gr. Süd*, including *A. Gr. Balck/6. Armee*. Summarizing the past year's events, he stated:

> Soldiers of the Army Group! For us, 1944 was a difficult year. It brought us heavy and sustained fighting and despite all of our exertions, many of our hopes were unfulfilled. Despite this, we can look back at the year 1944 with pride. Despite their overwhelming superiority in men and material, the Bolshevists were unable to smash our front and force us from our positions. You have inflicted heavy losses on them through your bravery and perseverance, which will make themselves felt decisively in the coming battles. In recognition of this [achievement] you have my sincerest appreciation and thanks. Despite all the efforts of our enemies, the power of our nation has remained unbroken. In the West, the German *Wehrmacht* has launched a major surprise attack and dealt the enemy heavy blows. Also in our own area, the *Führer* will order the attack to liberate [Budapest] when the time has come. Then the hour of liberation of our Hungarian comrades will strike. But for now, it is necessary to stop the enemy by our determined resistance and to create the conditions for our own attack later on. In firm belief in our leader and trusting in the indestructible strength of the German people, we continue to fight until victory! This is our vow for the year 1945. Long live the *Führer*! Signed, Wöhler, *General der Infanterie*[42]

While this can hardly be considered a joyful expression of good wishes for the coming year, it is indicative of the mood prevailing in the various headquarters at the time. Balck, in his inimitably terse style, issued his own New Year's proclamation to the German and Hungarian troops in his *Armeegruppe* the following morning, distributed down to the *Kompanie* level of every unit in his command. Using rather less flowery terms than his army group commander had, he simply wrote, "To the troops of the *Armeegruppe!* I give you my best wishes for the New Year! This will be a year of decision, and I know that each and every one of you will make the supreme effort to achieve final victory. Hail to the *Führer!*"[43]

During his visit to Gille's newly established forward headquarters at Nagyigmánd the following day (the *Quartiermeister* and *Adjutantur* had remained in Acs), Wöhler met with Gille, Becker, Ullrich, and Harrendorf to review the plan and to ensure that each commander understood what was expected of him. According to the official record, no new points of discussion were brought forth and few, if any, questions were aired. All of those present expressed their hopes that Breith's feint towards Ösi would succeed, thus drawing away Soviet attention from the main attack in the north, which they were confident would succeed. Wöhler, in his evening report, later noted, "It is to be hoped that the deceptive measures regarding the point of attack will have the desired effect."[44] Much depended on the element of surprise to achieve the hoped-for victory.

Apparently, Wöhler paid this visit to Gille's headquarters without being accompanied by the commander of the army responsible for making the attack. According to the accounts of Maier, Strassner, Klapdor, and Vopersal, Balck did not visit Gille's headquarters before *Unternehmen Konrad* began. Even Balck himself fails to mention having visited the headquarters of *IV. SS-Pz.Korps* before the attack, but in all fairness, the commander of *A.Gr. Balck/6. Armee* had a lot on his hands during the last week of December 1944.[45] Most likely, his chief of staff, *Gen.Maj.* Gaedke, did visit Gille at Acs between 26 and 31 December, though there is no record of that either. After leaving Gille, Wöhler returned to his own headquarters, where he hosted a New Year's reception at the Esterháza palace, inviting 350 men from his army group, including 80 Hungarians. It is not known whether he invited anyone from *IV. SS-Pz.Korps* to this event; in any case, Gille and his troops had far more urgent things to concern themselves with that day.

Some units, as they struggled to prepare for the upcoming operation, found themselves diverted for other purposes. For example, on 29 December, the *Totenkopf* Division was tasked by *A.Gr. Balck/6. Armee* to send a reinforced regimental *Kampfgruppe* to the town of Füzitö, 10 kilometers east of Komorn, to protect a still-operating oil refinery located next to the Danube by establishing a secondary defense line behind the front. The only redeeming feature of this duty was that it positioned this regiment a mere 4 kilometers west of the designated line of departure for its impending attack. For command and control purposes, this regiment, *Pz.Gren.Rgt. Eicke*, was temporarily placed under *Div.Gr. Pape* of *III. Pz.Korps* for the next three days. On the morning of 1 January, the *Eicke* Regiment was relieved by two *Gneisenau* battalions, *2./XVIII* and *16./XVII*, which assumed responsibility for protecting the refinery, thus freeing up the regiment for its mission scheduled to begin that evening.[46]

Another interesting event was the arrival on the scene of one of the most colorful units that would ever serve under the *IV. SS-Pz.Korps*. This unit, the

2,000-strong *SS-Regiment Ney*, was composed of anti-communist Hungarian veterans of the Eastern Front who had been disavowed by the *Honvéd* (the Royal Hungarian Army) and estranged from Szalási's Arrow Cross party. Adopted by Heinrich Himmler, this regiment had been organized at first under the rubric of "Special Troops of the *Reichsführer-SS*," intended for internal security purposes and operations behind enemy lines, and was not initially viewed as part of the *Waffen-SS*. The regiment's commander, *Stubaf.* Károly ("Karl") Ney, had established a good working relationship with Himmler, who agreed to arm, equip, and train his regiment, which at first was composed of two infantry battalions. On 29 December, *A. Gr. Balck/6. Armee* attached the regiment to the *III. Pz.Korps* for the opening phase of *Unternehmen Konrad*, specifically for use in "front-line combat."[47] Shortly afterwards, each of its two battalions would be attached separately to the *Totenkopf* and *Wiking* Divisions and would participate in most of the *Konrad* relief attempts. Ney and his men had wanted to fight against the Soviet Union, and they would soon get their wish.

While many of Gille's troops had no time to ring in the New Year, some of the early-arriving battalions from the *Wiking* and *Totenkopf* Divisions that had been settled in for the past three days took advantage of the opportunity to enjoy themselves. According to one NCO, *Oscha.* Hugo Zährl from the *Eicke* Regiment, "The last hours of the year we wanted to let off steam one last time, we wanted to forget everything that had happened, but also not to think about the future, because who knows what the year 1945 will bring?"[48] Before celebrations had gone too far, his battalion set off after midnight for the front lines near the village of Szöny, where they occupied their forward assembly area, relieving a battalion from *Div. Gr. Pape*. Soldiers from *II. Abt./SS-Pz.Rgt. 5* of the *Wiking* Division, quartered in Komorn, celebrated the holiday on the evening of 31 December in "their typically positive approach."[49]

The staff company of *SS-Pz.Jag.Abt. 3* celebrated in grand style, as did the men from *IV. Abt./SS-Pz.Art.Rgt. 3*, who found to their surprise that the Hungarian wine they were drinking was much stronger than what they were used to. One participant, *Unterscharführer* Söhrmann, later wrote that the "alcohol flowed freely, and our motto was, enjoy the war, because the peace afterwards will be terrible!"[50] Several battalions conducted one last formal assembly, where commanders wished their men a happy New Year and good luck for the upcoming operation. Although they had no fireworks of their own to welcome in the New Year, a few dozen kilometers to their southeast, the men could see the glow of tracers, explosions, and signal flares, signs that the diversionary attacks by *III. Pz.Korps* had already begun.[51]

That evening, Balck sat down at this desk and wrote in his journal, "The front is stabilized, it is actually a miracle. Now comes the relief operation of Budapest."[52] Balck himself was not overly optimistic about the chances of success, later writing:

One thing was clear: even after the attachment of the *IV. SS-Panzerkorps*, the correlation of forces was not in our favor ... with these force ratios we could only succeed if we either managed to surprise the Russians [*sic*] and unhinge them for a short time, or if we hit them in short order with destructive strikes that inflicted such losses that they would break off the siege. Neither course of action had much chance of succeeding.

Regardless of what their army commander thought, the men of Gille's corps would give their all; seeing all of the German troops and tanks closely gathered in such a small area, they naturally thought they would win. They had to succeed—70,000 German and Hungarian troops and 800,000 civilians were counting on them. To highlight the seriousness of the situation, a telex from *IX. SS-Geb.Korps* in Budapest arrived at the headquarters of *A.Gr. Balck/6. Armee* on 30 December. Its single-sentence message simply asked, "When is Gille coming?"[53]

CHAPTER 5

The First Relief Attempt of Budapest—*Konrad I* 1–8 January 1945

Despite postwar accounts to the contrary, *Unternehmen Konrad* did not begin on 1 January 1945, but the previous day, when *Korpsgruppe Breith*'s *III. Pz.Korps* launched its diversionary attack towards Ösi. This village, 8 kilometers southeast of the important crossroads town of Várpalota, had been the scene of see-saw fighting since 29 December, when *Gen.Maj.* Thünert's *1. Pz.Div.* and the Hungarian *20. Inf. Div.* had been battling against the XXI Guards Rifle Corps for its possession. Control of Ösi was essential for the protection of the large oil refinery at Pétfürdő, a mere 6 kilometers west of the town, which incredibly continued producing petroleum products even while the fighting raged only a short distance away.

The first attack by the armored *Kampfgruppe* from *1. Pz.Div.*, launched at 3. p.m. on 31 December, failed to take Ösi, despite close air support provided by *Luftflotte 4*, which launched 100 sorties carried out by *FW-190s* of the Hungarian 1st Squadron of the 102nd Fighter-Bomber Group and the tank-busting *Stukas* of *Oberst* Rudel's *Schlachtgeschwader 2*. For the loss of six of their own tanks and assault guns out of 55 *panzers* employed, Thünert's troops were only able to claim the destruction of four SU-76 assault guns and the killing of an estimated 200 Soviet troops from the 69th Guards Rifle Division.[1] Thünert himself tried again that evening to take Ösi at the head of a much larger force, consisting of *Kampfgruppe Elias* from *Pz.Rgt. 1* with over 36 tanks and assault guns, *Kampfgruppe Huppert*, a *Panzergrenadier* battalion from *Pz.Gren.Rgt. 113*, the guns of *I. Abt./Pz.Art.Rgt. 73*, and five *Jagd.Pz. 38t Hetzers* attached to *SS-Reiter Schwadron Sparwasser*, which also contributed troops.[2]

This attack, which *1. Pz.Div.* initiated at 11:45 p.m. after a 10-minute artillery barrage that rang in the New Year, finally succeeded in taking Ösi by 4:30 a.m. on 1 January. Soviet and German land mines caused more casualties than enemy fire, which had repeatedly forced the battlegroup's *Pioniere* to dismount from their *SPWs* to clear lanes through the minefields in the dark. After suffering the temporary loss of three *panzers* damaged by mines and antitank guns, the armor—with the exception of the *Hetzers*—withdrew to Várpalota, while the *Panzergrenadier* battalion of the *Kampfgruppe*, including the SS men under *Ustuf.* Heinrich Sparwasser's command, occupied Ösi and the vineyard-covered hill to the south of the town.[3] Here, the men of *K.Gr. Huppert*'s *I. Btl./Pz.Gren.Rgt. 113* prepared for the inevitable Soviet counterattack, which began shortly after the German armor withdrew.

This counterattack, launched by two regiments from the 69th Guards Rifle Division, retook Ösi from *K.Gr. Huppert* after heavy fighting and continued advancing to the west towards Pétfürdő, but the Soviets were driven back before they reached the oil refinery or the *1. Pz.Div.* main defense line at Berhida. The Germans managed to retain ownership of the commanding position to the south of the town, digging into the vineyards on the hillside, where they prepared to repel any attempt to force them off the hill.[4] These two German attacks on 31 December and 1 January, while not as successful as hoped, did succeed in temporarily drawing the attention of General Zakharov of the 4th Guards Army, who had located his headquarters in Stuhlweissenburg, less than 30 kilometers away. Thünert's attacks had also pushed the front lines a few more kilometers away from the oil refinery, which continued its operations unhindered.

While the *1. Pz.Div.* and the 69th Guards Rifle Division fought for possession of Ösi that day, 25 kilometers to the northwest of Stuhlweissenburg, Lt.Gen. S. I. Gorshkov's V Guards Cavalry Corps continued in its attempt to take Mór from Harteneck's *I. Kav.Korps*. Mór was a tactically important town whose possession controlled the Sárviz River valley through the Bakony Forest, and the V Guards Cavalry Corps had been assigned the mission of taking it. Possession of the town would enable Gorshkov's corps, followed by other elements of the 4th Guards Army, to access the open plains stretching to the north beyond, which led directly to Raab and the Danube valley. Had they succeeded, the V Guards Cavalry Corps might have outflanked Gille's attack before it began. Despite the best efforts of the two Soviet divisions engaged, on 1 January they were not able to penetrate the front lines of the *23. Pz.Div.* or the *4. Kav.Brig.*, the latter having been reinforced by five *Pz.Kfw. VI* "King" Tiger II tanks from *s.Pz.Abt. 503*. After carrying out numerous determined assaults, particularly in the Csólkakő area, the Soviet attempt to take Mór was brought to a halt after suffering heavy losses. Undeterred, Gorshkov intended to continue his attack the following day with a third division.[5]

The large-scale attack against Ösi by *1. Pz.Div.* on New Year's Eve and the following morning apparently confirmed Zakharov's belief that a German counteroffensive aimed towards recapturing that city—the most likely enemy course of action—was about to unfold. This also explains why his army's reserve, consisting of the 16th Mechanized Brigade from the VII Mechanized Corps and the 41st Guards Rifle Division, was kept there instead of being positioned further to the north.[6] After all, the reasoning went (as the Germans hoped it would), anyone trying to launch a major attack through the rugged Gerecse and Vértes Mountains in the middle of winter would have to be incredibly foolish or desperate. Although the Red Army was aware of the departure of the *IV. SS-Pz.Korps* from the Warsaw area, and that it had been sent to Hungary, its intelligence services had not yet been able to determine its exact whereabouts.[7]

As evidence of the *1. Pz.Div.* diversionary attack's success, the intelligence summary of the 4th Guards Army issued on the evening of 1 January ended with the following statement: "The enemy is striving to hold its present positions with all its forces; on separate sectors of the front, the adversary is undertaking attacks for reconnaissance purposes and with the aim of improving local positions."[8] With the minimal conditions having been apparently met for the *IV. SS-Pz.Korps* to begin its own surprise attack that very evening, the stage was now set for the dramatic events about to unfold nearly 60 kilometers to the north.

On *A.Gr.Balck*'s left, Kirchner's *LVII. Pz.Korps* stated in its daily *Ic* report for 1 January that the *6. Pz.Div.* in the corps' center sector had observed Soviet engineers assembling a pontoon bridge on the far side of the Gran River south of Kicind (Kicsind), which it disrupted with artillery fire. The division also reported warding off a company-sized reconnaissance force a few kilometers away at Kam.-Darmoty (Köhid-Gyarmat). On Kirchner's left flank, *Div.Gr. von Rintelen* (formed from remnants of the *357. Inf.Div.*) reported that a battalion-sized Soviet force had crossed the Gran and achieved a local penetration in its defensive positions north of the Czech town of Garam-Mikola (modern-day Mikula), though a counterattack had already been launched to "clean it up" and restore the former position. Otherwise, nothing serious was reported.[9]

In Budapest itself, the situation was tense. In the *Ic* evening report for 1 January, the *IX. SS-Geb.Korps* stated that the Second Ukrainian Front had continued its concentric attack against the city's defenses, striking both the western and eastern bridgeheads of Buda and Pest with coordinated assaults, preceded in some areas by drumfire barrages. Elements of the 46th Army had been able that day to make a penetration in the western defenses that was 8 kilometers deep and 2–3 kilometers wide before they were driven back in a counterattack. Another Soviet breakthrough 1.5 kilometers west of Margareten Bridge was barely contained after heavy fighting. *Obergruppenführer* Pfeffer-Wildenbruch also reported that the enemy was able to widen their penetrations in the positions in the northeast corner of the eastern bridgehead in the vicinity of the towns of Rakoskeresztur and Rakoszentmihaly before they were contained by counterattacks that afternoon.[10] While aerial supply drops and evacuation of the *IX. SS-Geb.Korps'* wounded were continuing, these efforts were inadequate considering the daily demand for food, fuel, and ammunition, as well as the increasing number of medical cases needing to be airlifted out of the city.

For the troops of *IV. SS-Pz.Korps*, some still suffering from the aftereffects of their celebrations the night before, the morning and afternoon of 1 January 1945 was spent getting into position for the impending attack. The weather proved cooperative, with ground fog, light snowfall, and overcast skies concealing most of the final preparations from aerial observation and muffling the sounds of thousands of vehicles being driven forward. The daytime temperature hovered slightly above freezing, ensuring good mobility on unpaved roads or across farmers' fields, as the various companies, battalions, and regiments maneuvered their tanks, halftracks, and trucks into their forward assembly areas. Trains continued rolling in at the railyards in Raab, Acs, and Komorn, quickly discharging their cargoes of troops, vehicles, and weapons, and just as quickly departing.

Last-minute deliveries of rations, fuel, and ammunition continued right up to the moment when units began their assault. Communications wire was laid by the *Feldkabel Kompanie* of *SS-Nachr.Abt.104* from the corps headquarters to the *Gefechtstand* of each of the attacking divisions. Artillery fire plans and target coordinates were checked and checked again. Artillery ammunition and *Nebelwerfer* rockets were uncrated and positioned next to the guns and launchers in their concealed firing positions. Meanwhile, on the northern bank of the Danube, the troops from the two regiments of Harrendorf's *96. Inf.Div.* designated to take part in the division's river crossing operation that evening assembled their 100 assault craft and positioned them a few hundred meters beyond the river bank, out of sight.

As it grew dark, the weather turned bitterly cold (it reached a low of 26 degrees Fahrenheit or -3 Celsius that night) as the sky cleared, revealing a nearly full moon that would aid visibility for the attacking force. The curtain heralding the beginning of the first act of *Unternehmen Konrad* was raised on the north flank of the *IV. SS-Pz. Korps*, when the *96. Inf.Div.* began its river crossing without any artillery preparation. Originally scheduled to begin at 5:30 p.m., it was delayed for two-and-a-half hours after the troops of *Oberst* Erich Lorenz's *Gren.Rgt. 287* and *Oberstlt.* Hans-Dietrich von Böltzig's *Gren.Rgt. 283* discovered that many of the assault rafts and small boats were not riverworthy enough to risk a crossing (see Map 4).[11]

Due to the cold temperatures, the *Pioniere* operating the boats of the miniature landing fleet encountered difficulties when trying to start their engines, further delaying the operation.[12] After reshuffling the infantry platoons and remaining operational boats, the three assault groups set out in the darkness towards their objectives of Sütto, Labatlan, and Nyerges Ujfalu (Objectives 1, 2, and 3, respectively) on the southern bank. Large floes of ice on the river, which at this point was between 600 and 800 meters wide, proved to be an unexpected obstacle, endangering the flimsy assault craft.

When the assault group from *I. Btl./Gren.Rgt. 287* assigned the task of taking Objective 2, the village of Labatlan, tried to land, it was met by heavy defensive fire that forced Lorenz to abandon this attempt and move his troops to the third crossing point at Nyerges Ujfalu.[13] To the west of Lorenz's regiment, von Böltzig's *Gren.Rgt. 283* made an unopposed crossing at Mocs, landing to the west of Sütto unobserved. During the night and early morning hours, enough troops from Harrendorf's regiments managed to establish footholds at these two crossing points, enabling them to take both Sütto and Nyerges Ujfalu after overwhelming the defending troops from the 4th Guards Rifle Division in house-to-house fighting and forcing the remainder to withdraw uphill to the south into the Gerecse Mountains.[14] At this point, no Soviet tanks had yet been detected.

With two crossing sites thus secured, the remaining troops from the regiments of Lorenz and Böltzig, including their regimental heavy weapons companies, were ferried across by the division's *Pionier* battalion, as the regiments' infantry battalions fanned out to the east and west to widen the bridgehead, successively eliminating Soviet positions they encountered along the way and working their way into the rear areas of the 4th and 80th Guards Rifle Divisions. The division's third regiment, *Maj.* Christoph Magawly's *Gren.Rgt. 284*, would move forward on foot across the bridge at Komorn and along the southern bank of the Danube to join the rest of the division as soon as its trains arrived at the railroad yard in Neuhäusel.[15]

The success of *Oberst* Harrendorf's operation was recorded in the war diary of *H.Gr. Süd* late that evening, which stated, "During the [Danube] crossing of elements of the *96. Infanterie-Division*, no sound of fighting was heard. It would appear that the surprise was complete."[16] The chief of staff of *A.Gr. Balck*, *Gen.Maj.* Gaedke, described this feat as a *Kabinettstück* (an old-fashioned term describing a particularly clever, successful approach or action).[17] Along with the apparent success of the *1. Pz.Div.* diversionary attack, the second condition necessary for *Unternehmen Konrad* to proceed had been met. From this point onwards, it was the turn of the men in the armored spearheads from the *Totenkopf* and *Wiking* Divisions, as well as *Div.Gr. Pape*, patiently waiting in the darkness in their assault positions or in their idling armored vehicles, to play their role in the opening act of the drama.

While the river crossing was still ongoing, the lead elements of the *Totenkopf* and *Wiking* Divisions began crossing the line of departure at 7:30 p.m., roughly demarcated by the north–south course of the Altaler (Tatai) River–Kühltrieber Bach (creek), which emptied into the Danube. On the corps' left flank, the *Totenkopf* Division's attack began when *Hstuf.* Christian Bachmann's *II. Bataillon* of the *Totenkopf* Regiment waded the ice-cold Kühltrieber Creek, which in some places rose up to the men's chest. Soaking wet, his men climbed the opposite bank and continued their advance unnoticed by the defenders. Taking advantage of the full moon's illumination and a light snowfall, the battalion formed up and began their attack. The surprise was complete; the defending troops from the 217th Rifle Regiment had not expected an advance from this direction and were quickly overwhelmed by Bachmann's troops or forced to retreat towards the eastern hills.[18]

Not pausing to dry out or rest, Bachmann urged his battalion forward towards Hill 294, a snow-covered prominence that rose above the creek in the ghostly landscape. Against little resistance, the battalion soon occupied the hill that commanded the approaches to the village of Dunaalmas, their first objective, lying less than a kilometer to the north. Continuing without pause, the men from *II. Btl./ Totenkopf* continued their attack and soon broke into the southern outskirts of the village, catching the defenders from the 80th Guards Rifle Division completely by surprise. After securing the village, which straddled the river road leading to Sütto and Nyerges Ujfalu, Bachmann ordered his troops to dig in to await the arrival of the armored spearhead.

The armored group, with 11 Tigers of *9. Kp./SS-Pz.Rgt. 3* in the lead followed by the Panthers of *Stubaf.* Erwin Meierdress' *I. Abteilung*, departed its forward assembly area at Szöny at 11 p.m. With the enemy front-line position outflanked and dispersed by Bachmann's enveloping attack, the tank column reached Dunaalmas by midnight after encountering little sign of the enemy. After linking up with Bachmann's battalion, the *Totenkopf* Division's *Panzergruppe* passed through the village and continued its advance to the east, where it would clear the highway and join the regiment of the *96. Inf.Div.* defending Sütto.

However, shortly after departing Dunaalmas, the lead tank, Tiger 902, was knocked out and another disabled when its right running gear was struck by antitank gunfire. This brought the entire column to a halt, forcing the accompanying *Panzergrenadiere* to dismount and begin clearing the obstacle, which consisted of a strong position held by a number of T-34s from the 170th Tank Brigade, SU-85s from the 1348th Self-Propelled Artillery Regiment, and the guns of the 1000th Antitank Artillery Regiment. The *Totenkopf* Division had finally located the exact position of the XXXI Rifle Corps' elusive reserve force, and had no recourse but to fight through it if it were to reach its initial division objective on time.

In the center of Gille's attack, *K. Gr. Dorr*, formed from *SS-Pz.Gren.Rgt. 9 Germania*, and *Panzergruppe (Pz.Gr.) Darges*, consisting of *SS-Pz.Rgt. 5* and *II. Btl./ Germania*, began their attacks at the same time as the *Totenkopf* did. Since *Oberf.* Ullrich had not yet arrived at the division's *vorgeschobener Gefechtsstand* (forward command post) at Tata, Dorr initiated the attack without him, acting in the capacity as the senior-most officer on the scene. Before the armor could initiate its breakthrough attack along the Tata–Tarjan road, a penetration first had to be made in the Soviet lines by the infantry of *K.Gr. Dorr*.

To do this, they had to overwhelm the defenses of the 232nd Guard Rifle Regiment of the 80th Guards Rifle Division arrayed in the hills astride the towns of Szomód, Agostyán, and Baj in order to gain control of the paved highway leading through Agostyán. This was even more difficult than it sounds, for in order for the *I.* and *III. Bataillone* of the *Germania* Regiment to carry out this assault, they first had to ford the Kühltrieber Creek at Tóvarós opposite the town of Tata and force their way through the Soviet outpost line after negotiating a minefield in the darkness. This took several hours, and *K.Gr. Dorr* did not begin its general assault until 11 p.m., when *II. Btl./Germania* under *Hstuf.* Franz Pleiner—operating on *K.Gr. Dorr*'s right flank—pushed through the other two battalions of the regiment and attacked Baj, which fell quickly. Pleiner reported that his assault had interrupted the holiday celebrations of the Soviet defenders, who were caught completely by surprise.[19]

At the same time, *I.* and *II. Bataillone* assaulted Szomód and Agostyán to clear the route for the armor. At some point during the fighting for Agostyán, Pleiner was seriously wounded. The *II. Bataillon* then continued pushing eastwards up the *Heuberg* (Hill 537), and then cross-country to their initial objective, the village of Tolna, where it would cover the right flank of *Pz. Gr. Darges*.[20] Pleiner was replaced by *Stubaf.* Heinrich Amberg, who served in an acting capacity until confirmed as *Kommandeur* the following month.[21]

With the thinly occupied Soviet line now thoroughly overcome by the *Germania* Regiment's assault, *Pz. Gr. Darges*, joined by the *SPW*-equipped *III. Btl./Germania* commanded by *Hstuf.* Helmut Schumacher, was finally able to play its part. With *Hstuf.* Hans Flügel's *II. Abt./SS-Pz.Rgt.* 5 in the lead, Darges' tanks and mounted *Panzergrenadiers* began rolling along the highway towards Agostyán at midnight. The lead Panther from *6. Kompanie*, commanded by *Ustuf.* Günther Stelz, had nearly reached the western edge of Agostyán when he was shot in the head by a sniper, dying instantly. He was the first of many men from *SS-Pz.Rgt.* 5 to die in Hungary. Nevertheless, the armored assault continued and Agostyán was quickly taken. Their next objective, the large town of Tarján, appeared ripe for the picking. Once past Agostyán, troops from *K. Gr. Westland* noticed the bodies of German and Hungarian dead lying along the roadside leading out of the town. Whether they had been killed in action during the last week of December while fleeing from the advancing Soviets or been executed after capture, no one knew for certain, but many SS men assumed the worst.[22]

Throughout their advance, German and Hungarian troops had been welcomed as liberators by the civilian population that had decided to remain in their homes after the 4th Guards Army overran the forces defending the area during the last week of December 1944. Initially glad to see the Germans leave, the civilians soon learned the harsh realities of Soviet rule. Confiscations, outright plundering, physical abuse, and sexual assault had become the norm, and any attempt to report misbehavior by the occupying force was met with harsh reprimands by senior Red Army officers. The abuses and cases of arbitrary executions and rape are too long to go into here, but it puts the lie to the notion expressed in a book about the last 100 days of the war that "Ivan" was nothing more than a child-loving, teddy-bear gifting humanitarian.[23] If anything, the horrible treatment meted out to the Hungarian population confirmed their intention to continue supporting the German and Hungarian alliance.

While the *Wiking* Division consolidated it gains and continued moving forward, on its right, *Div. Gr. Pape* began its own assault at 8:30 p.m. when its two armored *Kampfgruppen*, *K. Gr. Philipp* (*I. Abt./Pz.Rgt. 11* and *II. Btl./Pz.Gren.Rgt. 114*) and *K. Gr. Knoop* (*I. Btl./Pz.Gren.Rgt. 98 and 3. Kp./Pz.Abt. 208*), advanced towards their initial objectives, the towns of Tatabanya and Bánhida, which lay along the highway that led through a narrow valley towards their intermediate objective, the industrial area of Felsőgalla. Once *Gen. Maj.* Pape's troops had taken this town, the division would stop and establish a defensive line oriented towards the south in order to cover the right flank of Ullrich's *Wiking* Division and protect it against the expected Soviet counterattack, while Ullrich continued his advance towards Bicske. Bánhida quickly fell to one *Kampfgruppe*, while the other pushed on ahead towards the intermediate objective of Tatabanya. For the first time on the Eastern Front after three months of steady retreat and defeat, a major German offensive was once again underway.

The records of the 4th Guards Army indicate that the Soviet command did not become aware of the German offensive until 2:30 a.m. on 2 January, six hours after it had begun. Describing Gille's attack as a surprise, it went on to ascribe its initial success to their enemy's "enormous superiority" in men, artillery, and armored vehicles, as well as the "unready state" of their defenses. This judgement, of course, is correct; against approximately 8,000 widely dispersed troops occupying a 48-kilometer-wide, incompletely prepared main defense line backed up by less than 50 tanks and assault guns, the Germans had hurled over 25,000 men, 320 tanks and assault guns, and 57 artillery batteries, achieving overwhelming odds of three or four to one against the defenders at the points of main effort. Due to this superiority, the Soviets reported, "the enemy managed to break through the first line of our defense and push back our units, capture Labatlan and Piszke and link up with the 96th Infantry Division's landing in the Nyerges Ujfalu area."[24]

Shortly after the first German success was reported, the 4th Guards Army's commander wasted no time in developing a counter to it. Though his army had few reserves of its own that could be immediately sent to the threatened area, General Zakharov skillfully deployed what he had. The first thing he did was to send a rifle battalion from the XXXI Rifle Corps' reserve as well as the entire 407th Light Artillery Regiment to reinforce the troops defending Agostyán, which he viewed as the most threatened area at the time, to be followed by combat engineer battalions and antitank gun batteries as soon as they could be brought up.[25] There was not much that Zakharov could do at this early point in the fighting to assist the 80th or 4th Guards Rifle Divisions; they would have to do the best they could and buy time until he could muster a more powerful response, including requesting additional assistance from Tolbukhin's Third Ukrainian Front. The first reinforcements that Tolbukhin dispatched to Zakharov was the 86th Guards Rifle Division (quickly transferred from the 46th Army of the Second Ukrainian Front), the 2nd Engineer Brigade, and the 12th (Separate) Antitank Artillery Regiment, but it would take half a day before the first troops would arrive.[26]

Meanwhile, as 2 January turned from night into day, Gille's advance continued. On the left, *Oberst* Harrendorf's *96. Inf.Div.* continued expanding its bridgehead along the southern bank of the Danube, as more troops were ferried across from the two regiments that had landed, including the rest of the battalion heavy weapons companies and regimental infantry howitzer and antitank companies. With the initial objective successfully accomplished, the division's artillery emplaced on the opposite bank could now be brought to bear to help drive the stubborn defenders from Nyerges Ujfalu and other pockets of resistance along the southern banks of the river in order to completely free up the highway for the approaching armor from the *Totenkopf* Division.

A few kilometers west of the bridgehead at Sütto, the *Totenkopf* Division's armor was engaged in heavy combat between Dunaalmas and Neszmely. The unexpected encounter with 18 T-34s from the 170th Tank Brigade, as well as the assault guns and antitank *Pakfront* erected east of Dunaalmas, meant that *Ostubaf.* Anton Laackmann's armored *Kampfgruppe* from *SS-Pz.Rgt. 3* would have to stop, deploy its supporting infantry from *Hstuf.* Hans Endress' *II. Btl./Eicke* Regiment, and fight its way through. To pin down the antitank gunners and force the Soviet infantry to seek cover, calls for artillery fire from *Stubaf.* Fritz Messerle's *IV. Abt./SS-Pz.Art.Rgt. 3* were radioed in, beginning at 5 a.m., increasing the already deafening volume of the hellish din as tanks dueled with one another and artillery fell upon the targets called in by forward observers.[27] When the lead Panther of his battalion was knocked out, *Stubaf.* Meierdress ordered his driver to pull around it and take the lead with his own tank, Panther 101. *Uscha.* Söhrmann, Meierdress' radio operator in the vehicle's hull, left his graphic account describing what happened next:

> One Tiger after another fell out. *Sturmbannführer* Meierdress took the lead. Behind him followed *Ostuf.* Strobl, the battalion adjutant in his tank. It was still dark, and up to this point we had not fired a shot. Suddenly *Stubaf.* Meierdress ordered "Halt!" and jumped out of the tank and disappeared. After a while, other tank crewmen came up to our tank and asked "what's going on?" ... "Why are we just sitting here?" asked *Ostuf.* Alfred Quilitz, the battalion *Nachrichten Offizier* [signals officer] ... after a short while, the commander climbed back in. It was now daylight. One glance at my watch: it was now 6:45 a.m. Meierdress gave his command, "Let's move out Sepp!" At that same moment, a terrible impact shook our tank. Inside the fighting compartment, everything turned red and it became terribly hot. Bail out! The turret was turned to the one o'clock position. I managed to crank my hatch open, which had been stuck ... Sepp Hirsch and I found ourselves in a roadside ditch. We saw that our tank was still running and Sepp climbed in again and brought the vehicle to a stop. Everyone inside the turret was dead.[28]

A hidden SU-85 assault gun, concealed in a house on the roadside, had fired the fatal shot that immediately killed Meierdress. Word of the death of the highly respected battalion commander quickly spread along the column of tanks and *SPWs*.

A hunt immediately began for the Soviet assault gun, which was finally spotted and destroyed a few minutes later by Panther 103, commanded by *Uscha.* Arp. In the melee that followed, the remaining *panzers* and Endress' *Panzergrenadier* battalion, backed up by *SS-Pz.Aufkl.Abt. 3*, combed through the remaining houses and woods alongside the road, locating and destroying the remaining Soviet tanks, antitank guns, and infantry. One eyewitness later wrote, "The men from *Rgt. Eicke* repeatedly attacked the enemy in a most grim fashion. Finally they penetrated into the last enemy position. The Russians [*sic*] withdrew slowly ... one [Soviet] tank after another was knocked out, seven by *Panzergrenadiers* using *Panzerfausts*. We also knocked out a few ourselves."[29]

With this last obstacle overcome, the armored column rapidly pushed eastwards along the road, with three eight-wheeled *Panzerspähwagen* (armored cars) of *SS-Pz.Aufkl.Abt. 3* now in the lead. To their right, the surviving infantry from the 80th Guards Rifle Division who had taken refuge in the hills overlooking the road fired at the Germans with everything they had, but without tanks or antitank guns, all they could do was harass the *Totenkopf* armored columns with small-arms fire as they roared past. Moments later, the armored cars of *Ustuf.* Wilhelm Goertz, with the tanks following closely behind, linked up with the troops from *Gren.Rgt. 283* of the *96. Inf.Div.* in Sütto. A task force from the *Rgt. Eicke* was then sent back to comb through the woods and eliminate the Soviet holdouts who had taken refuge there. After a short rest, the armored column kept pushing onwards. By 9 a.m., the spearhead had reached the outskirts of Piszke, approximately 10 kilometers east of the line of departure.[30] By all appearances, the *Totenkopf* Division had broken through the enemy's defenses and was now poised to begin exploiting its success.

While the *Totenkopf* Division continued its deep attack after overcoming tough Soviet resistance, the *Wiking* Division's assault, spearheaded by *K.Gr. Dorr*, continued pressing forward towards the town of Agostyán, which also served as the headquarters of 80th Guards Rifle Division. Dorr's and Darges's tanks and *Panzergrenadiers* soon overwhelmed the hasty Soviet defense arrayed before Agostyán, which quickly collapsed in the face of the concerted German attack, which featured enveloping attacks carried out by both the *I.* and *III. Bataillone* of the *Germania* Regiment that approached the town from behind. According to the after-action report filed by Col. Tishkov, the commander of the 80th Guards Rifle Division, command and control of his division had been "disrupted" by the German attack; truly an understatement.

While the easy taking of Agostyán was due more to a stroke of luck than anything else, *K.Gr. Dorr* had no time to stop and savor its success, for it still had to fight its way to the town of Tarján. To reach this intermediate objective, which lay 13 kilometers to the southeast, the armored spearhead would have to advance through the Vértes Mountains. The single road they would have to follow passed through heavily wooded areas, mountain passes, and steep defiles, ideal terrain for any defender intent on blocking an attack or launching an ambush. Once Tarján had been taken, the terrain would open up more to allow Dorr's forces to deploy along a wider front as they strove towards the next objective, the important crossroads town of Bicske, less than 20 kilometers away.

On the right of the *Wiking* Division, *Div.Gr. Pape* was experiencing difficulties as it attempted to prosecute its attack. The *Kampfgruppe* on the left became bogged down in a large antitank minefield only 500 meters short of the northwestern edge of Tatabanya, a situation that became worse when its leading vehicles came under fire from concealed antitank guns. On the right, the other *Kampfgruppe* was able to reach the hillside south of Tatabanya, where it too ran into such heavy resistance that it was unable to take or bypass the town. For all intents, the attack by *Div. Gr. Pape* had stalled in the face of the stubborn defense put up by the 34th Guards Rifle Division, made more manifest by its own lack of infantry to suppress Soviet antitank guns and clear populated areas by fighting house to house. Sandwiched between the *Wiking* and *Totenkopf* Divisions, Pape's *K.Gr. Bieber*—consisting of the remnants of the *271. V.G.D.* reinforced by *Pz.Abt. 208*, *M.G. Btl. Mark*, and *Marsch-Btl. FHH*—carried out its own attack eastwards towards Szomód, beginning at 4 p.m., dispersing scattered Soviet elements that had been bypassed earlier that day and seizing the town before nightfall.[31]

The failure of *Div.Gr. Pape*'s attack on 2 January signaled the first indication that the troops engaged in *Unternehmen Konrad* would experience a far more difficult time in the mountains than was first believed before the *IV. SS-Pz.Korps* could break through to Budapest. *Obergruppenführer* Gille, who had moved his corps forward headquarters next to the *Wiking* Division's *Gefechtstand* 5 kilometers west of Tata, was relying almost exclusively by this point on wireless message traffic or messengers to keep abreast of the situation. Since the spearheads of three of the four divisions under his control were now in the mountains, a natural phenomenon that interfered with radio signals, the flow of information would become even more constricted the longer the offensive continued.

Dispatch riders became the only reliable means to relay messages and situation reports, using motorcycles or *Kübelwagen*, but even highway travel had its hazards. An attempt by *Oberf.* Ullrich, who had just arrived after travelling from Raab, to drive to Dorr's forward command post on 2 January was stymied when his staff car was involved in a traffic accident. Although Ullrich was unhurt, his *Ia, Maj.* Otto Kleine, was serious injured, necessitating his evacuation and temporary replacement by *Stubaf.* Günther Braun, who was reassigned from the corps staff the following day to serve as the acting *Ia* until a permanent one could be assigned.[32] The roads were so bad, often impassable due to ice or deep mud, that travel or the delivery of time-sensitive dispatches could be delayed by six or even 12 hours, a lifetime on a fluid battlefield where one's forces were heavily engaged with the enemy and where the scenario was constantly changing.

Gille's first important decision since the attack began was to order the two armored *Kampfgruppen* of *Div.Gr. Pape* to cease their attack towards Felsőgalla and disengage. He instructed them to hand over the limited amount of territory they had gained to an infantry unit from *K.Gr. Bieber* and move north to Tata. Here, the two *Kampfgruppen* would fall in behind the *Wiking* Division—to which they would be temporarily attached—and follow it until Dorr's troops took Tarján, at which point the two battlegroups from *Div.Gr. Pape* would strike out towards the southwest and attack Tatabanya and Felsőgalla from behind. However, the problem of who would cover the right flank of the *Wiking* Division remained. To address this shortfall after discussing it with Gille, *Gen.d.Pz.Tr.* Balck authorized the transfer of the main body of the *6. Pz.Div.* from its position north of the Danube, where it was still holding a static front with the *LVII. Pz.Korps*, to join *Div.Gr. Pape*, beginning the following day. With nearly all of the *6. Pz.Div.* reassembled for the first time in over two weeks, it would bring a welcome addition to Gille's combat power.[33]

While the two *Kampfgruppen* from *Div.Gr. Pape* struggled to extricate themselves from the battlefield at Tatabanya and Alsógalla, the fighting continued elsewhere. Along the northern wing of Gille's corps, the advance by the *Totenkopf* Division, aided by the *96. Inf.Div.*, began to pick up momentum. When the armored spearhead of the division encountered a blocking position defended by up to 16 T-34s east of Labatlan, a fierce tank battle immediately ensued, featuring the employment of the four remaining Tiger tanks (seven others had fallen out due to battle damage or mechanical failure) and the Panthers from *I. Abt./SS-Pz.Rgt. 3*, supported by *Panzergrenadiers* with *Panzerfausts*. These Soviet tanks from the 170th Tank Brigade were quickly destroyed, with no German tanks being lost. By noon, the *Totenkopf* Division's lead element had linked up with the *96. Inf.Div.* bridgehead at Nyerges Ujfalu, whose *Gren.Rgt. 287* had lost 139 men taking the town, including Hill 200 a kilometer to the south.[34]

This marked a critical juncture in the *Totenkopf* Division's mission; with Nyerges Ujfalu now under German control, a portion of the division's *Panzergruppe*, joined by *II. Btl./Eicke*, veered south at 2:10 p.m. along the road to Bajót, executing the right turning movement that was a key component of the plan. The remainder of the division would continue moving along the river road until it arrived at the intersection east of the village of Táth, where it would begin its own wheeling movement to the south. With the area between Nyerges Ujfalu and Dunaalmas cleared of enemy troops, with the exception of those who had retreated into the hills, the rest of the *Totenkopf* Division could now deploy along a wider front.

Bajót fell that evening to an attack led by *Hstuf.* Heinz Müller's *III. Btl./Eicke*, reinforced by the Tigers and eight *Pz. IVs* from *Ostuf.* Gerhard Wenke's *5. Kompanie* of *II. Abt./SS-Pz.Rgt. 3*. One eyewitness later described it thus: "It was night as we drove through the burning village of Bajót. Our tanks had done good work here. At the road intersection south of the village, it looked pretty bad … burning Soviet tanks, guns and vehicles of every description lay all over the place."[35] Another participant, *Panzerfunker* (radio operator) Edelmann, riding in *Panzer 501* commanded by *Uscha.* Jupp Windisch, later wrote:

> As soon as we turned right at the road junction [south of Nyerges Ujfalu], we immediately began receiving well-aimed antitank and artillery fire, forcing us to stop to fire and then resume our advance. Then the assault seemed to unfold like one from the good old days. With gusto, firing from all barrels, we reached Bajót and fought our way into and through it.[36]

From Bajót, a small reconnaissance team was sent onwards to Bajna, where they encountered Hungarian civilians, who provided information that the Soviets had fled from that town hours earlier and described the horrors they had endured during their brief period of Soviet occupation. When a T-34 roared past them in the dark, the team's leader, *Unterscharführer* Marienfeld, quickly determined that their information, though well-intended, was not correct. A few minutes before this had happened, his two armored cars had captured an American-made Jeep after scattering its Soviet occupants with a burst of his machine pistol. The Jeep and its crew had somehow managed to get in between the two German vehicles in the dark, not knowing they were following German troops. With Soviet troops seemingly everywhere, Marienfeld decided to hide and wait until dawn before moving forward again, since a further advance in the darkness was deemed too risky. The lone tank that had passed him was dealt with a few minutes later when it ran into a roadblock manned by the reconnaissance battalion's motorcycle company, which had been warned in advance by Marienfeld via radio.

When the division's other armored spearhead reached the crossroads at Táth, the reinforced division reconnaissance battalion took the lead and began the turn to the southeast. Less than 4 kilometers past the intersection, it ran up against a strong Soviet defensive position, most likely manned by the 4th Guards Rifle Division, whose troops and antitank guns were spread out along the highway in front of the sugar factory 2 kilometers northeast of Tokod. Here, the advance was brought temporarily to a halt for the night by the heavy fire of the defenders until the main body of the *Panzergruppe* could arrive.[37] In the interim, *Brig.Fhr.* Becker's forward headquarters moved forward from Mocs to Nyerges Ujfalu, where the division commander could command and control his division more effectively. Overall, the first full day of fighting had gone well and Becker's *Totenkopf* Division had achieved all of its objectives, thanks in large part to the active role played by Harrendorf's *96. Inf.Div.* in carrying out a risky night amphibious assault, followed by its envelopment attack.

Within the area of operations of the *Wiking* Division, the advance was proceeding far more slowly, due to the inhospitable terrain as much as enemy resistance. Another factor inhibiting its operations was the absence of more than half of its combat units, which were still arriving at the railheads in Komorn and Raab. All that *Oberf.* Ullrich had at his disposal on 2 January was *K.Gr. Dorr* with three *Panzergrenadier* battalions, two half-strength tank battalions, and one self-propelled artillery battalion, much less than what the *Totenkopf* Division had sent into battle. While the battalion from *K.Gr. Bieber*, reinforced by a tank battalion, operating on Ullrich's left flank had taken Szomód, the two *Kampfgruppen* from *Div.Gr. Pape* on his right had made only limited progress, leaving this flank exposed to a Soviet counterattack.

After enjoying success at Agostyán, *K.Gr. Dorr*'s armored spearhead, led by *Ostuf.* Karl-Heinz Lichte and his *5. Kompanie*, prepared to advance down the forest road towards Tarján in the late afternoon. Engineers leading the column frequently had to dismount to remove antitank mines laid across the road. Before his tanks had gone 2 kilometers, Lichte's company was ambushed by a *Pakfront* composed of guns from the 1000th Antitank Artillery Regiment, arrayed in the woods east of Agostyán. After losing one Panther to enemy fire and being unable to deploy his company due to the terrain that kept his tanks road-bound, Lichte had to request help from the accompanying *Panzergrenadiers* from *III. Btl./Germania*, who dismounted from their *SPWs* and fanned out into the woods to eliminate the antitank gun belt. At the same time, Soviet troops from 80th Guards Rifle Division attacked the column from the steep hillsides abutting the road, slowing the pace of advance even further.

This was to become the prevailing pattern of the *Wiking* Division's attack through the Vértes Mountains—advance, encounter ambush, dismount infantry, fight through roadblocks with an outflanking maneuver, remount, and continue moving. The situation was further complicated by the need to drop off security elements to keep the road open as the spearhead continued its advance, decreasing the strength of the lead units, but there was no other choice. Large numbers of Soviet troops from the 80th Guards Rifle Division, ranging in size from rifle companies to entire battalions, were bypassed during the breakthrough and had taken refuge in the forest. They soon proved to be more than a mere nuisance. Instead of trying to break out from encirclement, as was usually the case, these stay-behinds aggressively attacked the German columns strung out along the highway, slowing them down as Dorr's troops were forced to defend themselves and launch counterattacks of their own to clear the highway. It was to prove an exhausting, costly, and time-consuming process.

Artillery support, so necessary for the success of any attack, was brought back into play after the initial attacks went forth. Once *K. Gr. Dorr* went into the hills east of Tata though, when it was needed the most to suppress or destroy the numerous antitank barriers that the 80th Guards Rifle Division had erected in their path (at least 20 between Tata and Tarján), it was either unavailable or ineffective. The dense woods, steep terrain, and numerous defiles the leading columns had to pass through during their advance to Tarján made it exceedingly difficult for *Staf.* Karl-Heinz Bühler's *II. Abt./SS-Pz.Art.Rgt. 5* to accurately target the enemy's positions.[38] The topographic interference with transmission and reception of radio messages did not help either, often delaying the relaying of important requests for fire support. No light observation aircraft were available to observe or correct fire either, as was common with American and British forces. Effective artillery support would not be available until both *Kampfgruppe Dorr* and *Hack* finally broke out of the wooded mountains southeast of Tarján and reached level terrain.

By nightfall on 2 January, the *Panzerspitze* (tank spearhead) of the *Wiking* Division had reached a point 6 kilometers southeast of Agostyán, where it halted for the night within sight of the village of Tolna. By this point, its attack had been underway for over 24 hours.[39] To complicate the situation that the *Wiking* Division faced, Soviet troops had reoccupied the town of Baj, through which ran a portion of the division's main supply route. To remedy the situation, Ullrich, who had by this point arrived on the scene, dispatched the division's combat engineer battalion—*Hstuf.* Eberhard Heder's *SS-Pz.Pio.Btl. 5*—which promptly drove out the enemy and restored it to German control.

That evening, the *IV. SS-Pz.Korps* in its *Tagesmeldung* (daily report) summarized the events of the day and the status of its attack to *A.Gr. Balck/6. Armee*:

> After overcoming strong enemy resistance, the *Kampfgruppe* attacking through Agostyán ejected the enemy from Tardos and pushed him as far back as Tolna. The mopping up of scattered enemy elements from the area around Szomód is still underway. Despite large sheets of melting ice and minimal initial enemy resistance, our own troops [*96. Inf.Div.*] were able to surprise [the enemy] and widen and unite our own bridgeheads along the southern banks of the Danube, despite the enemy's efforts to hinder us. The river road has been cleared of the [Soviets] as far as the eastern outskirts of Nyerges Ujfalu. Several enemy counterattacks against that town were driven off. The enemy was forced to give up Labatlan, and against increasingly tough enemy resistance, the fighting for Bajót is still underway.[40]

In his own diary, Gille complained that the division attacking on his right, *Div.Gr. Pape*, had failed to carry out its own assault, threatening the security on his southern flank and forcing the *Wiking* Division to divert some of its own limited combat power for that purpose.[41]

Although Gille's staff did not mention it in its evening report, the first trains of the *711. Inf.Div.* had begun to arrive on 2 January, though it would take two more days before the entire division would be ready for employment. Once he had assembled his division, *Gen.Lt.* Reichert would lead them into the Gerecse Mountains in the wake of the *Totenkopf* Division, with the mission of combing the woods and hills to eliminate the substantial number of Soviet troops from the 80th and 4th Guards Rifle Divisions who had been bypassed during the initial assault. Then, once it caught up with the German spearhead, the *711. Inf.Div.* would join up with the *96. Inf.Div.* and continue the advance towards Gran.

To the right of Gille's corps, *Korpsgruppe Breith* also summarized its operations that day in its own *Tagesmeldung* to *A.Gr. Balck/6. Armee*, writing that "on the center and middle of the *Korpsgruppe* sector, the day passed quietly ... against tough enemy resistance and strong antitank barriers, our own attack against the western and northern edge of Alsógalla [Tatabanya area] was temporarily brought to a halt."[42] One is left to wonder why the diversionary attack by the *1. Pz.Div.* was not continued that day, for had it done so, it possibly would have forced the 4th Guards Army to keep more of its units in place to the benefit of Gille's attack.

On Gille's left flank, the situation on the northern bank of the Danube had not significantly changed, thereby creating the impression at Balck's headquarters that it was safe to pull out most of the *6. Pz.Div.* from *LVII. Pz.Korps* and send it over the river the next day. *Generalleutnant* Kirchner's operations staff reported that evening:

A two-battalion strong enemy attack against Kam. Darmoty was driven off, and a weak enemy force is still holding out on the west bank [of the Gran] in the oxbow lake east of the village [of Kam. Darmoty]. [Our troops are] fighting against a weak enemy group as they try to mop up the western bank [of the river] near Garamvezekeny and Szodo, but this action is not yet completed.[43]

This seemingly minor Soviet bridgehead at Gran would soon prove to be more than an insignificant headache.

In Budapest, the *IX. SS-Geb.Korps* reported that evening that "heavy fighting was continuing with the focal point being the northeast sector and the elimination of the deep [enemy] penetration in Kispest during the night. Two T-34s were destroyed with close-combat weapons." No other significant activity occurred that day, except the garrison reported constant bombing and strafing runs by Soviet ground-attack aircraft in groups as large as 15 at a time, predominantly IL-2, A-20 Boston bombers, and Lagg-3s, supported by fighter escorts, that focused their attacks against front-line positions and the center of the city.

The *IX. SS-Geb.Korps* reported that 19 *Junkers Ju-52s* had landed within Budapest and evacuated 268 wounded from the garrison, while 73.5 tons of ammunition and 925 gallons of gasoline were dropped from 56 *Heinkel He-111s*, barely enough to meet daily requirements. A supply ship that had set out down the Danube from Komorn with supplies had run aground behind Soviet lines and its daring crew of volunteers were hurriedly attempting to transfer the materials onto smaller vessels to take it to Budapest. This effort was only partly successful.[44]

The evening summary by *Gen.d.Pz.Tr.* Balck's *Ic* to his own higher headquarters, *H.Gr. Süd*, described the progress by Gille's corps:

Against our own attack south of the Danube, which is slowly gaining ground, the enemy has committed his XXXI Guards Rifle Corps and a portion of the XVIII Tank Corps, which are offering tough resistance against our forces. The regrouping of enemy forces against our own attack spearheads has not yet been identified, but we expect that we will have to reckon that the enemy will commit his local reserves [portions of the XVIII Tank Corps] away from the western front of Budapest as well as forces from the southern area of the Vértes Mountains, especially mobile units, which will be thrown against our own forces to slow down their attack.[45]

Balck's own intelligence section was especially concerned about the status of the 6th Guards Tank Army, which was undergoing a reconstitution period east of the Gran River a few dozen kilometers behind the front line opposite Kirchner's *LVII. Pz.Korps*.

Although no signs of its imminent movement had been reported, the *6. Armee's Ic* deputy, *Hauptmann* von Pander, wrote that evening that "we must expect that this reconstitution will end soon, and when it does, and because of our own offensive, it may be brought into action sooner than expected to stop us or may be used at a later point in time to continue its operations towards the west."[46] Removing the *6. Pz.Div.* from Kirschner's *Korpsgruppe* on 3 January might soon prove to be a riskier move than originally believed.

As far as the Third Ukrainian Front was concerned, something *was* happening along the Danube west of Gran and in the mountains east of Tata, but the size and scope of the German action was yet unknown. Initial reports from the front lines were conflicting, and the loss of communications with some units in XXXI Guards Rifle Corps and the XVIII Tank Corps (170th Tank Brigade) that had been cut off made the situation even more uncertain. Whether it was a full-scale offensive or merely a local attack was not yet known, but as previously mentioned, both the 4th Guards Army and its Front headquarters began reacting less than six hours after the attack began.

The most powerful trump card of all, besides the 86th Guards Rifle Division and antitank regiments that the 4th Guards Army had already sent, were the three other brigades of the XVIII Tank Corps that had been positioned west of Budapest to block any German relief attempt of Budapest coming from the Lake Velencze–Stuhlweissenburg area. Though these brigades had suffered heavy losses during the past month of fighting, on 2 January the two remaining tank brigades (the 110th and 181st) combined still had 80 operational T-34s and the 363rd Heavy Artillery Regiment had 19 SU-122 self-propelled guns. During the evening, these brigades were ordered forward and to be in position in front of Bajna and Tokod by the next morning in order to counter the *Totenkopf* Division's thrust.[47] In addition, Gorshkov's V Guards Cavalry Corps was ordered that same evening to begin displacing from the Mór area to the northeast, with the leading division, the 12th Guards Cavalry Davison, being initially directed towards Felsőgalla.

Even more fortuitously, both tank brigades were arrayed in positions between Bicske and Zsámbék, the objectives of the *Wiking* and *Totenkopf* Divisions, respectively. The 32nd Motorized Rifle Brigade was positioned in nearby Csabdi between both tank brigades. They could not have been more advantageously placed there even had General Zakharov known that two crack SS *panzer* divisions were heading directly towards them. They would soon be ordered by the 4th Guards Army to form a new defensive belt to block any advance aimed towards Budapest. Somehow, the *H. Gr. Süd* intelligence staff had not detected these units' precise locations; otherwise, it would be difficult to believe that the German high command would have selected *Konrad* as the course of action taken. However, their presence would not be known for three more days, during which a great deal of fighting would take place as the Soviet defensive effort began to coalesce.

That evening, *H. Gr. Süd* issued additional guidance it had received from the *OKH Führungsstab* for the continuation of the attack towards Budapest. Three additional instructions were included in the order that would impact *A. Gr. Balck/6. Armee*, and by extension, *IV. SS-Pz. Korps*. These included the requirement to retake all of the old *Margarethestellung*, specified as the "final objective" of the offensive (which implied that at some point, Gille's corps would be shifted to the south); guidance to the encircled garrison to break out "only in case of extreme necessity," subject to

OKH approval; and the elimination of the nascent Soviet bridgehead west of the Gran River that was currently being contained by Kirschner's *LVII. Pz.Korps*.[48] Truly, this was a battle that was being micromanaged at the highest command levels of the German Armed Forces.

Though *Ogruf.* Gille may have been satisfied with the results of the day's fighting, *Gen.d.Inf.* Wöhler and *Gen.d.Pz.Tr.* Balck apparently were not. In a telephone discussion between the two at 10:10 p.m. on 2 January, Balck opined that the assault divisions had attacked along too narrow a front, and that this "mistake" was responsible for what he judged as the slow pace of the advance.[49] Given that both the *Totenkopf* Division and the *96. Inf.Div.* had achieved their objectives for the day, and that the *Wiking* Division had attacked with less than half of its combat strength along a single axis of advance into the mountains where the enemy was easily able to erect blocking positions, this would seem to be a most unfair assessment. *Divisiongruppe Pape*, a unit composed of army personnel, came into no such criticism despite the fact that it had made almost no progress at all during its attack towards Felsőgalla, including its failure to take its initial objective, Tatabanya.

This negative view of the *IV. SS-Pz.Korps* by the command and staff of both *A.Gr. Balck/6. Armee* and *H.Gr. Süd* would continue to manifest itself during the operation. As a further example, an hour after the commanders spoke, Balck's and Wöhler's chiefs of staff conducted their own telephone conversation and were much more critical. According to the war diary of *H.Gr. Süd*, *Gen.Maj.* Gaedke told his counterpart at the army group headquarters:

> The general impression is that nothing occurred to the commanders and their subordinates [of the *IV. SS-Pz.Korps*] to do after reaching their first objective. In contrast to the better-trained leaders of 1941 and 1942, they lacked the initiative to exploit successes on their own and drive relentlessly ahead. This is apparently based on a certain insecurity in acting on their own responsibility without detailed guidance.[50]

To say that such an assessment was grossly unfair is an understatement. The evidence is very persuasive that both the *Wiking* and *Totenkopf* Divisions pursued their objectives very aggressively.

It has already been stated that the two SS divisions conducted their attacks with little time to prepare, and in some cases units attacked immediately after detraining. Adding to this unfavorable situation was that they had to attack at night, with no opportunities to conduct a reconnaissance, in the winter, through mountains along narrow roads at less than full strength, and with no artillery preparation. Based on these facts, it is evident that neither division could have attacked across a wide front, at least during this early stage of the offensive. It is a wonder that they had accomplished anything at all. In addition, the Red Army they faced in 1945 was not the same one that the *Wehrmacht* had fought in 1941, for it had evolved into a tough, relatively efficient, flexible, well-equipped fighting machine led by competent men.

Therefore, any comparison between the leaders and troops of 1941 and 1945 was gratuitous and an indication of the existing prejudice that Gaedke and Balck held against Gille and his troops. Interestingly, the only unit whose performance Gaedke praised was Harrendorf's *96. Inf.Div.*, whose amphibious assault Gaedke praised as a masterstroke of senior and mid-grade leadership.[51] However, without the timely arrival of *Brig.Fhr.* Becker's armored *Kampfgruppe*, Harrendorf's division may well have been wiped out in short order. Such high-level sniping against the performance of Gille and his troops would soon become the norm.

While the commanders and key staff officers of *A.Gr. Balck/6. Armee* and *H.Gr. Süd* continued their criticism of the conduct of *Unternehmen Konrad* and discussed the future course of the operation, the fighting continued almost unabated that night, with the temperature hovering around 27 degrees Fahrenheit. On the far left flank of the *IV. SS-Pz.Korps*, the *96. Inf.Div.* kept up its efforts to consolidate its hold on the southern bank of the Danube, while its easternmost regiment, *Oberst* Lorenz's *Gren.Rgt. 287*, conducted an enveloping attack east of Nyerges Ujfalu in an attempt to overcome Soviet defenses erected around the sugar factory northeast of Tokod, while *Oberstlt.* von Böltzig's *Gren.Rgt. 283* took up defensive positions on Lorenz's right, oriented towards the area south of Táth. The division's third regiment, *Gren.Rgt. 284*, was hurrying on foot to link up with the rest of the division, where it would initially become the division reserve.[52]

To the right and south of Harrendorf's troops, Becker continued his division's deep attack towards Zsámbék. Its lead column on the right flank, Laackmann's *Panzergruppe*, assaulted Bajna from the north and executed an enveloping attack from the town's east and west. Just when it seemed the town was in German hands, a large-scale Soviet counterattack consisting of up to 26 tanks and other armored fighting vehicles pushed through Bajna from the south. In the wild tank battle that ensued in the town, the attacking force—the 110th Tank Brigade from the XVIII Tank Corps—was thrown back after losing 11 tanks, including six knocked out by *Panzergrenadiers* with *Panzerfausts*, against the loss of one *Pz. VI* Tiger damaged and one Panther destroyed.

During the German attack against Bajna, Soviet close air-support aircraft strafed and bombed the follow-on column of the *Kampfgruppe* formed around the rest of the *Eicke* Regiment, destroying several vehicles and creating a column of black smoke visible at a distance. The command *SPW* of *III. Btl./Eicke* was struck during this air attack, mortally wounding the battalion commander, *Hstuf.* Ewald Ehlers. A successor, *Stubaf.* Ernst Kiklasch, would be duly appointed, but in the meantime, the attack continued.

Falling back to the heights southeast of Bajna, the Soviet forces quickly erected a *Pakfront* reinforced by the surviving tanks and SU-122 self-propelled howitzers that kept up a withering fire on the town's new occupants. Writing afterwards, one of the participants in the battle, *SS-Funker* Edelmann, described the scene:

We receive tank fire from the entrance of Bajna. We take up line formation … a concealed assault gun fires but misses and is quickly taken out. Otto Grimminger, our gunner, is an ace! "Forward! Move out!" Thus we enter Bajna where the 12.2cm assault gun stands just where he knocked it out … A Tiger tries to break through. It returns after being hit. The same happens with a Panther. *Obersturmführer* Wenke [his company commander] asks me if we have radio contact with any close-support aircraft. I try my hand on several frequencies using our 10-Watt transmitter. After a few minutes, I am able to establish radio contact with one of the aircraft. I am then told [by the pilot] "expect us in about 10 minutes! Throw out orange smoke markers!" We waited for a little while, and suddenly two *Junkers Ju-88*s start circling around the village and fired at the enemy using their on-board cannon, setting an enemy tank on fire.[53]

Following this rare instance of successful close air support, the town was once more in German hands. As it consolidated its position, the *Panzergruppe* from *SS-Pz.Rgt. 3* prepared to continue its advance, though for the time being it was brought to a halt by the *Pakfront* south of the town. While the *Totenkopf* Division had been able to defeat this counterattack, the appearance of the 110th Tank Brigade was an ominous sign that the Soviet reaction was already in full swing.

The other *Kampfgruppe* of the *Totenkopf* Division, formed around *Pz.Gren.Rgt. 5 Totenkopf*, was operating 3 kilometers to the east and parallel to the one from the *SS-Pz.Rgt. 3*, separated by a long ridgeline. This battlegroup took the town of Nagysáp that morning against no resistance (the Soviet defenders having withdrawn earlier) and continued advancing until it arrived at a point due east of Bajna and west of the neighboring village of Sarisap (Sarisán). The division's reconnaissance battalion, *Hstuf.* Eberhard Zech's *SS-Pz.Aufkl.Abt. 3*, operating on the division's left flank, bypassed the enemy-occupied village of Szarkás, leaving the *96. Inf.Div.* to clear it of its Soviet defenders, and continued its advance 6 kilometers down the highway towards Sarisap.

That was as far as Zech's battalion got before it got the order to veer to the southwest to come to the aid of the *Kampfgruppe* fighting in Bajna. It arrived at roughly the same time in the afternoon when tank and mechanized brigades from both the XVIII Tank and VII Mechanized Corps, the latter recently diverted from the 46th Army, began a coordinated counterattack along the line Sarisap–Nagysáp–Bajna. Heavy fighting ensued that effectively halted the *Totenkopf* Division's advance for the remainder of the day, including a tank-led attempt to retake Nagysáp in the afternoon that was only stopped after *SS-Pz.Jäg.Abt. 3* destroyed three T-34s.[54] The division took advantage of this brief pause to carry out badly needed replenishment of fuel and ammunition, and to reorganize its units before continuing its attack early the following morning.

To the right of the *Totenkopf* Division, the *Wiking* Division continued its advance towards Tarján before sunrise. The remainder of the bypassed Soviet troops in Tolna (also called Vértestolna in some accounts) were eliminated in house-to-house fighting by *Stubaf.* Amberg's *II. Btl./Germania* during the evening of 2–3 January, while the rest of *K.Gr. Dorr* pressed its attack towards Tarján shortly after midnight. To cover the left flank of his advance until the division was able to link up with Becker's troops, Dorr directed *Hstuf.* Martin Kruse's *I. Btl./Germania* to take the village of Tardos, which it did in an enveloping attack under the cover of darkness. Likewise, to neutralize any Soviet forces in the neighboring village of Héreg 5 kilometers southeast of Tardos, the main body of Kruse's battalion continued its advance to the southeast, after leaving troops behind to secure Tardos. Héreg fell after a brief struggle, though with each town along the flanks now needing some sort of security force to prevent them from returning to enemy control, they had to be taken from *K.Gr. Dorr.* As these flank protection detachments were left behind, the *Wiking* Division's spearhead grew weaker the deeper it penetrated into the mountains.

To get to Tarján, *Ostubaf.* Dorr's *Kampfgruppe* would attack along the road leading southeast out of Tolna, which lay in a narrow valley between two forests. This meant that the tanks from *Pz.Gr. Darges* would have to move along an ice-covered road, up steep Mount Peskő (Hill 400), and through heavily wooded terrain before Darges's tanks reached open ground west of Tarján. Such an approach would work to the defender's favor, offering numerous opportunities to spring ambushes against the lead tanks in the column, which could not maneuver off the narrow road. A reconnaissance patrol sent up the road also reported that a strong Soviet antitank *Pakfront* was lying in wait only 1 kilometer southeast of Tolna. Clearly, if the *panzers* attempted to move in that direction, they would encounter great difficulties before they could fight their way through to Tarján.

Not satisfied with this course of action, *Ostubaf.* Darges suggested to Dorr and Ullrich (who had moved his command post forward to be near the front of the column) that his *Panzergruppe* should be allowed to outflank the *Pakfront* instead. Turning to the right from the Tolna–Bajna road out of sight of the enemy, Darges's tanks closely followed a narrow track along the wood line to the left of the Soviet position. Once abreast of the antitank gun barrier, the lead tank company deployed and immediately struck the surprised Soviet gunners on its left flank, quickly rolling up their position and capturing or destroying 17 antitank guns.[55] With this initial obstacle to Tarján now eliminated, the German force still had to get over the mountain and fight its way through the woods.

Panzergruppe Darges wasted no time in resuming its advance, following the kilometer-long serpentine road leading through the mountains. Encountering several Soviet tanks concealed in the forest, these were quickly destroyed by the tanks of the lead company, Lichte's *5. Kompanie/SS-Pz.Rgt. 5*, which continued pressing forward. Once clear of the woods, Lichte's tanks made a sharp right turn and barreled towards Tarján, only 2 kilometers away. When the column drew abreast of Lake Szúnyog, located on the right side of the road, a concealed Soviet self-propelled gun fired at the lead vehicles from a range of approximately 500 meters. The shot struck the second Panther in the column, commanded by *Oscha.* Männer, the leader of Lichte's *2. Zug. Obersturmführer* Lichte, riding in the lead tank, responded in kind, destroying the enemy vehicle with a shell from his 7.5cm cannon. Unfortunately, Männer died later from his wounds, but the road to Tarján was now clear.[56]

In the early afternoon, the advance towards Tarján was pressed forwards, with the tanks and SPWs of K.Gr. Dorr now able to deploy in open terrain for the first time since the offensive began. Arrayed against this force, which according to Soviet records consisted of 35–40 tanks and other armored vehicles, stood troops of the 93rd Rifle Division, which had only arrived a few hours earlier.[57] This division had been pulled out of the line from its positions at Pusztavám, where it had been fighting against the 4. Kav.Brig., and in a forced march had covered over 45 kilometers to be in its new positions by dawn on 3 January.[58] Before it had an opportunity to adequately prepare its defenses, the regiment in front of Tarján was overwhelmed by the Wiking Division's attack. By 3 p.m., most of the town had fallen into the hands of Ullrich's division, though heavy fighting on the southern outskirts continued for several more hours as the Soviet troops resisted bitterly before they were finally thrown back.[59]

Not pausing to rest, Dorr pressed his attack forward and by 4:30 p.m., his Kampfgruppe had advanced to a point 5 kilometers southeast of Tarján. Throughout the battle, attacks by Soviet aircraft (a menace that Gille characterized as "constant") harassed and bombed the German column, though antiaircraft fire rendered most of the Red Air Force's attempts to stop their advance ineffective. By 5 p.m., the situation was judged to be stable enough to warrant the transfer of the division's forward command post from Tolna, where it had reached the night before, to Tarján, where it would remain for the next several days.[60]

On that same day, Stubaf. Braun arrived to temporarily take up the reins of Division Ia. The news that Stubaf. Fritz Vogt's I. Btl./Norge had detrained in Komorn and was en route to join with Dorr's Germania was a welcomed development; it would become a badly needed addition to the regiment's dwindling infantry strength. To add to this bit of positive news, the transportation officer for the 6. Armee reported that 23 trains loaded with troops and equipment from the Wiking Division had arrived in Komorn and Raab that day, including major elements of the Westland Regiment.[61]

Closely associated with the Wiking Division's movement on 3 January was the progress made by the Div.Gr. Pape, whose two armored Kampfgruppen (K.Gr. Philipp and Knoop)—including at least 20 tanks—followed Ullrich's division during its advance that day. After the troops of K.Gr. Dorr had captured Tarján and while they were still consolidating their position before resuming their attack, K.Gr. Philipp veered to the southwest and approached Tatabanya along the highway from the northeast. Finding themselves behind the positions of the 34th Rifle Division and astride the far-left flank of the newly arrived 93rd Rifle Division, K.Gr. Philipp shot up a Soviet supply column before it was halted at the pass in the mountains overlooking Tatabanya and Alsógalla, a mere 2 kilometers northeast of their objective, due to strong Soviet resistance as much as the approaching darkness.[62]

Unless they withdrew quickly, the defenders in the valley below risked being encircled the following day if the troops and tanks from *Div. Gr. Pape* aggressively prosecuted their attack, and if *K. Gr. Bieber* attacked from the west. Their situation would only become worse, especially if the other armored battlegroup, *K. Gr. Knoop*, caught up with *K. Gr. Philipp* and joined the fight. Undeterred by this threat, the Soviet troops holding Tatabanya and Felsőgalla held firm and continued their staunch defense of the mountain pass. So far, *Div. Gr. Pape* had not achieved any of their objectives, and would prove to be a continuing disappointment to Gille.

Another highlight of 3 January was the movement of *6. Pz. Div.* from its positions north of the Danube. Tasked with reinforcing *IV. SS-Pz. Korps*, it would not be completely formed up at Tata until the following day, at which point it would move into the mountains to take up its new position to the right of the *Wiking* Division. The division's acting commander, *Oberst* Friedrich-Wilhelm Jürgens, would have to catch up with *Oberf.* Ullrich in order for him to closely coordinate the activities of his division with those of his new partner.

Oberst Jürgen's first task was to clear the main supply route of the *Wiking* Division from Tata to Tarján of bypassed elements of the 80th Guards Rifle Division, whose troops were continuing to harass Ullrich's logistics convoys as they passed through the hills and forests of the Gerecse Mountains. A benefit of this arrangement was that Jürgens's division would finally be rejoined by *K. Gr. Philipp*, which had most of the division's operational tanks and *SPWs*. Once reunited, the division would establish its forward command post at Héreg, cover the right flank of the *Wiking* Division, and ensure the connectivity between it and the neighboring *Div. Gr. Pape*. Even if it did not storm Tatabanya, *K. Gr. Philipp* was ideally positioned to protect the right flank of the *Wiking* Division against any Soviet attack from that direction.

Although the fighting that day occupied center stage, another noteworthy event that occurred on 3 January was the personal visit by *Gen. d. Inf.* Wöhler to Gille's corps forward headquarters in Nagyigmánd that morning. His intent was to see for himself why the advance had been proceeding so slowly, based on what he had heard from von Grolman, his chief of staff, who himself had probably been influenced by Gaedke's negative impression of the *IV. SS-Pz. Korps'* performance thus far. Since Gille had gone forward himself to confer with Ullrich at the *Wiking* Division's *Gefechtstand* (still located at that point in Tata), Wöhler—after speaking with *Ostubaf.* Schönfelder at Nagyigmánd—was driven to Tata to meet with both commanders. Along the way, the *H. Gr. Süd* commander gained a greater understanding of what Ullrich's and Dorr's troops had endured while having to fight their way through rough terrain against such a determined opponent. One eyewitness to the visit was *Ostuf.* Jahnke, the division's *O1*, who wrote that evening in his personal diary:

> Visit today by the corps commander and the army group commander at the division forward command post … according to him [Wöhler], things were proceeding too slowly. In spite of the difficulties with the terrain and the way the enemy was able to slow us down using relatively

simple antitank defenses emplaced in well-sited blocking positions, our spearhead was able to reach Vértestollna [Tolna] ... The commanders, after seeing with their own eyes the difficulty posed by the terrain, came away satisfied with the progress achieved by the division so far.[63]

Wöhler and Gille concluded their meeting with Ullrich in Tata after urging him to keep moving forward as quickly as he could in order to maintain the tempo of the operation. By this point, three days into the operation, *Gen.d.Pz.Tr.* Balck had yet to visit Gille's *Hauptquartier*, which was most uncharacteristic of a commander who at one time during the early stages of the campaign in the Soviet Union had been renowned for his frequent visits to the front line to see the situation "up front" for himself.

Jahnke and the rest of the division staff displaced forward to Tolna during the early afternoon, as previously described. Wöhler and Gille shortly afterwards returned to their own headquarters, each with their own interpretation of events so far. After returning to his own headquarters at the Esterhazy castle, Wöhler wrote in the war diary of the army group's *Führungsabteilung* his own impression of the visit, including notes about the units he visited:

> *IV. SS-Pz.Korps*: I emphasized to the corps chief of staff today the necessity for the attack to be pressed forward without delay; otherwise, the enemy would gain too much time to regroup his forces. I had the impression that everything possible was being done and that yesterday's limited success was no fault of either the corps or the divisions. *SS-Obergruppenführer* Gille was forward with the *5. SS-Pz.Div. Wiking*.
>
> The *96. Infanterie-Division*: The *Ia* was still in the [division's] old command post at Bucs, while the division commander had crossed over to the south bank of the Danube about two hours earlier ... I let him know quite unmistakably that the situation was critical and required the greatest possible speed in the attack and for bringing in those forces which are still far to the rear.[64]

In general, Gille was satisfied with his troops' performance. That evening, *IV. SS-Pz. Korps* reported in its *Tagesmeldung* the following:

> Due to our attacks, the enemy gave up Tarján and Héreg. In the Bajna–Nyerges Ujfalu sector, the enemy's resistance increased. Enemy armored forces, which had temporarily forced their way into Bajna and Nagysáp, were thrown back to the high ground to the east. The enemy was able to fend off our own attack against the [sugar] factory [east of] Nyerges Ujfalu. The fighting is still going on.

While the *Totenkopf* Division would face even more fighting the next day as the XVIII Tank Corps heightened its attack, the way appeared open for the *Wiking* Division to reach Bicske, which it expected to do by the evening of 3–4 January.

Although its report did not mention it, ground attacks by up to 300 aircraft sorties from the Soviet's 17th Air Army had noticeably increased in the *IV. SS-Pz.Korps* area of operations on 3 January, making life difficult for any German columns moving along the roads in open terrain.[65] Rather than providing overwhelming close air support to the advancing units, *Luftflotte 4* had been forced to battle for air parity, dedicating many of its available sorties to combating Soviet fighter aircraft, shooting down 35 that day alone. The air fleet's *Stukas* and *Henschel He-129* tank busters that did break through Soviet fighter cover on 3 January managed to destroy 29 enemy tanks and carry out 190 bombing sorties that evening.[66]

Korpsgruppe Breith had not been idle that day either, reporting that battalion- to regimental-sized attacks by the XXI Guards Rifle Corps had been launched against the positions of the *1. Pz.Div.* east of Czajag, a village on the eastern shore of Lake Balaton. These attacks were still underway when the report was submitted. At the same time, *Korpsgruppe Breith* reported attacks in similar strength were being conducted against the positions held by *K.Gr. Knoop* of *Div.Gr. Pape* in Bánhida, 2 kilometers northwest of Tatabanya.

An additional company-size attack by Soviet troops was reported against the positions at Pusztavám held by elements of the *4. Kav.Brig.*, but this was successfully repulsed. The report made no mention of the progress of *K.Gr. Philipp* or *Knoop*. Surprisingly, the successful counterattack that day by the *4. Kav.Brig.* to seize Pusztavám, a town north of Mór defended by the 93rd Rifle Division, was not mentioned in the daily report, only the small-scale Soviet attack mentioned above. Though a relatively minor attack compared to the action being carried out by the *Wiking* or *Totenkopf* Divisions 60 kilometers to its north, the *4. Kav.Brig.* was able to push its main defense line as far forward at the western bank of the Altaler River and liberate most of the town.[67]

North of the Danube, *Korpsgruppe Kirschner* (*LVII. Pz.Korps*) that evening reported that with the exception of localized fighting conducted to eliminate the small Soviet bridgehead on the western bank of the Gran River at Garam Vezekény, no combat activity took place throughout the rest of the corps' defensive sector. Interestingly, the report made no mention at all of the much larger Soviet bridgehead west of the city of Gran at Parkány, which had been dormant since it was established the week before. This bridgehead, mutually contained by the *3. Pz.Div.* and the Hungarian *2. Pz.Div.*, was held by the 53rd Guards Rifle Division of the XXV Guards Rifle Corps, which had not yet committed the bulk of its forces west of the Gran. Except for the occasional foot patrolling and exchange of artillery fire, there was no combat activity worth mentioning. Perhaps this lack of activity on the part of the 7th Guards Army had lulled the Germans into a sense of complacency.

On 3 January, for the first time since the encirclement began, the fighting within *Festung Budapest* slackened noticeably. This was primarily due to the Third Ukrainian Front's need to take forces from the city's inner and outer western encirclement rings and form reserves to halt the advance of the *IV. SS-Pz.Korps*. Some of these forces had already made their appearance in front of the *Totenkopf* Division at Bajna and Sarisap. Accordingly, the 46th Army, responsible for carrying out the attacks against Budapest from the west, was ordered to halt its offensive against the city and to go over to the defense.[68]

Though it did not submit a *Tagesmeldung* that evening, the *IX. SS-Geb.Korps* had not been neglected by either side. To make up for the slackening of ground combat activity, the Red Air Force's 5th Air Army dedicated a significant amount of its available sorties against the city, carrying out a number of low-level bombing and strafing attacks against important targets such as troop concentrations, individual tanks, and identified headquarters locations. At the same time, the *Luftwaffe* flew 93 resupply sorties to the city, using 34 *Junkers Ju-52*s and 59 *Heinkel He-111s*.

The *A.Gr. Balck/6. Armee* intelligence summary reported the results of air reconnaissance flown that day by the *Luftwaffe* behind Soviet lines. The pilots had spotted the movement of a significant amount of troops away from Budapest and towards the German lines to the west and northwest of the city, but their precise destination was unclear. Some of these Soviet troops were assessed as being from the II Guards Mechanized Corps and the 86th Guards Rifle Division. The *6. Armee Ic* continued:

> Furthermore, it appears that the enemy, after regrouping between Mór and Bánhida, is preparing to attack again to the west or northwest. In the course of this regrouping, it cannot be ruled out that the VII Mechanized Corps may be directed to the Bánhida area in the southern part of the Vértes Mountains … The withdrawal of forces from the western front of Budapest had not yet made a measurable impact on the concentration of forces in the course of the battle so far … North of the Danube the shifting of the enemy forces to the west makes the regrouping of the XXIV Guards Rifle Corps closer to the Gran Front a possibility. The [Soviet] air force deployment to the Ipolysag [the Slovak town of Šahy, north of the Danube] area confirms a newly identified enemy center of gravity with implications for his future intentions.[69]

In its own *Tagesmeldung* for *H.Gr. Süd*, submitted by the *A.Gr. Balck/6. Armee* chief of staff himself, *Gen.Maj.* Gaedke concluded with an updated estimate of the situation:

> The general impression of the course of today's attack is that things went well for the *5. SS-Pz. Div. Wiking*. Otherwise, the enemy seems to have concentrated his forces in two areas: one in front of the *3. SS-Pz.Div. Totenkopf* south of Bajna as far as to the southwest of Gran; the other southwest of Bicske. It is to be hoped that a vacuum lies in front of the present attack of the [*Wiking*] and that the enemy has lost his cohesion in the area around Bicske. The presence of the II Guards Mechanized Corps is not yet confirmed, but from the large number of enemy tanks which have appeared, it would seem to have entered the fight. The two armored divisions have lost a valuable day before they became [accustomed] to the peculiarities of mountainous terrain. Now they seem to have mastered them. The relief of Budapest is still expected. The 86th Guards Rifle Division, previously confirmed outside of Budapest, has now appeared on the Danube west of Gran.[70]

That same evening, at 10:10 p.m., Wöhler and Balck spoke to one another over the field telephone, discussing the overall situation and the progress of *Unternehmen Konrad* thus far. According to the transcribed record of the conversation, Wöhler asked what his intent was for the coming days and Balck replied as follows:

It was to be hoped that during the night [the *Wiking* Division] would be able to advance a considerable distance towards Bicske. The *3. SS-Pz.Div. Totenkopf* was involved in heavy fighting. The *96. Inf.Div.*, which did not advance very far today, was to assume the left flank-guard mission for the *Totenkopf* Division against the enemy concentrating to the southwest of Gran. *Divisionsgruppe Pape* was to be directed against enemy forces concentrating west of Bicske and also in Alsógalla [Tatabanya area], where they were apparently growing stronger. He wanted to place the *6. Pz.Div.*, which was to be across the [Danube] River by morning, into the line to the right of the *5. SS-Pz.Div. Wiking*. The *711. Inf.Div.* was to be brought forward to mop up.

When Wöhler asked him for his estimate of the situation thus far, the conversation concluded after Balck stated that he was "quite pleased with today's results. The forces needed 24 hours to come to terms with armored fighting in the mountains. Now they have the hang of it. In addition, the *Armeegruppe* was continuing to plan. [He] intended to pull the *4. Kav.Brig.* out of the line from the Vértes Mountains front and use it in the attack."[71]

Prior to retiring for the night, Balck issued instructions to the *IV. SS-Pz.Korps* for the following day's operations. His orders made it clear that the two *panzer* divisions of Gille's corps were expected to reach the initial objectives of Bicske and Zsámbék by that evening and to conduct operations throughout the evening to take advantage of the attack's momentum and to keep the enemy off balance. The *96. Inf.Div.* was ordered to take the sugar factory northeast of Tokod and continue pushing east towards Gran via the crossroads village of Öröktarna. Once it had done this, it would veer to the southeast and continue covering the left flank of the *Totenkopf* Division via the Körteles–Dorog axis. At this point, no mention had been made of cancelling *Konrad*; the prevailing opinion among the army and army group commanders seemed to be one in which they would "wait and see" how the next several days of fighting turned out before they would take the next step. The following day, Thursday, 4 January, would therefore be a crucial one.

After a freezing night, the day would not get much warmer than 25 degrees Fahrenheit and the skies would be mostly overcast with moderate visibility. In the mountains, the roads would be icy, with temperatures even lower than in the lowlands. The soldiers of both sides would be forced to sleep outdoors in these conditions, and no campfires were allowed. Food, when issued, would probably have cooled off between the time it was cooked and when it was brought forward to troops in the front lines. Hot coffee was a scarce commodity. Most armored vehicles, except for Panthers and Tigers, lacked any kind of heating system for the crew compartment, and crew members or troops riding in most other kinds of vehicles, whether *SPWs*, armored cars, or trucks, had no option but to bundle up with as many layers of clothing as possible.

By this point of the war, the *Wehrmacht* and *Waffen-SS* had developed and issued adequate winter clothing for its troops, but this would only keep them from freezing to death, not make them comfortable while fighting outdoors in the elements. If they were fortunate, some troops—whether German, Hungarian, or Soviet—would commandeer a farmhouse or barn for shelter, but most were not afforded this luxury. The widespread use of alcoholic beverages—usually wine, vodka, slivovitz, or *Julischka*—provided only temporary relief from the cold and, when abused, only made a soldier's individual situation worse, particularly if it clouded the judgement of his leaders or his own reflexes in combat.

Nevertheless, the attack rolled on. That morning on the corps' left flank, the *96. Inf.Div.*, urged on by the *H.Gr. Süd* commander during his visit the previous day, pressed forward at 3 a.m. with renewed determination. It had good reason to, for the division had been singled out by *Gen.d. Inf.* Wöhler for special criticism on 3 January. In a *Fernschreiber* message sent to Balck, Gille, and all of his division commanders at 3:45 p.m., Wöhler wrote:

> I have serious cause for concern [about the pace of the operation] and must demand the utmost speed and momentum from the attacking corps. The *Ia* of the *96. Inf.Div.* was not clear today even at 10:00 a.m. whether the division had started its attack to the east or not. I remind everyone that our attack is a day and night continuously connected fighting action. The faster we advance, the less opportunity the enemy has to regroup. It is necessary to park all vehicles that are not indispensable; otherwise, the few roads will inevitably be blocked. Exercise tight traffic control day and night.[72]

After a severe tongue-lashing by his army group commander, the division's *Ia*, *Maj.* Ulf Burchardt, would have made haste to gain as much situational awareness as quickly as possible. However, with his division commander on the other side of the river, he would have to rely on wireless communication or messengers using one of the ferries running at Sütto or Nyerges Ujfalu to make contact with Harrendorf.

Nevertheless, with all three regiments of the division plus its *Füsilier* battalion, assault gun battery, *Pionier* battalion, and artillery regiment now present on the field, *Oberst* Harrendorf now had sufficient combat power to carry out his mission. On the left, making the division's main effort that day, *Oberst* Lorenz's *Gren.Rgt. 287* advanced 1 kilometer past Öröktarna and, following a three-hour battle, took possession of Táth after overcoming resistance by two regiments of the 86th Guards Rifle Division, capturing 14 guns and 12 trucks of the 1255th Antitank Artillery Regiment in the process.[73]

After a brief consolidation of his two battalions, Lorenz continued his attack at 10 a.m., reaching the Tokod railway station after overcoming determined Soviet defenses. Five of the *StuG III* assault guns supporting his attack were hit by antitank gunfire, with two being completely destroyed. As his regiment continued its advance, it encountered a very strong Soviet position outside of Dorog held by one regiment from the 86th Guards Rifle Division, supported by several T-34s from the 37th Guards Tank Brigade and JS-II Stalin tanks of the 30th Guards Heavy Tank Regiment.[74] This was simply too much to overcome without tanks of his own.

Until his regiment could be reinforced, Lorenz ordered his men to dig in astride the Dorog–Körteles road.

On the division's right, *Maj.* Magawly's *Gren.Rgt. 284* almost reached Sarisap (Sarisán), where it made contact with *SS-Pz.Aufkl.Abt. 3.* In the middle, *Oberstlt.* von Böltzig's *Gren.Rgt. 283* maintained connectivity with both flanking regiments, clearing any Soviet positions it found along the way. That same day, *Gen.Lt.* Reichert's *711. Inf.Div.* had advanced 10 kilometers through the Gerecse Mountains, clearing the woods of the enemy, until it reached the town of Dunaszentmiklós by nightfall. It would continue its mission and catch up with the *96. Inf.Div.*, which had moved its division *Gefechtstand* to Nyerges Ujfalu, by the end of the following day.[75] As Reichert's division marched through Szomód, the troops from *K.Gr. Bieber* from *Div.Gr. Pape*, who had taken the town two days before, were relieved of their security mission, allowing them to march south to rejoin *K.Gr. Pape* near Bánhida.

Oberst Harrendorf's division, charged with the responsibility of protecting the left flank of the *Totenkopf* Division, was moving forward as quickly as it could, but his regiments found keeping up with Becker's division's movement quite a challenge. Not only did they have to keep pace with a rapidly advancing *panzer* division without much armor of their own, but the non-motorized *Grenadiere* had to fight their way through a series of oncoming Soviet reserves and antitank barriers that were being pushed forward to halt the German advance in its tracks. To further complicate the situation, Soviet artillery was beginning to be employed more accurately and in greater amounts, whereas up to this point, it had been scattered and ineffectual. To better coordinate the efforts of the two divisions, Becker moved his forward headquarters to Nyerges Ujfalu, adjacent to Harrendorf's. Such close proximity enabled both commanders and their staffs to confer face-to-face and allowed both divisions to gain and maintain a better sense of how each of their battles were unfolding, at least for the few days they were co-located in the riverside town.

That day, the *Totenkopf* Division was experiencing its heaviest fighting since the offensive began, with its troops having to fight their way through a series of hasty defenses erected by the reserves from the XVIII Tank Corps, some of which had begun appearing the previous day, as already mentioned. On the southern outskirts of Bajna on the division's right flank, its forces faced off against elements of the 110th Tank Brigade, supported by several assault guns of the 363rd Heavy SP Artillery Regiment. During the early morning of 4 January, taking advantage of a snowstorm, *Panzergrenadiers* from *III. Btl./Eicke* were able to infiltrate the Soviet positions in the dark and managed to destroy three T-34s and one JSU-122 using hand-held antitank weapons. With few supporting infantry of their own to provide close-in protection from such attacks, the remaining tanks withdrew 5 kilometers south along the main road to the chapel at Csima, where they halted and regrouped.[76]

The point of main effort that day for Becker's division was not to be a continued defense of Bajna, but the seizure of Szomor, a sizeable town approximately 8 kilometers to the south and the same distance north of its intermediate objective, Zsámbék. Before dawn, as the *Totenkopf* Division's *Panzergruppe* formed up to continue its assault from Bajna, the Soviet antitank positions atop the hills straddling the road to Szomor were eliminated in hand-to-hand combat or with *Panzerfausts* and hand grenades by troops from the *Eicke* Regiment, who took advantage of the lingering darkness to approach the guns unobserved, often wading through deep snowdrifts.

The way to Szomor now clear, the *Panzergruppe* advanced to the south, its tanks sliding and skating along the ice-covered road as they roared full-speed to their objective. Every now and then, they would stop and fire at Soviet antitank positions or *Panzergrenadiers* would dismount and deal with dug-in infantry by enveloping them. The column would keep moving onwards after each successive roadblock was eliminated, while the hills on either side of the road reverberated with their detonations.

Finally, after overcoming several well-laid tank ambushes along the way, the advance was brought to a halt a mere 4 kilometers short of Szomor when it encountered a well-entrenched antitank barrier positioned along a ridgeline centered on Hill 184, a prominence that provided a commanding view of the highway. Because this *Pakfront* could not be overcome by a frontal assault, *Ostubaf.* Laackmann, commander of SS-Pz.Rgt. 3, decided to bypass it, leaving it to the accompanying *Panzergrenadiers* to deal with it. Turning to the south, Laackmann ordered his tank column to leave the road and continue its advance overland out of range of the enemy's guns, taking advantage of the relatively open terrain to deploy in a standard *Panzerkeil* (armor spearhead) formation.

After progressing 3 kilometers against negligible resistance, Laackmann's *panzers* entered the village of Gyermely from the north, 1 kilometer west of Szomor, completely outflanking the units from the XVIII Tank Corps arrayed to the east. When the lead German tank approached the outskirts of the neighboring town, it encountered a well-emplaced *Pakfront* that would have made any attempt to take Szomor without infantry support suicidal. To further convince the *Totenköpfler* that an attack against Szomor that afternoon was a bad idea, as Laackmann's tanks approached Szomor they were counterattacked by the 181st Tank Brigade, which had only arrived in the town hours before.

Turning around after losing several tanks to Soviet fire, Laackmann ordered his *Panzergruppe* to return to Gyermely to await the arrival of the rest of the column. After conferring with his fellow commanders, Laackmann planned to assault the position at Szomor during the night using a combined tank–infantry team. That day, the *Panzergruppe* had advanced over 9 kilometers, the most rapid rate of progress the division had achieved in a single day up to that point, and had put to flight both a tank and a mechanized infantry brigade.

To the left of Bajna, the division's other armored *Kampfgruppe*—formed around *III. Btl./Totenkopf*, *II. Abt./Pz.Rgt. 3* (equipped with *Pz.Kfw. IV*s), and *SS-Pz.Jag. Abt. 3*—was embroiled in heavy defensive fighting south of the village of Nagysáp. During the early hours, *III. Btl./Totenkopf* was relieved in the line by *Stubaf.* Ludwig Schwermann's *SS-Pio.Btl. 3* in order for it to move forward towards the village of Epöl alongside the left flank of the other *Panzergruppe* in Bajna. Upon encountering a strong Soviet *Pakfront* supported by infantry on the northern edge of Epöl, *III. Btl./ Totenkopf* enveloped the village and quickly took possession of it after overcoming an initially determined defense. While this battalion consolidated in Epöl, one of its sister battalions, *II. Btl./Totenkopf*, moved through the village and pushed forward towards Szomor to continue the flank protection mission to the left of Laackmann's *Panzergruppe*.[77]

On the division's far left flank, the reconnaissance battalion, reinforced by *SS-Pz. Jäg.Abt. 3*, seized Sarisap proper and was preparing to continue its advance when it was struck by a company-sized infantry attack supported by armored vehicles originating from the village of Dag. After repelling this effort to block their advance, *Hstuf.* Zech's *SS-Pz.Aufkl.Abt. 3* departed Sarisap that afternoon and continued pushing south towards Kirva, its objective for the day. Responsibility for securing Sarisap was handed over to the *96. Inf.Div.* in order to free up all of the *Totenkopf* Division's units to continue its mission to get to Zsámbék that evening.

As darkness fell, the reconnaissance battalion reached the outskirts at Kirva (modern-day Máriahalom), but was given a warm reception by the defenders, who had established yet another *Pakfront* to block the battalion's advance. With this attack stalled, just like that on the division's right flank at Szomor, fighting on 4 January drew to a close, as the *Totenkopf* Division focused on refueling, restocking ammunition, and reorganization in preparation for another grueling day of operations.

As the *Totenkopf* Division's columns ran the gauntlet of Soviet roadblocks from Bajna to Szomor, at the same time the *Wiking* Division initiated its own attack from Tarján. Its advance was to prove the most impressive achievement that day, with Darge's *Panzergruppe* fighting its way nearly 17 kilometers southeast to the village of Mány, a mere 4.5 kilometers northeast of its intermediate objective of Bicske.[78] Setting off at 1 a.m. on 4 January, the *Wiking* Division's armored spearheaded encountered little to no resistance as it barreled its way down the snow-covered road towards Bicske. The advance came to a halt an hour later, when the lead vehicles in the column were confronted in the dark near Esztermajor, a village 3 kilometers northwest of Mány, by armored vehicles from the 16th Mechanized Brigade of the VII Mechanized Corps approaching from the opposite direction.

In the short but sharp tank battle that ensued, Hans Flügel's *II. Abt./SS-Pz.Rgt. 5* knocked out five enemy tanks against the loss of none of its own, though Flügel was wounded seriously enough to require evacuation while he was conducting a reconnaissance on foot in search of the command post of *II. Btl./Germania*.

Obersturmbannführer Darges immediately replaced Flügel with *Ostuf.* Karl-Heinz Lichte, commander of the *5. Kompanie*, to serve as the acting *Bataillons-Führer* until a permanent one could be appointed. Together with *Stubaf.* Amberg's *II. Btl./ Germania*, moving to the right of the *Panzergruppe*, the advancing armored column continued moving south towards Bicske.

Darge's *Panzergruppe* was carrying its own infantry escort aboard his tanks, consisting of *Stubaf.* Vogt's *I. Btl./Nordland*, which had only arrived in Tarján the previous day. To the right lay Dorr's *Germania* Regiment, which had established flank security positions between Tarjan and Gyarmatpuszta with its *I.* and *III. Btl./ Germania*, reinforced by five or six tanks from *SS-Pz.Rgt. 5*. Beyond these forces, there was no connection with any German units on the division's right flank, and no sign of *K.Gr. Philipp* or the *6. Pz.Div.*, for that matter.[79]

At the same time, the Soviet 16th Mechanized Brigade and the 41st Guards Rifle Division, soon followed by the 12th Guards Cavalry Division, had begun to establish a coherent defense line, featuring integrated antitank gun defenses manned by the 1289th Antitank Artillery Regiment, to block any attempt by the *Wiking* Division to reach Bicske. Centered in the area between Szár on the left and Mány on the right, the heart of the defense was concentrated before the village of Csabdi, which controlled access to Bicske from the north.[80]

Although the Soviet reserves had only arrived the previous evening, they had already established a formidable defensive barrier to block the *Wiking* Division's further progress. Sufficient Soviet artillery (four regiments' worth) had been brought forward to provide a gun density of up to 40 barrels per kilometer of front, to further stymie the *Wiking*'s advance.[81] Although Amberg's *II. Btl./Germania* had taken Vasztély, it had been stopped by the increasingly stiff Soviet defenses 4.5 kilometers northwest of Mány and could go no further. German artillery support was minimal at this point, since the attacking columns had left most of the batteries far behind.

Recognizing the strength of the Soviet position, *Oberf.* Ullrich, who was riding in his *SPW* close to the head of the column, ordered a halt as it grew dark. With his forces widely scattered and running low on fuel and ammunition, he decided instead to resume the attack early in the morning, once the vanguard of *Ostubaf.* Hack's *Westland* Regiment had arrived. The plan was simple: with both regiments on line and the artillery having caught up and able to provide fire support, the division would advance early the following morning as far as the highway running from the southwest to the northeast between Bicske and Zsámbék. There, once Bicske had fallen, Ullrich intended to wait until the *Totenkopf* Division came abreast on his division's left flank, which surely must occur within the next day, and then both divisions would advance in tandem towards Budapest, less than 21 kilometers away.

Rather than hurl all of his forces in a head-on attack into the Soviet defensive positions, Ullrich intended to outflank Bicske from the east using the bulk of the *panzer* regiment. *Panzergruppe* Darges would launch its attack with approximately

20 Panthers and *Pz. IV*s, along with an SPW company from *SS-Pz.Aufkl.Abt. 5* and Vogt's *I. Btl./Norge* in support. Once Darges's tanks crossed the highway between Zsámbék and Mány, they would swing to the southwest and hit the defenders in the flank. After destroying enemy antitank defenses from behind, the *Germania* and *Westland* Regiments, with artillery support, would press the attack home and seize Bicske. With supply columns now established close by in Tarján, Ullrich's troops would use the opportunity to rearm and refuel in preparation for the next day's operations.[82]

While the *Wiking, Totenkopf,* and *96. Inf.Div.* were all embroiled in heavy fighting on 4 January, the same could not be said of *Div.Gr. Pape* or the *6. Pz.Div.* In the case of the *6. Pz.Div.*, it had only recently arrived and had not yet assembled all of its forces to play its intended role. One of the armored *Kampfgruppe* from *Div.Gr. Pape* that had been following the *Wiking* Division attempted to work its way through the mountain pass northeast of Alsógalla, but was unable to fight its way through. Another was able to make its way through Tarján and attack southeast towards the important rail station at Szár, but only got as far as Nagynémetegyház before it was stopped by a counterattack launched by the 16th Mechanized Brigade, which had been sent to prevent the Germans from approaching along the Bánhida–Tatabanya–Felsőgalla corridor. Although this combat group (most likely *K.Gr. Philipp*) had destroyed seven tanks, one SP gun, and 14 antitank guns, it had fallen far short of its mission of covering the right flank of the *Wiking* Division, whose commander continually complained about the lack of support from that direction.[83]

That evening, in the *IV. SS-Pz.Korps'* nightly *Ia Tagesmeldung* for 4 January, it reported the following to headquarters of *A.Gr. Balck/6. Armee*, a copy of which was also sent to *H.Gr. Süd*:

> On the left flank of the attack, the *96. Inf.Div.* broke loose past the sugar factory east of Nyerges Ujfalu, took the railroad crossing at Tokod and advanced to a point five kilometers west of Körteles. The *711. Inf.Div.* began mopping up actions in the mountains to the rear of the assault groups. It succeeded in taking the village of Dunaszentmiklós, where there had been fighting since the beginning of the attack on 1 January … The *3. SS-Pz.Div. Totenkopf* continues to engage a stubbornly defended antitank gun belt and infantry positions south, southwest, and west of Bajna. However, during the day, it fought through to the northwest side of Szomor, while the division reconnaissance battalion protected the left flank by taking Sarisán. The [division] was again faced with the strongest enemy armor force … As on the previous day, the *5. SS-Pz. Div. Wiking* made the best progress of all the assault elements of the [corps]. Although even today it failed to reach the initial objective of its attack, Bicske, its main group approached the village of Mány about 4.5 kilometers to the northwest of the objective, along and to the east of the Tarján–Bicske road. Its reconnaissance battalion advanced to a point five kilometers west of Bicske. The enemy had constructed another strong antitank gun belt front outside of Mány … [in the *Div.Gr. Pape* area], unbroken enemy forces are still holding the pass at Alsógalla on the right flank of the attack group. They could not be thrown out of their positions on the preceding days by frontal attacks from the north and northwest, and today it turned out that they could not be successfully tackled from the east either … The *6. Pz.Div.* has completed crossing the Danube and is moving up behind the *5. SS-Pz.Div. Wiking* at Tarján.

At this point in the battle, the troops carrying out *Unternehmen Konrad* had fought halfway to Budapest, which still lay 21 kilometers away. Gille closed his daily report in his typically taciturn, no-frills style, describing his intentions for the following day: "The battle will continue."

This was also the first day where results of the first four days of the offensive were reported. According to the records, the *IV. SS-Pz.Korps* from 1–4 January had knocked out or destroyed 79 Soviet tanks and assault guns (40 on 4 January alone), 106 artillery pieces, 107 antitank guns, 27 mortars, and 40 antitank rifles, among other items including trucks, horse-drawn wagons, and field kitchens. The corps also reported capturing 138 prisoners. The *I. Flieger-Korps*, which was providing the bulk of the close air support missions on behalf of *Luftflotte 4*, claimed separately that its aircraft had destroyed 48 tanks, three armored cars, two assault guns, and 177 trucks. It also reported that its fighters had shot down 87 Soviet aircraft.[84] On 4 January alone, *Luftflotte 4* and the Hungarian Air Force's 102nd Air Brigade flew 500 sorties, shot down 25 Soviet aircraft against the loss of 11 of their own, and knocked out 15 enemy armored vehicles. By comparison, the Red Air Force flew over 700 sorties that day against both air and ground targets.[85]

General der Panzertruppe Balck was so pleased with the accomplishments of the *IV. SS-Pz.Korps* that day that he sent a hand-written letter to Ullrich and Becker, congratulating them on the performance of the *Wiking* and *Totenkopf* Divisions: "I congratulate you on your preliminary success [this day]. Now you must continue your attacks relentlessly and your troops must be [on the lookout for] the opportunity to carry out more local enveloping attacks. Signed, Balck, *Oberbefehlshaber*."[86] He did not send a congratulatory note addressed to Gille, however.

On the left of the *IV. SS-Pz.Korps*, *Gen.Lt.* Kirchner's headquarters reported that besides reconnaissance and combat patrol activity carried out by both sides, the day passed without *LVII. Pz.Korps* having anything significant to report. To Gille's right, *Korpsgruppe Breith/III. Pz.Korps* reported that south of Ösi, several battalion-sized attacks supported by as many as five assault guns had been launched that day by the enemy, but all were driven off by the *1. Pz.Div.* Breith also reported that the entire village of Pusztavám, which had been taken by the *4. Kav.Brig.* the previous day, had been retaken by the enemy in a counterattack. On the rest of his corps group's front, he reported no significant large-scale fighting as having occurred.

In Budapest, the situation had not improved much, despite the departure of at least one Soviet corps and portions of another from the encircling ring on the western side of the city (Buda), which were sent to reinforce the troops being sent to prevent Gille's troops from reaching Bicske and Zsámbék. According to one report,

The enemy attacked around the clock, especially the eastern bridgehead [at Pest], and gave the defenders no rest. The continuous attacks caused ammunition to be expended faster than it could be replaced. During the day, the last possibility for landing aircraft was lost. Air supply was then possible only by means of airdrops, and it was no longer possible to evacuate the wounded.

[The *IX. SS-Geb.Korps*] intended to establish a new airhead. Elements of the *22. SS-Freiwilligen Kav.Div. Maria Theresa* were to attempt to retake the old landing field [on Csepel island].[87]

During the day, *Gen.O.* Guderian learned that the two railroad bridges over the Danube in the city center had been blown up, putting the eastern bridgehead in Pest at great risk of being cut off, an event that prompted him to order that all demolition be stopped. However, his orders came too late, as by that point, all except three of the remaining Danube bridges (out of seven original crossings) had been destroyed. He forbade any further demolition of bridges in the city, requiring approval from *OKH*.[88] At least when the time came to abandon Pest, there would hopefully still be a few bridges left to allow the defenders to withdraw into Buda in good order.

The *Ic Tagesmeldung* for 4 January from *A.Gr. Balck/6. Armee* expressed some notes of alarm. The *Ic/AO, Hptm.* von Pander, wrote:

> To the west of the Danube, the enemy is constantly throwing more forces, which come from the south-western front of the Vértes Mountains [i.e., from the Stuhlweissenburg area], towards our own attack spearheads. In addition to infantry units, the enemy has regrouped the mass of the V Guard Cavalry Corps and parts of the VII Mech. Corps to the north. According to aerial reconnaissance, [the enemy's forces] are no longer being sent to the area south of Stuhlweissenburg. After recognizing the danger threatening west of the Danube, the enemy is making every effort to bring our own attack to a halt by bringing up additional forces, perhaps even from the depths of his reserves. The regrouping of the 6th Guard Tank Army, [according to our] aerial reconnaissance reinforces our belief that he has abandoned his previous operative intention ... [and instead] we expect that he may make a push with the 6th Guard Tank Army across the Danube to the south, or, what is more likely, from the bridgehead at Parkány to the west.

According to the *H.Gr. Süd Ic*, the Second and Third Ukrainian Fronts by this point in the battle had committed 230 tanks and assault guns, of which 127 had been destroyed or knocked out of action. Of more concern was the tally of new Soviet units identified so far, which included one tank corps, two mechanized corps, and one cavalry corps, with a total of six tank brigades and seven mechanized infantry brigades, as well as seven rifle divisions.[89] More of every category was on their way.

In his own summary of the day's activities and his intent for the following day, Balck (or Gaedke, writing for his commander), echoing some of the *Ic* estimate, stated:

> Our attack is now also forcing the enemy to shift forces [from] north of the Danube. Air reconnaissance confirms strong enemy mechanized forces east of the Gran that are marching to the south in two columns. The enemy may intend to move these forces across the Danube to counterattack the left flank of our attack at Gran and from the Pilis Mountains, or he could swing west and mount an operation to the west from his bridgehead at the mouth of the Gran at Parkány. As yet, there is no basis for determining which of these two options he will select.[90]

Balck did not yet think that the developing situation north of the Danube had grown so critical that *Konrad* should be called off; the offensive would continue. To that effect, that night he issued additional guidance for the following day, with instructions for each of corps in his *Armeegruppe*:

IV. SS-Pz.Korps. Continue the attack towards the southeast and break through along the Stuhlweissenburg–Budapest highway with the *Wiking* through Bicske towards Martonvasár and the *Totenkopf* through Zsámbék towards Tárnok and Érd; additionally, the *96. Inf.Div.* would continue its attack through Dorog (Körteles) and Pilisvörösvár; and the *711. Inf.Div.* would advance through Táth and depending on how the situation developed, would seize Gran (Esztergom) and continue advancing through Pilisszentkereszt or insert itself between the *Totenkopf* and *96. Inf.Div.* to ensure connectivity as they advanced towards Budapest.

Div.Gr. Pape. With the subordinated *6. Pz.Div.*, open as quickly as possible the narrow pass and highway at Alsógalla and Felsőgalla, and take Felcsút next. Continue the assault onwards through Vértes–Acsa towards Kápolnás-Nyek. By this evening, start pulling out all the remaining [armored] elements of the *8. Pz.Div.* and get it moving [north] through Komorn towards the Nagy Salló area. Send the division commander immediately to the *LVII. Pz.Korps* headquarters in Urdvard. Get them moving through Komorn and report their strength immediately.

Korpsgruppe Breith. Pull out the entire *4. Kav.Brig.* and relieve them in the line with the Hungarian *Inf.Rgt. 1* and *Pz.Aufkl.Abt. 23* [of the *23. Pz.Div.*]. The brigade is to be ready at a moment's notice to carry out any counterattack should the enemy break through. The *23. Pz.Div.* is to be moved so it is better positioned to carry out an attack … Begin preparing plans to carry out an attack from the sector held by the *23. Pz.Div.* using *Pz.Gr. Weymann* (reinforced by all the tanks and assault guns from the *1.* and *23. Pz.Div.*) and the *4. Kav. Brig.*, using two possible avenues of approach a) via Zámoly towards the northeast to join up with *Div.Gr. Pape* and b) in an east–southeast direction towards Pákozd while avoiding Stuhlweissenburg. The goal of either course of action is to cut off the enemy's forces in the Vértes Mountains.[91]

In evaluating this order, two things quickly become evident, especially after a brief look at the existing map dated 4 January depicting each of the division's zones of attack (see Map 4).

The first is that the projected southeast direction of advance of the *IV. SS-Pz. Korps'* attack no longer made any sense, in that even if both the *Totenkopf* and *Wiking* Divisions achieved their assigned objectives, they would arrive at a point 10–15 kilometers *southwest* of Budapest. At this point in the siege, the perimeter of the Budapest garrison's outer defense line had shrunk considerably, and Balck must have known this. The only way that *Unternehmen Konrad* could succeed, then, was if the garrison broke out in that direction—i.e., to the southwest. Yet the garrison had been specifically ordered not to do this except on the expressed orders of *OKH* (i.e., Hitler). Essentially, even if Gille's corps reached its final terrain objectives, it would be striking into thin air.

The other curious aspect of this order is that Balck apparently assumed that the 6th Guards Tank Army would remain static where it was in the corner east of the confluence between the Danube and Gran Rivers, with a foothold still on the west bank at Parkány. This, despite dire warnings from the *Armeegruppe Ic* that the indications did not support this. Balck himself even raises this possibility, though he admits that he is not certain what course of action the enemy would take. A subsequent order issued that evening directed *LVII. Pz.Korps* to pull the *3. Pz.Div.* out of the front lines and replace it with the Hungarian *Szent László* Division and the understrength *211. V.G.D.* near Parkány. It was then to move through Komorn into an assembly area centered around the town of Bakony immediately behind the *23. Pz. Div.* Here, it was to be reunited with its own armored elements, primarily *Pz. Rgt. 6* and *Gruppe Weymann*, led by *Oberstlt.* Martin Weymann. The reason given for this transfer was the need to reconstitute it as a reinforcement for a future assault group.

Therefore, the movement of the *3.* and *8. Pz. Div.* away from the front opposite the city of Gran—where they were the last divisions of any substance in the *LVII. Pz. Korps* defensive sector that could block any action by the 6th Guards Tank Army—makes no sense at all, especially given that the *6. Pz. Div.* had already departed. Admittedly, the portion of the order concerned the movement of the *8. Pz. Div.*'s tank regiment, *Pz. Rgt. 10*, and one *SPW* battalion from *Pz. Gren. Rgt. 98* that was still operating under *Div. Gr. Pape.* However, the movement of the rest of the *8. Pz. Div.* to a point 30 kilometers north to the far left flank of the *LVII. Pz. Korps* and away from the Parkány bridgehead, as well as the movement of the *3. Pz. Div.* entirely from the corps' order of battle, would only leave a mish-mash of infantry divisions, including two Hungarian divisions, to face the steadily growing power of a reconstituted Guards tank army.

What can be seen in this order, and subsequent orders issued that day and the next, was the beginning on an outline of a future plan—one that would not only incorporate the ongoing offensive being prosecuted by the *IV. SS-Pz. Korps* and *Div. Gr. Pape*, but a more ambitious one that would involve most of the divisions of Breith's *III. Pz. Korps* (including the *I. Kav. Korps*) in a complimentary attack from the Stuhlweissenburg area to the northeast, taking the form of a classic pincer movement. This was a hallmark of Balck's thinking and an indication that he was beginning to realize that Gille's corps could not carry out the relief of Budapest on its own. While such an attack had been contemplated as an essential part of the next phase of *Unternehmen Konrad*, it was to have taken place after the siege of Budapest was lifted; it was now to be carried out in conjunction with that operation, but the decision to execute it, as well as the date, had not yet been approved by *H. Gr. Süd* or the *OKH*.

Regardless of the rationale behind Balck's orders, the attack by the *IV. SS-Pz. Korps* was to go forward shortly after midnight the following day, as previously described. But after four days of intense activity, including heavy combat, many of the units in Gille's corps had been brought to the "point of exhaustion," according to one source.[92] Fortunately, by midnight on 4 January, most of the attacking units involved in *Unternehmen Konrad*, except for the *711. Inf. Div.*, had all arrived. The unit that benefitted the most from the past four days of rail shipments was the *Wiking* Division, whose *Westland* and artillery regiments had arrived mostly intact.

With the addition of three other artillery battalions from *Ostubaf.* Bünning's *SS-Pz. Art. Rgt. 5* to augment the two battalions supporting the *Wiking* Division thus far, the division would finally have the means to both destroy or suppress Soviet defensive positions and would also be able to conduct counter-battery fire against the increasingly strong enemy artillery concentrations. Unfortunately, because the artillery battalions of both the *Wiking* and *Totenkopf* Divisions—as well as that of the *96. Inf.Div.*—were so widely dispersed, the commander of *SS-ARKO 504*, *Oberführer* Kurt Brasack, was unable to exercise the same degree of coordination as he had when the corps was fighting around Modlin, rendering it less effective than formerly. Additionally, *Div.Gr. Pape* had no appreciable artillery of its own, though when it had finished assembling behind the *Wiking* Division, *6. Pz.Div.* at least would be able to contribute its own division artillery, a total of 31 guns.

In recognition of this arrival of its own artillery to augment its firepower, the *IV. SS-Pz.Korps* was directed that same day to relinquish control of *I. Abt./Pz.Art.Rgt. 80* and send it back to its parent *8. Pz.Div.* However, despite the fact that all of the two SS divisions' antiaircraft battalions had arrived by this point, their light and heavy *Flak* batteries had proved insufficient to deal with the burgeoning number of Soviet air attacks that had repeatedly attacked and slowed down the attacking columns. To help remedy this situation, *A. Gr. Balck* authorized the attachment of the *leichte-Flak Abteilung 77* from the *15. Flak-Div.* to the *IV. SS-Pz.Korps*, beginning on 5 January.[93] Once it arrived, the battalion would be split up and its batteries attached to the forward-most attacking units to protect them against low-level air attack by the dreaded IL-2 *Sturmoviks* and LaGG-3s. That same day, the corps' *Flak* assets would be further augmented by the arrival of the Hungarian *102. Flak-Art.Abt.*

As 5 January began, on the corps' left flank, the leading elements of the *711. Inf. Div.* had advanced as far as Tokod. *Generalleutnant* von Reichert had already established his division's forward headquarters in Tata, close to Gille's own *Hauptquartier*. His division had been given the mission of advancing towards Gran and taking that city as well as the heights overlooking it to the immediate south. Pursuant to these orders, one of his battalions initiated an attack to the northeast from the Tokod railway station toward the northeast, oriented along the highway parallel to the river leading to Gran, while the *96. Inf.Div.* was to conduct an attack to seize Dorog (Körteles) on its right. One battalion was tasked with seizing the village of Zsidódi-Puszta 5 kilometers northeast of the Tokod train station and establishing a strong antitank barrier to block any Soviet tank attacks emanating from Gran. Details of its attacks were still forthcoming that evening. Once the division's forces had taken Gran, *Gen. Lt.* von Reichert would move his headquarters forward to Tokod.[94]

In the *96. Inf.Div.* area of operations to the right of the *711. Inf.Div.*, *Oberst* Harrendorf initiated his attack early that morning and his troops immediately encountered tough enemy resistance. Despite the freezing temperatures (the day's average was 22–25 degrees Fahrenheit), *Gren.Rgt. 283*, attacking from Szarkás on the division's right, quickly seized the cloth guild's hall and the mill in Tokod, and continued its attack southeast towards Hill 457, possession of which provided a commanding view of the division's entire battle area. On the left, both *Gren.Rgt.*

287 and *284* advanced from the northern outskirts of Tokod towards the town of Dorog, held by elements of the II Guards Mechanized Corps.[95] Both attacks were brought to a standstill after suffering heavy losses while attempting to overcome the Soviet defensive position from the northwest and southwest. During the attack by *Gren.Rgt. 287*, its attack faltered after the dynamic commander of the lead *II. Bataillon, Hptm.* Sturm, was seriously wounded.

By mid-morning, it had become apparent that the Soviet defenses in Dorog could not be overcome; the defenders had dug in several JS-II Stalin tanks from the 30th Guards Heavy Tank Regiment that simply could not be knocked out by infantry weapons alone, prompting the grenadiers to ask the whereabouts of their own tanks. Most of the division's assault guns by this time had been temporarily rendered inoperable or destroyed, and the *Totenkopf* Division could not spare any of its own. The attack by the third regiment, *Gren.Rgt. 283*, continued towards Bajna via Nagysáp, where it was to link up with the left flank of the *Totenkopf* Division. The attack initially bogged down in heavy fighting and only succeeded after its infantry companies had suffered heavy losses while accomplishing their objective.[96]

Though the attacks on the corps' left flank by the two infantry divisions were important, the actions in the center fought that day by the two SS *panzer* divisions were the most vital if *Konrad* were to succeed. The several major engagements that took place that day were characterized by determined German attacks to fight their way towards their objectives of Zsámbék and Bicske, while the Soviet defenders rushed more and more armored and mechanized forces—as well as employing artillery and air attacks—to block them. In many ways, the fighting on 5 January can be considered the high water mark of the first relief attempt. It was on this day that the offensive reached its culminating point, because the *IV. SS-Pz.Korps* had suffered such heavy losses in men and matériel that it could proceed no further with the forces remaining.

During this stage, *Ogruf.* Gille was able to exercise little control of the actual fighting due to the distance between his command post in Tata and the forward elements of his corps, as well as the compartmentalization of the battlefield due to the particularities of the terrain. The best he could do was to ensure a constant flow of ammunition, fuel, and food to the leading units. Although he carried out as many of his customary daily visits to the headquarters of each division as he could, the distances involved—by this point, his corps frontage was approximately 60 kilometers wide—as well as the always-present threat of enemy ambushes along the way, caused his visits beyond the division command posts to be few and far between. Instead, this day was characterized by a series of local engagements fought according to the individual initiative of regimental, battalion, and company commanders, often in isolation from one another.

For the *Totenkopf* Division, the fighting on 5 January can be summed up in one word: Szomor. Although it was not the only locality fought over that day, it was the most important. *Brigadeführer* Becker's troops had advanced to the western edge of the town before they were driven off by a Soviet counterattack, but had managed to take the neighboring village of Gyermely. Soviet forces had dug in less than a kilometer to the south, threatening any movement from Gyermely to Szomor with artillery and antitank gunfire. During the early stages of Becker's attack on 5 January, *K. Gr. Eicke*, consisting of the bulk of *SS-Pz. Gren. Rgt. 6*, approached Szomor from the north along the road from Bajna, overcoming Soviet blocking units "every step along the way like a shuffling boxer" before finally seizing the northern entrance of Szomor as well as the northwestern portion of the town.[97]

As the *Kampfgruppe* prepared to fight its way into the town proper, its two leading Panthers burst into flames when struck by accurate antitank fire. An attempt that foggy morning to have some of its escorting infantry work their way into the town failed with great loss, leaving the northern streets of the town, according to one eyewitness, "literally covered with the bodies of the fallen."[98] The commander later estimated that his troops had faced as many as 45 Soviet tanks and a large number of antitank guns inside the town and the surrounding area. To the southwest, up to 18 enemy tanks and a *Pakfront* were observed occupying the high ground between Szomor and Gyermely, the latter town still being held by the division's *Panzergruppe*. Also unknown to the Germans, the 22 surviving tanks and SP artillery from the 170th Tank Brigade and 1438th SP Artillery Regiment (with a combined 11 T-34s and 11 SU-85s) were preparing an ambush 3 kilometers south of Szomor along the road to Zsámbék, near the village of Felsoörpuszta.[99]

Becker ordered a coordinated enveloping attack, using *K. Gr. Eicke*, the *Panzergruppe*, and a similar sized *Kampfgruppe* from *II. Btl./Pz. Gren. Rgt. 5 Totenkopf*. Approaching Szomor from the north, east, and west, the two battlegroups pushed quickly into the town and were just as swiftly involved in house-to-house fighting against the determined defenders from the 49th Guards Rifle Division, whose supporting tanks fought German *panzers* at point-blank range. Soviet antitank guns were seemingly hidden around every corner, waiting to ambush the *panzers* as they slowly advanced down the town's narrow streets. Grenadiers stalked individual Soviet tanks with *Panzerfausts* and hand grenade bundles, while Soviet troops sought to do likewise. Tank commanders watched in mounting alarm as tracers arced over their heads and bullets pinged against their protecting armor, but to button-up completely meant limiting their observation of approaching threats. Hand-to-hand fighting was reported and losses on both sides were heavy, as artillery fire from both sides rained down indiscriminately. The *Totenkopf* Division had not fought such a pitched battle since it had successfully defended Siedlce six months previously.

As the *Kampfgruppe* from the *Eicke* Regiment continued the fight for possession of the town that lasted until the evening, the battlegroup from the *Totenkopf* Regiment with its supporting armor pushed its way through the town and continued advancing to the southeast. It then wheeled to the southwest to link up with the *II. Bataillon* of the *Westland* Regiment that had been holding the position west of Gyermely taken earlier in the day, forcing the retreat of the troops from the 49th Guards Rifle Division holding the position south of the town.

With Szomor now in German hands, its new owners prepared for the inevitable Soviet counterattack, which arrived shortly thereafter in the form of the 5th Guards Mechanized Brigade from the newly arrived II Guards Mechanized Corps. The two leading tanks of the brigade were quickly knocked out, one by a Tiger tank of *9. Kp./ SS-Pz.Rgt. 3* and the other by an 8.8cm antiaircraft gun manned by the Hungarian *102. Flak-Art.Btl.* that was accompanying the *Kampfgruppe*. Three further Soviet tanks were destroyed by infantry, while four more were accounted for by German and Hungarian antitank guns, forcing the withdrawal of the mechanized brigade to a position 1.5 kilometers south of Szomor.

While the battle for Szomor was raging, *III. Bataillon* of the *Totenkopf* Regiment, operating on the division's left flank, advanced from the village of Epöl and was able to successfully block the north–south road at a point 2.5 kilometers south of Sarisap, denying it to Soviet forces from the 6th Guards Mechanized Brigade attempting to conduct their own advance to Sarisap from the village of Kirva. An attack by the division's reconnaissance battalion, *SS-Pz.Aufkl.Abt. 3*—operating 7 kilometers east of Epöl—was carried out at 1 p.m. to take the town of Dag, but it failed when its troops encountered a much larger Soviet force from the 4th Guards Mechanized Brigade and the 86th Guards Rifle Division emplaced behind a strong *Pakfront* on the high ground northwest of the town. Although the reconnaissance battalion destroyed one SU-76 assault gun and forced the abandonment of two others, its forces were not strong enough to prevail against the enemy position and were forced to withdraw.[100]

With the way to the south apparently clear, the *Totenkopf* Division's *Panzergruppe* resumed its advance towards Zsámbék that afternoon. As it proceeded down the Szomor–Zsámbék road, its lead elements were fired upon by the 170th Tank Brigade concealed in the woods near the village of Felsoörpuszta from a range of approximately 1 kilometer. The column was forced to deploy from the road, but the heavy fire from the concealed Soviet armored fighting vehicles could not be overcome. Although it made four attempts to fight its way through, the *Panzergruppe* was not able to go any further.

The commander of *SS-Pz.Rgt. 3* (as well as the *Panzergruppe*), *Ostubaf.* Anton Laackmann, was seriously wounded during this engagement, requiring his medical evacuation, which forced his temporary replacement by *Stubaf.* Boris Kraas, the commander of the division's armored artillery battalion, *I. Abt./SS-Pz.Art.Rgt.3*.[101] That evening, the *Totenkopf* Division consolidated its gains from the day, replenished badly needed fuel and ammunition (often siphoning fuel from abandoned Soviet vehicles), evacuated its wounded, and counted its many dead. But despite its best efforts, the *Totenkopf* Division would not reach Zsámbék that day.

For Ullrich's *Wiking* Division, the high point of the fighting that day centered around the seizure of the Hegyikastely (Hegyks Castle Estate) atop Hill 214. To get there, however, his troops had to fight their way through the strong infantry and antitank barriers being set up by the reconstituted XXXI Guards Rifle Corps, the forward elements of the approaching XXIII Rifle Corps, and the left flank of the XVIII Tank Corps, in addition to several antitank regiments, all supported by increasingly numerous artillery regiments. One member of the division described the Soviet antitank defenses as being arranged like a chessboard, with *Ratsch-bum* (German slang for Soviet antitank guns) arrayed in mutually supporting fashion, making it extremely difficult to overcome unless several were assaulted simultaneously by tanks and infantry with artillery support.[102] Most of the fighting swirled around the towns of Csabdi on the right flank and Mány on the left, with the Hegyks Estate in the center.

On the right (western) flank of the division, the bulk of *Stubaf.* Heinz Wagner's *SS-Pz.Aufkl.Abt.* 5, along with a *Kampfgruppe* from the *Westland* Regiment, were relieved after a brief Soviet encirclement by an element of the neighboring *6. Pz.Div.* Once freed, the reconnaissance battalion attacked towards the southwest to seize a large farming estate 3 kilometers northwest of Csabdi, a task that it accomplished late in the evening. The main body of Dorr's *Germania* Regiment (less one battalion) attacked the towns of Csabdi and Mány, while Hack's newly arrived *Westland* Regiment with its two remaining battalions covered the division's open left flank between Gyermely and Mány. This required one of the *Westland* Regiment's battalions (*Hstuf.* Ernst Heindl's *II. Btl./Westland*) to conduct an attack in the early hours of the day to seize an enemy-occupied hill 2 kilometers west of Gyermely that provided a commanding view of the area as far as Szomor.

Hauptsturmführer Heindl's troops obediently climbed the steep hill, laden with hand grenades and *Panzerfausts*, and took it after heavy fighting, only to find themselves under heavy artillery fire once they reached its summit.[103] Here, they were able to observe and protect the right flank of the *Totenkopf* Division, which was embroiled in heavy fighting at the same time between Gyermely and Szomor. Shortly afterwards, they successfully repulsed a Soviet attack that was launched from the area south of Gyermely, though the *Totenkopf* Division was still holding on to the town itself.[104] Later that day, *II. Btl./Westland* took over the town completely from the *Totenkopf* and assumed responsibility for its defense.

The main burden of the *Wiking* Division's advance that day was borne by *Panzergruppe Darges*, consisting of the regiment's remaining tanks (approximately 20), Vogt's *I. Btl./Norge*, and an *SPW* company from the division's reconnaissance battalion. During the pre-dawn hours before it began operations, *Panzergruppe Darges* refueled and rearmed in the village of Vasztély, taken the day before by Amberg's *II. Btl./Germania*. Simply to get to Vasztély was a struggle in itself. The roads were so steep and ice-covered that the tanks could not drive uphill on their own, requiring assistance from tank recovery vehicles to reach it.[105] Darges then initiated his attack at 6 a.m. in the general direction of the gap between Csabdi and Mány, 5 kilometers to the southeast. Within an hour, the *Panzergruppe* had broken through the hasty defenses of the newly arrived 41st Guards Rifle Division and 10 minutes later had crossed the Bicske–Zsámbék road near Hill 214, which commanded the highway in either direction. A dense fog had settled in during the early morning, limiting observation by both sides, but in this particular instance it worked to the benefit of the *Panzergruppe*.

Here, Darges's lead tanks encountered a column of Soviet trucks towing antitank guns which were unaware of the Germans' presence on account of the fog. After shooting up several of them, the *Panzergruppe* captured 15 along with their guns and prepared to continue moving towards its objective to the south, the town of Bicske. Before it moved on, Darges sent one tank platoon of five Panthers from Lichte's *5. Kompanie*, commanded by *Ustuf.* Heinrich Kerkhoff, to reconnoiter the road to Bicske and look for any hidden enemy positions, while the rest of the column waited. They did not get far. Approximately halfway to their objective, the fog lifted, exposing the platoon to fire by a *Pakfront* set up by the 595th (Separate) Antitank Artillery Regiment east of Bicske. In a matter of minutes, two Panthers were struck by antitank shells and went up in flames. The other three fired off their smoke grenades and beat a hasty retreat back to Hill 214, taking the crews from the two destroyed tanks along with them, some of whom were badly wounded.[106]

Rather than continue with his attack or fight his way back through Soviet lines to rejoin the rest of the division, Darges decided on the spot to pull back to a more defensible position and await developments. He most likely expected the rest of the division to catch up with him shortly. After all, the *Germania* and *Westland* Regiments were both attacking at the same time he began his own advance. Unfortunately, his radio communications were sporadic at best, so he was not able to provide timely situation reports to Ullrich's command post in Tarján. Attempts by small patrols to probe towards Bicske and Zsámbék were driven back. After considering his situation, Darges decided that he did not have enough troops and tanks to take Bicske on his own, so he would defend his present position until the rest of the division caught up. Shortly afterwards, he received a radio message from Ullrich informing him that *A. Gr. Balck/6. Armee* wanted the *Panzergruppe* to stay where it was and continue blocking the road until told otherwise.

The site he chose to establish the blocking position was the Hegyks Castle Estate, built in the 18th century by the Batthyány family. A large, solidly built three-story country manor (not an actual castle despite the name), it boasted a compound 200 meters long and 150 meters wide, surrounded by a high wall on three sides, with the northeastern side being open. Perched atop the ridgeline encompassing Hill 214, it was a natural defensive position featuring a stone observation tower that provided a commanding view in all directions. When Darges and his force began approaching the estate, its occupants—a group of staff personnel from either the XXXI Guards Rifle Corps or the 41st Guards Rifle Division—immediately fled to safety, leaving behind many of their maps and other assorted paraphernalia in their haste.

Within this position, the commander of *SS-Pz.Rgt.* 5 emplaced his remaining 18 tanks and dozen or so *SPW*s in a so-called *Igelstellung* (hedgehog position). The escorting infantry from Vogt's *Norge* battalion established a blocking position astride the Bicske–Mány road, while the company from *SS-Pz.Aufkl.Abt.* 5 and Vogt's elite assault platoon dug in around the position outside the walls of the compound (see Figure 2).[107] Here they waited for the next Soviet move, while Dorr and Vogt made their headquarters inside the castle, safe from everything except a direct hit. They did not have to wait long.

Shortly after establishing their position, the estate was attacked by 20 tanks of the 181st Tank Brigade from the direction of Mány, after a Soviet reconnaissance

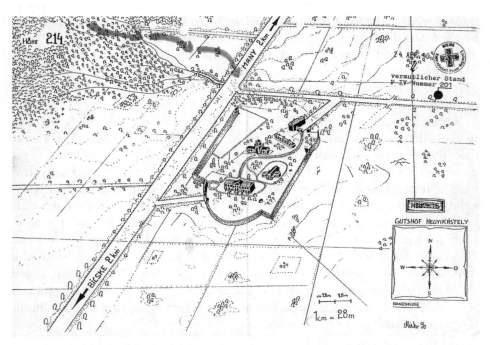

Figure 2. A hand-drawn sketch of the Hegyk Castle Estate east of Bicske, which was seized by the *Panzergruppe* of the 5. *SS-Pz.Div. Wiking* on 5 January 1945. Between 5 and 12 January 1945, it was defended by 20 tanks of *SS-Pz.Rgt.* 5 led by *SS-Ostubaf.* Fritz Darges, *I. Btl./SS-Pz.Gren.Rgt. 23 Norge* led by *SS-Stubaf.* Fritz Vogt, and several smaller units, including elements of the division's engineer and armored reconnaissance battalions. Despite numerous attacks by Soviet armored units, air attacks, and constant shelling, the *Panzergruppe* defended this isolated position until ordered to withdraw. Known as the "Fort of the Unbreakables," it was completely destroyed during the fighting. (Courtesy of Mirko Bayerl).

patrol sent to Hegyks failed to return. After one of the T-34s was knocked out by a direct hit from a Panther, the rest turned back. Thus the stage was set for a week-long battle, reminiscent of the famous last stand at the Alamo during the War for Texas Independence in 1836. Being neither able to advance nor allowed to retreat, *Panzergruppe Darges* was subjected to unrelenting attacks and artillery barrages until finally ordered to retire on 12 January. By that point, the fighting had moved elsewhere. From time to time, a supply column was able to infiltrate Soviet lines using a farm track and evacuate wounded, but it was subject to intermittent enemy fire and could only be done at night.

A war correspondent from the *Wiking* Division's *SS-Kriegsberichter* platoon, who was present on the scene, later wrote a colorful description of the fighting at the Hegyks Estate that was published in *Das Schwarze Korps*, the official news magazine of the SS:

> Next to the road, surrounded by an old wall, rose a Hungarian castle in the Hegyks estate. It became the core of the *Gruppe's* hedgehog position. The Grenadiers placed their security positions outside the wall. Behind the wall, only sixty meters from it, *Ostubaf.* Darges set up his command post. The enemy had spotted the movements of the German troops. He began to fire … An enemy reconnaissance party was reported at the south of the wall. It was shot up by several of our men. Shortly afterwards, 20 Soviet tanks attacked. They ran into the waiting Panthers. A short combat, the closest T-34 lost its turret, the rest turn away. Before darkness fell, *Hstuf.* [sic] Vogt made the necessary infantry preparations. In the darkness the *Panzers* can see little, therefore, the burden of the fighting will fall on the shoulders of the Grenadiers. The exposed MG posts are brought back within the wall. The *Panzers* are placed so that they can provide artillery support for the Grenadiers' defensive battle. The first attack on the castle began shortly before midnight. After a heavy preparatory artillery barrage, enemy infantry simultaneously stormed the wall from two sides. At the wall there was wild hand to hand fighting and hand grenade duels.[108]

While the *Panzergruppe* made its soon-to-be famous "last stand" at the Hegyks Estate, fighting continued elsewhere throughout the division's zone of attack, with no appreciable ground gained during the rest of the day by the *Westland* or the *Germania* Regiments, neither of which were able to make any noteworthy progress. Soviet reinforcements continued flowing into the area, strengthening the defense line between Zsámbék and Bicske, especially with artillery and antitank troops. The division's *01*, *Ostuf.* Jahnke, later wrote:

> In the morning hours the division attacked with two infantry [sic] regiments and artillery support towards the south. The division was able to cross over the line [Bicske–Mány–Zsámbék] despite increasingly stiffening enemy resistance and advanced directly towards Bicske. The terrain became increasingly level. Once the enemy recognized the intentions of our attack's objective—Budapest—he constantly moved strong forces, especially antitank weapons, into our path. Our own losses were considerable. Around evening, the attack had to be called off. [We experienced] the usual amount of enemy air activity.

The day's actions were summed up by the corps commander quite succinctly, who wrote afterwards, "The divisions reached the line Bicske–Zsámbék. The enemy reinforced his forces there constantly, with especially strong antitank defenses and counterattacks. At about sundown, our attack had to be halted [because] our losses were too great."[109] The Soviet official account agrees, stating that "5 January was the turning point in the fighting ... during the fighting, [the enemy] achieved only insignificant territorial successes, which were not justified by the losses incurred ... [he] enjoyed no success on this day along the 4th Guards Army Front."[110]

On the right flank of the *Wiking* Division, the *6. Pz.Div.*, with its 28 tanks and tank destroyers reinforced by 10 *Pz. Vs* from *I. Abt./Pz.Rgt. 26* detached from *Div.Gr. Pape*, finally began to swing into action.[111] On the same day, both it and *Div.Gr. Pape* were formally placed under the operational and administrative control of *IV. SS-Pz.Korps*, an action that should have been done with the latter division before the offensive even began, for it undoubtedly would have led to better coordination with the *Wiking* Division and may have led to more success at Tatabanya and Felsőgalla than what it achieved on its own. Most of *K.Gr. Bieber*, consisting of the headquarters of the *271. V.G.D.* and *I. Abt./Pz.Lehr-Rgt. 130*, was taken away from *Div.Gr. Pape* and reassigned to Breith's *III. Pz.Korps*, where both units would undergo eventual reconstitution.[112] In the meantime, it was elevated in status to *Div.Gr. Bieber*, with two attached German machine-gun battalions (*Btl. Lausitz* and *Mark*) and four infantry battalions from the Hungarian *25. Inf.Div.*

Shortly after repositioning itself to operate on the corps' right flank, one unit of the *6. Pz.Div.*, *Maj.* Fritz Biermann's *II. Btl./Pz.Gren.Rgt. 4*, found itself under attack by troops from the 34th Guards Rifle Division against its positions atop Hill 300, 3 kilometers north of Felsőgalla. After a short but sharp action, the battalion was thrown off the hill but immediately counterattacked and drove off the assailants, who abandoned five of their antitank guns during the action when the Germans retook the ground lost earlier in the day. However, Felsőgalla still remained out of reach because Biermann's battalion lacked the strength to continue pushing through the pass and to take the town without significant reinforcements.

The rest of the *6. Pz.Div.*, including *K.Gr. Philipp*, continued supporting the *Wiking* Division's attack that day. *Kampfgruppe Philipp*, with approximately 40 armored vehicles, continued its advance from the village of Nagynémetegyház, which it had taken the previous day. While conducting a wheeling movement northeast of the latter town, *K.Gr. Philipp* ran into the forward elements of the 16th Mechanized Brigade, advancing in the opposite direction. In the meeting engagement that followed, the Soviet force was compelled to retreat to the town of Tükrös, where it attempted to set up a hasty defense, but to no avail.

Kampfgruppe Philipp pressed its attack in conjunction with a battalion from the *Westland* Regiment, took Tükrös by storm, and advanced in a southeast direction towards the western environs of the town of Csabdi, knocking out five Soviet tanks in the process. After occupying the town that evening, the *6. Pz.Div.* attack was called to a halt. Though its actions that day were successful, Tatabanya and Felsőgalla still remained in enemy hands, continuing to block the best high-speed avenue of approach to Budapest.[113] In its evening situation report, the *IV. SS-Pz. Korps* summarized its operations that day:

> In the difficult terrain of the Vértes Mountains, hard fighting continued all day against tough enemy resistance … the enemy was thrown off a hill three kilometers north of Felsőgalla and also had to give up a hill he had temporarily gained control of before our own counterattack … Through an enveloping attack near [the towns of] Nagynémetegyház and Kisnemetegyház (seven kilometers southeast of Felsőgalla), the enemy lost 10 tanks and one assault gun, and 14 antitank guns were captured. The enemy, who tried to hold his ground in Csabdi, was pushed back to the northwestern edge of Bicske after our own forces overcame numerous antitank barriers despite tough resistance. Enemy resistance north of Szomor was broken, though localized fighting was still ongoing. In addition, the enemy was thrown back from the heights northwest of Sarisap as well as from the southwestern edge of Dorog [Körteles]. The fighting is still ongoing.

On the left, the *LVII. Pz.Korps* (*Korpsgruppe Kirschner*) reported: "Except for an unsuccessful enemy combat patrol in platoon strength near Zseliz [in the *Div.Gr. Rintelen* sector], along the rest of the corps' front there was no combat activity or enemy movement of significance worth reporting."

Korpsgruppe Breith reported: "In the sector between Lake Balaton and Környe, no combat activity was reported to have taken place." The Hungarian *3. Armee*, responsible for defending the northern shore of Lake Balaton, reported "A minimal amount of artillery harassing fire by both sides … during the late morning hours, we observed substantial enemy motor vehicle traffic along the southern shore from the west towards the east," a sure sign that additional Soviet reinforcements were on the way.[114]

The situation in Budapest was in stark contrast to that reported by most of *A.Gr. Balck/6. Armee*, which except for the *IV. SS-Pz.Korps*, was experiencing very little fighting. That night, the *IX. SS-Geb.Korps* reported:

> During the night there was a substantial amount of enemy disrupting [artillery] fire. An enemy assembly area was smashed by our own artillery fire. Several local breakthrough points were successfully defeated by our own assault troops … we have received no [front-line] reports since … [over] Budapest the enemy carried out individual bombing raids and attacks by close air support and fighter aircraft, using bombs and on-board weapons.

Due to bad weather, no airdrops over Budapest could be carried out during the evening, a shortfall that further deepened the already disastrous supply situation. Several thousand wounded still awaited evacuation, and without an airfield to land upon, their chances of being flown out for medical treatment were slim. Front-line units, especially holding the eastern salient in Pest, had to shorten their lines because they could not defend what they had with the little ammunition available.[115]

In regards to the overall enemy situation, the *6. Armee Ic* was not sanguine. The signs were plainly evident that the Third Ukrainian Front was responding robustly to the threat posed by *Unternehmen Konrad*. Despite the progress that the *IV. SS-Pz. Korps* had achieved that day, the *A.Gr. Balck/6. Armee* Deputy *Ic* wrote:

> The enemy is now fighting against our breakthrough area with the II Guards Mechanized Corps, the XVIII Tank Corps, the bulk of the V Guards Cavalry Corps, and a portion of the VII Mechanized Corps, as well as six to eight rifle divisions. According to a reliable agent report, the employment of another large mechanized formation, the V Tank Corps, is to be expected soon. Our aerial reconnaissance has also identified the regrouping of additional parts of the 46th Army away from the western front of Budapest. Against the eastern front around Budapest, additional infantry forces have been fed into the battle, including the 36th Gds. Rifle Div. and the 297th Rifle Division.

That was not all of the bad news, for the *Ic* was even more concerned about the signs of the increasingly unfavorable situation developing north of the Danube:

> North of the Danube in the Gran area, the enemy appears to be regrouping his infantry forces. According to a reliable agent, the XXVII Guards Rifle Corps has expanded the area along the front under its control and has relieved parts of the IV G.C.C. [Guards Cavalry Corps] in the line west of Leva ... The cavalry corps of the Plieyev Army has been identified as taking part in an attack on the northern flank of the *LVII. Pz.Korps*. A high-level intelligence source has reported that the 6th Guards Tank Army is readying its forces in preparation for an attack ... in comparison to a previous estimate of its task organization, an attack towards the west is to be expected. However, the possibility of this army conducting a crossing of the Danube towards the south cannot be completely ruled out.[116]

Clearly, the window of opportunity for rescuing Budapest and restoring the *Margarethestellung* was rapidly closing. Not only was the fate of the Budapest garrison and its 800,000 civilian inhabitants at stake, but if the negative trend continued, the relief force itself might find itself in dire straits as well. According to the initial estimates before the operation began, the city was to have been relieved by this point, yet the relieving forces of *Unternehmen Konrad* were still 21 kilometers away. Time was not on Balck's side, and the longer it took to reach Budapest, the further chances of relief receded and the more imperiled his forces would become.

On 5 January, the first official tally of the results of the *Konrad* offensive in terms of damage inflicted on the Red Army's 4th Guards Army was released by *A.Gr. Balck/6. Armee*. Between 1 and 5 January, based on reports from divisions, aerial observation, and agents inserted behind enemy lines, the *6. Armee Ic* estimated that the *IV. SS-Pz.Korps* and *III. Pz.Korps* had destroyed 191 Soviet tanks and assault guns, 624 artillery and antitank pieces of all calibers, 50 mortars (12cm and larger), 147 wheeled vehicles, and 166 horse-drawn vehicles. In addition, it claimed to have captured 565 Soviet troops, though the number of bodies counted or those estimated to have been killed were not released. The antiaircraft units of the corps reported having shot down 16 enemy aircraft.

These numbers reflected the destruction of the XXXI Guards Rifle Corps and its three divisions, the damage inflicted on the first troops sent as reinforcements from the XVIII Tank Corps, as well as the 86th Guards and 93rd Rifle Divisions.[117] What the report did not mention was that several thousand stragglers from the XXXI Guards Rifle Corps and the 170th Tank Brigade of the XVIII Tank Corps had managed to escape the net being drawn around them and make it safely back to their own lines, having evaded German attempts to hunt them down. Reports on the *IV. SS-Pz.Korps'* own losses thus far would not be released until 7 January.

Amidst all of the developments, *Gen.O.* Guderian, chief of staff of the *OKH* and the one individual answerable to Hitler for conduct of operations on the Eastern Front, arrived that day via his command train at *H.Gr. Süd* headquarters at Esterháza. The purpose of his three-day visit was to speak to the various commanders on the spot (from the army group's *6.* and *8. Armee* and the *2. Pz.Armee*) and to gain a better appreciation of the situation there, as well as to pay a visit to the Hungarian minister of defense. That afternoon, during his visit with *Gen.d.Inf.* Wöhler, he enquired as to the reason why the relief operation was proceeding so slowly, especially after it had shown so much promise at the beginning. Wöhler responded that the primary reason was that "the initial success won during the night attack of January 1st had not been exploited with sufficient boldness to constitute a breakthrough on the following night."[118]

Guderian later wrote that the German armed forces, especially during this operation, no longer had the type of leaders or the same quality of troops that it had in 1940. Had the *Wehrmacht* (and by extension the *Waffen-SS*) still possessed these qualities, Guderian believed that *Konrad* would have succeeded and that troops could then have been freed up for employment elsewhere (one participant sarcastically noted that the *Wehrmacht* did not have the same caliber of senior commanders of 1940, either).[119] Clearly, his thinking was still more focused on the thin front line in Poland held by *H.Gr. Mitte* and he believed that the earlier Wöhler finished with the Budapest operation, the sooner that "excess" *panzer* divisions could be transferred to the most threatened areas on the Eastern Front where he expected the great Soviet winter offensive to begin in a week's time (in particular the Baranov bridgehead). After all, *H.Gr. Süd* was employing 10 *panzer* divisions in Hungary alone (the *1., 3., 6., 8., 13., 23., 24., FHH*, and the *3.* and *5. SS*), almost as many as the three other army groups on the *Ostfront* were assigned, which had to defend a front line that was over 800 kilometers long, compared to the main defense line in Hungary which was less than half that width.

That evening, Guderian, Wöhler, and Balck, along with their chiefs of staff, met to discuss the continuation of *Konrad*. By this point, it was becoming evident that the relief operation was running out of steam on account of the unexpectedly rapid response of the 4th Guards Army, aided by Tolbukhin's and Malinovsky's mutual decision to aid Zakharov's army by detaching units fighting on the western encircling ring around the city. It was time, they agreed, to initiate Phase II of *Konrad*, the attack to restore the *Margarethestellung*. Though this phase of the operation would have to be initiated earlier than originally planned, if it were to have any chance of success at all it had to begin as soon as possible. The commander of *A. Gr. Balck/6. Armee* also knew that the threat of a move by the 6th Guards Tank Army north of the Danube across the Gran River could not be ignored for very long and was well aware that Guderian wanted the operation to be concluded as fast as possible to free up *panzer* divisions as reserves for *H. Gr. Mitte*. The fate of the encircled forces in Budapest, as well as concern for the city's civilian population, were other factors weighing on the minds of the German commanders, as well as the minds of the leaders of the newly installed pro-Fascist Hungarian government.

Therefore, without waiting for Gille's attack to take Bicske and Zsámbék, Phase II of the attack would begin as early as 7 January. Its prosecution would be the responsibility of *Gen.d.Pz.Tr.* Hermann Breith's *III. Pz.Korps*, using the *1.* and *23. Pz.Div.* and the *4. Kav.Brig.*, reinforced by the addition of 46 Panthers left behind by the withdrawing *I. Abt./Pz.Lehr-Rgt. 130*, which was being transferred back to the Western Front to be reunited with its parent *Panzer-Lehr* Division and issued new vehicles. A corps artillery brigade—*Volks-Art.Korps 403* with 87 guns—would provide additional supporting fire for this attack.

The *4. Kav.Brig.* would hand over its positions in the Mór corridor to the Hungarian *1. Hussar* Division (formerly known as the *1. ung.Kav.Div.*) of the Hungarian *20. Armee-Korps*, reinforced by a German unit, *M.G. Btl. Lausitz* (a *Geneisenau* unit), and move to an assembly area west of Mór. The *3. Pz.Div.*, which was undergoing reconstitution behind the lines of Kirschner's *LVII. Pz.Korps*, was being brought down to Bakony-Czerny to complete its rebuilding process by 7 January in the rear area of the *23. Pz.Div.* This was a calculated risk, because if the 6th Guards Tank Army did begin an attack to the west from the Parkány bridgehead, there would be few armored units available north of the Danube to staunch it. To remedy this situation, the immediate transfer of *20. Pz.Div.* from the front in Slovakia in the *H. Gr. A* area to the *LVII. Pz.Korps* was recommended.

Generaloberst Guderian and Wöhler had different opinions about the direction of attack—should it go south of Lake Velencze, with the *1. Pz.Div.* forming the *Schwerpunkt* on the right, or should it go north of Lake Velencze between Stuhlweissenburg and Mór, with the *4. Kav.Brig.* or *23. Pz.Div.* making the main effort on the left in a drive towards Zámoly? Both commanders agreed that the focal point of Breith's attack should be aimed towards a link-up with the right flank of the *IV. SS-Pz.Korps* in the Bicske area. Such an attack would do two things: reestablish most of the old *Margarethestellung* and destroy a large proportion of the enemy's forces trapped in the ensuing pocket. Once this task was accomplished, both corps would advance side by side directly east to Budapest and relieve the encircled garrison. Despite Guderian's preference for the former course of action, he approved Balck's plan to attack north through Zámoly.

Obergruppenführer Gille, who was not present at these discussions, aired his own opinion to his army commander that evening. He felt that the attempt to reach Budapest via Bicske would ultimately fail unless something was done immediately to ease the pressure being brought against the *Totenkopf* Division, which was experiencing great difficulty in keeping abreast of the *Wiking* Division and could not break through the increasingly strong Soviet defensive barrier being erected along the line Gyermely–Szomor–Kirva. To resolve this dilemma, Gille proposed to send a *Kampfgruppe* from the *Wiking* Division to the *Totenkopf* Division's aid by moving to the northeast and attacking the Soviet forces arrayed at Szomor in the flank and destroying them.[120] Then, Gille reasoned, the *Totenkopf* could catch up with the *Wiking* Division and both divisions would continue their attack towards Zsámbék and Bicske, respectively.

This proposal Balck rejected, stating that the *Schwerpunkt* of the offensive would shift to the south and that Gille would devote his efforts once Breith's attack began to extending his own right flank westwards to enable the success of Breith's upcoming attack by creating more maneuver space for the *Wiking* and *6. Panzer* Divisions. The *Panzergruppe* under Darges, holding the Hegyks Castle Estate, was ordered to stay where it was and continue blocking the highway between Zsámbék and Mány. Gille was specifically instructed by *A.Gr. Balck*'s chief of staff to forbid Darges's tanks from attacking towards the former town to assist with the *Totenkopf* Division's attack. Gille was further instructed to direct the *Germania* Regiment to conduct an attack northwest towards Csabdi to assist the forward progress of the *6. Pz.Div.*, an order that would effectively tie the hands of the *Wiking* Division's commander and ensure that it would make little progress the following day or provide any relief to Darges's isolated regiment.[121] The field army was now directing the employment of individual battalions!

The last instruction Gille received that evening was to form an artillery group using gun batteries from both the *96.* and *711. Inf.Div.* in order to provide additional fire support to the Hungarian *Szent László* Division on the other side of the Danube. This division, which had undergone a brief reconstitution after being mauled the previous month, did not possess much artillery of its own and was being brought back into the front lines opposite the Parkány bridgehead due to the withdrawal of the *6. Pz.Div.* Although the *8. Pz.Div.* had already attached one of its four artillery battalions to this division, it was insufficient to provide the degree of support the situation warranted, especially if the 6th Guards Tank Army did carry out an attack from the Parkány bridgehead. While neither of Gille's two infantry divisions were actually required to move assets north of the Danube, they were expected to cooperate closely with the Hungarian division, which was virtually next door on the other side of the river. To this end, the *IV. SS-Pz.Korps* was ordered to send an artillery observation team to the *Szent László*'s headquarters in the village of Bela.[122]

This requirement was somewhat tempered by the news that Gille's corps would be augmented on 7 January by the attachment of the Hungarian *23. Res.Div.*, whose commander, *Gen.Maj.* Géza Fehér, had been directed to report to Tata to meet with Gille on 6 January no later than 8 a.m. This second-rate Hungarian infantry division, which was still under the administrative control of the Hungarian *3. Armee*, was being sent to assume the rear-area security mission of the *711. Inf.Div.*, part of which was still combing the woods and hills between Szomód and Nyerges Ujfalu looking for Soviet stragglers bypassed during the initial attack.[123] Once this division arrived, it would enable *Gen.Lt.* Reichert to employ all three of his regiments in his drive towards Gran, scheduled to begin on 7 January. Thus ended 5 January, a day characterized by both failure and success, with time running out for the defenders and citizens of Budapest, as well as the troops riding to their rescue.

Saturday, 6 January marked the sixth day of Operation *Konrad*. As it had the past several days, temperatures dropped to a low of 25 degrees Fahrenheit (–3 degrees Centigrade) as the snow continued to fall. Roads were as hazardous as ever and icy conditions made travel in any kind of vehicle, whether wheeled or tracked, a challenge for even the most experienced drivers. Though the lead elements of the divisions had for the most part entered into more level and negotiable terrain, the supply columns still had to move through the Vértes and Gerecse Mountains, ever alert not only for hazardous road conditions, but for Soviet stragglers from the XXXI Rifle Corps seeking to strike back at their tormentors.

Obergruppenführer Gille's mission for 6 January remained unchanged—relieve Budapest. For the *Wiking* and *Totenkopf* Divisions, it meant that on this day they must seize Bicske and Zsámbék, respectively. The newly arrived *6. Pz.Div.*, along with *K.Gr. Philipp*, was still expected to protect the right flank of the corps by seizing Tatabanya and Felsőgalla, while advancing as far as Szár on the *Wiking* Division's right flank. On the left, the *96. Inf.Div.* would continue its attempt to take Dorog and Csolnok, while on the corps' far left, the newly arrived *711. Inf.Div.* would initiate its own advance towards Gran, seize the heights above that key town, as well as establish a blocking position at Zsidódi. Though exhaustion was beginning to set in, expectations and hopes were still high among the fighting troops that this would be the day when the sought-after breakthrough would be achieved; once that had taken place, Budapest's western outskirts and the entrapped *IX. SS-Geb.Korps* were still only 21 tantalizing kilometers away.

For their part, the commanders and troops of the 4th Guards and 46th Armies were equally determined that the hated "Hitlerites" would be stopped before they got that far. After it had become apparent that no additional attacks were coming from the Ösi area and that the one coming from the Tata–Felsőgalla area was the Germans' main effort, Marshal Tolbukhin wasted no time in ordering additional mechanized and rifle corps to be moved from other areas within his sphere of operations to the most-threatened points. Here, these reserves would not only launch counterattacks to delay the oncoming *panzers*, but construct a new defense line a few kilometers beyond the Szár–Bicske–Zsámbék line. Even should Gille's troops break through this Soviet defense line, another one at least equally as strong would be ready and waiting for them.

Equally important, from the Soviet perspective, was that the Second Ukrainian Front was positioning elements of the 6th Guards Tank Army deployed north of the Danube in order to conduct a spoiling or diversionary attack across the Gran, using the V Guards Tank and the VIII and IV Guards Mechanized Corps, supported by the front-line troops of the XXV Guards Rifle Corps of the 7th Guards Army. While the intelligence staffs of *A. Gr. Balck/6. Armee* and *H. Gr. Süd* had discussed the possibility of a spoiling attack originating from this sector, both Wöhler and Balck had discounted it. Neither the commanders nor their *Ic* staffs had any idea of the size of the Soviet force being arrayed there, however.[124]

Once operations commenced before dawn, it quickly became apparent that the *6. Pz. Div.* attack would not get very far that day. Though the division's lead elements were able to seize the village of Csordakút and the high ground 3 kilometers northwest of Bicske (Hill 256) while *K. Gr. Philipp* took the village of Nagynémetegyház on the division's right flank, it was able to advance no further in the face of fierce resistance given by the 11th Guards Cavalry Division of Gorshkov's V Guards Cavalry Corps and the 16th Mechanized Brigade. As the division continued its push to the southeast, troops from the Soviet LXVIII Rifle Corps, primarily the 34th Guards Rifle Division, launched counterattacks northeast from Alsógalla towards Tolna, threatening the supply lines of the *6. Pz. Div.*[125] Although these attacks were contained by *Div. Gr. Pape* (which was exercising tactical control of the division), the vulnerability of *6. Pz. Div.* to future attacks from this direction must have weighed heavily on the mind of its commander, *Oberst* Jürgens, who was forced to continually strengthen the area around Alsógalla–Felsőgalla at the expense of weakening his lead attack elements.

To the left of the *6. Pz. Div.*, the *Wiking* Division struggled to maintain its attack's momentum and its units found themselves under constant assault as more and more Soviet brigades and divisions were thrown into their path. On the division's right, adjacent to the *6. Pz. Div.*, *Ostubaf.* Dorr's *Germania* Regiment attacked Csabdi from the west, north, and east, but was unable to penetrate the stout defenses of the 12th Guards Cavalry Division and 16th Mechanized Brigade. On the division's left, *Ostubaf.* Hack's *Westland* Regiment advanced as far as the forest 1 kilometer west of Mány but was able to go no further due to counterattacks launched by the 41st Guards Rifle Division and portions of the 181st Tank Brigade of the XVIII Tank Corps. Both sides claimed a number of tanks destroyed; the XVIII Tank Corps claiming 19 German armored vehicles destroyed, while admitting to losing eight of its own, though this most likely reflected the number of tanks completely destroyed, as opposed to those damaged but repairable.[126]

The focus of the fighting that day in the *Wiking* Division's advance remained the blocking position erected along the Bicske–Zsámbék highway established by the division's *Panzergruppe*, led by *Ostubaf.* Darges, which held a very tenuous connection with the *Westland* Regiment on the northern side of the highway. Throughout that day, Darges's miniscule force of 18 tanks—including Vogt's understrength *I. Btl./Norge*—held the Hegyks Castle Estate against numerous attempts by Soviet forces to capture it, which would have freed up the highway for movement of their own supplies and troops. The position at Hegyks was subjected to overwhelming artillery fire during daylight hours, as the XXXI Guards Rifle Corps and XVIII Tank Corps sought to pulverize Darges's battlegroup.

While the artillery shelled the German position indiscriminately, tanks from the 181st Tank and the 16th Mechanized Brigade stood back and pounded holes in the wall surrounding the estate with high-explosive shells. The unrelenting fire forced most of Vogt's infantry into the grounds of the estate, with many seeking shelter within the thick walls of the castle's ground floor or in its large basement. The tanks themselves were primarily used as the *Panzergruppe*'s artillery, contributing to the castle's defense using their 7.5cm high-explosive shells in indirect fire mode.

Occasionally, Darges's *panzers* made forays against the Soviet tanks positioned several hundred meters beyond the walls, and claimed to have destroyed 12 Soviet armored fighting vehicles on 6 January alone. One platoon of six tanks even made a reconnaissance in force towards Mány, but was driven back by the overwhelming Soviet response after losing no tanks of its own, though it claimed to have knocked out five T-34s and two heavy guns.[127] At night, the tanks withdrew back inside the walls of the estate, while Vogt's infantry assumed responsibility for repelling the nightly attacks by Soviet riflemen, three on the night of 6/7 January alone. Soviet aircraft attacked the position both day and night, conducting strafing and bombing attacks to add to the destructive power of the artillery and mortar fire.

Somehow, a supply convoy, consisting mostly of armored vehicles, managed to find their way through Soviet lines to Hegyks during the evening, delivering enough fuel and ammunition to allow Darges and his troops to keep fighting, quashing any thoughts of the necessity for breaking out. Whenever possible, the wounded were evacuated in *SPWs*, although *Hstuf.* Willi Hein, the battalion commander of the regiment's *I. Abteilung*—who had been wounded in the lower leg by a mortar shell while he was standing in the front doorway of the castle—refused to leave. Since he was incapacitated, command devolved to *Ostuf.* Bauer, who would lead the battalion for the next several weeks.[128] Despite the seemingly precarious situation, Darges was instructed to remain where he was and continue blocking the Bicske–Zsámbék highway. Though he did not know it, the advance by his force marked the farthest point reached during Operation *Konrad I.*

To the *Wiking* Division's left, Becker's *Totenkopf* Division was having an equally difficult time reaching its objective of Zsámbék. Though it had successfully taken

Szomor the previous day, the introduction of numerous Soviet reserves on 6 January would keep its goal out of reach. The division's *Panzergruppe*, now led by *Stubaf.* Kraas, continued moving down the road from Szomor to Zsámbék early in the morning. By 9 a.m., it had reached Hill 290, a mere 4 kilometers northwest of the town. But it would get no further, having come up against the defenses of the newly arrived 170th Tank Brigade, which quickly destroyed four of Kraas's *panzers* near the village of Felsoörpuszta.

With the *Panzergruppe* momentarily blocked, action then shifted to the division's left flank, where Becker directed two battalions from the *SS-Pz. Gren. Rgt. 5 Totenkopf*, along with the division's armored reconnaissance battalion, to make an attempt to approach Zsámbék from the northeast via the towns of Dag and Kirva. This attempt also failed, having run up against two guards mechanized brigades (the 5th and 6th) as well as several rifle divisions. In the division's center, *SS-Pz. Gren. Rgt. 6 Eicke* also tried to punch south between Szomor and Kirva, but this attempt was stymied too. Early in the afternoon, the *Panzergruppe* tried once more, attacking towards Mány. After proceeding approximately 900 meters northeast of Felsoörpuszta, the lead tanks ran up against a *Pakfront*. Two *Pz. VI* Tigers from *9. Kp./SS-Pz.Rgt. 3* were damaged as well as one *Pz. IV*, but the latter tank had to be destroyed by its crew because it was deemed irrecoverable.

Once again blocked by the ever-strengthening Soviet defenses, Becker ordered the *Panzergruppe* to move to the division's eastern flank late in the afternoon to try an enveloping movement east of Zsámbék via Dag, but this attempt came up short as well when the armored group's spearhead encountered antitank guns and T-34s. These were from the 4th Guards Mechanized Brigade of the II Guards Mechanized Corps, which a few hours before had been arrayed along the ridgeline encompassing Hills 234 and 220 northwest of Dag.[129] The lead tank, a Tiger, was knocked out of commission by an antitank gun, as was a Panther that moved forward to take its place. One participant in this action, *Sturmmann* Erich Lehmkuhl, later described what happened:

> By 2300 hours, we finally began the attack along a road. As we approached a bend in the road, we came under heavy defensive fire. I felt a heavy impact on my left foot. We had been hit by a round that had penetrated the hull. My first thought was that I had lost my right foot. I opened the radio operator's hatch and climbed out and slid down into the snow ... I took cover in a ditch next to the road. I had my leg held against the clear sky, and I saw my foot was gone up to the Achilles heel ... I don't know how long I was lying there, but the next thing I remember was a medic standing over me with a syringe and another man saying he was going to take me away on a motorcycle sidecar combination ... [In Komarn] I was the first to be operated on. Afterwards I was visited by the company *Spiess, Hauptscharführer* Beneke, who awarded me the Iron Cross, First Class and gave me a small package with some chocolate in it.[130]

Having achieved no significant success that day for the loss of at least six *panzers* from his dwindling armored strength, Becker decided to regroup and make another try for Zsámbék the next morning.

To the left of Becker's division, *Oberst* Harrendorf's *96. Inf.Div.* was not finding the going that day any easier. The division's northernmost *Kampfgruppe*, formed around *Gren.Rgt. 283*, continued its effort to capture Dorog, but to no avail. With none of the division antitank battalion's *Sturmgeschütze* operational, the *Kampfgruppe* simply could not overcome the firepower of the dug-in tanks from the 37th Tank Brigade and the 30th Guards Heavy Tank Regiment. The situation was developing slightly more favorably to the south, where *Gren.Rgt. 283* was able to seize the high ground 1 kilometer west of Csolnok as well as the village of Kohlenberg (now incorporated into modern-day Csolnok) 1.5 kilometers to the north, including Hill 340, before being brought to a halt by the defenses of the 86th Guards Rifle Division.

On the division's right flank, the third regiment—*Gren.Rgt. 284*—sought to maintain the tenuous contact with the neighboring *Totenkopf* Division in the vicinity of Sarisap. In addition to the significant challenges posed by the continual arrival of Soviet reserves, the *96. Inf.Div.* now had to contend with increasing attention from the Red Air Force, whose aerial interdiction efforts grew more bothersome with each passing day. At least all of the division's artillery was now in action, allowing its new commander, *Oberstlt.* Dr. Koch to bring all four of his battalions into action to support the three infantry regiments. On that same day, *Oberst* Harrendorf moved his division command post forward to the mill in Tokod (Tokod-Mühle) to be closer to the fighting.

The biggest surprise of the day came from a quarter where no one expected much success—the zone of attack of the recently arrived *711. Inf.Div.* on the corps' far-left flank along the Danube. Its infantry regiments composed predominately of recent draftees and transfers from the *Luftwaffe* and *Kriegsmarine*, it not only successfully took the village of Zsidódi in the afternoon, but the high ground that lay several kilometers to the east a few hours later, including Hill 309. At roughly the same time, an infantry company sent out to reconnoiter towards Gran entered the town uncontested, surprising and overcoming the small Soviet garrison defending it. Upon hearing the news of this success, the commander of *III. Btl./ Gren.Rgt. 744*, *Hptm.* Eduard Post, continued the attack on his own initiative and swept through Gran as far as the hill mass dominating the eastern approaches to the town, where he stopped and began establishing a strong defensive position that dominated the approaches to the town from the east. For this deed, *Hptm.* Post was later awarded the Knight's Cross in a separate order issued by *A.Gr. Balck/6. Armee.*[131]

When apprised of this development, *Ogruf.* Gille ordered *Gen.Lt.* Reichert to send all available forces into Gran and the area south of the town to begin exploiting this success by attacking to the south and southeast. The only other development in the *IV. SS-Pz.Korps* area that day was the arrival of the Hungarian *23. Inf.Div.*, with its three infantry battalions, to begin the thankless task of mopping up bypassed Soviet stragglers and performing security duties in the areas behind the front lines between Szomód and Nyerges Ujfalu. Overall, neither Gille nor Balck were satisfied with the progress that day. Gille's chief of staff, Manfred Schönfelder, later wrote in his diary summing up the events of 6 January:

> The attack is stuck. The enemy has brought up eight rifle divisions and three mechanized units to defend against us. The armored battlegroup of the *Wiking* has had to defend itself between Mány and Bicske against attacks from all sides and can no longer advance. The terrain itself does not allow for an enveloping attacking by our mechanized forces along the road Bicske–Zsámbék and [Dorog].

All that Gille could add was a terse statement: "The divisions have reached the line Bicske–Zsámbék. The opponent is strengthening himself constantly, especially with powerful antitank defenses and counterattacks. Around the evening hours, the offensive had to be called to a halt, our losses were too great."[132] According to one contemporary knowledgeable observer, "All in all, the results of this day of fighting were unsatisfactory for the *IV. SS-Pz.Korps*. The idea began to grow in the corps headquarters that the attack could be resumed and achieve final success only by shifting the *Schwerpunkt* to the still mobile left flank [to exploit the success achieved that day by the *711. Inf.Div*]."[133]

As the troops and tanks of the *IV. SS-Pz.Korps* were doing their utmost that day to succeed in their mission, the divisions and brigades of *Korpsgruppe Breith* were preparing to carry out their own attack the following day. The attack, to be carried out using the *3. and 23. Pz.Div.* and the *4. Kav.Brig.*, was to be directed, as previously described, towards a link-up with Gille's corps in the southern Vértes Mountains along the highway linking Csákvár, Bicske, and Zsámbék. Overall control of the operation would be exercised by *Gen.d.Kav.* Harteneck's *I. Kav.Korps*. Most of 6 January was used by the units to move into their forward assembly areas in preparation for the attack, scheduled to begin the next morning. Both Generals Breith and Harteneck evidently believed that this attack would help the *IV. SS-Pz.Korps* continue with its attack, but in retrospect they were embarking on an impossible task, for Gille's attack—at least in the southeast—had culminated.

In Budapest, the perimeter continued to shrink, especially the eastern bridgehead in Pest. Though Soviet artillery fire and air attacks did not noticeably slacken, thanks to the efforts of the *22. SS-Fw.Kav.Div. Maria Theresa* the previous day, sufficient ground had been retaken on Csepel Island to reestablish a landing field for aircraft. During the evening of 5–6 January, 23 *Ju-52* transports were able to land on this field, disgorging their cargo of 38 tons of ammunition and other supplies. During the evening, they also evacuated 228 casualties who required urgent treatment. Additional airdrops by 49 *He-111s* and nine *Ju-52s* were able to deliver 40 more tons of ammunition, rations, and fuel. However, the airfield once again came under enemy fire, rendering it unusable by the evening of 6/7 January. Despite receiving this badly needed aid, the headquarters of the *IX. SS-Geb.Korps* pessimistically reported:

Artillery ammunition gone; almost out of infantry ammunition, which will last only under firing restrictions. Fuel is almost gone. Rations can be stretched to 7 January only by severe rationing. Situation of the wounded is catastrophic. Army [i.e., *6. Armee*] must make arrangements for the evacuation of 3,000 wounded. As the newly established landing strip on Csepel Island is no longer usable because of enemy action, supplies can only be air dropped tonight, weather permitting.

As grim as the situation in Budapest appeared, the situation on *A. Gr. Balck/6. Armee*'s left flank north of the Danube, where Kirchner's *LVII Pz.Korps* was positioned, became just as bad.

On that day, the 6th Guards Tank Army initiated its own offensive, with the support of the 7th Guards Army, when its leading elements began crossing the Gran River at 3 a.m. and attacked out of the Parkány bridgehead without any artillery preparation, achieving complete surprise. Evidently, until this point, both the *H. Gr. Süd* commander and his chief of staff had believed that the 6th Guards Tank Army was located further to the east in an assembly area, where it was reconstituting its forces, and was not likely to participate in a large-scale offensive while *Konrad* was still underway (see Map 4).

The intelligence staffs of both *H. Gr. Süd* and *A. Gr. Balck* had been raising warnings about the possibility of such an attack by the 6th Guards Tank Army or the 7th Guards Army for the past three days, but their fears had not been seriously considered by either Balck or Wöhler. In fact, Balck had been stripping divisions from Kirchner's corps and using them to reinforce both Gille's and Breith's corps, believing that *LVII. Pz.Korps* still had sufficient combat power to deal with any attempt by the 7th Guards Army to cross the Gran.

All that Kirchner now had to defend his sector against an overwhelmingly powerful attack by not one but two Soviet armies along a 15-kilometer-wide front by two Soviet rifle corps, two mechanized corps, and one tank corps was an understrength *panzer* division (the *8.*), an equally understrength *Volks-Grenadier Division* (the *211.*), and the recently reconstituted Hungarian *Szent László* Division, as well as a smattering of small *Alarm* units. The only appreciable forces in his rear area were elements of the *Luftwaffe*'s *15. Flak Division* defending the bridge and railyards at Komorn.

Needless to say, Kirchner's forces were not strong enough to hold back the attackers, who managed to push forward 16 kilometers on the attack's first day. Clearly, Komorn and Neuhäusel were their immediate objectives; if they fell, it would put not only *LVII. Pz.Korps* in jeopardy, but would threaten Gille's *IV. SS-Pz. Korps* with envelopment should the Soviets establish a bridgehead over the Danube in the corps' rear area. Several German and Hungarian *Kampfgruppen* were quickly surrounded, the *Szent László* Division scattered, and the *8. Pz.Div.* and *211. V.G.D.* were fighting desperately to reestablish some sort of continuous defense line, but to no avail.

Suddenly, the Hungarian Front offered an arresting paradox: both opponents were attacking at the same time in opposite directions—the Soviets north of the Danube heading west, the Germans and their Hungarian allies south of the Danube heading east! In the evening summary for 6 January concerning this attack, the *H. Gr. Süd Ia* dryly noted in the *Kriegstagebuch*, "During the night, the enemy launched his expected (!) attack with the 6th Guards Tank Army in the direction of Komorn ... the penetration has not yet been sealed off. Resumption of the enemy's attack is to be expected on 7 January."[134]

This was the situation confronting Guderian when he visited the headquarters of the *IV. SS-Pz. Korps* in Tata later that morning. Accompanied by the *OKH* operations chief, *Oberst i. G.* Bogislaw von Bonin, Guderian was given a briefing by Gille outlining the progress of the offensive so far. Their visit was a brief one; according to Schönfelder, who was present, Guderian and von Bonin returned to the *A. Gr. Balck/6. Armee* headquarters in Martinsberg soon thereafter, because "of the danger to his person from enemy air attack at the corps' location."[135] Here, they would receive a similar briefing by Balck and Gaedke, his chief of staff outlining the field army's perspective of how the operation was progressing.

During his briefing to Guderian and von Bonin, Gille essentially told them that the *IV. SS-Pz. Korps* attack had stalled in the face of formidable Soviet antitank defenses being erected along the line Tatabanya–Felsőgalla–Csabdi–Bicske–Zsámbék–Kirva–Csolnok–Dorog, which created a distinctive bulge in the main defense line of the 4th Guards Army. Not only were his *panzer* divisions finding these positions tough to crack, but newly brought up Soviet armored and mechanized formations were launching numerous counterattacks that had to be warded off, further slowing his rate of advance.

Based on the developing situation, Gille stated that he expected no further forward progress at Bicske and Zsámbék. Instead, he recommended to Guderian and von Bonin that *IV. SS-Pz. Korps* should be allowed to reinforce the area where his troops were enjoying success—namely, along his left flank at Gran, where the *711. Inf. Div.* had made significant advances earlier that day. While some of his divisions would remain where they were to freeze the Soviet reinforcements in place, Gille recommended pulling out and sending at least one armored division to the north to spearhead the advance from Gran.

Before Guderian departed Gille's headquarters, he received a telephone call from Balck who gave him a brief description of the developing situation north of the Danube in *LVII Pz. Korps'* sector. During the conversation, Balck proposed bringing down the *20. Pz. Div.* now, as had been earlier suggested, instead of keeping it at Altsohl in Slovakia, and assigning it to Kirschner's corps before it was too late. At 10:10 a.m., von Bonin contacted *Gen.d.Pz. Tr.* Wenck, his boss on the *OKH Führungsstab* in Zossen, to let him know that Guderian had approved Balck's idea. Wenck quickly sent orders to the *20. Pz. Div.* to immediately begin loading for rail movement to Neuhäusel. Once it arrived, it would conduct a counterattack to stop the attack by the 6th Guards Tank Army before it reached Komorn. Evidently,

Guderian was far more concerned about events unfolding north of the Danube than he was with the status of the attempt to relieve Budapest.

When Guderian and von Bonin arrived at Balck's headquarters, located aboard the command train in Martinsberg, after their brief visit to the front, Balck and Gaedke briefed them further on the plan to carry out the supporting attack by the *I. Kav.Korps* the following day that would go through Zámoly and link up with Gille's right flank somewhere near Csakvár. Rather than consider Gille's suggestion to shift the *Schwerpunkt* to his corps' left flank at Gran, the assembled generals discussed taking away the *6. Pz.Div.* from Gille and using it to reinforce the attack by the *I. Kav.Korps*. After weighing the pros and cons of this idea, by unanimous consent they finally rejected it, opting to leave it in place for now, if for no other reason than to "broaden its spearhead" to close the distance that *I. Kav.Korps* would have to travel in order to effect the linkup with *IV. SS-Pz.Korps*.

To his credit, Balck did briefly consider shifting the *6. Pz.Div.* to reinforce the northern flank at Gran, but after weighing the alternatives, he ultimately rejected this idea. Evidently, he and the other officers present placed greater confidence in the attack by Harteneck's corps that would allow the attack of Gille's corps "to get moving again." The following day would prove whether this confidence was misplaced. The only other item that Guderian and Balck discussed was what could be done until the arrival of the *20. Pz.Div.* to shore up Kirchner's *LVII. Pz.Korps*.

With *Korpsgruppe Breith* and its *I. Kav.Div.* about to commence its attack towards Zámoly on 7 January, and Gille's corps decisively engaged, the only thing that Balck could spare was *Pz.Abt. 208*, which could be detached from *Div.Gr. Pape* at Bánhida. Thus, the following day the battalion, with its 38 tanks and assault guns (of which 29 were operational), was sent over the Danube bridge in Komorn to join the *8. Pz.Div.* and do what it could to help delay the rapidly approaching Soviet assault.

When Gille learned that evening that his proposal to shift his corps' point of main effort from the south to the northern flank at Gran had been rejected by his field army and army group commanders, he became extremely frustrated. He felt so strongly that both Balck and Wöhler were making a mistake that he called Hitler's headquarters at the *OKW* directly and requested that Guderian, as chief of the *OKH*, be allowed to present the case directly to the *Führer* on Gille's behalf in order to convince him that the attack by the *IV. SS-Pz.Korps* had to be shifted to the north. According to Schönfelder, Gille received no response from Hitler, though perhaps he had planted the seed of an idea that would come to fruition several days later.[136] In his memoir, Guderian made no mention of having heard of this request, but his notes for this period are rather sparse, his main focus being the looming Soviet offensive in Poland and what could be done at this late stage to prepare for it.

Day seven of *Konrad* was marked by heavy fighting in the south, with no appreciable gains being made, while in the north, the *711. Inf.Div.*, a unit initially held in low esteem, continued to surprise everyone with the speed of its advance.

One reason why *Gen.Lt.* Reichert's division was enjoying such success was that it was at nearly full strength and was relatively fresh when it arrived—after all, 6 January marked the first day that the division had been involved in actual combat. Furthermore, it had faced only rear echelon Soviet troops with few heavy weapons of their own. In contrast, the other four divisions in the *IV. SS-Pz.Korps* had been fighting almost non-stop since 1 January, suffering substantial losses in manpower and material during their advance, reflected in the dwindling numbers in their *Kampfstärke* as well as their vehicle readiness rates.

After seven days of constant combat, horrific road conditions, and mountains that had to be overcome, the readiness rates of armored fighting vehicles had declined propitiously, particularly that of the corps' *panzers*. That day also marked the first opportunity to compile and submit the mandatory weekly report on available armored vehicle strength to the field army, which Gille's *Ia, Stubaf.* Wilhelm Klose, assembled with the assistance of the corps' *Technischer Führer für das Kraftfahrwesen* (*TFK*, or G-4 Maintenance Officer), *Stubaf.* Otto Brandt. The status reports are quite revealing and clearly illustrate how rapidly the combat power of the corps had eroded (see Figures 3 and 4 for the status of both divisions as of 1 January 1945).

Of the 320 armored fighting vehicles (including tanks, tank destroyers, and assault guns) that were on hand as of 1 January (of which 285 were deemed "mission ready"), only 112 were still operational at the close of 6 January. Thus, Gille's corps was conducting operations with roughly a third of the number of ready *panzers* of all types that it had when it began *Konrad*. Of the 201 that had fallen out for various reasons from 1–6 January, only 39 had been deemed a total loss due to the vehicle's complete destruction by the enemy or by its crew. Many others had been damaged in battle, which maintenance crews were hurriedly trying to restore to a semblance of operational readiness.

On 6 January, the *3. SS-Pz.Div. Totenkopf* reported having 44 armored fighting vehicles operational, including eight *Pz. IVs*, 10 *Pz. V* Panthers, four *Pz. VI* Tigers, 13 *StuGs*, and nine *Jg.Pz. IVs*, though it still fielded 53 operational guns in its artillery regiment. The *5. SS-Pz.Div. Wiking* was in far worse shape, with only eight *Pz. IVs*, eight Panthers, one *StuG*, and four *Jg.Pz. IV* tank destroyers, for a total of only 21 able to go into battle, slightly more than a tank company in size, but its artillery regiment still had 47 guns. The *6. Pz.Div.*, which had reabsorbed *K.Gr. Philipp* into its ranks, was slightly better off, with eight *Pz. IVs*, 35 Panthers, and four *Jg.Pz. IVs*, giving it a total of 47 tanks and tanks destroyers, as well as 31 artillery tubes.

None of the armored vehicles from the *96. Inf.Div.* were operational, though its horse-drawn artillery regiment still possessed 12 batteries' worth of guns. On the other hand, the *711. Inf.Div.* still had seven operational *Jg.Pz. 38t* tank destroyers but only 19 artillery pieces. Another factor that had further weakened Gille's available armor strength was Balck's decision on 6 January to transfer *Pz.Abt. 208* from *Div. Gr. Pape* to *LVII. Pz.Korps*, taking with it 22 operational *Pz. IVs* and seven *StuGs*,

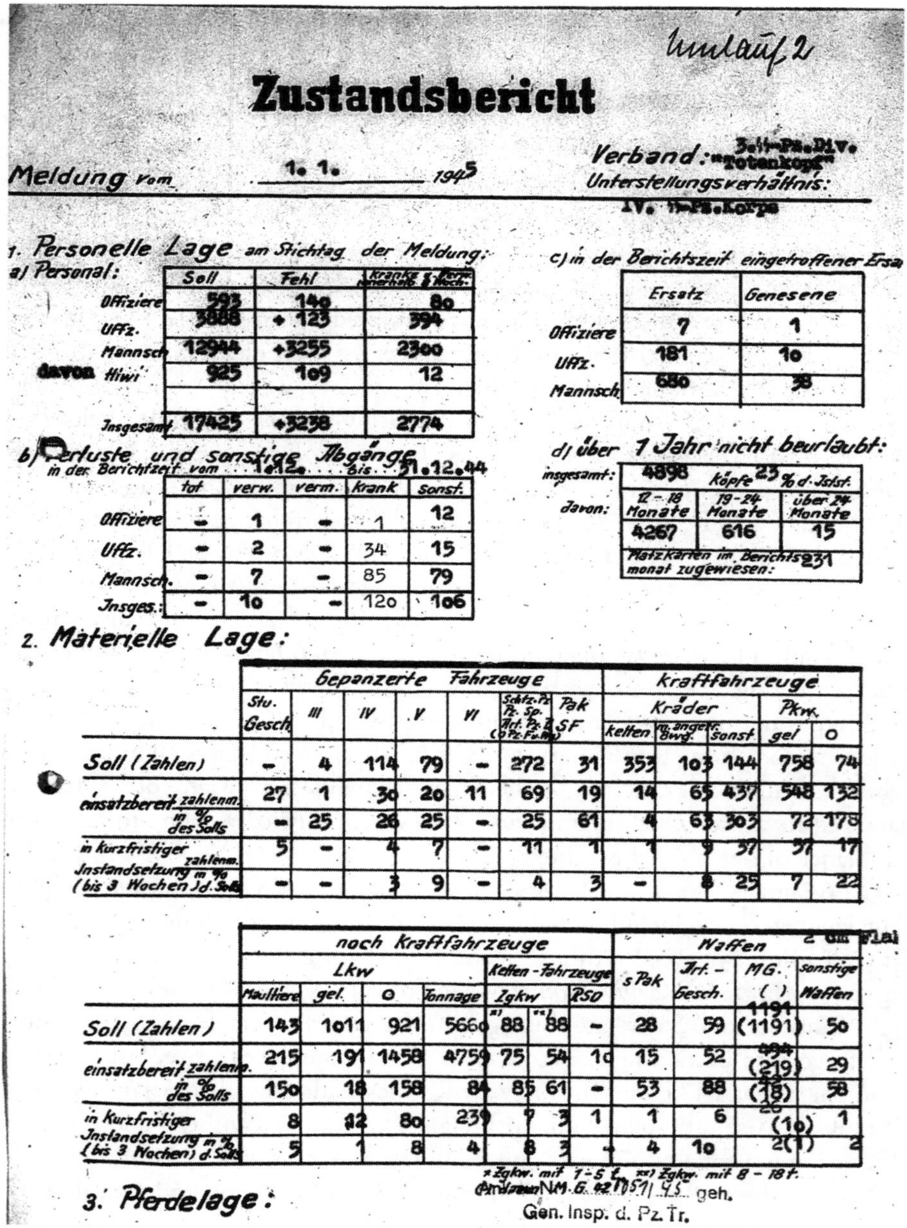

Umlauf 2

Zustandsbericht

Meldung vom 1. 1. 1945

Verband: 3. SS-Pz.Div. "Totenkopf"

Unterstellungsverhältnis: IV. SS-Pz.Korps

1. Personelle Lage am Stichtag der Meldung:

a) Personal:

	Soll	Fehl	Kranke u. Verw. innerhalb 8 Woch.
Offiziere	593	140	80
Uffz.	3888	+ 123	394
Mannsch.	12944	+3255	2300
davon Hiwi	925	109	12
Insgesamt	17425	+3238	2774

b) Verluste und sonstige Abgänge in der Berichtzeit vom 1.12. bis 31.12.44

	tot	verw.	verm.	krank	sonst.
Offiziere	–	1	–	1	12
Uffz.	–	2	–	34	15
Mannsch.	–	7	–	85	79
Insges.:	–	10	–	120	106

c) in der Berichtszeit eingetroffener Ersatz

	Ersatz	Genesene
Offiziere	7	1
Uffz.	181	10
Mannsch.	680	38

d) über 1 Jahr nicht beurlaubt:

insgesamt:	4898 Köpfe	25 % d. Istst.	
davon:	12–18 Monate	19–24 Monate	über 24 Monate
	4267	616	15
	Platzkarten im Berichtsmonat zugewiesen: 231		

2. Materielle Lage:

	Gepanzerte Fahrzeuge							Kraftfahrzeuge				
								Kräder			Pkw.	
	Stu. Gesch.	III	IV	V	VI	Schtz.Pz. Pz.Sp. Art.Pz.B. (o.Pz.Fu.Wg.)	Pak SF	Ketten	m. angetr. Bwg.	sonst.	gel.	O
Soll (Zahlen)	–	4	114	79	–	272	31	353	103	144	758	74
einsatzbereit zahlenm.	27	1	30	20	11	69	19	14	65	437	548	132
einsatzbereit in % des Solls	–	25	26	25	–	25	61	4	63	303	72	178
in kurzfristiger Instandsetzung (bis 3 Wochen) zahlenm.	5	–	4	7	–	11	1	1	9	37	37	17
in kurzfristiger Instandsetzung (bis 3 Wochen) in % d. Solls	–	–	3	9	–	4	3	–	8	25	7	22

	noch Kraftfahrzeuge							Waffen			
	Lkw				Ketten-Fahrzeuge						
	Maultiere	gel.	O	Tonnage	Zgkw [x]	Zgkw [xx]	RSO	s Pak	Art.-Gesch.	MG. ( )	sonstige Waffen
Soll (Zahlen)	143	1011	921	5660	88	88	–	28	59	1191 (1191)	50
einsatzbereit zahlenm.	215	191	1458	4759	75	54	10	15	52	494 (219)	29
einsatzbereit in % des Solls	150	18	158	84	85	61	–	53	88	42 (18)	58
in kurzfristiger Instandsetzung (bis 3 Wochen) zahlenm.	8	12	80	239	7	3	1	1	6	26 (10)	1
in kurzfristiger Instandsetzung (bis 3 Wochen) in % d. Solls	5	1	8	4	8	3	–	4	10	2(1)	2

2 cm Flak

x Zgkw. mit 1–5 t. xx) Zgkw. mit 8–18 t.

Anlagen NM.G. 42 11.5.1.45 geh.

Gen. Insp. d. Pz.Tr.

3. Pferdelage:

Figure 3. The monthly *Zustandbericht* (status report) of the *3. SS-Pz.Div. Totenkopf* for the month of December 1944, compiled on 1 January 1945. These reports were submitted to the German Army's Inspectorate of *Panzer* Troops in Berlin, which was responsible for the doctrine, organization, training, manpower procurement, infrastructure, and leadership development of all *panzer* troops, regardless of whether they were from the *Heer*, *Waffen-SS*, or *Luftwaffe*. (Courtesy of Martin Block)

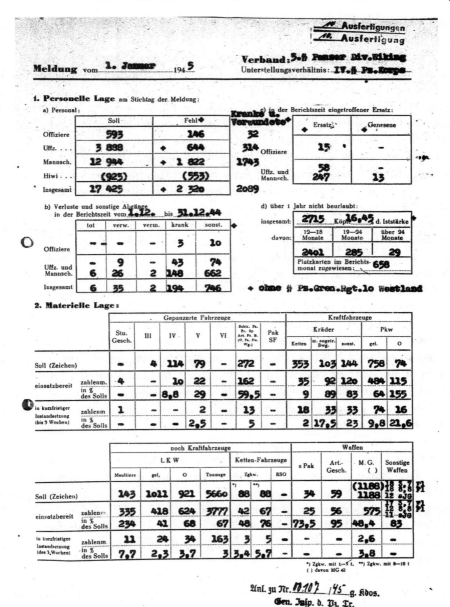

Figure 4. The monthly *Zustandbericht* (status report) of the 5. SS-Pz.Div. Wiking for December 1944, compiled on 1 January 1945. The monthly report provided information on both personnel and material readiness, including the number of casualties suffered, replacements assigned, actual unit strength, and amount of armored fighting vehicles and other vehicles needed to enable a *panzer* division to operate as intended. The reverse side was used by commanders to express certain issues that influenced their combat readiness. (Courtesy of Martin Block)

leaving *Gen.Maj.* Pape with no armor remaining in his makeshift command except *StuG.Brig. 239.*

At the same time that the corps' *Ia* and *TFK* were tabulating their statistics on vehicle readiness, the corps' *Adjutant* or *IIa* (personnel officer), *Stubaf.* Karl-Willi Schulze, and his assistants were compiling the number of casualties suffered by all elements of the corps since 1 January. Losses in killed, wounded, and missing in action had been considerable. For instance, from 1–6 January the *Totenkopf* Division had suffered the loss of 242 men killed, 1,064 wounded, and 54 declared missing in action, not counting those reporting sick or injured. This loss—1,360 men in all categories, less those reporting sick—represents roughly a third of the division's initial *Kampfstärke* before the offensive began, which by this date had shrunk to 2,858 men, though still a respectable number.

In comparison, the *Wiking* Division had lost 1,070 men, including 166 killed, 791 wounded, and 113 missing, leaving it with a respectable *Kampfstärke* of 3,318 men, not counting the two other battalions, *I. Btl./Norge* and *I. Btl./Danmark*, which consisted of 390 and 509 men, respectively. Its slightly lower losses are attributable to the late arrival of the *Westland* Regiment, which had not completed its rail movement from Poland until 4 January. The *96. Inf.Div.*, which had been in the thick of the fighting since the very beginning, had lost 110 men killed, 674 wounded, and 185 missing in action, a total of 969 men, leaving it with a remaining *Kampfstärke* of only 1,700, a reflection of the hard fighting it had done without the benefit of much armor support and the fact that it had not enjoyed a period of rest behind the front lines in Slovakia like the other divisions had. The *711. Inf.Div.*, which had only just arrived, did not submit a report, though at this early stage its losses would have been minimal.

Losses suffered by *Oberst* Jürgen's *6. Pz.Div.*, including *K.Gr. Philipp*, amounted to only five killed, 70 wounded, and six missing, reflecting its late arrival as well as the fact that it had not yet been involved in any really hard fighting. Most of these losses would have been confined to its *K.Gr. Philipp*. Now completely assembled except for minor elements left behind in the *LVII Pz.Korps* sector, the division mustered 1,307 men in its *Kampfstärke*, less than average for a *panzer* division and a reflection of the hard fighting it had experienced since the previous November.

Divisionsgruppe Pape—which was now a division in name only, having been stripped of most of its armor—could only submit an incomplete casualty report for the period concerned, totaling just eight men killed and wounded. This is hardly a reflection of the heavy fighting it had experienced since 1 January, but the transfer of most of its fighting units had caused Pape to lose contact with them, making it difficult to obtain their status reports. Its two remaining battalions, including a 186-man battalion consisting of remnants of the *271. V.G.D.*, resulted in a total *Kampfstärke* of only 430 men for the *Divisionsgruppe*.[137]

All told, the *IV. SS-Pz.Korps* now had a combined *Kampfstärke* of only 13,451 men (not counting *Korps-* or *Heerestruppen*) as of the evening of 6 January, after losing 3,512 effectives, almost 21 percent of its combined *Kampfstärke* when the offensive began.[138] With this greatly weakened collection of forces, including his remaining 112 operational armored fighting vehicles, Gille was still expected to relieve Budapest. Still, *Gen.d.Pz.Tr.* Balck and his chief of staff optimistically believed that once the attack by *I. Kav.Korps* had begun on 7 January, the attack by the *IV. SS-Pz.Korps* would become "unstuck," thereby freeing it up to continue its part in the relief of Budapest.

That morning, before major operations commenced, Gille issued an order of the day that specifically mentioned Guderian's visit on 6 January and repeated Hitler's expectations for the success of the relief operation as well as the urgent necessity for doing so:

> On the occasion of the visit of the Chief of the General Staff of the Army, *Generaloberst* Guderian, to the General Command on January 6, 1945, he once again emphasized the decisive importance of the thrust of the *IV. SS-Panzerkorps* into the Budapest area. Beside the military necessity, namely fighting for freedom of the occupation and reclaiming the area of Budapest, there is the political necessity, because Budapest means Hungary. Moreover, this operation, if fully successful, can bring about a turn of the struggle in the Hungarian area and possibly decisively influence the fighting on the entire Eastern front.
>
> ... The *Führer* has given this task to the *IV. SS-Panzerkorps* and expects his divisions to carry it out to the last man and to achieve the goals set for them under all circumstances by an unrestrained, unstoppable urge to advance and an iron necessity. The first goal of the fighting, to penetrate the forest mountains, has almost been reached. The substantial booty we have taken testifies to the severity of the fighting and the heavy losses of the enemy. We continue to strive towards the ultimate goal, for it must and will be achieved. The brave, hard fighting garrison of Budapest are looking towards us in anticipation.

One observer from the *96. Inf.Div.*, *Hptm.* Hartwig Pohlmann, a staff officer who had witnessed the fighting since 1 January and was well aware of the odds stacked against the German and Hungarian forces, was not impressed with such bombast. After the war, he wrote:

> This order was ... indicative of Hitler's unrealistic assessment of the situation during this period of the war and its inevitable effect on the command of the higher leadership. That everything was being done to liberate the trapped comrades in Budapest was, of course, in keeping with the views of everyone from the youngest Grenadier on up.[139]

Gille was most likely quite aware of the true situation, having made his daily visits to the headquarters of his divisions and as far forward to the front line as possible, as was his custom whenever the security situation permitted. His sincerity for the rescue of the Budapest garrison was genuine. As also was his custom, he did not openly question seemingly mindless orders from above, but in the case of the relief of Budapest, even Gille's acceptance of such orders had its limits, as will be seen.

Whether Hitler's expectations were realistic or not, the offensive to relieve Budapest continued. In the area of the northern attack group (*IV. SS-Pz.Korps*), road conditions worsened as the snow continued to fall and freezing temperatures prevailed, while to the south, *Korpsgruppe Breith*'s *I. Kav.Korps*, now designated the southern attack group, initiated its attack towards Zámoly on more level and open ground, where the weather had less impact. On the far right in Gille's zone of attack, the much-weakened *Div.Gr. Pape* successfully held back a Soviet reconnaissance in force from the 34th Guards Rifle Division originating from Felsőgalla. To its left, the *6. Pz.Div.*, after heavy fighting, took Hill 256 (known locally as Dobogó), the high ground dominating the town of Csabdi 3 kilometers northwest of Bicske, and successfully held it throughout the day as it fended off numerous tank-supported counterattacks launched by elements of the 16th Mechanized Brigade.

Adjacent to the *6. Pz.Div.*, Ullrich's *Wiking* Division was involved in seemingly interminable see-saw fighting as its two *Panzergrenadier* regiments bitterly fought over Csabdi and Mány. After overcoming the stubborn resistance offered by troops from the 41st Guards Rifle Division and tanks from the 16th Mechanized Brigade, which included house-to-house fighting and tank-versus-infantry duels in the streets, the troops from the *Germania* Regiment in Csabdi finally prevailed. This enabled them to open up a relief corridor for the encircled *Panzergruppe* holed up in the Hegyks Castle Estate and begin delivering additional fuel and ammunition for Darges's beleaguered force, which had been fighting off numerous attempts by Soviet tanks and infantry to storm the estate during the past 48 hours.

Instead of being allowed to break out, Darges's and Vogt's accompanying infantry battalion from the *Norge* Regiment were ordered to continue holding their position. Now reinforced by Vogt's heavy weapons company (*4. Kp./Norge*), the battered *Panzergruppe* fended off several counterattacks launched from Bicske by the 32nd Mechanized Brigade and 181st Tank Brigade. On the division's left flank, the *Westland* Regiment, including a small force of supporting armored vehicles (estimated by the Soviets at between seven and 12 tanks), struggled to take Mány, each attempt failing in the face of heavy defensive fire from a battalion of the 181st Tank Brigade and the guns of the 595th Antitank Artillery Regiment. The most the *II. Bataillon* of Hack's *Westland* Regiment was able to accomplish was to seize and regain possession of the wooded area 1 kilometer west of Mány, after being initially ejected by a Soviet counterattack carried out by the 181st Tank Brigade. This was the most the division was able to accomplish that day; the situation was becoming hopeless. That night, the *Wiking* Division's *O1*, Günther Jahnke, wrote in his diary:

> A further attack is out of the question … the division must dedicate more and more of its forces to strengthening its flanks … we're going to have to pull our lead assault element back … [we are fighting] vigorous defensive battles all along our entire front. The enemy keeps attacking us in regimental strength. Only by conducting counterattacks, can we continue holding our position. On account of having to dedicate so much of our forces to flank protection, our front

line is too long and our own forces too weak. Our neighbors [both left and right] are not able to keep up. Tonight we will have another ongoing discussion about the future course of the offensive for the coming days.[140]

The division's left-hand neighbor, Becker's *Totenkopf* Division, was finding the going equally as tough as it slowly fought its way towards Zsámbék. Hill 317 (referred to as Hill 315 in Soviet accounts), a summit only 1 kilometer northwest of the key town, was taken during a costly attack carried out by a *Kampfgruppe* from the *Eicke* Regiment, supported by Panthers from *I. Abt./SS-Pz.Rgt. 3*.

After reportedly losing 11 of its tanks, including nine Panthers (as claimed by the Soviets), the battlegroup finally succeeded in taking the hill after destroying as many as 17 Soviet tanks and assault guns that day, including 11 SU-100s from the 382nd Guards SP Art.Rgt. After the hill was finally in German hands, its defense was left to *Ustuf.* Herbert Häger's *9. Kp./SS-Pz.Gren.Rgt. 6 Eicke*, whose troops successfully defended it against numerous attacks for the rest of the day. This represents the closest that Becker's division would ever get to its goal.

Along the rest of the division's vulnerable flank stretching from Zsámbék to Sarisap, its units struggled to keep the vigorously attacking Soviet forces at bay, while trying at the same time to secure more advantageous defensive positions. Two kilometers northeast of Szomor, *II. Btl/Eicke* was engaged in a deadly defensive battle against units of the 49th Guards Rifle Division and 5th Guards Mechanized Brigade attacking towards the west from the direction of Somodor Puszta. One participant in this engagement, *Sturmmann* Weyer, later wrote a letter home describing the battle:

> From the east approached a strong [enemy] infantry force supported by tanks. Our own supporting tanks fired at the mounted Russian [*sic*] units. The clumps of brown-clad troops scatter across the snow and retreat back into the forest and back up to the heights. The explosive shells of our tanks blow the Russian troops apart with massive explosions. The Soviet tanks drive around aimlessly through the area.[141]

To the north of Weyer's battalion, the division's reconnaissance battalion, *Hstuf.* Zech's *SS-Pz.Aufkl.Abt. 3*, was involved in heavy fighting in the vicinity of Kirva and was surprisingly able to advance 5 kilometers to the southeast that afternoon, the division's greatest advance that day, though this gain did little to ease the pressure being exerted upon its comrades fighting to take Zsámbék to the south.

On the division's left flank near Sarisap, *III. Btl./SS-Pz.Gren.Rgt. 5 Totenkopf* was forced to withdraw from its exposed position on Hill 234 (known locally as Kopar Hegy) 1 kilometer northwest of Dag when it was confronted by a large-scale attack carried out by elements of the II Guards Mechanized Corps. The battalion hastily dug in on the ridgeline on the eastern edge of Sarisap and immediately repelled an attack carried out by the 86th Guards Rifle Division. The attack by infantry having failed, the Soviet commander on the scene sent tanks into Sarisap, which overran the *Grenadiere* but were stopped by a counterattack initiated by *Ostuf.* Paul Sima, with a few *Jg.Pz. IVs* from his *1. Kp./SS-Pz.Jag.Abt. 3*. After three

T-34s were knocked out in short order, the remaining Soviet tanks withdraw in the direction of Dag. A portion of the division's combat engineer battalion, *SS-Pz. Pio.Btl. 3*, was moved to Sarisap to reinforce the defenses there in recognition of the town's importance.

Should Sarisap fall, the division's rear area logistics installations would be directly threatened and its lead units fighting at Zsámbék could have been cut off. The more the division's flanks had to be safeguarded at the expense of its *Schwerpunkt*, the smaller its chances of achieving its mission's purpose became; but it had no other choice but to do so. Interestingly, one armored car platoon from *SS-Pz.Aufkl.Abt. 3* was ordered to move from its security position at Tokod, where it had been relieved by a unit from the *96. Inf.Div.*, along the highway towards Dorog. While in Tokod earlier that day, its platoon leader, *Uscha.* Marienfeld, had observed the Soviet attack take place on the opposite bank of the river. He wrote later that, "At Tokod we saw the Russians [*sic*] advancing towards Komorn on the other side of the Danube. It was a strange feeling to watch the troop movements of our opponents."[142]

Between Sarisap and Dorog, the *96. Inf.Div.* was fighting its own battle, almost in isolation from the rest of the *IV. SS-Pz.Korps*. On its right, the defenses at Sarisap by *Gren.Rgt. 284* were hard pressed by repeated company- and battalion-level attacks as it maintained its connection to the left flank of the *Totenkopf* Division; in the center of the division's defense line at Csolnok, *Hptm.* Klaus Pipo's *Füs.Btl. 96* held firm; on the division's left, both *Gren.Rgt. 283* and *287* carried out the division's main effort, the assault on Dorog.

Although the division had nearly surrounded the town, its defenders from the II Guards Mechanized Corps refused to yield, forcing both Grenadier regiments to carry out a succession of bloody assaults to take it. By early afternoon, *Gren.Rgt. 283*, attacking from the south, and *Gren.Rgt. 287*, attacking from the west and northwest, had penetrated into the center of Dorog. With victory nearly in sight, the *96. Inf.Div.* was about to complete its seizure of the town when the defenders from the 37th Tank Brigade launched a large-scale counterattack in the afternoon, hurling the attackers back to the western outskirts. Despite the division's best efforts, its troops could not take Dorog, although it continued trying for another week with nothing to show for it except a long list of dead, wounded, and missing.[143]

To balance these discouraging developments, Reichert's *711. Inf.Div.* continued its advance against negligible opposition. In addition to consolidating its seizure of the hill mass 2.5 kilometers east-southeast of Zsidódi, at the same time the division began pushing out of Gran towards the south along the road leading through the Pilis Mountains to the town of Pilisszentlélek, which fell to the leading unit of the division by 11 p.m. after an advance of nearly 10 kilometers. This in turn created the opportunity to take Dorog from the east, as the attempts to seize the town from the opposite direction by the *96. Inf.Div.* had not been successful. The division was duly ordered to send a *Kampfgruppe* in that direction to complete the encirclement, though it had not yet covered the distance by nightfall. Suddenly, in Gille's mind at least, the game had changed. It was now up to the senior leadership of *A. Gr. Balck/6. Armee* and *H. Gr. Süd* to realize what an opportunity had just fallen into their lap.

However, the focus of Balck and Wöhler was not on the *IV. SS-Pz. Korps* that day—instead, they were concentrating on the fighting taking place on the far left and far right flanks of *6. Armee*. On the right, 7 January marked the beginning of the operation by the *I. Kav. Korps* of *Korpsgruppe Breith* to take Zámoly and link up with the right flank of Gille's corps. *General der Kavallerie* Harteneck's cavalry corps was strong enough—it consisted of the *3.* and *23. Pz. Div.*, the *4. Kav. Brig.*, a *Panzergruppe* from the *1. Pz. Div.* (*K. Gr. Huppert*), and *schw. Pz. Abt. FHH*, with 137 tanks in all, including 13 Tiger IIs.

Making its combat debut during this operation was *SS-Regiment Ney*, which had been attached to the *IV. SS-Pz. Korps* until this point. Previously engaged in rear area and route security duties in support of the *Totenkopf* and *Wiking* Divisions, it was attached to *K. Gr. Huppert* of the *1. Pz. Div.* to bolster its infantry strength for the attack towards Zámoly. Composed on two battalions at this point, it had a combined *Kampfstärke* of 420 men, and would be led into battle not by Ney, but by his deputy, *Hstuf.* Pál Vadon. A light infantry battalion in regards to armament, it lacked any heavy weapons of its own but would be extremely useful in upcoming operations involving clearing built-up areas defended by the enemy, where *panzer* divisions were at their most vulnerable.[144]

The defending 5th Guards Airborne and 84th Rifle Divisions of the XX Guards Rifle Corps had erected minefields and numerous *Pakfronts* along the corps' axis of advance. Furthermore, they had nearly two weeks to strengthen their defensive positions, especially in the aftermath of the *1. Pz. Div.* diversionary attack at Ösi on 31 December/1 January. Unknown to the Germans, both the I and VII Mechanized Corps occupied assembly areas only 10 kilometers away from Harteneck's *Schwerpunkt*. When the attack by *I. Kav. Korps* began in the early hours, the 4th Guards Army commander believed that the actual relief attack towards Budapest had finally begun and was ready for it.

After a preliminary artillery and rocket barrage that lit up the snow-flecked gloomy morning sky and smashed the Soviet forward positions, the troops of Harteneck's corps jumped off from their line of departure and made slow but steady progress, with advances of 3–10 kilometers being reported on that first day alone. The Germans' *panzers* and *Panzergrenadiere* were able to punch through the front lines held by the 11th and 16th Guards Airborne Rifle Regiments of the 5th Guards Airborne Division and soon advanced towards Zámoly, Sárkeresztes, and Csákberény.

The *3. Pz. Div.* had nearly enveloped Zámoly from the south by 4 p.m., when the Soviet mobile reserves finally began to come into play. Counterattacks by the 41st Guards Tank Brigade and the 63rd and 64th Guards Mechanized Brigades of the arriving VII Mechanized Corps, and the 63rd and 93rd Rifle Divisions, combined to slow the rate of advance and inflict heavy casualties on the attackers, who continued advancing. As an indicator of the intensity of the fighting, on that day alone, *A. Gr. Balck/6. Armee* reported *I. Kav.Korps* had destroyed 30 Soviet tanks, 45 antitank guns, 14 artillery pieces, and five captured German 8.8cm antiaircraft guns, while the Soviets claimed to have destroyed at least 40 German armored vehicles. The attack would continue the following day, when Balck expected that Zámoly would fall, opening up the highway leading to Bicske and Harteneck's corps uniting with Gille's.

General der Panzertruppe Balck was also concerned about developments unfolding on his *Armeegruppe* left flank, where the attack by the 6th Guards Tank Army was continuing to unfold. Swatting aside German and Hungarian attempts to stem its progress, including counterattacks launched by *Pz.Aufkl.Abt. 8* of the *8. Pz.Div.*, the lead echelon from the V Guards Tank Corps had approached to within 15 kilometers of Komorn and the IX Guards Mechanized Corps had advanced a similar distance to the equally important rail junction at Neuhäusel.

The relatively ineffective deployment of the *8. Pz.Div.*, the LVII. *Pz.Korps'* only significant reserve, had resulted in the relief of its commander, *Gen.Maj.* Gottfried Fröhlich, the previous day and his temporary replacement until 25 January by *Gen. Maj.* Emmo von Roden, who had been assigned to the *H.Gr. Süd Führerreserve* since relinquishing his position as *Kampfkommandant* of the town of Káloz when it was overrun two weeks before. To prevent his own *Hauptquartier* in Udvard from being taken by the advancing Soviet spearheads, Kirchner was forced to move his command post 20 kilometers to the southwest, taking over the installation in Gúta formerly inhabited by *Korück 593*.

To bolster Komorn's defenses, Balck ordered the Flak regiments from the *V Flak-Korps* stationed there to be employed in the direct fire role on the city's eastern outskirts, against the protests of the *Luftwaffe*. Several *Gneisenau* infantry battalions conducting rear area security between the Danube and Mór were rushed to Komorn to bolster its defenses. Fortunately, the forward elements of the *20. Pz.Div.* had already begun to arrive by train in Neuhäusel and would begin conducting counterattacks the following day.

To everyone's relief, due to the narrow width of the attack and the fact that the 7th Guards Army had not joined in as part of a general offensive except for one rifle corps, the leadership of *H.Gr. Süd* concluded that the attack by Col.Gen. Andrei Kravchenko's 6th Guards Tank Army was a limited one, designed to forestall or divert German attention away from attempts to relieve Budapest, and was not a direct threat to Vienna or the integrity of *H.Gr. Süd*, as had been originally feared. However, since the northern bank of the Danube was now under Soviet control from the Gran River as far west as Sütto, most of the left flank of Gille's corps was exposed and threatened with Soviet direct and indirect fire. Fortunately, no attempt was made by the 6th Guards Tank Army to carry out a river crossing, no doubt to the vast relief of the command and staff of the *IV. SS-Pz.Korps.*

By this time, Gille had completed his assessment of the situation and had developed a change to the original concept of operations, in which he envisioned pulling out the *Wiking* Division, replacing it with the *6. Pz.Div.* (which would have to extend its own lines to the left or east), and inserting Ullrich's division in the same zone of attack as the *711. Inf.Div.* in order to reinforce the success attained that day. He had already been ordered to consider other possible courses of action by *A. Gr. Balck/6. Armee,* whose chief of staff envisioned using the *6. Pz.Div.* in this role. In addition, Gille wanted the *Totenkopf* Division to remain where it was and go over to a defensive posture.[145] But first, he would have to gain Balck's and Wöhler's approval for such a redirecting of his corps' *Schwerpunkt.*

In Budapest itself, the relief of which was the goal of the entire operation, 7 January was another bad day. In its *Tagesmeldung* for that day, *IX. SS-Geb.Korps* reported:

> The intensity of the fighting around Budapest is increasing in severity from hour to hour, placing ever-heavier demands on the garrison. As on previous days, the eastern sector is the focal point on this 11th day of the battle for Budapest. The enemy has managed to break open friendly defensive lines with heavy use of artillery, tanks, and ground attack aircraft at a high cost in casualties to both sides. Bitter street fighting rages in Kis-Pest. South of the east railroad station, two penetrations were sealed off in counterattacks. The front line, manned in strongpoint fashion, is becoming ever thinner because of the high casualties in spite of rigorously combing out staff and rear-area service personnel. [The] supply situation has become highly critical, especially for ammunition ... total casualties from 24 December to 6 January: 5,621 men. *Flak-Regiment 12* with attached Hungarian antiaircraft units is successfully supporting the infantry in ground combat and has shot down 15 enemy planes.[146]

Shortly after sending that report, Pfeffer-Wildenbruch, the commander of the *IX. SS-Geb.Korps,* followed up with an urgent radio message, stating that "relief of Budapest has to take place as soon as possible. The population is becoming hostile; Hungarian troops are deserting to the enemy. Supply has ceased. There are 4,000 wounded in the city."

At the headquarters of *OKH, H.Gr. Süd,* and *A.Gr. Balck/6. Armee,* a great deal of debate took place that evening about the future course of operations in Hungary. Though relief of Budapest and reestablishment of the *Margarethestellung* remained a priority, each of these levels of command had different ideas as to what the main priority ought to be and how to go about accomplishing it. The *OKH* chief of operations, *Gen.d.Pz. Tr.* Wenck, believed that the attack towards Zámoly should be shut down immediately and *Korpsgruppe Breith* moved to the northern bank of the Danube to protect Komorn. Wöhler believed that the introduction of the *20. Pz.Div.* into the fight there would be sufficient, while Balck wanted to continue attacking at Zámoly but was also considering Gille's proposal to shift the *Schwerpunkt* of his corps' attack to the north. Balck even entertained Gaedke's idea of taking the *II. Batallion* of the *Pz.Gren.Div. FHH,* which had arrived in Komorn on 2 January after completing its activation in Germany, and sending it to the *711. Inf.Div.* to lead an attack along the river road parallel to the Danube and have it lead the breakthrough from Gran to Budapest.[147]

All were unanimous in believing that the time had come for the *IX. SS-Geb. Korps* to withdraw to the west bank of the Danube and abandon Pest, while at the same time believing that the encircled garrison needed to prepare an attack to the northwest to link up with the approaching troops of *IV. SS-Pz.Korps* in the Pilis Mountains. Guderian, who was still visiting Wöhler at his headquarters (he departed for a visit to *H.Gr. A* the next morning), said he would raise the matter with Hitler, who was the only person in the chain of command who could permit a withdrawal and breakout.

Before the day ended, Guderian, Wöhler, Balck, and their chiefs of staff agreed to give the attack by *I. Kav.Korps* another day to see how the assault at Zámoly would turn out; the rate of advance that first day had been less than impressive, especially given that so many *panzers* (over 100) had been committed to the fight. The same went for Gille's attack—a "wait and see" attitude prevailed, but if Harteneck's attack failed, then "a more encompassing decision" would have to be made after 8 January. But it was clear to nearly every leader in the *IV. SS-Pz.Korps* that their attack was not going to succeed, at least not along the Bicske–Zsámbék avenue of approach. The Soviet defenses had simply become too strong.

The crucial day of 8 January dawned as the previous several days had, with temperatures below freezing, continuing snow showers, and deep cloud cover that would initially limit air operations by both sides. Roads in the Vértes, Gerecse, and Pilis Mountains were still icy and difficult to negotiate, restricting the mobility of both combatants. Still, the offensive ground on, in both Gille's and Harteneck's zones of attack. North of the Danube, the counteroffensive by the 6th Guards Tank Army continued into its third day, barely slowed by the makeshift efforts of the *LVII. Pz.Korps* to stop it. Both sides hoped to achieve decisive results that day, but when it ended, neither the Soviets nor the Germans were able to completely achieve their goals.

Until he was given permission by his field army commander to carry out his proposal, Gille had no choice but to continue following the original plan, but his three mobile divisions had been compelled to transition to the defense nearly everywhere. An early morning attack by the *6. Pz.Div.* ran afoul of a large antitank minefield backed up by a *Pakfront* a mere 1.5 kilometers northeast of Bicske. An attempt by one of the division's *Kampfgruppe* to push its right flank closer to the *I. Kav.Korps'* oncoming spearheads in the west only got as far as Hill 223 north of Obarok Puszta, where it was forced to halt and defend itself against numerous counterattacks by the two divisions of the V Guards Cavalry Corps. That marked the limit of its advance that day.

To its left, the *Wiking* Division found itself embroiled in repelling numerous attempts by the XXXI Rifle Corps and the XVIII Tank Corps to penetrate its positions all along its front between Csabdi and Mány. The only effort it was able to mount and keep moving the ball forward was an attempt by Darges's *Panzergruppe* at 12:30 a.m. to advance towards Bicske. Although the tank-led night assault along ice-choked roads got as far as the northern edge of Bicske, reaching the city cemetery, a Soviet counterattack carried out at noon from the opposite direction by elements of the 32nd Mechanized and 181st Tank Brigades out of Mány forced Darges to order a withdrawal to the Hegyks Castle Estate before his troops were encircled.

That evening, the *O1* of the division summed up the fighting that day in his diary: "The enemy has had eight days to strengthen his forces. Our own forces are too weak. Without reinforcements, a relief of Budapest from this direction is not possible. [We have suffered] considerable losses of our own. [We face] very strong enemy tank and artillery defenses."[148] On the same day, the commander of *III. Btl./ Germania, Hstuf.* Helmut Schumacher, was killed in action. His place was temporarily filled by *Hstuf.* Paul Scholven. Schumacher would be missed; a close friend of Franz Hack, he had been with the *Wiking* Division since its inception.

Similarly, the *Totenkopf* Division found itself facing increasingly strong opposition along its extended front line running from the northern outskirts of Zsámbék to a position east of Szomor, then to Kirva, and thence to the western outskirts of Sarisap, where its left flank was still tied in with the right of the neighboring *96. Inf.Div. Brigadeführer* Becker, whose division *Gefechtstand* was located in Bajna, had to orchestrate the employment of his dwindling number of *panzers* and assault guns to counter numerous Soviet attacks throughout the day, while still attempting to carry out the seizure of his original objective, Zsámbék.

In this, his troops nearly succeeded that day, when between 7 and 9 a.m. that morning, a *Kampfgruppe* from *I. Btl./Eicke*, supported by 10 armored vehicles, managed to fight its way through a *Pakfront* blocking the approaches to Hill 265, 500 meters west of Zsámbék-Hegy (Hill 317) and approached to within 300 meters of the road leading west to Mány, only 1 kilometer west of Zsámbék. Another *Kampfgruppe* to the east assaulted downhill from Zsámbék-Hegy and nearly reached the town's northern outskirts before they were finally brought to a halt by the 49th Guards Rifle Division, supported by tanks from the 110th Tank Brigade and the 363rd SP Artillery Regiment. After bitter fighting, the *Totenköpfler* were driven back with the loss of three of their armored fighting vehicles, according to Soviet sources. On the right, an attempt by *III. Btl./Eicke* to take the village of Felsőörs-Puszta finally succeeded after losing four tanks in order to overpower the troops of the 19th Rifle Division, which lost two T-34s and two SU-85 assault guns of their own in the ensuing engagement.

Elsewhere, the *Totenkopf* Division's troops were caught up in heavy fighting along the division's long eastern flank at such places as Tök (2 kilometers north of

Zsámbék) and Kirva. Soviet artillery and mortar fire was increasing in strength, as were the density of their antitank defenses. Infantry attacks against German positions had also noticeably increased. The best that the *Totenkopf* Division could do at this point was to hold its current positions. That day alone, the XVIII Tank Corps claimed to have destroyed 134 *IV. SS-Pz.Korps* armored vehicles (which includes tanks, halftracks, and armored cars) and killed as many as 300 German troops, but this must be viewed skeptically since at the end of the day their opponent still had possession of the field. Still, it was an indicator of the seriousness of the fighting.[149]

To the left of the *Totenkopf* Division, the advance by *Oberst* Harrendorf's *96. Inf.Div.* had come to a complete standstill. Like Becker, Harrendorf found himself completely occupied in defending the gains his regiments had made during the past several days. His troops were hard pressed by Soviet counterattacks at Sarisap, Csolnok, and Dorog, but were able to hold their ground. The division's strength was slowly beginning to drain away, with later estimates showing that it had suffered the loss of 1,200 men from all causes between 1 and 10 January.

To make the division's situation more acute, Gille ordered Harrendorf to send a grenadier regiment to Gran, where it was to relieve the regiment from Reichert's *711. Inf.Div.* defending the town that was being sent away to the south to support an attack by another regiment of the division. This diversion of forces left the defense of Harrendorf's sector in the hands of his five remaining battalions. He could at least have drawn some satisfaction from the fact that they were backed up by a still-powerful *Art.Rgt. 96*; thanks to its guns, his division was still able to hold its ground. Harrendorf's greatest worry was that the Soviet attack along the northern bank of the Danube endangered his own division's main supply route, which ran along the river road in clear view of the enemy on the other side.

During the day, the leading regimental *Kampfgruppe* of the *711. Inf.Div.* continued to consolidate the position at Pilisszentlélek that it had seized the night before, while the other *Kampfgruppe* on its right began pushing onwards to its next objective, the village of Kesztölc, which would complete the encirclement of Dorog. A long hill mass running parallel to both regiments stretching from Zsidódi to Pilisszentkereszt prevented either regiment from cooperating with the other, which became painfully evident when the road linking Gran to Pilisszentlélek was closed off later that day by Soviet infantry after the initial assault element of the division had passed through the previous evening.

Once the regiment holding Gran had been relieved by *Gren.Rgt. 284* of the *96. Inf.Div.*, its two battalions were able to clear the vitally important route that evening. At the same time, the regiment attacking Kesztölc was stopped and flung back to its starting point by the 99th Rifle Division. Meanwhile, additional Soviet forces were brought up from the Budapest area to set up a strong blocking position 4 kilometers east-southeast of Gran to prevent any German attempt to exploit the Budapest–Gran road as a high-speed avenue of approach to carry out the assault on the city. No matter what Gille may have thought about the ease with which his point of main effort could be switched to the left flank, it was clear that the going would not be as easy as previously estimated.

That night (8 January), the *Ic* of Gille's corps submitted his daily report. Summarizing the day's activities, *Stubaf.* Herbert Jankuhn wrote:

> The fighting in the Bicske–[Sarisap] sector did not change the [corps] situation during the day. The enemy opposed our own attacking groups with strong resistance and tried to counter them with unsuccessful counterattacks. The enemy advancing northwest from Kesztölc was able to take a position eastwards of Zsidódi and block the road leading from Gran to Pilisszentlélek. Our own counterattack [by the *711. Inf.Div.*] has already begun.[150]

Not mentioned in his diary was that within the *IV. SS-Pz.Korps'* area of operations alone, between 18 and 20 Soviet independent antitank regiments had already been deployed during the past several days, with more on the way.

Without waiting for permission, Gille had already ordered his *Führungsabteilung* to begin planning the transfer of the *Wiking* Division from the Bicske area to the corps' far left. This would entail ordering Ullrich to pull his troops back to the start line at Tata and move behind the *711. Inf.Div.*, while having three of his other divisions—the *6. Pz.Div.*, the *Totenkopf,* and the *96. Infanterie* Divisions—transition to a wholly defensive posture. Meanwhile, the *Wiking* Division, using a reinforced regimental-sized *Kampfgruppe*, would advance through the Pilis Mountains and relieve Budapest from the northwest. Gille would find the challenge of convincing his field army commander of the rightness of this course of action to be easier than he first believed.

The fighting was just as heavy in the other corps' area of operations as it was for the *IV. SS-Pz.Korps*. On the right, the counteroffensive by *I. Kav.Korps* towards Zámoly failed to gather momentum. The *Korpsgruppe Breith's Ic* reported that evening:

> In extremely heavy fighting, the enemy's forces east of Sárkeresztes and those located astride the Stuhlweissenburg–Zámoly highway were thrown back. Further attacks [by our forces] were brought to a standstill in front of strong antitank gun barriers. In Zámoly, the enemy continues to reinforce and was observed at this point sending in approximately 60 tanks. Along the rest of the *Korpsgruppe's* front, no combat activity occurred worth mentioning.

This somewhat bland statement obscures the fact that the VII Mechanized Corps, the reserve of the 4th Guards Army, was fully committed to battle that day, with noticeable impact upon the rate of advance of the *I. Kav.Korps*, which was reduced to a slow crawl. To add to the seriousness of the situation, the I Guards Mechanized Corps had also been identified moving into position east of Zámoly. Nevertheless, Balck insisted on giving the attack one more day to achieve results, even as *Unternehmen Konrad I* morphed into *Konrad II*.

On the *A.Gr. Balck* left flank across the Danube, Kirchner's *LVII. Pz.Korps Ic* reported in his *Tagesmeldung*:

Weak [enemy] tank attacks against our bridgehead at Komorn and stronger tank-supported attacks originating from the area southeast of Neuhäusel have been warded off; Additionally, repeated enemy attacks against the northwestern portion of Bátor-Keszy [held by a *Kampfgruppe* of the *8. Pz.Div.*] were unsuccessful. Northeast of Köbölkut the enemy punched through several [of our] positions, took [the town of] Seldin [held by the *211. V.G.D.*] and pushed onwards towards Bart from the south. According to a recent report, during the course of the day 27 enemy tanks were destroyed ... according to observer reports, during the afternoon as many as 130 [enemy] motor vehicles were seen moving from Parkány [bridgehead] to the west.[151]

This was interpreted as an indicator that the IV Guards Mechanized Corps was being introduced to the battle, a worrying development. Both the XXIV and XXV Guards Rifle Corps of the 7th Guards Army were also following in the wake of the attack by the 6th Guards Tank Army, but had been left behind by the tanks to deal with the German and Hungarian defenses still in position along the Gran to the north of Parkány.

However, the lead elements of the *20. Pz.Div.* that arrived that day in Neuhäusel by rail had already begun conducting counterattacks, effectively slowing the advance by the IX Guards Mechanized Corps headed towards that railway nexus. With the *20. Pz.Div.* now on the scene, both Balck and Wöhler breathed a little easier that day; the crisis that they had feared the most—the loss of Komorn and an attack into the rear of the *IV. SS-Pz.Korps*—had not transpired after all. With this situation beginning to stabilize, Operation *Konrad* could continue without having to divert major combat elements from *Korpsgruppe Breith* to stem the counteroffensive north of the Danube.

With the outcome of the first iteration of *Konrad* still undetermined at noon, it is worth reminding the reader of the continuing crisis within *Festung Budapest*. The *Tagesmeldung* submitted by the *IX. SS-Geb.Korps Ia* reported:

> The enemy succeeded in continuous heavy fighting in making penetrations into the northern section of Kis-Pest [the suburb southeast of Pest], south of the east railroad station and on the southern edge of Pestujhely. Countermeasures were put into effect. The southern portion of the sector of the *22. SS-Fw.Kav.Div. Maria Theresa* was pulled back to the northern edge of Csepel–northwest section of Kis-Pest. The day passed without major enemy action on the western front of the bridgehead.[152]

Despite the bad flying weather, the *Luftwaffe* managed to conduct up to 450 sorties on 8 January, many of which were launched to stem the advance of the 6th Guards Tank Army north of the Danube.

During these aerial attacks, *Luftflotte 4* reported destroying as many as 27 Soviet tanks and self-propelled guns between the Gran River and Komorn. In comparison, the Red Air Force flew 102 sorties over the Zámoly area alone, harassing the advancing elements of the *1., 3.,* and *23. Pz.Div.*, as well as the *4. Kav.Brig.*, with air-ground attacks by IL-2 *Sturmoviks* and LaGG-3s.[153] No resupply missions were flown in support of the Budapest garrison on account of the weather, nor were any landings made due to the lack of an adequate airfield.

Later that afternoon and into the evening, a series of back-and-forth conversations took place between the commanders and chiefs of staff of *H. Gr. Süd* and *A. Gr. Balck/6. Armee*, including at least one telephone discussion involving select individuals from the *OKH Führungsstab* in Zossen. The records do not indicate to what degree Gille or any of the other corps commanders participated in these discussions, but based on the decisions made and the orders issued that evening, it is very likely that Gille's proposals were given a fair hearing, since many of them were adopted before the day ended. Everyone was aware that time was running out for the Budapest garrison.

By the evening of 8 January, it had become apparent to all concerned that *Konrad* had foundered. The attack by *I. Kav.Korps* had gained little ground that day, and prospects for future success were minimal. The attack by the *IV. SS-Pz.Korps* had been stalled along the line Bicske–Zsámbék since 5 January, and except for the success achieved on 7/8 January by the *711. Inf.Div.* on the corps' far-left flank, it had become evident that *Unternehmen Konrad* failed. Though the counteroffensive north of the Danube by the 6th Guards Tank Army against the *LVII. Pz.Korps* was still dangerous, measures taken that day to counter it were beginning to have their impact, and the immediate threat seemed to have passed.

Based on these realities, the commanders of *H. Gr. Süd* and *A. Gr. Balck* finally came around to accepting Gille's proposal to shift a *panzer* division to his corps' left flank and reinforce the success achieved that day at Gran. The idea to use the *Wiking* Division to accomplish this was finally approved, though *Gen.Maj.* Gaedke persisted in his idea to use the *6. Pz.Div.* for this purpose before Balck finally overruled him. As the staffs of the various commands worked throughout the evening to develop the plan of what would soon be called *Unternehmen Konrad II*, the news arrived that at 7:30 p.m., Hitler had disapproved the proposal to allow *IX. SS-Geb.Korps* to withdraw from the eastern bank of the Danube around Pest and move into positions in the portion of the city on the western bank. This was a setback, as the various staffs believed that Pfeffer-Wildenbruch and his encircled troops only stood a chance of linking up with the approaching relief force if it could concentrate its remaining troops in Buda. They would now have to adjust their plans accordingly.

So, after eight days of extremely heavy fighting in appalling conditions, *Konrad I* came to a disappointing close. Although the *IV. SS-Pz.Korps* had made impressive initial progress, its divisions had still not been able to attain its immediate objective, the line Bicske–Zsámbék, which was deemed essential for the relief of Budapest. The reasons why it did not succeed are readily apparent, and were evident even before the offensive began: they included the decision to launch it before all of Gille's corps had arrived and the failure of *Div.Gr. Pape* to take Felsőgalla, which lay astride the most suitable avenue of approach through the mountains. Another reason was the short duration of the diversionary attack by the *1. Pz.Div.* towards Ösi, which lasted less than 24 hours.

The efforts of the troops involved during the operation did not go unnoticed by the *Führer*, however. In recognition of the accomplishments of the troops from the *III. Pz.Korps* and *IV. SS-Pz.Korps*, the *Wehrmacht* communique issued on 8 January 1945 stated:

> In Hungary, troops of the *Heer* and *Waffen-SS* were able to punch their way through enemy positions arrayed between Lake Balaton and the Danube after difficult offensive fighting lasting several days ... north of the Vértes Mountains [our troops] were able to advance to the east for a distance of 40 kilometers.[154]

As satisfying as hearing about the troops' heroic deeds may have felt, such glowing words of praise were no substitute for the reinforcements and additional supplies the situation warranted. Still, it was better than nothing at all, and soldiers could always write home to their families and brag about it if they wished.

Based on the rapid reaction of the 4th Guards Army to the attack by the *I. Kav.Korps* towards Zámoly on 7 January, it would have been more beneficial had *Korpsgruppe Breith's* operation been carried out in conjunction with that by the *1. Pz.Div.* on 1 January and continued for as long as possible. This would actually have tied down Soviet reserves later used to block the *IV. SS-Pz.Korps* assault. Instead, launching the Zámoly attack a week later, after Gille's attack had already stalled, achieved absolutely nothing except the destruction of numerous armored vehicles and the loss of hundreds of soldiers that *Korpsgruppe Breith* could ill afford in exchange for the few kilometers gained.

In their memoirs, *Gen.d.Pz.Tr.* Balck and his chief of staff, as well as *Gen.O.* Guderian, placed the blame on the shoulders of the troops conducting the fighting, whom they deemed to lack the same "offensive spirit" that the *Wehrmacht* had in 1940. It was indeed no longer 1940, but the records indicate that the men of *IV. SS-Pz.Korps* had given every ounce of effort to relieve Budapest, despite having to fight their way through increasingly strong Soviet defensive belts. If *Konrad I* failed, it was not because of the troops or their unit leaders.

Blame, if there is to be any, has to be apportioned among the senior leadership concerned, from field army to army group level, and as high up as the senior leadership at the *OKH*, including Hitler himself and Guderian. In particular, Hitler's decision to deny the request by *H.Gr. Süd* to allow the evacuation of the eastern portion of Budapest, as well as his disapproval of any early breakout attempt, probably doomed the city. None of these worthies were able to agree on a single course of action, and their decision to launch *Konrad I* can be seen in retrospect as a default option, which no one seemed very enthusiastic about. That is evident from reading the official record, where indecision at nearly every step of *Konrad I* doomed it to fail. Perhaps *Konrad II* would correct these errors and lead to the successful relief of Budapest.

Another point worth mentioning is the striking similarities between *Unternehmen Konrad I* and *Wacht am Rhein*, the German offensive through the Ardennes intended to strike towards the city of Antwerp, launched on 16 December 1944. Both were launched in secret, in the dead of winter, through a heavily wooded, mountainous area with a less-than-ideal road network. Both were spearheaded by troops of the *Waffen-SS*, Hitler's elite guard. Neither offensive had sufficient fuel to reach their objectives, nor had the units involved sufficient time to prepare, on account of the great secrecy involved. Both offensives involved units recently reconstituted with large numbers of recent draftees and involuntary transfers from the *Luftwaffe* and *Kriegsmarine*, with far too few NCOs and junior officers. In neither operation did the units involved have the authorized numbers of armored vehicles to perform their assigned doctrinal role. The list goes on.

Another similarity worth mentioning is that both offensives struck their opponent in a quiet sector of their front lines, where exhausted units occupied thinly spaced and insufficiently prepared defenses. Bad weather neutralized much of their opponents' massive air power. However, both offensives also quickly faced an alerted opponent after the first several days' success, opponents who quickly rallied and shifted powerful reserves to slow and finally stop the Germans' advance. Like the *Wacht am Rhein* offensive, the entire *Konrad I* operation was a massive gamble, and one that failed. It was now up to the same troops and leaders, exhausted after eight days of bitter fighting, to do everything possible to succeed where it had previously failed, and thus *Konrad II* was born.

CHAPTER 6

The Second Relief Attempt of Budapest—*Konrad II* 9–13 January 1945

By 8 January 1945, the *Heeresgruppe Süd* commander and his counterpart at *A. Gr. Balck/6. Armee* had realized that the first Budapest relief operation had clearly failed. Not only that, but the attack towards Zámoly initiated on 7 January by *Korpsgruppe Breith* was also just as likely to fail, having encountered a stronger than anticipated reaction by the 4th Guards Army. By the close of 8 January, after two days of heavy fighting, it was obvious that any further progress in the Zámoly area of operations was not likely to justify the cost in lives lost and *panzers* destroyed, no matter how many Soviet tanks were knocked out. It seemed as if the only German commander who was still determined that *Konrad* should continue was the commander of *IV. SS-Pz. Korps*, Herbert Gille, whom Hermann Balck had already written off as a Nazi fanatic.

The German high command in Hungary issued no official announcement stating when *Unternehmen Konrad I* had ended, but it had clearly run out of steam by the eighth day of the offensive. *Obergruppenführer* Gille believed it failed for two reasons; first, that it was attempted before all the forces designated to take part had arrived, thus denying the commander concerned (Gille) the combat power the plan was predicated upon; and second, that the forces providing the flank protection needed to ensure its success, provided by *Div. Gr. Pape* and the *96. Inf.Div.*, were unable to keep pace with the two SS *panzer* divisions comprising the main effort. This left the *Schwerpunkt* extremely vulnerable to enemy counterattacks and forced the *Totenkopf* and *Wiking* Divisions to detach their own units to protect the flanks along their route of advance, further weakening the combat power of the armored spearheads, which Gille had already deemed insufficient.[1]

Added to these two factors was that the fact that the commanders and operations staffs at *H. Gr. Süd* and *A. Gr. Balck/6. Armee* had underestimated how quickly the 4th Guards Army would react to the offensive, nullifying what little advantage there had been in achieving the element of surprise on 1 January. In addition, the diversionary attack at Ösi by the *1. Pz.Div.* had been of too short a duration; a modern-day observer might find it puzzling why it was discontinued after a mere 24 hours. That the attack towards Zámoly would not succeed should also have surprised no one;

that it was continued for several more days after *Konrad I* had failed quickly became an exercise in sheer futility. Had these two attacks been combined into one larger effort specifically designed to tie up Soviet reserves, *Konrad I* might have worked, but it does not seem to have been considered by the commanders responsible for the broader aspects of the offensive, specifically Wöhler and Balck.

However, the successful action by the *711. Inf.Div.* from 6–8 January on Gille's far left flank was the single ray of hope upon which the fortunes of what was soon to be designated *Konrad II* was based. *Obergruppenführer* Gille had already been mulling over changing the direction of his corps' *Schwerpunkt* since 6 January, when the attacks by his two SS divisions had stalled at Bicske and Zsámbék. The seemingly effortless seizure of the town of Gran on 7 January by Reichert's underestimated division had opened a window of possibilities that cemented in Gille's mind the idea that if his corps were to rescue the garrison of Budapest, then he must shift a division to that flank to reinforce this success while the opportunity still presented itself. [2]

Towards this end, as previously outlined, he had already begun drafting a concept plan that would consist of shifting the *Wiking* Division, beginning with a reinforced regiment, to the far left, where it would occupy a forward assembly area immediately to the rear of the *711. Inf.Div.* in the vicinity of Gran. Then, leading with an armored battlegroup, the *Wiking* Division would pass through Gran and move into the Pilis Mountains towards the southeast along the road leading through the valley towards the town of Pilisszentlélek, taken by the *711. Inf.Div.* on 8 January. This force would then conduct an attack towards its intermediate objective, the town of Pilisszentkereszt, which lay only 21 kilometers north-northwest of Budapest. From there, the ground gradually sloped downhill and become more favorable for the commitment of tanks, which would provide the necessary preconditions for the *Kampfgruppe* to reach the final objective, the town of Pomáz 12 kilometers to the southeast. Taking advantage of the military airfield near this location, relief supplies for the Budapest garrison could be brought in and wounded flown out once contact with the city's defenders was reestablished (see Map 5).

There were several advantages to this plan. In addition to the surprise Gille hoped to capitalize upon, there were few Soviet forces positioned within this area at that moment, as had been demonstrated by the surprisingly rapid advance of Reichert's foot-bound infantry division. Most of the Soviet troops occupying ground in this area were rear-echelon units of the 46th Army, which was investing Budapest's western defenses. The bulk of the 4th Guards Army and the elements of the 46th Army sent to reinforce it were fighting west of the Pilis Mountains between Dorog and Kirva, where they were preventing the *Totenkopf* Division and the *96. Inf. Div.* from advancing. Furthermore, the *Wiking* Division's lead regiment would be protected on either side by the physical barrier of the Pilis Mountains themselves, which would hinder the 4th Guards or 46th Armies from launching any flanking attacks with armored forces.

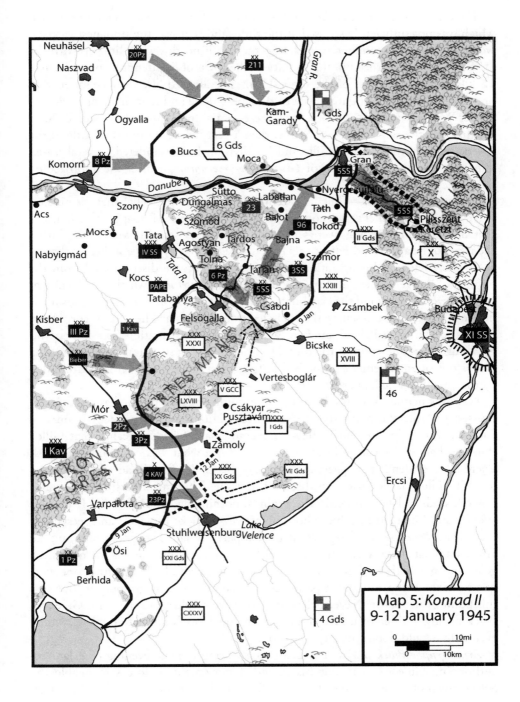

Map 5: *Konrad II*
9-12 January 1945

There was one additional precondition in order for this relief attack to succeed, which was not sufficiently stressed at the time, and that was the Budapest garrison would also have to conduct an attack to the north-northwest to link up with the *IV. SS-Pz.Korps* spearhead in the vicinity of the town of Szentendre, approximately 12 kilometers northwest of the city's defenses. Gille had already recognized that one division could not fight its way to Budapest alone and that the cooperation of Pfeffer-Wildenbruch's *IX. SS-Geb.Korps* was essential for *Konrad II* to succeed. After all, that was the same plan that had worked a year before during the battle of the Cherkassy Pocket, in which Gille and his division had "wandered" several dozen kilometers along with the rest of *Gruppe Stemmermann* to meet the approaching relief force.

This was a key point—Gille had seemingly arrived at the belief that his mission had evolved into a relief attack conducted solely to rescue the Budapest garrison, and that all other considerations were secondary. Nearly every step he would take during the next four days would reflect this belief. In addition, evidence indicates that he most likely felt that his operation had necessarily become disconnected from the original objective of reestablishing the old *Margarethestellung*, which Gille's chief of staff believed was beyond the capability of *A. Gr. Balck/6 Armee* anyway. Gille's focus now was strictly upon rescuing the encircled troops. Why had he and his corps been brought down from Poland anyway? Was that not his reputation, as a leader who got things done and could turn around hopeless-seeming situations, such as leading troops out of encirclement (as he had at Cherkassy) or relieving cities surrounded by the enemy (as he had at Kovel)?[3]

However, neither Balck nor his army group commander seemed to have sufficiently stressed to Gille the point that these two operations were dependent upon one another. This helps to explain how they could have failed to realize that Gille's thinking had evolved in a different direction from what was originally intended. There is no evidence to suggest that Balck or his chief of staff had taken the time to visit Gille's headquarters to discuss this issue. This misunderstanding would sow the seeds of later failure. In their minds, nothing had changed, and Balck and Wöhler still intended to achieve both objectives—relieve Budapest and reestablish the former *Margarethestellung*. What they apparently failed to understand, unlike Gille, was that there were only sufficient forces to carry out one of the offensive's goals, but not both, and even then, the odds of successfully doing either one were questionable. Perhaps all of the parties concerned were already grasping at straws by this point in the battle. Nevertheless, the offensive would continue, with Gille and Balck having a different understanding of the operation's ultimate purpose, which eventually would doom the city's garrison.

Armeegruppe Balck/6. Armee issued orders during the late evening of 8 January authorizing Gille to carry out his intended movement of forces to enable the *Schwerpunkt* of his attack to shift to his left or northern flank. Essentially, his attack would entail pulling out the *Wiking* Division incrementally, beginning with Hack's *Westland* Regiment. To provide sufficient combat power to carry out its assignment, Hack's task force would be reinforced with a self-propelled artillery battalion, a *Panzerjäger* company, two *Nebelwerfer* batteries, and a company from *SS-Pz.Aufkl. Abt. 5*, thus forming *K.Gr. Westland*. The movement to Gran and assembling for the attack would require at least 24 hours; the earliest that Hack could begin his attack would be the late evening of 9 January.

To cover the *Wiking* Division's defensive sector as it withdrew, the *6. Pz.Div.* would have to extend its own left flank as far as Mány, link up with the *Totenkopf* Division, and transition to the defense. The *Wiking* Division's *Panzergruppe*—with its 16 operational tanks and *I. Btl./Norge*—would remain where it was at the Hegyks Castle Estate and continue blocking the Bicske–Mány road for the time being, at least until a portion of it (its *II. Abteilung*) could be withdrawn and sent north. The *Totenkopf* Division would also transition to a defensive posture, as would the *6. Pz.Div.* As part of the plan, *Oberst* Harrendorf and his *96. Inf.Div.* was ordered to temporarily attach one of his regiments, *Gren.Rgt. 284*, to Reichert's division and assume responsibility for defending Gran while freeing up *Gren.Rgt. 744* of the *711. Inf.Div.* In order to carry out this task, Harrendorf's other two regiments and the division's *Füsilier* battalion would have to extend their own flanks to cover the sector being vacated by the transfer of *Maj.* Magawly's regiment. The *711. Inf.Div.* would continue its own attack, focusing on the envelopment of Dorog from the east and clearing bypassed Soviet forces in the wake of *K.Gr. Westland's* advance.[4]

One unanticipated aspect of the plan was Balck's approval of Gaedke's ambitious suggestion to use the recently arrived *II. Btl./Pz.Gren.Rgt. FHH*—reinforced by nearly a dozen armored vehicles from the *Totenkopf* Division—in a solitary attack along the river road towards Budapest. This daring effort would be led by the indispensable *Oberstlt.* Ernst Philipp, who would be detached from leadership of the other *Kampfgruppe* bearing his name in the *6. Pz.Div.* His battlegroup would strike out towards Szentendre along the Danube, bringing along a convoy of trucks carrying 200 tons of relief supplies for the encircled garrison. *Generalmajor* Gaedke, believing that the ineffective resistance the Soviets offered against the attack by the *711. Inf.Div.* was a sign of general weakness, had been advocating this operation, which had attracted Guderian's attention during this visit, for the past two days. When Hitler learned of this audacious plan from Guderian, he took a great interest in it, enthusiastically describing the concept as a *Husarenritt* (Hussar ride). Once it began, Hitler insisted on being updated every half an hour on its progress. This attack was scheduled to begin at 10 p.m. on 9 January.[5]

It is worth noting that Gille and Philipp themselves were not in favor of the plan, believing that it stood little chance of success, while another observer declared it suicidal. Gille even begged Balck to use this task force instead to reinforce the *Wiking* Division's attack, but his field army commander turned down his request, most likely because Hitler was now enamored of the idea.[6] Gille and his chief of staff knew that *K.Gr. Philipp* would be exposed to Soviet fire from the opposite bank of the Danube during its entire advance, and it would take very little effort on the enemy's part to stop its advance or cut it off at any point during the 46-kilometer route. Because the *Feldherrenhalle* battalion was already occupying an assembly area near Komorn, it began its own movement earlier in the day and had arrived in Gran before sundown on 8 January, where it met with the other elements tasked to accompany it. Philipp's *Kampfgruppe* was not required to wait for the arrival of *K.Gr. Westland*, and its advance would begin as soon as *Gren.Rgt. 284* could initiate an attack east of Gran to clear a Soviet blocking position erected 4 kilometers from the town.[7]

For *Unternehmen Konrad II* to succeed, Balck and Wöhler believed it was imperative for Harteneck's *I. Kav.Korps* to continue its attack towards Zámoly, even if chances for its success were minimal by this point. Based on the vigorous Soviet response against Harteneck's offensive so far, they thought that by doing so, *I. Kav. Korps* would continue to tie down the I and VII Guards Mechanized Cordps, which otherwise might be free to attack *IV. SS-Pz.Korps'* exposed right flank. To improve the chances that Harteneck's holding action would succeed, Balck instructed Breith to use the newly arrived Hungarian *1. Hus.Div.* and the *3. Kav.Brig.*, being brought up from the *2. Pz.Armee* area, as well as *Div.Gr. Bieber*, to conduct a separate, rather ambitious (under the circumstances) attack between Mór and Kecskéd, designed to bring the forested area on the western edge of the Vértes Mountains north of Zámoly under German and Hungarian control. This attack, controlled directly by *Korpsgruppe Breith*, was to begin by the morning of 9 January at the latest.[8]

North of the Danube, on 9 January, the *LVII. Pz.Korps* would continue its counterattack against Kravchenko's 6th Guards Tank Army, with Kirchner attempting a double envelopment of the Soviet tank spearheads using the *20. Pz.Div.* attacking southeast out of Neuhäusel and the *8. Pz.Div.* attacking to the northeast from Komorn. The *211. V.G.D.*, which had refused its right flank when it was attacked by a rifle corps from the 7th Guards Army, would conduct counterattacks of its own towards the south to begin constricting the width of the Soviet penetration along the Gran. Should Kirchner succeed with his counterattack, Balck instructed him to push the attackers back across the Gran while destroying as much of their armored strength as possible and to reestablish the main defense line that had existed prior to Kravchenko's attack.

The *Luftwaffe* was tasked to conduct as many ground-attack sorties as it could possibly carry out. Fortunately for Balck, the senior *Luftwaffe* officer on the scene, *Gen.Maj.* Hans-Detlef von Rohden, who was serving on Göring's *Luftwaffe* general staff in Berlin, was conducting a tour of the area at the time; as an old friend of Balck's, he did what he could to ensure good air-ground cooperation. *Generalmajor* von Rohden had already assisted Balck two days before when, on his own authority, he overruled the local commander of the *Luftwaffe* units stationed in Komorn from the *V. Flak Korps*, who had wanted to withdraw all of his batteries from the front lines, at a time when Balck wanted to employ their 8.8cm antiaircraft guns in the direct-fire role against approaching Soviet tanks.[9] Von Rohden had put a stop to this withdrawal, much to Balck's satisfaction.

When 9 January dawned, the units comprising the right flank of the *IV. SS-Pz. Korps*—the *Totenkopf* and *6. Panzer* Divisions—were already transitioning to a defensive posture. This process involved instituting various active and passive defensive measures, including digging fighting positions, preparing mutually supporting fire plans, laying minefields, and constructing other obstacles designed to slow or force the enemy to deploy into pre-planned kill zones. *Oberst* Jürgen's *6. Pz.Div.* began the relief in place of the *Westland* Regiment shortly after midnight. This went rather quickly, since Hack's regiment was already in position on the *Wiking* Division's right flank in the Csabdi area. The relief in place of Dorr's *Germania* Regiment would initially prove problematic because his three battalions—arrayed between Csabdi, Mány, and Gyermely—were located several kilometers southwest and forward of the *Totenkopf* Division, which had been unsuccessful in extending its own flank far enough to cover the gap. Therefore, the *6. Pz.Div.* would have to take control of this area as well, temporarily subordinating Dorr's regiment to its command for several days until the relief in place was finished.

When Jürgen's division assumed full responsibility for the defense of the *Wiking* Division's former sector at midnight, the only substantive elements of the division remaining in its old positions were Darges's *Panzergruppe*, which would continue holding its position at the Hegyks Castle Estate until 12 January, and at least two battalions of Dorr's *Germania*, along with his regimental headquarters. The new defensive sector was so wide that the *6. Pz.Div.* lacked sufficient strength to establish a continuous defense line (on 6 January it had a *Kampfstärke* of only 1,305 men and 47 *panzers*), so it was forced instead to occupy it with a series of strongpoints, with only a series of thinly manned outposts connecting them. Much of the gaps between strongpoints would have to be covered by artillery fire alone, forcing the already overextended *SS-ARKO 504* to realign its existing artillery assets to cover both the defensive front of the corps in the south as well as the new attack being planned in the north. Active German defensive measures included conducting strong reconnaissance in force tactics whenever possible, using tank-led *Kampfgruppen* to attack and disperse any Soviet assembly areas before they could launch attacks of their own.[10]

The *Wiking* Division, with Hack's *Westland* Regiment being relieved first, would move to its new assembly area southwest of Gran via the road running from Gyermely–Tarján–Bajna (where the headquarters of the *Totenkopf* Division was located) –Nagysáp–Tokod. Ullrich's own divisional *Gefechtstand* would depart from Tarján, which would become the headquarters of the *6. Pz.Div.*, and move along the route via Tarján–Héreg–Bajót. *Oberführer* Ullrich would co-locate his new headquarters with that of the *711. Inf.Div.* in Gran. When the lead column of the *Westland* Regiment began moving north at 3 p.m., most of its units were concealed by the heavy fog, freezing rain, and snow that made observation by the enemy difficult.

By midnight, the division's combat elements, including most of the *Westland* Regiment, had arrived in their designated assembly areas a few kilometers southwest of Gran without having lost any vehicles or troops along the way to enemy action. Movement along the ice-covered roads was difficult, especially during the hours of darkness. The fact that this had all been accomplished without the division having to issue any detailed march orders or being detected by the enemy was attributed to the "demonstrated spirit and readiness for action of all ranks," according to one eyewitness, but the detailed concept plan that Gille's corps staff had prepared the previous day no doubt contributed to the movement's success.[11]

While the *Wiking* Division was being relieved in the lines by *6. Pz.Div.*, the fighting along the entire corps' front was undiminished. On this day, the forces of the 4th Guards Army initiated a series of counterattacks designed to push the Germans away from the Bicske–Mány–Zsámbék area. From the left to the right, the reconstituted XXXI Guards Rifle Corps, supported by the XXI Guards Rifle Corps, attacked the *6. Pz.Div.* in a northwesterly direction from Szár and Bicske, but *Oberst* Jürgen's division held its ground. The XVIII Tank Corps, supported by the XXIII Rifle Corps, pushed hard against the *Totenkopf* Division from the direction of Mány and Zsámbék, particularly against the position held by *III. Btl./Eicke* on Hill 317 1 kilometer northwest of Zsámbék.

One Soviet assault against Sarisap, most likely made by the 86th Guards Rifle Division, supported by tanks from the VI Guards Mechanized Corps, was the greatest threat the *Totenkopf* Division faced that day. When the defending *Panzergrenadiere* from *II. Btl./Pz.Gren.Rgt. 5 Totenkopf* were nearly overrun by Soviet tanks, a platoon from *SS-Pz.Jag.Abt. 3*, commanded by *Ostuf.* Bernt Lubich von Milovan, conducted a counterattack with three *Jg.Pz. IV*s. While Milovan's tank destroyer and another calmly took aim and destroyed several Soviet tanks at close range, the third vehicle, commanded by a newly assigned *Oberjunker* (officer candidate), continued charging up the hill alone. An eyewitness described what happened:

> As soon as it reached the hill, we heard a loud crack; [his vehicle] was hit in the left drive sprocket. The crew bailed out … a second shell hit one of the left return rollers. When that happened, a piece of the roller [broke off], striking *Rttf.* Erich Urban in the hip and killed him on the spot … the *Oberjunker* was wounded as well. Sergeants Müller and Hinz placed the body of Urban under the vehicle on a shelter quarter but since the Russians [sic] were approaching, they had to leave it behind … a later attempt to retrieve his body failed, but during this attempt, *Hascha.* Hanräder was killed and *Uscha.* Uhle was seriously wounded.[12]

South of Sarisap, *SS-Pz.Aufkl.Abt. 3* did what it could to screen the wide area stretching between that locality and Kirva, warding off several attempts by their opponents to send patrols through German lines. Though costlier in terms of ammunition and fuel expended, at least the transition from offensive to active defensive operations allowed the troops from the *Totenkopf* and *6. Pz.Div.* to let the Soviets carry out attacks for a change, where the Germans' heavy weapons and artillery could exact a heavy toll.

To the left of the *Totenkopf* Division, the *96. Inf.Div.* detached as ordered its *Gren.Rgt. 284*, which was pulled out of the line and sent marching towards Gran, where it would relieve *Oberst* Jobst Hilmar von Bose's *Gren.Rgt. 744* of the *711. Inf.Div.* This would enable *Gen.Lt.* Reichert to employ all three of his regiments to continue the advance beyond Pilisszentlélek, as well as complete the encirclement of Dorog from the east. Although the regiment attacking Dorog (von Bose's *Gren. Rgt. 744*) made little progress that day, the two regiments (*Gren.Rgt. 731* and *763*) pushing down the valley managed to advance 3 kilometers beyond Pilisszentlélek before they halted for the day.

They also managed to seize Hill 423, which sat atop the mountain ridge separating the towns of Pilisszentlélek and Kesztölc. *Major* Magawly's *Gren.Rgt. 284*, now responsible for the all-round defense of Gran, began preparing its attack to clear the Soviet roadblock lying 5 kilometers to the southeast in order for *K.Gr. Philipp* to begin its push down the river highway that evening. The battalion charged with carrying out this mission, *II. Btl./Gren.Rgt. 284*, duly reported that it had done so by midnight. As it turned out, this was a false report, but that was not known at the time.

That evening, Gille conducted an orders briefing at 8 p.m. at the headquarters of the *711. Inf.Div.* in Gran that included the commanders of the *Wiking*, *96.*, and *711*. Divisions, as well as *K.Gr. Philipp*. In broad terms, Gille outlined the mission of *K.Gr. Westland* and *K.Gr. Philipp*, what their objectives were, and the importance of maintaining the tempo of their advance. The artillery fire support plan would have been briefed to the participants, as well as what was known of the enemy's situation. By midnight, all of the forces designated to take part in the initial stage of the impending assault were in their forward attack positions and ready to go. Troop morale was described as good, as described by a participant, who later wrote that "Everyone knew that within the encircled city, there were thousands of German and Hungarian comrades, as well as 2,000 female *Wehrmacht* auxiliaries" who were depending upon the success of their relief mission.[13] Due to difficulties experienced by some units in getting into their forward positions, the attack was delayed until 1 a.m. on 10 January.

To the right of the *IV. SS-Pz.Korps*, the newly formed *Div.Gr. Bieber* initiated its own attack on the morning of 9 January between Mór and Kecskéd towards the forested Vértes Mountains lying to the east and southeast. Although the *3. Kav.Brig.* had yet to arrive to lend its considerable weight, the attack went forward anyway using elements of three Hungarian divisions (their *2. Pz.Div.*, *25. Inf.Div.*, and

1. Hus.Div.) and four German infantry battalions. After advancing 2 or 3 kilometers in the face of heavy resistance by three understrength divisions of the Soviet LXVIII Rifle Corps, the most that the German and Hungarian troops were able to accomplish was the recapture of Pusztavám by the Hungarian *Inf.Rgt. 1* before the attack was brought to a halt on the western edge of the forest. To add insult to injury, 146 Hungarian soldiers, taking advantage of the chaos inherent in combat, went over to the enemy.

In another related development virtually unnoticed at the time, a new *Kampfgruppe* was in the process of being established on 9 January that would take over the shrinking defensive sector located between the *6. Pz.Div.* and *Div.Gr. Bieber*, still held by *Div.Gr. Pape*. This unit, named *K.Gr. Bundesmann* after the commander of *Heeres-StuG Brig. 239*, Hptm. Günther Bundesmann, would relieve the commander and staff of *Div.Gr. Pape* on 10 January, which was scheduled to be withdrawn the following day to begin the planned reconstitution of *Pz.Div. Feldherrnhalle*, the main body of which was still encircled in Budapest.[14] Besides the 28 assault guns of the brigade (of which only six were operational), this battlegroup would also have five Hungarian battalions to defend the 8-kilometer sector between Tata and Környe. Command of *K.Gr. Bundesmann* would initially be exercised by the *IV. SS-Pz.Korps.*

Despite the vigorous combat activity taking place throughout the *Kampfraum* (combat area) of *A.Gr. Balck/6. Armee* on 9 January, the heaviest fighting occurred in the Zámoly area, where the *I. Kav.Korps* was valiantly holding its ground in the face of savage and unremitting counterattacks by the I and VII Guards Mechanized Corps. After grinding through Soviet defenses while enduring heavy losses in personnel and armored vehicles to mines and artillery fire, by noon, any further advance by Harteneck's troops was out of the question, especially considering the heavy snowfall obscuring the battlefield. Holding what ground they had gained would require a supreme effort by the men of the *1., 3.,* and *23. Pz.Div.* and the *4. Kav.Brig.* In confusing, back-and-forth fighting that day, both sides sustained heavy losses. It could have been even worse; the counterattack by the two Soviet mechanized corps went forward with insufficient preparation, particularly in regards to the amount of artillery allocated to the attacking units, and the lack of a common understanding of the operation's objectives led to a series of piecemeal assaults that the Germans were able beat back.[15] The heavy snowfall contributed to the confusion, due to the inability of commanders to exercise visual control of their units.

Because of the unexpectedly strong counterattacks by the I and VII Mechanized Corps, that inflicted heavy losses on the *panzer* units, Breith had to give up any further idea of attacking that day and ordered Harteneck to do what he could to prevent the Soviet tanks and mechanized forces from rupturing his front line and completely breaking through. When 9 January finally ended, the *I. Kav.Korps* claimed to have knocked out 74 Soviet tanks that day alone, while the 4th Guards Army admitted to losing only 46. Still, this was half of the number of Soviet tanks committed to battle that day. German losses were not insignificant, though not reported. The Third Ukrainian Front later claimed to have inflicted "enormous losses as a result of our counterblow."[16]

One participant in the fighting that day, Maj.Gen. Ivan N. Russianov, commander of the I Guards Mechanized Corps, later wrote:

> The combat on 9 January was hard and prolonged. The discharge of heavy guns, the explosion of shells, mines, and grenades, and the chatter of long machine-gun bursts continued until nightfall on the snow-covered rolling plains south and west of the Hungarian villages of Zámoly, Csala, and Patka. Around noon, the enemy launched strong tank counterattacks out of the area of Gyula. The Fascists and Soviet armored vehicles became intermingled at almost point-blank range. The victor was the one who managed to get off the first shot.[17]

According to inflated Soviet estimates, their troops knocked out 45 German tanks on 7 January, claimed another 16 on 8 January, and 20 more destroyed the following day, which, if true, amounted to over 90 tanks and tank destroyers lost in three days of fighting, over three-quarters of what the Germans had begun their offensive with.

At this pace, the Germans would run out of operational *panzers* before the Soviets did, which would hand the advantage over to their opponents. Breith, as instructed by Balck, was ordered that evening to instruct Harteneck to cease his attack and temporarily transition to the defense across this *Korpsgruppe*'s wide sector. Russianov received a similar call at 10 p.m. from Tolbukhin, who instructed him to halt his corps' assault too.[18] Although *Korpsgruppe Breith* had destroyed far more tanks than it had lost, the German offensive towards Zámoly by the *I. Kav.Korps*, like *Konrad I*, was beginning to appear a failure.

On the *A. Gr. Balck/6. Armee* left flank north of the Danube, the German defensive measures taken during the past two days had begun to take effect, and the attacks by the 6th Guards Tank Army and the two rifle corps from the 7th Guards Army had noticeably slowed. The two-division counterattack that Kirchner had been instructed to carry out with this *LVII Pz.Korps* had to wait another day when Balck learned that the railroad line being used by the *20. Pz.Div.* to transport the rest of its units to Neuhäusel had been damaged by partisans near the Slovak town of Zilina and would require 24 hours to repair. In the meantime, those elements of the division that had arrived continued establishing blocking positions south and southeast of the town. The *8. Pz.Div.*, reinforced by *Pz.Abt. 208* and the remnants of the Hungarian *Szent László* Division, was holding firm in and around Komorn, but was ready to play its part in the operation. Thus, Kirchner's counterattack would not get fully underway until 10 January.[19]

Fighting in Budapest continued. That evening, the *IX. SS-Geb.Korps* radioed, "In the western bridgehead, the days passed quietly, with the exception of mortar and antitank gun fire. In the center sector of the eastern bridgehead [i.e., Pest] enemy attacks continued. In the enemy breakthrough sector southwest of Pestujhely, the situation was unclear."[20] The corps also reported that the enemy was using flame-throwing tanks in the attack of both sides of the eastern railroad station, its troops were involved in house-to-house fighting there, and both sides had suffered heavy casualties.

Due to the horrible flying weather, the *Luftwaffe* was unable to conduct any air supply drops. Pfeffer-Wildenbruch estimated that his corps' supply of ammunition for all types of weapons would be completely exhausted by 11 January unless more was flown in. Rations would run out that same day. In addition, there were 3,880 wounded to care for, including 1,400 litter-born patients who could not care for themselves. The situation in the city had indeed grown dire, and was getting more desperate with each passing day.[21]

With *Unternehmen Konrad II* about to begin in mere hours, the German high command once again began to exhibit doubts, especially Hitler. Though the *Führer* was enthusiastic about Philipp's impending *Husarenritt* along the Danube, he seemed to have little appetite for continuing the attack along the *IV. SS-Pz.Korps'* left flank. In a series of back-and-forth communications later that day between Guderian and Wöhler, in which Balck also took part, Hitler appeared to be leaning increasingly towards calling off *Konrad II* completely because he felt that the odds of it succeeding were diminishing. Instead, he advocated transferring Gille's corps to the far right flank of *A.Gr. Balck/6. Armee*, where it would again serve as the main effort in a variation of the original *Unternehmen Paula* plan, attacking south of Stuhlweissenburg between Lakes Balaton and Velencze.

It was all that Guderian, Wöhler, and Balck could do to argue that it would take too long—between five and eight days—to effect the transfer of Gille's corps to the far right, a distance of over 150 kilometers by road or rail, and that such a delay would only increase the odds that Budapest would have fallen during the interim, not to mention the increased distance the relief force would have to travel as it fought its way through to the city, roughly 90 kilometers. With Guderian acting as a sympathetic intermediary, Wöhler implored Hitler to give the operation a chance, stressing the fact that there was still a small window of opportunity in which to exploit the success of the *711. Inf.Div.* using both the *Wiking* Division and *K.Gr. Philipp*.

Guderian, in his last telephone conversation with *H.Gr. Süd* on 9 January, attempted to explain the true situation at the *Führerhauptquartier* as clearly as possible to Wöhler and Balck. He told them that Hitler's decision was subject to change at a moment's notice:

> [The] *Heeresgruppe* should be prepared for the *Führer* to order the *IV. SS-Pz.Korps* to regroup with *Korpsgruppe Breith* for a new attack to the south. The attack should take place as far south as possible, in an area where the enemy would not expect it … The commander in chief [i.e., Hitler] expressed another concern: the *IV. SS-Pz.Korps* was constantly under attack. One had to be able to replace it [note: in its current sector] with something, otherwise everything accomplished by the attack so far would be thrown away.[22]

Guderian closed this conversation by asking Wöhler whether the *3. Kav.Brig.*, supported by a *Volks-Artillerie Korps*, would suffice to cover the defensive sector being given up by Gille's corps. However, this unit had not yet arrived in enough strength to carry out such an ambitious assignment.

Unstated in this conversation was that the plan required the *6. Pz.Div.* and the *96.* and *711. Inf.Div.* to remain in their current positions; with the addition of the *3. Kav.Brig.*, with its six infantry battalions and the extra artillery, Guderian thought it would be enough to hold the ground taken between 1 and 8 January. After all, it would only be replacing the *Wiking* and *Totenkopf* Divisions, not all five of Gille's divisions. Although this suggestion was still a concept plan, not a directive, Wöhler and Balck set their staffs to work on developing it in more detail over the next several days. The commander and staff of the *IV. SS-Pz.Korps* would remain unaware of these developments for a least two more days.

Finally, at 1 a.m. on 10 January, Guderian secured Hitler's reluctant permission to allow the offensive to proceed, but the two most important questions were left unanswered: would Hitler allow the garrison in Budapest to withdraw to the west bank of the Danube, and would he allow it to conduct a limited attack designed to establish contact with the relief column? The topic of abandoning Budapest altogether was not even brought up, perhaps because all parties concerned knew what Hitler's answer would be. It was clear that he intended to hold on to Budapest come what may, and no one—not even Guderian—wanted to risk incurring his wrath for broaching the topic. This understanding was apparently not communicated clearly to Gille, whose thinking—as previously mentioned—had evolved to the point where he and his subordinate commanders believed that they were carrying out a rescue operation that would deliver the garrison of Budapest to safety through the Pilis Mountains once contact was established north of the city.

Unternehmen Konrad II was originally scheduled to commence at 10 p.m. on 9 January with the attack by *K.Gr. Philipp*, but as previously mentioned, the units involved experienced difficulties in moving into their attack positions due to the limited visibility and the deep snow, which signaled that the attack would not go forward until 1 a.m. on 10 January at the earliest. In addition to this unforeseen complication, the last-minute telephone call from the *OKH Führungsstab* authorizing *A.Gr. Balck/6. Armee* to order the attack to commence did not arrive at Balck's headquarters train in Martinsberg until 1 a.m. on 10 January. However, the *OKH Führungsstab* attached conditions to the operation—it had to succeed quickly, in two days at the most. If it did not, then *A.Gr. Balck/6. Armee* would be forced to withdraw the *IV. SS-Pz.Korps* and move it to the south to carry out the plan that Hitler favored. Thus, *Konrad II* would be under enormous pressure and compelled to show quick results as it raced against the clock.

The delay in issuing the order had set in motion a series of contradicting communications that reverberated up and down the entire chain of command, from

A. Gr. Balck/ 6. Armee headquarters to the lowest infantry companies in the *IV. SS-Pz. Korps* as they sat waiting in their forward positions for the signal to attack. As late as 3 a.m. on 10 January, Gille, who was visiting Ullrich's command post in Gran, stated that he still did not know when he would receive permission to begin the attack. Ullrich told Gille that the attack needed to go forward as soon as possible, without any further delays.[23] But the corps commander's hands were tied. The *O1* of the *Wiking* Division, *Ostuf.* Jahnke, wrote in his diary with signs of frustration, "All elements of the division have assembled for the attack by 2400 hours. However, at 0100 hours [on 10 January], the order arrived: Attack postponed. Is it perhaps a *Führerbefehl?* The element of surprise could be lost."[24]

This delay by the *OKH Führungsstab* in issuing the order authorizing the attack to go ahead would cost Gille's command precious time. It does not seem to have been a deliberate act to lessen the operation's chances of success, which would have been sabotage (as Gille alleged after the war), but was most likely due to misunderstandings at every level of command between the divisions of the *IV. SS-Pz. Korps* on the front lines and the *Führerhauptquartier* in Ziegenberg.[25] Hitler's own indecision cannot be ruled out as a cause of the delay, but Guderian, who would have known, made no comment in his book about the incident. Finally, in the late morning or early afternoon, *H. Gr. Süd* received permission to authorize Gille's attack to go forward, representing a delay of 15 hours.

The first action of *Unternehmen Konrad II* began with an attack by *Gren.Rgt. 731* of the *711. Inf.Div.* at 3 p.m. to continue pushing past Pilisszentlélek in order to create a breach in the Soviet defensive positions wide enough to enable *K.Gr. Westland* to begin its penetration. The temperature was still below freezing, the snow continued to fall, and paved roads throughout the area had patches of black ice that inhibited movement. In these conditions, the attack by Reichert's troops ground forward slowly, as his men had to fight their way through the thick snow-covered forest on the slopes on either side of the road held by the determined troops of the 99th Rifle Division. When the *711. Inf.Div.* had finally achieved its objectives for the day, Gille was able to give the green light for the *Wiking* Division's attack to begin at 8:30 p.m. In the interim, the time lost was put to good use, since it allowed Ullrich to bring up more elements of his division from their previous sector. It also gave the units taking part in the attack time to more thoroughly prepare their troops and equipment, including the emplacement of artillery batteries needed to support the initial stages of the operation.

Kampfgruppe Philipp, which was supposed to commence its own attack at 10 p.m. on 9 January before the general assault began, finally began its operation at approximately the same time that the *711. Inf.Div.* started its attack. After departing Gran in the early hours, its lead element—consisting of three armored cars from *1. Kp./SS-Pz.Aufkl.Abt. 3* led by *Ustuf.* Wilhelm Goertz—moved forward quickly along the river road, expecting easy passage through the lines of *II. Btl./Gren.Rgt. 284.*

The battlegroup was brought to an abrupt halt, however, when the lead armored car reported to *Oberstlt.* Philipp that the Soviets were still blocking the road at the narrows where the hillside sloped down to the river. Two *SPWs* carrying combat engineers moved forward in the darkness to clear an obstacle blocking the road, but were both damaged when they struck antitank mines concealed in the snow. Enemy fire began to erupt, halting the entire affair.

Apparently, the attack carried out the previous day by *Maj.* Hillermann's *II. Btl./ Gren. Rgt. 284* that was supposed to clear the roadblock erected along the Danube road had not been successful after all, despite a previous report to the contrary. Therefore, Philipp's attack could not go forward until this enemy-held position had been eliminated. Quickly sizing up the situation, Philipp ordered Hillermann's battalion to bypass the enemy position by going around the southern slopes of Hill 308 using a forest track at the base of the hill, while the rest of his *Kampfgruppe* waited on the road. Caught from behind, the Soviet position quickly fell to *II. Btl./Gren. Rgt. 284*'s assault by 11:40 a.m. With this obstacle removed, the motorized elements of *K.Gr. Philipp* finally resumed their advance, but precious hours had been lost.

Continuing down the highway, Philipp's *Husarenritt* had barely progressed a kilometer when it encountered yet another Soviet roadblock, which the assault guns from the *Totenkopf* Division forming the *Kampfgruppe* spearhead were able to overcome after destroying it with direct fire. After advancing less than 9 kilometers that day, *K.Gr. Philipp* was finally forced to a halt along the road 3 kilometers northwest of the village of Pilismarót on account of heavy and accurate fire from the opposite bank of the Danube, only 750 meters away. Unbeknownst to Philipp, or Gille for that matter, the 93rd Guards Rifle Division from the Second Ukrainian Front had arrived in the village of Szob the previous evening and had begun ferrying its troops across the river during the night and early morning.

The *Ic* of *H.Gr. Süd* had known that this division had been detected moving into Szob the day before and had sent word to *A.Gr. Balck/6. Armee* that this was occurring, but *Gen.Maj.* Gaedke evidently discounted the report and did not pass it along to the *IV. SS-Pz.Korps.* Throughout the day, the 93rd Guards Rifle Division was able to get enough of its troops across the river in time to block any further progress by Philipp's battlegroup. Thus stymied, the German spearhead was compelled to pull back and take up a defensive position in Basaharc, a cluster of farmhouses 500 meters south of the river's edge, out of range of most of the enemy's direct fire weapons. Here, Philipp and the troops from *II. Btl/Pz.Gren.Rgt. FHH* dug in while he planned his next move. This marked the limit of his advance on 10 January.[26]

Once it had become clear that the *711. Inf.Div.* had done all that it could to enable *K.Gr. Westland* to break through the Soviet defensive positions southeast of Pilisszentlélek, *Ostubaf.* Hack was finally given permission to initiate his own oft-delayed movement into the Pilis Mountains towards the town at 3 p.m., which took several hours to reach over the snow- and ice-covered road between Gran and

Pilisszentlélek. According to the division's *O1*, who was monitoring radio message traffic emanating from Hack's command vehicle as he sat in the division's forward command post in Gran, it seemed that the attack, which did not get underway until 8:30 p.m., was progressing very rapidly after surprising and overcoming initially weak enemy defenses. Jahnke wrote in his diary later that evening:

> Difficult mountainous terrain, resembles the foothills of the Alps in character … [after] midnight, first reports of success, prisoners, mostly rear-area personnel from divisions surrounding Budapest … [encountering] defensive antitank and mortar fire. No casualties of our own [so far]. *Westland* moving forward well. *Germania* is still being delayed.[27]

While little of consequence occurred on 10 January in the sector held by the *96. Inf.Div.*, the situation in the *Totenkopf* Division's defensive sector was anything but quiet. Throughout the course of the day, its positions were attacked numerous times by Soviet tank and infantry forces, in particular at Zsámbék, where the *Eicke* Regiment destroyed seven tanks that day alone.

This signified something of a milestone, for by 10 January, Becker's division had destroyed or rendered inoperable 145 Soviet tanks and other armored fighting vehicles since it began its attack on 1 January. Sarisap, defended by the *III. Btl.* of *SS-Pz.Gren.Rgt. 5 Totenkopf*, was also attacked by strong enemy forces that were attempting to push their way through the front lines between Sarisap and Szomor. Reinforced by the division's *Begleitkompanie* (escort company), an 8.8cm battery from *SS-Pz.Flak-Abt. 3*, and *3.Kp./SS-Pio.Btl. 3*, the town's defenders, led by *Ostuf.* Wolfgang Knorr, fought determinedly against successive enemy assaults, but found themselves encircled by the day's end.[28] The following day, the division would launch an effort to restore the front line and relieve the embattled defenders.

In the defensive sector held by the *6. Pz.Div.*, including the elements of the *Wiking* Division that had not yet been relieved, local counterattacks continued throughout the day, emanating chiefly from Bicske and Mány. The V Guards Cavalry Corps, the 16th and 32nd Guards Mechanized Brigades, and the 62nd Guards Rifle Division, despite all suffering heavy casualties, persisted in their efforts in the face of heavy German resistance. Soviet artillery fire was heavy and continuous. Much of it was focused against the position held by *Pz.Gr. Darges* at the Hegyks Castle Estate, whose thick walls had been reduced to ruins by this point, though Darges and Vogt hung on despite enemy pressure. On the corps' far right flank, *K.Gr. Bundesmann* assumed responsibility for defending the sector formerly held by *Div. Gr. Pape*, though it reported no combat activity worth mentioning.

To the right of *IV. SS-Pz.Korps*, the attack by *Div.Gr. Bieber*, launched with such high expectations the previous day, achieved very little. Against strong enemy resistance, only a few meters of insignificant ground were gained and a battalion-sized Soviet attack even managed to penetrate that afternoon into the northern portion of Pusztavám. Even inserting the *Kampfgruppe* from the Hungarian *1. Hus.Div.*

Fighting in Hungary, January–February 1945

During the movement to Hungary, all of the corps' units were moved by rail. Here, troops from the Headquarters, *IV. SS-Panzer-Korps* are shown after unloading from the trains that brought them down from Modlin, late December 1944. (Lange)

Another photo depicting troops from the corps' *Hauptquartier* dining "al fresco," late December 1944. Many of the troops traveled in unheated box cars with no latrine facilities. (Lange)

The same troops observed during their lunch. Most of these men are either officers or NCOs from the corps' headquarters and supply company. (Lange)

Panther from *Stabskompanie, I. Abteilung, SS-Pz.Rgt. 3 Totenkopf* east of Nyerges Ujfalu, early January 1945. (*SS-KB* Hermann Grönert, courtesy of Mirko Bayerl)

An *Sd.Kfz. 251 Schützenpanzerwagen* (most likely from *K.Gr. Dorr*) passes a burning fuel truck somewhere in the Gerecse Mountains, early January 1945. (Jarolim)

Troops from the *96. Inf.Div.* cross the Danube on a ferry after seizing the southern bank of the river between Gran and Nyerges Ujfalu, early January 1945. (Kern)

Kampfgruppe Dorr, spearheaded by *SS-Panzer-Regiment 5*, wind their way through the Gerecse Mountains, early January 1945. (Jarolim)

An artillery battery from the *Wiking* Division, equipped with 10.5cm self-propelled *Wespen* ("Wasps") howitzers, preceded by *Sd.Kfz. 251* carrying *Panzergrenadiere* traveling south of Tarján during *Konrad I*, early January 1945. In the background, a *Pz. III* artillery observation vehicle can be seen. (Jarolim)

A column of vehicles from the *Wiking* Division pass a knocked-out Soviet 7.62cm antitank gun during *Konrad I* in January 1945 while moving south from Tarján. (Jarolim)

Troops from *K.Gr. Hack* of the *Wiking* Division advance through the Pilis Mountains en route to Pilisszentkereszt during *Konrad II*, January 1945. Bodies of German soldiers killed in earlier fighting, most likely from the *711. Inf.Div.*, lie unburied on the roadside. (Jarolim)

Troops from *K.Gr. Hack* during the withdrawal from Pilisszentkereszt after the cancellation of *Konrad II*, 12 or 13 January 1945. Note the completely iced-over road, which made travel difficult for wheeled and armored vehicles alike. (Jarolim)

A *Grille* ("Cricket" 15cm self-propelled gun) from the regimental infantry howitzer company of *K.Gr. Hack* during the withdrawal from Pilisszentkereszt, 12 or 13 January 1945. On the left, an ancient Krupp *Protze* ("Boxer") has stopped due to mechanical trouble. (Jarolim)

SS troops from the *Wiking* Division or *I. Btl./SS-Pz.Gren.Rgt. Norge* pass the carcasses of several dead horses from a Soviet supply column shot up during *Konrad I*, early January 1945, near the southern outskirts of Tarján. (Jarolim)

SS troops from the *Totenkopf* Division rest on the northern outskirts of Szomor during *Konrad I* in early January 1945. (Grönert)

Two SS troops from the *Totenkopf* Division share a friendly moment somewhere north of Szomor, January 1945. The soldier leaning against the rear idler wheel of a *Pz. IV* may be a wire layer, evidenced by the large spool of communications wire lying next to him. The other soldier has a *Panzerfaust* antitank projectile launcher balanced on his right shoulder. (Grönert)

SS troops from the *Totenkopf* Division passing through Szomor, early January 1945. In the foreground, an *Sd.Kfz. 10 leichter Zugkraftwagen* half-track tows a captured Soviet 7.62cm antitank gun, a valued addition to the division's antitank defenses. (Grönert)

Gille and Becker converse during a snowstorm, mid-January 1945. It appears that both men are wearing *Luftwaffe* insulated flight boots. (Photographer unknown, courtesy of Mirko Bayerl)

The defenders of the "Fort of the Unbreakables," Hegyks Castle Estate, sometime between 6 and 11 January 1945. Front row (from left to right): *Ustuf.* Werner Liebald (*4. Kp, I. Btl./Norge*) and *Stubaf.* Fritz Vogt (*I. Btl./Norge*). Back row (left to right): *Ostuf.* Ernst Kiefer (*4. Kp, I. Btl./Norge*), *Ostuf.* Helmut Bauer (*3. Kp./SS-Pz.Rgt. 5*); *Hstuf.* Willi Hein (*I. Abt./SS-Pz.Rgt. 5*); *Ostubaf.* Fritz Darges (*SS-Pz. Rgt. 5*); unidentified officer from *II. Abt./SS-Pz.Rgt. 5*; *Hstuf.* Karl-Heinz Lichte (with cigarette, *5. Kp./SS-Pz.Rgt. 5*); and *Ostuf.* Hans Weerts (*4. Kp./SS-Pz.Rgt. 5*). (Photographer unknown, courtesy of Günther Lange)

Several tanks from *SS-Panzer Regiment 3*, including *Pz. IV*s, *Pz. V* Panthers with infantry mounted aboard, and *StuG III*s moving through Szomor on their way to Zsámbék in early January 1945. The road in the background running uphill leads to Gyermely, which was captured by the *Westland* Regiment. (Grönert)

Fritz Darges speaking to *SS-Stubaf.* Heinz Wagner, the commander of *SS-Aufkl.Abt. 5*, at the regimental command post during *Konrad III*, January 1945. (Lange)

Willi Hein's *Befehlspanzer* (command tank) *Pz. IVH* of *I. Abt./SS-Pz.Rgt. 5*, parked in front of the Hegyks Castle, January 1945. (Photographer unknown, courtesy of Hans Fischer)

The commander of *SS-Aufkl.Abt. 5*, *SS-Stubaf.* Wagner, stands beside the commander of his *1. Kompanie*, *SS-Hstuf.* Hermann Kaufmann, near the *SS-Pz.Rgt. 5* command post, January 1945. (Lange)

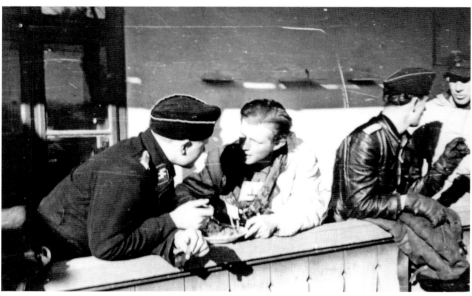

Officers from *SS-Pz.Rgt. 5* at the regimental command post of *SS-Pz.Rgt. 5*, January 1945. (Lange)

An *SS-Unterscharführer* from *SS-Pz.Rgt. 5* issuing supplies in January 1945. (Lange)

Several *StuG III* assault guns from *Sturm-Art. Brig. 303* during *Konrad III*, between 18 and 28 January 1945, while the brigade was attached to the *Wiking* Division. (*SS-Kriegsberichter* Kok, courtesy of Mirko Bayerl)

SS-Obersturmbannführer Dorr in his command vehicle during *Konrad I* shortly before his fatal wounding, January 1945. (Jarolim)

A *StuG III* from the *Totenkopf* Division near Szomor during *Konrad I*, early January 1945. (Photographer unknown, courtesy of Mirko Bayerl)

SS troops fire on Soviet positions in the Pilis Mountains during *Konrad II*, late January 1945. (Photographer unknown, courtesy of Mirko Bayerl)

An SS *Jagd.Pz. IV/L48* during *Konrad I*, January 1945. An abandoned Soviet 7.62cm antitank gun lies in the foreground. (Jarolim)

Troops from the *Totenkopf* or *Wiking* Division talk to a Hungarian woman near Baraczka or Pettend during *Konrad III*. (Grönert, courtesy of Mirko Bayerl)

Troops from the *6. Pz.Div.* prepare for their assault near Csabdi during *Konrad III*, 23 January 1945. (Photographer unknown, courtesy of Mirko Bayerl)

Troops from the *6. Pz.Div.* prepare for their assault near Csabdi during *Konrad III*, 23 January 1945. (Photographer unknown, courtesy of Mirko Bayerl)

SS-Obersturmbannführer Fritz Darges in his command post near Stuhlweissenburg during late February or early March 1945. (Kern)

Survivors of the Budapest garrison, including a mixture of *Heer* and *Waffen-SS* troops, being taken to the rear on top of a *6. Pz.Div.*-provided *Sd.Kfz. 251 Schützenpanzerwagen* after being rescued near Szomor, 15 February 1945. (Author)

During the lead up to the *Frühlingserwachen* Offensive, Sepp Dietrich visits Gille's headquarters in Inota, early March 1945, to discuss the upcoming operation. From left to right, Manfred Schönfelder, Gille, Dietrich, and Friedrich Rauch, Gille's *Ia*. (Lange)

failed to move the ball forward. By this point, the divisions of Maj.Gen. Nikolai N. Shkodonovich's LVIII Rifle Corps had been strengthening their defensive positions for nearly three weeks and had erected a formidable barrier against any attacking force, especially one lacking any appreciable armor of its own to lend support.

Korpsgruppe Breith's main effort, the renewed attack by *I. Kav.Korps* towards Zámoly, had devolved into a stalemate in the face of continuing counterattacks by the I and VII Mechanized Corps. That evening, Breith's headquarters reported:

> An enemy attack against our own *Kampfgruppe* east of Sárkeresztes was unsuccessful ... Along the highway towards Zámoly, the enemy was pushed back slightly to the north. Local enemy thrusts from Zámoly towards the south and southwest ultimately failed to achieve any gains worth mentioning ... the enemy was able to ward off our own counterattack aimed at destroying their breakthrough southwest of Csákbérény. An enemy attack in the strength of two battalions against Söréd failed. An enemy assembly area north of Zámoly and east of Mór was struck by our own [concentrated] artillery fire.[29]

The report failed to mention the impact that heavily drifting snow and icy roads had on operations, as both opponents grappled in a life-and-death struggle for Zámoly.

According to some reports, Hill 225, located 2 kilometers northeast of the village of Söréd, changed hands five times, ending up in Soviet hands by the end of the day. At least nine Soviet tanks were knocked out that day by *K.Gr. Weymann* of the *3. Pz.Div.*, including three M4A2 Shermans by *Leutnant* Schenck of *2. Kp./Pz.Rgt. 6*. This was practically the only noteworthy success achieved by the *I. Kav.Korps* that day; the other units of the corps had run afoul of minefields and *Pakfronts* whenever they tried to counterattack, only reinforcing the realization that both sides were at a stalemate.[30]

On the north side of the Danube, the two-division counterattack by Kirchner's *LVII. Pz.Korps* against the overextended armored spearheads of the 6th Guards Tank Army began to gather momentum. With almost all of the *20. Pz.Div.* combat elements now on the ground, it attacked out of Neuhäusel towards the south and southeast with nearly its entire weight. Similarly, a now-rejuvenated *8. Pz.Div.* under the energetic leadership of acting commander *Gen.Maj.* von Roden, attacked out of Komorn to the northeast was also enjoying success in stopping and pushing back Soviet troops and tanks from the 6th Guards Tank Army.

A *Kampfgruppe* from *20. Pz.Div.* attacked south from Perbete and threw Soviet troops out of Komaromszentpeter, while another battlegroup destroyed 10 Soviet tanks attempting to storm the town of Kürt, 10 kilometers east of Perbete. The only question remaining unanswered was the future course of action by Col.Gen. Kravchenko's sole uncommitted element, the IV Guards Mechanized Corps. Would it advance to the west to reinforce his army's other two corps? With the course of the fighting now going against Soviet forces north of the Danube, this remained an open question for the next several days. The rest of the front along the Gran River was described as quiet, signifying that no major offensive activity was planned or imminent.[31]

Of course, things in Budapest were not nearly as rosy; in fact, the situation was quite the opposite and the situation in the city seemed to be getting out of hand. In his nightly report, Pfeffer-Wildenbruch stated:

> The civilian population of Budapest is in a very critical position. Most are practically without food. Major areas of the city are without water and light. The total lack of leadership, due to the flight of all noteworthy party and administrative officials, adds to the increasing dissatisfaction. There are already visible signs of unrest, which previously could only be suppressed by reference to the approaching relief forces.

Throughout that day, attacking Soviet forces continued to force the defenders on the eastern side of the city to withdraw block by block into an ever-shrinking perimeter. Three city districts were abandoned that day alone by the defenders, due to a lack of sufficient infantry to hold the ground as well as shortages of even small-arms ammunition.

According to reports, only 20 *Luftwaffe* resupply sorties were flown on 10 January. Due to inclement weather, their loads of relief supplies were dropped blindly, with most of them falling behind Soviet lines causing the remainder of the resupply missions scheduled that day to be cancelled.[32] In fact, the weather was so bad that air activity throughout the entire area of operations of *H.Gr. Süd* and *A.Gr. Balck/6. Armee*, as well as Red Air Force sorties, was minimal.

While these dramatic events were unfolding, that afternoon *Gen.d.Inf.* Wöhler paid a visit to *Gen.d.Pz.Tr.* Balck at his headquarters in Martinsberg to discuss the progress of *Konrad II* so far, as well as options for future operations. Accompanied by his army group *Ia, Oberstlt. i.G.* Wilhelm Schäfer, Wöhler discussed the situation at length for several hours with Balck and his staff. One result of this meeting, besides a clearer understanding of the current status of the ongoing fighting, was an updated estimate of the situation or commander's assessment prepared by the *H.Gr. Süd* operations staff for the official record and for their counterparts at *A.Gr. Balck/6. Armee* headquarters. As ably summarized by Maier in his book, *Drama between Budapest and Vienna*, five key points in this situation estimate stood out:

1. Although an attack by the regrouped *IV. SS-Pz.Korps* from the area southwest of Stuhlweissenburg [note: the plan advocated by Hitler] promised greater results—since it would simultaneously cut off enemy forces west of Budapest—it would be necessary to interrupt the fighting for at least five days [in order to get the corps into position].
2. It seemed doubtful whether the Budapest garrison could hold out until such an operation achieved effective results.
3. During the time before relieving forces could arrive, the enemy could strengthen his forces and reduce the Budapest bridgeheads.
4. The planned operation would thus only be possible once Budapest was relieved.
5. The intention of forcing a breakthrough through the Pilis Mountains [note: by *IV. SS-Pz. Korps*] must be maintained, since it was the shortest way to Budapest and the terrain favored a subsequent breakout by the garrison.[33]

Evidently, this document was either sent to Guderian's headquarters in Zossen via *Hellschreiber* or Wöhler gave it to him verbally over the telephone, for shortly afterwards Guderian instructed his deputy, *Gen.d.Pz.Tr.* Wenck, to contact Wöhler's headquarters to point out that if the attack by the *IV. SS-Pz.Korps* through the Pilis Mountains did not succeed by the night of 10–11 January and threatened to become a "long, drawn-out affair," then Hitler would order the regrouping towards Stuhlweissenburg without any further ado.[34]

This response arrived when the attack by *K.Gr. Westland* was only several hours old and had not yet achieved any measureable results. It seems as if the *OKH* chief of staff and his chief of operations had already concluded that Gille's attack through the Pilis Mountains would fail and that its movement to Stuhlweissenburg was inevitable. Why, then, would they seem to be humoring Wöhler and Balck? Possibly, both Guderian and Wenck were only allowing the attack by the *Wiking* Division to continue, even with such slim hopes of success, because that was what both Balck and Wöhler wanted and, despite the odds, it just might succeed. In other words, the senior leaders at *OKH* were hedging their bets. After all, they knew Hitler's mind better than anyone else and probably believed that *der Führer* had already made his decision to go with the southern course of action. They also knew one other thing—that Hitler still clung to the stubborn idea that Budapest would continue to be held, to the last man and last bullet if necessary.

While the leaders at *OKH*, *H.Gr. Süd*, and *A.Gr. Balck/6. Armee* continued arguing the advantages and disadvantages of the attack through the Pilis Mountains as well as the wisdom of canceling it altogether, the troops involved continued to perform their duty as weather conditions began to deteriorate. On the morning of 11 January, the temperatures began to rise above freezing for the first time in weeks, setting into motion a thawing trend that turned previously ice-caked roads into mud- and slush-covered quagmires as several feet of snow began to melt. Snow and rain began to fall throughout the day, adding further to the misery felt by attackers and defenders alike, who were forced to live and fight in these horrific conditions.

On the corps' left flank, *K.Gr. Philipp* made another attempt to continue its push down the highway towards Szentendre. Although the inclement weather was not as much of a factor inhibiting his *Kampfgruppe's* mobility along the river highway as it was to the *Westland* Regiment fighting its way through the mountains, *Oberstlt.* Philipp and his troops had to contend again with enemy fire coming from the opposite bank of the river, where the 93rd Guards Rifle Division had arrayed its heavy weapons. Later that day, *K.Gr. Philipp* advanced as far as the northern outskirts of the town of Pilismarót against determined opposition by elements of the 93rd that had been ferried across, but this marked the furthest extent of the *Husarenritt*. Philipp's battalion-sized *Kampfgruppe* was simply too small to overcome the enemy's defenses. The convoy of trucks carrying the 200 tons of relief supplies for the Budapest garrison never got beyond Gran. Soviet counterattacks throughout the day forced Philipp to first order his troops to fall back to Basaharc again before finally withdrawing that evening to the narrows 5 kilometers east of Gran where they had encountered the first roadblock during the early hours of the previous day.

The news from *K.Gr. Westland* was more positive. Having begun its attack late in the evening on 10 January, *Ostubaf.* Hack, leading from the front in his command vehicle, drove his men hard to make up for lost time. By sunrise on 11 January, they had covered the 5 kilometers of ground between Pilisszentlélek and Pilisszentkereszt after negligible resistance. After the war, Franz Hack described the advance:

> We are withdrawn and regrouped; *Kampfgruppe Westland* in the lead, reinforced by *panzer* artillery and the combat engineer battalion. We march in the direction of the Danube and the Pilis Mountains. The motor road is trafficable. We come to mountain country with pine forests, steep hills and hairpin turns. The village of Pilisszentlélek appears in front of us. Our reconnaissance troops have made contact with the enemy. Everyone halts. The *1. Bataillon* [of the *Westland*] gets ready for attack. Pushing forwards along both sides of the road, we overcome one Soviet outpost after another during the night. Along the road lay German trucks, some abandoned, some driven into the ditch. They carry the tactical markings of the *Feldherrnhalle* Division. In between there are abandoned German weapons and heaps of equipment, as well as discarded piles of supplies, all evidence of the fighting to get through to Budapest … numerous Soviet troops use these [abandoned] vehicles as cover; in many cases we have to fight them with hand grenades. After daybreak, it continues. We have reached Pilisszentlélek.[35]

Augmented by the newly arrived *SS-Sturmjäger Rgt. 1*, a unit composed of Hungarian SS volunteers activated in Tata only three days before, the men of *K.Gr. Westland* fought their way towards the larger town of Pilisszentkereszt that evening against the determined defense of the three understrength regiments of the 99th Rifle Division which had been reportedly reinforced by several armored vehicles. By early morning on 12 January, Pilisszentkereszt was completely in German and Hungarian hands and the defenders had been thrown back 2 kilometers southeast of the town. During the fighting, the Hungarian SS men, commanded by *Stubaf.* Kelemen Ridegh, sustained heavy casualties in their first sustained combat action, as they struggled against their Soviet opponents.[36]

In the wake of the attack, a regiment of the *711. Inf.Div.* continued to mop up bypassed Soviet troops along both sides of the route, eliminating or pushing them back further into the mountains, where they would be unable to hinder the advance of Hack's regiment. One kilometer east of the highway between Pilisszentlélek and Pilisszentkereszt, a battalion from *Gren.Rgt. 731* scouted towards Dobogókó, a *Kurort* (health resort) located at the top of a steep hill at the end of a winding mountain road. To their surprise, the battalion discovered that within the Dobogókó resort itself lay a German field hospital, which had been captured two weeks before when the area was first overrun by Soviet troops between 26 and 28 December.[37]

Perhaps due to its isolation as well as a lack of means, the occupying force had not yet had time to evacuate the hospital's inhabitants to a prisoner of war camp.

Thus, a number of German and Hungarian wounded—up to a thousand according to some sources, but probably far fewer—as well as the German medical staff, including one Hungarian nurse, were liberated, much to the relief of everyone involved.[38] While doctors, nurses, and other medical personnel taken prisoner by Soviet forces, as well as walking wounded, were usually sent to temporary camps set up in occupied areas in Eastern Europe during this stage of the war, non-ambulatory enemy wounded were most often administered a *Genickschuss* (mercy killing via a bullet in the back of the neck) on the spot. Dobogókó, the highest peak in the Pilis Mountains at 700 meters above sea level, provided a commanding view of the bend in the Danube north of Budapest. On the evening of 11/12 January, the final goal of *Unternehmen Konrad II* seemed tantalizingly within reach. To add to Gille's optimism, the first elements of Dorr's *Germania* Regiment had begun to arrive in the vicinity of Gran and were being sent forward to reinforce *K.Gr. Westland.*

To the right of and behind *K.Gr. Westland,* west of the ridgeline separating the two divisions, *Gren.Rgt. 744* from *Gen.Lt.* Reichert's *711. Inf.Div.* moved into position east of Dorog in preparation for another assault the following day by the *96. Inf.Div.,* being temporarily attached to it for that purpose. The rest of Reichert's division was either employed in consolidating control of the ground recently taken, establishing defensive positions in the hills southeast of Gran, or supporting the attack by the battlegroup of the *Wiking* Division with *Gren.Rgt. 731. Oberst* Harrendorf's *96. Inf. Div.,* less its *Gren.Rgt. 284*—which was still defending Gran and supporting the advance of *K.Gr. Philipp*—was not involved in any significant fighting that day, but Harrendorf had once again been given the mission of taking Dorog on 12 January using its *Gren.Rgt. 283* and *287.*

On the corps' right flank, the *Totenkopf* Division and *6. Pz.Div.* continued to hold their ground. *Oberst* Jürgen's troops from the *6. Pz.Div.* warded off numerous localized Soviet attacks directed from Csabdi and the Mány area west of Zsámbék, while the *Eicke* Regiment maintained its defenses north of Zsámbék. The division's reconnaissance battalion, *SS-Pz.Aufkl.Abt. 3,* warded off several attempt to retake Kirva, while *III. Btl./Totenkopf* successfully defended Sarisap. A significant portion of the *Germania* Regiment (perhaps a battalion) had already been withdrawn by this point and sent marching north to join the rest of the *Wiking* Division. An order directing *Pz.Gr. Darges* to withdraw its *II. Abteilung* was also issued that day, leaving only the *I. Abteilung,* with less than a dozen *Pz. IVs* and assault guns, to continue holding the Hegyks Castle Estate along with Vogt's *I. Btl./Norge.*[39] On the corps' far right, *K.Gr. Bundesmann* reported no combat activity worth mentioning. German intelligence reports detected that the 4th Guards Army was shifting units away from the Bicske–Zsámbék area and towards either flank to combat the German attacks in the north and south, which likely contributed to the easing of pressure against Becker's and Jürgen's divisions.[40]

While *IV. SS-Pz.Korps* was savoring the relative success achieved that day on its left, the same cannot be said for *Korpsgruppe Breith*, which was experiencing another day of heavy fighting with mixed results to show for its troops' efforts. The evening before, Balck had directed Breith to resume his attack, in the belief that it would relieve some of the pressure being exerted against the advance through the Pilis Mountains by the *Wiking* Division. On the left of Breith's *Korpsgruppe*, sandwiched between the *IV. SS-Pz.Korps* and *I Kav.Korps*, *Div.Gr. Bieber* attempted to continue its attack begun the previous day to ease some of the pressure against the divisions attacking towards Zámoly, but the few assault troops that went forward from the Hungarian *1. Hus.Div.* and *2. Pz.Div.* between Bokod and Pusztavám made little headway. During their attack, another 150 Hungarians from their armored division deserted to the enemy, which must have been a very discouraging sign to their comrades who remained behind to defend their homeland.

As for Harteneck's *I. Kav.Korps*, which was also directed to resume its attack, the highlight of the day was the taking of Zámoly, which had been the corps' objective for the past four days. Preceded by a heavy artillery and rocket barrage, the *4. Kav. Brig.* conducted an enveloping attack against the town from the north, while the *23. Pz.Div.*, spearheaded by *K.Gr. Weymann*—now reinforced by *s.Pz.Abt. 503 Feldherrnhalle*—attacked from the south. On the corps' left flank, the *3. Pz.Div.* was able to take Felsőmajor after heavy fighting. Zámoly's defenders, including the 5th Guards Airborne Division and 93rd Rifle Division, fiercely resisted the German onslaught, forcing the attackers to take the town house-by-house.

Of the 13 *Pz. VI* Tiger II tanks employed by *s.Pz.Abt. 503* in the attack on 11 January, all but three were destroyed or rendered temporarily inoperable during the fighting. In exchange, of the numerous T-34 and JS-II heavy tanks the battalion encountered that day, they claimed the destruction of 21 tanks and self-propelled guns and 20 antitank guns. In a quirk of fate, the battalion also destroyed three Soviet troop-carrying gliders that had mistakenly landed at the airfield northwest of Zámoly, in the belief that they were behind friendly lines. That day, *I. Kav.Korps* claimed the destruction of 31 Soviet tanks and the same number of antitank guns. In return, Soviet forces claimed that they had destroyed 38 German tanks and armored vehicles.[41]

For all intents and purposes, this marked the culmination of Harteneck's attack. Although his corps had finally taken Zámoly, the hoped-for breakthrough towards Bicske, the link-up with the right flank of the *IV. SS-Pz.Korps*, and the encirclement of the bulk of the Soviet defenders arrayed between both corps did not occur. Not only did Harteneck's three-division attack lack sufficient infantry to protect the armor and hold the ground that had been gained, but the rapid countermeasures taken by the Third Ukrainian Front and 4th Guards Army commanders, including the commitment of the I and VII Mechanized Corps, had proved too much to overcome. The terrible weather throughout had also greatly hampered operations by either side. By the end of 11 January, both sides claimed victory; in reality, all they had achieved was a temporary stalemate.

Zámoly had indeed finally been taken, but at a high cost. German sources indicate that *I. Kav.Korps* lost approximately 1,200 men in the armor battle at Zámoly; reliable figures for their armor losses are not available. The 4th Guards Army official records claimed the destruction of 139 enemy tanks and tank destroyers, as well as 50 *SPWs*, which if true would be more than the Germans began their offensive with. *Korpsgruppe Breith* afterwards claimed that between 7 and 11 January, its divisions had destroyed or disabled 169 Soviet tanks and self-propelled guns, which tallies closely with the number the Soviets declared as total losses (117). According to their own records, 2,900 Soviet soldiers were killed, wounded, and missing during the battle.[42] While Zakharov could claim that his army had stopped the relief of Budapest at Zámoly (not the actual intent of Harteneck's attack), the Germans could also claim that their offensive had tied up two powerful mechanized units that could have been used to attack the right flank of the *IV. SS-Pz.Korps*. Thus, with neither side having achieved victory, the stage was set for the next attempt to relieve Budapest.

North of the Danube, the counterattack by Kirchner's forces rolled onwards, though not as rapidly as originally hoped. While the spearheads of the 6th Guards Tank Army had been prevented from taking the key transport hubs of Komorn and Neuhäusel, they clung stubbornly to the ground they had taken, forcing the *20. Pz.Div.* and *8. Pz.Div.* to carry out a number of small, costly engagements to pry Soviet troops out of the towns of Bagota, Bajcs, Perbete, Ujgyalla, and Komaromszentpeter. Kravchenko's tank army still had a lot of fight left in it, though it was obvious to German intelligence that its attack no longer posed a serious threat to the survival of *A.Gr. Balck* and that *Korpsgruppe Breith* would not have to send more of its own forces across the river to help stop it.[43]

One of Wöhler's greatest concerns expressed that evening relating to the situation north of the Danube, was that unless the Soviet forces that had crossed the Gran were eliminated, the Second Ukrainian Front would have a large enough foothold to continue the advance towards it ultimate objective of Vienna. However, Kirchner's corps was not strong enough to carry out an assignment of that magnitude for the time being. Balck's staff was primarily concerned in getting the railway line between Neuhäusel and Komorn back into operation. The elimination of the Gran bridgehead would have to wait another month.

With the railway line cut and temporarily out of service, supplies for *6. Armee* would be delayed, since the trains carrying them to the terminus at Komorn, Acs, and Raab would now have to follow a slow, roundabout path far to the west in order to avoid the battle area. This unwelcome event had occurred at a time when Balck's embattled forces needed all of the ammunition and fuel supplies they could get. Gille, for his part, was concerned that his corps' left flank along the Danube was vulnerable to Soviet interdiction at any point along the 50-kilometer stretch of the river between Gran and Komorn. His supply trucks were already being fired upon from the opposite bank as they drove along the Danube river highway. At some point, a more comprehensive plan would have to be drawn up, but for the moment *H. Gr. Süd* and *A. Gr. Balck/6. Armee* were still preoccupied with the relief of Budapest.

In Budapest, the fighting continued undiminished. A direct hit on the Elisabeth Bridge connecting the east and west portions of the city destroyed a large portion of it, rendering it unusable for armored vehicles, leaving only two intact bridges. By this point, Marshal Malinovsky was becoming anxious about the delay in seizing the city. It was taking far too long and was consuming far more of his forces than he had anticipated. Considering it a "thorn in his side," the sooner it could be eliminated the better because it was delaying the preparations needed to continue his Front's movement towards Vienna.[44] On 11 January, he directed the Red Air Force to unleash its ground-attack aircraft to harass and bomb every identifiable German and Hungarian position in the city.

The 46th Army's artillery and mortar fire increased in its intensity in a bid to more quickly overcome the defenders. Accordingly, the casualties suffered by *IX. SS-Geb. Korps* began to rise, forcing Pfeffer-Wildenbruch to order the front lines to withdraw even further into the city.[45] Soviet loudspeaker broadcasts to Hungarian troops were inducing more and more of them to surrender or defect. Ammunition continued to be strictly rationed; no successful airdrops by the *Luftwaffe* took place that day. However, the city's defenders still held out, in the hope that Gille's relief attack would succeed, an event which they believed was imminent.

While the fighting flared along the entire front line of *A. Gr. Balck/6. Armee*, events equally as dramatic were once again taking place from the level of Gille's corps headquarters to the field army, army group, and finally Hitler's own headquarters. It seems that Hitler was growing impatient with the delays taking place on Gille's left flank, where his units were doing their utmost to overcome the weather as much as they were the Soviet defenders. As they had the previous day, a series of telephone or radio conversations took place between Gille's forward command post in Gran, Balck's in Martinsburg, Wöhler's in Esterháza, and Guderian's in Zossen.

While Guderian had been able to get the *Führer* to accede to a temporary delay in the movement of the *IV. SS-Pz. Korps* to prosecute the *Südlösung* (which would soon become *Unternehmen Konrad III*), Gille's troops had to show quick results. Evidently, the progress by *K. Gr. Westland* during the evening of 11 January had not been enough to convince the dictator that the plan was working. The failure of *K. Gr. Philipp*'s "Hussar ride" along the banks of the Danube was also another disappointment, of which Hitler was undoubtedly aware since he was supposed to be informed every hour on the status of its progress. Wöhler and Balck begged Guderian for more time; for his part, Guderian was most likely growing weary of having to serve as an intermediary, especially since he had never been in favor of *Konrad* in the first place.

To lend some impetus to the *Wiking* Division's attack, that evening Balck directed the *Totenkopf* Division to carry out an attack on the morning of 12 January aimed towards the town of Pilisvörösvár, where it would link up with the right flank of Ullrich's division. The *Wiking* Division, in turn, would use elements of the slowly arriving *Germania* Regiment to conduct an attack to the southwest from Pilisszentkereszt to link up with approaching elements of the *Totenkopf*. But it was all a fantasy and stood no chance of success whatsoever. The *Totenkopf* Division was in no condition at the moment to conduct such an attack along a 15-kilometer avenue of approach defended by at least five divisions from two enemy rifle corps.

Balck had been right about one thing, though—these *were* not the same divisions that he had gone into the Soviet Union with four years earlier. Unlike the full-strength, well-trained, and well-equipped *panzer* divisions of 1941, those he was directing in January 1945 were half-strength, filled with poorly trained recruits, without air cover, and lacking a secure supply line to provide them the munitions and fuel they needed. Unfortunately for Balck, he seemed to have regarded them to be just as capable as his forces had been in his glory days, which were now long past, but he still held them responsible when they failed to achieve his lofty objectives. However, the front-line troops would be the ones to pay the price for his unrealistic optimism, as out of place in 1945 as defeatism would have been in 1941. Still, to their credit, the German *Landser* kept fighting, if for nothing else than to rescue their comrades trapped in Budapest.

At 2 a.m. on 11 January, *Gen.d.Pz.Tr.* Wenck at *OKH* headquarters had notified the chief of staff at *H.Gr. Süd* that he had been arguing with Hitler for two hours to gain his permission to grant the authority for *Gen.d.Inf.* Wöhler to make his own decisions involving the disposition of the forces and future course of action in Budapest. His efforts were all in vain, for Hitler categorically denied Wenck's requests. Not only would Pfeffer-Wildenbruch's *IX. SS-Geb.Korps* continue defending *Festung* Budapest, but Wöhler was denied the authority to order it to withdraw to the Danube's western bank without *der Führer*'s expressed permission.

Wenck also informed von Grolman that unless Gille's attempt to reach Budapest through the Pilis Mountains succeeded quickly, it would have to regroup towards the south beginning on 12 January. When von Grolman asked him how the Budapest garrison could continue fighting when air delivery of supplies had failed, Wenck assured him that more efforts would be made to resupply, including increased use of gliders to bring in fuel and ammunition. Shortly after this conversation took place, von Grolman contacted *Gen.Maj.* Gaedke at *A.Gr. Balck/6. Armee* headquarters to give him the bad news, including reaffirming the order for Pfeffer-Wildenbruch to defend Budapest to the last round. Without the freedom of action to order the *IX. SS-Geb.Korps* to give up the eastern bank of the city—a necessary prerequisite for any link-up with the approaching relief force—or the authority to order the garrison to break out, there was little that Wöhler could do to help Balck. Hitler held all of the cards, and Gille's attack had now become a dead end, though he did not yet know this.

The order that informed him that the effort to relieve Budapest was nearing its end arrived at Gille's forward headquarters in Gran at 8:40 p.m. on 11 January, shortly before Hack's battlegroup successfully assaulted Pilisszentkereszt. This order, described as a *Führer-Entscheidung* emanating directly from Hitler's headquarters, instructed Gille to break off his attack and immediately begin moving the *IV. SS-Pz.Korps* to the area southwest of Stuhlweissenburg. Less than three hours later, bypassing *A.Gr. Balck*, Gille radioed directly to *H.Gr. Süd* at 11:40 p.m., informing its chief of staff that his troops had taken Pilisszentkereszt and were enjoying further success. He told von Grolman that he should be allowed to continue with his attack the following day and that it promised to be the best chance to rescue the city's garrison.

In response, the *H.Gr. Süd* chief of staff stated that he should begin regrouping that very evening, as he had been ordered. Gille then told him that he felt certain the advance by Ullrich's troops would shortly achieve the desired result; after that, he would have a better idea of the future chances of his mission's success. With the arrival of the rest of the *Germania* Regiment, which he (incorrectly) understood was being replaced at that moment by the *3. Kav.Brig.*, Gille argued that he would then have sufficient forces to reach his objective in three days at the latest. Von Grolman hesitated, seemingly convinced by the logic of Gille's argument, and backed off his insistence that the *IV. SS-Pz.Korps* begin moving to its new assembly area, at least for the time being. Granted a temporary reprieve, *Unternehmen Konrad II* would continue for a few more hours.

This conversation, of course, did not settle the argument, even though at that moment Gille felt certain that success lay within his grasp and that the logic of his case would finally win out. At midnight on 11 January, *H.Gr. Süd* passed on Gille's comment to *OKH*, to which Wenck replied only 30 minutes later that the *Führer* order still stood; the regrouping must go ahead. *Heeresgruppe Süd* then notified Gille directly, bypassing Balck's headquarters as well, even though this may have encouraged Gille to continue "jumping" his chain of command. This tendency of Gille's to go around the established channels, a practice frowned upon in the *Heer* but common among *Waffen-SS* senior officers, infuriated officers of the old school like Balck, but in this particular case, Balck seems to have distanced himself. Three hours after this exchange of messages, Gille's headquarters was notified that the *IV. SS-Pz.Korps* must start displacing immediately towards the Stuhlweissenburg area, beginning with the *Germania* Regiment, portions of which were still under *6. Pz.Div.* control.[46] The matter did not end there, for Gille had ordered the attack by the *Wiking* Division to continue, despite orders to the contrary, and 11 January passed into history.

While the senior commanders haggled with one another and with Hitler throughout the evening of 11 January and the early hours of the following day, Ullrich continued pressing forward with his attack. Though *K.Gr. Philipp*'s attempt to reach Budapest had been a complete failure, *K.Gr. Westland*—after consolidating its grip on Pilisszentkereszt—would resume its successful advance to the south with its *I. Bataillon* in the lead. Defeated for the moment, the troops from the Soviet 197th Rifle Regiment of the 99th Rifle Division were compelled to fall back to a blocking position 2 kilometers southeast of the town, leaving behind a large amount of weapons and equipment as well as a number of its troops taken prisoner.[47] The way ahead to Budapest appeared to be clear of the enemy; victory seemed at hand.

With Pilisszentkereszt taken, on 12 January, the *Wiking* Division's commander could now contemplate sending elements of Dorr's *Germania* Regiment as soon as they arrived in a southwesterly thrust along the road leading to the town of Pilisszántó, barely 3 kilometers away. Should the attack by the *Totenkopf* Division get underway that same day, possession of this village would enable the *Wiking* Division to link up with Becker's troops in Pilisvörösvár, 6 kilometers further to the south. *Obersturmbannführer* Hack, who had been wounded in the thigh by a grenade splinter the day before, took advantage of the relative calm after the battle while his troops mopped up to have his wound examined at the regimental dressing station.

After the splinter was removed and his leg bandaged, he briefly rested, since he had probably been awake for most of the past 48 hours. Refreshed, he made his way back to his command post several hours later. He later wrote, "I wanted to get back to my troops, for I knew that the commander of the fortified city of Budapest was *Brigadeführer* Jochen Rumohr, commander of the *8. SS-Kav.Div. Florian Geyer*, and I was very eager to do what I could to help him."[48] A *Westland* foot patrol was sent to reconnoiter the route to Pilisszántó and made it as far as the fork in the road 1.5 kilometers southwest of their own lines. The route appeared to be clear. However, this patrol unknowingly marked the farthest point that *Unternehmen Konrad II* would reach.[49]

Behind the *Wiking* Division, the *711.* and *96. Inf.Div.* continued to battle bypassed Soviet forces. Their main effort on 12 January was the big assault against Dorog, which, if allowed to remain in enemy hands, threatened the *Wiking* Division's supply lines running along the narrow corridor 5 kilometers to the east. Reinforced by *Oberst* von Bose's *Gren.Rgt. 744*, Harrendorf's troops from *Gren.Rgt. 283* and *287* at first made good headway, despite his protests that his men had insufficient time to prepare for their attack and that the deep snow hindered their movement. Although his regiments managed to once again seize the northern portion of the town, defended by the 86th Guards Rifle Division, they were unable to advance any further. Supported by the remaining tanks of the 37th Tank Brigade and the 30th Heavy Tank Regiment, the 263rd Rifle Regiment counterattacked that afternoon, driving the German troops back to their line of departure. Concerning the assault at Dorog that day, the *96. Inf.Div.* historian later commented, "It was an intense, costly day of fighting, especially for the men of *Gren.Rgt. 283*, without [the division] having achieved any success worth mentioning."[50]

In the rest of the *IV. SS-Pz.Korps* area of operations, enemy pressure appeared to have eased, though it had not ceased altogether. On 12 January, both the *Totenkopf* Division and *6. Pz.Div.* reported only localized enemy attacks, which they were able to ward off without much loss to themselves. *SS-Pz.Gren.Rgt. 6 Eicke* was able to thwart several attempts by Soviet troops to conduct armed reconnaissance along the regiment's long defense line stretching between Sarisap and Szomor. Thanks to its reinforcement by the division's reconnaissance, *Flak*, and combat engineer battalions, the *Eicke* Regiment was able to hold its ground, with ample indirect fire support provided by *SS-Pz.Art.Rgt. 3* that destroyed or dispersed Soviet attempts to attack during daylight hours.[51]

As yet, the *Totenkopf* Division most likely had no inkling of the level of indecision affecting the corps headquarters, as well as every other level of command between the field army and the *Führer's* headquarters. Although the orders had been issued the previous day for Becker's division to conduct a supporting attack towards Pilismarót in conjunction with one from the opposite direction by the *Wiking* Division, nothing seems to have come of it and it is not mentioned in any of the division's histories. Upon receipt of the order, Becker may well have laughed at its implausibility, for at that point, he would have known that his division was incapable of carrying out an attack of such magnitude. The only plausible explanation as to why the attack towards Pilismarót was even considered must be laid at the doorstep of Hermann Balck, who by this point was beginning to express an unrealistic degree of optimism bordering on fantasy. At any rate, even had Becker tried to carry out the operation, it would have been cancelled that evening anyway, at the same time the *Wiking* Division's attack was likewise called off.

On the right of the *IV. SS-Pz.Korps*, the various elements of *Korpsgruppe Breith* continued operations, though at a lower tempo than the day before. The thaw was continuing as scattered rain showers pelted the area. During the early morning, black ice on paved roadways proved a continuing hazard for motor vehicle traffic. Off-road movement was slowed considerably due to the deep mud. *Divisionsgruppe Bieber* reported no combat activity at all, except noting that its forward outposts had observed Soviet units moving in and out of their positions, signifying that some sort of relief in place was occurring. No Hungarians were reported as having deserted to the enemy that day.

In the *I. Kav.Korps* area, Harteneck's divisions continued to carry out small unit-level attacks designed to keep the enemy off-balance, particularly whenever the Soviets attempted to erect obstacles along the paved highways leading northeast out of the towns of Zámoly, Stuhlweissenburg, and Sárkeresztes. Southwest of Csakvár, an attempt by Soviet infantry, reinforced by nine tanks, to move down the highway towards Zámoly was thwarted and dispersed by the well-aimed artillery fire of the *3. Pz.Div.* On the corps' left boundary it shared with *Div.Gr. Bieber*, an enemy force was able to penetrate into the town of Csólkakő, but a counterattack mounted by the *3. Pz.Div.* in conjunction with the Hungarian *2. Pz.Div.* was able to retake it and ward off a subsequent attack. The *I. Kav.Korps* had already been notified that its headquarters would be replacing that of the *IV. SS-Pz.Korps* in Tata and would assume responsibility for the defense of the ground gained in the Vértes, Gerecse, and Pilis Mountains during *Konrad I* and *II*.

On the left flank of the *IV. SS-Pz.Korps* north of the Danube, operations in the *LVII. Pz.Korps* area of operations were considerably more dynamic. Company-sized armor engagement took place throughout the day, as the *panzers* of the 8. and 20. *Pz.Div.* tangled with the few remaining tanks available in Kravenchenko's tank army. Six T-34s were destroyed on 12 January alone by the *20. Pz.Div.* in the area north of Komaromszentpeter, while numerous other attempts to continue the sputtering Soviet counteroffensive were warded off by Kirschner's troops at Baty Kesy, Kis-Konkoly, and Ogyalla. A few battalion-sized infantry attacks were attempted at Seldin, the area north of Bart, and northwest of Gina, but except for one local penetration north of Seldin, all of the other attempts were defeated. Kirchner expected the one at Seldin to be cleared out the following day.[52]

In Budapest, *IX. SS-Geb.Korps* was notified of the *Führerbefehl* that stated there would be no withdrawal, no breakout, and no attempt to link up with an approaching relief force, and that they were expected to fight to the last bullet. The high expectations that the German and Hungarian troops had felt until this point were dashed once the news filtered down to the rank and file. At any rate, they had little time to ponder their fate, at least on the eastern bank of the Danube, which experienced unrelenting attacks against the southeastern corner of the bridgehead that led to deep penetrations in their defense line. Artillery fire and air attacks continued in an attempt to destroy the two remaining bridges over the Danube.

Just as the previous day, only a few aerial resupply missions were attempted due to the weather and increasingly strong Red Air Force patrols. A successful effort to salvage some of the supplies from the Danube steamer that had been sunk downriver the week before was carried out by a daring team of volunteers using small boats, but the amount of ammunition they brought back was barely enough to sustain the garrison for another day. Pfeffer-Wildenbruch had requested more reinforcements to be flown in, but this was turned down due to the inability of the *Luftwaffe* to land in the meadow below the castle, which was under fire during the day by Soviet artillery.[53] Soon, the garrison would have no other resources other than what it could provide itself.

However, 12 January was not yet over. Late in the afternoon, when Hack returned to his command post in Pilisszentkereszt after medical treatment, he was in for a nasty surprise:

Scarcely had I arrived back at the regiment, when I received a fresh piece of bad news through an order from *Panzer* Army [*sic*] Balck: Division *Wiking* is immediately to break off further advance; new assembly area Veszprém, further instructions follows … What can that possibly mean? What were the generals thinking of? Have all our efforts to help the hard-pressed soldiers in Budapest been in vain? We do not get an answer from anyone; head-shaking everywhere.[54]

How had the situation changed so dramatically? While Hack could be forgiven for his lack of knowledge of what was occurring behind the scenes, Gille had been actively negotiating for more time to prosecute his attack, despite the clear orders from Hitler to cease operations and move his corps. Certain that time was running out to rescue Budapest, he had been doing everything in his power to convince his chain of command to allow him to continue *Konrad II*, which he thought was on the verge of major success.

Bypassing *A. Gr. Balck/6. Armee* repeatedly throughout the day, Gille dealt directly with the *H. Gr. Süd* chief of staff in a series of exchanges in which he repeatedly implored von Grolman to keep trying to win over anyone at *OKH* to his point of view. Von Grolman spoke to Wenck, von Bonin, and even Guderian, but they all remained frustratingly unhelpful, repeating the refrain that "the *Führer* has made up his mind and cannot be persuaded otherwise." While von Grolman was sympathetic to Gille's situation, there was only so much that he could do. The only way that his argument would win out and possibly convince Hitler to allow the attack to continue was if the *Wiking* Division was able to demonstrate a noteworthy success that day. Apparently, taking Pilisszentkereszt did not meet that lofty standard.[55] Unfortunately for Gille, resistance by the 99th Rifle Division was beginning to stiffen east and southeast of Pilisszentkereszt by the late afternoon, slowing the advance of *K. Gr. Westland* to a crawl.

Earlier that day, Gille had even contacted Heinrich Himmler by telephone and asked the *Reichsführer-SS* if he could speak to Hitler directly on his behalf and beg him to allow more time for his attack to develop. Gille reminded the leader of the SS empire that an entire SS corps—after all, his own troops!—was encircled in Budapest and another one was trying to relieve it; if *Konrad II* failed and the city's garrison was lost, it would be a tremendous humiliation for the SS. Never before had such a large portion of the *Waffen-SS* been threatened with a defeat of this magnitude, an event that would have greatly lessened its prestige. If this argument could not sway the vain Himmler, nothing would.

To his credit, Himmler did try to intervene, but Hitler was still adamant—he had indulged *H. Gr. Süd* and his *OKH* staff long enough and had run out of patience. To Hitler's way of thinking, *Konrad II* stood no chance of succeeding, so the longer Gille's corps remained in the Pilis Mountains, the more it jeopardized the much larger operation that *der Führer* wanted to carry out in the south.[56] All other means of persuasion had been exhausted. Thus, the order stood: the *IV. SS-Pz.Korps* must immediately begin moving to the south and the *IX. SS-Geb.Korps* must fight to the last round.

Like Hack's, the disappointment that everyone else involved in the operation felt was immense. Even the corps commander was not immune. According to eyewitnesses, upon receipt of the order at 7 p.m., after reading it through twice, he reportedly gritted his teeth in anger and frustration.[57] Having run out of options, he had no other choice but to order that Ullrich's attack be brought to a halt. In the order he sent to the *Wiking* Division's commander, he laconically wrote:

> Command from the *6. Armee*: halt your attack immediately. Move your corps to the area north of Lake Balaton. A new attack from there towards Budapest (90 kilometers away!). And we are now standing only 18 kilometers from the city. All [of our] arguments were unsuccessful. The corps has to relocate.[58]

Others were not as reserved as the corps commander when they received their new orders. When he was notified an hour later, the *O1* of the *Wiking* Division later wrote:

> [The order passed down by *IV. SS-Pz.Korps*] was completely incomprehensible. [The] Division considers further advance on Budapest as entirely possible and promises success. A weakened and outnumbered enemy lay in front of us. Flank attacks by [enemy] tanks are not expected because of the terrain, not even possible. By following these two valleys we can storm our way to Budapest. Everyone is of the opinion that we can reach the city in another day at the most if the encircled troops break out towards us ... we made all of our arguments, the commanding general [Gille] even spoke with the *Führerhauptquartier*, but with no success. So now, in sight of the church towers of Budapest, we have to call off our attack so close to the goal that lay in front of our very eyes—safely opening the pocket and thus the relief of a large part of the encircled troops.[59]

Gille's chief of staff, Manfred Schönfelder, also expressed his opinion: "The city was about 17 kilometers ahead of our spearhead. In this situation, the order to break off the attack fell like a bomb and destroyed all hope. And it wasn't Balck who had to resist it with all his strength, but Gille." Schönfelder later expounded upon this point, stating that it was Gille who provided the motivating force to keep the attack going, following the commander's intent expressed in Balck's original order directing the *IV. SS-Pz.Korps* to carry out *Konrad II*.

But Gille's chief of staff did not stop there. In 1981, he wrote that he believed both Balck and Wöhler were responsible for the failure of the attack because it was their duty to disobey Hitler's order and allow the attack through the Pilis Mountains to continue past 12 January. After all, other senior leaders had disobeyed orders from Hitler and had achieved success, including von Manstein, Model, and even Balck himself. This may be a harsh assessment; there was no guarantee that the 46th Army would not redouble its efforts to block the *Wiking* Division (there were signs this was already occurring), and while Wöhler and Balck on their own authority could have theoretically ordered Pfeffer-Wildenbruch to launch a breakout towards them, both seemed disinclined to do so.[60]

In his own autobiography, Balck makes no mention of any inner turmoil he may have experienced when confronted with this "no-win" situation; instead, he blamed the commander of the *IV. SS-Pz.Korps* for the failure of *Konrad II*:

Gille at the time thought that a further thrust of the [corps] was impossible, only to state afterwards that he would have gone farther. Hitler finally ended our internal argument and ordered us to regroup. In this case, Hitler's intervention was appropriate.[61]

Not only is this untrue (the official records of *H. Gr. Süd* clearly shows that Gille all along was the plan's strongest and most consistent proponent), but Balck's *Order in Chaos* conceals the fact that Balck did very little to assist Gille, nor did he apparently make any attempt to persuade Hitler to change his mind. Perhaps cynically, Balck felt that neither *Konrad I* nor *Konrad II* ever stood much chance of success (after all, he did favor *Unternehmen Paula* and declared himself against *Konrad* from the beginning) and most likely wanted to avoid blame when both attempts failed. In this case, Balck successfully dodged any responsibility for his failure as a field army commander and managed to preserve his reputation, at least for a few more months.

For their part, the fighting troops in the Pilis Mountains were unaware of any of these machinations, but glumly went about their duties after they received the discouraging order to cease their attacks and begin preparing for their new assignment. *Kampfgruppe Westland* called in its patrols and began setting up a defense line in the town of Pilisszentkereszt, which would be handed over to the *711. Inf. Div.* early the following morning, 13 January. While *Gren. Rgt. 731* would hold the town as long as possible, Hack's regiment would begin withdrawing towards Gran early in the morning, beginning with supply elements. Before departing, Günther Jahnke and several of his fellow staff officers from the *Wiking* Division drove up to the peak of Dobogókó Mountain for one last look at what they believed to be the church spires of Budapest, remotely visible in the distance through the morning mist. With a sigh, they turned around and began their long journey to Veszprém.[62] *Unternehmen Konrad II*, after only four days, was over.

CHAPTER 7

Change of Mission
13–17 January 1945

While *Ogruf.* Gille and three of his five divisions (the *96.* and *711. Inf.Div.* and the *Wiking* Division) were struggling to reach Budapest through the Pilis Mountains from 9–12 January, plans to move the *IV. SS-Pz.Korps* south to Veszprém were being concurrently developed by *Gen.d.Pz.Tr.* Balck's operations staff, as alluded to in the previous chapter. By 10 January, *A.Gr. Balck/6. Armee* had already received the *Führerbefehl* from *OKH* that ordered the change in the relief operation's *Schwerpunkt* towards the south, following the outline of the original plan drawn up for *Unternehmen Paula.* As the troops engaged in *Unternehmen Konrad II* struggled against the elements as much as against the Red Army, a complex follow-on plan involving nearly every element of *A.Gr. Balck/6. Armee* positioned south of the Danube River was being crafted, independent of whether Gille's attack succeeded or not. *Heeresgruppe Süd* quickly dubbed the plan *Unternehmen Konrad III* to distinguish it from the earlier *Paula* plan.

How much of Balck's attention and intellectual energy was focused on the development of this plan at the expense of *Konrad II* is not known; what is known is that he had been in favor of the *Südlösung* or *Paula* since his arrival in Hungary three weeks before, which could explain why he had not used his much-bragged-about influence with Hitler to argue for the continuation of Gille's attack.[1] One senior member of Gille's staff asserted after the war that Balck wanted *Konrad II* to fail, which may shed light on why he did not lobby in support of Gille's urgent request to allow the *Wiking* Division to continue its push through the Pilis Mountains.[2] Indeed, the records of official communications contained in the *H.Gr. Süd* war diary for the period 9–12 January reveals that Balck's headquarters played a surprisingly passive role in the debate, leaving it up to the *H.Gr. Süd* commander to advocate for Gille's point of view; on several occasions, Gille pressed for it himself, going as far as to cajole Himmler into arguing his case directly with Hitler. Regardless of Balck's motivations, when the *IV. SS-Pz.Korps* received its new orders during the late evening of 12 January, the very same day that *Konrad II* was beginning to enjoy its first tactical success, the plan for *Unternehmen Konrad III* was already complete and had been distributed to all of the units within the *A.Gr. Balck/6. Armee* designated to take part.

Actually, three separate orders were issued on 12 January. The first was *Führerbefehl* Number 450008/45, issued earlier by the *OKH Führungsabteilung* to *H.Gr. Süd*, titled "Order for New Starting Point for the Operation," that stated, "The *Führer* has ordered that the *Schwerpunkt* of the offensive operations of the 6. *Armee* is to be shifted immediately to its right wing," followed by a brief description of the concept of the operation, troops involved, artillery support, and supporting role to be played by Kirchner's *LVII. Pz.Korps* north of the Danube.[3] This order was immediately supplemented by a more detailed warning order issued by *H.Gr. Süd* addressed to *A.Gr. Balck/6. Armee* that stated, among other things:

> The objective of the new operation is to cut off the enemy forces positioned between the Danube and the Vértes Mountains from contact with their rear area and to reestablish contact with the Budapest garrison. It is imperative to penetrate to the Danube as quickly as possible so that we can then wheel to the north to continue the attack while screening to the south ... Decisive for the success of the operation is preserving the element of surprise. For this purpose, the retention of the previous intent [i.e., *Konrad II*] is to be simulated by continuing to attack at the previous offensive points of main effort. The objectives already obtained in the attack, especially by the spearhead in the Pilis Mountains, are to be held.[4]

In essence, *Konrad II* had been relegated to the status of a deception operation meant to keep the enemy's attention focused away from where *Konrad III* was to take place, though apparently Gille was not notified of this change in the plan. The *A.Gr. Balck/6. Armee* order also provided a list of additional units that would be shipped to Hungary in order to reinforce the main effort of this attack, which would again be carried out by the *IV. SS-Pz.Korps*, including two separate tank battalions, a rocket launcher brigade, a *Sturmartillerie* (assault gun artillery) brigade, and a special flame-throwing tank company.

What was most noteworthy about this operations order was the broadened objectives of the offensive. Rather than merely reestablishing contact with Budapest and reoccupying the former *Margarethestellung* west of the city—as had been the original intent of the *Konrad I*, *Konrad II*, and *Paula* plans—the plan for *Konrad III* was far more ambitious. In addition to accomplishing the previously named objectives, the new operation was also aimed at nothing less than encircling and destroying the bulk of the Soviet forces located west of the Danube, including most of the 4th Guards and 46th Armies (see Map 6).

The identity of the person at *OKH* who tasked *H.Gr. Süd* with this additional objective is unknown, but most likely the plan was envisioned by Hitler himself after looking over the situation map in his headquarters, which would have been replete with flags showing all of the locations of German, Hungarian, and Soviet units. The front lines would have been drawn in, as with any standard situation map, and would have also shown what appeared to the naked eye to be an opportunity for an easy victory west of Budapest, with Soviet units positioned in such a way that would have made them vulnerable to a pincer attack. Guderian, in his own

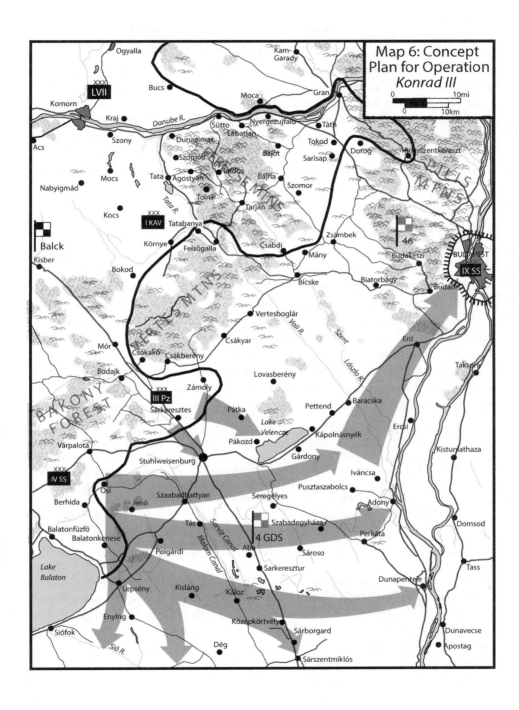

Map 6: Concept Plan for Operation *Konrad III*

memoirs, distanced himself from the plan, considering it to be "ill begotten" at best, though to be fair he was far more concerned about the Soviet winter offensive about to erupt in central Poland than events unfolding in Hungary.[5]

Taking at face value the flags on the map representing German and Hungarian armies, corps, and divisions—as he was often wont to do—Hitler would have imagined them as being full-strength organizations with the same or greater capabilities that they possessed earlier in the war. In his own memoirs, Balck—who should have known better—expressed his enthusiasm towards this alteration of the original *Paula* plan, doubtless because the *OKH* concept conformed to his own vision of the same kind of large-scale encirclement operations by armored forces that he had so often successfully carried out while commanding a *panzer* corps on the Eastern Front.

The miscalculation of ends versus the means needed to achieve all of these ambitious goals would shortly come back to haunt Balck, but when the plan was drawn up he expressed no such reservations. In fact, he later wrote in his memoir that it "was imperative for us to take advantage of every opportunity to encircle the Russian [*sic*] forces and destroy them. The relief of Budapest would only be possible after all the Russian forces had been defeated." He did state after the war that he harbored some doubts at the time, including the possibility that the attacking force might become trapped between the two Soviet armies should the offensive fail, but the actual records of *H.Gr. Süd* do not reflect his apprehension.[6]

In a letter to Hungarian author Peter Gosztony 17 years later, Gille himself reflected on the reasoning behind the unpopular decision to call off *Konrad II* and Hitler's unrealistic demand to substitute a much more ambitious objective:

> On January 10, Hitler had already decided to replace the deadlocked *Nordlösung* with the *Südlösung* and accordingly transfer the *IV. SS-Panzerkorps* to the south wing of *A.Gr. Balck*. The center of gravity—[Hitler] determined—was to be south of Lake Velencze; the further away from the previous attack point of *Gruppe Breith* [i.e.., *III. Pz.Korps*], the better. From there, it was to advance south past Stuhlweissenburg towards Budapest, together with army units. Although Generals Wöhler and Balck strongly opposed this plan, since they believed that the Budapest garrison should be relieved first [in his memoir, Balck stated the exact opposite], Hitler insisted on his idea, which he hoped would cut off the enemy forces in the Danube Bend and destroy them. The "small success" (the relief of Budapest) was probably not enough for him, and so he had to move on to the bigger blow [i.e.., the *Südlösung*].[7]

What is noteworthy in this statement is that Gille did not seek to cast blame or aspersions upon Balck or Wöhler, placing the guilt for the failure of *Konrad I* and *II* squarely where he felt (and where contemporary evidence shows) it belonged—upon Hitler. If only Balck had been able to do the same 20 years later, but he chose instead to blame a subordinate commander for the operations' failure, long after Gille had passed away.

Faced with a *fait accompli* emanating from Hitler's *Führerhauptquartier, A.Gr. Balck/6. Armee* put the finishing touches on its own order, which would be the one actually used by all of the elements of his army taking part in the upcoming operation. This order, *Ia Nummer 5/45*, was issued to the three corps concerned by midnight on 12 January. It was simply titled "Timetable, Movements, Task Organization and Attack Time for *Konrad III*." Although all of the units involved had already received their own copies of the warning order issued by *H. Gr. Süd*, they would base their own plans on that of the field army, which would exercise immediate control of the operation. All three of the German corps located south of the Danube—the *I. Kav. Korps*, *III. Pz. Korps*, and *IV. SS-Pz. Korps*—as well as the Hungarian *VIII. Armee-Korps*, would play a direct or supporting role in the attack.[8] At some point after 17 January, the attacking forces were supposed to be augmented by the *44. Reichs-Gren. Div. Hoch und Deutschmeister* (*HuD*), an experienced unit primarily composed of Austrians. A supplemental order assigning individual tasks to each of the corps participating in the operation would be issued the following day.

In its essence, the operation—scheduled to commence on 18 January, six days after the order was issued—would consist of an attack in a southeasterly direction between Lakes Balaton and Velencze by the *IV. SS-Pz. Korps*, constituting the main effort with four *panzer* divisions (*3.* and *5. SS-Pz. Div.*, and *1.* and *3. Pz. Div.*). After penetrating the main Soviet defense line between the two lakes, the corps would execute a left turn, pivoting to the northeast and orienting towards the towns of Ercsi and Rackeresztur on the west bank of the Danube, with its left flank protected by Lake Velencze . Once the spearhead reached the Danube, it would pivot once again to the north, with its right flank bounded by the Danube and its vanguard orienting on the southern outskirts of the city, where it would then establish contact with the encircled *IX. SS-Geb. Korps*.

To the left of the *IV. SS-Pz. Korps*, the *III. Pz. Korps* would conduct a supporting attack one day earlier than the main assault with the *23. Pz. Div.* and the *4. Kav. Brig.*, along with the attached Hungarian *VIII. Armee-Korps*. It would push eastwards from the area between Zámoly and Stuhlweissenburg, seize the high ground north of the latter city, and continue its advance oriented towards a point northeast of Lake Velencze, where it would link up with the left flank of Gille's corps, enabling *A. Gr. Balck/6. Armee* to destroy a substantial portion of the 4th Guards Army in the ensuing encirclement.

In the north, the *I. Kav. Korps*, assuming responsibility for the sector formerly held by the *IV. SS-Pz. Korps*, would defend the front line established during *Konrad I* and *II* and tie down as many of the Soviets' reserves as possible using the *6. Pz. Div.*, *3. Kav. Brig.*, *96. Inf. Div.*, *711. Inf. Div.*, and *K. Gr. Bundesmann*. On the right of *IV. SS-Pz. Korps*, a *Kampfgruppe* composed of the reconnaissance battalions from the *1.*, *3.*, and *23. Pz. Div.* (later augmented by the Hungarian *25. Inf. Div.*) would screen Gille's exposed southern flank and provide early warning of any counter reaction by Soviet forces, though this decision did deprive the *panzer* divisions of their accustomed "eyes and ears." *Luftflotte 4* would continue to provide both air support for the attack and aerial resupply of the Budapest garrison, and would even attempt to achieve local air superiority. Upon receipt of this order on 12 January, units in both *I. Kav. Korps* and *III. Pz.Korps* began positioning for their new mission, even while *K.Gr. Hack* was still consolidating its gains in the wake of its seizure of Pilisszentkereszt.

For the impending operation, in addition to the divisions described above, the *IV. SS-Pz.Korps* would be reinforced by *s.Pz.Abt. 509, I. Abt./Pz.Rgt. 24* (with *Pz. V* Panthers), the three aforementioned *Panzer-Aufklärungs Abteilungen, StuG-Abt. 303, Sturm-Pz.Abt. 219, Volks-Art.Korps 403*, and *Volks-Werfer Brig. 17*, along with additional *Heerestruppen* such as engineer, *Flak*, and rear area security battalions. Although not mentioned in the order, the move of Gille's corps to the Veszprém area would require it to disconnect from its previous logistical support establishment centered in the Komorn–Raab–Acs area, where its units drew their rations, fuel, and ammunition, and establish new connections with other *6. Armee* logistical units located in the area north of Lake Balaton.

Most of the corps and division field hospitals would remain for the time being in Komorn and Raab, though field dressing stations and ambulance companies would relocate to the Veszprém area by 18 January. The *1.* and *3. Pz.Div.*, since no movement was required of either of them, would continue relying on their already established logistical relationships. In addition, the *3. Pz.Div.* would be pulled out of the line near Zámoly at the same time and sent to the Várpalota area to carry out a hasty reconstitution in order to restore a semblance of its combat power in time for *Konrad III*. The *4. Kav.Brig.* would assume responsibility for the *3. Pz.Div.* sector by extending its lines to the north.

The continuation of the Budapest relief operation would place even greater demands on the *6. Armee* logistics infrastructure than it was already experiencing. The severing of the railroad line between Neuhäusel and Komorn north of the Danube forced trains to take a roundabout journey that extended the time it normally took by at least a day, causing a ripple effect that not only delayed train schedules, but also slowed deliveries of supplies to forward units. Shortage of cargo trucks, weather conditions that made road movement hazardous, and fuel shortages all contributed to the already strained logistics situation. To add to the shortages in nearly every category of supply, the enormous expenditure of artillery ammunition on 9 and 10 January by all units of *A.Gr. Balck* (2,370 metric tons, equivalent to 2,612 short tons), created a one-day shortfall in this category of ammunition that could not be made good until the rail network could be fully restored.[9]

Another category of supply that would affect *Konrad III* (and subsequent operations) was the increasingly constrained supply of gasoline, vital for an army so dependent upon its mobility for battlefield success. After 10 January, the *Oberquartiermeister* of the *6. Armee* could no longer guarantee the minimum amount of gasoline required to fuel all of the army's combat fighting vehicles, estimated to be 320 cubic meters (84,535 gallons) a day. Even wood needed to fuel the 450 trucks powered by wood-gas generators was in short supply, forcing a number of these badly needed cargo vehicles to be immobilized until the specially cut wood could be obtained. The Soviet advance north of the Danube from 5–10 January had also sidelined the small oil refineries at Szöny and Füzitö, now vulnerable to artillery fire from the opposite bank of the river.

The 6. *Armee Oberquartiermeister* had established an ambitious goal of building up to a two-fold *Verbrauchsatz*, or basic load of fuel, before *Konrad III* began. This equaled the minimal amount needed to sustain a *panzer* division for a full day of movement, estimated to be the equivalent of driving 161 kilometers.[10] However, for the reasons already listed, attaining a gasoline stockpile of this magnitude would prove to be nearly impossible. All of these unanticipated events contributed to the worsening supply situation for the month of January, adding an extra sense of urgency to the operation, not to mention the knowledge of the dwindling ability of the encircled forces in Budapest, whose time was running out, to supply their own combat troops. *A.Gr. Balck/6. Armee* issued several orders concerning the need to economize on fuel, including a requirement to park all motor vehicles not specifically needed for the upcoming attack, though this would not have amounted to more than a trickle of fuel saved in comparison to what was needed. Still, every liter of fuel saved was another liter to keep the *panzers* running a little longer.[11]

A report submitted by the *Oberquartiermeister*, dated 11 January, did not go into any detail concerning how the addition of the *IV. SS-Pz.Korps* and its two *panzer* divisions to the already strained logistics infrastructure north of Lake Balaton would be remedied; apparently, this was covered in a subsequent order.[12] Nevertheless, *Konrad III* would be conducted on a logistical shoestring, the knowledge of which undoubtedly influenced the thinking of all the commanders involved. In addition to Balck's orders to conserve fuel, *H.Gr. Süd* called for the implementation of even more stringent economizing measures, including limiting movement of motor vehicles unless absolutely necessary. For a field army composed primarily of *panzer* divisions completely reliant on gasoline and diesel fuel for their every move, as opposed to one composed chiefly of horse-drawn infantry divisions, this was a drastic measure indeed. In contrast, the Red Army would have no such problems—its troops, tanks, and guns would have everything they needed in abundance when the German attack began.

While Gille's own *Quartiermeister*, *Ostubaf.* Hans Scharf, was forced to wrestle with the logistical implications of the *Unternehmen Konrad III* operations plan and the development of his own supporting plan, the corps' *Führungsabteilung*—led by *Ostubaf.* Schönfelder and *Stubaf.* Klose—would have conducted the mission analysis to identify the specific and implied tasks inherent in the order, simultaneously having to direct the continuation of *Konrad II*, which until the evening of 12 January they still believed to be an ongoing affair.[13] The supplement to the operations plan for *Konrad III*, issued by *H.Gr. Süd* at 3:25 p.m. the following day, provided additional detailed guidance for each of the corps involved.

The mission order provided to the *IV. SS-Pz.Korps* was very specific, though it did allow Gille some latitude in exercising his commander's discretion in carrying out his assignment. The paragraph describing specified tasks for each major unit, titled *Ansatz der Kräfte*, stated that on 18 January 1945,

a): *IV. SS-Pz.Korps* attacks to the east from the sector of the *1. Pz.Div.* to initially establish bridgeheads across the Sárviz Canal, with the *5. SS-Pz.Div. Wiking* at Sárkeresztur–Aba, with the *3. SS-Pz.Div. Totenkopf* on both sides of Fövenyipuszta and the *1. Pz.Div.* south of Stuhlweissenburg. The right flank of the assault forces is to be covered by attacks by *Pz.Aufkl.Abt. 1, 3,* and *23* to take the Sió Canal between Lake Balaton and Simontornya. The *4. Kav.Brig.* will follow up behind the main effort (the *3.* and *5. SS-Pz.Div.*) to give infantry support to the attack and eliminate remaining nests of enemy resistance [note: as events were to reveal, the *4. Kav.Brig.* was relieved of this task before the offensive began].

b): The attack by the *III. Pz.Korps* is intended to be conducted one day in advance of the main effort described above with the massed forces of the *3. Pz.Div.* and the *23. Pz.Div.* to capture the high ground north of Stuhlweissenburg.

c): Continuation of the attack of the *IV. SS-Pz.Korps* to the northeast after passing to the south of Lake Velencze : the *5. SS-Pz.Div.* and the *3. SS-Pz.Div.* in the area of Ercsi–Rackeresztur and the *1. Pz.Div.* in the area of Baraczka.[14]

With this information in hand, Schönfelder and Klose could then begin determining individual specified and implied tasks for each division, including *Ablauflinie* (phase lines), *Zwischenziele und Angriffsziele* (intermediate and final objectives), *Angriffsachse* (avenues of approach), and the other myriad details involved in conducting operations with a force now consisting of four divisions and at least 60,000 men.

In the limited time available, they would also have war-gamed various courses of action to achieve their objectives, determine priorities of support for artillery fire, logistics (in cooperation with Scharf and his *Quartiermeister* staff), where to designate main supply routes, and how best to integrate the limited amount of *Luftwaffe* close air support into the overall scheme of maneuver. Having received this order on 13 January shortly after midnight, Gille's staff would then have five days to develop and issue one of their own, which followed the standard format outlined in the pertinent *Heer* doctrinal manuals and would have been issued in sufficient time to allow the individual divisions to develop their own operations orders. To ensure rapid transmission of the corps order's details as they were being developed, liaison officers from each division would make frequent visits to the corps' *Führungsabteilung* to glean whatever information they could from the *Ia* or *O1* so they could further refine their own plans. Dispatch riders would also have been employed to deliver copies of orders and maps produced by the corps *Kartenstelle* to the units involved.

The supplemental order 5/45, issued by *A.Gr. Balck/6. Armee* on 12 January, also designated new assembly areas for the units of the *IV. SS-Pz.Korps* when they arrived in their new area of operations, as well as the unit movement schedule. First, the corps *Hauptquartier* would begin moving on 13 January and would displace to a wooded area near Balatonfüzfő, a village located on the shore of Lake Balaton 10 kilometers east-southeast of the city of Veszprém, where it would become operational the following day. The *Wiking* and *Totenkopf* Divisions would move into their designated assembly areas in the region between the town of Zirc and Veszprém between 13 January and the evening of 16/17 January, with their headquarters in Balatonalmádi and Hajmáskér, respectively.

These actions would require both divisions and corps troops to move by road and rail; the average road distance from Tata to Veszprém was 100 kilometers, and from Gran to Veszprém was over 150 kilometers, most of it along ice- and snow-covered roads. Movement by rail would require a trip of over 200 kilometers, though it would take less time to cover the distance. Units whose armored vehicles were too far away from railroad yards would have to drive to Veszprém, risking mechanical breakdown. The shortest rail movement from Komorn to Veszprém would take four hours in peacetime, though in January 1945 that same journey would take twice as long, having to go through the rail nexus at Raab. The *1.* and *3. Pz.Div.*, since they were already located in the area, would remain where they were. All four divisions were to be ready to initiate their attacks on the morning of 18 January.

The termination of *Konrad II* and the issuing of instructions ordering a change of mission for the *IV. SS-Pz.Korps* were not the only major events occurring on 12 January. In the Ardennes, the *Wacht am Rhein* offensive (the battle of the Bulge) had run its course and the Western Allies were preparing a counteroffensive of their own to restore the front line and destroy any German forces trapped in the ensuing attempt to encircle *G.F.M.* Model's *H.Gr. B*. In Alsace-Lorraine, the *Nordwind* offensive—which was launched by *Gen.O.* Blaskowitz's *H.Gr. G* with 17 divisions on 31 December 1944—was close to reaching its own culminating point, though the fighting would continue until 25 January with little to show for the heavy losses suffered by Blaskowitz's forces. The Allied bombing campaign against German cities continued unabated, which the new wonder weapons, including the jet-powered *Me-262* fighter, were unable to stop.

But the most important event of 12 January, one that cast the others into the shadows, was the initiation of the long-anticipated and much-feared Soviet winter offensive. Codenamed the Vistula-Oder Operation, five Soviet army groups—from north to south, the Third, Second, and First Belorussian Fronts, and the First and Fourth Ukrainian Fronts—attacked along a nearly 800-kilometer front stretching from Königsberg in the north to the Carpathian Mountains in the south. Erupting from the bridgeheads at Magnuszew, Puławy, and Sandomierz/Baranov, the two leading army groups—Marshal Zhukov's First Belorussian Front and Marshal Konev's First Ukrainian Front—spearheaded by four tank armies, quickly blasted through the thinly manned German defenses and completely unhinged the entire defensive framework of *H.Gr. Mitte* and *H.Gr. A*.

With a 3.9 to 1 superiority in troops, 3.4 to 1 in artillery, and 4.7 to 1 in armor, the 2.2 million troops, 6,464 tanks, and 46,000 artillery pieces in the two attacking Fronts forming the Red Army's main effort simply obliterated German front-line defenses erected by the *9.*, *17.*, and *4. Pz.Armee*.[15] The "Wet Triangle," defended by the *IV. SS-Pz.Korps* for three months during the previous autumn, was abandoned with hardly a fight. Poland's capital city, retaken from the *Armia Krajowa* at such great cost during the Warsaw Uprising, was given up by 15 January, despite its status as a *Festung* that required it to be defended to the last man. What Guderian had foretold on 9 January had come to pass with a vengeance; when pushed hard, the entire Eastern Front began collapsing like a house of cards.[16] From this point onwards, nearly all of Guderian's efforts were directed towards stopping the Soviet offensive and rebuilding a semblance of a front line. Any diversion of forces to other fronts, including Hungary, he saw as pointless.

Incredibly, Hitler did not fully share Guderian's concern. Guderian wanted to pull *SS-Oberstgruf.* Sepp Dietrich's *6. Pz.Armee* out of the Ardennes, where its attack had failed, and send it to the Eastern Front. Though Hitler recognized that the Soviet Vistula–Oder offensive posed an existential threat to the Third Reich unless brought to a halt, he still coveted the Hungarian oil fields even more. Rather than sending Dietrich's army to where it was most desperately needed, he indicated his desire to ship it to Hungary instead, where it would spearhead yet another offensive designed to retake Budapest and safeguard the oil fields. Despite Guderian's entreaties and protests, Hitler would insist that his own plan be carried out, ignoring the advice of his most experienced and talented *panzer* commander. Thus, the stage was set for the debacle that would unfold over the next six weeks, which would not end until the Red Army had reached the banks of the Oder River less than 100 kilometers from Berlin.

None of this was known by the men of the *IV. SS-Pz.Korps* at the time, though as the days went by, the periodic *Wehrmachtbericht* began to mention the names of towns thought to be safely within Germany's borders that were now in the front line, a sign that the Soviet juggernaut was relentlessly rolling westwards. The corps and division commanders, staffs, and troops were far too busy preparing for their new mission to take much notice anyway; much work remained to be done before they could begin their attack on 18 January. One of the most important tasks looming before the corps on 12 January was to extricate all of the corps' units, primarily the *3.* and *5. SS-Pz.Div.*, from the front lines between Csabdi, Zsámbék, and Gran, and get them moving to the west and then south while turning over their positions to the incoming *3. Kav.Brig.* or adjacent units already holding ground in the area.

All of the movement from the north to the south would be accomplished during evening hours in order to maintain operational security. Movement of other forces, such as the *3. Kav.Brig.*, from the south to the north would be conducted during daylight hours to deceive Soviet intelligence into believing that these signified additional reinforcements being sent in support of *Konrad II*. Because the *Hauptquartier* of the *IV. SS-Pz.Korps* was required to be operational in its new location by the morning of 14 January, command and control of the *Totenkopf* and *Wiking* Divisions during their relief in place would be temporarily exercised by *Gen.d.Kav.* Harteneck's *I. Kav.Korps*, which would move from Isztimér on 13 January in order to take over the forward command post in Tata currently occupied by Gille's corps.[17] Once Becker's and Ullrich's divisions had departed the area and arrived in their new locations north of Lake Balaton, they would once more revert to the control of the *IV. SS-Pz.Korps*.

While the Soviet winter offensive began to gather momentum hundreds of kilometers to the north and the *OKH* scrambled to seal off the enormous holes being torn in the front lines of *H.Gr. Mitte* and *H.Gr. A*, the period between 13 and 17 January witnessed the movement of the *IV. SS-Pz.Korps*, its two SS divisions, and other units into the Veszprém area, taking over responsibility for the defensive sector held by the *1. Pz.Div.*, which would be aligned under Gille's order of battle. Following the movement instructions detailed in the supplementary order issued during the late evening of 12 January, the first unit affected was the *3. Kav. Brig.*, which began moving into the Tata area on the night of 12/13 January from its former positions southwest of Lake Balaton, where it had been fighting with the *2. Pz.Armee* since the end of November 1944.[18]

This veteran brigade, commanded by *Oberst* Peter von der Groeben, would relieve the *Totenkopf* Division, allowing Becker and his troops to withdraw and prepare for their movement to the south. Composed of two *Reiter* (mounted infantry) regiments of two battalions each, the *3. Kav.Brig.* would bring an artillery regiment (*Art.Rgt. 869*), an antitank battalion with 24 assault guns and tank destroyers, an armored reconnaissance battalion, and other brigade troops, making it nearly the size of a *panzer* division, though lacking tanks. Reporting a respectable *Kampfstärke* of 2,148 men on 13 January, it would move into the Vértes Mountains and take up the defensive positions of the *Totenkopf* Division, replacing it sequentially over the next several days.

Reportedly, *Brig.Fhr.* Becker had been just as surprised to get the news to withdraw to Veszprém as his compatriot Ullrich had been at Pilisszentkereszt on 12 January. According to *Standartenoberjunker* (officer candidate) Peter Renold, a platoon leader in *II. Btl./SS-Pz.Gren.Rgt. 5 Totenkopf*, Becker learned about the new orders to pull his division out during a visit to the *II. Bataillon* command post near Szomor on 13 January. Renold, who was on the scene, said the telephone rang while Becker was speaking to the battalion commander, *Stubaf.* Christian Bachmann. It was the division headquarters with the news about the order from *A.Gr. Balck/6. Armee* that had just been passed on by *IV. SS-Pz.Korps*. Upon hearing the news, Becker immediately launched into an "unforgettable angry outburst" concerning the regrouping. After regaining his composure, he gave the order, "Back to the old staging area!"[19]

Per the same order, the *Germania* Regiment of the *Wiking* Division, since it was the closest regiment to the railroad yard in Tata, would also begin moving out during the evening of 12/13 January. All but one battalion of Dorr's regiment had already been relieved in the line by the *6. Pz.Div.*, and most of his men were en route to Gran when he received his new orders at the regimental command post at Vasztély. The battalion located northeast of Csabdi would be temporarily held back until relieved by a battalion from the *3. Kav.Brig.*[20] Portions of the regiment that had already reached the Tokod area to support *Konrad II* would have to turn about and rejoin the rest of the regiment at a temporary assembly area west of Nagyigmánd, using the road running along the southern bank of the Danube. That same evening, the *Westland* Regiment would disengage from the Pilisszentkereszt area and hand over its positions to *Gren.Rgt. 731* of the *711. Inf.Div.* in order to begin its own displacement to an assembly area west of Gran during the evening.[21]

During the night of 13/14 January, the rest of the *Wiking* Division would be relieved, as well as roughly half of the *Totenkopf* Division, by the *3. Kav.Brig.* A portion of Becker's artillery regiment and other division heavy weapons would be temporarily held back until all of the *3. Kav.Brig.* heavy weapons had arrived, thus guaranteeing continuous artillery, *Flak*, and antitank support throughout the conduct of the relief in place. By the morning of 14 January, all of the *Germania* Regiment was supposed to have arrived by a road march at its new assembly area north of Veszprém. That same evening, the *Westland* Regiment would begin its movement to Nagyigmánd using the river road from the area west of Gran.

According to the movement order, the rest of the *Totenkopf* Division—except one *Panzergrenadier* battalion—would be withdrawn the following day, leaving the *3. Kav.Brig.* in control of its former defensive sector. *Obersturmbannführer* Hack's *Westland* Regiment, after departing Nagyigmánd, would arrive by the end of the day in the division's assembly area near Zirc, while the remainder of the *Wiking* Division and the lead elements of the *Totenkopf* Division would arrive in the area that the *Westland* Regiment had just vacated. The following evening of 15/16 January, the rest of the *Totenkopf* and *Wiking* Divisions would depart the Nagyigmánd area and travel by road to their respective assembly areas to the south. The remaining battalions under the temporary control of the *3. Kav.Brig.* would finally be relieved in the line on 16 January and be allowed to rejoin their regiments near Zirc and Veszprém. By the evening of 16/17 January, if all went according to plan, both divisions would be completely assembled and back under the control of *IV. SS-Pz.Korps*, ready to begin the attack the following morning.

One unit of the *Wiking* Division ordered to withdraw from the front lines during this time was *Ostubaf.* Fritz Darges's *Panzergruppe* from *SS-Pz.Rgt. 5*, which until 12 January was still defending an isolated position within the Hegyks Castle Estate. By this point, its *II. Abteilung* had already departed, leaving only the regimental headquarters and the few remaining vehicles of the *I. Abteilung*, along with *Stubaf.*

Fritz Vogt's depleted *I. Btl./Norge*, to hold this critical position. With a portion of the *Germania* Regiment having already departed and the remainder preparing to leave, there was no longer any reason for staying, since the commander of the *6. Pz.Div.* saw no point in continuing to hold the cratered and shell-riddled ruin, isolated as it was beyond the division's forward defenses arrayed between Csabdi and Mány.

Connected to the *6. Pz.Div.* only by a tenuous supply line in an old sunken road running through no-man's land between Mány and Bicske that could only be traversed at night, Darges and Vogt made the joint decision to pull out that evening. Loading up the regiment's wounded aboard some trucks and the two remaining operational *Pz. IVs*, including the injured *Hstuf.* Willi Hein who was seated in his own command tank, the group managed to slip between the Soviet cordon surrounding their position. After a few hours, they made it back to the command post of the *Germania* Regiment in the village of Vasztély, where Darges, Vogt, and Hein were personally greeting by Hans Dorr.

Their escape had not been without incident; one captured Soviet GMC truck loaded with some of the regiment's wounded was destroyed by a round fired by an enemy antitank gun, killing everyone aboard.[22] A sapper platoon stayed behind to destroy the remaining tanks that could not be repaired and blow up what was left of the castle, before making their own way back to Vasztély. Darges and the other exhausted survivors were instructed to move to Tata and begin preparing their vehicles for movement to Veszprém; Willi Hein was sent to the division's field hospital in Komorn to have his leg wound treated and never actively served again, spending the rest of the war recovering in a hospital. Vogt and his decimated battalion were instructed to remain in the Csabdi area under the temporary control of the *3. Kav.Brig.*[23] Thus, the epic defense of the Hegyks Castle "fort" by the *Unbeugsamen* (the unbreakable ones) faded from the pages of history and passed immediately into *Waffen-SS* legend.

Conducted at night, the movement of both divisions from the front lines between Bicske and Gran proceeded without interference from the enemy, except for random bombing by Soviet aircraft that usually missed their target. Road conditions, fatigue, darkness, and weather combined to make the trip hazardous. Traffic accidents were frequent, as long lines of vehicles struggled to make their way north without adequate lighting due to blackout conditions. Inoperable vehicles would have been towed out of the temporary repair yards set up in division rear areas to be repaired once they arrived in Veszprém. Some vehicles slid off the road and into ditches or ravines and were abandoned, especially in the Gerecse Mountains. Heavily burdened infantry marched along rutted roads, often calf-deep in mud or slush.

Often wet, exhausted, and always cold, the men struggled on as best they could. Rest stops were set up along the movement routes to provide the troops respite, with the issue of hot coffee and food, as harried *Feldgendarmes* struggled to maintain control of traffic. Wounded troops who would recover from their injuries within two or three weeks were evacuated from division field dressing stations to hospitals in the corps or army rear areas until they were well enough to rejoin their units. Those who would not, like Willi Hein, were sent back to hospitals in the Reich. Tracked vehicles—especially tanks, assault guns, and tank destroyers—were supposed to be loaded on trains in Komorn or Raab, but the shortage of special rail cars designed to carry heavy vehicles limited the number of trains bound to Veszprém to two each day, a factor that virtually guaranteed it would take at least five days to move all of both divisions' armor.[24]

The first armored vehicles from the *Totenkopf* Division arrived at the railyard at Komorn to begin loading on the evening of 13 January. To their dismay, the crews from *SS-Pz.Jäg.Abt. 3* discovered that the rail cars positioned there had a load capacity of only 15 tons, far less than what was required to transports tanks, assault guns, and tank destroyers, most of which weighed 30 tons or more. The railway personnel told them that only two trains a day with the proper railcars were available to move the entire corps.[25]

The division commander, upon learning of the situation, decided to send most of his armored fighting vehicles to Veszprém via a 100-kilometer circular route that followed the highway linking the towns of Nagyigmánd, Bana, and Gyorszadhegy, and then along the road leading through the steep hills of the Bakony Forest through Varsany–Bakonyszentkiraly–Oszlop–Veszprém before finally terminating at Zirc.[26] Consequently, a large number of the *Totenkopf* Division's tanks and other armored vehicles fell out during the two-day march due to mechanical problems or lack of fuel, forcing the maintenance company of *SS-Pz.Rgt. 3* to tow them to their final destination, where they would be repaired if possible or refueled on the spot. By 17 January, most of the regiment had reached its assembly area near Zirc, but late-arriving vehicles and crews had less than 24 hours to prepare for the demanding offensive operation scheduled for the following day.

Operational security was enhanced by an order issued by *A.Gr. Balck/6. Armee* on 12 January directing all of the units involved in the movement to conceal their identity by covering up their vehicles' license plates or division insignia that would have made it easy for Soviet agents to identify their particular SS division or regiment, including SS division cuff titles. Apparently, this order was not being obeyed uniformly, as *Gen.d.Inf.* Wöhler learned to his disappointment when he visited *Gen.d.Pz.Tr.* Balck's headquarters during the morning of 14 January.[27] Wöhler took Balck to task over this apparently widespread infraction, after he had seen with his own eyes SS vehicles moving on the roads still sporting their division insignia. He also spotted numerous vehicles from virtually every unit in the *IV. SS-Pz.Korps* and *III. Pz.Korps* driving about with uncovered license plates. This led to another order being issued the following day directing the field police and *Streifendienst* units responsible for traffic regulation to stop any vehicle or individual in violation of this order and direct them to camouflage their vehicle's plates or tactical insignia on the spot.[28]

Despite the best efforts of Becker and Ullrich's men to conceal their withdrawal and movement to Veszprém, Soviet troops on the opposite side of the Danube were able to observe their departure, especially along the river road leading from Gran to Komorn. This portion of the highway lay under the very noses of troops from the 6th Guards Tank Army located on the opposite bank less than 1 kilometer away. Although they would not be able to directly observe the movement of German troops in the darkness, they would have heard it, especially when large numbers of armored vehicles were involved. The sound of tank treads would have carried for long distances; the direction of movement could also be inferred simply by following the sound's change of direction. German and Hungarian prisoners, as well as a handful of deserters, had also revealed to their Red Army captors that the SS corps was being relieved and headed west.[29] Despite the best efforts of their pilots, Soviet aerial reconnaissance could not confirm the transfer of the corps, due to inclement weather that made it nearly impossible to see what was happening on the ground.

Fortunately for Gille's corps, Soviet intelligence drew the wrong conclusion, based on the little evidence they were able to glean. Rather than suspecting that the movement signified the corps' relocation to Veszprém, their intelligence organs logically concluded that the *IV. SS-Pz.Korps* was being pulled out and sent north via Komorn and Raab to reinforce *H.Gr. A* or *H.Gr. Mitte*, then involved in the early stages of countering the Vistula–Oder offensive or to prepare the defense of Berlin. The fact that this movement signified merely a continuation of the relief attempt of Budapest does not seem to have occurred to them. Therefore, while Balck's forces were unable to maintain strict operational security, they could still deceive the Third Ukrainian Front sufficiently to ensure that *Unternehmen Konrad III* would achieve the element of surprise when it began on 18 January.[30]

The *OKH* actually did consider sending Gille and his two divisions to reinforce *Gen.O.* Harpe's *H.Gr. A*. At 11 p.m. on 14 January, *Gen.d.Pz.Tr.* Wenck, chief of the *OKH Führungsabteilung*, contacted the chief of staff of *H.Gr. Süd* by telephone to enquire whether the *IV. SS-Pz.Korps* could be spared to help relieve the Soviet pressure being exerted on the neighboring army group. Wenck reminded *Gen.Lt.* von Grolman that his army group, on paper at least, was the strongest one on the Eastern Front and implied that it could afford to spare a corps for employment elsewhere. Von Grolman responded that the only way that *Gen.d.Inf.* Wöhler could accede to such a demand would be if Hitler gave the army group commander permission to exercise local command authority over the encircled Budapest garrison, which would enable Wöhler to issue an order to break out and abandon the city. Wenck told him he would consult with Guderian and call back.

Four hours later, the *OKH* notified *H.Gr. Süd* that it could keep Gille's corps, but Hitler had not yet decided whether to grant Wöhler the authority over Budapest that he requested (and the situation demanded). Three days later, the *OKH* called *H. Gr. Süd* once again, notifying Wöhler and his staff that it had still not settled the matter of whether to withdraw the *IV. SS-Pz.Korps* and to order the army group to cancel *Konrad III* altogether. If this plan was carried out, Gille would have had to turn his corps around and order his divisions to drive their wheeled vehicles north to Pressburg (modern-day Bratislava) by road while moving their armored vehicles by rail from Raab.

Apparently, Guderian had not given up his attempts to gather forces to stop the Soviet winter offensive, but his efforts in this particular instance were in vain (his own memoir makes no mention of this incident). At 6:25 p.m. that same day, *H. Gr. Süd* received the message from *OKH* that the *Führer* had ordered that the "Field army-group [i.e., *A. Gr. Balck/6. Armee*] would carry out the orders issued for the coming attack."[31] Instead, both the *8.* and *20. Pz.Div.*, still operating north of the Danube against the shattered 6th Guards Tank Army, would be sent to aid *H. Gr. A* and their place taken by an infantry division. Thus, the *IV. SS-Pz.Korps* would remain where it was and *Konrad III* would proceed on schedule.[32]

Between 13 and 17 January, over 35,000 men from the *IV. SS-Pz.Korps* laboriously made their way out of the Gerecse and Pilis Mountains, where they had been fighting for the past two weeks, to their new assembly areas around Veszprém, leaving a trail of broken-down vehicles along the way to mark their passage. By 15 January, all of the corps' *Hauptquartier* and *SS-Nachr.Abt. 104* had arrived, as well as all of *SS-Werf.Abt. 504* and one of the corps' transportation companies. Most of the *Totenkopf* Division had arrived, though two *Panzergrenadier* battalions from the *Eicke* Regiment were still en route, as well as one battalion from the *Panzergrenadier* Regiment *Totenkopf* and three of its artillery battalions left behind until the relief in place by the *3. Kav.Brig.* was complete. On 15 January, its *panzer* regiment reported 42 operational vehicles, including 10 *Pz. IV*s, seven *Pz. V* Panthers, four *Pz. VI* Tiger Is, and 15 *StuG*s. The division's tank-destroyer battalion, *SS-Pz.Jag.Abt. 3*, reported six combat-ready *Jg.Pz. IV/L48*s, thus giving the division a total of 42 combat-ready tanks, assault guns, and tank destroyers.[33]

The *Wiking* Division, although it had farther to travel, had almost completely arrived in its assembly areas by 15 January, lacking only two battalions from the *Westland* Regiment, still making their way back from Gran. *Obersturmbannführer* Darges's *SS-Pz.Rgt. 5* had not yet been joined by its *I. Abteilung* and its three operational *Pz. IV*s, though all of the Panther-equipped *II. Abteilung* had arrived, bringing with it only eight *Pz. V*s, of which five were operational. Only two *Jagd.Pz. IV*s were combat ready, out of 13 on hand; thus, on 15 January, the division had only 10 operational armored fighting vehicles. Many other non-operational tanks and other armored vehicles were in repair yards located in Tata or south of Komorn and would straggle into the Veszprém area after the offensive had begun. On that same day, only one of *SS-Pz.Art.Rgt. 5*'s artillery battalions was still on the road moving to its assembly area.

Two days later, all of the *Korpstruppen* were present, but some elements of the corps' two divisions were still absent, placing them in danger of not arriving in time before *Konrad III* began the following day. The *III. Btl./SS-Pz.Gren.Rgt. 5 Totenkopf* was still occupying its positions north of Zsámbék under the control of the *3. Kav. Brig.*, as was *II. Abt./SS-Pz.Art.Rgt. 3*. In addition, a more accurate count of the division's non-operational tanks in repair status was taken, which amounted to 16 *Pz. IV*s, 14 *Pz. V* Panthers, 11 *Pz. VI* Tigers, 12 *StuG*s, and five *Jg.Pz. IV*s, a total of 58 non-operational armored fighting vehicles that would soon be badly needed.

The *Wiking* Division still lacked half of its *panzer* regiment's remaining tanks; on the evening of 17 January, it reported only seven operational *Pz. IV*s, 12 *Pz. V* Panthers, and seven *StuG*s, a total of 26 armored fighting vehicles, barely enough to equip a single tank company and a far cry from the number it was authorized. All of the division's other elements had either arrived or were on the road and expected to arrive by the evening of 17 January. The only exception was *I. Btl./Danmark* and *I. Btl./Norge*, which were still in Tata. The *I. Btl./Danmark* had been attached to the *6. Pz.Div.* since 10 January and would not be able to rejoin the *IV. SS-Pz.Korps* until 21 January, three days after the offensive had already begun. Both battalions would serve as the *IV. SS-Pz.Korps'* reserve during the initial stages of the operation (see Appendix B, Selected Orders of Battle).

In regards to the armored fighting vehicle situation in the *1. Pz.Div.*, it was in relatively good shape. On 17 January, *Gen.Maj.* Thünert's *panzer* regiment could muster 12 operational *Pz. IV*s, 35 *Pz. V* Panthers, and 11 assault guns and tank destroyers, for a total of 58 out of 87 assigned. *Oberstleutnant* Philipp had been released from his assignment as commander of the *Kampfgruppe* bearing his name that had attempted the ill-fated *Husarenritt* along the Danube east of Gran, and was able to resume command of his regiment, *Pz.Rgt. 1*. The *3. Pz.Div.* also had a significant number of operational armored fighting vehicles on hand, including 21 *Pz. IV*s, 27 *Pz. V* Panthers, and 19 assault guns, a total of 67 out of 95 assigned.

Though the available number of SS *panzers* was hardly encouraging, the overall armor strength of the *IV. SS-Pz.Korps* would improve with the attachment of the two separate tank battalions previously mentioned—*s.Pz.Abt. 509* (Tiger IIs) with 45 heavy tanks and the still-arriving *I. Abt./Pz.Rgt. 24* (Panthers) with 14 tanks initially—as well as the 45 *StuG III/IV* assault guns assigned to the newly reconstituted *Sturm-Art.Brig. 303*.[34] A tally of German armor conducted on 17 January on the eve of the offensive revealed that the *IV. SS-Pz.Korps*, serving as the main effort, would begin *Konrad III* with a total of 483 tanks, assault guns, tank destroyers, and SP antitank guns, of which 311 were considered to be operational, including 46 *Pz. VI* Tiger I and IIs (of 56 assigned).

On the other hand, the *III. Pz.Korps*, serving in the role of the supporting effort on Gille's left, was a relatively weak armored force. The *23. Pz.Div.* and the *4. Kav. Brig.* reported a total of only 45 operational armored fighting vehicles out of 122 on hand, including only two operational *Pz. VI* Tiger IIs in the attached *s.Pz.Abt. 503 FHH* (out of 13 assigned). Soviet records dating from the same time assessed that the *III. Pz.Korps* and *IV-SS Panzer Korps* had a combined strength of 644 available tanks, assault guns, and tank destroyers (including some Hungarian tanks), roughly equal to the German count, though the Red Army generally counted every enemy armored vehicle as being operational. Thus, they believed the Germans were nearly twice as strong in available armor as they actually were.[35]

What the reports fails to make clear is that Gille's corps (indeed, every corps in Balck's army) was woefully short of infantrymen. This had been a chronic problem with the *6. Armee* since the loss of most of its infantry divisions during the debacle in Rumania the previous August and September. Heavy in armored units, the *6. Armee* lacked enough ground troops to securely hold front-line positions, attack entrenched enemy infantry, or support the armor during an attack. This had forced Balck and his predecessor, Fretter-Pico, to use *panzer* divisions or a field training division in their stead. Having only four *Panzergrenadier* battalions in each division, as opposed to seven in the standard infantry division of the period, a *panzer* division defending the same amount of ground as an infantry division was at a distinct disadvantage. To perform the same mission, a *panzer* division would have to disperse its troops widely, resulting in thinly defended main defense lines, though backed up by tanks and artillery when necessary to repel any enemy penetrations.

Infantry divisions were also needed to follow in the wake of *panzer* divisions during an offensive operation, where they would consolidate the ground recently gained, eliminate any bypassed enemy pockets of resistance, and protect the flanks of the breakthrough while the tanks continued their advance. It was the lack of supporting infantry divisions that had hobbled the advance of Gille's corps during *Konrad I*. The need to secure their flanks had forced the *Totenkopf* and *Wiking* Divisions to detach elements of their own *Panzergrenadier* battalions to perform this mission, a necessity that weakened the armored spearheads the deeper they plunged into enemy-held territory. As of 17 January, there were only two German infantry divisions in *A.Gr. Balck/6. Armee* operating south of the Danube, the *96.* and *711. Inf.Div.*, and neither would directly participate in *Konrad III*. Although the *44. Reichs-Gren.Div. HuD* was being shipped from *2. Pz.Armee* to join *A.Gr. Balck*, it would not arrive until the offensive was well under way. Most of the newly formed *Volks-Grenadier* divisions had been sent west to support the failed Ardennes offensive, where they had suffered heavy losses, and the two in the *H.Gr. Süd* order of battle, the *211.* and *271. V.G.D.*, had both sustained heavy casualties and were in need of reconstitution themselves.

Thus, individual Hungarian infantry battalions were being increasingly inserted into the front lines between German units as a stopgap measure, though their combat power was less than that of their German counterparts and some of them suffered from high desertion rates.[36] In regards to the Hungarians, by this point in the war their reliability had become a source of concern to German senior commanders, except for the most elite units, such as the *1. Hus.Div.*, the *2. Pz.Div.*, or the *Szent László* Division. In his memoir, Balck wrote that he thought *Honvéd* troops were unsuited for defense, but did well in the attack, stating, "My intent was to use our less-capable allies in a way that exploited their strength."[37] Ironically, the Hungarian units participating in *Konrad III* would be used primarily in a defensive role, where they performed tolerably well, despite Balck's prejudicial comments to the contrary.

To build up the capability and reliability of the Hungarian Army, *H.Gr. Süd* had undertaken several initiatives to improve their morale, such as equipping units with German matériel (especially weapons) and a more liberal policy in regards to their eligibility for German awards for valor, as well as more positive coverage in the German press and front-line newspapers.[38] Although the remaining patriotic Hungarian commanders and troops probably appreciated this new-found attention, preserving their men's morale was a tall order, given that two-thirds of their country was now occupied by the Red Army and that their capital city of Budapest was clearly about to fall into enemy hands. Consequently, the shortage of ordinary *Landser* to hold the line in Hungary and elsewhere would continue to be an unsolvable problem.

On 13 January, *A.Gr. Balck/6. Armee* reported the *Kampfstärke* of all its German and Hungarian units to *H.Gr. Süd*, except that of the *IV. SS-Pz.Korps*, whose units were listed as being "on the march" and thus unable to report their combat strength. The latter's last strength report was submitted on 6 January, only a week into *Konrad I*, and the corps' *Kampfstärke* would not have markedly increased, especially since both the *Totenkopf* and *Wiking* Divisions had been involved in heavy fighting between 7 and 12 January. By this point, both divisions would have absorbed their *Feld-Ersatz* (field replacement) battalions into their line companies, which would have provided a limited number of replacements for the men killed or wounded in combat. Their next division weekly status reports would not be submitted until 21 January, three days into the *Konrad III* offensive. The monthly report, which would provide both the number of men counted as casualties and replacements, would not be assembled until the end of the month, 10 days away.

The strength of the *1.* and *3. Pz.Div.* on the eve of *Konrad III* in terms of manpower are both known, however. As of 13 January, *Gen.Maj.* Thünert's *1. Pz.Div.* reported that it had a *Kampfstärke* of 2,857 men, including 1,302 from its own ranks, 532 attached Hungarian troops, 130 men from *Gren.Ers.Rgt. 44*, and 893 men from *SS-Regiment Ney*.[39] The *3. Pz.Div.*, commanded by *Oberst* Wilhelm Söth since 1 January 1945 (already well-known by the staff of the *IV. SS-Pz.Korps* from the time he commanded *Gren.Brig. 1131* east of Warsaw), had received no attachments from other units and reported a *Kampfstärke* of only 1,165 men.[40] Though at that point in time still serving under the *6. Pz.Div.* in the *I. Kav.Korps* area of operations, the *I. Btl./SS-Pz.Gren.Rgt. Danmark* reported having a *Kampfstärke* of 517 men, an indication that it had not yet seen any heavy fighting. It would finally rejoin *IV. SS-Pz.Korps* on 21 January. Thus, not counting either the *Totenkopf* or *Wiking* Divisions, Gille would have 4,022 additional soldiers from the *Heer* and *Honvéd* serving under him. Assuming that the combined *Kampfstärke* of the two SS divisions were roughly equal to those reported by the *1.* and *3. Pz.Div.*, the *IV. SS-Pz.Korps* would have had approximately 8,000 foot soldiers (infantry, combat engineers, and reconnaissance troops) ready for battle.

The *III. Pz.Korps*, which would conduct its own attack to the left of the *IV. SS-Pz.Korps* during *Konrad III*, was composed of the *23. Pz.Div.* and the *4. Kav. Brig.*, as well as the Hungarian *VIII. Armee-Korps*. On 13 January, the *23. Pz.Div.*, commanded by *Gen.Maj.* Josef von Radowitz, reported a relatively robust combat strength of 2,398 men, including 2,247 of its own as well as 151 Hungarian troops from *Bataillon Bartha*. The *4. Kav.Brig.*, commanded by *Gen.Maj.* Rudolf Holste, reported having 1,668 combat troops. The corps' reserve from the Hungarian *VIII. Armee-Korps* reported a *Kampfstärke* of 1,108 men arrayed in four infantry battalions from the *23.* and *25. Inf.Div.*, and *Pio.Btl. II*. Thus, *Korpsgruppe Breith/III. Pz.Korps* would commit 5,174 combat troops for *Konrad III*, not counting *panzer* or artillery crewmen. All told, Soviet intelligence staffs estimated that *A.Gr. Balck/6. Armee*, along with the two attacking corps, would commit 54,000 men from all combat branches to the operation.[41]

One bright spot, at least in regards to combat power, was the amount of artillery the Germans and Hungarians would bring to bear in support of the offensive. Including mortars, infantry howitzers, field howitzers, and cannons, the *IV. SS-Pz. Korps* boasted 406 indirect fire weapons with which to support the attack. This number included 87 guns of various calibers, ranging in size from 10.5cm howitzers to the massive 21cm mortars to be provided by the attached *Volks-Art.Korps 403* with its six battalions.[42] The *Totenkopf* and *Wiking* Divisions had 60 and 56 artillery pieces respectively, though not all of them were operational. In two weeks, the corps would also be joined by *SS-s.Art.Abt. 504* with 15 heavy field guns. Besides artillery, the corps had 24 *Nebelwerfer* rocket launchers in *SS-Werf.Abt. 504* and 108 additional rocket launchers assigned to *Volks-Werf.Brig. 17*, ranging in size from the 15cm to 30cm *Werfer*.

However, the corps initially lacked an artillery observation battalion, upon which *Oberführer* Kurt Brasack had relied for the tremendous success of the corps' artillery during the fighting at Warsaw and Modlin during the previous autumn. When the *IV. SS-Pz.Korps* arrived in Hungary after Christmas, the *6. Armee's Artillerie-Führer*, *Gen.Lt.* Friedrich von Scotti, lacked sufficient artillery observation battalions in his *Höh.Art.Kdr. (HARKO) 306* to provide Brasack with one, leaving Gille's *ARKO* commander no option but to make the best of what personnel and equipment he had, which was not much. Neither the *Totenkopf* nor *Wiking* Divisions had an observation unit of their own, and the corps' *SS-Beob.Abt. 504* would not arrive on the scene for two more weeks. The lack of an artillery observation battalion would limit the *IV. SS-Pz.Korps'* ability to get the maximum effect out of its artillery during the initial days of the upcoming offensive, so a *Heer* unit—*lei.Beob.Abt. 32*—was loaned to *SS-ARKO 504* until the arrival of the corps' designated SS artillery observation battalion during the first week of February.

Korpsgruppe Breith/III. Pz.Korps' artillery headquarters, *ARKO 3*, had proportionately fewer artillery and rocket artillery units assigned or attached, though it possessed in all 95 different mortar, artillery, and rocket-launching batteries of various sizes and capability, including *II. Abt./Heeres-Art.Brig. 959* and *Volks-Werf. Brig. 19*, approximately 370 guns in all. However, roughly half of *Korpsgruppe Breith's* available artillery was under the control of Harteneck's *I. Kav.Korps*. Breith's corps at least had its own artillery observation battalion, *leichte Art.Beob.Abt. 29*, but it had to continue supporting Harteneck's corps as well as Breith's with sound- and flash-ranging capability. Overall control of *A.Gr. Balck/6. Armee's* artillery would be exercised by *Gen.Lt.* von Scotti's *HARKO 306*.

Though not usually listed as being a component of the artillery arm, Gille's corps alone had 83 towed and self-propelled 7.5cm antitank guns on hand, including 16 in the *Totenkopf* Division and 24 in the *Wiking* Division, which could also be used in the indirect-fire role if needed. The units of *III. Pz.Korps* taking part in the attack had 36 similar *Panzerabwehrkanone*. Though of limited utility during the initial stages of an offensive operation, antitank guns were necessary for the protection of the flanks after a penetration had been achieved by the armor, as well as to provide the infantry with the means to destroy any enemy tanks during defensive operations. In a pinch, these guns could also carry out indirect-fire missions, much like the artillery, provided that they were issued appropriate high-explosive ammunition.

To augment the corps' antiaircraft capability, two *Luftwaffe* units—*lei.Flak-Abt. 77* and *lei.Flak-Abt. 91* from *Flak-Sturm Rgt. 133*—were attached to initially defend the corps' artillery firing positions, including *Volks-Art.Korps 403*, against the strong Red Air Force ground-attack response that was anticipated. Once the corps' vanguard had penetrated the Soviet main defense line, these two battalions would be attached to the *Totenkopf* and *1. Pz.Div.*, respectively. Their 2cm and 3.7cm antiaircraft guns could also be used in the direct-fire mode against ground targets, should the need arise.[43]

Taking into account the terrain that lay before *IV. SS-Pz.Korps*, which was crisscrossed by many streams and canals (some as wide as 30 meters) that could become obstacles to its rapid advance, *A.Gr. Balck/6.Armee* sent a significant amount of combat engineers and bridge-building units from its reserve of *Heerestruppen* to Veszprém between 14 and 16 January. These consisted of *Brücken-Kolonne B* (Light Bridging Column) *929*, two companies (*1.* and *3.*) from *Brückenbau* (Bridge Construction) *Btl. 552*, *Brücken-Kolonne K* (Medium Bridging Column) *4*, *2. Kp./ Heeres-Pionier Brig. (mot.) 52*, and *1. Kp./Heeres-Pionier Btl. 255*. Taken together, these engineer units would be able to emplace light and medium pre-fabricated steel bridges that would accommodate most vehicles, though bridges strong enough to withstand the weight of the corps' 54-ton *Pz. VI* Tiger Is and 70-ton giant Tiger IIs would have to be specially constructed.[44] In order to be prepared to carry out their assignment as quickly as possible, these units would have to be positioned near the head of the attacking columns.

None of the German units taking part in the upcoming offensive could be characterized as being "fresh," for all had been engaged in combat more or less constantly since their arrival in the Hungarian theater of operations, whether from the beginning in September 1944 or as late as the first week of January. Whether fighting in the Vértes or Pilis Mountains as part of *Konrad I* and *II*, or engaged in the abortive attack towards Zámoly with the *I. Kav.Korps*, the German and Hungarian troops of *III. Pz.Korps* and *IV. SS-Pz.Korps* had been fighting in harsh winter conditions against a seemingly inexhaustible opponent with little respite. Even the *3. Pz.Div.*, which was being pulled out of the line for a brief reconstitution and refreshment period after suffering heavy losses, would have only two or three days to rest. The number of replacements that had arrived for the thousands of men who had been killed or wounded in *A. Gr. Balck/6. Armee* since 1 January were not enough to increase the *Kampfstärke* of any of the units concerned to their *Sollstärke* (authorized strength).

Not only were the men tired and needing rest, but their equipment, including individual weapons and uniforms, were badly in need of repair and replacement. The poor condition of some men's combat boots was a topic of concern of the *Oberquartiermeister* of the *6. Armee*. Tanks and other armored vehicles that were lost in battle were not replaced; those still remaining needed several days to be restored to minimum operating condition, as reflected by the equal numbers of vehicles out of service compared to those that still qualified as "runners." The only units that could be considered rested and fully equipped were *s.Pz.Abt. 509* and *Sturm-Art.Brig. 303*, both fresh from a lengthy rebuild and re-equipping process in Germany.

Of course, the Soviet troops that would receive the brunt of the German assault were not exactly fresh either, especially those opposite Zámoly, the scene of heavy fighting during the previous week. Most of the troops of the 4th Guards Army had been conducting operations without a break since October 1944, and were just as exhausted as the Germans. They had suffered heavy casualties and most of the regiments, brigades, and divisions were operating at half-strength or less. Though tanks and antitank guns could be quickly replaced, the strain on the Red Army's personnel replacement system was beginning to show the effects of four years of war, demonstrating that there were limits even to the Soviet Union's seemingly inexhaustible manpower reserves. By this stage of the Great Patriotic War, units were lucky if half of their casualties were replaced. To exacerbate the situation, priority for replacement of losses had been given to Marshal Zhukov's and Koniev's army groups of the Second and Third Ukrainian Fronts that were leading the winter offensive to the north.

Opposite Zámoly, the XX Rifle and XXI Guards Rifle Corps, commanded by Maj.Gen. I. M. Afonin and Lt.Gen. P. I. Fomenko, respectively, still barred the way in front of the *III. Pz.Korps*. Although they had been forced to yield ground during the previous week, by 18 January their subordinate units—the 5th and 7th Guards Airborne Divisions, the 63rd, 84th, and 93rd Rifle Divisions, and the 41st, 69th, and 80th Guards Rifle Divisions—would have nearly a week to recover from the fighting and redouble their efforts to strengthen their defensive positions before *Unternehmen Konrad III* began.[45] Additional artillery and antitank units had been brought in, miles of barbed-wire entanglements had been strung up by sappers, and thousands of infantry and antitank mines had been laid along the most likely avenues of approach. Several kilometers to the rear of the front lines, the I Guards Mechanized and VII Mechanized Corps had been occupying reserve positions, where both corps lay in readiness, with a total of 133 tanks and 37 of the new SU-100 self-propelling guns, awaiting the call to respond should the hated "Hitlerites" make another attempt to break through towards Budapest.[46]

In the path of the *IV. SS-Pz.Korps'* assault were troops from Maj.Gen. P. V. Gnedin's CXXXV Guards Rifle Corps, consisting of Maj.Gen. I. A. Gorbachev's 252nd Rifle Division and Maj.Gen. Nikitin's 1st Guards Fortified Region. Though this portion of the Soviet line had not been attacked since the Germans' abortive *Spätlese* offensive three weeks before, and was less densely held than the area east of Zámoly, its defenders had used the time wisely, reinforcing their obstacle belts, fortifying their defensive positions, and emplacing additional artillery and antitank guns. Unlike the units arrayed east of Zámoly, however, the Soviet troops opposite the *IV. SS-Pz.Korps* were not backed up by any appreciable armored reserves to parry or block an attack by German armored forces, except a rifle battalion from the 63rd Mechanized Brigade that had suffered heavy losses the week before near Zámoly and 20 SU-76 lightly armored assault guns from the 1202nd SP Artillery Regiment.[47]

If *Unternehmen Konrad II* and the *I. Kav.Korps* attack against Zámoly had indeed failed, at least both had successfully drawn off a significant amount of the 4th Guards Army's and 46th Army's reserves away from the point where the main effort of *Konrad III* would be directed, including the V Guards Cavalry, I Guards Mechanized, and X Rifle Corps. The commander of the 46th Army, assigned to Malinovsky's Second Ukrainian Front, was also concerned about a possible breakout from Budapest towards the Bicske–Zsámbék area, so additional forces were moved across the Danube to that location. The only significant reserve possessed at this time by the Third Ukrainian Front was the CXXXIII Rifle Corps with three rifle divisions, recently released from the *STAVKA* strategic reserve. When the German offensive began on 18 January, it was still busily engaged in crossing the Danube south of Budapest and was moving into an assembly area between Seregélyes and

Perkáta. The Front also had the 10th AT Artillery Brigade in reserve at Baraczka, a considerable defensive force.[48]

Though each rifle or guards rifle division in the path of the German attack was operating at roughly 50 percent of its authorized strength (on average 4,800 men or less), this weakness was compensated for by the attachment of army-level field artillery units.[49] For example, the XXI Guards Rifle Corps was reinforced by two artillery regiments and an antitank artillery regiment. Each rifle or mechanized corps was supported by additional army-level combat engineer, antiaircraft, and road construction units. The greatest weakness of the Soviet defenses was not the quality or armament of their units, but the width of the front that each division was expected to defend, especially in the area east of Lake Balaton, where Gille's assault would begin.

While the forces in the Zámoly area were relatively concentrated along narrow frontages, the CXXXV Rifle Corps—squarely in the path of the *IV. SS-Pz.Korps'* spearheads—was not. Gille's assault would strike the leftmost regiment of the 252nd Rifle Division, the 928th Rifle Regiment, holding a frontage of 5 kilometers, and the 1st Guards Fortified Region, with a frontage of 13 kilometers.[50] A fortified region was a static defensive unit, used by the Red Army as an economy-of-force measure. Though low in the number of troops assigned, consisting of only five artillery-machine-gun battalions, this organization, with a total assigned strength of 3,122 men, was equipped with a large amount of heavy machine guns and more than the usual amount of artillery and antitank guns.[51] In front of the *IV. SS-Pz. Korps*, the 1st Guards Fortified Region had also emplaced deep minefields, electrified barbed-wire entanglements (a deadly novelty), and antitank gun concentrations.

This 18-kilometer sector, held by less than 4,817 men, would soon by confronted by the bulk of four *panzer* divisions, with a nearly 10-to-one advantage in the number of troops committed, an advantage the Germans rarely enjoyed by this point in the war. There were actually fewer Soviet troops in this breakthrough area than German intelligence had initially estimated.[52] The *A.Gr. Balck/6. Armee* and the *IV. SS-Pz.Korps Ic* both believed that the area was defended by three rifle divisions and one fortified region, but there was only the one rifle division and the aforementioned fortified region; the other two divisions had been shifted to the northeast after 8 January to block the initial German attack towards Bicske and Zsámbék.[53] Still, Gille's troops would find the initial attack more difficult than they originally estimated.

As previously mentioned, *Gen.O.* Otto Dessloch's *Luftflotte 4*, augmented by the Hungarian *102. Luft-Brigade*, would provide fighter, ground-attack, bomber, transport, and reconnaissance aircraft in support of *Konrad III*. To ensure sufficient support during the first several days of the offensive, when it was needed most, its subordinate unit, *General der Flieger* Paul Deichmann's *1. Fliegerkorps*, would "surge" as many sorties as possible, depending upon the weather. The result would be a situation where, for the first times in months, large numbers of German and Hungarian aircraft would strafe and bomb Red Army positions and columns moving on the roads in daylight, to a degree that had not been experienced by Soviet troops since the opening days of Operation *Barbarossa*, according to an official Soviet report.[54]

As of 10 January 1945, *Luftflotte 4* was prepared to commit three fighter squadrons, four bomber squadrons, eight ground-attack squadrons, and three transport squadrons, with 731 aircraft in all, of which approximately 553 were operational. Furthermore, the Hungarian Air Force had 125 operational aircraft that would support the offensive, including 97 fighter aircraft consisting mostly of German-built *Messerschmitt Me-109* fighter-bombers.[55] How long the *Luftwaffe* could sustain such a high sortie rate was an open question; but without dedicated air support, the offensive could not hope to succeed, especially if the Red Air Force went unchallenged.

Luftflotte 4's Soviet counterpart, Marshal of Aviation Vladimir A. Sudets's 17th Air Army, had been operating in the Budapest–Lake Balaton area for several months, and during numerous aerial battles since October 1944 had lost hundreds of aircraft to the guns of German and Hungarian fighters and *Flak*. Undaunted, Sudets's airmen would force the German and Hungarian aircrew to fight hard for their relatively brief control of the skies during the initial stages of *Konrad III*. As of 17 January, the 17th Air Army had 808 operational aircraft, with an additional 122 under repair. Of this number, 372 were ground-attack aircraft, predominately IL-2 *Sturmoviks* and Douglas A-20 Bostons. Due to lessons learned in combat against the *Luftwaffe* during the past year, the number of fighter aircraft in the air fleet had been increased, with 154 Yak-3 and Yak-9 fighters, and 148 of the newer Lavochkin La-5 aircraft, for a total of 302 considered operational. The relative robustness and simplicity of Soviet-built aircraft, compared to those of the Germans, as well as their well-known capability of operating from primitive airfields, would allow the 17th Air Army to establish and maintain a high sortie rate, which German and Hungarian aviation units were unable to match the longer the battle continued.[56]

The *IV. SS-Pz.Korps*' two SS divisions would be fighting in unfamiliar terrain for the first time since they had arrived in Hungary. For the *1.* and *3. Pz.Div.*, which had both been engaged in battle west of Budapest for over a month, it was nothing new, but for the tankers from the *Totenkopf* and *Wiking* Divisions, it was a welcome change. Instead of fighting up and down the forests, valleys, and steep hills of the Gerecse, Vértes, and Pilis Mountains, their *panzer* battalions would now be attacking across the *Puszta*, the wide-open, rolling plains of Hungary. Ideal tank country, the area between Lake Balaton and the Danube consisted of mostly level farmland, interspersed with occasional small patches of woods and sturdily built villages. The road network was good and included many stretches of paved highway that would facilitate movement, especially for tanks. The peculiarities of the terrain and the road network, of course, would equally benefit the 4th Guards Army when it began to counter the German offensive.

Besides the greater distance that the relief forces would have to fight through in order to get to Budapest (approximately 90–100 kilometers), there was one other limiting factor to the *Konrad III* offensive plan. Due to the landforms in this region of Hungary, most of the streams and rivers originating in the Vértes, Gerecse, and Pilis Mountains drained in a southeasterly direction towards the Danube, as did Lake Balaton. These rivers or canals—from west to east, the Sió, Malom, and Sárviz (Nádor) Canals, and the Gaja, Csikolai, Váli, and finally the Szent Laszlo Rivers—all combined to pose a series of natural obstacles lying perpendicular to the German direction of attack.

These would have to be crossed before any force could reach Budapest, hopefully by capturing as many existing bridges as possible. If not, field-expedient bridges would have to be constructed quickly. In addition to these larger drainage features that amounted to key terrain that could influence the outcome of battle, there were dozens of smaller creeks, streams, and rivulets that would force advancing units to bridge, go around, or seek fording sites, steps that would all require additional time. The challenges posed by the terrain had already been recognized by the *A. Gr. Balck* staff engineer officer, *Oberst* Victor Gerber, hence the attachment of such a large amount of engineer and bridging assets to the *IV. SS-Pz. Korps*. If employed properly under the guidance of the corps' engineer, *Ostubaf.* Fritz Braune, these special-purpose troops could tremendously enhance the corps' mobility and allow the armored units to adhere to their rigid time schedule.

Another limiting factor of this route of advance was the weather, especially during the late winter and spring. A significant amount of snow had fallen during the past month, and portions of the *Puszta* between Lake Balaton and the Danube were still covered by drifts. The brief thaw that had set in during the beginning of the second week of January had caused a portion of it to melt, leaving standing pools of water that concealed the soft, boggy soil underneath. Fortunately for the attacking force, freezing temperatures had returned after the middle of the month, once more making possible off-road movement by tanks. *Divisionsgruppe Pape* of the *III. Pz. Korps* had already experienced how the wet Hungarian soil had interfered with the abortive *Spätlese* offensive the previous month, and no one on Balck's or Gille's staff wanted to see that happen again. As luck would have it, the *Luftwaffe*'s weather service forecast continuing freezing temperatures for at least the first week of the offensive.

Between 13 January and the evening of 17 January, *IV. SS-Pz. Korps* units continued to arrive in their new assembly areas around Veszprém, some rolling in at the last minute. Units laid communications wire, constructed camouflaged positions, stockpiled artillery ammunition, topped off their vehicles with precious fuel, and drew an issue of iron rations. Field kitchens served up what would be the last hot meal the assault troops would receive for the next several days. What little time that remained was put to good use. Troops mended their clothes as best they could or took them to the corps' *Bekleidung-Instandsetzungs Kompanie* (Clothing repair and maintenance company) to be repaired. Soldiers wrote letters home and caught up with reading the mail that had arrived while they were fighting in *Konrad I* and *II*. Tank mechanics worked feverishly to get as many vehicles operational as time and the spare part situation would allow. Weapons were cleaned, small-arms ammunition and hand grenades were issued, and troops tried to get as much rest as possible while they could.

The last units to be released from the *3. Kav.Brig.* and sent on their way to rejoin their division were *Hstuf.* Heinrich Bock's *III. Bataillon* of the *Totenkopf* Regiment and *Stubaf.* Friedrich Messerle's *IV. Abt./SS-Pz.Art.Rgt. 3*, both of which arrived on 18 January after *Konrad III* had already begun, following a harrowing journey along the ice-covered highway running through the Bakony forest. Difficulties in being relieved in place by the *3. Kav.Brig.* had caused the delay, slowed even further by the terrible traffic situation along the icy or snow-covered roads. They would constitute a substantial addition to the combat power of the *Totenkopf* Division when they finally rejoined it.

On 16 January, Gille and Breith were summoned to Balck's headquarters in Martinsberg for a final operations briefing by the *A.Gr. Balck/6. Armee* staff. Later that evening, Gille met with the commanders of his four divisions that would be serving together during the impending offensive.[57] Perhaps as a result of the meeting with his corps commanders, Balck decided to issue an order of the day, addressed to the troops about to take part in the offensive:

> Soldiers of the *6. Armee*!
>
> *Der Führer* has ordered the final destruction of the Russian [*sic*] units trapped to the west of Budapest between the Danube and the Vértes Mountains, thus clearing the way for your comrades in Budapest.
>
> In execution of this order, all preparations have been made by the leadership for a successful outcome: a large number of [artillery] batteries, [rocket] launchers and planes are ready to support you. The Russian before you has not yet recovered from his losses of tanks and men after the previous battles.
>
> It is only up to you to use these advantages. Drive like lightning into the enemy, push unperturbed around [his] flanks and take advantage of every success by pushing on immediately! Keep in mind the target of our attack: Budapest!
>
> The slogan is "Forward!"[58]

Though there are no records recounting how this order was perceived by the troops when it was later read to them, it summed up the prevailing attitude felt by tens of thousands of troops arrayed between Stuhlweissenburg and Lake Balaton. Surely, the soldiers must have thought, we will break through and relieve Budapest this time. According to one participant, "Once again, the troops were seized with an almost indescribable enthusiasm. After all the terrible months of fighting ... despite their heroic resistance, [we] had had to withdraw again and again in order to fend off the enemy … and after two [initially] successful but nevertheless futile attempts to relieve [Budapest], the troops should now finally be attacking on a broad front."[59]

As the final preparations for *Konrad III* were being made, the front lines from Gran to Zámoly were relatively quiet between 13 and 17 January. A major exception was the Soviet counterattack against the German troops defending Pilisszentkereszt, the village that had marked the farthest point of the *Wiking* Division's advance on 12 January during *Konrad II*. Beginning on the morning of 14 January, battalions from the 99th Rifle and 11th Guards Cavalry Divisions carried out an assault against the outnumbered troops of *Oberst* von Limburg-Hetlingen's *Gren.Rgt. 731* from the *711. Inf.Div.* that were holding the town. After four days of heavy fighting, Limburg-Hetlingen's regiment was forced to relinquish Pilisszentkereszt and withdraw north to its former positions astride the road at Pilisszentlélek. Having retaken the ground they had lost the week before, X Guards Rifle Corps, responsible for the operation, transitioned to the defense on 18 January.[60]

Meanwhile, the siege of Budapest continued unabated. Great pressure was being exerted against the eastern bridgehead in Pest, whose defenders were being continuously forced to surrender ground in the face of the Red Army's overwhelming numerical superiority. As the garrison withdrew into an ever-tighter perimeter around the two remaining bridges, it appeared likely that Pest would fall within a week, if not in two or three days. Pfeffer-Wildenbruch's pleas for ammunition and medical supplies were partially answered on the night of 14/15 January, when *Luftflotte 4* flew 84 resupply sorties over the city. Though this was the greatest effort in nearly two weeks, the amount delivered was still insufficient. The *Luftwaffe* could not continue operating at this level in the face of Soviet antiaircraft fire and aerial intercept missions flown by the 5th and 17th Air Armies without losing an inordinate amount of the slow and ungainly *Ju-52* transports. The following evening, only 5.6 tons of supplies were dropped, an amount grossly insufficient to meet the demand. Bad flying weather continued to be just as much an impediment to aerial resupply operations as Soviet fighters and *Flak*.[61]

While the troops that would take part in *Konrad III* were still assembling, *H.Gr. Süd* continued its thankless effort to convince *OKH* that the *Führer* needed to grant permission for the *IX. SS-Geb.Korps* to break out. Finally, on 17 January, Hitler agreed to allow Pfeffer-Wildenbruch to order his troops on the eastern bank of the Danube to withdraw to the western side of the city, but no more than that. By this point, Pest was defended by remnants of the *8.* and *22. SS-Kav.Div.*, the *13. Pz.Div.*, and *Pz.Div. FHH*, plus a smattering of Hungarian units.

Carrying out a plan that had been drawn up weeks before, the survivors, accompanied by thousands of civilians, withdrew across the river during the night of 17/18 January while subjected to heavy Soviet artillery barrages that indiscriminately killed soldiers and civilians alike. After the rearguard had crossed, engineers blew up the Chain and Elisabeth Bridges to deny them to the enemy early the next morning.[62]

With Pest having been given up, the addition of the several thousand German and Hungarian troops who had escaped would correspondingly increase the defensive capability of the Buda garrison, which in turn would enable the *IX. SS-Geb.Korps* to hold out for several more weeks. Therefore, there was still a garrison requiring relief and *Konrad III* could go forward as intended, though it would have made more sense at this point to authorize a break out, but Hitler was having none of that.

Meanwhile, final preparations went forward as planned. During the morning of 17 January, commanders from corps headquarters, the *Totenkopf*, and *Wiking* were allowed to go to the front lines dressed in Romanian uniforms in order to view their designated *Verfügungsraum* (attack or "jump off" positions) for the following day and to see up-close the *Hauptkampflinie* currently held by the *1. Pz.Div.* and the attached *SS-Rgt. Ney*. Why they were given Romanian and not Hungarian uniforms to wear was not explained, though this was undoubtedly intended as part of the *Konrad III* operational deception plan. During the evening, the forward headquarters of Ullrich's division moved forward to the village of Papkeszi, while that of Becker's was moved up to a position within the village of Hajmáskér. From these forward locations, they could observe and control the initial assault of their respective divisions.

General der Panzertruppe Balck was disappointed to learn earlier that day that the *44. Reichs-Gren.Div. HuD* was being moved on *OKH* orders from a position where it could support either corps taking part in *Konrad III* to a new location north of the Danube, where it would replace both the *8.* and *20. Pz.Div.*, which had been ordered to begin moving that same day by rail to the north, where they would reinforce *H.Gr. A.*[63] Thus, the largest and most capable infantry unit designated to support the new offensive had been taken out of the game before the attack had even begun.

Instead, the Hungarian *25. Inf.Div.* would be substituted several days after the operation began, something which neither side welcomed, though *A.Gr. Balck* had no choice since the *44. Reichs-Gren.Div.* had already been sent elsewhere. Once the Hungarian division was committed on the right flank of the *IV. SS-Pz.Korps*, per German practice, *Wehrmacht* units (in this case, the three aforementioned armored reconnaissance battalions) would initially be inserted between individual Hungarian battalions to serve as "corset stays" to ensure that their erstwhile allies would not run away when the first Soviet response was encountered.[64] For their part, the proud Hungarian officer corps considered this German standard operating procedure as humiliating, though recent experience with Hungarian defections and desertions had shown it to be a prudent measure.

That evening at 7 p.m., Gille's headquarters issued the final version of the corps' operations order for what it had dubbed *Unternehmen Kräutergarden* (Operation *Herbal Garden*), the subordinate plan of *Konrad III* that pertained to the *IV. SS-Pz. Korps'* role in the offensive. The order, titled "Deployment for the relief attack on Budapest from the area west of Stuhlweissenburg," stated:

On 18 January 1945, *IV. SS-Pz.Korps* breaks through the enemy's position between Lake Balaton and Lake Velencze and strikes in a northeast direction to the river Danube, then establishes contact with the troops encircled in Budapest.

The follow-on task of the army [*A. Gr. Balck/6. Armee*] will be to destroy the enemy located in the region west and northwest of Budapest.

The corps' tasks and individual division tasks were outlined as follows:

1. The divisions of the corps, together with units already occupying the front line will break through the enemy's positions on a wide front and strike towards the Malom and Sárviz Canals, where they will seize bridgeheads so that they can subsequently use them to continue the offensive in a northeast direction.
2. After suppressing the initial resistance of the enemy, the *5. SS-Pz.Div.*, *3. SS-Pz.Div.*, and *1. Pz.Div.*, ignoring the threat to their flanks, will advance to the lines of the Sárviz Canal and seize bridgeheads in order to prevent the enemy from consolidating on the canal and will carry out a crossing of our own force to the opposite bank with the aim of continuing the offensive.
3. The primary task of the *3. Pz.Div.* is to quickly move forward together with the attached reconnaissance squadrons and capture the most important crossings along the line of the Sió Canal, thereby covering the right flank of the corps.
4. The *1. Pz.Div.* with its units facing to the north will cover the corps [left flank] against the enemy forces in the Stuhlweissenburg region. Division commanders are authorized to issue this order to troops in the zone of attack beginning at 8 p.m. on 17 January 1945.[65]

The order included a command and control paragraph at the end that listed the authorized flare signals used by the attacking units, including green flares to signify the need to shift artillery fire, purple to warn of enemy tanks approaching, and so forth. It then listed the initial locations of each unit's forward command post. The order concluded with a reminder of the importance of all units to promptly submit situation reports, with divisions required to do so every three hours, stressing, "In this operation, rapid reporting is of great importance for the deployment of our tank forces and corps artillery in critical areas."

The order itself was drafted by *Stubaf.* Fritz Rentrop, who had replaced *Stubaf.* Willi Klose as the corps' new *Ia* that day.[66] With the arrival of Rentrop, Klose was posted to the *Wiking* Division to take up his new duties as that division's *Ia*. In turn, *Stubaf.* Günther Braun—who had been serving as the acting *Ia* of the *Wiking* Division since 2 January after *Maj.* Otto Kleine was injured in an automobile accident—was reassigned to the *Totenkopf* Division instead of returning to his previous position on the *IV. SS-Pz.Korps* staff. Rentrop was a highly decorated officer who had been awarded the Knight's Cross in Russia on 15 October 1941 while commanding a *Flak* battery in *Pz.Gren.Div. Das Reich*. He was also a recent graduate of the 15th wartime *Generalstabslehrgang* and a previous instructor at the *SS Junkerschule* in Braunschweig. A highly experienced and dedicated officer, he was a welcome addition to the corps' *Führungsabteilung*, where great things were expected of him.

After receiving the final copies of the order from Gille at his forward headquarters in Balatonfüzfő, division commanders returned to their command posts and set their staffs to work towards making any necessary adjustments to their own plans. At 11:10 p.m., all preparations were reported to be complete, when the units carrying out the initial phases of the attack had finished occupying their jump-off positions immediately behind the front lines, no more than 1,500 meters away from the enemy. The *Totenkopf* and *Wiking* Divisions' combat engineer battalion commanders obtained information from their counterparts in the *1. Pz.Div.* about the location of its minefields as well as those of the enemy. Sappers cleared lanes through German minefields during the night to enable the passage of armored vehicles, though clearing of Soviet minefields would have to wait until the attack began due to the need for secrecy. At the same time, troops from the *III. Pz.Korps* a few kilometers to the north were also carrying out the same last-minute preparations for their own supporting attack. Due to delays experienced in moving up its unit, the preliminary attack by the *III. Pz.Korps* would take place one day later, coinciding with that of the *IV. SS-Pz.Korps.*

The front, according to Soviet reports that night, became "unsettlingly calm," with none of the usual German artillery harassment fire being reported. Stranger still, the daily flow of Hungarian deserters also ceased. Because the sounds of motor vehicles and human voices being carried by the wind could be heard opposite their lines, the *Frontovniks* from the 1st Guards Fortified Region and the 252nd Rifle Division could only surmise that Hungarian units had been replaced in the line by German ones. Other than that, there was no reason to suspect that anything out of the ordinary was about to occur.[67] They would soon face a rude awakening.

The Third Relief Attempt of Budapest—*Konrad III* Part I: The Initial Drive, 18–23 January 1945

On the last night before the beginning of *Konrad III*, the front lines east of Lake Balaton were strangely quiet. Infantry patrols sent out by the 1st Guards Fortified Region to determine the cause of this unaccustomed lull were unsuccessful in their attempts to determine what this signified, finding the German troops on the opposite side of the Soviet lines fully alert and ready to repel any attempt to take prisoners or tap telephone lines. Things finally settled down after midnight, as the temperature dropped to 24 degrees Fahrenheit (–5 degrees Celsius). German meteorologists reported lightly scattered snow showers throughout the area and cloudy, misty weather that hindered both aerial and ground observation. Roads continued to be icy and dangerous for movement of both tracked and wheeled vehicles.[1]

Along the *IV. SS-Pz.Korps'* 32-kilometer front line, in dozens of camouflaged jump-off positions ranging from those near Csór in the northeast to the edge of Balantonakarattya on the shores of Lake Balaton to the southwest, nearly 65,000 German and Hungarian troops—*Panzergrenadiere*, tank crews, artillerymen, sappers, reconnaissance troops, and many others—awaited the dawn. Some smoked their last cigarette, others tried to snatch a few moments of rest, while officers reviewed their maps one last time. By 4 a.m., everything was ready. Half an hour later, over 400 German and Hungarian guns, mortars, and rocket launchers began the preparatory barrage upon identified and suspected Soviet positions, which ranged back and forth across the front held by the CXXXV Guards Rifle Corps for 30 minutes. At 5 a.m., the ground assault began and the final attempt to relieve Budapest was underway. Like the *Wacht am Rhein* counteroffensive in the Ardennes, which was also carried out in complete secrecy, surprise was total (see Map 7).

The evening summary of the day's operations submitted by the *IV. SS-Pz.Korps* reported that despite encountering numerous *Pakfronts*, heavily mined approaches, electrified barbed-wire entanglements, and deeply echeloned enemy defensive positions, its attacking divisions were able to successfully break through the line held

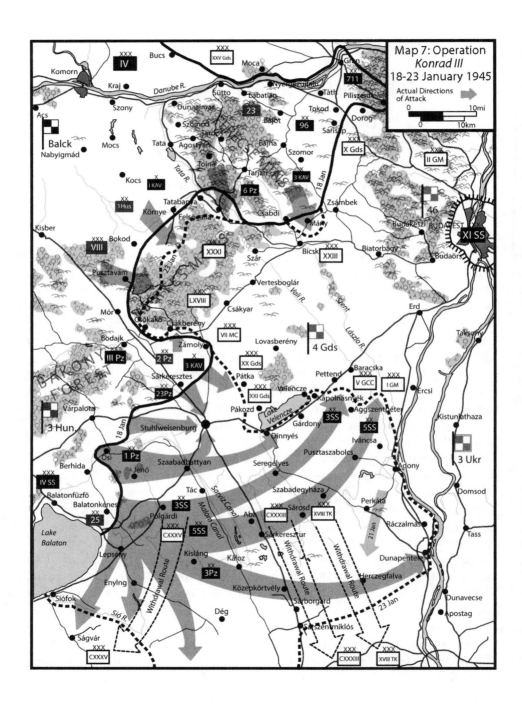

Map 7: Operation *Konrad III* 18-23 January 1945

by the 1st Guards Fortified Region and the 252nd Rifle Division in several places. In some areas, though not all, very tough enemy resistance was encountered during the initial stages of the attack that could only be overcome after heavy fighting. Gille's headquarters reported that despite the Soviets' attempt to block the advance by his armored spearheads, his troops were able to seize the town of Balatonfökajar and the heights south of Lepsény.[2]

Continuing onwards, his troops advanced as far as the town of Dégh and were able to seize two bridgeheads over the Sárviz Canal, one near the town of Tác and the other southeast of Sárszent-Mihály, despite enemy efforts to stop them. Scattered Soviet units bypassed earlier were proving to be a problem, as they attempted to withdraw and establish a new defense line. To prevent this from occurring, *IV. SS-Pz. Korps* was forced to detach units to eliminate them before the enemy troops could disrupt the supply lines of advancing German formations. In addition, Soviet troops were forced to withdraw from the western portion of Falubattyán (modern-day Szabadbattyán) after launching an unsuccessful counterattack. As an indication of the severity of the fighting that day, *IV. SS-Pz.Korps* reported capturing or destroying 80 antitank guns, 20 self-propelled guns, and nine tanks.[3]

This brief and succinct report, submitted via land-line telephone to the headquarters of *A.Gr. Balck/6. Armee* by the corps' *Führungsabteilung* (after being reviewed by Gille and/or his chief of staff), seems rather clean and bloodless, but on the ground it was anything but. The right-most unit of *IV. SS-Pz.Korps*, the *3.Pz. Div.*, had the easiest time of it that day, as its tanks and *Panzergrenadiers* surged forward through the left flank of the 1st Guards Fortified Region resting on the eastern shores of Lake Balaton. Earlier that morning, *Oberst* Söth's *Panzerpioniere* had breached three successive obstacle belts including minefields in a five-hour operation, including having to negotiate electrified barbed-wire entanglements, which proved to be a dangerous novelty. With the sappers having cleared lanes through these obstacles, the division's armor was now able to pass through a narrow gap in the Soviet lines near the village of Lepsény, while its grenadiers widened the breach to the left and right by aggressively rolling up Soviet trench lines and fortified positions.

Less than five hours later, the division's spearhead—a *Kampfgruppe* formed around *I. Abt./Pz.Rgt. 6* and *Pz.Gren.Rgt. 3*—was able to push through into the rear area of the CXXXV Guards Rifle Corps and reach the town of Dégh around 3:30 p.m. Two-and-a-half hours later, the division's spearhead had reached the Sárviz Canal west of Sár Szentmiklós, after encountering and destroying Soviet supply units. After a brief pause to consolidate, the *Kampfgruppe* crossed the canal and established a small bridgehead, while the rest of the division caught up. On the division's right flank, its *Pz.Gren.Rgt. 394* deployed to ward off any Soviet countermeasures, while the three armored reconnaissance battalions—*Pz.Aufkl.Abt. 1, 3,* and *23*—fanned out to the south and southwest along the Sió River between Siófok and Simontornya to provide early warning should the 57th Army to their west begin moving units in their direction.[4]

To the left of the *3. Pz.Div.*, *Oberf.* Ullrich's *5. SS-Pz.Div. Wiking* found the going much tougher than anticipated. After painfully slow progress through the extensive minefields and wire obstacles barring entry in front of the Soviet positions, the division's *Germania* Regiment (minus its *III. Bataillon*), reinforced by *I. Btl./Norge*, had to fight hard to overcome strong resistance offered by the machine gunners, artillerymen, and infantry of the 1st Guards Fortified Region near the village of Balatonfőkajar. Enemy mortar fire was particularly accurate and German losses were heavy. When the *Wiking* Division's slowly developing attack was threatening to upset the offensive's timetable, *Ogruf.* Gille went in person to Ullrich's headquarters to see what was causing the delay. Gille grumbled that *Gen.Maj.* Gaedke, *A.Gr. Balck's* chief of staff, had visited his own forward command post shortly beforehand, and was described as being "quite upset" about how the battle was going so far.[5]

Gille urged his division commander to get things moving. Ullrich, feeling the pressure from above, ordered *Ostubaf.* Dorr to employ Darges's *Panzergruppe* in the attack to lend the weight of his armor against the enemy's defenses, even though this was supposed to occur only after the infantry had already broken though. Dorr's armored battlegroup—consisting of *III. Btl./Germania*, all of the remaining tanks of Darges's *SS-Pz.Rgt. 5*, and the attached assault guns of *Sturm-Art.Brig. 303*—was finally able to pierce the Soviet main defense line by sundown after heavy fighting. Having broken through the thin defensive crust of the 1st Guards Fortified Region, the enemy's resistance lessened considerably, allowing *K.Gr. Dorr* to strike deeply into the rear area of the CXXXV Guards Rifle Corps. After overrunning Lepsény, it pushed through the village of Kisláng, capturing a large amount of war matériel in the process before halting for the evening along the Malom Canal at Káloz, where its lead elements were able to establish a small bridgehead on the opposite bank.[6]

To the left of the *Wiking* Division, the *3. SS-Pz.Div. Totenkopf* attacked out of the area along both sides of the town of Berhida towards the southeast. After quickly fighting their way through the Soviet obstacle belt, the division's lead elements (*K.Gr. Eckert* and *Kleffner*) achieved their initial penetration in the main defense line between the villages of Füle and Jenö, despite having to ward off flank attacks by the enemy while doing so. By 2 p.m., its leading element—a small armored *Kampfgruppe* led by *Stubaf.* Kraas—took the town of Tác and was able to establish a small bridgehead over the Malom Canal, due west of the parallel Sárviz Canal. The assault group on the left, spearheaded by *SS-Pz.Jäg.Abt. 3*, fought its way into the town of Falubattyán, located at the northern confluence of the canals, where it encountered the first Soviet tanks from the VII Mechanized Corps' 63rd Mechanized Brigade. Shallow bridgeheads were established at both locations, consisting solely of infantry from *SS-Pz.Gren.Rgt. 5 Totenkopf*, who were supported on the opposite bank of the canal by the regiment's heavy weapons companies and division artillery.

Because the *Totenkopf* Division's two lead elements were unable to get any armored vehicles across either canal, since the bridges at both locations had been damaged or destroyed by retreating Soviet troops, *Brig.Fhr.* Becker ordered them to spread their troops along the canal towards the north and south, eliminating any resistance encountered along the way, destroying at least one T-34 in the process. With Soviet resistance stiffening on the opposite bank of the Malom Canal at both Tác and Falubattyán, Becker decided to wait until nightfall to order a crossing, since doing so in daylight entailed a great deal of risk. These bridges would have to be shored up and reinforced before the attack could proceed much further anyway, so he set his *SS-Pz.Pio.Btl. 3* to work.[7]

On the division's left flank, the attached heavy tank battalion, *s.Pz.Abt. 509*, was experiencing a great deal of difficulty in overcoming Soviet minefields, bad road conditions, and determined resistance, especially that offered by antitank guns of the 1st Guards Fortified Region and SU-76s of the 1202nd SP Artillery Regiment. The Soviet defenders were only overcome after coordinated action by *Maj.* Hans-Jürgen Burmester's Tiger IIs, *Hstuf.* Zech's *SS-Pz.Aufkl.Abt. 3*, and assault guns of *SS-StuG Abt. 3*. Several JS-II heavy tanks from the 78th Guards Heavy Tank Regiment made their appearance, adding additional backbone to the defense. Finally, after fierce fighting, Soviet resistance on the western bank of the Malom Canal was overcome, but only after *s.Pz.Abt. 509* was reduced to just 18 operational *panzers* due to battle damage or mechanical failure. Even worse than the loss of 24 vehicles, however temporary, the battalion suffered a number of casualties among its officers, including *Maj.* Burmester, who was wounded in action. He was replaced by *Hauptmann* König, commander of the battalion's *2. Kompanie.*[8]

On the corps' left flank, *Gen.Maj.* Thünert's *1. Pz.Div.*, reinforced by *Rittmeister* Weidemann's *I. Abt./Pz.Rgt. 24*, also encountered challenges in overcoming the defenses prepared by the 252nd Rifle Division, but after its sappers had cleared lanes through the minefields, its lead elements quickly passed through and were able to seize the town of Ösi by midday and advance on the right as far as the Sárviz Canal at Sárszent Mihaly. Once here, Thünert's leading *Kampfgruppe* formed around *Oberstlt.* Philipp's *Pz.Rgt. 1* quickly established a bridgehead, but the bridge over the canal was soon found to be too flimsy to accommodate 45-ton Panthers, though lighter *SPW*s carrying *Panzergrenadiers* could cross. Combat engineers were set to work to reinforce it in order to continue the advance early the next morning.[9]

On the division's left, its other *Kampfgruppe* from *Hauptmann* Heinle's *I. Btl./ Pz.Gren.Rgt. 1* that was advancing due south of Stuhlweissenburg, was able to reach the railway station at Palmajor after encountering tanks from the 16th and 64th Mechanized Brigades of the Soviet VII Mechanized Corps, which were being sent in response to the German attack. In an engagement against Soviet tanks fought near Nádasdladány, the *3. Schwadron* (equivalent of a *panzer Kompanie*) from *I. Abt./Pz.Rgt. 24* destroyed four T-34s and 12 antitank guns against the loss of one

Panther before halting for the night at the canal near Sárszent Mihaly. Throughout the advance, *Gen.Maj.* Thünert, as was his habit, accompanied the division's spearhead riding in his command vehicle (an *SPW*), enabling him to make rapid decisions on the spot aimed at taking advantage of the situation and continuing the attack. Overall, despite high losses in some of its units, especially in the *Wiking* and *Totenkopf* Divisions, the *IV. SS-Pz.Korps* had achieved all of its first-day objectives and reached the Sárviz and Malom Canals along a 30-kilometer wide front stretching from Sárszent Mihaly to Káloz. Everything still appeared to be on schedule to continue the corps' advance the following morning.

In the *III Pz.Korps* attacking zone on Gille's left, between Stuhlweissenburg and Zámoly, Breith's troops were able to seize comparatively little ground and were finally brought to a halt after encountering extremely tough Soviet resistance south and southeast of the town of Sárkeresztes. In the fighting around the heights 3 kilometers southeast of that town, six enemy tanks were destroyed, along with 13 antitank guns, and 100 Soviet troops captured. Prior to the attack, Hungarian units on Breith's left were unable to prevent Red Army troops south of Kecskéd from penetrating 2 kilometers into their own positions. A counterattack launched by German troops supporting the Hungarians was able to throw their opponent back and restore the front lines, but only after suffering heavy casualties.

In the *I. Kav.Korps* defensive sector, Soviet troops were able to finally take the heights 5 kilometers northwest of Bicske after repeated battalion-sized attacks, and were able to expand their penetration into the lines of the *6. Pz.Div.* to a depth of 2 kilometers. To the north, in the *3. Kav.Brig.* sector, a Soviet penetration made into the brigade's lines in the southwestern portion of Sarisap was eliminated and the previous front line restored. Near Dorog, a Soviet attack in regimental strength was able to seize the commanding heights northeast of the town, prompting a large-scale counterattack by the *96. Inf.Div.* which was still underway that evening. Another similarly sized attack was launched against the positions of *Gren.Rgt. 731* of the *711. Inf.Div.* northwest of Pilisszentlélek, but was driven off after the defenders held firm.

On the northern side of the Danube in the *LVII. Pz.Korps* sector, an attack by troops from the *8. Pz.Div.* was able to force troops from the 6th Guards Tank Army off a key hill 5 kilometers northeast of the town of Mocs. A few kilometers to the north, a Soviet counterattack southwest of Bucs was warded off by the *20. Pz.Div.*, but attacks persisted well into the evening, with indecisive results. Across the rest of the front along the Gran, *Gen.Lt.* Kirschner reported no other combat activity worth mentioning. These were some of the last actions fought by these two *panzer* divisions before they were replaced by the *44. Reichs-Gren.Div. HuD* and shipped to reinforce the battered *H.Gr. A* hundreds of kilometers to the north. Their combat power would soon be sorely missed.

In Budapest, the *IX. SS-Geb.Korps'* evacuation of the eastern bridgehead in Pest was reported to have been completed during the evening of 17/18 January without being pressed very closely by the enemy, though artillery fire throughout the withdrawal was intense. Most of the defenders' heavy weapons and armored vehicles were abandoned or blown up to prevent their capture. On the western bridgehead in Buda, Pfeffer-Wildenbruch reported that Soviet troops attempted to penetrate the front lines at numerous locations, but were driven back by the defenders, who suffered heavy losses while doing so. During these attacks, two Red Army tanks were destroyed by German infantrymen using hand-held antitank weapons.

That evening, *Luftwaffe* efforts to resupply Pfeffer-Wildenbruch's force enjoyed a measurable degree of success. Despite the snow and strong winds over the city, the aircrews of *Luftflotte 4*, flying primarily from their air base at Papa, were able to drop 41.75 metric tons (46 short tons) of German and 2.5 tons of Hungarian munitions over the city by parachute, as well as 0.12 tons (275lb) of medical supplies. Troops in the city reported difficulty in recovering the supply canisters due to the deep snowdrifts that hampered efforts to transport their precious contents back to supply points. These badly needed supplies would enable the garrison to continue fighting for several more days. Given the opportunity, the crews flying the ancient *Ju-52* transports and *He-111* bombers converted to cargo carriers could work miracles, and the night of 18/19 January witnessed one of them.[10]

In the air above the attacking forces of *A. Gr. Balck/6. Armee*, very strong Soviet aerial activity was reported against the units of the *IV. SS-Pz.Korps*, including numerous sorties flown by ground-attack aircraft using low-level bombing and strafing runs against Gille's advancing units, sometimes targeting individual vehicles. German aerial reconnaissance was able to report that long convoys of as many as 50 trucks were observed moving east along the road that ran along the southern shore of Lake Balaton, with some vehicles towing antitank guns. Even though the *Luftwaffe* was unable to fly as many scouting sorties as the situation demanded, this report signified that infantry elements from the neighboring 57th Army were being sent east to reinforce the CXXXV Guards Rifle Corps.

Overall, *A. Gr. Balck* was satisfied with the day's progress. With the exception of the attack by the *III. Pz.Korps*, whose *23. Pz.Div.* had been able to push forward only 3 kilometers towards the heights east of the Stuhlweissenburg–Sárkeresztes road, the four divisions of the *IV. SS-Pz.Korps* had achieved all of their assigned objectives. The *I. Kav.Korps* had held its positions, and the attack by *LVII Pz.Korps* was steadily pushing the forces of the 6th Guards Tank and 7th Guards Armies back to the starting point where their offensive began nearly two weeks earlier. Therefore, Gille's corps needed to take advantage of its success gained that day and continue pushing onwards the next morning before the 4th Guards Army could craft a unified response. At this point, Balck and his commanders had learned how quickly the Third Ukrainian Front could react and seemingly conjure reserves out of thin air.

Consequently, Balck's headquarters issued additional guidance for the following day in a teletype message sent out at midnight to his four army corps and his Hungarian allies. Balck directed his troops to:

1. Continue the breakthrough attack that same night [i.e., 18/19 January] from the bridgeheads established on the Sárviz Canal to the east and northeast to the narrows between Ercsi and Lake Velencze to take the Váli [Canal] sector and build bridgeheads over the canal;
2. Gain and hold the Sió [River] sector with the armored reconnaissance battalions to establish bridgeheads for the protection of the extended south flank;
3. *I. Kav.Korps* to launch attacks north of Mány to fix the enemy and hinder the withdrawal of his forces to bind him in place; and
4. Prepare a breakout from the southern sector of the western bridgehead in Budapest to the southwest to take the Budaörs airport, while simultaneously holding the current defensive lines. This is to be carried out only by special order issued by the *Armeegruppe*.

This last task, which amounted to an "on-order" type of mission, had not yet been cleared with *OKH* headquarters, meaning Hitler. However, it did signify that *Gen.d.Pz.Tr.* Balck was contemplating ordering the *IX. SS-Geb.Korps* to carry out a partial breakout, if only to link up with the relief force.

If nothing else, this would allow Pfeffer-Wildenbruch's wounded to be evacuated, though the city would still have to be held. By this point, there was very little of the city in German and Hungarian hands still to hold. But spirits were high among the attacking troops, casualties in Gille's corps had been relatively light, and the signs seemed promising for the following day's attack. After a brief pause to rearm and refuel, as well as giving artillery and other supporting arms an opportunity to reposition forward to continue providing dedicated fire support, the four attacking divisions of the *IV. SS-Pz.Korps* prepared to continue their attack at first light the next morning.

As mentioned earlier, both the 4th Guards Army and its higher command, the Third Ukrainian Front, were caught off guard by the attack that morning. German deception operations had been highly successful. Both Zakharov and Tolbukhin were convinced that the *IV. SS-Pz.Korps* had been shipped out of Hungary and was no longer a threat to be reckoned with. The only German actions they considered as possible dangers were an unlikely resumption of the attack by the *I. Kav.Korps* towards Zámoly and some sort of continuation of the attack towards the southeast out of Gran, combined with a breakout attempt from Budapest. Most of the corresponding Soviet responses being considered or actively underway between 12 and 17 January involved moving forces around to reinforce the center and right flank of the 4th Guards Army, at the expense of the army's left flank, where the German blow actually fell on 18 January. The only available force that could be initially committed to counter this attack was the VII Mechanized Corps, which was already in position northeast of Stuhlweissenburg and had begun to send portions of its four brigades to reinforce the LXXXV Guards Rifle Corps in the south.

It would take several more days for the Soviet commanders to actually identify *A. Gr. Balck*'s point of main effort; until then, most of their responses were tentative and insufficiently powerful. Zakharov's army had already committed most of its reserves and would have to depend upon Tolbukhin's ability to acquire additional forces from the *STAVKA*'s strategic reserve to fully counter the attack by the *IV. SS-Pz.Korps*.[11] A German intelligence assessment that evening of possible Soviet countermoves stated, "It remains to be seen whether the enemy will intensify his attacks to relieve the situation or regroup his mobile units to the south to avoid being cut off from his supply lines."[12] Unless quick action was taken, it was possible the German attack might penetrate into the operational depths of the 4th Guards Army the next day and cut it off on the west bank of the Danube.

The *Konrad III* offensive resumed before daybreak the following morning. Weather conditions were almost identical to the previous day, except that the fog that prevailed on 18 January had given way to snow. This was good news for the Germans; not only would the freezing conditions allow tanks and other armored vehicles to continuing to maneuver cross-country, but the snowfall would make it difficult for the Red Air Force to locate and attack German ground targets, though it would also hamper *Luftwaffe* attempts to provide close air support to the attacking tank columns.

While this was welcome news for the commanders charged with leading the ground attacks, the harsh weather conditions made life difficult for those taking part. On 19 January, an *SS-Kriegsberichter* "embedded" with the *Totenkopf* Division reported:

> The cold has become even harder, over the foothills of the Bakony Forest and the Vértes Mountains an icy wind blows down and brushes furiously over the ice of Lake Balaton and the open foreland. It covers vehicles and tanks with smooth layers of frozen snow, biting the lungs of the *Panzergrenadiere* and turning their winter clothing into crinkled parchment.[13]

In many instances, troops had to bed down for the night in the open, scooping up enough snow around their positions to form a windbreak against the biting cold. Fires in these conditions were strictly forbidden, lest it reveal their positions, leaving Gille's men no alternative other than to huddle together for warmth as best they could and long for the morning sun.

Describing the action that day in its evening summary, Gille's *Führungsabteilung* continued its upbeat assessment of the results of the offensive thus far. In dry official language, the *Korps Ic* reported:

> Weak enemy forces were thrown out of Siófok and forced back across the Sió Canal. Corps reconnaissance assets [i.e., *Pz.Aufkl.Abt. 1, 3,* and *23*] reported that in the tactical zone located along both sides of Simontornya, enemy forces appeared to be getting reinforced by an unknown number of armored fighting vehicles. One of our own armored groups attacked into the town of Sárbogárd via Herczegfalva towards the northeast and in so doing, reached the Danube at Dunapentele. At this location [our units are] fighting with a reinforced enemy unit that is still under way. Attacking out of Sárkeresztur, our own advancing forces crossed the railroad

embankment five kilometers south of Sárosd. West of Aba, the enemy was still offering tough resistance. Near Fövenyipuszta, our forces were able to overcome a strong enemy antitank barrier after heavy fighting and threw the enemy out of Seregélyes. Also during the late afternoon, we were able to force the enemy back across the railroad line six kilometers west-southwest of the southwest corner of Lake Velencze.[14]

The most significant point in the entire report was the news that the corps' spearhead had already reached the Danube ahead of schedule; what was not reported was that this effectively cut the 4th Guards Army in half. It would take approximately 24 hours for the Soviet command to become aware of this fact. For his part, Gille described the events of the day in his usual prosaic, matter-of-fact style, writing, "The attack made good progress despite enemy counterattacks. By 3 a.m., the *Wiking* Division had already reached Kisláng south of Stuhlweissenburg after having advanced 40 kilometers beyond the *HKL*. By the middle of the day, it had already crossed the [Sárviz] canal at Káloz. The other divisions are lagging behind."[15]

Despite the progress made that day, Balck was far from satisfied with the performance of Gille's corps, singling out both the *Wiking* and *Totenkopf* Divisions for criticism. Despite the possibility that both divisions were experiencing communications difficulties, Balck believed that the status of their attacks' progress was being unreported due to negligence, leaving both Gille and Balck in the dark as to where Ullrich's and Becker's forward elements were actually located. It prompted Balck to order Gille to move forward to determine for himself what was happening, though Gille hardly needed urging to do what was his usual practice anyway. Despite this, Balck verbally complained about the unresponsiveness of the *IV. SS-Pz.Korps* to Wöhler at 5:15 p.m. that afternoon.[16]

Upon examination of the official records, including the transcriptions of radio message traffic received by the *Führungsabteilung* of *A.Gr. Balck/6. Armee*, it can be seen that the *Totenkopf* and *Wiking* Divisions were sending a steady stream of situation reports throughout that day, belying Balck's assertions to the contrary. In all, 18 such radio messages were recorded in the *A.Gr. Balck/6. Armee* war diary as having been received that day, including reports stating the precise location of the *Wiking* and *Totenkopf* Divisions' forward elements, ongoing combat activity, and actions of the enemy. It must be taken into account that the spearheads of both SS divisions were now over 50 kilometers away from Gille's headquarters, a distance where the standard FM communications systems were beginning to reach the limit of their operational range. In addition, atmospheric factors might have influenced the transmission of any kind of electronic communications, whether FM, AM, or short-wave.

In retrospect, Balck's frustration may be a simple case of improper or negligent sharing of information within his own headquarters, or perhaps within the headquarters of Gille's corps or by the radiomen of *SS-Nachr.Abt. 104*. Regardless, when he spoke with Wöhler at 9 p.m. that evening, he was asked by his superior for more information about this incident. Balck simply told him that he had found out what he needed to know, stating that he was simply expressing a *vorsorglich* (precautionary) expression of annoyance. Such pettiness on Balck's part had become standard operating procedure when dealing with the *IV. SS-Pz. Korps.*[17]

Again, down at the division level, things did not appear so cut and dried, for the fighting was heavy all along the line when the assault was resumed that morning. While the three armored reconnaissance battalions secured the corps' 75-kilometer right flank along the Sió River to the west and south, the *3.Pz.Div.* resumed its attack towards the northeast at first light. It soon took the town of Herczegfalva by storm and pushed as far as Dunapentele, where the enemy put up stiff resistance.[18] With this move, *Oberst* Söth's division cut the supply lines of the CXXXIII Rifle Corps, separating it from its artillery and logistics services, which were still crossing the Danube at this point.

Alongside Söth's division, Ullrich's *Wiking* Division also made rapid progress. Both men had worked closely together during August 1944 east of Warsaw, and their previous relationship was put to good use during this battle. After the Sárkeresztur bridge east of the Sárviz Canal had been reinforced, at 5:30 a.m. the division's lead element burst forth in a headlong assault towards the east. A tank-supported Soviet counterattack was launched from the direction of Seregélyes against the division's left flank, but this was warded off.

By late afternoon, the division's assault group on the right reached the area 5 kilometers east of the town of Sárosd, roughly halfway towards its intermediate objective of Perkáta. During the afternoon, despite tough enemy resistance, the *Kampfgruppe* on the left was able to take the town of Aba, but could not advance any farther that day. With his division having taken a large swath of enemy territory, Ullrich decided at 12:40 p.m. to move his *Gefechtstand* closer to the front lines, selecting the village of Kisláng for his forward headquarters. Because the pace of the *Wiking* Division's advance had outstripped that of its left-hand neighbor, Becker's *Totenkopf* Division, Ullrich was forced to deploy *Stubaf.* Wagner's *SS-Pz.Aufkl.Abt.* 5 to cover his wide-open left flank.

It took a little longer for the *Totenkopf* Division to resume its advance because of the work needed to repair the bridges over the Malom and Sárviz Canals at Tác and Falubattyán, which had been disabled by retreating Soviet troops the day before. It was not until 7:45 a.m. that Becker was able to get all of his division across and moving again, but when it did, it struck eastwards with a vengeance. Near the village of Fövenyi Puszta, its vanguard element ran up against a well-constructed Soviet *Pakfront*, forcing its tanks to deploy in order to overcome the defenses. After heavy fighting, the Soviet antitank gunners were forced to abandon their guns, suffering heavy losses, clearing the way for the *Totenkopf* Division's tanks to finally break through into the clear. The division's spearhead halted for the night at a position approximately 4 kilometers west of Seregélyes, its intermediate objective.[19] By this point, Becker's troops had advanced 30 kilometers since the previous morning when the offensive began.

On the corps' left flank, the *1. Pz.Div.* pushed south of Stuhlweissenburg after overcoming initially strong resistance offered by the 252nd Rifle Division. Skirting the southern edge of the city, *Gen.Maj.* Thünert's spearhead reached the southwestern tip of Lake Velencze by the afternoon, taking the town of Dinnyés that evening. That same day, the division's commander was forced to divert a significant portion of his forces to cover the ever-expanding exposed left flank between Lake Velencze and Palmajor (over 20 kilometers wide by this point) in order to protect it against enemy counterattacks emanating from the direction of Stuhlweissenburg, which was still in the hands of the enemy. Fortunately for the *1. Pz.Div.*, these Soviet counterattacks were local in nature and not part of any concerted, organized effort to stop its assault.[20]

At the close of 19 January, Breith's *III. Pz.Korps* reported that it had not yet taken Stuhlweissenburg. Northwest of the city, the enemy appeared to be strengthening his front-line defenses and a battalion-sized attack was launched against German troops east of the town of Sárkeresztes, achieving local penetrations before being thrown back in a counterattack. South of the town of Környe, another battalion-sized Soviet infantry assault achieved another short-lived breakthrough before being defeated and ultimately driven back. A portion of the front lines seized by enemy troops the day before was ironed out by a German counterattack and the previous position restored.

While these represented German defensive successes by the *23. Pz.Div.*, the *4. Kav.Brig.*, and the Hungarian *2. Pz.Div.*, this was not Breith's mission, which was to attack in support of the *A.Gr. Balck/6. Armee* main effort north of Lake Velencze by seizing key terrain and gaining control of Stuhlweissenburg. The failure or inability to strengthen Breith's corps to carry out this important mission was to have dire consequences a week later, though this was not sufficiently appreciated when the offensive was being planned seven days earlier. Nevertheless, the *III. Pz.Korps* was ordered to renew its attack at 7:30 p.m. that evening, with the *23. Pz.Div.* renewing its effort to take Stuhlweissenburg and *Div.Gr. Holste* (*4. Kav.Brig.*) carrying out a supporting attack to the north.

To Breith's left, Harteneck's *I. Kav.Korps* reported that the *6. Pz.Div.*, after overcoming tough enemy resistance, had been able to clear out a dangerous penetration of its front line in the forest 5 kilometers northwest of Bicske. This area, located on the hilltop west of Csabdi, had been taken by the *Wiking* Division nearly two weeks earlier and its loss the previous evening had threatened to undermine the integrity of Harteneck's entire right flank. On his left, Soviet troops continued to attack the forward positions of the *711. Inf.Div.* east of the town of Kesztölc and northwest of Pilisszentlélek in a bid to force *Gen.Lt.* Reichert's troops back into Gran. In the heavy fighting that took place that day, a number of key hills changed hands several times, with the outcome still uncertain when the evening report was submitted. In the areas held by the *3. Kav. Brig.* and the *96. Inf. Div.*—both arrayed in the center of the *I. Kav. Korps* defensive sector—no combat action worth mentioning was reported, a sign that Soviet forces opposite them were either being relieved or repositioned.

On the northern bank of the Danube, the *LVII. Pz. Korps* was trying to get the most offensive action out of its two *panzer* divisions before they were recalled and sent north. *Generalleutnant* Kirchner's aggressive attacks against Col. Gen. Kravchenko's battered 6th Guards Tank Army were paying off; in two or three days, if he did not withdraw his three tank and mechanized corps across the Gran River in time, the 6th Guards Tank Army's commander ran the risk of losing most of his force. However, on 19 January, Kirchner found out that this was not going to be easy; that day, an armored battlegroup from *8. Pz. Div.* was forced back to its starting point when its attack against an enemy-occupied patch of woods north-northeast of Karva was counterattacked by a tank-supported Soviet force of battalion size originating from the neighboring town of Mužla.[21]

Ten kilometers northwest of Karva, an attack by the *Kampfgruppe* from the *20. Pz. Div.* threw defending Soviet troops out of their positions southwest of Bucs. To counter this German success, a Soviet tank brigade with its few remaining tanks attempted an attack of its own out of Bucs and Bátorove Kesy, but was beaten back without having gained any ground. Along the rest of the corps front, as had been reported the previous day, no combat worth mentioning took place in the defensive sectors held by the *211. V.G.D.* and its neighbor to the north, *K. Gr. Staubwasser*, an ad-hoc unit formed from the remnants of the *357. Inf. Div.* Although not mentioned in the daily summary, by this point in the campaign the railroad line between Neuhäusel and Komorn had been freed up, thus allowing railway construction battalions to begin repairing the line and putting it back into service.

In Budapest, the *IX. SS-Geb. Korps* reported that during the early hours of 19 January, a Soviet combat patrol of at least company strength had been able to cross over the eastern arm of the frozen Danube in the vicinity of the northern tip of Margaret Island and seize a small bridgehead. Margaret Island, situated as it was between both banks of the Danube, was still being defended as a bulwark against any Soviet river crossing attempt.[22] Recognizing the danger, *Ogruf.* Pfeffer-Wildenbruch sent an SS battalion, reinforced by a Hungarian infantry company and four antitank guns, to throw them back across the river. Although this force was strong enough to push the Soviet patrol back to the abutments of the unfinished Árpád Bridge, it was not powerful enough to completely wipe out the attackers or force them to withdraw back across the river.[23] The Soviets would be back to try again the following night after receiving reinforcements. Along the rest of *Festung Budapest's* defensive line, both sides carried out numerous armed reconnaissance forays; with the exception of the usual artillery and mortar fire, everything else passed relatively uneventfully.

On 19 January, Red Air Force activity increased considerably, with the squadrons of the 17th Air Army reporting 718 individual sorties being flown that day.[24] In the skies above the *IV. SS-Pz.Korps* and the *LVII. Pz.Korps*, Soviet ground-attack and fighter aircraft sought out the German spearheads and subjected them to multiple bombing and strafing runs. These attacks did not go unchallenged; on 19 January alone, the *Totenkopf* Division reported shooting down two IL-2 *Stormoviks*.[25] In contrast, over *III. Pz.Korps* and *I. Kav.Korps*, only enemy reconnaissance aircraft were reported.[26] Twelve IL-2 *Sturmoviks* from the 615th Ground Attack Aircraft Regiment, flying as low as 400 feet, attacked the Tigers of *s.Pz.Abt. 509* as the battalion was crossing the Nador Canal in the afternoon, but despite the use of PTAB tank-destroyer bombs, only one Tiger was damaged by a lucky hit on the barrel.

The *I. Fliegerkorps*, though most of its aircraft were grounded in the morning by the weather, began operating in the afternoon, with its *Stukas*, *Me-109*s, and *Fw-190*s flying 270 sorties against retreating Soviet columns and subjecting them to a pounding such as they had not experienced in a very long while. *Messerschmitt Me-210*s of the Royal Hungarian Air Force also flew a number of sorties against Soviet ground targets. Throughout the day, the Germans and Hungarian *Jäger* shot down 21 Soviet aircraft.[27] There was no shortage of targets; German reconnaissance aircraft reported over 800 Soviet vehicles moving in an easterly direction towards the lower Danube bridges, indications of a large-scale retreat.

In the field army's daily intelligence summary, Balcks' Deputy *Ic*, *Hptm.* von Pander, reported that the enemy appeared to be regrouping the VII Mechanized Corps and XVIII Tank Corps in the area between Stuhlweissenburg and the Danube in order to defend against *A.Gr. Balck*'s attack group. Pander reported that Soviet infantry and numerous artillery units were being moved towards the south via Stuhlweissenburg. Aerial reconnaissance detected additional movement from the north headed towards the area between Lake Velencze and the Danube. From the front south of Lake Balaton held by the Soviet 57th Army, additional forces—presumably from the 61st Guards Rifle Division—were observed moving to the east. Based on these reports, the deputy *Ic* assessed that the most likely course of action of the 4th Guards Army was to smash the attacking German spearhead and safeguard the connections to their own supply lines by concentrating all available forces from the north and partly also from the south.

Upon reviewing the day's events that evening, *Gen.d.Pz.Tr.* Balck informed the *H.Gr. Süd* commander that he believed the 4th Guards Army had been beaten and was retreating in disarray. The success of the day's actions had evidently exceeded his initially negative expectations. After the war, Balck stated in his memoir, "We had prepared for the attack with great care because ... I had serious doubts about it." Even in his personal diary at the time, he wrote before the battle, "Our hopes of getting the [troops in Budapest] out are little more than minuscule. Nobody should have any illusions on that point."[28] With the successful outcome of day two of *Konrad III*, Balck had changed his mind and was now chasing illusions of his own.

For his part, *Gen.d.Inf.* Wöhler did not share the same opinion. As previously noted in the *6. Armee* daily intelligence estimate, a great deal of enemy movement had been detected by German reconnaissance aircraft. An updated intelligence estimate was drafted early that evening, which stated:

> There was still no clear picture of the enemy [situation gained] from aerial reconnaissance ... [which had] confirmed 2,000 enemy vehicles moving from the area in front of [our] attack north towards Budapest and 600 vehicles moving in the opposite direction to the south. In the first case, it was possibly a question of [logistics] elements fleeing; in the second case, it was the moving up of forces.[29]

The logical conclusion that Wöhler drew was that while the rear echelon elements of the CXXXV Rifle Corps were indeed pulling out to avoid encirclement, at the same time Soviet reserves—including tank and mechanized units—were being rushed in the opposite direction to plug the "deep and wide" hole that had been blasted in the front lines of Tolbukhin's army group, as well as to insert additional forces into Stuhlweissenburg to prevent it from falling into the hands of the German and Hungarian forces.[30]

With the exception of the understrength CXXXIII Rifle Corps, which on 19 January was still in the process of moving into its assembly area near Perkáta after crossing the Danube near Dunaföldvar, the only reserves available to the Third Ukrainian Front to plug the hole was the XVIII Tank Corps, which had played an important role in slowing the advance of the *IV. SS-Pz.Korps* during *Konrad I.* After a week's rest, the brigades of Maj.Gen. Govorunenko's corps had been partially reequipped with a number of armored fighting vehicles to replace what had been lost in battle during the past two weeks. On 17 January, it reported having 79 operational vehicles within its three brigades, including 66 T-34s, eight JSU-122 assault guns, and five SU-85 SP tank destroyers, making it still a potent force.[31]

During this brief period of rest, the corps had been positioned southwest of Budapest to block any attempt by the garrison to break out, but the danger of that occurring was outweighed by the much more serious situation unfolding south of Lake Velencze. Zakharov had already alerted Govorunenko the previous evening of his new mission, and the XVIII Tank Corps began moving south during the night of 18/19 January. The initial intent was to set up a new defense line at the Sárviz Canal, provided that the corps arrived in time, but this plan was overcome by events on the ground before it had even departed its rest area. In any case, the next day promised a great deal of heavy fighting, but until these reserves arrived, the most that Maj.Gen. Gnedin's CXXXV Guards Rifle Corps could hope to accomplish was to delay the attackers as long as possible and prevent them from establishing bridgeheads over the Malom and Sárviz Canals.

After conferencing that afternoon with Wöhler concerning the progress of the past two days of fighting, Balck issued additional guidance to his forces for the following day's operations that modified the original *Konrad III* plan. Sensing an opportunity to achieve even greater results than what the operation was originally intended to achieve, Balck directed the Hungarian *3. Armee* to carry out an amphibious operation across Lake Balaton to the opposite bank, adjacent to the Sió River screen line established by *Pz.Aufkl.Abt. 1*.[32]

The unit chosen to carry out this operation, the Hungarian *25. Inf.Div.*, was to ferry two of its battalions during the night of 20/21 January and seize the town of Zamárdi, then attack to the east and trap any Soviet units between the landing site and Siófok, held by its reconnassiance battalion.[33] Once it had linked up with the force holding Siófok, the remaining regiments of the *25. Inf.Div.* would either be ferried across the lake or brought down to the Sió River along the eastern shore of Lake Balaton, where they would assume responsibility for defending the wide defensive sector, freeing up the three German armored reconnaissance battalions for further assignment or to return to their units.

For its part, the *IV. SS-Pz.Korps* was to continue its own assault to seize the narrows between the Danube and Lake Velencze, the corps' intermediate objective, with the *1. Pz.Div.* and the two SS divisions. A crucial element of this entailed seizing a bridgehead over the Váli River. This would create the necessary conditions for the advance towards Budapest, the ultimate goal of the offensive. Breith's *III. Pz.Korps* would continue its attack to seize Stuhlweissenburg and bring the northern shore of Lake Velencze under German control.

The adjacent *I. Kav.Korps* was given the most ambitious task of all. This consisted of concentrating both the *6. Pz.Div.* and *3. Kav.Brig.* into a powerful armored task force that would strike in a southeasterly direction towards the gap between Bicske and Zsámbék, with the twin goals of tying up or diverting Soviet reserves away from the attack by the *IV. SS-Pz.Korps* as well as forming the northern arm of a pincer designed to trap the better part of the 4th Guards Army. To achieve this massing of combat power, Harteneck would have to ruthlessly strip nearly all of his mobile units from the rest of his front line between Felsőgalla and Gran, causing considerable risk when the defense of most of his corps' defensive sector would be handed off to the depleted *96.* and *711. Inf.Div.* The regrouping of these forces would begin early the next day in the area east of Csabdi. As for the *LVII. Pz.Korps*, it would transition to the defense, since the replacement of both of its *panzer* divisions by the *44. Reichs-Gren.Div.* had already begun, a move that would limit the corps' ability to conduct mobile operations.

In evaluating his intentions for the following day, one cannot help but notice that the practical goals of *Konrad III* were being outstripped by Balck's ambitions. While the landing operation by the Hungarians at Lake Balaton would affect nothing if it failed (they could simply be redirected around the lake's eastern shore to get to the Sió River), any failure by the *I. Kav.Korps* to achieve its objectives, or the *III. Pz.Korps* for that matter, would have wide-ranging consequences. In addition, none of the units concerned had enough combat power to carry out what they were being ordered to do. Nevertheless, Wöhler approved the modifications to Balck's plan, which went out to the units involved by *Fernschreiber* that evening. As for the units concerned, Gille's four divisions had been fighting almost continuously for the past 48 hours; with little time for rest, his men used the opportunity during the night to replenish ammunition, fuel their vehicles, and evacuate the wounded. Tank recovery teams would retrieve any damaged armored vehicles and work through the day to place as many as possible back into operation.

The third day of Operation *Konrad III* would involve just as much heavy fighting as the previous two days, but would also see the continuation of the *IV. SS-Pz.Korps'* advance, albeit at a slower pace. On 20 January, the weather still hovered around freezing, snow and ice continued to affect mobility for wheeled and tracked vehicles, and low-hanging clouds hampered air operations by both sides. With Budapest only 50 kilometers away, Gille's troops redoubled their efforts, well aware that time was running short. The commanders of the 4th Guards Army and the Third Ukrainian Front had already begun to see Balck's true intentions and were beginning to craft a response, a trait that the Red Army had repeatedly demonstrated throughout the campaign in Hungary. On 20 January, this took the form of Govorunenko's XVIII Tank Corps, whose brigades attacked aggressively into the face of the German main attack and soon found themselves surrounded. This fight would become the major tactical event of the day.

In its summary of the day's events, the *IV. SS-Pz.Korps* reported to *A.Gr. Balck/6. Armee* in the evening that despite heavy fighting, including a number of Soviet counterattacks, things were going according to plan. The corps' *Ic, Stubaf.* Jankuhn, wrote:

> The enemy penetration north of Felsőnyék was in the process of being eliminated ... Előszállás, as well as the heights west and northwest are still occupied by the enemy. Our own *Panzergruppe* is advancing along the Danube River road without any noticeable enemy resistance as far as Radicsa Puszta. The enemy was forced to abandon Perkáta ... Our troops fought all day long for the possession of Sárosd and Aba. Tank-supported enemy forces were able to ward off our own assaults against these towns, though an enemy counterattack from Sárosd toward the southeast and south failed. Heavy fighting [for these towns] continues. Strong enemy resistance east of Fövenyi Puszta was finally broken around mid-afternoon and his forces were thrown out of Seregélyes. The enemy was unable to hinder the advance of our attacking columns in the area 6 kilometers northwest of Puszta Szabolcs and Agárd Puszta. [34]

Jankuhn also mentioned that a reconnaissance was carried out by troops from *Pz.Aufkl.Abt. 1* towards Zamárdi, and found it free of the enemy. Nevertheless, the Hungarian *3. Armee* decided to scrap the amphibious operation because of the heavy ice on the lake and bring the *25. Inf.Div.* around to the Sió defensive sector by truck instead, where it began relieving *Pz.Aufkl.Abt. 1* between Siófok and Mezö Komárom later in the day. To simplify command and control of the Hungarian *25. Inf.Div.*, *Gen.d.Pz.Tr.* Balck decided to attach it to the *IV. SS-Pz.Korps*, instead of leaving it under the Hungarian *3. Armee* as originally intended.

On the corps' 120-kilometer right flank along the Sió River sector, the three armored reconnaissance battalions, bolstered by the arrival of lead elements from the Hungarian 25. *Inf.Div*, reported a number of Soviet units cautiously approaching from the south. Both Balck and Gille knew that the defense of this vulnerable sector was exceedingly thin and it would be expecting too much for the *3. Pz.Div.* to defend this sector and continue its attack north along the Danube. A better command and control arrangement needed to be made quickly to relieve *Oberst* Söth of this responsibility.

A Soviet probe across the Sió River at Mezö Komárom earlier that morning had already been driven back by *Pz.Aukfl.Abt. 1* as its last official act before handing off its sector to the Hungarians; more enemy forces had been spotted assembling in the area south of Simontornya and Czecze, where the Sió River and Sárviz Canal intersected. This area marked the boundary between *Pz.Aufkl.Abt. 23* on the western side of the Sárviz and *Pz.Aufkl.Abt. 3* on the east. While the size of the approaching Soviet force was unknown, one thing was certain—there were insufficient forces to stop them from attacking to the north if they chose to do so. Three armored reconnaissance battalions and a reinforced Hungarian infantry division were simply not enough to screen, much less hold, such a wide frontage.[35]

In the aforementioned *3. Pz.Div.* zone of attack, while its *Pz.Aufkl.Abt 3* screened its extended right flank between Czecze and the area south of Dunapentele, *Oberst* Söth's armored spearhead, *Pz.Gr. Weymann*—composed of the bulk of *Pz.Rgt. 6, I. Btl.(gep.)/Pz.Gren.Rgt. 3, Pz.Jäg.Abt. 543*, and *II. Abt/Pz.Art.Rgt. 75*—continued pushing north along the west bank of the Danube. By 3:15 p.m., it had reached the road and rail intersection 5 kilometers south of Adony, after overrunning Soviet rear-area units at Perkáta and Rácalmás. The only enemy resistance that *Oberstlt.* Weymann reported encountering along the way were ineffectual air attacks against his leading columns. At Adony, his forces were brought to a halt by a minefield and *Pakfront* erected by the 41st Guards Cavalry Regiment from the V Guards Cavalry Corps and the 1255th Separate Antitank Regiment. Here, Weymann and his troops halted for the remainder of the day as they waited for the rest of their column to catch up before making an organized assault the following morning.

At the same time, *K.Gr. Medicus*—comprising the reinforced *II. Btl./Pz.Gren.Rgt. 3*, which had been left behind to guard the Danube ford at Dunapentele—reported that it had shot up a Soviet river crossing attempt at that location, sinking five river tug boats and a barge carrying troops in the process. As the division continued its drive north, it had to drop off numerous detachments along the river to observe and report any additional enemy attempts to cross, thereby weakening the division's leading elements even further. Söth had already been forced to detach one battalion from *Pz.Gren.Rgt. 394* to protect the division's exposed southern flank between Dunapentele and Herczegfalva. The lack of sufficient infantry to occupy the ground gained by the advancing *panzer* divisions was now being acutely felt.[36]

The *3. Pz.Div.* left-hand neighbor, the *Wiking* Division, experienced its share of heavy fighting that day, as the arrival of Soviet reserves along the Sárviz Canal began to influence the battle. In several places in the division's rear area between Sárosd and Aba, Soviet mechanized forces from all four of the XVIII Tank Corps' brigades—the 110th, 170th, and 181st Tank Brigades, and the 32nd Motorized Rifle Brigade—and the CXXXIII Rifle Corps, along with supporting arms, were able to punch their way through the *Totenkopf* and the left flank of the *Wiking* Division and advance far enough to the south to sever its attack group's supply lines.

In turn, Dorr's *Panzergruppe* severed one of the Soviet supply columns, shooting up or capturing a large number of trucks at 9 a.m., and reported reaching the town of Perkáta by 2 p.m., which Balck later disputed.[37] Shortly afterwards, Dorr and Darges quickly found their *Panzergruppe* under attack from all sides, forcing them to temporarily form a hedgehog position to avoid being overrun by a large enemy force. Due to the condition of the ground, which was covered by deep snowdrifts, the approaching Soviet troops and tanks had to take the crossroads town in order to continue their move to the south, but each attempt was rebuffed with heavy losses.

Throughout the rest of that day, the encircled *Panzergruppe* and other division elements successfully fought off a number of enemy attacks, knocking out as many as eight enemy tanks that day. As the Soviet force continued with its attack against Perkáta, Ullrich's entire division was forced to temporarily revert to a defensive posture along the line Perkáta–Sárosd–Sárkeresztur, facing to the north. In one tank engagement earlier that morning, *Ostuf.* Karl-Heinz Lichte, the acting commander of *5. Kp./SS-Pz.Rgt. 5*, was wounded in action near Sárosd when his command tank was struck by an enemy shell, perhaps fired by a JS-II heavy tank. After being rescued from his burning tank by his old friend Alfred Grossrock, he was driven directly to the regiment's field dressing station, where its surgeon, Dr Edwin Kalbskopf, saved his life. He was quickly replaced as company commander by *Ostuf.* Heinrich Kerckhoff.[38] Another long-time *Wiking* officer was killed that same day near Sárosd when his SP artillery battery from *5. Bttr./SS-Pz.Art.Rgt. 5* was overrun by two T-34s. *Hstuf.* Fritz Zäh had just emplaced his battery in its firing position when the *Wespe* he was commanding attempt to engage the onrushing enemy tanks with direct fire.[39] His remains were never recovered.

After heavy fighting, the town of Aba, 11 kilometers west of Sárosd, fell to Soviet troops during the early afternoon. Attempts by a portion of Franz Hack's *Westland* Regiment to retake it from the west were repulsed. Another attempt was made from the east by *I. Btl./Westland* a few hours later, but this too failed.[40] This was especially disconcerting, because this town was located far behind the front lines, and even behind Sárosd, which had been taken earlier. The loss of Aba, however temporarily, meant that the division's main supply route had been cut and that its forward spearheads operating east of the Sárviz Canal—primarily Dorr's *Panzergruppe*, the rest of the *Germania* Regiment, and *SS-Pz.Aufkl.Abt. 5*—would soon run out of fuel unless Aba was retaken, and quickly.

Apparently, throughout most of 20 January, neither Gille, Ullrich nor any of their subordinate commanders realized that the XVIII Tank Corps and CXXXIII Rifle Corps had given up their attempt to stop the *Wiking* or *Totenkopf* Divisions along the Sárviz Canal and had instead been given permission to break out to the south before they were completely encircled and destroyed. The fact that the *IV. SS-Pz.Korps* had bypassed or encircled a large number of Soviet units (at least four tank/mechanized brigades and two rifle divisions) fighting in the area encompassed by the towns of Sárkeresztur, Seregélyes, and Perkáta was not yet generally known when the *Korps* resumed its advance that morning, but by midday Gille, Ullrich, Becker, and Söth had become painfully aware of the true nature of the situation.

It became evident by the end of the day, however, that the general direction of movement of these trapped units was to the south, where they sought to make contact with the new front line rapidly being formed on the right flank of the *3. Pz.Div.*[41] These two Soviet corps could have just as easily reached the safety of the Danube by moving eastwards, but with no bridges or ferries available, the XVIII Tank Corps and CXXXIII Rifle Corps could have only escaped by abandoning all of their equipment, including Govorunenko's 64 remaining tanks and assault guns. Not wanting to establish bridgeheads on the western bank of the Danube yet again after seizing them at great cost the first time, Marshal Tolbukhin forbade this course of action, which left the southern escape route in the direction of Dunaföldvar as the two corps' only viable option.[42]

These developments forced *Oberf.* Ullrich to order some of the division's leading elements to turn about and eliminate this existential threat by "attacking to the rear." This was made all the more difficult because the bulk of the division's *panzers* were temporarily encircled 2 kilometers northwest of Perkáta. This "mopping up" process (it was far more than that), carried out predominately by the *Westland* Regiment, would require at least 24 hours to complete, slowing the *Wiking* Division's advance considerably. Once again, the lack of infantry divisions to secure the area just taken would demand a toll in terms of the attacking force's loss of momentum. Had the *Wiking* been followed by an infantry division, this task could have been delegated to it, leaving Ullrich's division free to continue its attack to the northeast.

Although the *Totenkopf* Division was embroiled in just as much heavy fighting on 20 January as the neighboring *Wiking*, its progress was greater, since it managed to avoid contact with the bulk of the enemy's encircled forces. The division's actions that day can be summed up in one word: Seregélyes. This key town, through which passed one of the main supply routes for the 4th Guards Army, had to be taken that day in order for *Konrad III* to remain on schedule. Because the swampy ground leading to the town's western approaches was deemed impassable for tanks despite the freezing temperatures, the division's armored spearhead was forced to go around the northern portion of the town, while *K.Gr. Eckert*, formed around *SS-Pz.Gren. Rgt. 5 Totenkopf*, attacked it instead. By 9 a.m., *Stubaf.* Eckert's assault had been driven back with heavy losses by the defenders, who were determined to hold on as long as possible.

This maneuver forced the *Panzergruppe* to temporarily move out of its designated zone of attack and move into the right flank of the neighboring *1. Pz.Div.*, whose commander apparently did not object to this incursion. However, *Gen.Maj.* Gaedke, the chief of staff of *A.Gr. Balck*, did object and complained loudly to his counterpart at *H.Gr. Süd* at 9:25 a.m., stating that once again Gille and the *IV. SS-Pz.Korps* were disobeying orders by not adhering to the plan. In his radio message, Gaedke stated, "This is contrary to the original order that directs the *3. SS-Pz.Div.* to fight in close cooperation with the *5. SS-Pz.Div.* in order to help them."[43] Considering the actual situation on the ground, this was a ridiculous accusation, given that once Seregélyes was in the hands of the *Totenkopf*, Becker's division would be able to continue moving towards the northeast as originally instructed, while still being able to assist the *Wiking* Division by launching a supporting attack to the south (which it did later in the day).[44]

While fighting in Seregélyes was still ongoing, the division's reconnaissance battalion, *SS-Pz.Aufkl.Abt. 3*, continued moving and had reached the village of Puszta Szabolcs by mid-afternoon. The *Panzergruppe*, moving closely alongside the right flank of the *1. Pz.Div.*, skirted the southern shore of Lake Velencze and took the town of Gárdony by the early afternoon. After seizing the village of Kis Velencze, located at the lake's eastern tip, the *Panzergruppe* halted for the evening after an advance of over 20 kilometers. While carrying out this maneuver, it leapfrogged ahead of Thünert's division, taking advantage of Soviet weakness in this area. Once again, Balck complained that the two SS divisions were failing to report their situation, insinuating that they were deliberately keeping him in the dark as to their actual locations and troop dispositions.

To remind Gille and his divisions of the importance of timely reporting their situation to the field army, Balck sent out a *Fernschreiber* telex message at 12:40 p.m., demanding that they comply with his directive immediately. Even Gille's chief of staff, Manfred Schönfelder, complained that radio and telephone communications with the divisions were erratic and insufficient,[45] despite the fact that the two SS divisions of Gille's corps had sent no less than 19 separate situation reports via radio that same day. While *Fernschreiber* and radio message traffic were generally reliable, the weather conditions were atrocious, affecting the range and quality of transmissions, leaving messengers and liaison officers as the only other reliable means to convey messages back and forth to *IV. SS-Pz.Korps* headquarters. Soviet units passing through the area could have intercepted or killed these men, while also severing any telephone cables they found, the Germans' only other reliable back-up communications mode.

After being stymied in its various attempts to seize Seregélyes for several hours, *K.Gr. Eckert* launched a two-pronged attack from both the north and south, beginning at 2 p.m. While *SS-Pz.Jäg.Abt. 3* under *Stubaf.* Boris Kraas attacked the town's northern outskirts, *Hstuf.* Peter Stienen's *I. Btl./Totenkopf* fought its way into the city from the south in the face of determined Soviet resistance. Reinforced by *Stubaf.* Fritz Vogt's *I. Btl./Norge*, which attacked the town from the southwest, Eckert's force was soon embroiled in house-to-house fighting. Two of Kraas's tank destroyers were knocked out in the melee that followed, in exchange for several T-34s. By 3:40 p.m., the town was finally in German hands. After any remaining Soviet resistance in Seregélyes was mopped up, Eckert's *Kampfgruppe* continued advancing to the northeast, leaving Vogt and his exhausted troops to consolidate control of the town.

They did not have long to complete this task before they were attacked by a much larger Soviet force that had slipped between Eckert's battlegroup and the left flank of the *Wiking* Division. The attackers, consisting of a mixed infantry and tank unit from the XVIII Tank Corps, swept into the town from the east, but their first attempt was brought to a halt after heavy fighting by Vogt and his mixed German-Norwegian battalion. The next attempt was more successful, forcing *I. Btl./Norge* to fall back after bitter hand-to-hand fighting. One participant, a Norwegian volunteer, later wrote, "The Russians [*sic*] drove us back towards the town's western edge. Our wounded, as well as our [battalion surgeon] Dr Storm and two medics, were murdered" by Soviet troops after the battalion aid station was overrun.[46] Finally, before the attackers could consolidate their own gains, *Stubaf.* Ludwig Schwermann's *SS-Pz.Pio.Btl. 3*, acting as Becker's division reserve, and Vogt's surviving troops conducted one last counterattack near sunset, retook Seregélyes, and assumed security for both the town and the surrounding area.

To the left of the *Totenkopf* Division, Thünert's veteran *1.Pz.Div.* continued to screen the corps' left flank, especially in the area south of Stuhlweissenburg. As *K.Gr. Philipp*, its forward element, began to skirt the southern shore of Lake Velencze as it advanced to the east, its flank would be protected along the lake's entire 15-kilometer length, but the area immediately south and southeast of the city would prove problematic. It was through this swampy area that a well-constructed, hard-surfaced highway ran along the stretch between Stuhlweissenburg and Seregélyes; this road was also one of the primary supply routes for the Soviet troops defending the former town and the primary reason why the *1. Pz.Div.* had constructed a blocking position to prevent enemy troops from using it.

This blocking position was defended by the division's *K.Gr. Huppert*, formed from *Pz.Gren.Rgt. 1* minus its *I. Bataillon*, reinforced by 10 *Pz. IV* tanks from *II. Abt./Pz.Rgt. 1*, some tank destroyers from *Pz.Jäg.Abt. 37*, and a 420-man battalion of Hungarian SS men from *SS-Rgt. Ney* under the command of *Hstuf.* Pál Vadon. On Huppert's right, the two battalions of *Maj.* Werner Marcks's *Pz.Gren.Rgt. 113* had established a defensive barrier facing to the north and east, where his regiment connected with Philipp's battlegroup. Throughout that day and into the evening, elements of the XXI Guards Rifle Corps continued their efforts to break through this blocking position, in vain as it turned out, for the *1. Pz.Div.* held firm. Meanwhile, the division's main assault element—Philipp's armored *Kampfgruppe* along with *I. Abt./Pz.Rgt. 24* and *I. Btl. (gep.)/Pz.Gren.Rgt. 1*—reached the town of Agárd on the southern shore of Lake Velencze at 8 p.m., marking the division's farthest advance for the day.[47]

In his notebook entry for 20 January, Gille described the dramatic events of the day in the barest of terms:

> The attack by the "T" [*Totenkopf* Division] reached the [Nador] Canal. The *1. Pz.Div.* also crossed the canal with the additional assignment of reorienting some of its units to the left. After the crossing of the canal by the "T", an armored enemy unit attacked to the south and cut off the spearhead of the "W" [*Wiking* Division], forcing it to form a hedgehog position, where it warded off all of the enemy's attacks. The *3. Pz.Div.* reached the Danube at Dunapentelek [*sic*] with its armored group but is still in the process of forming a solid flank facing to the south, which demands [the diversion] of much of its force. [It has] no neighbor to the right.[48]

This statement, while true, belies the ferocious nature of the fighting that took place that day. The arrival on the battlefield of the XVIII Tank Corps between the Danube and Lake Velencze, and the unexpected encounter with the newly arrived CXXXIII Rifle Corps, would shape the course of the battle for the next several days.

Summing up the day's activities, *III. Pz.Korps* reported that the attack by the *23. Pz.Div.* southeast of Sárkeresztes confronted strong Soviet resistance and was unable to seize any ground. During the late afternoon, a battalion-sized enemy counterattack began to unfold against German defenses in the town of Borbála Puszta, supported by strong artillery fire and a smoke screen. The outcome was still in doubt during the early evening, when the report was submitted. The *4. Kav.Brig.* reported that east of Zámoly, another Soviet attack took place that was able to gain additional ground in front of the brigade's defensive positions. West of Zámoly, Breith's *Ic* reported that two company-sized enemy attacks took place, but both were warded off. Another battalion-sized attack was able to penetrate defensive positions in the northern portion of the town of Csólkakő, nestled in the southern tip of the Vértes Mountains. Adding to the corps' dismal performance that day, three Hungarian assault groups from the *2. Pz.Div.*, attempting to attack Soviet positions north of Söréd, south of Pusztavám, and south of Kecskéd, were driven off without accomplishing anything, other than reporting that they were engaged by dug-in tanks serving in the artillery role at Kecskéd.

In the *I. Kav.Korps* sector, whose two mobile units (the *6. Pz.Div.* and *3. Kav. Brig.*) were regrouping for their important mission scheduled to begin the following morning, Soviet forces were extremely active. Five kilometers northwest of Bicske, a battalion-sized attack was launched against the front line of the *6. Pz.Div.*, which was able to fend it off without losing any ground. In the *3. Kav.Brig.* sector, the

Soviets launched a large-scale reconnaissance in force towards Szomor, without having achieved any success worth mentioning. On the left flank of the *3. Kav. Brig.*, the attackers had more success, managing to achieve a penetration in the lines held by the *96. Inf.Div.* in Sarisap after carrying out numerous company- and battalion-level assaults.

At Dorog, the Soviets launched battalion-sized attack against the troops of both the *96.* and *711. Inf.Div.*, after subjecting the defenders to a strong artillery barrage beforehand. After hand-to-hand fighting, the assailants were thrown back, though the defenders suffered heavy losses. Northwest of Pilisszentlélek, the hard-pressed troops of the *711. Inf.Div.* were attacked by a battalion-sized Soviet force supported by five tanks. The outcome of this engagement was still in doubt at the time of the report, though the *Ic* did not sound optimistic. By this point, the *96.* and *711. Inf.Div.* had only 11 operational armored fighting vehicles between them to defend their sectors against any determined enemy armored assault. The signs for the corps' large-scale attack scheduled for the following day were not auspicious. Further denuding the corps' left by requiring the *96. Inf.Div.* to extend its defense lines to Szomor would leave Harteneck's flank even more vulnerable.[49]

North of the Danube, combat activity in Kirschner's *LVII.Pz.Korps* had begun to wind down after the departure of portions of both the *8.* and *20. Pz.Div.* for their new assignment with *H.Gr. A.* The most important operation carried out that day was the continuation of the attack directed against Karva by the remaining *Kampfgruppe* from the *8. Pz.Div.*, the Hungarian *Szent Laszlo* Division, and *Pz.Abt. 208*. Despite strong enemy resistance, Kirschner reported that the attack was making progress. In other areas, the corps reported a number of company- and battalion-sized Soviet attacks against German positions east of Madar, west of Bátorove Kesy, and along the railroad embankment south of Kurt, but all were warded off by the last remaining *Kampfgruppe* from the *20. Pz.Div.* and the newly reconstituted *153. Ausbildungs* (training) *Division*, with no ground reported as having been given up.[50]

Within the ever-shrinking perimeter held by the German and Hungarian troops in Budapest, ground combat activity had slackened somewhat. The most significant tactical action of the day was the German counterattack carried out on the night of 19/20 January to retake the northern tip of Margaret Island, siezed the day before by Soviet troops. Despite the efforts of the predominately SS battalion that led the attack, it failed in the face of withering fire from the defenders, backed up by direct and indirect fire from the eastern bank of the river, now completely controlled by the Second Ukrainian Front's 46th Army. Elsewhere along the *IX. SS-Geb.Korps* perimeter, lively artillery and mortar fire was reported, but no serious infantry assaults took place. Shortly before noon, artillery observers within the perimeter spotted a large concentration of Soviet troops forming up in the railroad yard at Budaörs, 5 kilometers southwest of the city, as well as another one in the Budatétény area. While the reason for their activity could only be surmised by Pfeffer-Wildenbruch and his staff, these forces were most likely reserves from the 46th Army forming up to ride to the aid of the 4th Guards Army.

In the air, the *A. Gr. Balck/6. Armee Fliegerverbindungsoffizier* (*Flivo*, or liaison officer) reported that Red Air Force activity was heavy and widespread, despite the terrible flying weather. The efforts of the 17th Air Army appeared to focus, once again, upon the spearhead units of the *IV. SS-Pz. Korps* and the southwestern sector north of the Danube defended by the *LVII. Pz. Korps*. German forward units reported multiple bombing and strafing runs by Soviet aircraft against mobile units lined up on the highways and upon front-line positions. For its part, the Red Air Force claimed to have flown 450 daylight sorties, with a further 220–230 sorties that night.

German ground-attack aircraft, including *Henschel Hs-129* tank busters from *Schlachtgeschwader 9*, carried out only 150 sorties of their own, focusing most of their efforts against Soviet columns moving in either direction between the Danube–Lake Velencze gap. The *I. Flieger Korps'* declining readiness rate, coupled with its pilots' dependence on more favorable flying conditions, was slowly yielding the initiative to the Red Air Force.[51] Despite the terrible weather, 57 aerial supply missions were flown over Budapest, but the records do not indicate how many of their air drops landed within German and Hungarian lines.[52]

Nevertheless, German reconnaissance missions continued, but the results did not auger well for the future of *Konrad III*. The several photographic missions flown over the area southwest and southeast of Budapest confirmed the *IX. SS-Geb. Korps* reports, with a large amount of vehicular traffic spotted along the Danube and the roads leading out of the city. In addition, a great deal of ferry traffic was reported to be taking place at several locations along the Danube south of the city, an indication of some sort of enemy movement. Long columns of Red Army vehicles were photographed as they assembled on both sides of the river at each of these ferry sites. Whether they were retreating or were reserves being brought up could not be determined by examining the photographs.

The *6. Armee Ic* also reported that for the first time, the CXXXIII Rifle Corps, with four rifle divisions, had been identified in front of Gille's corps, along with the XVIII Tank Corps that had already been encountered along the Sárviz Canal, where it had carried out aggressive counterattacks. There were also indications that the Third Ukrainian Front's reserve, the 5th Guards Cavalry Corps, was being brought down from the Pilis Mountains sector where it had been fighting against the *711. Inf. Div.* Furthermore, the 113th Rifle Division, fresh from its assignment to the 57th Army, had been spotted heading towards the *IV. SS-Pz. Korps'* far right (or western) flank, a worrying development in view of the fact that this sector was being handed over to the Hungarians. But what caused the *Ic* the most worry was the possible future courses of action being contemplated for the I Guards Mechanized Corps, a powerful unit that had previously been identified fighting on the eastern face of the Budapest perimeter. Radio intercepts by the *H.Gr. Süd* signal intercept and decryption unit, *Kommandeur der Nachrichtenaufklärung 8* (*KONA 8*), had indicated that it was moving south along the eastern bank of the Danube; when and where it would arrive was unknown when 20 January came to a close.[53]

From Marshal Tolbukhin's perspective as a Front commander, the outlines of *A.Gr. Balck*'s plan appeared to be taking shape. Caught completely by surprise at first, he was now convinced that Balck's movements, especially the attack by the *IV. SS-Pz. Korps*, were designed to entrap a significant portion of the 4th Guards Army, as well as to enable the Budapest garrison to break out, a fairly accurate assessment. The attempted defense along the Sárviz Canal had failed, resulting in the encirclement of nearly all Soviet forces between Lake Velencze and the Sió River. The most they had done was to slow the German rate of advance.

Therefore, Tolbukhin's next course of action was to use his few remaining reserves to prevent the encirclement of the rest of Zakharov's army by establishing a new 17-kilometer defense line between the Danube and Lake Velencze. This not only entailed repositioning his existing forces, but would require reinforcement by elements of Malinovsky's Second Ukrainian Front as well from the *STAVKA* strategic reserve. As an indication of the general sense of alarm that *Konrad III* was generating among the leadership of the Third Ukrainian Front at that time, Tolbukhin recounted several months later:

> After the enemy breakthrough to the Danube, the situation for the troops of the Third Ukrainian Front became difficult for the first time. The southern flank ... was open [i.e., where the Germans had broken through] and this threatened the 57th Army, 1st Bulgarian Army, and 12th Yugoslav [Tito's forces], which were occupying positions southeast of Lake Balaton and along the Drava River with encirclement ... The Front's headquarters was in the town of Paks, and enemy *panzer* reconnaissance units were approaching ... Frankly speaking, the situation was dangerous.[54]

To assist Tolbukhin, the *STAVKA* handed complete responsibility for reducing the Budapest garrison to Malinovsky's Second Ukrainian Front, a task that would be carried out by his 46th Army. Pursuant to this, the X Guards Rifle Corps—the right flank unit of the 4th Guards Army—would be subordinated to the 46th Army, freeing the Third Ukrainian Front from having to fight two battles simultaneously. Tolbukhin also anticipated that the two other complementary operations that he thought *H.Gr. Süd* was developing would begin to unfold within the next several days, so he started taking the necessary steps to prepare to meet those too.

The first action the marshal expected was a breakout by the Budapest garrison towards the *IV. SS-Pz.Korps*' attacking column, which at that point was approaching rapidly from the south. By reinforcing the 4th Guards Army and assigning responsibility for preventing this from occurring to the 46th Army, this threat could be minimized. The next German course of action, and the more dangerous one from the Soviet perspective, was a complementary attack by the *2. Pz.Armee* from the western end of Lake Balaton towards the east, with the objective of linking up with the right flank of Balck's *6. Armee* and Hungarian forces, thereby encircling the 57th Army positioned south of the lake.

This would be even more dangerous if *H. Gr. F*, positioned along the Drava River to the south, supported the *2. Pz.Armee* by executing its own attack to the north to link up with either that army or *A. Gr. Balck* south of Lake Balaton. To prevent this from happening, Tolbukhin would have to delay the movement of Soviet and Bulgarian forces south of Lake Balaton that could assist the 4th Guards Army around Stuhlweissenburg. For the next several days, the actions of the Third Ukrainian Front would be guided by these assumptions, which would work to the Germans' advantage, at least initially. However, at some point, Tolbukhin would realize his error and begin responding with overwhelming force.[55]

Throughout the day, Balck began to realize that the evolving situation was becoming more than the *IV. SS-Pz.Korps* could manage on its own, in strict terms of its span of control, specifically concerning the area encompassing the attack zone of the *3. Pz.Div.* It was simply too big and *Oberst* Söth could no longer fight two separate battles while remaining focused on his primary task—the drive towards Budapest. It began to dawn on all the leaders concerned that constructing a viable defense along the Sió River sector to the west and to the south between Siófok and Simontornya would require a dedicated effort. The *3. Pz.Div.* could perform one of these tasks, but not both, and Gille could not spare anything from his other divisions to help either.

Consequently, Balck and Gaedke began formulating a plan that would assign responsibility for protecting the western flank to a separate headquarters and remove it from the *3. Pz.Div.* The Hungarian *25. Inf.Div.* was already in the process of moving the remainder of its regiments around the eastern shore of Lake Balaton to take up position along the Sió River defense line, but Balck recognized that this division would not be enough to perform this task by itself. To augment the Hungarian division, Balck wanted to keep the three armored reconnaissance battalions (*Pz. Aufkl.Abt. 1, 3*, and *23*) in place, since they were all heavily armed and 100 percent mobile. Because of his already expressed disdain for the general quality of Hungarian leadership, he felt that the *25. Inf.Div.* commander, *Oberst* Gyula Kalkó, would be unable to exercise sufficient command and control over his division and the three armored reconnaissance battalions.[56] In addition, Kalkó's communications battalion—co-located with the division headquarters in Enying—lacked the radio and *Fernschreiber* capability that the situation required, which was another strike against having a Hungarian unit assume full responsibility for this area.

To resolve this dilemma, Balck requested and secured the release later that evening from *H. Gr. Süd* of the commander and staff of *Pz. Gren.Div. FHH*, then undergoing the preliminary stages of conversion into a *panzer* division at its assembly area in the town of Bana, 15 kilometers east of Raab. Both the Hungarian *25. Inf. Div.* and the German reconnaissance units would be placed under its banner, and

Gen.Maj. Günther Pape, lately of *Div.Gr. Pape* fame, would lead it, signifying the reappearance of *Div.Gr. Pape* on the Hungarian battlefields. *Generalmajor* Pape and his conglomerate command would be subordinated to the *IV. SS-Pz.Korps* initially, though Wöhler and Balck discussed assigning it at a later date to the Hungarian *3. Armee*, commanded by *Gen.Lt. vitéz* József Heszlényi.[57]

Once Pape and his headquarters had been established at Mezöszentgyörgy, a small village 5 kilometers east of Lepseny, the responsibility for the *Sió-Abschnitt* (Sió River defensive sector) would transfer from the *3. Pz.Div.* to *Div.Gr. Pape.* Subsequent orders directing this change of division areas of responsibility went out that evening to all the parties concerned. One detail which Balck's order addressed was the lifting of the boundaries between the *IV. SS-Pz.Korps* and Heszlényi's *3. Armee.* This was especially curious, given that it delayed the decision to assign responsibility for defending the Sió River sector to the Hungarian *3. Armee.* In essence, it failed to designate the command and control boundary needed to cover this critical interim period, sewing needless confusion.[58]

At his headquarters in Martinsberg later that afternoon, Balck assessed the events of the day and the progress that had been made. He had already made a decision to reorganize the command and control of the Sió River sector by assigning this task to *Div.Gr. Pape.* In regards to the main effort of the ongoing operation, he expressed his intent for the following day in an order issued before he went to bed that evening. This *Auftrag* (mission statement) took into account the Soviet actions so far and what needed to be done to continue adhering to the operations timeline. This modification to the original *Konrad III* order assigned the following tasks:

a) Destruction of the enemy in the Aba–Sárosd area by the joint action of the *Wiking* and the bulk of the *Totenkopf* Division, as a precondition for the continuation of the advance towards Budapest.

b) Securing the northern flank of the [*IV. SS-Pz.Korps*] by the *1. Pz.Div.* in the area between the southern outskirts of Stuhlweissenburg and the western edge of Lake Velencze against an enemy breakthrough towards the south. In this regards, there must be a sufficient number of tanks and strong artillery [support].

c) Continuation of the aggressive attacks between the Danube and Lake Velencze by the *3. Pz.Div.* and elements of the *Totenkopf* in a northerly direction. Hinder any attempts by the enemy to reach this corridor from the north, especially any orderly attempt by him to construct a cohesive defense along this line [i.e., the gap between the Danube and Lake Velencze].

d) The *3. Pz.Div.* will block all attempts by the enemy to conduct any kind of river traffic by establishing a favorable position at Dunapentele using tanks, antitank guns, and artillery [here he was referring to Soviet attempts to ferry troops across the Danube].

e) Complete the relief of *Pz.Aufkl.Abt. 1* and *23* by the Hungarian *25. Inf.Div.* along the Sió River sector and send these reconnaissance battalions east to provide flank and rear area protection from the enemy in the area between Simontornya and Czecze and to prevent disruption of supply routes and the destruction of the rail line between Nagy Dorog and Czecze.[59]

Wöhler essentially rubber-stamped Balck's modifications to the original *Konrad III* order, since he had been following the events throughout the day and was in accordance with his field army commander's conclusions. He understood the need to call a brief halt, at least in the center of Gille's advance, in order to eliminate the threat posed by the large grouping of Soviet forces still occupying ground between Perkáta and the Seregélyes. Wöhler also seconded Balck's and Gille's assertions that more infantry divisions were needed to perform this task.

In a telephone conversation with *Gen.d.Pz.Tr.* Wenck, the head of the *OKH Führungsabteilung*, at 11:30 p.m., Wöhler asked for another infantry division to replace the *44. Reichs-Gren.Div.*, which had been shipped north of the Danube to fight with the *LVII. Pz.Korps* instead of with the *IV. SS-Pz.Korps* for *Konrad III*. *Heeresgruppe Süd* paraphrased Balck's wording in its own order and transmitted them to *OKH* headquarters to obtain Hitler's final approval. Surprisingly, Wenck relented and agreed to assign the *356. Inf.Div.* to *A.Gr.* Balck for "such duties in the rear area." This division was serving at the time with *H.Gr. C* in Italy, but Wöhler was able to convince Wenck to transfer it to *H.Gr. Süd.*

Wöhler also raised the topic for the first time of asking the *OKH* whether it could direct *H.Gr. F* to carry out a supporting attack to its north to link up with *A.Gr.* Balck south of Lake Balaton in order to encircle and destroy the Soviet 57th Army and Bulgarian 1st Army. This was the same move that Tolbukhin feared the most.[60] Fortunately for the commander of the Third Ukrainian Front, an attack of this scale would take weeks to plan and prepare, and *Konrad III* would be long over by then. Thus, the stage was set for the continuation of the offensive, which picked up the next morning where it had left off the evening before, with both sides tearing each other apart.

Sunday, 21 January marked the fourth day of Operation *Konrad III*. The weather had not changed appreciably, though the snowfall of the past several days had eased. The day dawned with a light frost, below-freezing temperatures, fog, and mist. During the night, brisk winds had caused deep snowdrifts to build up along roadways in some areas, forcing supply columns to halt and clear them before they could continue. The forecast for the afternoon was more promising, predicting bright, sunny weather with scattered clouds, but instead worsened as the day progressed, severely limited German and Soviet air activity. The white-painted combat vehicles of the *IV. SS-Pz.Korps* would still be difficult to detect as they moved cross-country over the relatively flat, snow-covered landscape of the *Puszta*. While the improved weather would benefit the German tank troops, who could take advantage of their superior optics and engage Soviet tanks at greater distances, it also meant that the Red Air Force would be present overhead in strength, to harass and bomb the German armored spearheads until the weather worsened.

The most important combat activity of the day featured the successful breakout from encirclement of the XVIII Tank and the CXXXIII Rifle Corps to the south and southeast, which paradoxically benefitted the *IV. SS-Pz.Korps'* drive to the north, at least initially. While the bulk of the Soviet units escaped, some remnants and stay-behind elements had to be eliminated, but when this was finally achieved, the immediate threat to Gille's supply lines had been overcome. That evening, Jankuhn, the corps *Ic*, summed up the day's activities:

> On the *Sió-Abschnitt*, no combat activity of significance was reported. In the area of Csösz, Aba, and Sárosd, after heavy fighting, the encircled enemy located there were destroyed and the localities mopped up of any remaining enemy forces. However, some enemy remnants, including a few tanks, were able to break out from the Sárosd area and make their way southeast to the Herczegfalva area. The tough enemy resistance south and southwest of Adony was broken and around midday their forces were thrown out of the town. Also, in heavy fighting, the enemy forces defending Kápolnás Nyék and Sukoró were forced to surrender. Combat operations are still in progress.[61]

His report, while essentially accurate, understated the size of the Soviet force that had escaped. Reflecting upon the day's event, Gille also underestimated the number of men his corps had encircled that day, later writing, "The enemy groupings that had broken through were surrounded and wiped out, only small portions of which were able to escape to the south."[62]

While much of their heavy weapons and equipment from the XVIII Tank and the CXXXIII Rifle Corps had indeed been left behind or destroyed, enough of their units had escaped intact to the south, where they could be quickly reconstituted south of Dunaföldvar. For example, the 110th Tank Brigade of the XVIII Tank Corps had been reduced to only 10 operational vehicles, but most of the crews who had lost their tanks due either to combat or lack of fuel had managed to escape, as well as most of their other troops. In fact, *IV. SS-Pz.Korps* reported taking only 1,175 Soviet prisoners of war between 18 and 21 January, a relatively low number considering the size of the units that had been encircled.[63] Gille's corps also claimed the destruction of 207 Soviet tanks and self-propelled guns, 229 artillery pieces, and 257 antitank guns during the same period, a significant amount by any standard, but the XVIII Tank Corps did not consider itself defeated.[64] The tank corps commander, Maj.Gen. Govorunenko, estimated the following day that he had lost half of the armored fighting vehicles he had gone into battle with on the night of 18/19 January. Still, even with the remaining 40 or 50 operational tanks, that was still more than the 34 tanks that the *3. Pz.Div.* reported as being operational at the time.

Another event of the day that was not mentioned in the evening *Ic* report was the movement of Gille's forward command post from Balatonfüzfő to Csösz, a "jump" of over 38 kilometers, placing Gille and the rest of his *Führungsabteilung* much closer to the front lines and within range of his divisions' radios, which in theory at least would alleviate some of the concerns his field army commander had about the inability (or alleged unwillingness) of the *Totenkopf* and *Wiking* Divisions to communicate. It would also allow *Ostubaf.* Hüppe's *SS-Nachr.Abt. 104* to lay field telephone cables all the way to the divisions' own forward headquarters, despite the risks this entailed. For the time being, the rest of the *Korps-Hauptquartier*, including the *Ib* (*Quartiermeister*) and the *Adjutantur*, would remain where they were in Balatonfüzfő until such time the situation was stable enough for them to move forward.

At the division level, Gille's units reported a number of significant developments that occurred on 21 January. The surge of escaping Soviet units, most of which streamed through the 10-kilometer gap between Herczegfalva and Előszállás during the night of 20/21 January, enormously complicated operations of the *3. Pz.Div.* the following day. While Govorunenko counted the number of remaining troops, tanks, and guns still under his command, *Oberst* Söth found himself now being torn in three different directions, with three different missions—defend along the Sió River sector, counterattack south to prevent the escaping Soviet units from coalescing, and continue his attack to the north. It soon became apparent that this was too much of a burden to place on the back of a single, widely dispersed division, which possessed a *Kampfstärke* of only 1,815 men, including those from the attached armored reconnaissance battalions from the *1.* and *23. Pz.Div.* (though not the Hungarian *25. Inf.Div.*).

After the division's armored battlegroup, *K.Gr. Weymann*—consisting of *I. Btl./ Pz.Gren.Rgt. 3* and *Graf* von der Schulenburg's *Pz.Rgt. 6*—finally took Adony at 12:25 p.m., it resumed its advance to the north, approaching the confluence of the Váli and Danube near Szinatelep later that day. Before it could prosecute its assault any further, the *Kampfgruppe's* commander, *Oberstlt.* Martin Weymann, was ordered to turn about that evening and conduct an attack against Herczegfalva, approximately 37 kilometers to his rear. While Weymann and his troops had been racing north alongside the right flank of the *Wiking* Division, the rest of *Pz.Gren.Rgt. 3*, along with *Pz.Gren.Rgt. 394*, had been contending with large numbers of Soviet troops continuing to break out to the south.[65]

This radical change in the *3. Pz.Div.* mission had come about on the orders of *Gen.d.Pz.Tr.* Balck, who, when informed on this unexpectedly negative development on Söth's right flank that morning, reacted by not only telling Gille to move *K.Gr. Weymann* to the south, but also ordering him that same morning to send a strong task force from the *Totenkopf* Division south to assist in destroying the Soviet forces assembly at Herczegfalva. Uncharacteristically (but correctly), Gille ignored this part of the order, choosing instead to allow Becker's division to continue pushing to the northeast with its full might. Unlike Balck, Gille more clearly understood the need to reach the Váli River as rapidly as possible before the V Guards Cavalry Corps could construct a cohesive defensive line, though time was quickly running out.[66]

At some point during the afternoon, an organized Soviet attempt, possibly by the 110th Tank Brigade, was undertaken from Herczegfalva towards the northwest in a move apparently designed to either sever the supply lines of Söth's division or assist the last trapped units attempting to escape from the pocket between Aba and Sárosd.[67] The unit defending that area, the division's *Pz.Aufkl.Abt. 3*, was unable to stop both the escape attempt and the relief attack by the 110th Tank Brigade, and urgently needed help. In addition, the forward elements of Lieutenant General Lasko's XXX Rifle Corps had begun arriving in Herczegfalva after being ferried across the Danube, where they immediately set about constructing defensive positions and establishing *Pakfronts*.

As previously related, Balck deemed this threat to be of such magnitude that he ordered the *3. Pz.Div.* spearhead to cease its advance, turn about, and counterattack to eliminate this threat with its *Panzergruppe*. Once again, the lack of follow-on infantry divisions to secure the ground taken was adversely impacting the progress of *Konrad III*. While Söth still had 34 operational tanks, assault guns, and tank destroyers by this date, they were no substitute for infantry—"boots on the ground"—who could hold or retake key terrain, or man a credible outpost line.

Returning to Adony, which was handed off to the *Wiking* Division late in the afternoon, Weymann and his mixed tank and infantry force moved immediately to the south by a night march and began preparing for their attack against Herczegfalva, scheduled to commence the next morning. As for the situation along the Sió River defense line to the west, aside from aggressive patrolling and random shelling by elements of the 57th Army, things were relatively quiet. More Hungarian troops had arrived throughout the day to fill in the gaps between the German reconnaissance battalions, but there were still not enough of them, nor were there sufficient artillery batteries to effectively cover the 50-kilometer sector. *Generalmajor* Pape and his staff had not yet arrived, but were expected to be operational by 22 January, at which point Söth could hand over responsibility for the defense of the *Sió-Abschnitt*.

On 21 January, the *Wiking* Division was once again able to resume its advance late in the day, ironically due in part to the escape of the two encircled Soviet corps during the evening of 20/21 January, an event that removed the threat against the division's supply lines. The majority of the division was employed throughout the day to eliminate a number of Soviet units that had not been able to escape towards the south. In the pocket between Aba and Sárosd, Hack's *Westland* Regiment—with help from a portion of Dorr's *Germania* Regiment—launched a pincer attack into the encircled enemy grouping and eliminated it by 2 p.m.

After assuming responsibility for the Adony–Iváncsa area following the relief-in-place of *K.Gr. Weymann*, Ullrich's division was once again able to mount a unified advance, exemplified by *Pz.Gr. Dorr*'s seizure of Puszta Szabolcs by 7 p.m. while en route to its next objective, the Váli River along the line Szinatelep–Puszta Aggszentpéter. Along the way, Dorr's tank/infantry team had eliminated as many as 14 hastily emplaced *Pakfronts* and destroyed 12 T-34 tanks at little loss to themselves.[68] While Dorr's armor halted at Puszta Szabolcs to take on fuel and ammunition, *SS-Pz. Aufkl.Abt. 5* continued its advance, feeling its way towards the Váli River.

Since the initiation of *Konrad III* three days before, the *Wiking* Division's armor and personnel strength had declined considerably. On the morning of 21 January, it reported having only three operational *Pz. IV*s, five *Pz. V* Panthers, and four *Jagd. Pz. IV*s, a total of 12 armored fighting vehicles ready for combat, not including *SPW*s. An undetermined number of its tanks and assault guns were in various stages of repair. The attached *Sturm-Art.Brig. 303* also reported having 34 operational assault guns out of 44, including eight vehicles equipped with the 10.5cm assault howitzer. The division's artillery was still in relatively good shape, reporting 41 pieces operational, including 25 10.5cm and 16 15cm guns, of which six were 10.5cm self-propelled *Wespen* (Wasps) and four 15cm *Hummeln* (Bumble Bees). It also had at least four serviceable 7.5cm towed antitank guns. In regards to the division's overall *Kampfstärke*, it counted 2,106 foot soldiers in its ranks, out of 9,436 men in the division present for duty. Ullrich rated his division as being only 45 percent mobile with a *Kampfwert* (combat value) of III, making it fully suitable for defensive, though not offensive, operations. In the present circumstances, this commander's evaluation meant little, because there was no other choice but to continue the offensive with the forces that were on hand.[69]

The division commander's greatest concern at that point was not so much its overall combat power evaluation, but the rather tenuous connection of his right flank with the *3. Pz.Div.*, made even shakier by the departure of nearly all of that division's combat elements to confront the groups of Soviet forces assembling between Dunaföldvar and Herczegfalva. By 4 p.m., the situation in the wide-open space between the front lines and the division's rear area had stabilized enough for the division's new *Ia, Stubaf.* Wilhelm Klose, to displace Ullrich's *Vorgeschobener Gefechtstand* to Sárosd from its previous location at Kisláng. That evening, shortly after the headquarters personnel had finished setting up, the forward command post was targeted by a Red Air Force night raid. While no one was killed, the bombers did manage to score a lucky hit on Ullrich's command *SPW*, though he was with one of the forward units at the time. It did temporarily disrupt wire and radio communications with Gille's headquarters, delaying the relaying of information for several hours.[70]

Perhaps the *Wiking* Division's greatest loss that day happened later in the evening, when *Ostubaf.* Dorr was holding an orders group meeting at his command post in Sárosd with several commanders and staff personnel from the various units comprising his *Kampfgruppe*. While discussing the mission for the following day, the command post suffered a direct hit by either an artillery round or a high explosive shell fired from a Soviet antitank gun. Dorr and many of those gathered about him were struck by the blast's fragments, seriously injuring him and killing or wounding several others. He was immediately evacuated to the division's field hospital at Veszprém for life-saving surgery. He was temporarily replaced as the commander of the *Panzergruppe* by Fritz Darges. Several days later, *Stubaf.* Helmut Müller, the former commander of *SS-Feld-Ers.Btl. 5*, assumed command and led the regiment for the next six weeks until he too was injured.

Dorr's wounding (his 16th) shook the men of his regiment; he had been considered one of the division's toughest and steadiest commanders, and his absence would be keenly felt in the days to come. When Günther Jahnke, the division's *O1* at the time, heard about the legendary officer's wounding, he wrote, "The Division lost one of its ablest and most beloved officers."[71] Even Gille was shaken, remarking in his journal, "Through a direct hit by a tank cannon on the regimental command post of the *Germania*, Dorr, the regiment's commander, and several other officers were seriously wounded."[72] The 33-year-old Dorr, reputed to be an almost-invulnerable "man of steel" by his troops, had finally run out of luck.

Indeed, Dorr had been with the *Germania* Regiment since 1938, and had held every leadership position, ranging from platoon leader to company commander, battalion commander and finally regimental commander. In recognition of his courageous and exemplary leadership, he had been presented with the Knight's Cross with Oak Leaves and Swords on 9 July 1944, one of the few to receive this prestigious award. He had also been awarded the Close Combat Badge in Silver, the Gold Wound Badge, and the German Cross in Gold. Remarkably, he had also been awarded two of the *Panzervernichtungsabzeichen* (tank destruction sleeve insignia) for single-handedly knocking out two enemy tanks with hand-held antitank weapons, a feat that few men—especially regimental commanders—ever achieved and lived to tell of.[73] Though Müller was a competent and brave officer, he could not replace someone as well-regarded and inspirational as Hans Dorr. Thus, the ranks of the original "Old Guard" of the *Waffen-SS* continued to thin as the war in Europe ground through its final months.

The same day, while the *Wiking* Division was mopping up the last remaining Soviet pockets in its rear area and resuming its advance to the north, the reconnaissance battalion of the *Totenkopf* Division, *Hstuf. Zech's SS-Pz.Aufkl.Abt. 3*, reached the Váli River northeast of Puszta Aggszentpéter. Once it arrived at this point, the battalion continued reconnoitering to the north as far as Baraczka, but did not cross the river. Zech reported optimistically, "We've reached the Váli-Sector, enemy resistance broken! We're continuing our attack."[74] This radio message was monitored by *A. Gr. Balck's* signal intelligence company in *Armee-Nachr.Rgt. 549*, which passed it on to Gaedke, the army's chief of staff. Upon reading it, Balck misinterpreted it to believe that it meant the entire *Totenkopf* Division had closed up to the Váli River in force, when in fact no such thing had occurred—only forward elements from its reconnaissance battalion had reached the river, and they did not remain there long since they could not possibly hold it. Balck's misreading of this report would lead to much trouble later.

Meanwhile, the bulk of the division, spearheaded by *Stubaf. Pitschellis's Panzergruppe*—built around 21 of his 30 still-operational tanks and assault guns from *SS-Pz.Rgt. 3* and the *Panzergrenadiers* from *III. Btl/Eicke*—fought its way into the town of Kápolnás Nyék at the far northeastern tip of Lake Velencze that morning. On the town's southern outskirts, Pitschellis and his troops encountered two regiments from the 63rd Guards Cavalry Division (the 214th and 223rd) and the 1st Guards Mechanized Brigade from the I Guards Mechanized Corps, reinforced by the 1453rd SP Artillery Regiment, equipped with SU-100 assault guns. These units had arrived just in time to turn Kápolnás Nyék into a veritable fortress that would force the Germans to take it street by street at the cost of heavy casualties. To the right of Pitschellis's battlegroup, Eckert's *Pz.Gren.Rgt. 5 Totenkopf* in the center and Kleffner's *Pz.Gren.Rgt. 6 Eicke* on the right tried to keep pace, while doing their best to maintain the connection with the *Wiking* Division near Puszta Aggszentpéter.

Like the *Wiking* Division, the combat worthiness of the *Totenkopf* Division had begun to show signs of strain after three weeks of virtually non-stop combat. Were it not for the attachment of the 42 remaining King Tigers of *Hptm.* König's *s.Pz.Abt. 509* (of which 27 were still operational on the morning of 21 January), along with the 49 Panthers of *I. Abt./Pz.Rgt. 24* (25 still operational), the *Totenkopf* would have had the approximate armor strength of a *Panzergrenadier* division. That morning, the division reported only 30 operational armored fighting vehicles out of 101 on hand: five *Pz. IV*s, one *Pz. V* Panther, four *Pz. VI* Tiger I, and 20 assault guns. By the close of that day's fighting, it would have even less, leaving a trail of broken-down or damaged vehicles trailing all the way back from the Váli River to Veszprém.[75]

In regards to its *Kampfstärke*, it was only slightly better off than the *Wiking* Division, reporting that morning that it had 2,154 men ready for battle in its eight battalions, with an average battalion strength of 269 men, not including support or logistics troops. This was approximately half of what they would normally have reported had they been operating at full strength. Besides the loss of men incurred in combat, the numbers in all of the divisions reporting sick were beginning to increase as well, an unavoidable consequence of having to live and fight in a winter environment characterized by freezing temperatures, rain or snow, lack of sleep, insufficient food, and a high degree of physical stress that left the men susceptible to diseases such as pneumonia. An unnamed *SS-Kriegsberichter*, travelling with Eckert's *Kampfgruppe*, left an illuminating account of what these conditions were like:

> The hands of my wristwatch showed 6:25 p.m. exactly. The cold is still bitingly sharp. The men have not been able to sleep for [more than] an hour since the morning they started, they look like hell and are half-frozen with cold. They all have a terrible hunger and are stingy with their last cigarette.[76]

Though the overall strength of Becker's infantry and combat engineer units were decreasing, in regards to available artillery the division still possessed 40 operational pieces of various calibers (out of 50 on hand), signifying that *SS-Pz.Art.Rgt. 3* was still nearly at its full *K.St.N* strength. It also reported that 13 of its 16 remaining 7.5cm antitank guns were still operational.[77]

Throughout the day, the *Totenkopf* Division's three regimental-sized *Kampfgruppen*, joined by *K.Gr. Philipp* of the *1. Pz.Div.* (which had been temporarily attached to Becker's division earlier that morning), battled their way towards the northeast between Kápolnás Nyék and Puszta Aggszentpéter. In the struggle to reach and then vault over the Váli River line, it became a race between Lt.Gen. Gorshkov's V Guards Cavalry Corps and Becker's *Totenkopf* Division to see who got there first. The Soviet cavalry got a head start, when its leading units begun arriving during the previous day, bringing with them up to 15 artillery, antitank, and antiaircraft regiments—an enormous amount to support a single corps. Gorshkov's defense line along the Váli was becoming more formidable with each passing hour, except on his far left flank along the Danube.

When Pitschellis's tanks and *Panzergrenadiers* became bogged down in heavy fighting in Kápolnás Nyék against Gorshkov's Cossacks, *K.Gr. Philipp* of the *1. Pz.Div.* avoided the town, bypassing it to the west and going around the eastern shore of Lake Velencze. His *Kampfgruppe* then headed west and northwest towards the towns of Sukoró, Velencze, and Nadap, threatening to cut off the Soviet forces defending Stuhlweissenburg from the rear. In doing so, *Oberstlt.* Philipp had acted contrary to Gille's orders, which had tasked him to attack towards the northeast, not in the opposite direction. After destroying as many as 150 Soviet soft-skinned vehicles coming from the direction of Stuhlweissenburg, Philipp turned about and renewed the advance as he had been directed. Unbeknownst to him, his freelancing had attracted the attention of the XXI Guards Rifle Corps in that city, which dispatched the 93rd Rifle Division towards Velencze to keep the highway open and prevent the corps' encirclement by establishing a defensive line. This was to have the salutary effect of weakening the XXI Guards Rifle Corps' defenses by a third, only a few hours before the town was attacked later that evening.[78]

Elsewhere, though Eckert's and Kleffner's battlegroups had seized a large amount of territory and had nearly advanced to the Váli River as far as Baraczka on the left and Nagy Halom on the right adjacent to the *Wiking* Division's left flank, the *Totenkopf* Division was unable to establish a bridgehead across the Váli due to fierce resistance offered by Soviet units dug in on the river's western bank. Gorshkov's force included the two remaining divisions of the V Guards Cavalry Corps, remnants of the VII Mechanized Corps, and the full-strength I Guards Mechanized Corps, as well as bits and pieces of other elements that had broken out or avoided encirclement, including portions of the XVIII Tank and CXXXV Guards Rifle Corps. In fierce tank battles around Kápolnás Nyék, Kis Velencze, Felsö Besnyö, and Kis Halom, the *Totenkopf* Division's *Kampfgruppen*, along with *s.Pz.Abt. 509* and *I. Abt./Pz.Rgt. 24*, lost approximately 18 tanks and 22 *SPW*s that day, including at least six *Pz. VI* Tiger IIs that fell out with mechanical problems and nine *Pz. V*s destroyed. In exchange, the *Totenkopf* and its attachments destroyed as many as seven Soviet tanks from the V Guards Cavalry Corps in Kápolnás Nyék and approximately 70 percent of the M4A2 Shermans assigned to two brigades of the I Guards Mechanized Corps that launched an unsuccessful counterattack between that town and Puszta Aggszentpéter shortly after 9 a.m.[79]

With the exception of *K.Gr. Philipp*, attached to the *Totenkopf* Division during the early hours, the rest of Thünert's *1. Pz.Div.* was involved in defensive operations south and southwest of Stuhlweissenburg on 21 January. Apart from scattered Soviet artillery fire upon their positions and numerous enemy stragglers wandering about the area trying to return to their lines, the men of *Pz.Gren.Rgt. 1* and *113*, *Pz.Pio. Btl. 37*—and up to 15 tanks from *Pz.Rgt. 1*—prepared for the division's main effort for that evening, the capture of Stuhlweissenburg. Earlier that day, *SS-Rgt. Ney* had been attached to the division for this purpose, where it would operate on the left flank adjacent to the neighboring *23. Pz.Div.* of *Korpsgruppe Breith*, which in turn was supposed to attack the town from the northwest. Gille had promised reinforcements in the form of Vogt's *I. Btl./Norge* and a few Tiger tanks, but neither had arrived by the time the operation was scheduled to begin at 8 p.m. that evening.[80]

In the *Korpsgruppe Breith/III. Pz.Korps* area of operations, the situation was much quieter. Breith's headquarters reported that except for German and Hungarian combat patrols in the centre and left portion of its sector, there was little combat activity of significance for the *23. Pz.Div.* or the *4. Kav.Brig.*, which were supposed to be attacking, not defending. In the area of Oroszlány, one of the corps' units reported that it had observed the withdrawal of about 250 enemy troops from their front-line positions, the significance of which was unknown. On the corps' far-left flank in the Környe–Bánhida area, a significant movement of enemy troops under the cover of a smokescreen was spotted by troops of the Hungarian *Inf.Rgt. 42*, but their forward observers could not determine whether the enemy was reinforcing his position or withdrawing.

The situation was a bit more tense in the sector defended by Harteneck's *I. Kav.Korps* to Breith's north. That evening, the corps' headquarters reported that the enemy carried out attacks in company- and battalion-strength and was able to achieve two penetrations along a 2-kilometer section of the main defense line in the vicinity of Sarisap defended by the *96. Inf.Div.* One of these penetrations, that in the southernmost portion of the *HKL*, was eliminated by a counterattack, but the other one in the north could not be pushed back, and to make matters worse, Soviet troops were able to widen the penetration. No combat activity was reported as having taken place on the corps' right flank, where the *6. Pz.Div.* and the *4. Kav.Brig.* were preparing for their attack towards the south, now scheduled for 22 January.

North of Kesztölc and northwest of Pilisszentlélek, the *711. Inf.Div.* reported that the enemy had renewed his attacks against its main defense line, but in both cases was unsuccessful. As if these assaults were not enough of a cause for concern, *Gen.Lt.* Reichert reported that his troops holding Gran were being continuously subjected to concentrated artillery and machine-gun fire from the opposite bank of the Danube. Shortly before noon, long convoys of Soviet trucks were observed moving north of the river in a northwesterly direction, but whether all of these activities reflected the possibility that the 6th Guards Tank Army or 7th Guards Army were planning a river crossing attempt could not be determined.

Though the *LVII. Pz.Korps* was having to give up its two *panzer* divisions, except for a *Kampfgruppe* from each being temporarily left behind to ease the transition to the newly arrived *44. Reichs-Gren.Div. HuD*, Kirschner continued his aggressive efforts to keep pushing back the 6th Guards Tank Army to the Gran River as far as possible. Augmented by the *153. Feld-Ausb.Div.*, remnants of the Hungarian *Szent Laszlo* Division, and *Pz.Abt. 208*, the *Hoch- und Deutschmeister* Division, commanded by *Gen.Lt.* Hans-Günther von Rost, was able to carry out a counterattack that threw Soviet troops out of the village of Lukavini, 3 kilometers northeast of Moĉa on the bank of the Danube. The enemy launched a tank-supported counterattack of his own to retake the village later that day, but all he had to show for his efforts was the loss of six tanks. Eight kilometers away to the northwest, another German attack pushed the defenders back 1 kilometer east of Madar, straightening out a small bulge that had been created in the *HKL* by a previous Soviet incursion.

That same day, Kirschner was informed that his corps headquarters would be replaced by *Gen.d.Pz.Tr.* Ulrich Kleemann's *IV. Pz.Korps* (not to be confused with the *IV. SS-Pz.Korps*) the following day. After being relieved by Kleemann, Kirschner and his headquarters would depart immediately by rail for *H.Gr. Mitte*, where it would be assigned to the *17. Armee* and assume control of the *8.* and *20. Pz.Div.*, both already fighting in Silesia. Kleemann would assume command over the units that were defending along the Gran River line, including the *211.* and *357. V.G.D.*, the *153. Feld-Ausb.Div.*, and the *44. Reichs-Gren.Div. HuD.*, as well as the Hungarian *Szent László* Division.[81]

One German formation benefitting from the movement of Soviet reserves was Pfeffer-Wildenbruch's *IX. SS-Geb.Korps*, which reported that day that the situation had been relatively quiet, with the only combat activity worth mentioning a number of failed company-sized attempts to penetrate the Buda defensive perimeter by Soviet troops during the previous evening. Other than that, all he had to report for 21 January was strong Soviet antitank and mortar harassing fire against the southwest corner of *Festung Budapest*. Plans were developed to make another effort to wipe out the enemy force that had dug itself in on the northern tip of Margaret Island the following day, after having already failed twice to do so. At least the logistical situation had improved markedly, as promised: on the night of 20/21 January, enough resupply sorties were flown by the pilots and aircrew of *Luftflotte 4* to deliver 117.5 metric tons (129.5 short tons) of fuel, ammunition, rations, and medical supplies to the garrison using parachute canisters, *DFS-230* gliders (which landed on the old parade ground at the foot of the castle), and *Fiesler Fe-156* "Storks."[82]

Due to the poor flying weather that prevailed during daylight hours (but which had improved overnight), there was relatively little enemy air activity, save for reconnaissance flights. The *Luftwaffe* did manage to generate 100 sorties by ground-attack aircraft, despite the weather, focusing most of their attention on the long columns of Soviet vehicles moving south from the Budapest area and river traffic near Dunaföldvar, where the XXX Rifle Corps was ferrying its units over to the western bank.[83] During the day, a large formation of American four-engined bombers was observed flying at a high altitude along the Danube headed west, but nothing came of it. German reconnaissance flights also observed a slackening of Soviet highway traffic along the north–south Danube highway, but reported a large number of enemy vehicles moving south from Budapest in the direction of the gap between the eastern tip of Lake Velencze and the Danube, roughly marked by the course of the Váli River.

Based on these aerial observations, reports from forward units, and radio intercepts by *Armee-Nachr.Rgt. 549*, as well as prisoner interrogations and agents operating behind enemy lines, the *A.Gr. Balck* intelligence officer assessed that the bulk of the Soviet XVIII Tank Corps and CXXXIII Rifle Corps had indeed escaped during the previous evening after breaking through a gap in the German lines between Herczegfalva and Előszállás in the *3. Pz.Div.* area, thus confirming what the troops on the ground already knew. Based on this development, the field army's *Ic* expected that these forces, once they had undergone a brief reorganization, would turn about and begin carrying out attacks along the southern flank of the *IV. SS-Pz. Korps*, where its lines were most extended, focusing on the logistics arteries of the attacking German units.

In the rest of Gille's area of operations, the *A.Gr. Balck/6. Armee Ic* observed that between Lake Velencze and the Danube, the 4th Guards Army was having difficulty in preventing a further advance by the *1.*, *Totenkopf*, and *Wiking panzer* divisions. Because of the rapid advance by the *Totenkopf* and *1. Pz. Div.* from around the northern tip of Lake Velencze to the northeast and to the west (the brief thrust by *K.Gr. Philipp*), the defenders were being forced to move units from other areas south, west, and north of Stuhlweissenburg into the city's environs to defend it against a possible German assault. As already noted, one Soviet unit, the 93rd Rifle Division, had begun moving east out of the city in the mid-afternoon to prepare a defense against any further attempts to encircle the city from the east, which would soon prove a serious mistake. Observations by troops in the *I. Kav.Korps* also made it appear that the enemy was withdrawing forces from the Vértes Mountains and sending them south and southeast in an effort to delay or stop the advance by the *IV. SS-Pz.Korps*.[84]

Whether the Soviet leadership realized it or not at the time, the escape of the XVIII Tank Corps and the CXXXIII Rifle Corps on the night of 20/21 January, combined with the arrival of the XXX Rifle Corps at Herczegfalva and the V Guards Cavalry Corps along the Váli River defense line, marked a turning point in the Red Army's fortunes in the region. The salvation of the first two mentioned corps, both of which were partially re-equipped in record time, signified that the Third Ukrainian Front, which had been virtually cut in half when Gille's spearheads reached the Danube, could begin to exert pressure on his southern flank. The shift of the *3. Pz.Div.* towards the south essentially robbed *Konrad III* of more than a quarter of its remaining armored strength. This decision of Balck's would also divert scarce German resources, such as fuel and ammunition, from the other three armored spearheads racing towards Budapest. To be fair, he had no other choice but to do so; there were no other forces available despite his pleas, and the *356. Inf.Div.* would not arrive for another week. The arrival of the V Guards Cavalry Corps along the Váli River on 20 instead of 21 January meant that the Germans would now have to conduct a deliberate attack to vault this obstacle, a process that would further slow their offensive.

But the most important event of that day was the combined decision of Marshal Tolbukhin and Lt.Gen. Sharokhin, commander of the 57th Army, to stay and fight. Faced with the specter of the loss of the greater part of the 4th Guards and 57th Armies, Stalin—who had been kept apprised of the situation by Marshal Timoshenko, his on-the-scene *STAVKA* coordinator—was initially disposed to allow Zakharov and Sharokhin to withdraw their troops across the Danube. Alarmed at the potential loss of such a large body of Soviet troops at the hands of what Red Army intelligence believed to be an overwhelming German force, Stalin was prepared to allow them to abandon all of their equipment if that was required to ensure their escape, since the pontoon bridges at Dunapentele and Dunaföldvar had been prematurely destroyed. The days when he could afford to sacrifice hundreds of thousands of men with hardly a thought were long past; he now needed his armies to compete in strength with those of the approaching Western Allies once the war ended.[85]

However, Stalin first sought the opinion of the commanders on the ground before making a decision. In a radio conversation between Tolbukhin and Stalin during the evening of 20/21 January, Stalin asked whether it was advisable to defend west of the Danube or to retreat to the eastern bank. This placed Tolbukhin in an awkward situation; should he recommend that both armies remain and keep fighting, his life would be forfeit if they failed to stop the Germans and were destroyed. Before making his recommendation, the commander of the Third Ukrainian Front contacted Lt.Gen. Sharokhin, the commander of the 57th Army, whose army was most threatened with encirclement. Sharokhin recommended that they stay and fight where they were, even if surrounded, because it would be more difficult to push on towards Vienna if they retreated across the Danube. Taking his advice, Tolbukhin courageously decided to stay; he then notified Stalin that his armies would hold their ground and fight it out. Stalin quickly assented.

To carry out this ambitious plan, Tolbukhin's army group would still need assistance in order to buy time to build up the defensive front being constructed along the Váli River. On that same day, in addition to committing the V Guards Cavalry Corps, which was already fighting there, the *STAVKA* also authorized the rapid commitment of the two remaining brigades of the I Guards Mechanized Corps (the other two had been parceled out elsewhere), as well as the 113th and 252nd Rifle Divisions. In the southern front between Herczegfalva and Előszállás, the reorganized XVIII Tank Corps and the CXXXIII Rifle Corps would go over to the attack as soon as they had been joined by other units being brought up elsewhere from the Trans-Danubian theater of operations, such as the XXX Rifle Corps. Unbeknownst to the Germans, Tolbukhin's decision and that of the *STAVKA* to support his Front with substantial reserves marked the turning point of Operation *Konrad III* in the Soviet Union's favor; but it would take another week before Wöhler, Balck, and Gille fully realized this.

From the perspective of the commanders of *A. Gr. Balck/6. Armee* and *H. Gr. Süd*, except for the events on the right flank of the *3. Pz. Div.*, the situation on 21 January appeared to be developing quite favorably, despite the seeming reluctance or inability of the SS units to submit situation reports promptly. To judge the situation first hand, *Gen.d.Inf.* Wöhler went forward and paid a personal visit to Gille's forward headquarters at Csösz that day, as well as to that of *Gen.Lt.* Wilhelm Raapke's *HARKO 306*. Both Gille and Schönfelder had gone forward to assess the situation, leaving the corps' new Ia, *Stubaf.* Rentrop, to brief the army group commander. Wöhler was unable to learn much about the current situation in the *IV. SS-Pz. Korps* area with the two principals being absent, leaving him to stress to Rentrop the importance of sending clear and frequent reports to the field army, without which made it "difficult [for Balck] to get a clear overview" of the situation. He afterwards concluded that *Waffen-SS* units intentionally submitted fewer reports than comparable *Heeres* formations, despite his belief that they possessed "considerably more and better radio equipment."[86]

Wöhler radioed Guderian at *OKH* headquarters at 7:25 p.m. that evening to inform him that the *Totenkopf* Division had broken through the Váli River defense line, implying that it had seized a bridgehead, though this had not occurred at all. True, the division's armored reconnaissance battalion had reached the river, but it had not crossed, let alone broken through the entrenched V Guards Cavalry Corps all by itself. Based on a single radio message, then, both Wöhler and Balck drew the erroneous conclusion that success was finally at hand. This was especially ironic, given that both men had been very vocal in their criticism of Gille and his two SS divisions for not submitting timely reports. That they would arrive at such a conclusion based on such flimsy evidence almost defies belief, but their optimism would sow the seeds of the following day's disappointments, despite the successful outcome of the battle for Stuhlweissenburg during the night.

Believing that *IV. SS-Pz.Korps* was on the brink of achieving the operational breakthrough that he had long sought, that evening Balck issued guidance to *A.Gr. Balck/6. Armee* for the following day, 22 January:

1) Continuation of the attack to the northeast on and across the Váli sector with the *Wiking* and *Totenkopf* Divisions, and the *Panzergruppe* of the *1. Pz.Div.* (*K.Gr. Philipp*);
2) Commitment of the *3. Pz.Div.* against the enemy forces being reinforced in the Dunaföldvar bridgehead;
3) Reinforcement of the covering forces in the *Sió-Abschnitt* with the addition of more Hungarian units;
4) Continuation of the attack on Stuhlweissenburg from the south and west by the *1. Pz.Div.* and the *23. Pz.Div.*; and
5) Initiation of the planned attack by the *I. Kav.Korps* towards the Váli [River], depending on developments in the situation.[87]

After consulting with Balck, Wöhler also decided that it was time for *Gen.d.Art.* Maximilian de Angelis's *2. Pz.Armee* on his army group's right flank to take action to assist Balck's *Armeegruppe*, though heretofore this idea had only been discussed, not planned.

This action evidently would take the form of an attack by one of its corps "in a few days" to the east to tie up elements of the Soviet 57th Army in the Kaposvár area, that might conceivably tie up the 1st Bulgarian Army as well. Wöhler brought up this idea during his conversation with Guderian that night, calling it a "long-range objective." Guderian was not enthusiastic, stating that he did not think the time was ripe for such an action; an understandable response, given that he was focused more on obtaining additional troops to shore up the collapsing *H.Gr. Mitte* and *Nord*. When Wöhler received no immediate response from Guderian, he directed von Grolman, his own chief of staff, to draw up plans for the *2. Pz.Armee* to conduct the attack anyway, leaving the date open.

Wöhler also aired his proposal that the *OKH* chief of the general staff (i.e., Guderian) should contact his counterpart at the *OKW*. The *OKW*, which exercised command authority over *H.Gr. F* in northern Yugoslavia, could order that army group—commanded by *G.F.M.* Maximilian Freiherr von Weichs—to launch a limited attack to the north across the Drava River in the direction of Fünfkirchen (Pecs). By doing so, it would draw off or tie up Soviet reserves that might be employed against the southern flank of *IV. SS-Pz.Korps*, thus working in concert to increase the chances that *Konrad III* would succeed. When Wöhler received no immediate response from Guderian, he directed his chief of staff to copy von Weichs in on the same planning order issued to de Angelis's *2. Pz.Armee*. Von Grolman also inserted a paragraph requesting that *H.Gr. F* study the plan and draw up possible courses of action, should *OKW* approve Guderian's request that the two army groups (*F* and *Süd*) be allowed to cooperate.[88] Unfortunately, approval of the proposal would lie within Hitler's purview, since he was acting as the head of both the *OKH* and *OKW*, yet it would still have to be staffed by each command separately, a process that could drag on for days if not weeks.

The official record also shows that about this same time, Wöhler began to consider the idea of detaching the corps fighting north of the Danube and assigning it to *Gen.d.Geb.Tr.* Hans Kreysing's neighboring *8. Armee* instead. This action would free Balck from the responsibility of having to fight two different battles simultaneously and would make a more appropriate geographical boundary between the *6.* and *8. Armee*, but no action was taken on this proposal yet.[89] Left unstated is whether Wöhler himself might have begun to suspect that Balck was not quite up to the challenge of commanding such a diverse and geographically separated organization as his bespoke *Armeegruppe*.

All things considered, successfully commanding a relatively static infantry-centric command like *H.Gr. G* on the Western Front can be judged as far less intellectually challenging than leading a field army consisting of three mechanized German corps (four, including the encircled *IX. SS-Geb.Korps*) and a Hungarian army against two Soviet army groups in a wide-ranging, free-for-all battle. In similar situations on the Eastern Front where he had led a *panzer* corps, Balck had done very well indeed, but leading an *Armeegruppe* in Hungary in January 1945 was an entirely different proposition. Certainly, both Wöhler and Balck had their doubts about Gille's competence, but the *Obergruppenführer* had led his corps as well as anyone could in the current situation, displaying the drive and determination that this fellow corps commanders, Hermann Breith and Gustav Harteneck, apparently lacked. Before any of these leadership considerations could be brought to bear in any consequential way, a considerable amount of hard fighting still remained to be done, as the men of the *IV. SS-Pz.Korps* would soon experience on Monday, 22 January.

That day would be marked by two primary events: the continuing drive towards Budapest by the *Wiking* and *Totenkopf* Divisions, as exemplified by their attempt to overcome the Váli River defense line, and the seizure of the city of Stuhlweissenburg by the *1. Pz.Div.* Summing up the day's events from the corps' perspective, Gille's *Ic* wrote in his evening report:

> The enemy was thrown out of Stuhlweissenburg after fierce street fighting in the morning hours. About 500 prisoners from five rifle divisions and large amount of booty were brought in. East and northeast of the city, fierce battles against stiffening enemy resistance continued in the vineyard area … There were no particular occurrences along the Sió Canal sector. Sárbogárd was cleared of enemy remnants. Separate attacks on Herczegfalva from southwest are underway. The Danube island east of Dunapentele is [still] under enemy occupation, the island near Adony has been cleared of the enemy … In the area southeast to northwest of Puszta Aggszentpéter, our own attack was brought to a halt in front of strong enemy *Pakfront*. Enemy deployments south of Kis Halom and west of Puszta Aggszentpéter were smashed by our troops, who destroyed four

tanks. An enemy force with about 30 tanks was thrown off the hill 2.5 kilometers southeast of Kápolnás-Nyek. During the day, there was fierce fighting for the possession of that village, and repeated enemy attacks from the northern part to the southwest were repelled. Sukoró is still occupied by the enemy.[90]

Schönfelder left a more realistic appraisal of that day's attacks, writing afterwards that "Stuhlweissenburg was taken by the *1. Pz.Div.* Upon reaching the Váli Sector, the combat power of our own units appeared to have been exhausted and was no longer sufficient for successfully continuing the attack." In regards to the order that Balck issued after the fall of Stuhlweissenburg that directed the *IV. SS-Pz.Korps* to redouble its efforts, he further wrote:

> The *IV. SS-Pz.Korps* was given the mission that we were to group together all three of our *panzer* divisions, including the *1. Pz.Div.* [though not including the *3. Pz.Div.*] in the narrows [between Lake Velencze and the Danube] and to deploy them together with the support of the *Volks-Art.Korps* for the breakthrough to the northeast. We were urged to avoid a delay by speeding up the regrouping of the artillery and the *1. Pz.Div.* after their successful attack against Stuhlweissenburg.[91]

Schönfelder was very aware of the corps' dwindling combat power, as Gille would have been too, perhaps even more so because, as the commander, he had been visiting the front lines frequently. After four days of continuous fighting, Schönfelder himself was beginning to doubt whether the *IV. SS-Pz.Korps* still had enough strength to continue the advance, given the stiff resistance it had encountered along the Váli River.

By midnight on 21 January, the corps possessed only 142 operational armored fighting vehicles, less than half of the 311 operational tanks, assault guns, and tank destroyers it had possessed when the offensive began on the morning of 18 January. A quarter of these AFVs were away to the south with *3. Pz.Div.*, which was fighting a little war of its own; after 4 p.m., this division would come under the control of the Hungarian *3. Armee*, permanently removing it from Gille's span of control. This was perhaps the corps chief of staff's first realization that unless quickly reinforced, *Konrad III* was probably doomed to fail.

At the division level, fighting that day was generally heavy. Despite the below-freezing weather, averaging 22 degrees Fahrenheit, the troops of Gille's corps did their utmost to achieve their objectives. As Jankuhn noted in his report, the *Sió-Abschnitt* had been relatively quiet, allowing the remaining elements of the Hungarian *25. Inf.Div.* to move into their defensive positions relatively undisturbed. In turn, this enabled *Oberst* Söth to pull *Pz.Aufkl.Abt. 23* out of the line and position it a dozen kilometers to the east along the Sárviz Canal in order to cover the right flank of the *3. Pz.Div.*, which was embroiled in heavy fighting around Herczegfalva. The attempt by *K.Gr. Weymann* to take that town and destroy the large group of Soviet units assembling there was thwarted when it met heavy resistance as it approached from the northeast.

Weymann made a second attempt after moving around to the southwest and achieved some minor success until 4 p.m., when he halted his attack at the town's outskirts to reorganize before making another attempt after nightfall with the assistance of a battalion from *Pz.Gren.Rgt. 394*. The renewed Soviet aggressiveness displayed at Herczegfalva and the difficulties encountered in retaking the town were partially compensated for when *Pz.Aufkl.Abt. 3* retook the neighboring town of Sárbogárd, 10 kilometers to the southwest. As of the evening reporting deadline, *Gen.Maj.* Pape and his division headquarters had finally arrived and had taken responsibility for leading the defense of the *Sió-Abschnitt*, which in turn relieved *Oberst* Söth of having to control it; now the *3. Pz.Div.* commander only had to control the 46-kilometer portion of the front line between the Danube at Kulcs and the Sárviz Canal at Örs Puszta.

The *Wiking* Division, now reunited and with the threat to its supply lines overcome, advanced on a wide front between Puszta Szabolcs on the left and Adony on the right. North of Adony, it encountered minefields that delayed its progress until its *Pionier* battalion could be brought forward to clear them. Ironically, this was the same ground easily covered by the *Panzergruppe* from the *3. Pz.Div.* the previous day before it was recalled and sent back to attack Herczegfalva. During the time that had lapsed between the hand-off from Söth to Ullrich's division, Soviet troops had apparently crept back in and began work on fortifying the area. Nevertheless, the division's *Panzergruppe* and its two *Panzergrenadier* regiments were able to push through this obstacle. The *Westland* Regiment captured Iváncsa and Szinatelep, advancing as far as the railroad station north of the town. Moving along the division's front, *Stubaf.* Wagner's *SS-Pz.Aufkl.Abt. 5* crossed the Váli River northeast of Puszta Aggszentpéter and established a small bridgehead, but could advance no further in the face of determined enemy resistance.

The rest of the division reached the western bank of the river, but did not cross because the defenders held the high ground on the opposite bank overlooking the river and dominated all of the crossing sites with direct and indirect fire.[92] Even the addition of several *Pz. VI* Tiger IIs from *s.Pz.Abt. 509*, operating on the division's left flank, did little to move the ball forward. Wagner's reconnaissance battalion was able to cling to its small bridgehead despite attempts by a regiment from the 12th Guards Cavalry Division to dislodge it. That evening, the division's *O1*, Günther Jahnke, summed up the day's activities, "The division has finally caught up, our spearhead is fighting its way slowly towards the [north]-east after repelling numerous enemy counterattacks in the area of Puszta Szabolcs. Our wire connections are frequently disrupted. Most of our communications are by radio."[93] Despite these challenges, Ullrich's headquarters was still able to transmit no fewer than six radio messages informing Gille of the progress of his attack.

After enjoying a considerable amount of success on 21 January, the *Totenkopf* Division made hardly any progress the next day. Although it had captured most of Kápolnás Nyék the day before, the northern edge of the town had remained in hands of Gorshkov's Cossacks, who launched several tank-supported counterattacks throughout the day in an attempt to retake it. Having destroyed or scattered a large group of enemy troops and knocked out five tanks occupying an assembly area 2.5 kilometers southeast of the town near the village of Gróftanya, Becker was able to get his division moving again in time to capture Hill 150 by late afternoon. The 12 remaining operational tanks from *s.Pz.Abt. 509* attached to the *Totenkopf* Division also managed to reach the Váli southeast of Baraczka next to the *Wiking* Division during the morning, but got no further than that. Unsatisfied with the battalion's performance, Pitschellis, the commander of *SS-Pz. Rgt. 3*, directed one of his own battalion commanders to take charge and lead it, infuriating *Hptm.* König, who wrote a strongly worded letter of protest several days later to Guderian himself.[94]

Not only were the requisite 70-ton bridges lacking, but so were the combat engineers who were expected to erect them, which was one of König's complaints (another was that the *Totenkopf* Division did not know how to properly employ an independent heavy tank battalion). Inhospitable terrain unsuitable for the employment of heavy tanks, compounded by the fire from Soviet antitank guns emplaced on the opposite bank, made any kind of daylight crossing unthinkable anyway. With the Soviet defenses along the Váli finally in place, it appeared that the opportunity to rapidly break through towards Budapest had been lost. To add to the division's disappointing showing that day, the commander of *SS-Pz.Jäg.Abt. 3*, *Stubaf.* Boris Kraas, was wounded in action near Nagy Halom when his vehicle was knocked out by a Soviet antitank shell. Evacuated to a field hospital, he died from his wounds in an SS hospital on 28 February 1945. He was immediately replaced as the tank destroyer battalion commander by *Ostuf.* Werner Kolbe.[95]

The only truly successful operation concluded that day was the seizure of Stuhlweissenburg by the *1. Pz.Div.* during the evening of 21/22 January. The continuing possession of this town by three understrength divisions of the XXI Guards Rifle Corps (the 84th Rifle Division and 41st and 69th Guards Rifle Divisions), reinforced by the 9th Guards Tank Brigade and 382nd Guards SP Artillery Regiment of the I Guards Mechanized Corps, had become such a threat to the flanks of the *IV. SS-Pz.Korps* that any advance by Gille's forces beyond the southern shore of Lake Velencze entailed enormous risk unless it was in German hands. Though *K.Gr. Philipp* with most of the division's tanks was still operating alongside the *Totenkopf* in the vicinity of Kápolnás Nyék (where Philipp's force tied down the 93rd Rifle Division), the rest of Thünert's division, reinforced by approximately 1,500–2,000 Hungarian troops from *SS-Regiment Ney*, initiated an attack from the south and southwest quadrants of the city.

At some point later in the fighting, they were joined by Fritz Vogt's *I. Btl./Norge*, though not by *s.Pz.Abt. 509*, which was tied up in fighting east of Kápolnás Nyék while still attached to the *Totenkopf* Division. Gille had assigned Thünert's attack the priority of his corps' artillery support, provided by *Volks-Art.Corps 403*, which supplemented the division's own artillery regiment, *Pz.Art.Rgt. 73*. Thus, over 100 guns of various calibers were to take part in the preparatory bombardment. Beginning at 8 p.m., the combined artillery began firing a 20-minute barrage directed against all known and suspected Soviet defensive positions that had been scouted the previous day by patrols sent out by the *1. Pz.Div.*

Thünert's attacking troops, grouped into two battlegroups—*K.Gr. Marcks* and *Huppert*—and supported by 13 *Pz. IV*s from *II. Abt./Pz.Rgt. 1* and several Panthers from the *4. Kompanie*, closely followed the barrage in their *SPW*s and charged into the town from the south, taking advantage of the almost complete darkness. From the northern outskirts of the town, which was supposed to have been attacked at the same time by the neighboring *23. Pz.Div.*, little could be heard. On the town's western outskirts, *SS-Rgt. Ney* began its own attack. Evidence indicates that the defending troops were caught almost completely by surprise by the rapidity and force of the German attack, which later became known as the *1. Pz.Div. Husarenstreich* (German for a *coup de main*); one source states that some Soviet troops were observed running about in their underwear, having been rousted from their beds by the gunfire. Soon, Ney's troops, as well as the *Panzergrenadiere* from the *1. Pz.Div.*, were involved in house-to-house fighting. Hungarian SS men hunted Soviet tanks with *Panzerfausts* and fought their mortal enemy hand-to-hand, while Thünert's tanks fought duels against T-34s and M4A2 Shermans along the city's narrow streets.[96]

Finally, the troops from the *23. Pz.Div.* initiated their own attack from the north, joined by one regiment from the *4. Kav.Brig.* operating on its left. Once this force had joined in the attack, the capture of Stuhlweissenburg and its northern environs became inevitable. Having recovered somewhat from their initial surprise, the commanders of the 84th Rifle and 69th Guards Rifle Divisions inside the city realized that they were in danger of being completely surrounded, so began a rapid and unplanned withdrawal towards the northeast and east before it was too late. The transfer of the 93rd Rifle Division out of Stuhlweissenburg the previous day prompted by *K.Gr. Philipp*'s unauthorized movement had worked to the benefit of the attackers, who enjoyed a slight numerical advantage. As German artillery fire pounded the center and eastern districts of the city, the withdrawal by the XXI Guards Rifle Corps soon turned into a panicked rout, as German troops and tanks fired into the close-packed columns of Soviet troops and trucks as they fought to escape from the rapidly closing trap. Soon the roads leading out of the city were clogged with burning Soviet tanks and trucks and the bodies of their troops.

In the mopping up that followed, Thünert's division claimed to have taken 800 prisoners and destroyed 40 tanks and SP guns, and recaptured a number of their own damaged tanks that were being prepared for rail shipment back to the Soviet Union as war trophies. The northern suburb of Kiskecskemet was also taken and

Die Erfolgseite

In der Zeit vom 1.2. bis 28.2. wurden
von unserer Division erbeutet od. vernichtet:

Panzer	110
Sturmgeschütze	1
Geschütze	4
Pak	100
Flak	1
Granatwerfer	7
s. M.-G.	26
le. M.-G.	45
Handfeuerwaffen	193
Flugzeuge	3
Lkw.	18
Minen	903
Wurfgranaten	10800
7,62cm Granaten	1000

Dazu wurden eine Anzahl Gefangene
eingebracht.

DRUCK: KARTENSTELLE   HERAUSGEBER ABT.VI.

Figure 5. The periodic *Erfolgseite* (Success Page) of the *3. SS-Pz.Div. Totenkopf,* published in the division's troop newspaper, the *Totenkopfmelder* (the *Death's Head Messenger*). This example lists the results of the division's combat action between 1 January and 28 February 1945, which portrays the amount of Red Army tanks, guns, and other weapons destroyed or captured by the division during that period. (Vopersal, Vol. Vb, 687)

a new defense line between Zámoly and the western tip of Lake Velencze was finally established. The Remnants of the city's defenders were forced to retreat nearly 10 kilometers to the northeast and east until they reached the town of Pákozd, where they turned around and dug in along the Császari River.

Strangely, neither the *23. Pz.Div.* nor the *1. Pz.Div.* followed up their victory by carrying out a pursuit aimed at preventing the XXI Guards Rifle Corps from establishing another defense line, nor was there any plan for *K.Gr. Philipp*, defending the town of Velencze less than 20 kilometers to the east, to attack the city from behind, which would have cut off any escape route. Had they done so, it would have benefitted the further progress of *Konrad III* by securing the left flank of *IV. SS-Pz.Korps* once it had advanced beyond the safety of Lake Velencze. Perhaps they did not act because of the heavy casualties the attackers had already suffered during the fighting, or because the troops themselves were simply exhausted.[97] Regardless, it reflects a missed opportunity that Balck, Gille, and Breith should have anticipated.

After mopping up Soviet remnants in Stuhlweissenburg, Thünert handed the city over to the control of the *23. Pz.Div.* as directed. The defense of the city then became the responsibility of Breith's *III. Pz.Korps* after 4 p.m. Early in the morning of 23 January, the *1. Pz.Div.* began moving to its new assembly area in the town of Gárdony on the southern shore of Lake Velencze, where it was joined by *K.Gr. Philipp*. The Hungarian *SS-Rgt. Ney* would remain behind with the *III. Pz.Korps*, where it would be incorporated into the new defense line being constructed by the *23. Pz.Div.* east of Stuhlweissenburg. Once the *1. Pz.Div.* had arrived in its assembly area, it would undergo a brief one-day period of rest and reorganization before it rejoined the two SS divisions in a renewed drive to overcome the Váli River defense line the next day.

Thünert's division's achievement did not go unnoticed; in recognition of the German victory, it was mentioned in the daily *OKW* bulletin, which stated on 23 January, "Stuhlweissenburg was conquered in a surprise night attack by a Thuringian–Hessian *panzer* division, 800 prisoners were taken and a great amount of booty was brought in." That evening, Gille laconically wrote, "Stuhlweissenburg taken, great amount of spoils."[98] Balck wasted no time in sending a self-congratulatory telegram at 1:20 p.m. that afternoon to Hungary's head of state, Ferenc Szalási, and his minister, *Gen.O.* Beregfy, stating, "During the night of 21/22 January, Szekesfehervar (Stuhlweissenburg) was stormed and retaken by German and Hungarian troops."[99] Oddly, the telegram was not routed through *H.Gr. Süd* as protocol dictated.

Within the *Korpsgruppe Breith/III Pz.Korps* area of operations, in addition to the already mentioned participation of the *23. Pz.Div.*, its Ic also reported that enemy forces east-southeast of Sárkeresztes were thrown back across the line demarcated by the Stuhlweissenburg–Zámoly highway. To the north of the *23. Pz.Div.*, an attempt by the *4. Kav.Brig.* to straighten out the front line west of Zámoly managed only to gain several hundred meters of ground in the face of strong enemy resistance. The *Korpsgruppe* also reported that assault troops from the Hungarian *1. Hus.Div.* had conducted two large-scale probing attacks, one east of Környe and the other from Bánhida to the south. These *Stosstruppen* managed to penetrate 1.5 kilometers into Soviet-held territory and were able to determine that the units suspected to be occupying the area had not been pulled out of their positions and sent elsewhere, but had remained in place.

North of Breith's *Korpsgruppe*, Harteneck's *I. Kav.Korps* reported a small-scale enemy breakthrough at Sarisap that was being "cleaned out" by *Gren.Rgt. 283* of the *96. Inf.Div.* at the time the evening report was submitted. Its *711. Inf.Div.* also reported weak local attacks against its positions northwest of Pilisszentlélek, which were all repulsed. The planned attack between Mány and Bicske by the *6. Pz.Div.* and *3. Kav.Brig.* was once again postponed until the following day. On Harteneck's left, the newly arrived *IV. Pz.Korps FHH*—which had taken up the reins as the headquarters responsible for operations on the northern bank of the Danube from the *LVII. Pz.Korps* that morning—reported that the enemy breakthrough reported northeast of Moĉa the previous day had been completely eliminated, resulting in the destruction of 17 tanks by antitank guns and hand-held antitank weapons by troops subordinated to the *44. Reichs-Gren.Div. HuD.*

Within Budapest itself, now experiencing the beginning of its fifth week under siege, the *IX. SS-Geb.Korps* reported that during the night of 21/22 January, the Soviets renewed their attack to gain complete control of Margaret Island from their bridgehead on the island's northern tip as well as across the frozen Danube from the eastern bank, making several penetrations in the German and Hungarian lines. All of these small gaps in the German lines were sealed off, and counterattacks by SS troops and the Hungarian student battalion to throw the Soviet assault troops back were still in progress at the report's time. Along the rest of the perimeter, Pfeffer-Wildenbruch reported only sporadic artillery and mortar harassment fire. Although the Budapest garrison did not report the results of any aerial deliveries, the *Oberquartiermeister* of *A.Gr. Balck/6. Armee* reported that 9.75 tons of munitions, 264 gallons of gasoline, and 275lb of radio equipment were parachuted over the city during the night of 21/22 January.[100]

In the air, the Budapest defenders reported strong Soviet attacks against the city center of Buda as well as front-line positions. The *IV. SS-Pz.Korps'* *Flivo* report had not arrived by the evening deadline, though the divisions noted a considerable amount of attacks against their positions. As for the rest of the *A.Gr. Balck* area of operations, only limited enemy air activity was reported, except for reconnaissance flights. The *Luftwaffe* was also very active that day. Taking advantage of the relatively favorable flying weather, *Luftflotte 4* reported that its squadrons had completed 400 sorties, mostly against Soviet troops columns and river ferrying operations, and had managed to down 31 enemy aircraft.

German reconnaissance flights observed a considerable amount of vehicular traffic between the area south of Lake Balaton and the Danube in the Soviet 57th Army area, as well as north of Lake Velencze. North of the Danube, *Aufklärer* report observing up to 3,000 Soviet vehicles moving towards the north and northwest, including approximately 150 tanks. Their ultimate objective could only be guessed at, but it appeared that this signified some sort of build-up against either the *8. Armee* or *H.Gr. Mitte*'s forces in Slovakia.[101]

The *A.Gr. Balck/6. Armee Ic* also reported that either the 5th Guards Mechanized Brigade or the 32nd Independent Guards Mechanized Brigade was reported moving from the area north of the Drava River towards the Sió River sector, which could pose a considerable threat to the Hungarian forces holding this defense line. More Soviet forces had been spotted moving towards the Váli River defense line from the area south of Budapest, and the presence there of the I Guards Mechanized Corps had been positively confirmed. Additional infantry formations had also been spotted moving down to the Váli line, a sign that the 4th Guards Army intended to hold it.

A general staff officer from the Third Ukrainian Front captured that day confirmed that Tolbukhin's army group was now beginning to draw most of its supplies and reinforcements from the neighboring Second Ukrainian Front, whose ferrying activities across the Danube using the reconstructed bridge at Csepel Island had not been disturbed despite German air attacks. Overall, a general regroupment on the Soviet side appeared to be occurring, a sign that the Third Ukrainian Front was quickly recovering from its initial setbacks of 18–21 January, and was consolidating and strengthening its defenses in a manner that did not bode well for *Konrad III*.

Despite the good news of the arrival of additional reserves, the mood within the Soviet camp appeared to be glum. The official Red Army general staff study only stated that "the XXI Guards Rifle Corps [was] forced to fall back under pressure from superior forces and abandon Stuhlweissenburg and fall back to the line Pátka–Kisfalud."[102] The unexpected loss of the city was unwelcome news. The Third Ukrainian Front's political officer, Commissar Katunin, reported:

> The overall disorderly retreat by the units of the 21st Guards Rifle Corps continued until nightfall [on 22 Janary]. Blocking detachments that were deployed restored order and returned those who were fleeing back to their units. Control over the troops at lower levels of command are as before absent; individual commanders, especially artillerymen, have lost their units.[103]

In its explanation of the causes of the disaster, Soviet apologists afterwards exaggerated the size of the attackers, stating that the XXI Guards Rifle Corps was assaulted by an overwhelming German force, consisting of the *Wiking* Division and the *1. Pz.Div.*, as well as the *23. Pz.Div.*, with over 180 tanks (in fact, there were fewer than 30 used).[104] To shore up this weakened area of the front line, the commander of the 4th Guards Army, General Zakharov, dispatched the 223rd Rifle Division, recently received from the 46th Army of the Second Ukrainian Front, to the area east of Stuhlweissenburg.

Elsewhere, Zakharov's forces—especially the V Guards Cavalry Corps and the 1st Guards Mechanized Brigade and 2nd Mechanized Brigade of the I Guards Mechanized Corps—continued to solidify and reinforce their defensive positions along the Váli River, while to the south, the XVIII Tank, CXXXIII Rifle, and XXX Rifle Corps continued to prepare an organized advance against the *3. Pz. Div.* along the line Dunaföldvar–Herczegfalva. A continuous front was also being assembled opposite the Hungarians and Germans along the Sió River south of Lake Balaton by additional elements of the 57th Army, which had placed the remnants of the CXXXV Guards Rifle Corps under its command. The Red Air Force had been particularly active that day, with its air armies (the 5th and 17th) flying as many as 1,034 sorties and claiming to have shot down 36 German and Hungarian aircraft.[105] The increasing strength of Soviet air power was becoming clearly evident, generating three times as many sorties as the *Luftwaffe* and Royal Hungarian Air Force.

Despite the success of the assault on Stuhlweissenburg, neither Balck nor Wöhler were pleased with the overall situation. Both finally realized that their assessment of the previous day had not been altogether accurate; they had been overly optimistic. The Váli River line had not after all been overcome by the *Totenkopf* Division in a rapid assault. Despite the hope engendered by the single report of its reconnaissance battalion, a closer examination of the message's contents reveals that it clearly stated that it had only reached, not crossed, the river. It also had become glaringly obvious that the reserves that the Third Ukrainian Front had dispatched to the 4th Guards Army in the form of the V Guards Cavalry Corps and I Guards Mechanized Corps had won the race to the Váli River and were able to establish a formidable defense line in less than two days. There would be no *Husarenritt* to Budapest; from this point onwards, it would be a hard slog.

Throughout the day, both leaders also become aware of the growing threat to the far right flank of Gille's corps, where the *3. Pz. Div.* found itself embroiled in combat against the bulk of three Soviet corps. While only one of these (the XXX Rifle Corps) was at nearly full strength, the other two (XVIII Tank and CXXXIII Rifle Corps), though battered during their escape from encirclement, were being rapidly re-equipped and resupplied, and were already mounting local attacks. While *Oberst* Söth's troops finally took Herczegfalva by 7:45 p.m. that evening after destroying seven Soviet tanks and eight antitank guns, it was clear that the 57th Army—which had taken control of Soviet units operating in the area—would begin to push back the *3. Pz. Div.* or even attempt to strike deeper to sever the *IV. SS-Pz. Korps'* supply line to the north.

That afternoon, *Gen. Maj.* Pape and his division headquarters finally arrived and was ordered to immediately assume responsibility for defending the Sió River line, including control of the Hungarian *25. Inf. Div.* and the two German armored reconnaissance battalions, *Pz.Aufkl.Abt. 1* and *23*. At the same time, *Div.Gr. Pape* was subordinated to the Hungarian *3. Armee*, which assigned it the entire defensive sector between the Sárviz Canal and Sió River, effective from 4 p.m. This had the advantage of relieving the *3. Pz.Div.* of this onerous responsibility, freeing it to concentrate on fighting the enemy between the Sárviz Canal and the Danube. To better exercise command and control, *Gen.O.* Vitéz-Heszleny's *3. Armee* headquarters displaced from the town of Farkasgyepű, 20 kilometers northwest of Veszprém, to Balaton-Füszfö, the same location used by the *Wiking* Division five days earlier.

Additionally, Balck decided at 4 p.m. to subordinate the *3. Pz.Div.* to the Hungarian *3. Armee* that same day in order to free Gille from having to control what had become a separate operation and allow the *IV. SS-Pz.Korps* to concentrate strictly on prosecuting the offensive along the Váli line. In addition to defending the line between the Danube and the Sárviz Canal, *Oberst* Söth was tasked with destroying the Soviet XVIII Tank Corps by conducting continuous attacks, which was beyond his division's ability. To better facilitate coordination of their division's activities, Pape's headquarters was initially co-located with Söth's in the town of Káloz.[106] The forces of Söth and Pape were both woefully inadequate for such a major task, but there were no other reserves available to reinforce them and they would simply have to do their best with what they had. The German liaison staff at Vitez-Heszleny's headquarters was increased in size to handle the larger amount of staff coordination that this mission entailed.

Another topic that occupied the attention of both Wöhler and Balck that day was their growing dissatisfaction with the performance of the *IV. SS-Pz.Korps*, specifically that of its commander. Balck was to claim later that he had not authorized Gille to take Stuhlweissenburg and that this action delayed the attack against the Váli defense line by at least two days, thereby guaranteeing *Konrad III*'s eventual failure.[107] Despite Balck's assertions, this had no basis in fact; throughout the operation, *IV. SS-Pz. Korps* kept *A.Gr. Balck/6. Armee* continuously apprised of the attack's progress via telephone and *Fernschreiber*. The repositioning of *Volks-Art.Korps 403* to support the attack would also not have gone unnoticed by *Gen.Lt.* Raapke, the commander of Balck's *HARKO 306*. Balck's signal intelligence company also monitored the radio messages being sent back and forth from Thünert's division to Gille's headquarters, so at the very least his *Armee-Nachrichtenführer* (army signals officer), *Oberst* Friedrich Boetzel, would have had a good appreciation of what was happening; it is inconceivable that this officer would not at least have kept Balck's chief of staff, *Gen.Maj.* Gaedke, apprised of the situation.

In addition, Gille had already expressed his intent to retake the city at least one day before the attack began, against which Balck expressed no objections at the time. While there is no evidence that he expressly condoned Gille's plan, neither is there any evidence that he raised any objections to it.[108] From a strictly military point of view, it made sense. Stuhlweissenburg had to be taken before the offensive could be continued because it was positioned like a wedge separating *IV. SS-Pz.Korps* from the *III. Pz.Korps*, limiting their close cooperation. By 21 January, the supply lines of the *IV. SS-Pz.Korps* had been forced to follow a long, circuitous route around the city that was subject to Soviet interdiction at several points.

Balck's own *Oberquartiermeister* had supported this course of action, stating in a report two days earlier, "In the area of combat operations southeast of Stuhlweissenburg, the movement of supplies is often interrupted due to the heavy action of hostile fire. Because of this, delays are being created in the delivery of food and ammunition." Thus, eliminating this concentration of enemy forces would both remove the threat to the flanks and shorten supply lines considerably, thereby speeding the delivery of rations, fuel, and ammunition to the fighting units.[109]

Regardless of Gille's successful action, both of his higher commanders remained unsatisfied. Wöhler felt so strongly about the lack of information flowing up from the corps that he sent one of his own officers with a radio set to Gille's *Gefechtsstand* to send reports directly to *H.Gr. Süd* headquarters. Wöhler even established a forward command post of his own in Zirc to be closer to the scene of the fighting. Whether this was a subtle swipe at Balck's performance was undisclosed.[110] That evening, feeling uncertain of the actual situation and stung by his overreliance on a single optimistic report—compounded by the perceived reluctance or inability of the corps headquarters and its divisions to send timely and accurate reports—Balck went forward to Gille's headquarters at Seregélyes to see for himself what was happening. Wöhler, who was also conducting his own commander's tour of the area, may have traveled with him because he expressed his desire to speak with the SS corps commander too.

The records are not clear whether the *Obergruppenführer* was there at the time of the visit, but if Balck did speak directly with Gille, he left no record of what might have been said. However, when he returned to his headquarters in Martinsburg at 9:45 p.m. that evening, he recorded his thoughts in his nightly situation estimate to *H.Gr. Süd*, stating that he had the impression that "the attack of the *IV. SS-Pz.Korps* was stuck fast. Contrary to previous reports, there was no one in Aggszentpéter [this was incorrect—it was occupied by the *Wiking* Division at the time] and nobody had reached the Váli sector, with perhaps the exception of individual combat patrols of reconnaissance battalions." This he should have already known. Recording his thoughts in his commander's situation report that evening, he wrote:

> To prevent a further splitting up of friendly forces, which could no longer lead to success against increasingly strong opposition, [I] issued orders to the *IV. SS-Pz.Korps* to assemble all three *panzer* divisions and the *Volks-Art.Korps* in the gap between the Danube and Lake Velencze and launch them together for the breakthrough to the northeast.[111]

Wöhler had also arrived at a more realistic appraisal of the situation, writing that same evening in his commander's report to *OKH*:

Our attack has developed into a time-consuming and casualty-intensive struggle as our widely dispersed attack groups seek to clear enemy obstacles and defeat groups of enemy forces. This manner of fighting seems to be even less supportable in light of the relief of Budapest becoming ever more urgent due to renewed enemy preparations to assault the western bridgehead [i.e., Buda]. This situation requires a new decision.[112]

Based on the developments of 22 January and the indications that the Soviet defense was stiffening, Balck and Wöhler realized that the Váli River line could only be overcome by a coordinated attack by all three of Gille's divisions, including the *1. Pz.Div.*, once it had completed its movement out of Stuhlweissenburg and hasty reorganization at Gárdony.

The *A.Gr. Balck/6. Armee* commander at first wanted to begin the attack during the early hours of 23 January, but due to the difficulties encountered in moving *Volks-Art.Korps 403* and *Pz.Art.Rgt. 73* out of their firing positions west and south of Stuhlweissenburg along the poor road network south of Lake Velencze to their new assembly areas, he decided to postpone the attack until that evening or the early morning of 24 January at the latest. Thus, nearly two more days were added to the already delayed timeline for *Konrad III*; two more days that the defenders put to good use, including the addition of more antitank mines, emplacing *Pakfronts*, and the construction of a secondary defense line behind the Váli.

In studying the situation, Balck concluded that the best way to overcome a deeply-echeloned defense such as the one being constructed by the V Guards Cavalry Corps and I Guards Mechanized Corps was to create an opening with a powerful artillery barrage. Only then would Gille's divisions be able to advance through the gap. Once again, this was a task normally assigned to infantry divisions, but since there were none available, the *panzer* divisions would have to pierce the Soviet front lines themselves with their own *Panzergrenadiere*. Combat engineers would have to be positioned close to the front to clear minefields, with *Brückenbau* units standing by to quickly build or repair bridges that Gille's tanks and other heavy armored vehicles needed to cross the river.

Schönfelder's account does not mention the visit by either Wöhler and Balck, but he did acknowledge receipt of the change to the operations plan, writing, "*IV. SS-Pz.Korps* received the mission that all three *panzer* divisions, including the *1. Pz.Div.* to assemble in the 'narrows' and with the support of the *Volks-Art.Korps* conduct a breakthrough attack towards the northeast."[113] Gille's corps was not the only one to attract the attention of the *Armeegruppe* commander. Regarding Breith's *Korpsgruppe*, Balck stated his intent for that organization as well, writing, "[I] intend the right wing of the *III. Pz.Korps* to participate in the attack by attacking the area northwest of Pákozd and, later, Lovasberény and Acsa."[114]

Despite Balck's growing discontent with Gille, at least they agreed on one thing: the need to relieve Budapest before it was too late. To reinforce this point, Balck concluded his estimate of the situation, writing that "it was all the more urgent for the attack to break through rapidly to the northeast, as the Budapest garrison has concluded from today's signs of enemy activity ... that the enemy wanted to reduce the bridgehead with all his strength at the last moment [before we can relieve it]." The troops themselves were firmly convinced on that point; they had been fighting for three weeks to relieve the capital and they now seemed closer than ever. One participant, *Ustuf.* Erich Kernmayr, wrote after the war:

> For the first time after long months, even years, German troops had wrested away from the enemy large areas that had long been occupied by the Red Army. It was symbolic that this fight in snow and ice, the last fight in which a victory could be credited to the German flag, was fought by the men of the *Heer* and the *Waffen-SS* together in brotherly comradeship.[115]

The other decision that Balck made was to instruct the *I. Kav.Korps* commander that he must begin his own attack between Mány and Bicske; it had been delayed long enough. In order to draw off Soviet forces holding the Váli River line in front of Gille's troops, Balck ordered Harteneck to initiate the attack by the *6. Pz.Div.* and *4. Kav.Brig.* that very evening, or by 2 a.m. on 23 January at the latest.[116] The Hungarian *VIII. Armee-Korps*, attached to *Korpsgruppe Breith*, was also ordered to begin its eastwards push into the Vértes Mountains on the morning of 23 January. Wherever the Soviets began to pull back or show signs of weakness, its leading unit, the *1. Hus.Div.*, was to exploit the situation and tie down as many Soviet troops as possible to prevent them from being sent to reinforce the troops opposite Gille's three *panzer* divisions massing at the eastern tip of Lake Velencze.

So much for the intentions of *A.Gr. Balck*'s commander. For his part, Wöhler would do what he could to support Balck's offensive. Although he had "embedded" one of his junior staff officers (a certain *Hauptmann* Jahns) with a radio in Gille's headquarters to facilitate the exchange of information, the *H.Gr. Süd* commander still trusted his subordinate to see the offensive through. One of the other actions that Wöhler took was to continue his efforts to convince the *OKH Führungsstab* of the urgency to approve the plan put forth that would have the *2. Pz.Armee* conduct an attack aimed at linking up with the *IV. SS-Pz.Korps'* right flank (to be held after the afternoon of 22 January by the Hungarian *3. Armee*) and encircling the 57th Army and portions of the Bulgarian *1. Armee*.

Even if this plan failed, it would still divert some of the Soviet forces being marshaled against Hungarian and German forces arrayed along the *Sió-Abschnitt*. Wöhler proposed that this attack, which his staff had code-named *Unternehmen Eisbrecher* (Operation *Icebreaker*), should begin no later than 26 January and would involve the recently transferred *356. Inf.Div.* Once this attack was concluded—optimistically estimated to take only two or three days—this division would be sent to reinforce *A.Gr. Balck/6. Armee*, a journey that would require at least another day to move by rail to Várpalota, where it would arrive by 26 January at the earliest.

Wöhler also continued urging Guderian to intervene on his behalf with *OKW* in order to involve *H. Gr. F* in the effort to draw off or prevent Soviet forces from interfering with *Konrad III*.[117] For his part, Guderian told Wöhler that Hitler wanted a "clean sweep" west of the Danube using the forces he had, and he should plan accordingly. *Der Führer* was beginning to show signs of impatience, stressing that the operation needed to be wrapped up as soon as possible so the forces could be sent elsewhere. Left unstated was Hitler's insistence that the Hungarian oil fields had to be defended at all costs, a mission that had been entrusted to the *2. Pz.Armee* since November 1944; any offensive task undertaken by that army had to be balanced against this requirement.

Guderian did not rule out the possibility that *H. Gr. F* might still be able to assist with a supporting attack, since Hitler did not specifically forbid this, but he did block sending additional forces to *H. Gr. Süd* to support *Konrad III*, other than what had already been sent.[118] Though he was still performing his duties as chief of the *OKH* general staff to the best of his ability, by 22 January, Guderian himself had come to realize that the situation concerning Budapest was hopeless. He later wrote, "On the Budapest front, the Germans recaptured Stuhlweissenburg, but we knew that our forces were insufficient to win a decisive victory there, and unfortunately, the Russians [*sic*] knew it too."[119] Thus ended 22 January, with more than the usual amount of anticipation and trepidation among the commanders and staffs of the headquarters concerned. As for the soldiers fighting on the snow-covered *Puszta*, they were unaware of the drama unfolding behind the scenes; they were only convinced that it meant one day closer to saving Budapest.

While the following day would be characterized by the regroupment of *A. Gr. Balck's* forces for their coordinated assault on 24 January, this did not mean that no heavy fighting took place. To the contrary, a considerable amount of combat was reported by nearly all of its units in the lead-up to the renewed offensive. As far as the staffs of the corps and divisions were concerned, they had less than a day to draft changes to their own operations orders and distribute them to their subordinate units. The *IV. SS-Pz.Korps* received the following modification of the original *Konrad III* order from *A. Gr. Balck* during the late evening of 22 January or early morning hours of 23 January:

> The corps [will break] through the enemy defensive front between the Danube and Lake Velencze early in the morning on 23 January by massing all three tank divisions and all available artillery. It is important, after a strong artillery preparation, to break through at a narrow point first and then widen the breach. After making a penetration, advance rapidly to seize the designated objectives.

This date was shortly afterwards changed to the night of 23/24 January in recognition of the time required to move the *1. Pz.Div.* and the corps artillery from the western end of Lake Velencze to the eastern edge. Otherwise, everything remained the same.

While the bulk of the *1. Pz.Div.* was not engaged with the enemy that day, the rest of the corps was, which explains the rather low overall armor strength of the *IV. SS-Pz.Korps* reported by the end of the day. On the evening of 22 January, the *Totenkopf* Division reported having only 18 of its own armored fighting vehicles ready for action—seven *Pz. IV*s, three *Pz. V* Panthers, one *Pz. VI* Tiger I, and seven assault guns. As low as this readiness rate was, that of the *Wiking* Division was even worse, with just six *Pz. IV*s and six *Pz. V*s. The *I. Abt./Pz.Rgt. 24*, attached to *K.Gr. Philipp*, reported 26 operational *Pz. V*s, making it the strongest tank battalion in the entire corps. The *1. Pz.Div.* reported four *Pz. IV*s, 18 *Pz. V*s, one assault gun, and six tank destroyers ready for action, a total of 29. The attached heavy tank battalion, *s.Pz.Abt. 509*, reported only 12 *Pz. VI* Tiger IIs operational, out of 45 authorized. Five days of fighting snow and mud, as well as a determined enemy and improper employment, had led to this dire situation.

Sturm-Artillerie Brigade 303, supporting the *Wiking* Division, still had 21 operational vehicles. Although not participating in the attack slated for 24 January (and in fact now part of the Hungarian *3. Armee*), the *3. Pz.Div.* reported seven operational *Pz. IV*s, 10 *Pz. V*s, and two assault guns, a total of only 19 operational vehicles, a woefully inadequate number to defend a front line of such magnitude in the shadow of a resurgent enemy. It also reported three operational *Sturmpanzer IV Brumbär* ("Grizzly Bear") from the attached *Sturm-Pz.Abt. 219*, but these were not of any use against enemy tanks. All told, *IV. SS-Pz.Korps* only fielded 118 operational AFVs (not including *SPW*s and armored cars), a relatively low number given the circumstances.[120] This force was roughly equivalent to the number of tanks fielded by a single *panzer* division at 80 percent strength.

Neither would the corps be able to count *StuG.Abt. 1335* among its number; that day, this battalion—which had served as part of Gille's corps reserve—was ordered to begin moving immediately to the north of the Danube, where it would join the *IV. Pz.Korps FHH*.[121] Though only seven of its 15 remaining vehicles were still operational on 20 January, these would be sorely missed. Once again, Gille's troops would have to keep fighting with what they had; no new *panzers* were on the way to replace those that had been lost, placing an increased burden on the harried maintenance troops who struggled in sub-freezing temperatures to repair as many damaged or broken-down armored vehicles as quickly as possible. Both the *Wiking* and *Totenkopf* Divisions had established repair facilities in Veszprém, and any armored vehicles that could not be fixed on the spot at the regimental level were towed all the way back there, where better-equipped maintenance teams would do what they could to restore them to fighting condition or, if they could not be repaired, use them as a source of spare parts.

While 23 January had been set aside as a day for the *IV. SS-Pz.Korps* to regroup and reorganize its forces in preparation for the attack scheduled for the following morning, by no means did this mean that the day was uneventful. In fact, quite a bit of heavy fighting took place all along the line, from the town of Velencze on the corps' left flank, to Baraczka to its northeast, and from there along the west bank of the Váli River, where the right flank finally came to rest near Szinatelep on the west bank of the Danube. The only penetration of the Soviet defenses from the previous day was the tiny bridgehead still held by the *Wiking* Division's reconnaissance battalion northeast of Aggszentpéter that had been hemmed in by enemy attacks.

In his evening status report for the corps, *Stubaf.* Jankuhn reported "strong enemy artillery fire originating from positions located west of the town of Raczkeve on Csepel Island," which primarily affected the *Wiking* Division. This was a significant development, because up to this point most of the Soviet artillery encountered had been sporadic and poorly coordinated. Continuing his report, Gille's *Ic* stated:

> German spearheads had been able to force Soviet forces as much as four kilometers back [across the Váli River] northeast of Iváncsa. Bitter fighting took place all day for the possession of the agricultural estate three kilometers northwest [of Nagyhalom] and the area southwest of Hill 157, wherein local penetrations by enemy forces were repeatedly repulsed. From the area of Sukoró towards Nadap [west of Velencze], a considerable amount of enemy movement was observed.[122]

With his corps *Vorgeschobener Gefechtstand* now located in Seregélyes, Gille was much closer to the fighting, enabling him to complete his visits to each division command post in less time, especially since he no longer had to concern himself with time-consuming visits to the far-flung command post of the *3. Pz. Div.* Relieved of that responsibility, he and his *Führungsabteilung* could now focus strictly on the tactical challenge of breaching the Váli defense line.

Meanwhile, the rest of the corps staff, now located in the town of Jenö nearly 30 kilometers west of Seregélyes, busied themselves with logistical and administrative matters, such as forecasting requirements and monitoring the movement of supplies from the depots in the Veszprém area all the way to the eastern tip of Lake Velencze as well as the evacuation of the wounded and damaged matériel in the opposite direction. It is a well-established fact that during an offensive by armored units, great amounts of supplies, particularly fuel and ammunition, are routinely used up. For example, on 22 January alone, the various units of *A. Gr. Balck* had expended 750 metric tons of ammunition (approximately 826 short tons).[123]

The most closely monitored (and the most precious) commodity remained gasoline, without which *H. Gr. Süd* had no hopes of relieving Budapest or even mounting any sort of credible defense against the Red Army. Logistics staffs at the division, corps, field army, and army group levels were obsessed with monitoring daily fuel shipments to local depots, stockage levels, and deliveries to the forward units. On 22 January, the field army's *Oberquartiermeister, Oberstlt.* Otto Mitlacher, reported that on that day alone, the troops engaged in *Konrad III* (primarily the four *panzer* divisions of the *IV. SS-Pz.Korps*) consumed 530 cubic meters of fuel, or approximately 140,000 gallons, slightly less than the 588 cubic meters (155,000 gallons) used the day before. This left just 1,619 cubic meters remaining in all of

A.Gr. Balck's fuel depots as of 23 January, estimated to be approximately two days' worth. This would be only enough to keep the *Armeegruppe* supplied until 25 January unless more fuel shipments arrived.[124] Quartermaster staffs were even tracking the movement of individual *Eisenbahnkesselwagen* (*E.K.W.*, or rail tank cars) from the refinery to the field, as well as the daily output of the Hungarian refineries, so constrained had this vital resource become.

Though this subject was of great interest to the individual staff officers concerned, the maneuver elements of the *IV. SS-Pz.Korps* were only interested in the sufficient and continuous delivery of this precious commodity, as well as ammunition and to a lesser extent food. Their goal remained focused on closing up along the entire length of the Váli River from the Danube to Baraczka. In the *Wiking* Division attack zone, its right wing, consisting of *Hstuf.* Gerhard Sacher's *I. Bataillon* of the *Westland* Regiment, continued pushing north along the Danube. Though it was bitterly cold, visibility was clear, allowing the accompanying tank crewmen to get the most out of their vehicles' superior cannons and optics. When Sacher's battalion reached the Vali, he found that the opposite bank had been occupied by strong enemy forces in a commanding position located on the high ground.

On the division's left in the area of Aggszentpéter, a Soviet armored force attacked in a southerly direction, forcing *K.Gr. Westland* to quickly transition from an attack formation to a hasty defense to stem the enemy's attack. Once this had been accomplished, Hack's regiment launched a counterattack of its own to drive the enemy back and regain the lost ground. One member of the *Panzergruppe*, *Ostuf.* Kerckhoff, later wrote, "We made slow progress against tough resistance ... the weather turned worse; rain and snow alternated and reduced visibility."[125] In the center of the division, a small *Kampfgruppe* from *Hstuf.* Sacher's *I. Btl./Westland*, supported by four assault guns and the attached Hungarian *I. Btl./Inf.Rgt. 54*, managed to advance northeast along both sides of the railway bed 2 kilometers southeast of Aggszentpéter and found two intact bridges over the Váli. Wasting no time, Sacher hurried his men across and established a bridgehead of their own, which the *Kampfgruppe* successfully held throughout the day despite numerous Soviet attempts to wipe it out.[126] On the division's left flank, a Soviet attack forced the *Germania* Regiment to temporarily give up its hold on a farmstead 3 kilometers southeast of Aggszentpéter, until it was retaken in a joint counterattack launched by the *Germania* and *Westland* Regiments.[127]

In the *Totenkopf* zone, two battalions from the *Eicke* Regiment were able to seize the Gróftanya agricultural estate 5 kilometers southeast of Kápolnás Nyék, which had been defended by a mixed tank and infantry force. After forcibly ejecting the enemy after a hard-fought struggle, the regiment had to almost immediately defend it against multiple southwest-oriented Soviet counterattacks approaching along both sides of the highway and rail line between that town and Baraczka. Fortunately, the stoutly built houses on the estate made excellent strongpoints, protecting its defenders against all but a direct hit from Soviet artillery fire. Despite the best efforts of the men from the *Totenkopf* Regiment involved, they were unable to prevent the nearby farmstead at Nagy Halom from falling into the hands of the enemy.

In Kápolnás Nyék, *III. Btl./Eicke* was able to finish the conquest of that town after overcoming the Cossack regiment holding its northern outskirts and holding it against several unsuccessful Soviet counterattacks. To relieve this battalion and allow it to rejoin the rest of the regiment, Gille sent Becker the *I. Btl./Norge* and *I. Btl./Danmark*, which were immediately tasked with the town's defense. Now assembled outside of the town, *III. Btl./Eicke* was ordered to probe in the direction of Puszta Pettend to determine whether there was a bridge over the Váli still intact east of the town. If they found it, its commander, *Hstuf.* Heinrich Bock, was ordered to seize it and hold it until the rest of the *Eicke* Regiment arrived. They never got that far; 4 kilometers southwest of the bridge, Bock and 50 of his troops were ambushed by a superior enemy force. Bock was killed in action, while the rest of his patrol was badly shot up and barely managed to make it back to their own lines.

Between Kápolnás Nyék and the town of Velencze, *Rittm.* Weidemann, the acting commander of *I. Abt./Pz.Rgt. 24* with 31 operational *Pz. V* Panthers, had relieved *K.Gr. Philipp*, which had returned to rejoin its division at Gárdony before it ran out of fuel. Weidemann's battalion was now manning a protective screen line oriented towards the west in the direction of Stuhlweissenburg. During the day, it warded off a Soviet reconnaissance in force aimed in their direction, driving it away after destroying four M4A2 Shermans. On that same day, the *Totenkopf*'s *9. Kp./SS-Pz. Rgt. 3* had only one operational *Pz. VI* Tiger I; the rest had all fallen out of service due to mechanical failures or battle damage, but were being repaired as quickly as possible. The 12 remaining operational *Pz. VI* Tiger IIs of *s.Pz.Abt. 509* did not participate in any fighting that day, having been withdrawn to Seregélyes to rejoin the rest of the battalion, which was working to get as many of its damaged or broken down vehicles back in operation. That same day, its commander, *Maj.* Burmester, returned to duty after being wounded four days earlier.

Throughout the day, the *1. Pz.Div.* did its best to prepare for the following day's attack in its assembly area between Gárdony and Agárd. The artillery battalions of *Volks-Art.Korps 403* and *SS-Werf.Abt. 504* moved into their firing positions southwest of Kápolnás Nyék, where they stockpiled ammunition and issued firing instructions for the next day's attack. Constant Soviet air activity forced the units to camouflage their vehicles and guns as much as possible, though in the snow-covered, wide-open plains south of Lake Velencze, this was a task easier said than done. Late that afternoon, Gille was especially brief when commenting in his notebook, "Division *Wiking* reached the Danube at Adony, then turned to the north." His thoughts on the prospects of the attack scheduled for the next day were not recorded.

No copies of the *IV. SS-Pz.Korps* operations order are known to exist, and *A. Gr. Balck's* records are similarly lacking. However, it is possible to reconstruct the general outline of the plan, based on notes made by Peter Gosztony, who had corresponded with Gille:

> On January 23, *SS-Obergruppenführer* Gille decided to break the Russian [*sic*] barricade [along the Váli River] by advancing north of Baraczka to the town of Vál in order to cross the Váli [River] at a convenient point and advance further east. He regrouped [his forces] and started the attack again. The general lack of advancing infantry that [should] have been used to clean up the fighting area and to shield the flanks became obvious. After covering the south and north flank [with the *3. Pz.Div.*], only the two SS *panzer* divisions, the *1. Panzer-Division* and the *Volks-Artilleriekorps 403* remained for the actual main thrust to Budapest, with which *General der Infanterie* Wöhler [who appeared personally at the command post of the *IV. SS-Panzerkorps*] tried to get the offensive going again.[128]

To accomplish this, the *1. Pz.Div.* would be aligned on the corps left and would attack towards Baraczka from Kápolnás-Nyek, veer to the north and cross the Váli south of Vál, and wheel to the east. The *Totenkopf* Division, in the center, after crossing the Váli would attack in the general direction of Rackeresztur, while on the right, the *Wiking* Division, which already had a small bridgehead, would orient on Ercsi. To facilitate the seizure of a bridgehead at Baraczka, the *1. Pz.Div.* would attack first during the late evening of 23 January, while the other two divisions would attack during the early hours of 24 January after the artillery barrage had "softened up" the enemy's forward positions.

In the neighboring *Korpsgruppe Breith/III Pz.Korps* area of operations, its troops continued their efforts to force the XX and XXI Guards Rifle Corps back across the Csäszari River. Five kilometers northeast of Stuhlweissenburg, a *Kampfgruppe* from the *23. Pz.Div.*, formed from *Pz.Gren.Rgt. 126* and supported on its right by the attached *Kav.Rgt. 41*, attacked southeast towards Csala, a village 4 kilometers northwest of Pákozd. This gained only a few kilometers of ground before being brought to a halt by stiff resistance from the reassembled 69th Guards Rifle Division. A similar attempt on its left by *Gruppe Holste*, consisting of *4. Kav. Brig.* and the Hungarian *2. Pz.Div.*, was also unsuccessful after discovering during their attack that the area south of Zámoly was strongly fortified. However, an assault group from the Hungarian *2. Pz.Div.* was able to penetrate into the town of Csákberény, north of Zámoly. In the area controlled by the Hungarian *VIII. Armee-Korps* on Holste's left, the *1. Hus.Div.* continued its advance into the western foothills of the Vértes Mountains. Between Pusztavám and Kecskéd, its cavalrymen were able to push the 52nd Rifle Division back several kilometers; it was even able to wrest control of the heights immediately south of Bánhida from the LXVIII Rifle Corps.[129]

On 23 January, Harteneck's *I.Kav.Korps* finally initiated its oft-postponed attack towards the southeast. Despite tough resistance, extensive minefields, obstacles, and roadblocks, the troops from the XXXI Guards Rifle Corps and XXIII Rifle Corps could not prevent the *Panzergruppe* from *Oberst* von der Groeben's *3. Kav.Brig.* from taking the town of Mány and advancing 4 kilometers southeast of Bicske. In an attempt to cut off von der Groeben's armored spearhead, the defenders launched several strong counterattacks with as many as 30 tanks against his troops from Zsámbék and south of Mány, but *Kav.Rgt. 31* and *32*—along with the Hungarian *Aufkl.Abt. 13*—were able to fend off most of them after heavy fighting. To the right of the *3. Kav.Brig.*, the *6. Pz.Div.* forced its way into Felsőgalla, a town that had remained frustratingly beyond its reach for the past three weeks, and began approaching Bicske from the northwest. On the corps' left flank, the *96.* and *711. Inf.Div.* reported only minor enemy activity in the vicinity of Szomor and Sarisap, though of course this would not have been considered "minor" by the troops involved, who had to constantly fight off enemy combat patrols.

On the northern bank of the Danube, the *IV. Pz.Korps FHH* reported no combat activity worth mentioning, with the exception of frequent Soviet foot patrols and intermittent artillery fire along the defensive sector between Seldin and Cata. This was to be the second-to-last day that this corps would be reporting to *A.Gr. Balck/6. Armee*; Wöhler had finally received permission from *OKH* to remove it from Balck's control and subordinate it to the neighboring *8. Armee*, a change that both had been seeking for the past several days. After 25 January, it would no longer send reports to Martinsberg, leaving Balck to concentrate his attention on the more vital *Kampfraum* south of the Danube.

On the *A.Gr. Balck/6. Armee* far right flank, *Div.Gr. Pape*, operating under the control of the Hungarian *3. Armee*, reported no significant combat activity along the *Sió-Abschnitt* worth mentioning. *Oberst* Söth's *3. Pz.Div.*, after losing possession of Herczegfalva to a Soviet counterattack by the XXX Guards Rifle Corps during the early hours, retook it again after launching an armored assault led by *K.Gr. Weymann*. Passing through the town, the *Kampfgruppe* continued pushing the enemy as far as the railroad–highway intersection located 4 kilometers to the southeast. Hard fighting was still going on when the evening report was submitted to the Hungarian *3. Armee*.

In Budapest, the *IX. SS-Geb.Korps* reported that during the previous evening, the Soviets launched numerous assaults, supported by heavy artillery fire, against the perimeter's northwest and northern defensive sectors and had made several minor penetrations. All of these attacks were successfully brought to a halt and the attackers thrown back with heavy losses, while any pockets of remaining enemy troops were eliminated. Soviet troops attempted two battalion-sized attacks against German and Hungarian forces from their beachhead on Margaret Island, but in each case were thrown back. The remainder of the day passed relatively quietly, with the exception of constant enemy air activity, consisting of strafing and bombing attacks by ground-attack aircraft. The *Luftwaffe* was able to mount 159 individual aerial resupply sorties over the city, parachuting or delivering by glider 130 tons of supplies, though the results of these heroic measures were not reported by Pfeffer-Wildenbruch's headquarters.[130]

In the air, the *A.Gr. Balck/6. Armee* intelligence staff reported constant and aggressive Soviet air activity over nearly the entire *Kampfraum* compared to previous days. Enemy fighter-bomber activity, involving strafing attacks and bombing of supply routes, front-line positions, and artillery installations, was particularly heavy above the right-most sector of the *III. Pz.Korps* in the Stuhlweissenburg area and over the *IV. SS-Pz.Korps*. In contrast, the *I. Kav.Korps* reported hardly any enemy air activity at all, with the exception of Soviet reconnaissance aircraft. According to records of the Soviet 5th and 17th Air Armies, their squadrons carried out more than 1,000 individual sorties and claimed to have shot down 36 German and Hungarian aircraft. German records indicate that in addition to the resupply missions flown over Budapest, *Luftflotte 4* flew 152 daylight missions, shooting down 31 enemy aircraft against the loss of nine of its own.[131]

German reconnaissance aircraft were very active on 23 January too, seeking to confirm the final destinations of the wide-ranging enemy troop movements and thereby to deduce the intentions of the Soviet commanders. A large amount of road movement was observed west and north of Budapest, though there was very little observed along the entire front of the Hungarian *3. Armee*. As for what all of this meant, it was difficult to tell, but in general—based on the recent arrival of large numbers of Bulgarian units between Lake Balaton and the Drava River—it was apparent that it signaled a certain proportion of the 57th Army had been shifted to the east, where it would most likely be brought to bear against the Hungarian *3. Armee*, including *Div.Gr. Pape* and the *3. Pz.Div.*

It was also clear that the 4th Guards Army was determined to hold the Váli sector between Lake Velencze and the Danube at all costs, based on traffic movement analysis, radio intercepts, and tactical intelligence gained by the divisions of the *IV. SS-Pz. Korps* and *III. Pz.Korps*. The stubborn resistance and continuing reinforcement by Zakharov's army was another sign that Tolbukhin was determined not to yield an inch. Additionally, the increase in effectiveness of Soviet resistance northeast of Stuhlweissenburg between Pákozd and Zámoly seems to have come as a bit of a surprise. A logical observer would have thought that Soviet forces defending this area, threatened with encirclement, should have been withdrawn. However, after the fighting that day, the two Soviet corps fighting in this area (the XX and XXI Guards Rifle Corps) made it plain that they were staying put. It was also becoming evident that the three divisions of the LXVIII Rifle Corps in the Vértes Mountains area were withdrawing voluntarily, as indicated by the all-too-easy advance of the Hungarian *VIII. Armee-Korps* between Bánhida and Pusztavám.

The *Armeegruppe Ic* concluded that these troops were being brought down to reinforce the two corps fighting east and northeast of Stuhlweissenburg along the line Pákozd–Csakvár–Bicske. But the most ominous report of all was the *Richard Meldung* (secret coded message) sent earlier that day by a German agent operating behind enemy lines that stated the XXIII Tank Corps, located east of Budapest on the far side of the Danube with as many as 150 operational tanks and SP guns (initially misidentified as the II Guards Mechanized Corps), was being regrouped and preparing for movement. Just as worryingly, German intelligence had completely missed the westward movement of the CIV Rifle Corps, which had also been ordered by the Second Ukrainian Front to begin crossing the Danube with its three rifle divisions to reinforce the 4th Guards Army.

The agent had also learned that portions of the battered VII Mechanized Corps had been pulled out of the line and the corps was undergoing a hasty reconstitution. Enemy action against the perimeter of the Budapest garrison by the 46th Army was interpreted as being mainly directed towards preventing Pfeffer-Wildenbruch's preparations for a breakout by attacking it from all points of the compass. The only other item in the *Ic* report that day was the disappearance of the 6th Guards Tank Army from where it had been fighting north of the Danube in the area west of Gran. Reconnaissance revealed that it had apparently moved out somewhere to the north, destination unknown, most likely to reinforce the other Fronts attacking *H.Gr. A* and *H.Gr. Mitte* after undergoing some form of reconstitution.

In regards to the Soviet situation, having arrived at a decision to stand and fight, the Red Army's commanders began to put these plans into effect with a characteristic cold-blooded efficiency that was becoming routine. By strengthening the Váli defense line, Tolbukhin would force Gille's *panzer* divisions to expend their remaining strength in a series of fruitless attacks, thereby creating the conditions for a counteroffensive as soon as he deemed the force ratios favorable. He had also decided to dedicate nearly all of the 4th Guards Army's artillery to this one narrow area of the front.

Because the Soviet intelligence apparatus had estimated that the Germans were much stronger than they actually were—for example, on 22 January, the 4th Guards Army believed that the *Wiking* Division still had 100 operational tanks and assault guns, when it actually had no more than 46, including the attached *303. Sturm-Art. Brig.*—Tolbukhin decided to wait for several more days to commit the XXIII Tank Corps and CIV Rifle Corps, when Gille's attack had played itself out. When the German attack was spent, Tolbukhin would strike.[132]

That evening there was a considerable amount of message traffic between the commanders of *H.Gr. Süd, A.Gr. Balck,* and the *OKH* chief of the general staff. *Generaloberst* Wöhler wanted more infantry divisions, as did Balck, whose chief of staff pressured the *OKH Führungsabteilung* for permission to expedite the movement of the *356. Inf.Div.* from the *10. Armee* in Triest to *A.Gr. Balck/6. Armee.* While sympathetic, both Guderian and his deputy, *Gen.d.Pz. Tr.* Wenck, were noncommittal. Although Harteneck's corps had gained as much as 10 kilometers that day between

Zsámbék and Bicske, Balck had already decided that no decisive breakthrough by *I. Kav.Korps* was in the offing.

That same evening, Balck asked Wöhler yet again for more forces in addition to the *356. Inf.Div.*, requesting that two or three extra assault gun brigades be immediately sent to reinforce his army's attack. This was clearly beyond Wöhler's ability to provide, since he had already given Balck nearly everything he had asked for and told him there was nothing else he could spare without *OKH* help. Neither the *2. Pz.Armee* nor *8. Armee* could afford giving up their few precious assault guns, lest their own fronts be denuded of mobile antitank defenses. Besides, Guderian still had his eyes on the *IV. SS-Pz.Korps* and had not completely given up on the idea of removing it from *H.Gr. Süd* as soon as Budapest was relieved.

Balck would have to be satisfied with relinquishing control of the north bank of the Danube, including the *IV. Pz.Korps FHH*, and all of the headaches that had involved. However, one piece of good news was that Guderian had been able to secure Hitler's agreement, in his role as head of the *OKW*, to order *G.F.M.* von Weichs, the commander of *H.Gr. F*, to employ "at least four divisions" to attack Soviet and Bulgarian forces deployed in southern Hungary, in conjunction with an attack by *2. Pz.Armee*.[133] Unfortunately, the earliest that this combined operation could take place was 6 February, by which point Operation *Konrad III* would have been concluded, one way or the other. For its part, the *2. Pz.Armee*, which Wöhler did control, had tentatively scheduled to launch its own attack on 26 January.

In addition to anticipating the beginning of the coordinated assault by the *IV. SS-Pz.Korps* that evening after a two-day delay, the *Armeegruppe* commander and his chief of staff occupied themselves with business that appears relatively petty in retrospect. Since his arrival in December, Balck had begun issuing a plethora of daily orders and instructions to his corps commanders that bordered on micromanagement, which must have chafed experienced subordinates such as Breith and Harteneck. With the arrival of Gille and his SS corps, this tendency appears to have increased. Whether prompted by Gaedke, whose antipathy towards the *Wiking* Division in general and Gille in particular has already been discussed, or by his own distaste for the *Waffen-SS*, Balck had increasingly singled out the *IV. SS-Pz.Korps* for special criticism, such as accusing Gille of deliberately withholding information, sending false reports, and tolerating lackadaisical staff work.

One example of this increasing tendency to distrust the SS stands out: Balck's skepticism concerning the accuracy of a *Wiking* Division radio message from 22 January reporting that most of the encircled Soviet troops between Sárosd and Aba had escaped during the evening of 21/22 January. Balck did not believe that this could have happened without a large tank battle, and suspected the *Wiking* Division of having failed to submit an accurate report. To prove his point, *A.Gr. Balck* dispatched *Maj.* Alfred Neuhaus, his headquarters' *Adjutant* or *IIa*, to the

Wiking Division's command post in Sárosd to carry out a physical count of every destroyed Soviet armored fighting vehicle in its area of operations.

When he arrived at Ullrich's headquarters, he was met by *Ostuf.* Jahnke, the division's *O1*, whom Neuhaus directed to lead him on a tour of the battlefield. When first questioned, Jahnke reaffirmed that no large tank battle had taken place, that only 16 enemy tanks had been knocked out or immobilized between 21 and 22 January, and that he was the officer who had sent this report. Both men then drove to the scenes where the fighting reportedly took place, Jahnke showing him the exact location of every destroyed or inoperable Soviet tank or assault gun between Sárosd and Aba. After visiting four widely dispersed locations, Neuhaus could count only 13 wrecked or bogged-down enemy tanks, though there were signs that at least one had been recovered by either German or Soviet troops. He also counted two completely destroyed German assault guns in the same general area. Based on his findings, Neuhaus reported back to *A.Gr. Balck/6. Armee* headquarters that the *Wiking* Division's report had been essentially accurate and concluded that no large-scale tank battle had taken place.[134]

Perhaps in imitation of Wöhler's order to place a *H.Gr. Süd* staff officer within Gille's headquarters, Balck followed suit by sending one of his own staff officers, *Maj. i.G.* Kurt-Wilhelm Müller-Gülich, with his own radio team to Stuhlweissenburg to monitor front-line communications. Sent allegedly to "facilitate reporting," he was to listen equally to radio message traffic by Gille's corps and Breith's *III. Pz.Korps* and forward any messages as appropriate. However, the bulk of the messages relayed to Gaedke in Martinsberg were from the *Wiking* and *Totenkopf* Divisions, belying Balck's true intent.[135]

Nevertheless on 23 January, Müller-Gülisch forwarded to Balck's headquarters 30 separate messages sent by both divisions to *IV. SS-Pz.Korps* and vice versa that day alone; whether due to the increased emphasis on timely reporting or the presence of the *A.Gr. Balck* staff officer in the local area can no longer be determined. Nevertheless, it did enable Balck and Gaedke to have a clearer understanding of the situation (to "see" the battle more clearly), though this amounted to yet another form of micromanaging. This tendency would only increase as *Konrad III* reached it culminating point and beyond, further fueling the distrust and animosity existing between Gille and Balck.

Although unappreciated at the time, one of the greatest instances of military micro-management in German history was about to unfold and would have a wide-reaching and deleterious impact on all of the *Wehrmacht*'s operations, not just those of *A.Gr. Balck*. This was embodied in a *Führerbefehl* issued on 21 January, rather lengthily titled *Rechtzeitige Meldung der Absichten, Erstattung wahrer Meldungen und Halten der Verbindungen unter drakonischer Strafandrohung* (Timely Reports of Intentions, Submission of True Reports and Maintenance of Communications under Threat of Draconian Punishment), otherwise known as *Befehl Hitlers über die Meldepflicht aller militärischen Entschlüsse* (Hitler's Order over Reporting Responsibility for all Military Decisions). Essentially, this order required that all military decisions affecting operations from division-level up to the highest level of command be approved in advance by Hitler himself. It effectively hamstrung nearly every commander in all three branches of the *Wehrmacht* and *Waffen-SS* by forcing them to submit every single decision of significance to a microscopic review by one of the world's most detail-obsessed and decision-adverse leaders in all of military history.

Copies of this order were widely circulated on all fronts, and subordinate commands were required to reprint and distribute it down to division level. *Heeresgruppe Süd* issued its own verbatim copy of this *Führerbefehl* on 23 January, the day before *Konrad III* was resumed. Most of its requirements were highly restrictive:

> [The] Commanders in Chief, the Commanding Generals, and the Divisional Commanders are personally responsible that the following are reported to me soon enough so that I can intervene and so that a possible countermanding order can still reach the most advanced troops in time:
>
> a. Every decision involving operational movements.
> b. Every attack contemplated for a division or larger unit, which is not part of operations ordered by the Supreme Command.
> c. Every offensive operation on quiet fronts, exceeding normal combat patrol activity, which is liable to draw the enemy's attention to that particular sector.
> d. Every retreat or withdrawal movement which is contemplated.
> e. Any plan to give up a position, a local strongpoint, or a fortress.[136]

The dispatch of the officer-led radio teams can certainly be interpreted in this light, for in addition to ensuring that communications were being processed in a timely manner, these officers would also be well-placed to observe whether the *Führerbefehl* was being strictly adhered to.

The manner in which this order was perceived by its recipients in *H. Gr. Süd* can only be surmised, but it had the practical effect of putting nearly every commander from the rank of *Oberst* to field marshal in a virtual straightjacket. It forced every one of them to confront a life-or-death quandary: obey it without question and carry out orders even though they violated every rational concept of the art or war, or disobey and risk criminal prosecution and even death. At the very least, it had a chilling effect. One paragraph of Hitler's order addressed this possibility:

> I shall hold the Commanders in Chief, the Commanding Generals, the Divisional Commanders, the Chiefs of the General Staffs, and every single General Staff officer and officer in the Operations Staffs responsible that every report submitted to me either directly or through channels contains the unvarnished truth. Hereafter I shall punish with draconian severity every attempt to conceal the facts, whether it was done intentionally or through negligence.

Thus, establishing and maintaining wire and radio communications assumed even greater importance, which most likely was an additional factor in Balck's decision. The order recognized this, when it expressly stated the following:

I [Hitler] must point out that the maintenance of communications is a prerequisite for directing operations, especially in difficult combat actions and critical situations. I shall hold all commanders responsible that connections with the higher echelons as well as with subordinate command posts are not interrupted and that continuous communications with both higher and lower echelons of command are assured in every situation by exhausting all means and at the risk of their own lives.

This order, received on the eve of the continuation of the attack against the Váli line scheduled for that very night, would not have overly concerned Gille. As a *Nursoldat* ("just a soldier"), he would have seen any order as sacrosanct and faithfully carried it out as a matter of course. Any problems concerning communications was a technical matter, not one of bad intent, though he would have most likely been irked by the presence of two "liaison" officers eavesdropping on the daily operation of his corps headquarters.

Though Gille's or Schönfelder's thoughts on the matter are not recorded, those of *Ostubaf.* Georg Maier, the *Ia* of Dietrich's *6. Pz.Armee* and a 9 May 1942 graduate of the fifth wartime class of the *Kriegsakademie*, are. Concerning the *Führerbefehl*, he later wrote:

[This order] very decidedly limited operational command, even for purely tactical measures, in that it required a "*Führer* approval" for practically any significant course of action. Ideas suitable for the trench warfare of World War I increasingly found expression in Hitler's orders and directives. The more difficult and hopeless the situation became, the more he sought refuge in vigorous words and "iron-hard" orders. He could change nothing that way, only possibly make things even worse than they already were.[137]

Left unstated was the way this order also tended to slow the decision-making process. By insisting that nearly every order of operational or tactical significance be routed through the *Führerhauptquartier* for Hitler's personal attention, actions that needed to be made based on developing situations might have to wait hours or even days for his decision, thereby sacrificing the initiative to the enemy. Only by pretending ignorance of orders or an "unexpected" failure of his headquarters' communications equipment could a commander exercise independent authority; even then, he still risked an investigation of his conduct, especially if his locally made decision resulted in a negative outcome.

The impact of this order cannot be overemphasized, for it was to color the decisions of nearly every German commander on every front for the remainder of the war. Though Guderian does not mention it specifically in his memoirs, Hitler's increasing meddling in the decision- making process becomes increasingly evident after 21 January and made Guderian's position much more difficult. Before that date, Hitler had occasionally interjected himself into operational decisions and second-guessed his commanders, but after this *Führerbefehl* was issued, this became a frequent, indeed routine practice, to the detriment of everything, including Germany's entire war effort. It can even be argued that this ill-conceived order hastened the end of the war nearly as much or more than the Allies' ULTRA code-breaking program did; though worthy of additional study, for the sake of brevity this topic will be left for another time.

On the evening of 23 January, the *1. Pz.Div.* began moving from its forward assembly area around Gárdony towards its designated jump-off position within the town of Kápolnás-Nyek. The attack would be led by *K.Gr. Philipp*, whose *II. Btl./Pz.Gren.Rgt. 1* under *Hptm.* Ellinger—supported by two Panther companies from *Pz.Rgt. 1*—would form the spearhead of the attacking formation. Their initial objective was Baraczka. While refueling and rearming near the village of Börgönd, *Rittm.* Weideman's *I. Abt./Pz.Rgt. 24*, which was supposed to support Philipp's attack, was targeted by Soviet fighter-bombers and ground-attack aircraft, thus delaying its entry onto the field.[138]

Poor camouflage discipline was to blame; apparently, the battalion had made itself too conspicuous in the snow-covered, wide-open landscape, and the ever-vigilant Red Air Force made Weidemann's men pay the price for his negligence in terms of killed and wounded, as well as the loss of several tanks damaged or destroyed. It was not an auspicious beginning to what would become the last, and the most promising, relief attempt of Budapest.

As the *1. Pz.Div.* began crossing the line of departure shortly before 11 p.m., to its right the *Totenkopf* and *Wiking* Divisions were making their own last-minute preparations, including eliminating remaining nests of Soviet troops who had been operating in their rear areas. Everyone now depended on the *1. Pz.Div.* and the progress of its attack. Everything had been done in the limited time available to prepare for a successful assault. Now it was up to the individual *Heer* or *Waffen-SS* tanker, infantryman, sapper, artilleryman, and reconnaissance scout of the *IV. SS-Pz. Korps* to do his duty. They would do their best not to disappoint.

The Third Relief Attempt of Budapest—*Konrad III* Part II: The Final Push, 24–28 January 1945

The final five days of Operation *Konrad III* was to prove a contest of wills between the commanders of *A.Gr. Balck* and the Third Ukrainian Front. Balck, aware of his army's rapidly dwindling strength, would strive for one last decisive victory, while Tolbukhin, his powerful adversary, would work equally as hard to thwart it. If the *IV. SS-Pz.Korps* could break through Soviet defenses arrayed along the Váli, it just might make it to Budapest and relieve the embattled garrison, while also safeguarding Germany's last significant oil reserves. If the 4th Guards Army could break Balck's most powerful force, this might force the *IX. SS-Geb.Korps* to capitulate and would also create the necessary conditions for the resumption of the offensive towards Vienna.

It was plainly evident to nearly everyone involved in the German decision-making process that *Konrad III* was slowing down and in danger of stopping altogether. The initial hopes of reaching Budapest in two or three days had faded. Therefore, it was vital that this final attempt succeed. After a nearly two-day operational pause, the *1. Pz.Div.* and *Volks-Art.Korps 403* had finally moved from Stuhlweissenburg to the eastern shore of Lake Velencze by nightfall on 23 January and were ready to bring their considerable firepower to bear that evening. The *Totenkopf* and *Wiking* Divisions had done the best they could to reposition their artillery regiments to be ready in time for their own attacks, which would take place several hours after that of the *1. Pz.Div.* had begun.

As the troops crouched in their jump-off positions, very few of them were aware of the dire situation that Germany faced at the end of the third week of January 1945. The Ardennes offensive had ended in a bloody failure as German troops were forced back step-by-step to their original starting positions, where they had begun with such high hopes on 16 December. Sepp Dietrich's *6. Pz.Armee* had already been completely withdrawn from the front and had gone into reserve to undergo a complete reconstitution. The offensive in Alsace had also accomplished little except further weakening the forces of *Gen.d.Pz.Tr.* Balck's previous command, *H.Gr. G.* Meanwhile, *Heerestruppe Nord*, soon to be renamed *H.Gr. Kurland*, was locked up in the Lithuanian peninsula, accomplishing nothing.

Worst of all, Soviet forces led by Marshals Zhukov and Konev were rapidly approaching the Oder River, the last natural barrier before Berlin, sweeping aside every feeble German attempt to stop them. Heinrich Himmler, appointed by Hitler himself to be the commander of the misnamed *H.Gr. Weichsel* (Vistula), was proving himself to be so militarily incompetent as a battle commander that his efforts were hastening, not slowing, the Soviet advance. Yet despite all of these disasters and impending defeats, Hitler's gaze remained firmly focused on events in Hungary. For the average *Landser* occupying an ice-cold foxhole in the front lines east of Lake Velencze, the watchwords still remained "On to Budapest!"

When Wednesday, 24 January dawned, it was bitterly cold. Temperatures hovered around 24 degrees Fahrenheit (-5 degrees Celsius), accentuated by cloudy and hazy weather. A heavy layer of snow had fallen during the night, resulting in deep drifts in some areas that plagued supply convoys bringing up fuel and ammunition and evacuating wounded. As described in the previous chapter, the first unit to attack was the *1. Pz.Div.*, followed shortly after by the *Totenkopf* and *Wiking* Divisions, which simply resumed operations they had begun the previous day. In general, progress was satisfactory, though not as rapid as anticipated, despite the preparatory artillery fire that rained down on Soviet positions, which had been reinforced considerably during the past two days with additional antitank guns, tanks, self-propelled guns, and infantry.

The evening corps status report, as delivered by the *Ic* to his counterpart at *A.Gr. Balck/6. Armee*, reflected this new reality:

> The heights southwest of Ercsi were fortified and occupied by the enemy ... Against strong enemy resistance, our own attacking groups northeast of Aggszentpéter were able to form a bridgehead over the Váli [River]. The enemy had to give up Kis Halom and the southern part of Baraczka after hard fighting. In Kápolnás Nyék, fierce fighting took place throughout the day, and several enemy attacks from the northern part of the town were repelled. Several [enemy] attacks in battalion strength were launched against Velencze but were also unsuccessful. Hard and difficult fighting is still ongoing.

What this somber report does not make clear is that by the end of the day, the corps' units had managed to close up along the entire sector from the confluence of the Váli River with the Danube on the right to Baraczka on the left, a front-line width of 20 kilometers.

Reflecting on this and the succeeding days, Gille's chief of staff simply wrote, "In the days that followed, it became clear that success cannot be achieved alone merely by issuing orders, not if the opponent is willing to invoke *das Gesetz des Handelns* (i.e., seize the initiative) and turn the tables to his advantage on account of his overwhelming force."[1] An American historian, Earl F. Ziemke, summed up the events of 24–27 January 1945 when he wrote 30 years later, "For the next three days the Russians [*sic*] fought hard to hold a front flanking Velencze Lake on both sides. The German *panzer* divisions chewed their way through … but by then they had lost most of their initial momentum."[2]

Despite having to overcome considerable enemy resistance, numerous counterattacks, and terrain that favored the defender, the *Wiking* Division pressed forward. A reconnaissance aircraft reported that along the heights lining the eastern bank of the Váli, deeply arrayed Soviet trench lines and *Pakfronts* could be seen, which would pose a challenge for the attackers once they had managed to cross the river. Supported by several tanks from the *Panzergruppe* and a powerful barrage by the division's artillery regiment, the *Westland* Regiment reported that by 6 p.m. it was able to establish a bridgehead across the Váli east of Aggszentpéter on the division's left that was 2 kilometers wide and 1 kilometer deep after capturing two bridges that the defenders failed to destroy in time. Although not as large as hoped, this bridgehead could serve as a basis for further operations, should additional reserves be provided to exploit it. The *Westland*'s troops that did make it across were subjected shortly thereafter to a number of Soviet counterattacks on their left flank by elements of the V Guards Cavalry Corps, but were able to hold their ground throughout the evening.[3] Soviet indirect fire was becoming increasingly heavy and accurate, an indication that the 4th Guards Army's artillery reserves had finally been moved into the area to reinforce the V Guards Cavalry Corps' defense of the Váli line.

On its right, the attack by the division's *Panzergruppe* and the *Germania* Regiment, that began at 10 a.m. from the tiny bridgehead seized the previous day by the division's reconnaissance battalion, broke through the thin defenses of the 11th Guards Cavalry Division and continued past the mouth of the Váli for an additional 4 kilometers, before being brought to a halt due to heavy enemy fire emanating from the heights immediately south of the town of Ercsi and from opposite bank of the Danube. Once its attack had stalled, a portion of the *Panzergruppe* and the *Germania* Regiment handed off its forward positions to the Hungarian *I. Btl./Inf. Rgt. 54* and shifted to the division's left flank, where they reinforced the *Westland* Regiment's attack along the railroad line north of Puszta Szabolcs, assisting Hack's regiment in the seizure of the two aforementioned bridges.

According to the division's history, its troops encountered stiffening Soviet resistance on the left flank of its newly taken bridgehead that day, and its attacks were made even more difficult by the awful weather conditions, which featured alternating snow and rain showers.[4] With the *3. Pz.Div.* now taking its order from a different tactical headquarters (though still logistically and administratively under the *IV. SS-Pz.Korps*), Ullrich's staff was growing increasingly worried about the situation on the division's right flank, which was unclear to say the least.[5] As a precaution, a two-company *Alarmbataillon* (an ad hoc unit assembled to respond to local emergencies) was formed from the division's supply units and sent to the town of Adony to supplement the division's *Begleitkompanie* already in operation there. If Adony fell, the division's right flank would be left wide open, a risk that *Oberf.* Ullrich did not want to take.

The *Totenkopf* Division's attack that day was focused on eliminating the forward defenses of the 93rd and 252nd Rifle Divisions west of the Váli, southeast of Baraczka near Hill 157. After an initial artillery barrage that lasted over an hour, *Kampfgruppe Eckert*, reinforced by the division's few remaining operational assault guns, attacked from the area north of Felső Besnyő. Eckert's troops were able to dislodge the enemy from their defensive positions around the hill after a considerable amount of hard fighting near the large farming estate at Nagy Halom, in the course of which Eckert's battlegroup sustained heavy losses. After the fighting, a commander of one of the *StuG III* assault guns described the scene:

> Bleeding Grenadiers dragged themselves past us headed towards the rear. In front of us, exploding shells and machine-gun salvoes hammer a farmhouse defended by the Russians [*sic*]. Again and again among the noises of battle we hear our attacking troops shout their battle cry—"Hurrah!"—echoed immediately by the cries of "*Urrah!*" by the defenders. Around midday, we take the first enemy position. The red glow of the burning farmhouse illuminates the snow-covered landscape ... we keep rolling onwards. To the left of us, a T-34 explodes in a flash of bluish flames. Tracers from a *Vierlingsflak* [four-barreled 2cm antiaircraft gun] chew into the building. Suddenly a storm of Russian mortar shells bursts among our advancing Grenadiers. Hot splinters tear ragged wounds. The screams and yells of the wounded are unbearable. We receive the order to bypass the farm. Shortly thereafter, we find ourselves behind the Russians.[6]

Two kilometers to the north of Hill 157, troops from *Hstuf.* Bachmann's *II. Btl./ Totenkopf* stormed the village of Kis Halom, forcing the defenders from the V Guards Cavalry Corps to withdraw in disorder. To Bachmann's left, the few remaining operational tanks of *s.Pz.Abt. 509* swung into action on the wide-open *Puszta* when they spotted a large force of Soviet tanks approaching. After a 20-minute battle, one Tiger crew knocked out a JS-II Stalin heavy tank and four antitank guns, while the rest of the battalion accounted for 14 enemy tanks and 46 antitank guns.[7]

On the division's left boundary with the *1. Pz.Div.*, the main body of Kleffner's *Eicke* Regiment teamed up with *Pz.Gren.Rgt. 113* and *I. Abt./Pz.Rgt. 24* to launch a combined attack against Baraczka during the morning of 24 January. *Obersturmbannführer* Kleffner's task was to seize a bridgehead over Váli at that location to enable the rest of the division to cross and continue its attack. Supported by the guns of *III. Abt./SS-Pz.Art.Rgt. 3*, Kleffner's *Kampfgruppe* initiated their attack from Annamajor after 10 a.m. and made good initial progress. Supported on their left by *Pz.Gren.Rgt. 113*, his troops were able to penetrate into the southern environs of Baraczka, but were soon drawn into house-to-house combat. After heavy fighting, by the close of the day *K.Gr. Kleffner* was unable to complete the occupation of the town or seize a crossing over the Váli. That would have to wait until 25 January.[8]

In the *1. Pz.Div.* zone of attack, after initial success, the division was brought to a halt before the village of Pettend by a strong defensive barrier, heavily reinforced with antitank guns. Before it could fight its way through this defense line, it was forced to fight off a number of tank-supported counterattacks against its flanks. Together with the 22 operational *Pz. V* Panthers of *Rittm.* Weidemann's *I. Abt./Pz.Rgt. 24*, *Pz.Gren.Rgt. 113*—under its acting commander *Maj.i.G.* Marcks—attacked towards Baraczka at 1:30 a.m. from its jump-off position on the eastern outskirts of Kápolnás Nyék after an artillery barrage lasting only half an hour. Quickly covering the 8 kilometers separating the towns against negligible resistance, Marcks's *Kampfgruppe* seized the villages of Mereymajor and Annamajor with hardly a fight, linking up with *K.Gr. Kleffner* on its right.

While his *II. Bataillon* remained behind to assist Kleffner in taking Baraczka, Marcks and the rest of this force, including the *Pz. VI* Tiger Is of *9. Kp./SS-Pz. Rgt. 3*, swung to the north to attack Pettend. Hampered with radio difficulties that made it impossible to communicate with his supporting artillery and unable to talk to *Rittm.* Weidemann for the same reason, Marcks directed his *Panzergrenadiers* to carry out a dismounted assault on the village anyway, hoping that darkness and the element of surprise would help win the day. It did not. Approaching to within 200 meters of the village, his troops were spotted by an alert defender, who raised the alarm. Soon, *Hptm.* Weber's *I. Btl./Pz.Gren.Rgt. 113* was enveloped in a storm of heavy defensive fire that drove them to ground. Shortly afterwards, Marcks was met by the division commander himself, who arrived on the scene in his command *SPW*.

Generalmajor Thünert directed Marcks to pull back to Mereymajor before sunrise, and let the tanks of the *Totenkopf* Division's *Panzergruppe* take over the attack against Pettend. *Major* Marcks's *Kampfgruppe* and Weidemann's tanks were redirected instead towards Baraczka to help *K.Gr. Kleffner* take that town. Here, while the *Panzergrenadiers* attacked towards the center of the town from the south, the tank battalion encountered a nest of antitank guns on the southwestern outskirts. After overcoming these, Weidemann's *panzers* pressed into Baraczka without any infantry support. In short order, seven Panthers of *I. Abt./Pz.Rgt. 24* were knocked out, four of which were complete losses, in exchange for the destruction of just two Soviet tanks and one assault gun.

Heavy fighting raged throughout the evening, as the men of both *Pz.Gren.Rgt. 113* and *K.Gr. Kleffner* attempted to wrest control of the town from the 252nd Rifle Division, but they had only occupied the southern half of the town by the time of the evening report. The *Panzergruppe* from the *Totenkopf*, which was supposed to continue the attack towards Pettend, had no luck at all. Throughout the day, it was subjected to numerous attacks by Soviet ground-attack aircraft as well as counterattacks by the 63rd Guards Cavalry Division. Two Panthers from *I. Abt./ SS-Pz.Rgt. 3* were knocked out along the Pettend–Baraczka road at 1 p.m., and a Tiger I from the *9. Kompanie* was hit 1.5 kilometers west of Pettend by two 8.5cm rounds that disabled its track and running gear. Although the crew managed to bail out safely, the tank was left in no-man's land and was subsequently declared a total loss, later becoming a Soviet war trophy.[9]

Although the gains that day had not been as great as expected, at least all three of Gille's divisions had closed up along the entire Váli and had eliminated the Soviet bridgehead north of Nagy Halom. Nearly 20 enemy armored vehicles were destroyed, as well as large numbers of antitank guns. The biggest setback was the failure that day of the *1. Pz.Div.* to take Pettend and continue pushing north towards the town of Váli, where the division was supposed to seize a bridgehead and begin its wheeling movement to the south to entrap the V Guards Cavalry Corps. Once again, Gille's thoughts on the day are brief. He simply stated, "Strong enemy attacks on the left flank of the 'W' [*Wiking*] where 'T' [*Totenkopf*] still has not taken the same heights; these [enemy counterattacks] were warded off after our own forces suffered heavy losses. An [enemy] breakthrough during the night was cleaned up."[10]

As the *IV. SS-Pz.Korps* chewed its way through enemy defenses, the supporting attack on its far left flank by the *III. Pz.Korps* made hardly any headway at all that day. That evening, the corps' *Ic* reported that the *23. Pz.Div.* had observed a considerable amount of enemy movement in the area held by the XXI Guards Rifle Corps along the high ground north of the town of Pákozd, while the *4. Kav.Brig.* of *Gruppe Holste* said it had observed the continuing reinforcement of the XX Guards Rifle Corps' defensive positions southwest of Zámoly. *Gruppe Holste* further reported that northwest of Zámoly, the Soviets had been thrown back up to 1 kilometer south of an important road intersection. West of Csákberény, the enemy force opposing the attack by the Hungarian *2. Pz.Div.* was still putting up a stiff fight. Further to the north, Soviet rear guards from the LXVIII Rifle Corps had pulled back as far as the middle of the Vértes Mountains, enabling the Hungarian *1. Hus.Div.* to completely clear the villages of Puszta Mindszent and Gesztes of Soviet troops.

The other supporting attack, launched by the *I. Kav.Korps*, intended to help relieve the pressure on the *IV. SS-Pz.Korps*, was brought to a standstill by repeated counterattacks carried out by divisions from the XXIII Rifle Corps and XXXI Guards Rifle Corps. Though Harteneck's troops had enjoyed considerable success when they began their attack the previous day, it had become obvious by the morning of 24 January that any further progress was questionable. *Oberst* von der Groeben's *3. Kav.Brig.*, after taking Mány and advancing up to 8 kilometers to the southeast, was unable to widen the shoulders of its penetration, rendering it nearly impossible to insert the additional troops needed to continue the advance.

Its spearhead unit, *Kav.Rgt. 31*, reinforced by the Hungarian *Aufkl.Abt. 13*, was counterattacked throughout the day by battalion-sized enemy formations from the southwest and southeast, which it was able to fend off. Similarly, an armor-supported Soviet attack that evening against von der Groeben's cavalrymen dug in along the railroad line east of Bicske was also smashed, leaving behind four burning tanks as the enemy troops withdrew. On the corps' right, the *6. Pz.Div.* finally cleared enemy defensive positions south of Felsőgalla and took the heights surrounding the city. Most likely, this was due to the advance of the neighboring Hungarian *1. Hus. Div.* and not to the lackluster performance of the *6. Pz.Div.* Its equally uninspiring commander, *Oberst* Jürgens, had been replaced by *Gen.Lt.* Rudolf *Freiherr* von Waldenfels on 20 January, but he had not had time to reimpose his style of leadership on the division in the midst of heavy fighting (he had previously commanded the same division until March 1944).[11] On Harteneck's far left flank, both the *96.* and *711. Inf.Div.* reported no combat activity worth mentioning. North of the Danube, the *IV. Pz.Korps FHH* also reported no significant enemy action as having taken place, nor had ground observation observed anything out of the ordinary occurring behind the lines.

On the *IV. SS-Pz.Korps'* right flank, defended by the Hungarian *3. Armee*, the situation was reported as being relatively quiet, except in the village of Sár Szentmiklós, several kilometers southeast of Sárbogárd. Here, an enemy force—most likely from the 68th Rifle Division—had penetrated into the town during the previous evening and was busily fortifying it before it was thrown out later that day by a *Kampfgruppe* from the *3. Pz.Div. Oberst* Söth also reported that evening that the garrison defending Dunapentele (*K.Gr. Medicus* of *Pz.Gren.Rgt. 3*) along the Danube had been attacked from the south several times that day, but these had all been successfully driven off. One of Söth's greatest concerns was the extremely thin line of German troops screening the Danube from Dunapentele to Adony, where his division linked arms with the *Wiking* Division. Should the Red Army attempt to cross the river at any point along this 22-kilometer portion of the German line, there would be nothing that the *3. Pz.Div.* could do about it, nor could the *Wiking* Division, except to send its recently formed *Alarmbataillon* from Adony.

In Budapest, the *IX. SS-Geb.Korps* reported that the situation was relatively unchanged from the day before, with only "normal" disruptive mortar and artillery fire along the northwest and northern defensive sectors of the bridgehead. Attempts to iron out two small-scale penetrations were still ongoing. A company-sized attack by Soviet troops on Margaret Island was once again attempted, but this met with no success when it failed to overcome the SS and Hungarian defensive fire. By this point, the northern half of the island had fallen to the attackers, and it would not be long before the Germans would have to give up the rest of it as well. If Pfeffer-Wildenbruch had drawn up or updated any plans of his own for a breakout, they were not mentioned.

That night, the *Luftwaffe* flew resupply 117 sorties over the city (Soviet records state the number as 178), delivering 84 tons of ammunition, 9 tons of flour, and 5 tons of fuel to the encircled garrison, including some flown in by six cargo gliders that miraculously were able to land safely on the castle's parade ground, the notorious *Blutwiese* ("bloody meadow") where medieval jousting tournaments were once staged. By this point, the commander reported over 8,000 wounded requiring medical evacuation.[12] Food was becoming scarce, forcing Pfeffer-Wildenbruch to reduce the ration once again. Hungarian citizens were left to starve because no provision for them had been made by Szalási's Arrow Cross-led government.

In the air, Soviet activity had decreased compared to the previous day due to bad flying weather. Despite this, the Red Air Force was still able to press home many of its attacks. In the skies above the *IV. SS-Pz.Korps*, its divisions reported attacks by at least 113 IL-2 *Sturmoviks*, 13 Yak-9 fighter-bombers, and three DB-3 aircraft, using a combination of aerial bombs and on-board weapons. Most of their attacks were directed against troops in the front line, localities such as Kápolnás Nyék and Stuhlweissenburg, and main supply routes. Over the rest of the *A. Gr. Balck/6. Armee* sector, very little Soviet air activity was observed, except that by reconnaissance aircraft. German daytime aerial reconnaissance was sparse, also owing to the foul weather, though *Luftwaffe* and Hungarian combat squadrons flew 358 day sorties compared to the 723 flown by the 5th and 17th Air Armies.[13]

In his daily intelligence assessment, the *Armeegruppe Ic* highlighted the strengthening of the Soviet defenses between the Danube and Lake Balaton, including the area west of the Sió River opposite the Hungarian *3. Armee*. Based on agent reports behind enemy lines, it appeared that the VII Mechanized Corps had been withdrawn completely from the front west of Budapest, apparently to undergo a hasty reconstitution to bring it back up to its established table of organization. *Hauptmann* von Pander, the deputy *Ic*, noted that despite the best efforts of the troops from the V Guards Cavalry Corps to hold on to the western bank of the Váli, they had not been able to stop the German advance, particularly in the areas southeast of Baraczka where the *Totenkopf* Division had made such gains that day. Ground observation of the eastern bank revealed that the Soviets had constructed deeply echeloned defenses, with a secondary main line of resistance already prepared. At Mány, additional enemy tank-supported attacks against the spearhead of the *4. Kav. Brig.* were expected to continue into the following day. Overall, there was nothing to indicate any radical change in the enemy's order of battle or his intentions.

In regards to how the Red Army perceived the situation that day, its commanders continued to focus on strengthening the Váli defenses by sending additional reinforcements to help buttress the secondary line behind the V Guards Cavalry Corps. Two rifle divisions—the 34th Guards and the refreshed 41st Guards Rifle Divisions—were pulled out of their positions and ordered to march south to join the 4th Guards Army. Additional artillery units were added to the defenses, including three cannon-artillery brigades to be controlled by a new long-range army artillery group headquarters, similar to a German *HARKO*. To the south, another rifle division was added to the new front being constructed in the area south of Herczegfalva in order to allow the 32nd Mechanized Brigade of the XVIII Tank Corps to be pulled out and reconstituted.[14] If Zakharov's army could hold out for two or three more days, Tolbukhin was confident that he could seize the initiative after the *IV. SS-Pz.*

Korps, Korpsgruppe Breith, and *I. Kav.Korps* had expended their remaining strength in frontal attacks.

As the 4th Guards Army and 57th Army fought for time, the *STAVKA* continued to construct a plan that would not only block any future attempts to relieve Budapest, but would also push *A.Gr. Balck* completely out of the Lake Balaton–Danube region. Based on a *STAVKA Verkhovnoe glavnokomandovani* (*VGK*, or Supreme High Command) Directive dated 22 January, the Third Ukrainian Front was assigned the following tasks: eliminate the German breakthrough by a counteroffensive; destroy the enemy forces that had broken through to the Danube; and prepare a retaliatory counterblow using its own forces (primarily the reinforced 4th Guards Army) and additional assets to be brought up from the *STAVKA* strategic reserve. This last item was important; Tolbukhin's Front would be augmented by the CIV Rifle Corps and Lt.Gen. A. I. Akhmanov's XXIII Tank Corps from the Second Ukrainian Front, which would give it at least a two-to-one numerical superiority.[15] The exact date that the counteroffensive would be initiated was situation-dependent, but at the rate the *IV. SS-Pz.Korps* was burning itself out, it would not be later than three or four days at the most, perhaps as early as 27 January.

Despite the successes gained that day, particularly along the Váli, that afternoon both Balck and Wöhler were disappointed, having expected far greater gains. This was puzzling, since Gille's attack had scarcely begun. While it was true that his three *panzer* divisions had encountered stiff resistance along the entire line, the *Wiking* Division had managed to hold on to and even slightly expand its two bridgeheads on the corps' right flank. The attack on the left by the *1. Pz.Div.* at Pettend and Baraczka had not yet fully developed, but would be continued during the early hours of the following morning. Despite this measureable progress, Wöhler noted that evening in the *H.Gr. Süd* war diary, "As experiences today have shown, conducting a frontal assault into strong and deeply echeloned enemy defenses behind the Váli offered no prospects for a successful breakthrough."[16] This should have been obvious to everyone before the attack was even contemplated, since there was really no other route into Budapest except the one already chosen.

Wöhler and Balck both arrived at this realization during a visit that day to Gille's headquarters in Seregélyes. Wöhler, who had established a temporary forward headquarters at Zirc, did not have far to travel, while Balck's unaccountably was still located in Martinsberg, far from the action, necessitating a three or four hour drive to reach Seregélyes. Gille was not present at first, since he was out visiting the command posts of his divisions observing first-hand the progress of their assaults. While waiting for Gille, the two commanders discussed with his chief of staff the progress the attack had made so far and possibilities for future operations. Apparently, both generals became discouraged at what they saw as the attack's slow progress, and most likely took counsel of their fears. One of the factors influencing their decision-making process was an assessment issued earlier that day by the

A. Gr. Balck and *H. Gr. Süd* intelligence staffs that a large regrouping of Soviet forces was taking place north of Lake Velencze.

Taking this intelligence assessment into consideration, Wöhler and Balck decided that a major alteration of the original *Konrad III* plan was urgently necessary. In laying out his rationale for this decision, Wöhler wrote that evening:

> [B]ecause the enemy massing northwest of Lake Velencze presented a considerable danger to the flanks of an attack to the northeast on Budapest, the decision was made to swing the attack group of the *IV. SS-Pz.Korps* to the northwest between Lake Velencze and the Váli in order to destroy the enemy west of the Váli. The attack group of the *III. Pz.Korps* and the Hungarian *VIII. Armee-Korps* pushing forward from the Vértes Mountains would also attack as part of this effort. After it eliminated the flanking enemy west of the Váli, the attack would resume to the northeast.

Evidently, the intelligence staffs and the commanders of *H. Gr. Süd* and *A. Gr. Balck/6. Armee* misinterpreted what was actually happening on the ground and consequently began to hedge their bets, leading to decisions that would adversely affect the future course of the operation.

Althrough the 4th Guards Army was repositioning forces between Lake Velencze and the northern edge of the Vértes Mountains, most of these moves were part of the unfolding plan to shorten their lines in front of the Hungarian *VIII. Armee-Korps* and the left flank *Korpsgruppe Breith* in order to free up some of these units to reinforce the defenses along the Váli to stop the *IV. SS-Pz.Korps*. Just as importantly, the withdrawal of the LVIII Rifle Corps and XX Guards Rifle Corps from their positions along the western edge of the Vértes Mountains would also prevent them from being encircled within their increasingly exposed salient. In contrast, the XXI Guards Rifle Corps was staying put along the Csäszari defense line between Pákozd and Pátka and showed no indication of pulling out any time soon.

So while it is true that these three corps superficially appeared to be "massing" to carry out an attack against the left flank of the *IV. SS-Pz.Korps*, in reality they were concentrating in order to continue their defense while limiting the risk of encirclement. All three of these corps had been heavily engaged in the same area for over three weeks and were far below full strength. A large amount of their army-level artillery assets had been repositioned to cover the Váli front, leaving them without the offensive firepower to launch a large-scale counterattack. Additionally, with the withdrawal of most of the battered VII Mechanized Corps after 22 January (with the exception of its 16th Mechanized Brigade), these three rifle corps were short of armored fighting vehicles of their own and thus were not well suited to carry out counterattacks against what was still the most powerful German armored corps in Hungary.

An additional fear was that the II Guards Mechanized Corps was suspected to still be in the Zámoly area, though this was an error; evidently, the *A. Gr. Ic* staff had confused this corps with the I Guards Mechanized Corps, which had begun shifting to the Váli River line as early as 19 January. As for the real II Guards Mechanized Corps, it was positioned in the Pilis Mountains northwest of Budapest and was still stationary as of 24 January. Therefore, upon closer examination, it is abundantly clear that Wöhler's and Balck's fears were unfounded, but their misinterpretation led them to decide to order Gille to radically reorient the direction of his attack from the northeast to the northwest at a point in the battle where the odds of success of the former course of action were actually increasing.

When Gille returned to his command post that afternoon after his tour of the front lines, Balck was preparing to depart (Wöhler had already left by that point), but he took the opportunity before he drove away to inform his corps commander face-to-face of his and Wöhler's mutual decision. He thereupon ordered Gille to cease his frontal attacks against the V Guards Cavalry Corps and redirect the armored elements of two of his three *panzer* divisions 90 degrees to the northwest, where they would conduct an attack beginning that same evening. Gille's new objective was to encircle the Soviet salient north of Lake Velencze and eliminate it in conjunction with a supporting attack by *Korpsgruppe Breith/III. Pz.Korps* through Acsa and Zámoly. This, Balck told him, would remove any risks to his *IV. SS-Pz.Korps* flank, thus allowing his corps to reorient to the northeast and continue its relief attack towards Budapest unimpeded (see Map 8).

Apparently, Gille was not pleased to receive this change of mission and argued with his army commander about the logic behind the decision. Gille continued to believe that rather than attacking to the northwest, the focus of his corps' attack should remain the relief of the encircled forces in Budapest. To do this, he argued, he proposed shifting the *Schwerpunkt* to his right flank instead, at the point along the Danube where the *Wiking* Division had already established two bridgeheads over the Váli. Regardless of the merits of his proposal, he was overridden on the spot by the *Armeegruppe* commander. This placed Gille in an unenviable position; for the third time during Operation *Konrad*, he would have to tell his subordinate commanders that they were to cease their heretofore successful attacks, then still in progress, and shift their efforts towards another direction, just when their goal of relieving Budapest again appeared to be within reach.

While Gille's immediate personal thoughts on this decision were not officially recorded, save for a typically laconic entry in his *Tagebuch* made two days later, those of his chief of staff, Manfred Schönfelder, were.[17] Describing the most pivotal event in *Konrad III*, Schönfelder later criticized this decision:

> The commands of the *Heeresgruppe* and *A.Gr.* are characterized by hectic behavior, exemplified by changing the direction of [our] thrust to the northwest, west, even to the south, followed by regroupings and deployments with renewed attacks towards the east. All this with exhausted troops, who were tied up in decisive combat [at that moment]. Differences of the intent [of the operation] between Balck and Gille occurred. Gille wanted to push on towards Budapest, Balck wanted to destroy the enemy in the west first.[18]

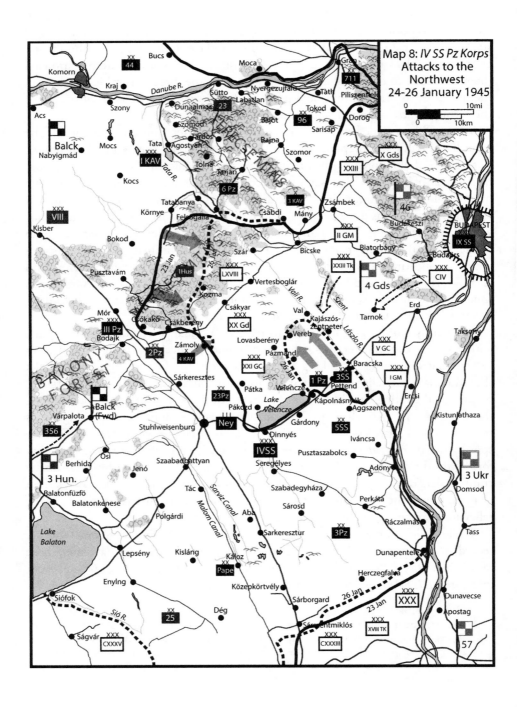

Of course, it must be said that neither Schönfelder nor Gille knew what was going on behind the scenes involving discussions between Wöhler, Balck, Guderian, and Hitler—as well as their respective chiefs of staff—and what was driving these decisions. Even if they had, however, it probably would not have caused them to change their minds—to their way of thinking, the objective still remained Budapest, and anything not focused on that immediate goal was a waste of effort.

In retrospect, it also seems that Balck did not go out of his way to keep Gille well informed about the reasoning behind his decisions. One might have asked, where was the legendary Hermann Balck, one of the *Wehrmacht*'s most daring and imaginative corps commanders, who was always up-to-date on the strengths and capabilities of his units, who always seemed to know what could and could not be accomplished? Stopping an ongoing attack and changing its direction in the middle of a battle when victory seemed to be within sight seems like a foolish decision, one taken with poor intelligence about the enemy situation, insufficient forces, and little preparation time, as if the Red Army of 1945 was the same one it had been in June 1941. In his self-justifying memoirs, Balck later wrote:

> We had to make a tough decision in the Valisz [*sic*] sector. The options were either an immediate advance toward Budapest, which is what Gille wanted to do, or first destroy the large enemy force on our left flank with the *IV. SS-Pz.Korps*, supported by the *III. Pz.Korps*. I decided first to destroy the enemy group on our left flank. If we moved on Budapest immediately, we would end up with two instead of one SS corps in the city, but there would be no forces to prevent the surviving Russian [*sic*] units from coming back at us. Gille was *incapable* [author's emphasis] of understanding this, which made the situation more difficult and cost us a precious twenty-four hour delay. By the time we finally launched the new attack, it was too late.[19]

This swipe at Gille's intelligence was entirely gratuitous, especially since the SS commander had a better understanding of the condition of his troops and what they could or could not achieve than his *Armeegruppe* commander did. It also illustrates what Gille clearly saw as the true goal of the entire operation—the relief of Budapest and the rescue of its garrison—while Balck and Wöhler had become fixated on conducting large-scale encirclement operations to destroy as many Soviet divisions as possible, a fantasy shared by Hitler. Schönfelder would have much more to say about this matter in the days to come, including comments about the deteriorating relationship between his corps commander and Balck.

Upon his return to Martinsberg, Balck was gladdened to hear from *H.Gr. Süd* that Guderian at *OKH* had approved the plan to shift the direction of the *IV. SS-Pz. Korps*' attack. However, should the attack to the northwest not yield quick results, Hitler was considering another plan to move Gille's corps around Lake Velencze to the Zámoly area and have it resume its attack from that direction, leaving one division to hold the entire west bank of the Váli between Lake Velencze and the Danube. Earlier that day, Guderian himself had contacted *A.Gr. Balck* by telephone and asked the chief of staff how and when his commander was going to finish "cleaning up" the area west of the Danube.

Apparently, Gaedke had answered the chief of staff of *OKH* satisfactorily. He replied that *A. Gr. Balck/6. Armee* would first clear the enemy in front of Budapest, clear out the enemy in front of the *2. Pz.Armee* south of Lake Balaton, and finally clear out the area along the Danube east of Gran. Gaedke concluded by stating, "As a prerequisite to this, however, one first has to be successful west of the Danube [i.e., along the Váli line] before the enemy can install himself in a strong defensive position along the Sió Front."[20] At some point during that afternoon, Balck had decided to move his forward command post nearer to the *IV. SS-Pz.Korps'* headquarters and accepted the recommendation of *1. Pz.Div.* that it be moved to the building in Várpalota where the Hungarian infantry school was formerly housed. Interestingly, Balck did not ask Gille's opinion as to where to plant his army commander's flag.[21]

One proposal made by the commander of *H. Gr. Süd* that was turned down by Guderian or Hitler was the plan by Wöhler and Balck to allow the *2. Pz.Armee* to initiate its own attack. This plan, *Unternehmen Eisbrecher*, was tentatively scheduled to begin on 26 January in order to relieve the pressure being exerted against *A. Gr. Balck*'s Hungarian *3. Armee*. Hitler was apparently concerned that this attack would draw off too many divisions (an infantry corps had been tasked with the mission) needed to protect the Nagykanizsa oil fields west of Lake Balaton, and instead proposed that the attack by *2. Pz.Armee* be carried out contingent upon the success of Gille's attack, that is, after Budapest was relieved.[22] This ruled out any immediate help in that direction, which would soon place the Hungarian *3. Armee*—including both *Div.Gr. Pape* and the *3. Pz.Div.*—in a precarious situation as elements of the 57th Army began to mass along the western bank of the Sió River and the southern flank between Dunapentele and Sárbogárd. With this and many other questions unresolved, the seventh day of Operation *Konrad III* drew to an inconclusive end.

Throughout the evening of 24/25 January, temperatures continued to hover below freezing and heavy snowfall was reported in some areas. Clearly, winter had not yet released its icy grip on this part of the *Puszta*. Cloud cover was very heavy and soldiers from both sides awoke that morning to find everything covered with a light frost. Crewmembers labored to start their vehicles in the icy weather and to warm up something to eat. Hot coffee was a rare commodity, a necessary item to sustain a soldier's alertness after another night spent out in the cold. Many of Gille's troops had not slept for more than three hours at a time during the past week, and were consequently on the verge of exhaustion. Upon receiving their orders to shift the direction of attack to the northwest at 4 p.m. on 24 January, all three of Gille's divisions labored overnight to comply with their orders and resume the attack.

This was easier said than done; the reconfiguration of the attacking units, which were to be composed primarily of armored units, would first require that the tank and assault gun battalions be rearmed and refueled to get ready for their new mission.

In some cases, units earmarked for this new attack were still in close contact with the enemy and would have to disengage while handing off their portion of the front lines to an infantry unit. During the remaining daylight hours of 24 January and until the sun's reappearance the next morning, Red Air Force ground-attack aircraft and fighter-bombers roamed the skies over the supply routes day and night between the Váli River and Stuhlweissenburg, machine gunning or bombing German truck columns carrying their precious loads of fuel and ammunition. They did not fly unchallenged; in the *Totenkopf* Division's area alone, its *SS-Flak-Abt. 3* shot down six Soviet aircraft that day.[23]

The units of the *IV. SS-Pz.Korps* spent most of 25 January involved either in ongoing defensive operations or moving forces into position to begin the attack towards the northwest. Balck was becoming impatient with the delay, which Gille's staff explained as being caused by logistics difficulties, the reasons for which, according to *H.Gr. Süd*, "were not really clear." Had anyone on the *H.Gr. Süd* staff taken the trouble to travel to the front lines to see actual conditions on the battlefield for himself, it would have immediately become clear why. Any movement—even of as short a duration as 10 or 20 kilometers—could take hours, given the state of the roads, enemy action, and poor visibility. Wöhler, who had appeared at Gille's headquarters that morning at 8 a.m., would have known, but apparently he said nothing to correct his staff's misperceptions.

The units that would provide the bulk of the forces for the attack would be the *1. Pz.Div.* and the *Totenkopf* Division, while the *Wiking* would hold the right flank between the area south of Baraczka and Adony. All of the *1. Pz.Div.* would take part, as would most of the *Totenkopf* Division, except for a battalion needed to consolidate the ground gained the previous day inside Baraczka. This battalion from the *Totenkopf* Regiment, assisted by several tanks, would continue its attempt to take all of Baraczka and secure a bridgehead over the Váli. As events would soon demonstrate, it would be unable to carry out these orders on account of the large number of troops the V Guards Cavalry Corps kept funneling into the town.

Beside the two divisions earmarked for the attack to the northwest, all of the corps' artillery battalions (except *SS-Werf.Abt. 504*, which remained with the *Wiking*) had finally established their firing positions between Kápolnás Nyék and Gárdony, having been "set" the day before, so no time would be lost in procuring fire support when needed. Wire communications networks had been set up by then to facilitate requests for artillery fire, thus avoiding some of the difficulties encountered the previous day when forward units, especially the *1. Pz.Div.*, attempted to request fire support by radio.

To reinforce the declining strength of *Pz.Gren.Rgt. 1* and *113* of the *1. Pz.Div.*, the *IV. SS-Pz.Korps* ordered the *Wiking* Division to send *Stubaf.* Vogt's *I. Btl./Norge*, as well as *Stubaf.* im Masche's *I. Btl./Danmark*, to support Thünert's division. All of *I. Abt./Pz.Rgt. 24* would participate, minus one *Schwadron* (equivalent to a tank

Kompanie) going to the *Totenkopf*, while the rest of the battalion would reinforce the *1. Pz.Div.* The *Wiking* Division's *Panzergruppe*, which had shrunk to only 11 combat-ready vehicles by the morning of 25 January, would remain with Ullrich's division. *Heeres-Sturm Art.Brig. 303*, with its 21 remaining operational vehicles, would be attached to the *Totenkopf* Division. The nine operational Tiger IIs from *s.Pz.Abt. 509* would also be attached in support of the *Totenkopf* Division, though at some point during the fighting that day, a portion of it was used in the assault on Pettend. In all, approximately 50 combat-ready tanks, assault guns, and tank destroyers would take part in the assault that day, roughly half of the remaining operational armored fighting vehicles in the *IV. SS-Pz.Korps*. Interestingly, the 4th Guards Army estimated that there were twice as many German armored fighting vehicles taking part in the attack that day, a common tendency among nearly every Red Army higher headquarters to overestimate the strength of their opponent.[24]

No copies of the modification to the *Konrad III* operations order issued by *A.Gr. Balck* or *H.Gr. Süd* for the attack on 25/26 January are known to exist except fragments; however, the *IV. SS-Pz.Korps'* supplemental order survived. It was not issued until 8:30 p.m. on 25 January, testimony to the delay caused by *A.Gr. Balck's* late issuance of its own order at 1:30 p.m. All three of Gille's divisions were encountering difficulties in repositioning their forces due to the weather, enemy action, and traffic control problems. Gille or Schönfelder most likely had already given subordinate commanders brief verbal instructions by telephone prior to the issuance of the written order, akin to a "warning order" issued by the armed forces of NATO nations today. The corps' written order, which referenced the *A.Gr. Balck* order for the attack issued seven hours earlier, was sent out to the units by *SS-Nachr. Abt. 104* via *Fernschreiber*. The order assigned each division its individual mission and supporting unit tasks, as described in the following paragraphs.

On the left, the *1. Pz.Div.*, with the exception of one *Panzergrenadier* battalion still engaged in the fighting in Baraczka, was ordered to advance from the area surrounding Pettend, including units positioned to the south and southwest of the village. Its mission was to attack through the Pazmánd–Vereb area towards the Vértes Mountains and seize Acsa. Once it had arrived at that point, it was to keep open the crossing sites to the west, north and south; then it was to screen the corps' left flank between Pazmánd and Vereb. On the right, the infantry elements of the *Totenkopf* Division still engaged along the Váli sector would be pulled out and reinforced by *s.Pz.Abt. 509*, *Sturm-Art.Brig. 303*, and a portion of *I. Abt./Pz.Rgt. 24* for a total of 38 vehicles. This division was ordered to advance to the northwest along the Váli River from the Baraczka area. Its mission was to attack towards Vál and *conduct a reconnaissance over the Váli River towards the east* (emphasis added by author) and block any crossing points. The *Wiking* Division was directed to relieve the *Totenkopf* Division along the Váli and secure the corps' deep right flank on the Danube and Váli Rivers between Adony and Baraczka.

Though decisive combat did not occur during most of the day, a significant amount of fighting still took place, most of it defensive. In his sparsely worded evening report, the corps' *Ic* relayed the following information to his counterpart at *A. Gr. Balck/6. Armee*:

> At 5 p.m., an enemy force of still-unknown size was able to cross the Danube and penetrate [into] Adony with several assault units. During the afternoon, an enemy force of battalion size moving south along the Danube river highway, with the support of several tanks, repeatedly attacked our bridgehead over the Váli northeast of Aggszentpéter. So far, all of these attacks were driven off. In difficult house-to-house fighting, the enemy was able to force our troops to pull back to the southern portion of Baraczka. Northwest of that location, our troops observed enemy reinforcement being moved up … The village of Pettend was completely cleared of the enemy.[25]

This report was so short and succinct, it would almost seem as if Gille had Herbert Jankuhn transcribing directly for him. In addition to its brevity, it gave no insight at all into the severity of the fighting at Pettend, which was as heavy as any the corps had encountered to date.

The corps' *Ia, Stubaf.* Rentrop, provided more information in his own nightly report to the *A. Gr. Balck Ia*. According to Rentrop, the *Wiking* Division on the right flank was busily engaged in warding off the attacks against its bridgehead adjacent to the Danube. Although the attacking unit, apparently from the newly arrived 122nd Rifle Division, failed to dislodge the troops from the *Germania* Regiment holding the small bridgehead, its defenders were subjected to heavy artillery and mortar fire throughout the day. One participant in the fighting was *Ostuf.* Kerckhoff, acting commander of *5. Kp./SS-Pz.Rgt. 5*, whose tanks, along with those of the neighboring *6. Kompanie*, made up the division's 11-tank *Panzergruppe*. Describing the action on 25 January, he later wrote:

> [The day began with] no attack; we screened. The weather turned worse and, as a result, the visibility. Late in the afternoon, we heard noise; the wind was [blowing] in our favor. Just before dark, the Russians [*sic*] attacked with tanks and infantry. Seven Russian tanks, almost all of them T-34s, were [soon] burning and gave us a view into the intentions of the Russians. We suffered no losses and still had 11 Panthers screening. Morale was good.[26]

Oberführer Ullrich was forced to commit the division's *Alarmbataillon* and *SS-Begleit Kp. 5* against the enemy force that had infiltrated Adony; the results of their counterattack were still unknown as of the evening reporting time. Throughout the afternoon, battalions and companies from the *Wiking* extended their lines towards the northwest in order to relieve similar-sized elements from the *Totenkopf* Division in time to allow them to move into their assembly areas for the attack that evening.

This placed a greater burden on the men of the *Germania* and *Westland* Regiments, as well as on divisional units, which had to accept lesser troop densities along their entire front, making them even more vulnerable to attacks. Whilst repulsing one of these attacks that day, *Hstuf.* Hermann Kaufmann, commander of *1. Kp./SS-Pz. Aufkl.Abt. 5*, was killed in action while leading his reconnaissance company in a counterattack along the Váli River. Kaufmann had been the last *Beglietoffizier/O5* for Gille when the latter was still commanding the *Wiking* Division. This was the price that had to be paid to enable *Konrad III* to continue going forward.

As can be imagined, action that day in the *Totenkopf* Division's area was considerably more dynamic. As its companies and battalions located south of Baraczka disengaged and were replaced by units from the *Wiking* Division, *Hstuf.* Heinz Müller's *III. Btl./Eicke*, along with six *Pz. V* Panthers from *I. Abt./Pz.Rgt. 24*, fought desperately to retain its foothold in Baraczka, but by noon had been pushed to the town's southern and southwestern edge by a series of fierce battalion-sized counterattacks launched by the 63rd Guards Cavalry Division. Artillery and mortar fire was reported to be intense, and casualties among Müller's battalion were heavy. To help his troops retake the town and reach the all-important bridging site over the Váli, a battalion from *Maj.* Marcks's *Kampfgruppe* of *Pz.Gren.Rgt. 113* joined Müller's battalion in a counterattack that afternoon. After a promising start, the attack was unable to reach its objective on account of the Soviet cavalrymen's stiff resistance, though they did manage to knock out two of their tanks.[27]

Southwest of Baraczka, the *1. Pz.Div.* was finally able to take Pettend after a day-long struggle. This village, insignificant except for its location, was stoutly defended by troops from the 93rd Rifle Division and an armored battlegroup from the I Guards Mechanized Corps, which had converted the village's strongly built houses and farm buildings into virtual fortresses. *Kampfgrupe Huppert*—which included *Pz.Rgt. 1, II. Btl./Pz.Gren.Rgt. 1, I. Btl./Norge*, and *I. Btl./Danmark*—struggled against its defenders from early morning until late afternoon before its commander was finally able to declare Pettend secure. Casualties were heavy on both sides. Thirty-one German tanks took part in the assault on Pettend, and their commanders learned the hard way that *Ivan* was no longer afraid of their *panzers*. According to one eyewitness, Soviets troops would seek shelter while German tanks roared overhead, then jump up and attack them from the rear once they had passed by.[28] Operating in villages or towns defended by enemy troops was suicidal unless tanks were supported by their own infantry to provide close-in protection.

The infantrymen from both sides stalked their enemy's tanks in the inferno among the houses and gardens of the village. One participant who survived the fighting in Pettend, *Uscha.* Jan Barstein from Vogt's *I. Btl./Norge*, left a very vivid account of the fighting:

> We fight from corner to corner, we don't have time to search the houses ... I run into a Soviet tank behind a barn; I seek cover behind the corner of a house, and shout for a *Panzerfaust*. But the armored vehicle is empty, its crew abandoned it ... its engine is still running ... We get through the village, and a vast open space lays in front of our eyes, full of burning tanks and the bodies of dead and wounded Soviets. On the right side of the road, parallel to it runs the railroad embankment and there sits a King Tiger, which has bypassed the Soviets and got in the rear from the left. Smoke columns emerge from the Soviet tanks, the *Ivan* retreats; the houses are burning behind us.[29]

Huppert's troops reported finding the bodies of several German and Hungarian troops who had been captured earlier. Many of them showed signs of having been tortured or mutilated by their captors, which may have been a factor in the increased bitterness that became evident during the fighting.

Unwilling to give up Pettend without a fight, the Soviets launched a number of unsuccessful counterattacks from the north and west of the village. All the attackers had to show for their persistence was the loss of 17 tanks from the I Guards Mechanized Brigade, including two T-34/85s and one JS-II Stalin.[30] Two kilometers to the northwest of Kápolnás Nyék, *Pz.Pio.Btl. 37*, augmented by a reconnaissance company from *Pz.Aufkl.Abt. 1* (the rest of the battalion was still attached to *Div.Gr. Pape*) and several tank destroyers from *Pz.Jäg.Abt. 37*, attempted to retake Velencze after giving it up two days before without a fight, but the battalion's attack failed to secure a foothold, forcing it to establish a screening line to cover the division's left flank east of the town instead.[31] Despite this setback, after two days of heavy fighting, Pettend was finally in German hands and the *1. Pz.Div.* attack scheduled for that evening would begin on time.

While the *IV. SS-Pz.Korps'* divisions did their utmost to get their troops into position by the deadline, the neighboring *Korpsgruppe Breith/III. Pz.Korps* continued its own operation. On its right flank, the *23.Pz.Div.*, supported by *SS-Rgt. Ney*, launched an attack against the salient held by the 69th Rifle Division on the western bank of the Császári River opposite Pákozd. This failed to achieve any measureable results and the units involved were forced to withdraw. *Divisionsgruppe Holste*, with the *4. Kav.Brig.* and the Hungarian *2. Pz.Div.*—supported by the few remaining Tiger IIs of *s.Pz.Abt. 503 FHH*—began its attack northeast of Zámoly and forced the defenders from the 80th Guards Rifle Division to withdraw to a new defense line 3 kilometers east of the town.

That afternoon, Holste's troops were able to observe the approach of Soviet reinforcements from their newly gained positions, that included a few tanks coming from the direction of Lovasberény. This was the vanguard of the 41st Guards Rifle Division, which was being sent to reinforce the XXI Rifle Corps' defenses, but it did not attack. On the left of *Div.Gr. Holste*, the Hungarian *2. Pz.Div.* reported that its attempt to take the commanding heights east of Csákberény had been thwarted by elements of the XX Guards Rifle Corps, but it had still managed to gain control of Hill 398 due north of the village of Gant as well as the village of Kozmá a few kilometers further north. Though most of the Vértes Mountains were now back in the hands of Hungarian troops, and the Soviet lines around Zámoly had been pushed back, these local successes did little to ease the pressure being placed on the *IV. SS-Pz.Korps*. Additionally, the approach of the 41st Guards Rifle Division may have reinforced Balck's own misperception that this unit was going to be used to attack Gille's left flank.

While Breith's corps had enjoyed a small degree of tactical success that day, Harteneck's *I. Kav.Korps* could make no such claims. The salient that the *3. Kav.*

Brig. had carved out of the Soviet lines between Csabdi and Zsámbék was subjected to a series of unsuccessful counterattacks throughout that day by troops and tanks from the south and east, with as many as 10 tanks at a time attacking. During the heavy fighting that raged back and forth, three Soviet tanks were knocked out, but *Oberst* von der Groeben's cavalry brigade gained no ground that day, and like the attack of its sister brigade fighting with *Div.Gr. Holste*, was not able to assist Gille's attack. The *6. Pz.Div.* attack towards the southeast ran into a strong enemy position 4 kilometers northwest of the town of Szár and got nowhere. In Harteneck's center, the *96. Inf.Div.* reported that the enemy had achieved a local breakthrough southwest of the town of Sarisap, which was eliminated by a counterattack, and on the corps' far left flank along the Danube, the *711. Inf.Div.* reported enemy ground reconnaissance activity north of Dorog, but little else.

North of the Danube, the *IV. Pz.Korps FHH* with its four divisions stopped reporting directly to *A.Gr. Balck/6. Armee* on 25 January, having been subordinated to the *8. Armee* from noon.[32] Wöhler had been seeking this change in Balck's order of battle for several days, which would ease the burden of the *6. Armee* commander and allow him to focus strictly on the relief of Budapest. The Soviets' Gran bridgehead, held by the 7th Guards Army and a few remaining elements of the 6th Guards Tank Army—which had figured so prominently in operations along the Danube during the first two weeks of January—would soon loom large again in *H.Gr. Süd* calculations, which will be revisited in a subsequent chapter.

On the *A.Gr. Balck* far right flank, the Hungarian *25. Inf.Div.* reported that its troops had spotted the southerly movement of a large body of enemy infantry departing the town of Ádánd, a few kilometers south of Siófok. Slightly more ominous was the report from *Div.Gr. Pape*, operating under the tactical control of the Hungarian *3. Armee*, which stated that troops from the Hungarian *Inf.Rgt. 26* manning the *Sió-Abschnitt* at Mezö Komárom had observed 15 tanks moving into the town of Szabadhidvég along the east–west highway. In the southeast corner of the *Div.Gr. Pape* sector at Simontornya, a reconnaissance company from *Pz.Aufkl.Abt. 3* reported that an estimated two companies of enemy foot soldiers had crossed the Sió River and taken the village of Jánosháza against negligible Hungarian resistance.

At the same time, a battalion-sized Soviet assault took the town of Sáregres on the western bank of the Sárviz Canal. At the reporting deadline, a joint German–Hungarian counterattack was still underway to retake it. *Panzeraufklärungs-Abteilung 3* also reported that the unoccupied town of Sár Szentmiklós south of its screen line had been taken over by enemy troops. It was becoming plainly obvious that there were insufficient troops to hold this far-reaching area of the front, and that a build-up by the 57th Army was underway.

In Budapest, the *IX. SS-Geb.Korps* reported that during the evening of 24/25 January, a company-sized attack by Soviet troops against the western perimeter of the Budapest bridgehead had been attempted, but had been fended off. German and Hungarian forces had attempted another counterattack against the slowly expanding Soviet beachhead on Margaret Island, but the results were still unknown at reporting time. German artillery observers located on the roofs of the tallest buildings in the city reported seeing a considerable amount of Soviet ferrying operations underway across the Danube 10 kilometers to the south at Budatétény, including the use of steam-powered vessels.

Although the German observers did not know this, their report most likely was the first sighting of the arriving XXIII Tank Corps, which was coming from the opposite side of the river where it had previously been operating under the Second Ukrainian Front. On that day, *IX. SS-Geb.Korps* reported the number of wounded being cared for within the bridgehead had swelled to nearly 10,000, an enormous total for the corps' few medical personnel to care for, given the chronic lack of medical supplies and shortages of nearly everything needed for their care, including food, potable water, and bedding. Due to the atrocious weather conditions and lack of suitable airfields, evacuation of the wounded had become practically impossible. The only thing the wounded could hope for now was the rapid approach of the *IV. SS-Pz.Korps*.

In the air, the *IV. SS-Pz.Korps* reported nearly 300 attacks by Soviet aircraft, including 200 by IL-2 *Sturmoviks* alone, making any daytime movement hazardous, especially by critical logistics units. Although not nearly as devastating as Allied air power on the Western Front, veterans of the Eastern Front found such a high level of activity by the Red Air Force disconcerting. In contrast, the *Luftwaffe* was able to generate only 60 sorties and shot down just one Soviet aircraft. Even individual tanks were targeted if they failed to properly conceal themselves with white camouflage paint or by hiding in built-up areas.

Elsewhere in the *A.Gr. Balck/6. Armee* area of operations, little enemy air activity was reported, save for omnipresent Soviet reconnaissance aircraft.[33] German reconnaissance aircraft were mostly grounded that day because of the weather; the few sorties flown reported inconclusive results, with the lone exception of one aircraft that photographed a large column of motorized vehicles crossing the Malom Canal west of Torbágy, a mere 21 kilometers northeast of the Soviet Váli defense line. Unfortunately, the pilot could not determine whether they were crossing to the west or to the east.

The bad flying weather and the inability of reconnaissance aircraft to take more photographs or obtain more precise information about the direction of movement of Soviet vehicular traffic was to have tremendous consequences. The evening intelligence summary for *A.Gr. Balck/6. Armee*, written by *Hptm.* von Pander, began with a recitation of the Soviet probes across the Sió River sector west of the Sárviz Canal already reported by the Hungarian *3. Armee*. Its tone then shifted to one of alarm, stating immediately after the somewhat blasé first sentence:

Throughout the entire [*A. Gr. Balck*] sector strong enemy attacks can be expected in the immediate future, after determining that 1) the enemy has had sufficient time to regroup the units that had broken out from encirclement [i.e., the XVIII Tank Corps and CXXXIII Rifle Corps] and realign them under the control of the 57th Army; and that 2) enemy units *formerly deployed on the eastern front of Budapest* [author's emphasis] have been detected. Besides these, according to a *Richard-Meldung*, the recently located VII Mechanized Corps can be expected to reappear once it completes its reconstitution.

The report made no mention concerning the whereabouts of the XXIII Tank Corps or CIV Rifle Corps. Following this statement, the deputy *A. Gr. Ic* resumed his normal tone, reporting the status of the enemy units identified along the Váli River that had been conducting counterattacks that day, as well as the small-scale river crossing at Adony that was the focus of *Alarm-Btl. Wiking's* attention that evening.

Hauptmann von Pander correctly assessed that the Soviets would continue their attempts to block any attempt by the *Panzergruppe* of the *IV. SS-Pz.Korps* to keep pushing towards the north after taking Pettend, which was the most obvious enemy course of action. What was yet to be seen, he wrote, was whether the 57th Army's impending attack from south of Lake Balaton would be conducted in tandem with a similar assault launched from the area between the Danube and Lake Velencze by the 4th Guards Army. The intelligence officer then concluded his daily report by stating that based on the observed movement of Soviet troops east of Zámoly, it appeared that the enemy was concentrating his forces northwest of Lake Velencze. He did not provide an assessment of what this meant, nor did he draw any conclusions as to what this intelligence signified, including the enemy's possible intentions. However, his last sentence evidently caught the eye of the commander of *A. Gr. Balck*, as well as that of his chief of staff.

The *Armeegruppe* deputy *Ic*'s assessment was mostly correct. What von Pander did not know was the date when the Third Ukrainian Front would initiate its counteroffensive, nor had he detected the approach of reinforcements from the Budapest area, although he had sensed that something was afoot. Had von Pander known that Tolbukhin's attack was originally intended to begin between 25 and 26 January, he would have been even more concerned than he already was. However, due to the *IV. SS-Pz.Korps'* advance to the Váli defensive line after overcoming the initial defenses west of the river, and the seizure of two bridgeheads between Aggszentpéter and the Danube by the *Wiking* Division, Marshal Tolbukhin's timetable was disrupted, which forced him to delay his attack until 27 or 28 January.

This two-day delay had the added benefit of providing more time for the XXIII Tank Corps and CIV Rifle Corps to completely close up into their respective forward assembly areas and to adequately prepare for their impending attacks. Until that time, however, the elements of the 4th Guards Army defending the approaches to Budapest—including the XX and XXI Guards Corps and the LXVIII Rifle Corps, as well as the V Guards Cavalry Corps and I Guards Mechanized Corps—were directed by the Third Ukrainian Front's military council to "stand to the death" and therefore were not earmarked to participate in the counteroffensive.[34] At this point, Tolbukhin as well as the *STAVKA* still believed that the attacking German force was numerically superior to their own, though as we have seen, this was not the case.

In the previously mentioned *STAVKA* Directive 11014, the general concept of the counteroffensive was outlined as follows: the 4th Guards Army, using the XXIII Tank Corps and CIV Rifle Corps, would attack from the north across the Váli in the direction of Sárosd while the 57th Army, with its XVIII Tank Corps, XXX Guards Rifle Corps , and CXXXIII Rifle Corps, would simultaneously carry out its own attack from the south, also aimed towards Sárosd.[35] Once they had linked up there, this action would have the desired effect of not only halting any German attempt to relieve Budapest for good, but would also encircle the bulk of the *IV. SS-Pz.Korps* and the *3. Pz.Div.* Finally, with the enemy's most dangerous force eliminated and the rest of Hungary wide open for exploitation, the *STAVKA*'s primary operational objective, the offensive towards Vienna, could be resumed. As for the rest of the 4th Guards Army, it too would "stand to the death" as ordered to prevent the Germans from breaking through to Budapest.

Despite his knowledge of the condition of Gille's divisions, *Gen.d.Pz.Tr.* Balck was expecting great things from the *IV. SS-Pz.Korps'* attack.[36] Still obsessed with the belief that the Soviet units concentrating north of Lake Velencze posed a greater threat than anything assembling beyond the Váli (though according to Soviet sources they were clearly not preparing an attack), Balck was intent on destroying this force of 40,000–50,000 men, even at the risk of compromising the offensive's primary objective—the relief of Budapest.

Although a complete copy of the *A.Gr. Balck/6. Armee*'s operations order for the attack has not survived, a captured fragment still exists, apparently corresponding to the same one issued at 1:30 p.m. that day. It clearly lays out Balck's own evolving intent for 26 January:

> Through an offensive by the forces of the *IV. SS-Pz.Korps* from the Pettend area in the direction of Acsa, and by concentrating the main forces of tanks, infantry, and artillery, in conjunction with the *III. Pz.Korps*, destroy the enemy forces located north of Lake Velencze. The forces of the *III. Pz.Korps* are to widen the breakthrough sector northeast and north of Zámoly, in order to develop the offensive from there, following the arrival of the artillery and *6. Pz.Div.*, to Csakvár.[37]

Worthy of note is that this order contains no mention of *I. Kav.Korps* continuing its attack between Csabdi and Zsámbék by the *3. Kav.Brig.*, a sign that Balck had given up hope that it would make any further progress. Instead, it implies that the *6. Pz.Div.* would have to be withdrawn from Harteneck's control and rapidly shift to the south to support *III. Pz.Korps'* attack at Zámoly. How a *panzer* division in contact with the enemy could be withdrawn in time, given the current weather and road conditions, and move to the area west of Zámoly to take part in the attack on 26 January is best left to the imagination, but Gille's own division commanders would have sympathized.

As if this was not enough to complicate the situation, both Wöhler and Balck were beginning to have doubts about Gille's ability as a corps commander to execute the orders he had been given, based on what they perceived as the slow pace of *IV. SS-Pz.Korps*' reorientation to the northwest. The reason why this was taking longer than they anticipated has already been explained, and was not due to any lack of leadership ability or intelligence on his part nor of his troops. Wöhler should have known that, since he had spent several hours that day with Gille and had observed with his own eyes the conditions on the ground. Nevertheless, Wöhler began transcribing records of his conversations with Gille that he would use against him several days later. Why Wöhler felt this way is unknown; previously, he had several *Waffen-SS* units serve under his command on the Eastern Front and had effusively praised their performance.[38]

For his part, Balck was already prejudiced against the SS commander and his judgement was possibly tainted by his expressed dislike of anything to do with the SS. Gaedke, his chief of staff, had loathed the *Wiking* Division in general—and Gille and Schönfelder in particular—ever since the Cherkassy Pocket, and his attitude may have reinforced his commanding general's tendencies, such as his outright dislike of Himmler or mistrust of anything emanating from the *IV. SS-Pz.Korps*' headquarters. In combination, these negative attitudes displayed by Gille's superior officers must have created a very hostile command environment for a leader who up to this point in his career had performed competently and steadfastly, if not brilliantly.

There was another incident that occurred on 25 January involving Wöhler and Gille that may shed additional light on the souring relationship between the two commanders. When Wöhler first arrived at Gille's headquarters that morning, the *IV. SS-Pz.Korps* commander gave his army group commander an informal situation briefing. Whether he was queried on the reasoning behind his delayed attack or not (it is impossible now to know), one of the first things that Gille brought to Wöhler's attention was the *1. Pz.Div.* and its tardy occupation of its forward assembly area, which Gille had ordered to be completed by 3:30 p.m. the previous day. This it had failed to do, which Gille considered a "failure of his expectations," an event that he believed had disrupted the timetable for his corps' attack that day.[39]

Upon being told this, Wöhler immediately contacted *Gen.Maj.* Thünert by field telephone from Gille's headquarters. Thünert explained that he had not considered Gille's directive to be an order at all, but rather "general information" concerning the upcoming operation. Besides, Thünert continued, a significant portion of his division had been tied up in combat in Baraczka and south of Pettend, and thus could not immediately break contact and move into a new assembly area at that moment. Wöhler then told Thünert that taking Pettend was extremely important as the movement towards Budapest was impossible until it was in German hands. It was, he told Thünert, something that *A.Gr. Balck* "absolutely had to have." This misunderstanding apparently reinforced Wöhler's impression that Gille's transmittal of instructions to his subordinate commanders left something to be desired and that he may not possess the skill needed to command a corps, especially in the current situation.

After speaking with the *1. Pz.Div.* commander, Wöhler told Gille that unless he got his corps moving immediately, there was a very real possibility that Hitler would order his corps pulled out and repositioned elsewhere, perhaps in the *III. Pz.Korps* area. Wöhler concluded by stating, "This made it all the more necessary to concentrate all friendly forces for one blow on one objective, so that we could at least fight through *somewhere* [emphasis added by author]. In the present situation, that was to the northwest." This was a curious thing for an army group commander to say to his subordinate, because it creates the impression that Wöhler was not convinced of his own reasoning why the attack towards the northwest was necessary. At any rate, the importance of the misunderstanding between Gille and Thünert appears to have been overinflated, and was not even mentioned by Schönfelder or in the otherwise meticulously detailed division history by *Maj.* Rolf Stoves, the division's operations officer at the time.[40] It does, however, provide a filter through which to view Wöhler's subsequent actions.

Another event that occurred at the same time was the divergence of opinions as to the purpose of the turn to the northwest. Evidence indicates that Gille thought it was only temporary and was needed to get past the V Guards Cavalry Corps by going through Pettend and around Gorshkov's right flank above the town of Vál; once having achieved this, he understood Balck's original intent as meaning that the *1. Pz.Div.* was expected to cross the Váli and attack southeast to get behind the Soviet defense line, thus opening the way for the rest of the corps to resume its advance. Perhaps Balck did not make his intent sufficiently clear; Wöhler certainly did not clarify the situation, even though he had several hours with Gille that morning to make that point.[41] Gille's focus remained upon the relief of Budapest, and any action that his corps took had to be directed towards that goal. Thus, one must greet with a certain amount of disbelief any claim that Gille and Schönfelder deliberately disobeyed orders the following day.

Gille called the *H.Gr. Süd* chief of staff at 4 p.m. that afternoon to request clarification of his orders—was his corps supposed to eliminate the enemy immediately west of the Váli and then resume his attack towards Budapest, or was he supposed to act in concert with the *III. Pz.Korps* and destroy the large enemy grouping north of Lake Velencze and then resume the attack towards Budapest? Gille then told von Grolman that his corps was suffering over 300 casualties a day, and that it only had enough remaining combat power to do one of these tasks, not both. Any concerted action with the *III. Pz.Korps* might destroy the XX Rifle Corps and XXI Guards Rifle Corps, but after completing that task (which he doubted the *III. Pz.Korps* was capable of), his corps would be too weak to continue to fight through the increasingly strong secondary defense line east of the Váli.[42] Of course, Gille was not even aware of the existence of the approaching XXIII Tank Corps and CIV Rifle Corps, and the threat that these forces represented. Had he known, he might have acted differently, but so would have Balck and Wöhler, who were just as ignorant of the actual enemy situation as Gille was.

Generalleutnant von Grolman called his counterpart at *A. Gr. Balck/6. Armee* immediately after speaking with Gille to obtain some sort of mutual agreement between the two chiefs of staff as to the purpose and phasing of this attack, since there were two competing versions. Gaedke told him, "The intent of the order was that this attack would be the first phase for the continued attack to the northeast." He went on to tell von Grolman that he had not yet issued orders to Gille to this effect, prompting the army group chief of staff to reply, "There is no indication that the northeast direction would be *taken up again* [emphasis added by author] after the completion of this mission. Otherwise the order is in agreement with the intent of the *Armeegruppe*."[43]

This was perhaps the first indication that *H. Gr. Süd* was beginning to believe that the loss of the Budapest garrison was a foregone conclusion. Gille, of course, had no knowledge of these deliberations, and the available evidence indicates that he was kept poorly informed as to what was really going on behind the scenes at the headquarters of his field army and army group. As always, he remained focused on the accomplishment of his mission, and anything that detracted from that he considered an unnecessary diversion of resources. He was perhaps the only remaining senior field commander at the time to understand what was truly at stake and why the operation had been launched in the first place.

To be fair, Wöhler was rather worried about the ominous developments on the right flank of *A. Gr. Balck/6. Armee* in the Hungarian *3. Armee* area of operations and possible signs of renewed enemy offensive activity north of the Danube in the *8. Armee* area. Wöhler ordered Balck to divert some of his *Armeegruppe*'s antitank units to Heszlényi's army, including an antitank battalion headquarters from the *23. Pz. Div.* and an antitank gun company from the *1. Pz. Div.* Along with other antitank assets coming out from *Heerestruppen* (including 14 tank destroyers), these assets would be attached to the *3. Pz. Div.*, which had the greatest need for them at the moment.[44] Wöhler also contemplated sending the entire *23. Pz. Div.* to the south, just as soon as *Konrad III* was completed.

One bit of good news was the arrival of the initial elements of *Oberst* Claus Kühl's *356. Inf. Div.* in Várpalota that day, where it would be "at the disposal" of *A. Gr. Balck/6. Armee*. It would take three more days for the entire division to arrive. Neither Wöhler nor Balck had yet agreed on how it would be employed (originally it was to be attached to the *IV. SS-Pz. Korps*), but at least one of the infantry divisions that they had so urgently requested the previous week was finally arriving.

To avoid any confusion and to dispel any misperceptions by any of its subordinate commanders, *A. Gr. Balck/6. Armee* sent out a final message at 11:10 p.m. that evening to *H.Gr. Süd* and all of the units within Balck's command. Stating the intent for the following day, 26 January, the message directed the *IV. SS-Pz.Korps* to "Attack with a concentrated force consisting of the bulk of its tanks, infantry, and artillery forces from the area of Pettend [northwest] in the direction of Acsa to destroy the enemy forces located north of Lake Velencze in cooperation with *III. Pz.Korps.*" It also told *III. Pz.Korps* to "widen the breakthrough area northeast and north of Zámoly gained the previous day and with the addition of the armored group from the *6. Pz.Div.* and newly attached artillery, renew your advance towards Csakvár. For further guidance refer above [to the paragraph concerning the *IV. SS-Pz.Korps*]."[45]

This clearly implied that the *III. Pz.Korps* was to link up with Gille's corps at Acsa, thereby completing the encirclement of the enemy's forces. It was an ambitious task, given the declining combat power of both corps and the unknown strength of the enemy. It remained to be seen whether they could carry it out. Gille, for one, was not happy with his assignment, as has already been noted. An officer who knew Gille later remarked:

> Everyone knew there was tension [between Gille and Balck;] in this case, the *IV. SS-Pz.Korps* was ordered to attack towards a point that looked like a trap. Gille said about this deployment: "It smells like a briefcase" [referring to Stauffenberg's assassination attempt of the previous 20 July]. Gille often quoted this line and everyone around him knew immediately what he meant [i.e.., that the "powers above," in this case Hermann Balck, were always trying to destroy Gille's corps through an act of treachery].[46]

Gille had a point. Although there is no evidence whatsoever that Balck was trying to destroy the *IV. SS-Pz.Korps*, nearly every mission the corps had been assigned since its activation the year before had seemed nearly impossible to carry out—including the three defensive battles east of Warsaw, holding the Wet Triangle, and the two previous relief attempts of Budapest, *Konrad I* and *II*. In each case, the corps had done what was expected but at great cost, and succeeded usually by a hair's breadth.

Friday, 26 January 1945—the ninth day of Operation *Konrad III*—was to prove the offensive's high water mark. Like the past several days, the weather was atrocious, with continuing snowfall alternating with rain, heralding the possible arrival of a short-term thaw. Roads were even worse than usual, with deep snowdrifts in some areas, punctuated by black ice on paved highways and muddy conditions on country roads. However, cross-country movement across the gently rolling fields of the *Puszta* by tracked vehicles remained good, even for the massive 70-ton *Pz. VI* Tiger IIs. Temperatures hovered around the freezing mark throughout most of the day. How Gille's troops endured such living conditions while having to fight against a determined (and equally suffering) enemy can only be imagined, but apparently some degree of "SS Spirit" still prevailed, for when they initiated their attack that day, they pressed it home with commendable enthusiasm.

The corps' attack, which began shortly after midnight following the departure of several *Kampfgruppen* from their forward assembly areas after 10 p.m., made good initial progress. While a portion of the *Totenkopf* Division, *III. Btl./Eicke*, prevented the enemy holding Baraczka from breaking out (though *Oscha.* Berger's Tiger I from *9. Kp./SS-Pz.Rgt. 3* was lost), the rest of the division, along with the *1. Pz.Div.*, surged to the northwest, keeping their right flank oriented on the northwest–southeast course of the Váli River.[47] All told, for this attack the *1. Pz.Div.* reported having 16 operational tanks, assault guns, and tank destroyers, the *Totenkopf* Division seven, *I. Abt./Pz.Rgt. 24* had 11, *s.Pz.Abt. 509* reported nine operational *Pz. VI* Tiger IIs, and the *Wiking* Division contributed seven. These 50 AFVs represented more than half of the *IV. SS-Pz.Korps'* remaining armor strength.[48] At some point during the morning, this number was augmented by the 21 operational assault guns of the *303. Sturm-Art.Brig.*

The corps' evening *Ic* report, which is somewhat understated, summed up the day's key events as follows, starting with the right flank and working its way to the left:

> A battalion-sized enemy attack northeast of Aggszentpéter was unsuccessful. An enemy attack of battalion size was able to throw back our forces that had established a bridgehead on the eastern bank of the Váli River at Kajászó Szent-Péter. Repeated enemy attacks from Vál towards the south were driven off. In the early morning hours, [our forces] threw the enemy out of Vereb and Pazmánd. The enemy launched strong tank-supported counterattacks towards Vereb from the northwest, west, and southwest, but were beaten back after we destroyed 10 of his tanks. At this moment, further enemy attacks are underway. In Pazmánd, our own units were forced to pull back from the center of the town after heavy fighting. In addition, at this same location during the late afternoon, the enemy renewed his counterattacks.[49]

Several things about this report stand out. The first, is that it does not mention two momentous events that occurred that day—a certain action by *K.Gr. Philipp* and the unexpected arrival on the battlefield of the Soviet XXIII Tank Corps.

Including the new areas it was to defend on its left flank stretching as far as the southern outskirts of Baraczka, Ullrich's *Wiking* Division now had to hold an *HKL* almost 25 kilometers long, an unbelievably wide frontage for such an understrength division. The division had already had to give up the *I. Btl./Norge* and the *I. Btl./ Danmark*, leaving its six remaining understrength *Panzergrenadier* battalions to defend it, forcing Ullrich to employ *Hstuf.* Eberhard Heder's *SS-Pio.Btl. 5* in the front line as infantry. The battalion-sized attack against Aggszentpéter mentioned in the evening report was driven off by *Hstuf.* Fritz Kruse's *I. Btl./Germania*. The division's only remaining reserve was *Stubaf.* Wagner's *SS-Pz.Aufkl.Abt. 5*. After sending what was left of the *panzer* regiment to join the attack on the corps' left flank, only two or three assault guns were left to support the infantry. The day's *Ic* report stated that the *Wiking* Division had to fight off several enemy attempts to penetrate its front line that day, an indication that the V Guards Cavalry Corps had no intention of easing the pressure against the Germans' front line along the Váli.

Another aspect of this report worth pointing out is that it downplays the tremendous progress the attack achieved during its initial stages. Initial reports revealed that the troops defending the area from the 63rd Guards Cavalry, 34th Guards Rifle, and 252nd Rifle Divisions—as well as elements of the I Guards Mechanized Corps—were caught completely by surprise. Even the headquarters of the XXI Guards Rifle Corps was nearly overrun at Vereb before all of its headquarters troops could be evacuated. Apparently, the inclement weather as well as the unexpected direction of the German attack had lulled the commanders on the scene into believing that Gille's troops would continue attempting to force a crossing of the Váli to the southeast of their position at Baraczka.

The forward headquarters of the 4th Guards Army was forced to evacuate from Vál when German armored reconnaissance vehicles were spotted on the town's southern outskirts, though the screen line erected by a regiment from the 34th Guards Rifle Division was sufficient to prevent their opponents from breaking through to the town. By daybreak, the *1. Pz.Div.* and the *Totenkopf* Division had advanced as far as 2 kilometers south of Vál on the right, the northern outskirts of Vereb in the center by 6:40 a.m., and the eastern outskirts of Pazmánd on the left by 2:50 a.m., representing an advance nearly 12 kilometers deep and 5 kilometers wide.[50] When they finally recovered from their surprise, the Soviets responded quickly and began to carry out a series of large-scale counterattack against Vereb, the first of which was beaten back after losing 10 tanks, as mentioned in the *Ic* report.

In order to keep providing the advance with continuous artillery fire, Gille ordered *Volks-Art.Korps 403* to begin displacing its firing batteries forward at 8:24 a.m., while leaving sufficient guns behind to support the *Wiking* Division in the area around Baraczka.[51] Not waiting for the corps artillery battalions to reposition themselves, the attacking columns kept moving, drawing fire support from the 10.5cm *Wespen* and 15cm *Hummeln* SP guns in the single armored artillery battalion of each division. The *I. Abt./Pz.Rgt. 24* reached Kajászó Szent Péter on the right flank and encountered a column of Soviet tanks approaching from the north, most likely from the I Guards Mechanized Corps. In the quick night battle that followed, the *Pz. V* Panthers of the battalion knocked out two T-34/85s, one JS-II Stalin, four M4A2 Shermans, and two antitank guns, for the loss of only two of its own tanks. It quickly took possession of the town, though it lacked any infantry of its own to hold it for long.

Hauptsturmführer Eberhard Zech's *SS-Pz.Aufkl.Abt 3*, hugging the western bank of the Váli, followed closely behind *I. Abt./Pz.Rgt. 24* as it moved north along the *Totenkopf* Division's right flank. While *Rittm.* Weidemann's Panther battalion hurried west to rejoin the rest of *K.Gr. Kleffner* after handing over Kajászó Szent Péter to Zech and his troops, Zech's battalion was able to seize the bridge over the Váli River at 3:20 a.m., which it managed to hold on to until mid-afternoon. Shortly after 6 a.m., two T-34s approached the battalion's positions from the village of Tordas, 2 kilometers to the northeast, and were quickly knocked out by the battalion's antitank guns. Although this action was unrelated to the corps' current mission to attack towards the west, the battalion commander was still acting on his previous mission-type orders to seize any bridge over the Váli should the opportunity present itself. After all, this would have proven useful once the direction of movement was shifted back again towards the original objective of Budapest. Gille would later be unfairly criticized for this action.

Once they had reached an imaginary line drawn west of Vál, both *panzer* divisions were supposed to pivot to the west-southwest (i.e., to their left) towards Pazmánd, leaving behind enough forces to hold the exposed right flank between Vál and Vereb. Pazmánd had already fallen to *K.Gr. Huppert* of the *1. Pz.Div.*, while Vereb was taken by *I. Btl./Pz.Gren.Rgt. 113* of *K.Gr. Philipp*. To the right of the *1. Pz.Div.*, *K.Gr. Kleffner* of the *Totenkopf* Division covered the attack's flank as the divisions prepared to make their turn to the west. Kleffner's own attack had initially been met by stiff opposition from a regiment of the 252nd Rifle Division and two battalions of the I Guards Mechanized Corps when it crossed the Budapest–Stuhlweissenburg highway that passed through Pettend shortly after midnight. An eyewitness, *Oberscharführer* Zährl attached to *Panzergruppe Pittschellis*, which composed part of *K.Gr. Kleffner*, later recounted that moment:

> At the head of our column rode *Stubaf.* Pitschellis … we soon crossed the main road at Pettend and began moving north. We immediately began to encounter strong enemy resistance. The Russians [*sic*] had emplaced a lot of antitank guns in strongly fortified positions. We were soon received by extremely heavy defensive fire. Several of our tanks were damaged … The Russian antitank gun crews vainly sought to bring our tanks and *SPWs* to a halt, but their situation was hopeless. Not wishing to be crushed along with their guns, they were forced to abandon them [and fled] … then we found a hole in the Russian defenses. The rest of our *Kampfgruppe* pushed through and in the thickly falling snow was able to drive deeper into the enemy's positions. We shot up enemy tanks and *Paks* [Pakfronts], took prisoners.[52]

The attack by *K.Gr. Kleffner* was so sudden, that *Stubaf.* Ernst Kiklasch's *III. Btl./Totenkopf* was able to capture eight Soviet field guns when it surprised their gun crews, who fled into the darkness. Upon reaching the outskirts of Vál, Kiklasch's battalion encountered stiff enemy resistance from dug-in infantry and heavy mortar fire, which brought its attack to a halt.

This came as a bit of a surprise. In the few hours since the attack began, a mixed task force from the 80th Guards Rifle Division had been rushed forward from the 4th Guards Army reserve to defend this position, emplacing at least one rifle regiment, an antitank artillery regiment, a heavy mortar regiment, and two artillery battalions to block the approaches to Vál. In conjunction with the neighboring 34th Guards Rifle Division, this task force began constructing a new defense line to contain the German attack.[53] The attack by *K.Gr. Eckert*, to the left of Kleffner's battlegroup, was also stuck fast. To make a bad situation worse, the temperature grew warmer, making cross-country movement across the sodden landscape by armored vehicles more difficult.[54]

With the first phase of his attack completed, *Gen.d.Pz.Tr.* Balck, who apparently spent most of the daylight hours with Gille at his forward headquarters, sent a radio message directly to Thünert and Becker later that morning ordering them to begin shifting the direction of their attack to the west by 1 p.m., with the instruction to "proceed directly towards the area north of Lovasberény in order to meet up with the assault spearhead of *Div.Gr. Holste* and destroy the enemy located in the heights between Lovasberény and Pátka [note: this would have been in the vicinity of the assembly area just occupied by the newly arrived 41st Guards Rifle Division]."[55]

This was somewhat unusual, given that Balck was leapfrogging Gille's headquarters and issuing commands directly to his subordinate commands from Gille's own *Vorgeschobener Gefechtstand*, something he acknowledged in his commander's report that evening.[56] This was yet another indicator of Balck's mistrust of the SS general and of his increasing tendency to micromanage, even though the *IV. SS-Pz.Korps'* actions had been in conformance with the operations plan and had been very successful so far that day. Having a field army commander issuing direct orders to his divisions while bypassing the chain of command must have chafed Gille, to say the least, not to mention Balck's tendency to talk to individual battalion commanders by radio while Gille was probably standing next to him.

At any rate, neither division was able to reorient their direction of attack at the moment, both having become embroiled in heavy fighting in Vereb, Pazmánd, and south of Vál. Quick to react, Zakharov had moved to seal off the German penetration later that morning by ordering the 93rd Rifle Division to counterattack the base of the salient at Pettend and Kápolnás Nyék from the west, and the 69th Rifle Division to advance to the Pazmánd area to begin its own attack. The 41st Guards Rifle Division, occupying its new assembly area between Pátka and Lovasberény, was also told to begin immediately launching counterattacks using one regiment against Vereb. The mission of these three rifle divisions was to stop Gille's attack and hold it in place until reinforcements could arrive.

During the see-saw fighting that ensued during the next several hours, both Vereb and Pazmánd changed hands several times. Elements of the *1. Pz.Div.* and *Totenkopf* Division became intermingled, as well as individual tank platoons from *s.Pz.Abt. 509* and *I. Abt./Pz.Rgt. 24*. What had begun as a successful attack soon turned into a slugging match, as individual German platoons, companies, battalions, and regiments found themselves embroiled in myriad one-on-one tank engagements, temporary encirclements, street fighting, and infantry assaults with their opponents. The snow and rain favored neither opponent, hindering observation and limiting the Germans' advantage in long-range tank gunnery. However, as he monitored radio transmissions, Balck gained the impression that the attack was proceeding as planned, even though this bore no relation to the actual situation.

As Kleffner's, Eckert's, Philipp's, Huppert's, and Marcks's *Kampfgruppen* struggled to regroup and hold on to the ground they had gained, losses mounted. The landscape was illuminated by the shimmering flames of burning towns and vehicles. Stricken tanks threw up columns of black smoke, punctuated by the sounds of their exploding ammunition and the screams of crewmembers trapped inside. Artillery fire from both sides impacted in a seemingly indiscriminate manner, killing friend and enemy alike, a sign that Soviet artillery, mortar, and rocket batteries were being committed to the fight. The small bridgehead over the Váli at Kajászó Szént Peter, seized early that morning by *I. Abt./Pz.Rgt. 24* and held since then by *Hstuf.* Zech's *SS-Pz.Aufkl.Abt. 3*, was given up after 3:30 p.m. when the battalion was attacked by the 135th Tank Brigade of the XXIII Tank Corps, forcing it to retreat. Earlier, this *Totenkopf* bridgehead had been the subject of much discussion between Balck and Gille, which will be covered shortly.

At approximately 10 a.m., two tank brigades from Akhmanov's XXIII Tank Corps, the 3rd and 39th, were ordered to advance from their assembly area near Torbágy–Eyték–Páty and destroy the enemy units that had broken through in the vicinity of Vereb. These two brigades were then to establish a new defense line by 2 p.m. between Pazmánd and Kajászó Szent Péter.[57] Earlier that day, the infantry of the 56th Mechanized Brigade had already been committed west of Vál between the task force from the 80th Guards Rifle Division and the regiment from the 41st Guards Rifle Division at the northwest corner of Vereb. All of its battalions were soon decisively engaged with German forces.[58] The entire brigade would soon be tied up in this engagement, upsetting plans for a future counteroffensive, but Tolbukhin believed this was to only way to stop the *IV. SS-Pz.Korps*.

Unaware of these developments, Balck believed that reports of approaching Soviet armored units signified the commitment of a brigade from the understrength II Guards Mechanized Corps, based on the scattered radio reports he had been receiving.[59] When Balck received a message that the *Totenkopf* Division had destroyed 15 Soviet tanks, he was not overly concerned, believing that the attack was continuing to proceed on schedule, and that this had only been a minor engagement. But as the Soviet pressure along the right flank of the attacking columns mounted, the *Totenkopf* Division was forced to divert more of its remaining armor to prevent the approaching Soviet force from interfering with the advance.

German casualties continued to mount. While conducting a midday counterattack in Vereb, the Panther of the commander of *SS-Pz.Rgt. 3*, *Stubaf.* Adolf Pittschellis, was disabled by an antitank gun. While transferring from his damaged *Befehlspanzer* to another in order to continue leading the attack, he was mortally wounded by enemy shell fragments or small-arms fire. He died 20 minutes later before he could be taken to a forward dressing station. His last words were reportedly "Keep on fighting!" Thus, at a critical moment, the *Totenkopf* Division lost another one of its "old-timers," who had been with the division since the beginning and had earned a reputation as a bold, decisive, and imaginative leader.

Like his predecessor Erwin Meierdress, the highly decorated Pittschellis was considered irreplaceable, but the battle would have to continue without him. His immediate successor on the battlefield was *Sturmbannführer* Meier, who was replaced shortly thereafter by *Ostubaf.* Dr Gerhard Adam, who had been serving on the staff of the *IV. SS-Pz.Korps* headquarters for the past 10 days.[60] Although he had commanded the regiment's *II. Abteilung* until 15 January, it must have required a significant mental adjustment on Adam's part to assume command of a *panzer* regiment in the middle of a heated battle. Pittschellis's remains were evacuated and buried in the ever-expanding *IV. SS-Pz.Korps* cemetery in Veszprém on 31 January.

It soon became obvious, even to Balck, that the *1. Pz.Div.* and the *Totenkopf* Division would not be able to begin their turn to the west and northwest at 1 p.m. as he had directed. Due to the mixing up of the two divisions' battlegroups, bad weather, and problems in obtaining fuel and ammunition, it would take several hours for all of the units concerned to reposition themselves in time for the next phase of the battle. In addition, the XXIII Tank Corps was beginning to exert pressure against the northern flank of *IV. SS-Pz.Korps* between Vereb and Vál, as well as between Vál and Kajászó Szént Péter along the Váli. Fighting in Baraczka had not died down either, tying down one battalion from *Totenkopf* Division as well as the leftmost battalion of the *Germania* Regiment.

The omens for continuing the attack towards the west could not have been worse. Nevertheless, Balck complained to *H.Gr. Süd* at 5:50 p.m. that afternoon that the "assault of the *IV. SS-Pz.Korps* towards the west has yet to begin."[61] A little over three hours later, the attack had still not begun, causing Balck to complain yet again to the commander of *H.Gr. Süd* that "the *IV. SS-Pz.Korps* still has not begun moving to the west." Finally, growing frustrated, Balck demanded an explanation from Gille why his attack had been continually delayed. Gille, who had moved forward at this time to be nearer to the fighting, replied that according to battlefield intelligence, his headquarters had determined that "the enemy has ordered his troops [in Vereb, Vál, and Pazmánd] to hold out, because [their] tanks are being brought forward."[62]

Balck was unmoved by this response, believing that Gille was taking counsel of his fears. He then told Gille, "In fact, [enemy] tanks have already appeared, of which a total of 15 have already been destroyed, but this should not have been an obstacle to the continuation of [your] attack; [you] could have pushed deeper into the enemy." That evening, when Balck relayed to Wöhler the substance of this conversation, which he suggested was yet more proof of lack of aggressiveness on Gille's part, Wöhler promised to call Guderian immediately to discuss the matter.[63] One prominent historian, Earl F. Ziemke of the U.S. Army's Center of Military History, summed up the toxic situation existing between the two commanders, channeling Balck 23 years later when he wrote:

> The commanding general, *Obergruppenführer* Herbert Gille, was a well-meaning bumbler who spent most of his time at the front. The chief of staff took a lighthearted attitude toward paper work, so lighthearted that on the 22nd [of January] Balck had to go out himself to find out where the front line was. Wöhler decided to keep Gille, who was at least something of a morale builder, and get rid of his chief of staff.[64]

A "well-meaning bumbler"? Gille had been labelled many things during his career while serving as a leader at the regimental, division, and corps level, but had never been accused of incompetence. His Knight's Cross with Oak Leaves, Swords, and Diamonds was sufficient testimony to that. Unfortunately, Ziemke's overly harsh and unfair evaluation has until now remained the "official" version of Gille's performance as a commander and what occurred on 26 January.

Late that evening, Balck, finally fed up with what he regarded as Gille's intolerably slow "regrouping," ordered the *IV. SS-Pz.Korps* to attack towards the west at 11 p.m. that night, excuses notwithstanding. Had Balck been able to monitor the radio net of *K.Gr. Kleffner* or *Pz.Gr. Pittschellis* earlier that day, he would have heard something quite different that would have challenged his previous perceptions and might even have caused him to reconsider launching the attack to the west at all. The 15 tanks that had been destroyed near Vereb were the vanguard of the onrushing 3rd Tank Brigade of the XXIII Tank Corps, not the remnants of the weary I Guards Mechanized Corps. Their appearance came as a nasty surprise to the *Totenkopf's* tankers. One eyewitness, *Oberscharführer* Zährl of *SS-Pz.Gren.Rgt. 6 Eicke* of *K.Gr. Kleffner*, remembered afterwards:

> Ivan constantly pushed forward with his tanks and infantry against the outskirts of the town [i.e.., Vereb]. Most of our own counterattacks were pinned down by heavy enemy fire. Radio message after radio message was sent and received, stating among other things that 40 [enemy] tanks had been spotted advancing on Vereb.[65]

Nevertheless, Zährl and his comrades were expected to somehow disengage from decisive combat with the enemy, re-form their assault columns, and continue their attack in a new direction, nearly 90 degrees to the west of their present position. It was a tall order, even for the *Totenkopf* Division, which had grown accustomed to impossible assignments.

Later that evening, Balck criticized Gille in yet another official report to *H.Gr. Süd* for "allowing" the *Totenkopf* Division's reconnaissance battalion to establish a bridgehead over the Váli, stating that this constituted a "dissipation" of the division's combat power, carried out without Balck's permission when the battalion was only supposed to screen the division's right flank. In his own lengthy postwar critique of Balck's action, Georg Maier, former *Ia* of the *6. SS-Pz.Armee*, stated that this mission *was* carried out in accordance with accepted tactical doctrine. It was merely one of the several tasks that armored reconnaissance battalions were routinely expected to perform, which was to screen the flanks of a *panzer* division. Seizing an undefended bridge when the opportunity presented itself was a logical move, especially when the original order to relieve Budapest still stood.[66]

That afternoon, at approximately the same time as *K.Gr. Kleffner* was beginning to tangle with the oncoming 3rd Tank Brigade, Gille ordered *K.Gr. Philipp* to carry out a counterattack from the Pazmánd area towards the Váli River south of the town of Vál. Its mission was to disrupt an enemy concentration reported to be assembling there in order to reduce Soviet pressure against *K.Gr. Kleffner* as it was attempting to regroup for the night attack. At that moment, *K.Gr. Philipp* consisted of elements of *I. Abt./Pz.Rgt. 1* and *I. Abt./Pz.Rgt. 24*—with fewer than a dozen Panthers combined—*2. Kp./Pz.Pio.Btl. 37*, and *I. Abt./Pz.Art.Rgt. 73*.[67] What followed was one of the most amazing incidents that characterized a campaign already laden with superlatives.

Rather than stick to his original orders—which stated that upon carrying out his mission, he was to rejoin the rest of the *1. Pz.Div.* for the night attack—Philipp disregarded them and decided to keep pushing to the northeast in the direction of Budapest instead, the original direction of the *Konrad III* offensive. Upon reaching the Váli at a point midway between Vál and Kajászó Szént Peter without encountering any significant enemy resistance, *Oberstleutnant* Philipp observed that the opposite bank was undefended. Because there was no bridge at this point, crossing the river (really a creek here) posed a problem as the hedge-lined opposite bank was too steep for his tanks to negotiate.

Undeterred, Philipp ordered his accompanying combat engineer company to level out a crossing point on that side of the creek using high explosives, which they quickly accomplished. He then ordered his battlegroup to ford the creek, beginning at 4 p.m., and assemble on the other side. Once they had accomplished this task, his *Kampfgruppe* began moving cautiously to the northeast. An element of the XXIII Tank Corps, most likely a tank company from the 39th Tank Brigade, launched a counterattack from the direction of Tordas, but Philipp's tanks quickly shot it up, destroying "a number" of T-34s and M4A2 Shermans.[68]

At long last, it seemed that *K.Gr. Philipp* was finally on its way to relieving Budapest, less than 18 kilometers away. Elements of the *Wiking* and *1. Pz.Div.* were already in radio contact with *Polizei-Kampfgruppe Dörner*, which was defending the southwest corner of the city's defense line. *Standartenführer* Helmut Dorner, in personal contact with Philipp, radioed, "Heartfelt well-wishes for your success and our liberation! Ten thousands of wounded men are awaiting [your arrival]!"[69]

Finally, Philipp was ready to stage his long-awaited *Husarenritt*, although with a much more powerful unit this time and along a much more straightforward route. One participant remembered the mood that day, "If at all possible, the men redoubled their efforts once more, [realizing that] they were only 15–18 kilometers away from the ring around Budapest!"[70] But it was not to be. Less than 2 kilometers west of the village of Gyúrómajor, one of Philipp's headquarters vehicles received a voice radio message that said, "Halt! Cease your attack! New orders to follow."

When Philipp, baffled by the order, directed the radioman to confirm the message to determine its authenticity, the sender—apparently from the headquarters of *A.Gr. Balck/6. Armee*—transmitted a new order that stated, "Return to your jump-off point and assemble near Vereb." Even Gille, the corps commander, who shortly afterwards arrived at the same crossing site to see the situation for himself, could not get the order reversed, having been told by Balck that he was ignorant of the context of the "overall situation," which would have explained why he could not continue pushing towards Budapest. Thus, the last and final opportunity for the relief of the great city passed with hardly a notice. Puzzled and disappointed, Philipp ordered his *Kampfgruppe* to turn around and return to their assembly area near Pettend.[71]

Nowhere in the *Kriegstagebuch* of *H.Gr. Süd* was there mention of this episode, which is curious, considering its significance. Whether the event was accidently omitted or deleted on purpose remains unknown, but earlier in the day, Balck had told Wöhler by field telephone that "any *Husarenritt* towards the northeast in the direction of Budapest would stall because of the II Guards Mechanized Corps assembled east of the Váli."[72] In reality, this was the much more powerful XXIII Tank Corps. Perhaps Balck remembered making this earlier statement when he learned of Philipp's attempt to strike out on his own towards Budapest. Strangely, Philipp was never punished for his unauthorized maneuver. Perhaps it was in keeping with his well-known reputation as a *Draufgänger* (daredevil), or because he wore the Knight's Cross with Oak Leaves. After all, Balck may have thought, why have him arrested for disobedience when no one knew when his skills would be needed again?

While the *IV. SS-Pz.Korps* was reorienting in order to continue its advance late that evening after a hard day of fighting, the complementary attack by *Korpsgruppe Breith/ III. Pz.Korps* got off to a rocky start. On Breith's right flank, *SS-Rgt. Ney* was tasked with seizing Hill 182, which meant attacking 5 kilometers towards Pákozd through the hilly wine-growing country that lay between that town and Stuhlweissenburg. As it began its advance, Ney's regiment of nearly 2,000 men was first brought up short by the effective defense of the 69th Rifle Division, which had strongly fortified its position four days after retreating from the latter town. Despite repeated attempts, Ney's SS regiment—now composed of three battalions of Hungarian volunteers—was driven back each time with heavy losses, before a final attack reached the top of Hill 182, where they dug in. One German officer, *Ustuf.* Erich Kernmayr, whose company was with the Hungarian regiment, afterwards reported:

> The vineyard became a practical volcano. Dozens of Soviet guns had apparently [pre-registered] their fire earlier and [their shell bursts] covered the top of these hills in dust and smoke. The Hungarian *Waffen-SS* suffered extremely heavy losses because they had only been able to partially dig themselves in; and for better or worse, the hill had to be abandoned again.[73]

Although Ney's troops were able to reach the summit of their objective, they were unable to hold it for long. The following day, the hill changed hands four times before the Hungarians were finally forced to withdraw after enduring several artillery-supported enemy counterattacks. *Untersturmführer* Kernmayr and his German SS men also pulled out; he and his troops from *SS-Kampfpropaganda-Zug Ungarn* were being sent elsewhere.

North of Stuhlweissenburg, the *23. Pz.Div.*, with its *K.Gr. Kujacinski* in the lead, attempted to penetrate the main defense line of the 84th Rifle Division beginning at 1:50 p.m. Departing from the village of Gyulamajor, *Hptm.* Norbert Kujacinski's battlegroup, along with six tanks from *Pz.Rgt. 23* and three tank destroyers from *Pz.Jäg.Abt. 128*, was tasked with supporting the neighboring attack of the *4. Kav. Brig.* by seizing the heights of Talliánmajor. After advancing less than 3 kilometers, Kujacinski's attack was blocked by heavy defensive fire from a *Pakfront*. After knocking out five antitank guns within a few minutes, the advance continued until it was finally brought to a halt when it was ambushed from both sides near Fülöpmajor. After losing two tanks destroyed and five more damaged to well-aimed antitank-gun fire, the battlegroup was forced to withdraw and return to its original starting line.

The corps' main effort by the *4. Kav.Brig.* southeast of Zámoly fared no better. A *Kampfgruppe* built around *s.Pz.Abt. 503 FHH*, composed of its three remaining operational *Pz. VI* Tiger IIs, 11 *Pz. V* Panthers, and four Hungarian SP antiaircraft guns—along with the Hungarian *Schützen-Btl. 5*, a *Panzergrenadier* battalion from the *23. Pz.Div.*, and two companies of Hungarian combat engineers—crossed the line of departure at 2 p.m. with the initial objective being the village of Borbálamajor, where it would link up in the vicinity with *K.Gr. Kujacinski*.

After breaking through the outer Soviet defense line and gaining several hundred meters of ground, *Kampfgruppe FHH*, led by *Hauptmann* von Diest-Körber, encountered the enemy's main defense line, held by troops from the 223rd Rifle Division, reinforced by elements of the 41st Guards Rifle Division. Here, the battlegroup faced several *Pakfronts*, which fought the Germans and Hungarians to a standstill. After defending the ground gained, the *Kampfgruppe's* commander decided that a further advance was impossible, so at 10 p.m. he ordered his men to withdraw to their starting line. With the failure of these attacks, German and Hungarian hopes that *Korpsgruppe Breith/III. Pz.Korps'* attack would advance far enough to meet the approaching spearheads of the *IV. SS-Pz.Korps* quickly began to fade.

On the left of the *4. Kav.Brig.*, the attack by the Hungarian *2. Pz.Div.* fared somewhat better, managing to push the front line northeast of Zámoly forward 2 kilometers and advancing as far as Forna Puszta before it stopped that evening. On the left boundary of *Korpsgruppe Breith/III. Pz.Korps*, the Hungarian *VIII. Armee-Korps'* attack gained some ground, as its *1. Hus.Div.* continued its push into the Vértes Mountains to complete its heretofore-successful occupation of the eastern slopes. After taking the village of Köhányás Puszta from a battalion from the 52nd Rifle Division, the cavalrymen managed to advance a further 2 kilometers before finally being stopped by an enemy counterattack. An adjacent attack by the attached Hungarian *Inf.Rgt. 42* fought its way into the neighboring village of Vérteskozma, but was unable to hold it and was soon forced to withdraw.[74]

Overall, the achievements of *Korpsgruppe Breith* that day—despite the performance of its troops—were much less than expected, and far less than what the situation required. In truth, the German units were far below their authorized strength in men and matériel, and exhausted after nearly four weeks of non-stop fighting, so the corps' failure should have come as a surprise to no one, especially Hermann Balck. The Hungarian troops, while spirited and motivated by their desire to regain lost home territory, lacked sufficient heavy weapons to achieve much more than what they already had, especially when facing an opponent numerically equal and far better equipped with weaponry than they were. And, of course, the steadfast defense of divisions of the Soviet XX and XXI Guards Corps and LVIII Rifle Corps deserve credit for defeating every German and Hungarian attempt to close the gap separating their two attacking *panzer* corps.

In the *I. Kav.Korps* sector, the *6. Pz.Div.*, minus its *Panzergruppe* (which was in transit to join up with the *III. Pz.Korps*), continued its advance towards the railway crossing 6 kilometers southeast of Felsőgalla, but was stopped by a battalion-sized counterattack in the afternoon, most likely carried out by elements of the 40th Guards Rifle Division. To the left of the *6. Pz.Div.*, the *3. Kav.Brig.* had transitioned to the defense, having gained no ground in the face of fierce enemy opposition the previous day. Unable to advance, it dug in and prepared to defend the small amount of territory that it had purchased at such great cost. Its only contribution to the fighting that day was to report the sighting of enemy movement out of an assembly area several kilometers southeast of Mány, which it tried to disperse with artillery fire. Whether the brigade's commander, *Oberst* von der Groeben, knew it or not, his troops were probably observing the departure of the XXIII Tank Corps as it began moving towards the south to attack the *IV. SS-Pz.Korps*.

On Harteneck's far left, the *96. Inf.Div.* successfully fought off two more company-sized attempts to retake Sarisap, while along the Danube, the *711. Inf.Div.* reported that Soviet forces, most likely from the X Guards Rifle Corps, had pushed in the division's outpost line northwest of Pilisszentlélek but had finally been halted at its *Hauptkampflinie*. Whether this signified the renewal of offensive activity by the 46th Army was unknown.

To the right of the *IV. SS-Pz.Korps*, the Hungarian *3. Armee* reported little of consequence occurring along the *Sió-Abschnitt* that day, though there were several company-sized engagements fought at Sáregres and Simontornya. The *3. Pz.Div.* was involved in heavy fighting east of the Sárviz Canal between Sárszent Miklós and Dunapentele. Confronted by three Soviet corps apparently carrying out strong combat patrols sent to probe German positions, Söth's troops were hard pressed to maintain contact with one another. Soviet troops were reported once again to have infiltrated Sár Szentmiklós, compelling the division to launch a counterattack that managed to throw them out by nightfall. Northeast of the village of Fejér Alap, a large concentration of enemy troops was observed assembling, but was successfully dispersed by artillery fire from *Pz.Art.Rgt. 75*.

Kampfgruppe Weymann, where most of the division's remaining armor was concentrated, carried out an attack from Herczegfalva against an enemy concentration located a few kilometers southwest of Szarvaspuszta, but became entangled in an extensive minefield backed up by a *Pakfront*. After his battlegroup had suffered heavy losses and his own command vehicle was knocked out by a direct hit, *Oberstlt.* Weymann was forced to order a withdrawal after destroying two Soviet assault guns and eight antitank guns. On the division's left between Herczegfalva and Dunapentele, a Soviet breakthrough at Nagyvenyim was thrown back and the hole in the line plugged up once again. While the efforts of the *3. Pz.Div.* to secure the southern flank of *A.Gr. Balck/6. Armee* were overall successful, the division's eroding strength made it unlikely that it would be able to hold the line should the three Soviet corps assembled opposite its position transition from the defense to a general offensive.

Already outnumbered by at least three-to-one, Söth's division simply lacked the combat power to do anything more than maintain a thin screening line. Fully aware of the division's situation, Balck had already begun taking steps to bolster its ability to withstand a large-scale attack. In addition to the attachment of the German antitank assets already mentioned, the commander of *A.Gr. Balck* was also planning to send it and the *Wiking* Division several *Luftwaffe* heavy *Flak* battalions from the *15. Flak-Div.* to serve in a ground combat role with their 8.8cm guns, as well as two Hungarian assault gun companies to reinforce their *25. Inf.Div.* Another event of consequence that day was the transfer of administrative and logistics responsibility from the *IV. SS-Pz.Korps* to the Hungarian *3. Armee*, which finally freed Hans Scharf, Gille's *Quartiermeister*, from the worry of having to supply the *3. Pz.Div.* This duty would now become the responsibility of the German liaison staff serving at Heszlényi's headquarters at Balatonfüzfő.

The *IX. SS-Geb.Korps* reported that during the previous evening, Soviet troops were able to achieve two deep breakthroughs in the western and northwestern portions of the pocket. A smaller attack launched against the southern portion of Budapest was unsuccessful. Throughout the day, the 46th Army stepped up its attacks against the entire perimeter of the pocket, in what seemed an obvious attempt to wipe it out once and for all. During the course of the day, the attackers were able to achieve a number of local breakthroughs, though were unsuccessful in gaining their larger objective. Pfeffer-Wildenbruch ordered counterattacks along the line to restore the situation, though the overall results of these were unknown by the evening reporting deadline.[75]

Once again, terrible flying weather limited the air operations of both sides. That night, the transports of *Luftflotte 4* were able to deliver only 24.4 metric tons of supplies over Budapest, not nearly enough. Muddy airfields and shortage of aviation fuel also contributed to the air fleet's inability to generate enough sorties to support the attacking corps, but German and Hungarian squadrons did manage to launch a number of ground-attack strikes against Soviet units. *Luftflotte 4* officially reported shooting up 19 Soviet aircraft on the ground and downing one in air-to-air combat, with 25 enemy vehicles destroyed in *Stuka* and fighter-bomber attacks. While the Red Air Force did manage to fly a number of sorties that day, the number was not given in official Soviet reports, though the *IV. SS-Pz.Korps* reported that its troops had been attacked by up to 70 IL-2s *Sturmoviks* and 22 fighter-bombers.[76] German aerial reconnaissance missions for the most part were unable to take off that day, and the few sorties that were flown were inconclusive. Once again, any opportunity to spot the approach of the XXIII Tank Corps and CIV Rifle Corps was lost.

In this situation, an accurate assessment of enemy intentions and capability became critically important, but with so few reconnaissance sorties being flown, both *H.Gr. Süd* and *A.Gr. Balck/6. Armee* were nearly blind, other than what front-line observations, POW interrogations, radio intercepts, and agents could provide. Apparently, the 4th Guards Army was maintaining strict radio listening silence, because German monitoring stations failed to pick up anything concerning the movement of Soviet reserves. In essence, by bringing the XXIII Tank Corps and CIV Rifle Corps into position northeast of the *IV. SS-Pz.Korps* undetected, Tolbukhin had managed to achieve a level of operational surprise that would put paid to any further German efforts to relieve Budapest.

The intelligence assessment of the evening of 26 January, written to inform command staff over anticipated enemy activity for the following day, was not completely incorrect though. *Hauptmann* von Pander, speaking for the *A.Gr. Ic*, *Oberstlt.* Wüstenberg, wrote:

> Between Lake Balaton and the Danube the enemy's situation and intentions are unchanged. According to a *Richard-Meldung*, the VII Mechanized Corps, whose quick reconstitution appears to have been completed, has been identified as moving across the Danube at Dunaföldvar. Between the Váli sector and Lake Velencze, the enemy, with divisions coming from the Vértes Mountains and from the area north of Lake Velencze, could not prevent a breakthrough by our attack, which surprised him by going to the northwest. During the day, according to an *Arno-Meldung* [another agent operating behind Soviet lines], newly identified enemy forces, including the II Guard Mechanized Corps approaching from the areas of Pákozd and Bicske, carried out several counter-attacks [against the *IV. SS-Pz.Korps*], demonstrating the enemy's plans to throw back our own attacking groups. Between Lake Velencze and the Danube, our own attacks could not gain any significant ground against the hard-fighting, tenacious enemy … The enemy's attacks against Budapest are increasing in intensity, evidence of his intention to smash our forces there as quickly as possible and to clear then out of his rear areas.[77]

What this assessment got wrong was that it completely missed the arrival of the XXIII Tank Corps and CIV Rifle Corps. Ironically, the tank corps had been mentioned three times during the evening before in the daily operations summary of *H.Gr. Süd*. With each mention, the designation of the corps had been correctly written using Roman numerals as "*XXIII Pz.Korps.*"

However, concerning this and the subsequent two mentions, a staff officer or *Ia Schreiber* (assistant operations NCO) within the army group's *Führungsabteilung* had crossed out "XXIII" and overwrote in pencil "*XVIII Pz.Korps*," which was known to be located to the south of Herczegfalva. By doing so, not once but three times, *H.Gr. Süd* inadvertently failed to gain a proper appreciation of the danger that the arrival of this corps posed to the *IV. SS-Pz.Korps* attack; having failed to recognize the threat, it had no cause to warn *A.Gr. Balck* and Gille's corps.[78] Thus, when the XXIII Tank Corps and its four brigades began moving out of its assembly area late in the morning and early afternoon of 26 January with over 165 tanks and self-propelled guns, it would have decisive effect on the course of *Konrad III*.[79] As previously mentioned, it had already begun to have an impact that afternoon, when General Zakharov was forced to prematurely commit three of its brigades against the *Totenkopf* Division west and south of Vál.

Soviet plans and intentions did not immediately change between 25 and 26 January, despite the threat of encirclement. The three corps of the 4th Guards Army (the XX and XXI Guards Corps and LXVIII Rifle Corps) were standing fast as ordered, between Pákozd and Szár. Although they had been forced to give up a few kilometers of ground to the *III. Pz.Korps*, the three corps and supporting artillery had inflicted heavy losses on *Div.Gr. Holste*, the *23. Pz.Div.*, and *SS-Rgt. Ney*, so much so that the *III. Pz.Korps'* remaining offensive strength had been bled away in successive minefields, antitank-gun belts, and crushing artillery fire.

In contrast, the attack to the northwest by the two *panzer* divisions of the *IV. SS-Pz.Korps* had come as a complete surprise to the commander of the 4th Guards Army, but the Germans' timetable was disrupted later than day when *Gen.d.Pz. Tr.* Balck insisted that the *1. Pz.Div.* and *Totenkopf* Division stop their hitherto successful advance and turn to the west and southwest instead in a quixotic attempt to link up with the *III. Pz.Korps* across 25 kilometers of heavily defended ground.

The ensuing delay as the two divisions struggled to re-orient their direction of attack bought the time that Tolbukhin needed to order Zakharov to bring the XXIII Tank Corps out of its assembly area and conduct a counterattack that slowed Gille's advance first to a crawl, then to a complete stop. Additional units from this corps would be brought forward that evening and the following morning to continue to fix and attrite Gille's forces. Balck unwittingly assisted the Soviets for a second time that day when he ordered *K.Gr. Philipp* to cease its drive towards Budapest and abandon its bridgehead over the Váli, thereby eliminating the last hope of ever rescuing the encircled garrison.

The premature commitment of Lt.Gen. Akhmanov's XXIII Tank Corps on 26 January delayed Tolbukhin's counteroffensive for three days. By the time it finally began on 29 January, the corps had already lost nearly half of its armor strength. However, the T-34s and M4A2 Shermans destroyed by the *IV. SS-Pz.Korps* between 26 and 28 January could soon be replaced, while those of Gille's corps could not. In contrast, none of the events occurring between the Váli River and Lake Velencze had any impact on the preparations for the attack against the southern flank of *A.Gr.*

Balck/6. Armee. While the 4th Guards Army fought the Germans and Hungarians to a standstill west of the Váli and put the finishing touches to the plan for its counteroffensive, the 57th Army with its three corps, soon to be joined by a fourth, was preparing to launch its own. By this point in the battle, not only did Marshal Tolbukhin and his army commanders begin to believe that they had stopped the last German relief of Budapest, but that the moment was coming soon when they would be able to drive them out of Hungary forever.

Reviewing the day's events, Balck was frustrated—not only with what he perceived as Gille's bungling of the attack, but with the apparent inability of *Korpsgruppe Breith/III. Pz.Korps* to achieve any measurable progress, though characteristically he did not express any criticism against Breith himself. Gille's attack towards Acsa and Zámoly was scheduled to resume at 11 p.m. that evening, although no one knew that this plan had already been overcome by events on the ground. Unaccountably, Balck still regarded the tank-heavy counterattacks from Vál against the right flank of the *Totenkopf* Division as a minor nuisance, despite all the evidence to the contrary, including the destruction of 15 Soviet tanks in a single engagement and a report about the approach of 40 more.

The combat power of Gille's corps had ebbed considerably since the previous day; a number of its remaining armored fighting vehicles had been destroyed or damaged during the fighting, while many had broken down or run out of fuel. What had saved the day on 26 January was the high morale and professionalism of the men of the three divisions in the *IV. SS-Pz.Korps*, who willingly sacrificed themselves towards what they saw as a worthy goal: the rescue of the men trapped in Budapest. Not even Balck's order to turn the direction of the attack to the west had staunched their enthusiasm, although Gille, Schönfelder, and many other SS commanders in the corps found it incomprehensible.

Another development that occurred on 26 January was the determination by both Wöhler and Balck that Gille was unsuited for the position of corps commander and that his chief of staff was incompetent. Wöhler even went so far as to write up a letter to be inserted into the official record of *H.Gr. Süd* concerning his dealings with Gille between 24 and 26 January and the reasons why he thought Gille needed to be relieved. None of the examples mentioned rose to the level where relief of command was the appropriate course of action, though Wöhler might have omitted those that did. Wöhler's main concern appears to be that Gille seemed unenthusiastic about attacking towards the west to link up with the *III. Pz.Korps*, had been slow in regrouping his corps, and allegedly did not understand that his forces needed to be concentrated for "a single blow against a single objective."

Yet neither Wöhler nor Balck seem to have taken into account Gille's growing concern about the significance of the sudden appearance of a large amount of enemy armor on his right flank. Gille probably had a better understanding than either Wöhler or Balck of what could be achieved with the rapidly dwindling force under his command. He also likely knew how Balck's (and Wöhler's) decision to deviate from the original plan had placed the *IV. SS-Pz.Korps* in an untenable situation. Gille and his chief of staff both adhered to their belief that the most important objective was still the relief of the Budapest garrison. Both knew that the diversion of their force towards the achievement of secondary gains, which were likely unobtainable, would further weaken the corps to the point where any relief of Budapest became impossible and its own survival would be in doubt.

Nevertheless, in his memorandum for the record in which he summarized his thoughts about Gille's performance, Wöhler concluded by stating his overall impression of the commander of the *IV. SS-Pz.Korps*:

> *SS-Obergruppenführer* Gille is not corps commander material. However, since he is very brave and is always on the move every day for hours on end, I would rather not recommend that he be relieved of command. His Chief of Staff, *SS-Obersturmbannführer* Schönfelder, is not suitable for his position. Staff work at the corps headquarters is poor. The reporting and command and control structures are not sufficient for moderate demands. For that reason, I must recommend that Schönfelder be relieved of his duties, as the upcoming missions are entirely too important.

Wöhler did not merely file this memorandum in the *H.Gr. Süd* war diary for posterity; he followed up by calling Guderian at *OKH* headquarters that evening to insist that Schönfelder be fired. Guderian told him that he would look into the matter, promising to investigate whether or not a change in the command structure of the *IV. SS-Pz.Korps* was warranted.[80]

Of course, since Gille and Schönfelder were both SS officers, jurisdiction in this matter lay solely in the hands of Heinrich Himmler, as head of the SS and the *Ersatzheer*, whose antipathy towards the "bourgeois" *Heer* general officer corps was well known. Assuming that Guderian did talk to the *Reichsführer-SS* about this matter (Guderian does not mention this event in his memoirs), Himmler took no action whatsoever and the two officers remained in their positions until the end of the war. This was not to be the last time that Balck would attempt to rid himself of his two troublesome subordinates.[81]

An eyewitness to the increasing friction between Balck and Gille, and himself a target of Balck's ire, Manfred Schönfelder painted a vivid portrayal of their relationship when he wrote after the war that Gille was being made the scapegoat for Balck's failure to relieve Budapest:

> [D]ifferences in intentions between Balck and Gille arose. Gille wanted to push on to Budapest, while Balck first wanted to destroy the enemy to the west. Balck accused Gille of not carrying out orders, an action bordering on disobedience, and held him responsible for the situation that has arisen on the northern front of the *Armeegruppe*. Balck's aversion against the leadership of the *IV. SS-Pz.Korps* was finally expressed in a memorandum in the *KTB* of the *Heeresgruppe*, which bore the signature of Wöhler.[82]

Interestingly, Gille did not learn about any of these attempts to replace him until after the war, since it was all being done behind his back and without his knowledge.

Neither did Gille's own notes mention anything about the incident. By this point, he had probably already become accustomed to Balck's carping and frequent overreaching of his authority, but there was little he could do about it. If Gille had ever complained directly to Himmler about the situation, as Balck alleged in his memoirs, no records of any such conversations are known to have survived.

But one other detail does stand out, one that Balck most likely was not aware of when he composed his memoirs in the late 1970s. If he had, he probably would have "remembered" the events somewhat differently. This concerns the transcriptions of two face-to-face conversations that took place between Balck and Gille on 26 January at 2:10 p.m. and 3 p.m. in the command post of the *IV. SS-Pz.Korps* at Seregélyes. It is not known who took the notes of the conversations, but it was most likely one of Gille's staff officers or his *Ia Schreiber*, *Oscha*. Schlemmer. These records were part of the corps' war diary captured by the Red Army a week later.

The first conversation at 2:10 p.m. concerned the bridgehead at Kajászó Szént Péter, which at that time was still being held by Zech's *SS-Pz.Aufkl.Abt. 3*. While both men were looking at the situation map in Gille's headquarters, the discussion that took place was recorded as follows:

> Balck: We must deal with the situation here [points to the map]. This is of vital importance. What is the situation here [at Kajászó Szént Péter]?
> Gille: This bridge, contrary to initial reports, is passable for tanks. We have a small bridgehead there.
> Balck rejoined: That is very good and very important. How is your advance going in this sector [i.e., the attack towards the west]?
> Gille: Contact was established between both *Kampfgruppen* at 12:10 p.m. The last dispatch arrived at 1:50 p.m.
> Balck, concluding: We must break through here. This will decide everything, otherwise we will lose. It is a shame that we wasted half a day here.[83]

What is remarkable about this conversation is that at that point in time, Balck did not criticize Gille's decision to keep the bridgehead at all (which was lost a few hours later), telling him that it was "very good and very important."

After all, the *Totenkopf* Division had been assigned the mission on 25 January by the *IV. SS-Pz.Korps* to conduct a reconnaissance over the Váli River towards the east and block any crossing points. A copy of this order had been sent to *A.Gr. Balck/6. Armee* headquarters the same day and entered into the official records as an *Anlage* (exhibit) in the *Kriegstagebuch* maintained by Balck's *Ia, Oberstlt.* Otto Marcks. However, later that evening in his conversation with Wöhler, Balck castigated Gille for dispersing his forces and disobeying orders by establishing a bridgehead at Kajászó Szént Péter, and wrote in his memoirs that Gille was "incapable of understanding" the importance of the attack to the west, as previously mentioned.[84]

The other conversation, though much longer, is even more illuminating. although too lengthy to be reproduced here, it is obvious that Balck thought that the *IV.*

SS-Pz.Korps was far stronger than it actually was. Besides the two principals, during this conversation they were joined by Schönfelder, Fritz Rentrop (the corps *Ia*), and Herbert Jankuhn (the corps *Ic*); in other words, the principal staff officers of the corps' *Führungsquartet*. In one exchange, Gille told Balck that the corps had not yet been able to determine the size and scope of the enemy forces massing on his right flank, but said "the enemy attempted a massive tank attack at 1:10 p.m. south of Vál."

Incredibly, this drew no request by Balck for more information about this alarming and highly significant report, and instead he asked Gille about the strength of the *1. Pz.Div.*, before adding, "You [i.e., *IV. SS-Pz.Korps*] have quite a significant body of troops." Gille countered this by saying, in a somewhat astonished manner, "With battalions of 80 men?" Somewhat cavalierly, Balck told him to "take soldiers away from the supply troops at once," implying that they should be assigned to the infantry.

When Schönfelder interjected that this would cripple the divisions' ability to sustain the fighting troops, Balck simply said, "I have seen personally that there are plenty of people in the *Nachschubtruppen*. These are young and tough." When both Gille and Schönfelder brought up the topic of relieving Budapest and the need to get through to it quickly, the *Armeegruppe* commander said authoritatively, "The *Führer* has already thought of these things, and has given out the order afterwards, therefore we need to act accordingly ... The *Führer* can only decide upon the facts that are reported to him."

Gille responded, "We have calculated [that our spearhead—i.e., *K.Gr. Philipp*] is only 14 kilometers away [from the city]." After a series of back-and-forth questions, Balck said, "I will do everything the *Führer* asks me to, and we shall at first complete this task here [i.e., the attack to the west]." To which Gille responded, in his last recorded remark, "Anyway, we are not going to get out of this nicely." "Nobody ever gets out of fighting nicely," replied Balck.[85]

For all the noble remarks in his memoirs about the need for commanders to act based on the dictates of their conscience, to make decisions based on the facts of the actual situation on the ground and in accordance with his instincts formed by battlefield experience and years of training, that Balck would justify his actions by quoting orders emanating from the *Führer* is at the very least ironic and provides an unfiltered view into his real character. It is all the more ironic that Balck was justifying his decision in such a manner in front of a gathering of senior officers of the *Waffen-SS*, who knew a thing or two about obedience to the *Führer*.

Left unsaid was any reference by Balck to the 23 January 1945 *Führerbefehl* that required unquestioning adherence to Hitler's orders at every level of command, under threat of draconian punishment. Oddly, on the single occasion when Balck mentions this order in his memoirs 35 years later, he dismissed it with the remark, "that [*Führer*] order had no effect whatsoever because it could not be implemented in the rapidly changing situations. It remained nothing but a piece of printed paper. I cannot remember that it ever played any role in our decisions."[86] It must be said that, based on the substance of the conversation recorded in Gille's headquarters on 26 January 1945, it most certainly did, at least in this case.

One last comment about this episode concerns Gille's seeming reluctance to change the direction of his attack. To Balck, this appeared to be little more than a deliberate attempt to forestall the attack. It is also possible that Gille had an instinctive feeling for what was about to happen, unlike Balck, who had discounted the possibility of a Soviet response. All of the warnings that Gille's command post had received that day from the front-line units, backed up by Gille's own personal observations on the scene, indicated that something big was about to happen on the battlefield between Vál and Vereb. At the time, he did not know that it was the XXIII Tank Corps heading his way (the intelligence chiefs still believed it was the much weaker II Guards Mechanized Corps). However, there had been too many sightings of approaching enemy forces, including large numbers of tanks and a steadily increasing volume of artillery fire, for Gille to believe anything other than that a major attack was about to unfold against what would be his exposed right flank should the *IV. SS-Pz.Korps* resume its attack to the west that evening.

Gille's instincts probably also led him to believe that whatever the enemy was about to throw at him, he would need everything at his disposal to counter it. In line with this thinking, he also must have felt in his bones that the attack towards the *III. Pz.Korps* stood no chance of success whatsoever and would achieve nothing except the further depletion of his already weakened forces or, even worse, might lead to Gille's corps being cut in half, which was Tolbukhin's stated intent. Since Gille could not openly disobey a direct order from Balck, all he could do to achieve the ends he sought was to drag out and delay the "repositioning" of his corps as long as possible, in the hope that it would buy the time needed to position his troops as best he could before the Soviet hammer blow fell. However, the reasoning behind Gille's actions must remain speculative, since he did not write about this incident after the war and Schönfelder's account only alludes to, but does not confirm, this unspoken decision.

Meanwhile, at the headquarters of *H.Gr. Süd*, besides interposing himself into the personnel issues of *A.Gr. Balck, Gen.d.Inf.* Wöhler had other concerns that were just as important as the fighting north of Lake Velencze. He had been frequently in contact with Guderian that day concerning several other issues, such as what to do concerning the developing situation southeast of Lake Balaton, where intelligence indicated that the 57th Army was preparing an offensive against the Hungarian *3. Armee* and the right flank of the *IV. SS-Pz.Korps*. He was also concerned about what was going on north of the Danube, where the formation holding his left flank, *Gen.d.Pz.Tr.* Hans Kreysing's *8. Armee*, faced an uncertain situation.

Speaking to Guderian, Wöhler expressed his concern that a rapid relief of Budapest was no longer possible, given that *Konrad III* was taking far longer than anticipated, agreeing with Balck that Gille's "delay" had cost 36 hours. If the attack towards Zámoly did succeed, Wöhler envisioned attaching the *23. Pz.Div.* to the *IV. SS-Pz.Korps* to allow the relief operation to resume, an unspoken admission that the joint attack towards Zámoly/Acsa by the *III. Pz.Korps* and *IV. SS-Pz.Korps* was probably already doomed to fail; without the *23. Pz.Div.*, the *III. Pz.Korps* did not have sufficient combat power to continue its attack.

For his part, Guderian thought this attack would be a waste of effort anyway, leaving the *H.Gr. Süd* commander with the impression that his superior at *OKH* had little confidence that the pincer operation by the *III. Pz.Korps* and *IV. SS-Pz.Korps* stood any chance of success. Rather, Guderian proposed that a new plan should be tried instead, one that involved an attack by *A.Gr. Balck/6. Armee* to the *south* in conjunction with one to the east by the *2. Pz.Armee*, with the rather ambitious goal of enveloping and destroying the 57th Army.

If successful, this plan—a resurrection of the since-cancelled *Unternehmen Eisbrecher*—would eliminate any threat to *H.Gr. Süd*'s southern flank. Then, once this task was completed, the relief attack towards Budapest could recommence. Wöhler asked Guderian whether the relief attack was still a priority, to which the chief of staff of the *OKH* replied in an affirmative manner, but Guderian added that *H.Gr. Süd* should still begin developing its plan for the southern attack immediately. Given that this process might take a week or more to plan and even more to carry out, it is worth pondering whether Guderian himself had also already written off Budapest by this point.[87]

The only other newsworthy event of that day was that Balck had decided to send the then-arriving *356. Inf.Div.* from Várpalota to Stuhlweissenburg to relieve the *23. Pz.Div.* This division would not be used to reinforce the *Konrad III* offensive after all, for it had arrived too late. Had it arrived by 18 January, as was originally intended, it would have significantly assisted the attacks by both the *Totenkopf* and *Wiking* Divisions, relieving them of the necessity of diverting significant portions of their combat power to mop up bypassed Soviet units. Instead, it would merely allow the *23. Pz.Div.* to be relieved in the line to be used elsewhere.

In turn, this would have allowed the SS divisions to concentrate more of their forces towards their objectives and increase the pace of the offensive. Since the *356. Inf.Div.* could not arrive any sooner than it did, through no fault of its own, the pending relief in place of the *23. Pz.Div.* signified the end of any effective participation in the relief of Budapest by the *III. Pz.Korps*. Where it would be used next had only been hinted at. Thus passed the remainder of 26 January, as the units of the *IV. SS-Pz.Korps* struggled to get into position to continue their now-pointless attack towards the west.

That evening and into the early morning, the *1. Pz.Div.* and *Totenkopf* Division struggled to reposition, rearm, and refuel their battalions in time for the renewed attack. The deadline of 11 p.m. came and went, but still there was no attack. As they carried out their last-minute preparations, at the same time both divisions had to repel Soviet attacks or carry out local counterattacks to retake their jump-off positions. On the right flank of *A. Gr. Balck/6. Armee* in the area of operations of the Hungarian *3. Armee*, the Soviet 57th Army began its anticipated counteroffensive. Saturday, 27 January was to prove a fateful day for the continuation of *Konrad III* and the relief of Budapest.

Worse weather conditions for launching any kind of large-scale offensive operation could not be imagined. On the night of 26/27 January, temperatures dropped as low as 25 degrees Fahrenheit (–3 degrees Centigrade) and over a foot of snow fell, accumulating in drifts several feet deep. Visibility was severely limited and most of the fighting that day occurred during near-blizzard conditions. On the far left flank of *A. Gr. Balck*, held by the severely weakened *711. Inf.Div.*, the Danube had frozen solid between Gran and Sütto to a thickness that would allow vehicular traffic, including light armor. Oddly, the 7th Guards Army on the north bank of the river (the 6th Guards Tank Army was in the process of pulling out by this point) took no action, other than sending foot patrols across the river during the night. Despite the momentary peaceful situation in the north, fighting throughout the rest of the *A. Gr. Balck/6. Armee Kampfraum* was extremely heavy.

In the *IV. SS-Pz.Korps* area of operations, the evening *Ic* report for 27 January was somewhat more descriptive than the previous day's. Reflecting the hard fighting the corps experienced that day, Jankuhn wrote:

> Southeast of Aggszentpéter, the enemy in regimental strength was able to force a 1.5 kilometer deep breakthrough that was sealed off; our defending forces were still in the process of clearing it out at the reporting deadline. Along the frontal arc of our penetration northeast of Lake Velencze, the enemy carried out a number of powerful tank attacks throughout the day. In Baraczka, the enemy was able to extend his control of the town as far as the southeast corner; Pettend changed hands twice ... Attacks along both sides of Kajászó Szent Peter north of F. Psz. Pettend by the enemy were partially repulsed by our own counterattacks. The ownership of Vereb was disputed several times, with varying degrees of success; Pazmánd was cleared of the enemy. In hard fighting throughout the course of the day, 44 enemy tanks were knocked out [note: this turned out to be an understatement].[88]

This report, though correct, barely conveys the dramatic events of the day. It seemed as if the commander of the Third Ukrainian Front also wanted to completely "clean things up" west of the Danube, but not in the way that Hitler or the commander of *A. Gr. Balck/6. Armee* had previously envisioned. The corps chief of staff later merely wrote, "The *IV. SS-Pz.Korps* alone knocked out 122 enemy tanks on 27 January," a stark expression of what happened that day.[89]

Before the assault by the *1. Pz.Div.* and *Totenkopf* to the northwest could even get underway, the Soviets launched an attack after midnight from Baraczka, spearheaded by the newly arrived 34th Rifle Division, assisted by the remnants of the 252nd Rifle Division and 11th Guards Cavalry Division. This attack struck the left flank of the *Wiking* Division, held by the *II.* and *III. Bataillon* of the *Germania* Regiment. After heavy fighting, *Stubaf.* Müller's regiment prevented their assailants from breaking out to the southwest and even managed to knock out four Soviet tanks in and outside Baraczka, forcing them to redirect their assault to the northwest of the town. As mentioned in the *Ic* report, the attack against Aggszentpéter, carried out by elements of the 122nd Rifle Division and 12th Cavalry Division, did manage to seize some ground, but the *Westland* Regiment, assisted by the Hungarian *I. Btl./Inf.Rgt. 54*, was able to contain it after launching a counterattack. As a result, the small bridgehead east of the town across the Váli remained in German hands.

It was now the only bridgehead. On the division's far right, the *I. Btl./Germania* and Hungarian troops were compelled to withdraw from the small bridgehead they held over the Váli north of Szinatelep after it was attacked by the 113th Rifle Division following a powerful artillery barrage. At the division's command post in Felsocikőla-Major, its *O1*, Günther Jahnke, wrote in his diary that day, "Strong enemy attacks against our left flank, where our left-hand neighbor [i.e., the *III. Pz.Korps*] was still hanging back. The Russians [*sic*] forced their way into Perkáta." This last item, reflecting the breakthrough of the 170th Tank Brigade from the XVIII Tank Corps, was a source of major concern to the division.

This town, on the division's rightmost or southern flank, was 16 kilometers northwest of Dunapentele and until that point in the battle was thought to be safely behind the front line held by the *3. Pz.Div.* to its south. Through it ran a paved highway leading to Seregélyes, the location of the corps' forward headquarters, and thence to Stuhlweissenburg. Should Perkáta fall to the enemy, it would expose the *Wiking* Division's main supply routes and the division itself to envelopment, at a most critical moment in the battle. Fortunately, the Soviet force, with at least 30 tanks, did not actually enter the town, but was satisfied to occupy the village of Mélykút 2 kilometers to the south, where it halted for the night.

To the left of the *Wiking* Division, the attack by the *1. Pz.Div.* and *Totenkopf* had been postponed yet again to 5 a.m., but even before that could finally get going, the village of Pettend was attacked by seven Soviet tanks from the 135th Tank Brigade and an infantry battalion an hour before the resumption of the German assault was scheduled. The village, located in the rear area of the *1. Pz.Div.*, was still occupied by Fritz Vogt's depleted *I. Btl./Norge*, which had seized it three days before after heavy fighting.[90] Nearby, a battery from *Pz.Art.Rgt. 73* of the *1. Pz.Div.* was occupying a firing position.

Though two of the attacking tanks were destroyed on Pettend's outskirts by the *Norge*'s antitank guns, the remaining tanks and accompanying infantry penetrated into the village's edge and were soon engaged in a bitter struggle with Vogt's battalion.[91] The artillery battery was overrun by the Soviet armored unit, which dispersed the gun crews and destroyed two of their howitzers, but not before the battery managed to knock out two tanks using direct fire. Vogt's two antitank guns were overrun and crushed under the tracks of enemy tanks along with their crews.

At roughly the same time, both the *1. Pz.Div.* and the *Totenkopf* found themselves under a concentric attack, as the XXIII Tank Corps, joined in the west by elements of the XXI Guards Rifle Corps and in the east by the V Guards Cavalry Corps, sought to squeeze them into the area between Baraczka, Kápolnás Nyék, Vereb, and Pazmánd. Here, the three Soviet corps intended to crush both divisions with over 100 tanks supported by overwhelming artillery and rocket fire. An overnight attack by a powerful enemy force achieved a deep penetration at Vereb, held by the *1. Pz.Div.* and *K.Gr. Kleffner*, which both units had still not been able to iron out by 6:30 a.m.

A second wave of attacks, including tanks from the 3rd Tank Brigade and the 56th Motorized Rifle Brigade, increased the size of the breach, forcing the *1. Pz. Div.* to cease any efforts to carry out its attack towards the west and deal with this threat, which, if not stopped, would drive all the way to Pazmánd. In Pazmánd, a single battalion from *Pz.Gren.Rgt. 113* was able to ward off an attempt to take the town by a regiment from the 69th Rifle Division that attacked from the west. To retake Vereb, the *1. Pz.Div.* assembled its three remaining *Panzergrenadier* battalions—all of them very weak—along with the 11 remaining Panthers from *Pz.Rgt. 1* under *K.Gr. Philipp.*[92]

Between Vereb and Kajászó Szént Péter, the rest of the *Totenkopf* Division held its ground against repeated attacks from the direction of Vál and the latter village. Here, near the spot where it had been thrown back across the Váli the previous afternoon, *SS-Pz.Aufkl.Abt. 3* stymied every attempt by the 104th Rifle Division to force a crossing. On the battalion's left, the *III. Bataillon* of the *Totenkopf* Regiment was able to thwart attempts by Soviet forces to drive southeast from Vál, which were able to make only negligible gains. Throughout the fighting, the *Totenkopf* Division's artillery regiment provided accurate and timely fire support, often in positions that were located completely out in the open and exposed to the enemy, without the benefit of any friendly infantry to protect the guns against Soviet attack. Consequently, each firing battery had to be prepared to engage tanks with direct fire if necessary.

The *IV. Abt./SS-Pz.Art.Rgt 3* was one such unit. Occupying a firing position a few kilometers south of *III. Btl./Totenkopf*, its men had just endured a freezing night out in the open. Its commander, *Stubaf.* Fritz Messerle, afterwards wrote:

> After a horrible night in the open air, the sun finally comes up. The barren landscape is covered in thick fog. The situation is still unclear, but it has become a bit quieter all around … therefore, the order to [continue the] attack is still valid. The confused situation is unsettling. Foot patrols are still out [looking for the enemy]. The battalion [*III. Btl./Totenkopf*], a fought-out bunch without any contact to the right and left, expects rather a strong enemy counterattack.[93]

After conferring with the battalion commander in the front lines, Messerle began driving back to his battalion command post in his Volkswagen *Schwimmwagen*. Suddenly, after he had travelled half the distance, he heard the sound of tanks off to his right. He later recalled, "A group of enemy tanks—T-34s and Shermans—emerged from the misty haze and roared in a single file towards the gun positions."[94]

After recovering from his surprise, Messerle ordered his driver to follow the tanks. Although he thought there was no chance to warn his men in time of what was coming, his driver looked for a chance to slip past the Soviet column. One of Messerle's men, *Unterscharführer* Wiese from the *9. Batterie*, picks up the story from there:

> Suddenly, from the row of bushes in front of our positions we see our battalion commander flying towards us at a high rate of speed. He is standing up bareheaded in his *Schwimmer*, waving his hands and shouting "Tanks to the front, tanks to the front!" What a devilish situation; we can't see anything, we've no cover. The firing mechanisms of our *Panzerfausts* are frozen … the only thing left to us is to surrender our loaded [howitzers]![95]

Before the guns crews could react, Soviet tanks, most likely from the 39th Tank Brigade, roared in through the fog and drove into the gun positions, weaving and firing in all directions with their machine guns. Firing at tanks with artillery at such a close range was impossible, since the shells would not have time to arm themselves after leaving the gun tubes and would be as much a danger to the gunners as to enemy tanks. One *Unterscharführer*, a gun commander, climbed aboard a T-34 in the hope of disabling it, but was shot off the turret by a neighboring tank. All seemed lost. Suddenly, just when a tank had turned its attention to Wiese's gun, "There was a loud bang—the T-34 is struck, it goes up in flames. A gun from the light battery [i.e.., 10.5cm] behind us has scored a direct hit."

Twenty minutes later, it was all over. Of the 14 T-34s that had broken through, 13 were enveloped in flames, destroyed either by the guns of the *8. (light) Batterie*, assault guns, or by crewmembers using infantry weapons. Only one tank got away. In the *9. Batterie*, two men were killed, six severely wounded. After that, calm settled on the battlefield. One participant in the fighting from the neighboring *8. Batterie*, *Unterscharführer* Fuhrmann, later wrote:

> The morning became surprisingly quiet; hardly any shots were heard being fired in the surrounding area. In front of our guns there lies an open, snow-covered field. In the background, blurred by fog, a row of hedges with a few trees stretches out in the distance. Here we have parked our prime movers. Some of our division's assault guns are in position there to provide cover.[96]

Throughout the day, the men of *K. Gr. Kleffner* and *Eckert* fought against the oncoming tide of Soviet tanks and infantry between Vál and Vereb, but were forced back bit by bit towards Pazmánd and Pettend by overwhelming enemy pressure.

Vereb changed hands several times that day, but by the evening, *K. Gr. Kleffner* was finally forced to withdraw after suffering heavy losses, though it was able to restore contact with *K.Gr. Eckert* on its right and the *1. Pz.Div.* on its left, after *Oberstlt.* Philipp sent five Panthers from the attached *I. Abt./Pz.Rgt. 24* to help out. *Obersturmbannführer* Kleffner radioed his commander, informing him that, "Connections [with adjacent units] have been restored. [Enemy] breakthrough has been cut off. [Have suffered] heavy losses. We urgently need more ammunition." The town had been completely reduced to rubble, its streets strewn with the bodies of German and Soviet soldiers and destroyed tanks. One eyewitness, *Oberscharführer* Zährl, later wrote, "It was a picture of complete devastation. It was war in the truest sense of the word."[97]

Throughout the area, packs of Soviet tanks roamed around seemingly without a sense of direction or plan, rendering them vulnerable to ambush by the tanks, assault guns, and tank destroyers from the two *panzer* divisions. Though greatly outnumbered, at least the Germans knew where they were and were still operating under the command and control of their division headquarters, while the Soviet units were not. Dozens of small-scale tank battles erupted, as two or three German armored fighting vehicles—sometimes joined by 8.8cm *Flak* batteries or antitank guns—took on dozens of T-34s or M4A2 Shermans. In the falling snow, numbers were not an advantage.

At Pettend, located at the base of the salient where General Zakharov hoped to cut off the German penetration from the day before, the attack was redoubled as troops from the 151st Rifle Division and 30 tanks from the 135th Tank Brigade surged against Vogt's meager defenses at approximately 10 a.m. Fortunately for Vogt and his bedraggled battalion of Norwegians, Germans, and *Volksdeutsche*, they had been reinforced in the meantime by three *Pz. VI* Tiger IIs from *s.Pz.Abt. 509*, led by *Feldwebel* Bauer. During the initial onslaught, Vogt's men and Bauer's tanks were forced to withdraw to the southwest due to the unrelenting pressure, leaving Pettend temporarily in Soviet hands.

Rallying along the railroad line southwest of Pettend, this tiny German force—reinforced by the Tiger II of the battalion commander, two *StuG IIIs* from *Pz.Jäg. Abt. 37*, and five Panthers from *I. Abt./Pz.Rgt. 24*—counterattacked. After a see-saw battle lasting several hours, the improvised task force was able to regain control of the town by 5 p.m. The men of *I. Abt./Norge* attacked the Soviet infantry and tanks with suicidal bravery, using whatever means at hand, including antitank mines, grenade bundles, and antitank guns to kill their opponents. Casualties on both sides were very heavy. Vogt himself accounted for six Soviet tanks with his own *Panzerfaust,* while in and around Pettend, 50 other enemy tanks were knocked out, including 13 by the rest of Vogt's battalion and 36 by the Tiger IIs of *s.Pz.Abt. 509*. Though necessary to prevent the *1. Pz.Div.* and the *Totenkopf* Division from being cut off, the recapture of Pettend by *I. Btl./Norge* was an unbelievable display of sacrificial courage, and one that came with a hefty price tag. During the fighting that day, Vogt's battalion was reduced to less than 50 men by the time reinforcements from the *1. Pz.Div.* arrived.[98]

The losses suffered by the four brigades of the XXIII Tank Corps that day were massive; in his after-action report, Lt.Gen. Akhmanov claimed that his corps lost 71 tanks and self-propelled guns that day, including 54 written off as total losses (roughly 43 percent of its total complement, including 380 casualties).[99] The *IV. SS-Pz.Korps* reported that it had knocked out nearly twice that number, though of course it was probably counting tanks from other Soviet units besides the XXIII Tank Corps that took part in the fighting that day, such as the I Guards Mechanized Corps, the V Guards Cavalry Corps, and the XXI Guards Rifle Corps, all of which had their own dedicated armored units. In the corps order written that evening, Gille described the events of the day:

> The enemy attacked our advanced tank detachments in the area of Vereb and south of Vál today with large forces of tanks and infantry. At dawn, the XXIII Tank Corps launched an offensive from the enemy's bridgehead in the Baraczka area in southwesterly and westerly directions, with the task of blocking the defile between the Váli River and Lake Velencze behind our advancing forward units. During fierce battles, a total of 122 enemy tanks were destroyed today.[100]

In truth, the *IV. SS-Pz.Korps* had narrowly avoided destruction, but only by a hair's breadth. Were it not for the hasty and haphazard commitment of the XXIII Tank Corps, it probably would have been worse. The after-action report of the 4th Guards Army, which had operational control of Akhmanov's tanks, stated:

> Units of the XXIII Tank Corps, upon entering the fighting, deployed in unfavorable conditions from the line of march under heavy enemy fire, particularly from his antitank artillery and fire from tanks and self-propelled guns in ambush [positions] ... Among the main shortcomings in the corps' combat operations were the following: poor knowledge of the enemy; cooperation with the artillery had been insufficiently worked out; a shortage of ammunition; and the absence of air support.[101]

All was not bad news in the wake of the counterattack's outcome, for the 4th Guards Army after-action report closed with this encouraging remark:

> However, this attack, in conjunction with offensive operations along the front's southern sector [i.e., against the *3. Pz.Div.*] was so sensitive for the enemy that as early as 27 January he was forced to switch from the offensive to the defensive. As a result of the XXIII Tank Corps' attack, the enemy's breakthrough sector was narrowed in the north to 1.5 to 2 kilometers and 3 to 4 kilometers in the south. The arrival of the 135th Tank Brigade in the Vegh area created the threat of encirclement for the enemy's breakthrough group [i.e., the *1. Pz.Div.* and *Totenkopf*].[102]

The attack had inflicted significant damage indeed, so much so that Gille recommended calling off the attack towards the west. At first, Balck did not agree at all, but blamed the "48-hour" delay of the attack (Balck had continued to keep score) on Gille's procrastination, ignoring the fact that had the *IV. SS-Pz.Korps* gone through with the attack, it would have been caught completely flat-footed by the XXIII Tank Corps' assault and possibly destroyed. Perhaps Gille "smelled a briefcase" in this affair as well.

As it was, it was bad enough. By the end of the day, the *Totenkopf* Davison reported its combat readiness status to the corps headquarters. Of its six *Panzergrenadier* battalions, only two were reported to possess average strength (200–300 men), while the other four were reported as "weak" (100–200 men). Its combat engineer battalion was reported as above-average strength (300–400), as was its *Feld-Ersatz* battalion, which was being used in a security role. The two attached battalions, *I. Btl./Norge* and *I. Btl./Danmark*, were rated as *abgekämpft* ("fought out," i.e., with a *Kampfstärke* of less than 100 men) and "above average," respectively. The readiness rate of its armored fighting vehicles was even worse. That evening, the division reported having only one operational Panther, one *Pz. IV*, and one Tiger I, as well as three still-operational assault guns.[103]

On the positive side of the scale, it still had 13 functioning heavy antitank guns (7.5cm), five heavy artillery batteries (15cm), and five light batteries (10.5cm). Rounding out the report, the division still reported its mobility as 90 percent, which meant that it could still move and fight, though without tanks it was no longer an offensive force. The dozens of damaged or broken-down tanks, assault guns, and tank destroyers that were strewn about the battlefield but still repairable (provided they could be recovered in time) would take days or weeks to be put back in operating condition. As a result of this report, *H. Gr. Süd* assigned Becker's division an overall combat rating of Category III, "Suitable for defensive assignments."[104]

The *Wiking* Division, which had not been as heavily engaged that day as the *Totenkopf*, was also rated as a Category III. It had fewer infantrymen than its sister division, with three of its battalions having been rated as "fought out" (less than 100 men). On the other hand, it had more available armored fighting vehicles, reporting three operational *Pz. IV*s, nine *Pz. V* Panthers, six *Jagdpanzer*, and two assault guns, for a total of 20. Its artillery regiment was in good shape (10 batteries), as was the number of antitank guns (12), though the shortage of trucks and halftracks earned it a mobility rating of only 42 percent.[105]

As the reports of the scale of the fighting began to reach the command post of both the *IV. SS-Pz.Korps* (which were forwarded by *Maj.* Müller-Gülich to Balck) and *A.Gr. Balck/6. Armee*, the German commanders at the field army and army group headquarters slowly began to realize what was happening. Gille, already well aware of how the battle was going, tried to get the attack called off completely. It took Balck a few more hours for reality to sink in. His first instinct was to call a temporary halt, then blame Gille for the failure of the attack towards the west on account of his "deliberate delays." However, as the reports from the fighting units continued coming in, Balck finally acknowledged that the resumption of the offensive could not be continued as intended and that, in fact, it was high time to cancel it and order a withdrawal, especially with the situation to the south of *IV. SS-Pz.Korps* developing so unfavorably.

To the left of the *IV. SS-Pz.Korps*, the *III. Pz.Korps/Korpsgruppe Breith* reported that very little fighting of consequence took place that day, since its attack towards the *IV. SS-Pz.Korps* had completely stalled the previous day. The only item of interest reported was that the enemy main defense line between Zámoly and Lake Velencze appeared to have been strongly reinforced. *SS-Regiment Ney* was thrown off Hill 182, 5 kilometers southwest of Stuhlweissenburg, after taking it the day before with such heavy losses.

Next to Ney's regiment, Balck's headquarters had ordered the *23. Pz.Div.* to begin pulling out of the area between Zámoly and Stuhlweissenburg that evening and prepare for movement to a new assembly area near Szabadbattyán, where it would become the *A.Gr. Balck* reserve for possible commitment in the south.[106] It was to be replaced in the line by the incoming *356. Inf.Div.* of *Div.Gr. Holste*, which would have to shift its front line to the south to cover the portion of the front line being given up. The *23. Pz.Div.* was ordered to leave its *Panzergruppe* behind as insurance until all of the *356. Inf.Div.* arrived. The armored *Kampfgruppe* from the *6. Pz.Div.*, which had been on the march from the Felsőgalla area since the previous afternoon, would join *Div.Gr. Holste* during the next day or so. The *4. Kav.Brig.* would remain in the Zámoly area, as would the Hungarian *2. Pz.Div.* On the rest of the corps front in the Hungarian *VIII. Armee-Korps* area, there was no significant combat reported except for local fighting in the Vértes Mountains near Hill 398 and north of Kozmá, where Hungarian forces were only able to make insignificant gains to the east.[107]

In the *I. Kav.Korps* area, Soviet troops were able to retake the heights south of the rail and highway intersection southeast of Felsőgalla, due primarily to the departure of the armored battlegroup from the *6. Pz.Div.* In the corps' center, held by the *3. Kav.Brig.* and the *96. Inf.Div.*, the day passed quietly. Along the southern bank of the Danube, the corps' screening force, consisting primarily of the *711. Inf.Div.* and Hungarian *23. Inf.Div.*, was keeping an eye on the activities of the 7th Guards Army, which had been relatively static for the past two weeks. An observation post of the *711. Inf.Div.* located on top of Szamár Hill, 4 kilometers east of Gran, reported a significant amount of motor vehicle traffic on the northern bank of the river leaving the town of Szob and heading towards the southeast; which unit or its destination could not be determined by ground observation.

On the *A.Gr. Balck/6. Armee*'s widely extended right or southern flank, held by the Hungarian *3. Armee*, Lt.Gen. Mikhail N. Sharokhin's 57th Army—with two rifle and one tank corps—finally launched its counteroffensive. Facing only the thinly dispersed *3. Pz.Div.* in the east, *Div.Gr. Pape* in the south, and the Hungarian *25. Inf.Div.* in the west along the Sió River sector, Sharokhin's troops focused most of their initial efforts against the salient in the south around Simontornya and the sector between the Sárviz Canal and the Danube, where they made rapid gains. At Simontornya, the 233rd Rifle Division of the CXXXIII Rifle Corps, taking advantage of small bridgeheads taken two days before, was sent across the Sió River and achieved a local penetration north of the town, but was stopped by a German and Hungarian counterattack south on the southern edge of the village of Igar. This setback was followed up by another attack by two Soviet rifle battalions towards the northwest. These two attacks failed after *Pz.Aufkl.Abt. 1* of the *1. Pz.Div.*, reinforced by two Hungarian battalions from their *26. Inf.Rgt.* and an assault gun battery, carried out a local counterattack.[108]

Between the Sárviz Canal and the Danube, the XVIII Tank Corps and XXX Rifle Corps attacked the *3. Pz.Div.* with no less than three rifle divisions and elements of three tank brigades. Employing as many as 60 tanks in the initial assault, the two corps (incorporated into the new 26th Army the following day) broke through the division's front at multiple locations. Sárbogárd, Herczegfalva, and Nagyvenyim fell in quick succession, while an armored spearhead continued pushing to the north. This force, comprising the bulk of the reconstituted XVIII Tank Corps, soon reached the area 2 kilometers south of the village of Nagy Lók, the heights northwest of Herczegfalva, and the outskirts of Mélykút, where they threatened Perkáta.

This was the attack that had set off alarm bells in the *Wiking* Division's headquarters later that day, as previously mentioned. Unless something was done quickly, the division's supply lines might soon be cut. At the time the *Ic* report was submitted, another tank-supported Soviet mechanized force was attacking towards the northeast out of Nagyvenyim, cutting off *K.Gr. Medicus* (*Pz.Jäg.Abt. 543* and *II. Btl./Pz.Gren. Rgt. 3*) in Dunapentele. *Oberst* Söth's regiments and battalions were forced to dash from one hotspot to another, as they desperately sought to staunch the irresistible flood of attacking tanks and infantrymen. It quickly became apparent that the offensive was seeking a much greater outcome than a mere local tactical victory. The very real threat arose that, unless brought to a halt, Soviet forces would reach Stuhlweissenburg within 24 hours, thus cutting off the entire *IV. SS-Pz.Korps* as well as the Hungarian *3. Armee*. Clearly, the *3. Pz.Div.* needed help, and immediately. This counteroffensive would soon have a wide-reaching impact that would reverberate far beyond the Hungarian theater of operations.[109]

Far removed from the carnage, the *Führerhauptquartier* at least appreciated the efforts the troops were making to relieve Budapest. In the daily *Wehrmachtsbericht* for 27 January, Hitler's headquarters announced that in Hungary "units of the *Heer* and the *Waffen-SS* broke through the enemy's defense line between Lake Velencze and the Váli sector in a night assault and surged forward towards the north. Soviet counterattacks were driven off … Hungarian assault formations pressed forward to complete the destruction of stubborn nests of enemy resistance all the way to the eastern edge of the Vértes Mountains."[110]

Meanwhile, throughout the day, the terrible situation in Budapest grew worse. During the night of 26/27 January, a battalion-sized Soviet attack against the northern perimeter defenses was reported, as well as several company-sized assaults against the western perimeter. All of these were pushed back, except for one in the middle sector of the defensive ring around the ever-shrinking *Festung*. Into this breach, the enemy poured in reinforcements that Pfeffer-Wildenbruch's dwindling forces attempted to seal off. At reporting time, the outcome of a counterattack against this position was not yet known. A concentration of Soviet troops observed forming up on the eastern bank of the river in Pest was attacked with artillery fire and scattered.

The *IX. SS-Geb.Korps*, clearly on its last legs, still had some fight left in it, but not for much longer. In a radio message that day, its commander reported:

> Last mobile elements of the *13. Pz.Div.* and the sector reserves committed to the fighting. Situation very serious … As we have no more reserves available, a loss of ground must occur corresponding to the increasing number of lost combatants … Use of armored elements in the streets and house-to-house fighting is only possible under certain circumstances. Drivers and *Panzergrenadiere* are fighting dismounted. Friendly losses are enormous. Number of wounded now exceeds the number of effectives.[111]

The most critically important aspect of his lengthy report, at least in regards to the logistical situation, concerned the loss of the last useable landing place in the city's western side. Pfeffer-Wildenbruch wrote:

> With the loss of the *Blutwiese*, the last possibility for landing cargo gliders, the supply situation is disastrous. Fate of the wounded horrifying. At this time about 34,000 German and Hungarian soldiers, along with more than 10,000 German wounded and 300,000 Hungarian civilians have been pushed together into an extremely small area.

As if to emphasize the corps commander's remarks, only 4.6 metric tons of supplies (5 short tons) were air dropped by the five aircraft from *Luftflotte 4* that managed to find their target, a pitifully insignificant amount.

Regarding other air activity, the *Luftwaffe* was able to generate only a minimum amount of sorties, which had no impact on the fighting. The horrible flying weather, due to a winter storm front that impacted any aircraft operating west of the Bakony Forest, meant that most never got off the ground. A few reconnaissance aircraft, operating from airfields beyond Hungary, managed to get airborne, as did the aerial resupply transports. The reconnaissance flights reported spotting 12 enemy tanks moving to the south from Waitzen (Vác), a town located on the eastern bank of the Danube between Szob and Budapest, as well as several trucks towing antitank guns moving in the same direction. Near Budafok on the southern outskirts of Budapest, German aircraft spotted two new pontoon bridges over the Danube, over which traffic was already flowing.[112]

One mission over Budapest that the *Luftwaffe* was able to fly was a leaflet mission, carried out to deliver a message to the troops from Hitler himself. The message, dated 27 January, was a daily order addressed to the "Defenders of Budapest." It read:

> The defenders of Budapest have repelled all attacks by the Bolshevists in the bloodiest battle since 16 December 1944 under their heroic commander *Obergruppenführer* Pfeffer-Wildenbruch.

For weeks, you have inflicted heavy casualties on the enemy in terms of both combat forces and material. The heroism and exemplary conduct of your commander and the resistance by the grenadiers of the *Heer*, the members of the *Waffen-SS*, and the Hungarian units fighting alongside you serve as an example for every soldier on every front. The German and the allied Hungarian people wish to express their gratitude to the men of Budapest for their bravery and willingness to sacrifice against the common enemy. You defenders of Budapest shall hold on until the hour of your relief arrives. Signed, Adolf Hitler.[113]

The Red Air Force was not engaged in morale-building activities that day, unless one counts the boost it provided its own troops by strafing and bombing the "Hitlerites."

Despite the wintry weather (the airfields of the 5th and 17th Air Armies on the other side of the Danube did not have to deal with the same cold front that the *Luftwaffe* did), IL-2s, Yaks, and A-20 Bostons managed to fly 260 sorties, concentrating most of their attention on the *IV. SS-Pz.Korps*, though its white-painted tanks were elusive targets in the snow.[114] However, one ground-attack mission did manage to strike the headquarters of *Pz.Rgt. 1* of the *1. Pz.Div.* in Gárdony, seriously wounding *Oberstlt.* Philipp. who had just returned from battle, and killing three officers and several enlisted men from *I. Abt./Pz.Rgt. 24* who had gathered at Philipp's command post. There would be no further "Hussar rides" by the bold *panzer* leader; he would be sidelined with his injuries until April.[115]

The *A.Gr. Balck/6. Armee* intelligence estimate was bleak. Now that the 57th Army had acted, and that the 4th Guards Army had thrown everything it had into blocking and then attempting to destroy the *IV. SS-Pz.Korps*, the enemy situation became crystal clear. Taking stock of its erroneous previous assessments, the field army's *Ic* was now able to view things more realistically. That night, *Hptm.* von Pander wrote:

> Between the Sárviz canal and the Danube, the enemy initiated his attack towards the north with the strength of approximately three to four rifle divisions and the XVIII Tank Corps. We expect this enemy attack to be reinforced at some point by the VII Mechanized Corps as well as the possible commitment of the 1st Bulgarian Army and other available forces of the 57th Army. At the same time, the enemy initiated a series of large-scale attacks along the western bank of the Sárviz Canal [at Simontornya] designed to tie down and bind up our forces there. We anticipate that similar attacks will be launched in the near future against the entire Sió River front.[116]

The *Ic* also commented on the extremely heavy fighting within the *IV. SS-Pz.Korps* attack zone that day:

> In connection with this attack in the south [by the 57th Army] the enemy launched a counterattack along the Váli sector with previously identified forces along with the newly arrived and completely refreshed XXIII Tank Corps. According to a *Richard-Meldung*, the enemy's first attack objective is to cut off our attack group [i.e., *IV. SS-Pz.Korps*] northeast of Lake Velencze from their logistics services and then destroy them. Based on aerial reconnaissance, the introduction of additional forces, possibly including the Pliyev Cavalry-Mechanized Group, is likely.[117]

In terms of what these intelligence reports, warnings, and indicators meant, von Pander was able to accurately deduce the Third Ukrainian Front's overarching goal:

> The overall objective of the enemy is to destroy our forces by conducting a pincer attack from both the north and south and to reestablish the connection between his forces located in the south. Along with these intentions, the enemy might also be seeking a breakthrough between Lake Velencze and the Danube, as well as a breakthrough between Lake Velencze and the Vértes Mountains. In order to carry out this latter objective, it appears that in addition to the troops already in position there, he is sending additional forces to this area ... against Budapest the enemy has once again introduced tanks with the apparent intention of speeding up the occupation of the bridgehead.

The German intelligence summary for 27 January was fairly accurate, though it came too late to be of much help. The inability to identify the arrival of the XXIII Tank Corps signified a significant lapse in *H. Gr. Süd's* intelligence collection effort, which *Gen.d.Pz. Tr.* Balck blamed on the *Luftwaffe's* failure to conduct continuous aerial surveillance.[118]

The *Luftwaffe* could still do many things, but it could not control the weather. However, it was *H. Gr. Süd* and *A. Gr. Balck/6. Armee* that failed to take adequate measures to assist the *3. Pz.Div.* in the south, knowing several days ahead of time that a large-scale attack was imminent. What reserves that were sent to assist Söth's division proved to be too little, too late. Outnumbered five or six-to-one, it was almost a miracle that Söth was able to keep his division together and that his troops were able to maintain a more or less continuous front line.

From the Soviet perspective, the 4th Guards Army and 57th Army had achieved several of its objectives that day. First, the XXIII Tank Corps' counterattack had stopped the attack by the *IV. SS-Pz.Korps* dead in its tracks. North of Stuhlweissenburg, the XX and XXI Guards Rifle Corps had prevented the attack by the *III. Pz.Korps* from even developing. Although the XXIII Tank Corps had suffered heavy losses, particularly in armored vehicles, the CIV Rifle Corps had hardly been committed at all and would be available to begin its attack the following day. This attack, whose general outline had already been revealed on 27 January, was aimed at cutting off the penetration north of Pettend at its base and would continue advancing to the south and west before transitioning to the larger objective of cutting off the entire *IV. SS-Pz.Korps* and *3. Pz.Div.* at Sárosd once it linked up with the three advancing corps of the 57th Army.

The latter army had made impressive gains that day, but this was only the beginning. Its forces had been directed to continue driving north until they met with the approaching spearheads of the 4th Guards Army at Sárosd, which, if successful, would complete the destruction of the bulk of *H. Gr. Süd's* forces west of the Danube. The only significant decision that Tolbukhin made that day, with the approval of the *STAVKA*, was to recommend a change to the command structure of the forces in the south. He recognized that Lt.Gen. Sharokhin's 57th Army was split into two components due to geographical features, which made command and control difficult; those forces west of the Sárviz Canal, including the Sió River sector, would remain with the 57th Army, while those located to the east of the canal would be placed under a new headquarters. Essentially, the three corps fighting east of the Sárviz (the XXX and CXXXIII Rifle Corps and the XVIII Tank Corps) would be detached from the 57th Army and placed under a new army headquarters, Lt.Gen. L. S. Skvirsky's 26th Army. This army headquarters had been brought out of *STAVKA* reserve, where it had been since the previous November after serving on the Finnish front. The change in command would become effective on 28 January.[119]

The events of the day had completely transformed the overall situation for the Germans for the worse, much to the disappointment of Hermann Balck, as well as nearly everyone else taking part in Operation *Konrad III*, to say nothing about what the men of the *3. Pz.Div.*—faced with imminent destruction—must have felt. To Balck's credit, he was able to sense what needed to be done, drawing upon the situational awareness skills that had made him such a successful *Panzerkorps* commander only a year before. Once he realized that Gille's attack had failed to materialize, and after he had recovered from the initial shock, he sensed that his army now found itself in mortal danger. Fully aware of his perilous situation, Balck made a quick assessment of the situation and understood what had to be done shortly before noon that day. The first decision he had to make was to determine how to stop the onrushing Soviet forces approaching from the south, using whatever means necessary.

He had already taken the first step when he ordered the *23. Pz.Div.* to begin pulling out of its positions north of Stuhlweissenburg. He planned to send this division south to aid the *3. Pz.Div.*, ideally followed by the *1. Pz.Div.* shortly thereafter. Unfortunately, Balck's command authority only extended so far; to take the additional steps, he needed permission from Wöhler, who in turn would need to secure the approval through *OKH* channels, meaning Hitler. At 2 p.m., Balck contacted *H.Gr. Süd* and requested permission to pull the *1. Pz.Div.* out of the line and reassign it to the *III. Pz.Korps*, which in turn would be withdrawn, handing over half of its sector to the *IV. SS-Pz.Korps* and the other half—the Hungarian *VIII. Armee-Korps*—to the *I. Kav.Korps*, which would be redesignated as *Korpsgruppe Harteneck*. General der Infanterie Wöhler's chief of staff, *Gen.Lt.* von Grolman, then contacted his counterpart at *OKH*, *Gen.d.Pz.Tr.* Wenck, who discussed the issue with Guderian.[120]

Apparently, shortly thereafter Guderian briefed Hitler, who gave his approval to the proposal, though with certain caveats. When Guderian contacted *H.Gr. Süd* at 5:25 p.m., he asked von Grolman whether the attack towards Budapest could be resumed; he was told that it was impossible ("definitely not"). Guderian then informed him that Hitler had ordered Stuhlweissenburg to be held at all costs until a suitable replacement for the *23. Pz.Div.* could be moved up. Until then, Guderian said, Hitler demanded that this division would have to leave a sufficient number of troops behind to hold the line until they could be replaced (i.e., its *Panzergruppe*). Five minutes later, *H. Gr. Süd*'s order, which Wöhler's staff had been working on for the past three hours, was sent out to *A. Gr. Balck/6. Armee*, which had already sent out two warning orders of its own. *Heeresgruppe Süd* "covered itself" by attaching Hitler's caveat to its order, stating:

> The *Führerbefehl* to the effect than an enemy breakthrough in the area of Stuhlweissenburg had to be prevented at all costs <u>must be rigidly obeyed</u> [emphasis in the original]. It would be better to take a chance in the south or in the north, than risk a failure in the gap of Stuhlweissenburg, for this would endanger the entire position.[121]

To fulfill this requirement yet allow the *23. Pz. Div.* to withdraw, an hour later *Gen. Lt.* von Grolman suggested to his counterpart at *A. Gr. Balck*, *Gen. Maj.* Gaedke, that the *Panzergruppe* from the *6. Pz. Div.* could be used to fulfill this requirement, since it was still technically "in transit" and could fill in for the *356. Inf. Div.* until it arrived. Finally, at 7:50 p.m. on 27 January, Balck's chief of staff made a series of calls over the landline telephone to all of the headquarters involved concerning the change of mission, followed up within an hour by a written confirmation sent via teletype and *Hellschreiber*.[122]

In its basic outlines, the order tasked the *III. Pz. Korps*—using the *1., 3.,* and *23. Pz. Div.*—to carry out a counterattack *en masse* to the south to destroy the enemy forces that had broken through and restore the old front-line positions of 26 January. *General der Panzertruppe* Breith was directed to establish his new headquarters in the area of Szabadbattyán and to be prepared to commence the attack, minus the *3. Pz. Div.*, which would remain in its current positions, no later than 28 January. *Divisions-Gruppe Holste* would fall under the command and control of the *IV. SS-Pz. Korps*, including its *4. Kav. Brig.*, *SS-Rgt. Ney*, and the Hungarian *2. Pz. Div.*

The *I. Kav. Korps*, now renamed *Korpsgruppe Harteneck*, would continue defending its current positions, including those of the Hungarian *VIII. Armee-Korps*, and extend its right boundary to the south along the line running through the towns of Mór, Gant, and Vértes Acsa. It would also give up the *Panzergruppe* from the *6. Pz. Div.* to the *IV. SS-Pz. Korps*. The Hungarian *3. Armee* would hand over control of the entire area east of the Sárviz Canal to the *III. Pz. Korps*.[123] There was no change to the missions of the *3. Kav. Brig.*, or those of the *96.* and *711. Inf. Div.*

In regards to the *IV. SS-Pz. Korps*, which was still heavily engaged in battle, *A. Gr. Balck/6. Armee* directed it to carry out the following tasks in *Fernschreiben Ia Nr. 727/45*:

> Cease present attacks and withdraw to the line west of the Váli River running from Baraczka to the northeastern corner of Lake Velencze [i.e., Kápolnás Nyék] where it will defend. Any bridgeheads over the Váli River must be held. The *Hauptkampflinie* between Baraczka and Lake Velencze is to be aligned in such a way, that the highway connecting Baraczka and Kápolnás Nyék be maintained for use by our own troops ... The *1. Pz. Div.* will be withdrawn during the night of 27/28 January and assemble in the area of Puszta Szabolcs. *Volks-Art. Korps 403*

will begin repositioning between Lake Velencze and the Vértes Mountains immediately. One SS division will be selected to provide a corps reserve consisting of one [infantry] battalion and five tanks to be positioned in the area immediately southwest of the southwest corner of Lake Velencze no later than the early morning of 28 January.[124]

Using this as a baseline order, Gille's *Führungsquartet* (Schönfelder, Rentrop, Jankuhn, and Velde) got to work to produce an order of their own that "nested" (i.e., conformed to) with that of the corps' higher headquarters. This order went out to the divisions before midnight on 27 January. Taking into account stated and implied missions, the order stated the following tasks:

> 5. *SS-Pz.Div. Wiking* defends along a section of the River Danube–Váli River between Adony and Baraczka and maintains the old front line of defense east of Adony–Szinatelep–Puszta Aggszentpéter. The bridgehead of Bévarmajor must be held back at all costs. Prepare material for the construction of a 70-ton bridge, so that, if necessary, using field-made elements of the framework, construction can begin immediately.
>
> 3. *SS-Pz.Div. Totenkopf*, in close cooperation with *1. Pz.Div.*, withdraws its units located northwest of the Baraczka–Kápolnás Nyék line and transitions to the defense. The *I. Btl./SS-Pz. Gren.Rgt. 24 Danmark* remains at its former positions subordinate to the division. The *I. Btl./ SS-Pz.Gren.Rgt. 23 Norge* withdraws from the front line and moves to Agárd–Gárdony area one kilometer southeast of Lake Velencze to be at the corps' disposal. The division should ensure the withdrawal of *s.Pz.Abt. 509*, *I. Abt./Pz.Rgt. 24*, and *303. Sturm-Art.Brig* when they will once again revert to become the reserve of the *Armeegruppe*. initially in the area south of Kápolnás Nyék, where they will initially be at the disposal of the corps. Upon reaching this area, the attachment of these units to the division is canceled. Transfer orders to these units will be handled through the headquarters of the division. New tasks for the three indicated units will be sent separately.[125]

Although it was to leave the framework of the *SS-Pz.Korps* in exchange for an immediate assignment to the *III. Pz.Korps*, the *1. Pz.Div.* also received the following tasks, since it would initially be assembling under Gille's administrative and logical control in the corps' rear area:

> 1 *Pz.Div.* in close cooperation with *3. SS-Pz.Div. Totenkopf*, withdraws its units, focusing first towards the northwest of the Baraczka–Kápolnás Nyék line during the night of 27/28 January in its entirety in order to concentrate in the Puszta Szabolcs area to be at the disposal of the *Armeegruppe*. Once it has arrived, the headquarters of the division joins the communication network of the command post of the *5. SS-Pz.Div. Wiking* in Felsocikőla-Puszta. Orders will be transmitted through the headquarters of *IV. SS-Pz.Korps*.

Divisionsgruppe Holste also received notification that it was to be joining the *IV. SS-Pz.Korps* order of battle the next day. It would be augmented on 28 January by the main body of the *356. Inf.Div.*, whose *Gren.Rgt. 871* had already arrived in Stuhlweissenburg, relieving the *I. Btl./Pz.Gren.Rgt. 126* of the *23. Pz.Div.*, which departed to rejoin the rest of its parent division immediately afterwards. The corps artillery and the corps' signal battalion also received additional guidance:

> Artillery: The artillery group of *ARKO 306 z.b.V.* will be echeloned for defense in such a way as to ensure firing in front of the left and central section of the *5. SS-Pz.Div.* and the right section of *3. SS-Pz.Div.* The *SS-Werf.Abt. 504* remains subordinated to *5. SS-Pz.Div. Wiking*.

Communications: *SS-Nachr.Abt. 104* will provide wire and radio communications with *5. SS-Pz.Div. Wiking* and *3. SS-Pz.Div. Totenkopf*, establish wire and radio communications with the *Div.Gr. Holste* and with *I. Btl./SS-Pz.Gren.Rgt. 23* in Agárd.

This order required that the units concerned had to carry out a number of other tasks that had to be accomplished very rapidly, especially the corps' three divisions. Not only was the *1. Pz.Div.* to be withdrawn completely from the corps' battle roster, but it and the *Totenkopf* Division both had to coordinate their withdrawals that evening from the Val–Vereb–Pazmánd salient to the new main defense line while still in contact with the enemy. By the next morning, *1. Pz.Div.* would hand over its positions to the *Totenkopf* Division, which in turn would have to extend its left flank as far as Kápolnás Nyék. The *Wiking* Division's task was relatively simple: hold its current positions.

The chief of the *OKH* General Staff issued an order at 1:10 a.m. on 28 January that officially cancelled *Unternehmen Konrad III*. The last attempt to relieve Budapest had irrevocably failed; the city was now to be abandoned to its fate and, except for what could be delivered by air, the garrison was on its own. *Obergruppenführer* Pfeffer-Wildenbruch's request for freedom of action had been denied; he and his men were left with no choice but to fight to the last man and the last bullet.[126] Amazingly, the German and Hungarian soldiers of the *IX. SS-Geb.Korps* would hold out for another two weeks in the face of numerous ground and air assaults and overwhelming artillery fire.

Simply ordering the cessation of the offensive did not mean that the fighting had ended; the following day, 28 January, witnessed myriad little battles, as the *1. Pz.Div.* and the *Totenkopf* Division struggled to disengage from the enemy and return to the line of departure from whence they had begun four days before. Typically, the Soviet forces, largely infantry by this point (since most of the tank units had been pulled back), pressed the withdrawing Germans as closely as possible, forcing the few remaining armored fighting vehicles and accompanying *Panzergrenadiere* to do an about-face and launch counterattacks to destroy them or at least force them to keep a respectful distance. The repositioning of most of *Volks-Art.Korps 403* forced the divisions to rely more heavily on their own artillery regiments during this interim period, not merely to carry out counterstrikes on advancing Soviet units and artillery, but to cover open ground where there were no troops available to hold it.

By this point in the winter, Lake Velencze had also mostly frozen over. Because there were no combat units available to cover the south shore of the lake should the XXI Guards Rifle Corps make an attempt to cross it with one of its divisions, Balck had already ordered Gille on 26 January to form *Alarmeinheiten* from corps troops and establish a series of outposts on the lake's southern shore to keep watch. This order included an instruction to the *IV. SS-Pz.Korps* that it was to tow any immobilized tanks then under repair and station them as strongpoints along the lake's shore to provide additional firepower if needed.[127] Fortunately, the Soviets made no attempt to cross the lake, but this order delayed the ability of Gille's *panzer* divisions to carry out timely repairs on its armored combat vehicles, especially when they were so widely dispersed from the repair facilities.

In his *Ic* situation report submitted on the evening of 28 January, Gille's intelligence officer wrote:

> Southeast of Aggszentpéter, a battalion-sized enemy force [most likely from the 12th Guards Cavalry Division or the 113th Rifle Division] penetrated the front lines, which was immediately repelled by a counterattack [probably by the *II. Btl./Westland*]. In heavy fighting, the enemy was able to take all of the southern portion of Baraczka and force his way into Pettend. There were further armor-supported enemy attacks in the Baraczka–Kápolnás Nyék sector but these were driven off. Along the highway connecting Stuhlweissenburg and Lovasberény, the enemy was able to achieve a breakthrough. Additional information is lacking at this time.[128]

His last line of the report was notable, because this occurred within the defensive sector of *Div.Gr. Holste*, as of midnight part of the *IV. SS-Pz.Korps*. It involved two Hungarian units—*Btl. Holczer* (composed of elements of two infantry battalions, from their *23. Inf.Div.* and *25. Inf.Div.*) and *SS-Rgt. Ney*, as well as a battalion from the *356. Inf.Div.* This marked the second time that Ney's regiment would fall under the command of Gille's corps.

At 9 p.m. the previous night, *K.Gr. Kleffer* of the *Totenkopf* Division had begun its withdrawal from Vereb. Its medical personnel loaded up the battlegroup's wounded in the few remaining vehicles and began moving slowly towards Pettend, through uncertain territory. Kleffner ordered that no rear guard was to be left behind, since there were not enough trucks or *SPW*s to retrieve them once they had accomplished their mission. If possible, the bodies of the men killed in the fighting were brought back as well. Shielded by the *Kampfgruppe*'s three remaining operational Panthers, the column reached the relative safety of the new front line at Pettend before sunrise on 28 January, after having to fight its way through a thin Soviet screen that had crept in after nightfall. Pettend was still held by Vogt's decimated *I. Btl./Norge, 3. Kp./ SS-Pz.Pio.Btl. 3*, and two of the three *Pz. VI* Tiger IIs from *s.Pz.Abt. 509* that had fought alongside Vogt's battalion the previous day.[129] Fortunately for Vogt and the few surviving men of his battalion, they were to be relieved by midnight and sent to a rest area to spend a few days reconstituting after being nearly wiped out in Pettend.

On the left flank, anchoring itself in Kápolnás Nyék, stood portions of the *Totenkopf* Regiment, reinforced by *I. Btl./Danmark*, while on the right flank, near the outskirts of Baraczka, most of the *Eicke* Regiment was emplaced, adjacent to the *II.* and *III. Btl./Germania*. What remained of *SS-Pz.Rgt. 3* was occupying a reserve position several kilometers southeast of Pettend. By this point, *Brig.Fhr.* Becker had established his division headquarters in Gárdony, close to the fighting. Like *Gen.Maj.* Thünert, he did not have much of a division left at this point, and what remained was widely scattered. *Standartenführer* Swientek's *SS-Pz.Art.Rgt. 3* had also been adversely impacted by the fighting. For example, its *IV. Abteilung* had lost most of its guns when it was overrun the previous day by Soviet tanks. Still, *Stubaf.* Messerle, its commander, had brought back everything he could, even damaged guns, as well as all of his dead and wounded. Most of his remaining serviceable guns were consolidated in his *10. Batterie.*[130]

That evening, Becker received another order, directing him to be prepared to move his division to Puszta Szabolcs, leaving behind the *Totenkopf* Regiment, which would fall under the temporary control of the *Wiking* Division. Apparently, Balck intended to send the *Totenkopf* Division south to join with the *III. Pz.Korps*, but nothing ever came of this directive, due to the intervention at 1:30 p.m. that day by *Oberstlt.* August Hermani of the *OKH Führungsabteilung.* Hermani reminded Balck's chief of staff of the long-standing prohibition that forbade the splitting up of SS units and removing them from the control of SS higher commands, such as a division or corps headquarters, without Himmler's permission.[131] Relenting, Balck ordered Gille instead to have Becker detach the *Totenkopf's* reconnaissance and combat engineer battalions and move them to the Stuhlweissenburg area to serve as the corps reserve, remaining well within the confines of the prohibition.

By the evening, all of the *Totenkopf* Division had managed to withdraw behind the Baraczka–Kápolnás Nyék highway. Because Becker's division was serving as the covering force, the *1. Pz.Div.* was able to withdraw in good order to its new assembly areas without incident, except for the aforementioned bombing of the headquarters of *Pz.Rgt. 1* at Gárdony that wounded *Oberstlt.* Philipp. Upon arrival in their designated areas at Gárdony, Puszta Szabolcs, and Felsocikőla Puszta, the division's units took stock and undertook a hasty reorganization to restore a semblance of combat capability as well as make any necessary adjustment to its task organization and chain of command.

Panzergrenadier Regiment 113 was so depleted by the heavy casualties it had suffered that each of its two battalions had been reduced in size to a company; in turn, these were combined into one small battalion-sized *Kampfgruppe* under *Maj.* Marcks. The same had been done with *Oberstlt.* Huppert's *Pz.Gren.Rgt. 1.* The rest of the division's battalion-sized elements had been similarly reduced in strength, and the few operational tanks of the *panzer* regiment had been grouped temporarily under the command of *Hptm.* Elias. Fortunately, during the evening of 28/29 January, the division received the attachment of *I. Abt./Pz.Rgt. 24* with 11 operational *Pz. V* Panthers and 15 *Pz. VI* Tiger IIs from *Maj.* Burmester's *s.Pz.Abt. 509*, which had managed to patch up a dozen of its tanks during the past several days. With these attachments, though low in infantry strength, the *1. Pz.Div.* at least possessed a semblance of offensive capability.[132]

On 28 January, the *Wiking* Division continued its defensive operations, thwarting several attempts by elements of the V Guards Cavalry Corps to penetrate its front line between the Danube and Baraczka. From left to right (i.e.., northwest to southeast), Ullrich had arrayed his division along the Váli front as follows: *II.* and *III. Btl./Germania* (Baraczka); *Alarmkompanie Wiking* (Kis Halom Puszta); *I.* and *II. Btl./Westland* and the Hungarian *I. Btl./Inf.Rgt. 54* (Aggszentpéter and bridgehead over the Váli); and *I. Btl./Germania* (on the far right flank next to the Danube). The division's reserve force, *III. Btl./Westland*, along with *SS-Pz.Aufkl.Abt. 5* and *SS-Pz. Rgt. 5*, occupied an assembly area in the vicinity of Nagy Halom. In Adony, two emergency companies composed of truck drivers and supply troops were joined by the division's *Begleitkompanie* to defend the town. Writing that evening, the division's *O1* described the events of the day:

> Once again the division finds itself in heavy defensive fighting. Enemy attacks [took place] from the northwest against Vogt [in Pettend], along the division's actual front line, from the east near Adony and from the south [near Perkáta]. The activity is constantly increasing, our opponent now appears to have sufficiently strong forces to bring to bear [against us].[133]

On the night of 27/28 January, Gille provided in his personal notebook a description of what had happened during the past two days and what he thought was about to happen. Having been made aware of what was heading his way, he wrote:

> [All] of the [corps] units began orienting themselves for the defense. The *Ic* reported that a strong enemy tank unit, a new tank corps, had assembled north of us. We expected an attack on our right flank. The army [headquarters] disputed this and demanded the continuation of the attack to the west. We had prepared ourselves to withstand the enemy's assault, which we expected to happen at any moment ... We were attacked by about 250 enemy tanks that attempted to drive as deep as the main highway [between Baraczka and Kápolnás Nyék]. At Pettend, there was a great tank battle, where on this day [27 January] alone 140 enemy tanks were taken care of. The *Norge* Battalion, composed of nearly all Norwegians, defended there and held its position; its commander, *Hstuf.* [*sic*] Vogt, accounted for six enemy tanks by himself. On account of the brave conduct of this battalion, the enemy was prevented from rolling up our [entire] front line.[134]

To the right of the *IV. SS-Pz.Korps*, Breith's *III. Pz.Korps* was already conducting operations, though mainly with the *3. Pz.Div.* and elements of *Gen.Maj. Radowitz's 23. Pz.Div.*, whose *Panzergruppe* was still in its old sector north of Stuhlweissenburg until it could be relieved by a similar one from the *6. Pz.Div.* It would be another day before the *1. Pz.Div.* would be able to join in with the *III. Pz.Korps'* counterattack.

General der Panzertruppe Breith's headquarters reported that Soviet troops, supported by eight tanks, had managed to penetrate the village of Gardamajor, 10 kilometers southeast of Sárkeresztur, where a counterattack by the leading element of the *23. Pz.Div.* was already underway. To its east, another Soviet attack, backed up by 25–35 tanks from the XVIII Tank Corps, threw *K.Gr. Weymann* out of Nagy Hantos, a mere 9 kilometers southeast of Sárosd and 11 kilometers southwest of Perkáta, and continued onwards until it had taken the heights several kilometers southwest of the latter town. An equally strong Soviet force was reported to be moving northwest along the road connecting Dunapentele with Perkáta.

Within Dunapentele itself, which *K.Gr. Medicus* continued to defend despite having been bypassed, two battalion-sized enemy attacks were driven back towards the southwest. Dunapentele was one of the most favorable crossing sites over the Danube, and the continuing possession of the town by the *3. Pz.Div.* was impacting Soviet logistical planning, so it had to be taken from the Germans as soon as possible. During the course of its counterattack that day, the *3. Pz.Div.* reporting knocking out 25 Soviet tanks (most likely from a brigade from the XVIII Tank Corps), a disturbing indicator of the size of the enemy force rushing towards the north. The situation was becoming increasingly dire, and as far as *Gen.d.Pz.Tr.* Balck was concerned, the rest of the *23. Pz.Div.* and the *1. Pz.Div.* could not get there quickly enough.

On the *A.Gr. Balck/6. Armee* left flank, *Korpsgruppe Harteneck/I. Kav.Korps* reported the only combat worth mentioning was an action that took place south of Felsőgalla, where Soviet forces continued slowly pushing towards the northwest, ejecting the defending forces of the Hungarian *II. Btl./Inf.Rgt. 54* from a large farmstead. Elsewhere along the corps' front, quiet reigned, except for artillery fire from the *711. Inf.Div.*, which it had managed to call down upon Szob in an attempt to disrupt the continuing southward movement of enemy forces along the highway leading through the town.

On the far right flank, the Hungarian *3. Armee* reported company- and battalion-sized penetrations in its front line along the Sió River in the area of the towns of Adand and Ozora, but these were eliminated during counterattacks by the Hungarian *25. Inf.Div.* Of much more concern was a division-sized assault supported by 10 tanks north of Simontornya, which managed to widen the penetration that Soviet forces had already made on the opposite bank of the bend in the Sió River over the past several days. The defending forces from *Div.Gr. Pape*—consisting of two battalions from the Hungarian *Inf.Rgt. 26*, an assault gun company, and *Pz.Aufkl. Abt 1* from the *1. Pz.Div.*—were unable to eject them from the village of Igar. Nor were they able to throw them back from the area south of Bacs Puszta or along the roadway running parallel to the Sárviz Canal near the village of Örs Puszta. The risky bet made by the commander of *A.Gr. Balck* at the outset of *Konrad III*, that relatively weak forces could hold the southern flank, had now been called in by the Soviet 26th and 57th Armies.

The evening report from *IX. SS-Geb.Korps* for 28 January was tinged with despair, though the garrison was not yet aware that *H.Gr. Süd* had written it off. Attacks along its northern, western, and southern perimeter continued to increase in intensity, while several blocks on the edge of the *Blutwiese* were lost during house-to-house fighting. Losses among the defenders continued to mount, forcing Pfeffer-Wildenbruch to order a withdrawal on the northern front as far as Szenvehegy Hill during the night of 28/29 January. Yet another attempt was made by Soviet troops to seize the rest of Margaret Island, but was beaten back by the dwindling German and Hungarian defenders. Air attacks against the Buda stronghold continued, though *Flak* troops managed to shoot down one aircraft. At least the *Luftwaffe* was able to airdrop a substantial amount of supplies that evening, delivering 130 tons of cargo, though the reports do not mention how much of it actually landed within friendly lines and how much on the Soviet side.

Due to improving weather conditions on 28 January, *Luftflotte 4* was able to launch a greatly increased number of sorties, flying 320 missions during the day against Soviet targets, claiming three tanks and 60 other vehicles destroyed, as well as damage to the pontoon bridge at Dunaföldvar. It also managed to fly 200 sorties during the night, focusing on assembly areas surrounding Budapest with conventional bombs and cluster munitions.[135] Bad weather at the high altitudes where most of the *Luftwaffe*'s reconnaissance aircraft operated rendered effective observation and photography of ground targets difficult. In the skies above Lake Velencze, the *III. Pz.Korps* reported being bombed and strafed by at least 46 IL-2 *Sturmoviks* and 14 LaGG-3 fighter-bombers, which focused on front-line positions and supply routes. The *OKW* war diary reported that on that day, the Red Air Force carried out 260 sorties.[136] Apparently, Soviet reconnaissance aircraft missed the redeployment of the *III. Pz.Korps* headquarters as well as the movement of the bulk of the *23. Pz.Div.* The *Flivo* attached to the *IV. SS-Pz.Korps* did not submit a report that evening, though enemy air activity must have been considerable.

The intelligence summary for that evening drew the inevitable conclusion that all of the signs indicated that the Soviets would continue their attacks between the Sárviz Canal and the Danube with the same order of battle that had become apparent during the past several days, but believed they still had several powerful cards to play, such as the VII Mechanized Corps, which had not yet been located west of the Danube.[137] Concerning other areas, *Hptm.* von Pander wrote:

> West of the Sárviz Canal, enemy assaults have intensified, apparently under the direction of the 57th Army using the newly introduced 233rd Rifle Division and the 32nd or the 5th Independent Guards Mechanized Brigade ... Between the Danube and Lake Velencze, the enemy continued with his attacks, but on account of the heavy losses in tanks he suffered during the previous [two] days, these attacks were of considerably less intensity. According to ground observation, the enemy's behavior, and a *Leo-Meldung* [yet another German agent inserted behind Soviet lines], the enemy apparently seems to be aiming towards the link-up of both of his assault groups from the north and the south towards an area immediately west of the Danube. Preparations for a strong enemy attack between Lake Velencze and the Vértes Mountains have not been reported, though attacks designed to tie up our forces in that area should not be ruled out ... according to a *Karl-Meldung*, the movement of the Pliyev Army [i.e., the I Guards Cavalry Mechanized Group] has been confirmed. However, it has not been established where the opponent intends to employ this army once it has crossed over the Danube.[138]

The plans for the further employment of the VII Mechanized Corps as well as the "Pliyev Army" at this point were conjectural and may have been influenced by Soviet disinformation or were part of a more comprehensive operational deception plan.

In fact, neither of these two units were present or envisioned to be employed west of the Danube in the near future. And what had been labeled as the "Pliyev Army," more formally known as the I Guards Cavalry-Mechanized Group, had been misidentified; what German agents had actually spotted without realizing it was the 6th Guards Tank Army, which had not been sent north after all, but had been moved to a reserve area east of Budapest for a month-long reconstitution as part of a longer-range offensive plan.[139]

As 28 January drew to a close, *H.Gr. Süd* could point to very little that *Unternehmen Konrad I–III* had actually achieved during the past four weeks of fighting. Although a significant amount of ground had been gained, *A.Gr. Balck/6. Armee* had failed to accomplish its main objectives, the liberation of Budapest and the restoration of the *Margarethestellung*. While Balck's *Armeegruppe* had destroyed a significant amount of Soviet armored vehicles during January, this had only a short-term beneficial effect. In fact, the *STAVKA* sent forward 566 replacement tanks and 283 self-propelled and assault guns to replace what had been lost in the Third Ukrainian Front area of operations that month alone.[140]

Despite the impressive number of enemy tanks destroyed and soldiers killed or wounded, *H.Gr. Süd* was in a worse position at the end of January than it was at the beginning. Nearly all of Balck's attacking units had been seriously depleted after four weeks of nearly constant combat operations. The six German panzer *divisions* and the one Hungarian one still part of *A.Gr. Balck*'s order of battle at the end of the month, including the two SS divisions, had all suffered heavy losses in nearly every category. Most of these losses were irreplaceable, including not only tanks and other armored vehicles, but the loss of experienced officers and NCOs as well. Two more *panzer* divisions were in the process of being destroyed in Budapest, as were two SS cavalry divisions. The question needed to be asked: was it worth it? Balck, 35 years later and with the benefit of hindsight, wrote:

> By the time we launched the new attack, it was too late. As I had feared, the Russians [*sic*] that had been pushed toward the south evaded destruction [i.e., the XVIII Tank Corps and CXXXIII Rifle Corps]. They were reinforced, they turned around and they wiped out the Hungarian Third Army ... with that, the fate of this relief attempt and the fate of Budapest were sealed. Reluctantly, we had to pull the *IV SS-Pz.Korps* back ... Despite heavy fighting, we were able to absorb the Russian attack between Lake Balaton and Lake Velencze. What would have happened if Gille had continued his move toward Budapest? All the courage of the troops, including the fanatically fighting *3.* and *5. SS-Panzer Divisions*, and all the efforts of the leadership had been in vain. The correlation of forces had been tilted too heavily against us.[141]

Two errors in this self-justifying statement are glaringly evident, based on the knowledge of what really occurred, knowledge that was available even then.

The first is that Balck makes it seem as if the Hungarian *3. Armee* was responsible for the defeat in the south, thus absolving him of any blame for what happened. In fact, as we now know, most of the combat power in the south was composed of the *3. Pz.Div.* and *Div.Gr. Pape*, with the Hungarian *25. Inf.Div.* fulfilling a static defense role along the Sió River. Balck also does not make it clear that the Hungarians were operating under his command, although it was called an *Armeegruppe* and not just the *6. Armee*, meaning that it was a combined German and Hungarian force under Balck's leadership.

The other aspect of this statement worth pointing out is that Balck does not mention that his ill-advised order to Gille to reorient his attack towards the west was responsible for the culmination of *IV. SS-Pz.Korps'* attack. Gille and his staff, as well as his three division commanders, instinctively knew that the only chance to relieve Budapest rested on a quick dash across the Váli River to the city and back. The corps had already seized two bridgeheads in the *Wiking* Division's attack zone. It would have made more sense to have shifted the *1. Pz.Div.* to the far right instead of directing Thünert's division to the west to attack towards Acsa along with the *Totenkopf* Division. By the morning of 28 January, all of this was moot; Gille's corps had spent itself repelling the counterattack by the XXIII Tank Corps and after that point, any *Husarenritt* towards Budapest was no longer possible.

Much has been made of the threat posed to the left flank of the *IV. SS-Pz.Korps* by the XX and XXI Guards Rifle Corps, but as we have seen, these forces were performing a defensive role, "standing to the last," against *Korpsgruppe Breith/III. Pz.Korps*. These corps' attacks from the west against the salient formed on 26 January by Gille's two attacking divisions were more of a reaction designed to slow or stop the German advance, rather than a move to cut it off. That was the mission assigned to the XXIII Tank Corps. In this regard, Balck was acting far more cautiously than the situation warranted. Had he stuck with his original plan, that is, continuing the drive to the northeast, the *1. Pz.Div.* and the *Totenkopf* Division may very well have reached Budapest.

Reaching Budapest did not equal the same thing as liberating it. The only way the plan could have succeeded was if the garrison had been given permission to break out on 26 January; indeed, Pfeffer-Wildenbruch had directed his staff to draft such a plan weeks earlier. As we now know, Hitler strictly forbade it, and repeated requests by Wöhler and Balck to grant them freedom of action to decide whether to authorize a breakout were denied. Evidence indicates that Gille was not aware of this crucial fact, but he did seem to know that his attack could only succeed if such a breakout by the *IX. SS-Geb.Korps* was in the offing. So, while it is quite possible that the relief forces could have reached Budapest, the only action beyond that point they were authorized to do was to link up with the encircled force.

Gille found it incomprehensible that a breakout order was not given; after all, only one year before *Generalfeldmarschall* von Manstein had defied Hitler and ordered *Gruppe Stemmermann* to break out from the Cherkassy Pocket on his own authority, and Gille had been there. However, neither Wöhler nor Balck possessed the moral courage of a von Manstein; apparently both leaders feared

Hitler's wrath more than they cared for the lives of their men. In one sense though, Balck was correct: had Gille reached Budapest, two SS corps would have been encircled, not just one. Had the *IV. SS-Pz.Korps* reached the city, and no breakout had taken place, his corps would have been stuck there, vulnerable to flank attacks along his entire route of advance (and retreat) by the XXIII Tank Corps and CIV Rifle Corps, the V Guards Cavalry Corps, and the I Guards Mechanized Corps.

With the relief operation now officially at an end, upon further analysis and with the benefit of hindsight, is it reasonable to ask whether there was ever any chance of relieving Budapest at all? Although the three iterations of *Unternehmen Konrad* had approached to within 14–22 kilometers of Budapest—depending upon whose version of the story told by participants you believe—without a corresponding attack from the city's garrison towards the relief force (while it still could do so), it is doubtful whether any of the three attempts would have succeeded. To identify the point where the plan went wrong, one has to go back to the end of December 1944, when Wöhler and Balck decided (reluctantly in Balck's case) to choose the *Nordlösung* through the Vértes Mountains over the southern approach. Gille's opinion in the matter was not solicited.

The primary limiting factor influencing this decision to attack in the north was time and fuel—it was thought that Budapest could not hold out longer than two weeks, so the generals decided that the quickest and most economical way to the city was better than the one that offered the greater chance of success. As it turned out, terrain, weather, and above all, enemy resistance finally forced Wöhler and Balck to cancel both *Konrad I* and *II*. Hitler's impatience was also a limiting factor, and as has been already discussed, he had been in favor of the *Südlösung* since the beginning. By the time that *Konrad III* began in the south two-and-a-half weeks after *Konrad I* started, the attacking forces had been seriously depleted; fuel was in short supply; its men were exhausted and they lacked sufficient combat power to reach the city, much less to overcome the formidable defenses erected by the 4th Guards Army. Besides these reasons, it must be mentioned that the *IX. SS-Geb.Korps* had declined in strength so much that it most likely could not have carried out an attack to meet the oncoming relief force by 26 January, even had its commander wished to.

However, had the *Südlösung* been selected from the outset and had begun on 3 or 4 January as originally envisioned, the chances for success would have been much better, especially had it been coupled with diversionary attacks in the north to draw off Tolbukhin and Zakharov's attention, not to mention a similar attack in the south by the *2. Pz.Armee*. Most of the attacking forces, especially Gille's two SS divisions, would have been at nearly full strength and relatively fresh. In addition, as events were to prove, making three separate relief attempts instead of one consumed far more fuel and ammunition than the original "southern solution."

By the time that *K.Gr. Philipp* reached within 14–18 kilometers from Budapest on 26 January, the *IX. SS-Geb.Korps* was too weak to break out; had the *1. Pz.Div.* reached the Váli River by 6 January, as was possible, it may have succeeded. But even then, Hitler would still have forbade such an attempt, because he wanted his forces to achieve far more than that—nothing short of restoring the front line to where it had been at the end of November 1944. So perhaps the relief of Budapest was never possible, no matter which course of action had been chosen. In one sense at least, the abandonment of the relief attempt was not all bad news, for it meant that *A.Gr. Balck/6. Armee* would now be able to concentrate strictly on fighting for its own survival, which by the evening of 28/29 January was not a sure thing.

CHAPTER 10

Battling to a Stalemate
29 January–4 February 1945

After the failure of *Unternehmen Konrad III*, the *IV. SS-Pz.Korps* did not have the opportunity to experience an "operational pause." Its divisions could not be granted time to take stock of the situation, to reorganize or to rest and reconstitute its weakened units. As if by the flick of a switch, Balck's mistimed and overly ambitious attempt to encircle Soviet forces north of Lake Velencze using the *IV. SS-Pz.Korps* was canceled and the corps' spearheads hastily withdrawn from the outskirts of Vál and the towns of Vereb and Pazmánd towards the Baraczka–Pettend–Kápolnás Nyék line, with the enemy following closely. Here, the *1. Pz.Div.* ended its two-week attachment to the corps, while the *Totenkopf* Division hung on for two more days until it too was forced to withdraw to the southeast corner of Lake Velencze. The *Wiking* Division clung as long as possible to the Váli River line until it began its own grudging withdrawal, its leaders believing until the last moment that Budapest could still be relieved.

The weather during this period, which became even more severe, took no notice of the fighting or of any human concerns, but rather continued its eons-old cycle of the seasons. On 29 January, the cold temperatures intensified, falling as low as –4 degrees Fahrenheit (–20 degrees Centigrade), rendering life—even survival—more difficult, especially for troops fighting out in the open. During the evening, soldiers from both sides sought shelter against the cold in Hungarian homes, outbuildings, and barns. Frostbite became common among the more exposed troops and Eastern Front veterans remarked that they had not seen anything as bad since the horrible winter of 1941–42. Rivers froze solid, as did the snow-blanketed *Puszta*, which at least eased cross-country movement by armored vehicles, provided that the crews could start their engines in the freezing weather. The day was interspersed with strong winds and occasional blizzards, which tended to drift up along the roadways. The skies remained partly cloudy; occasionally they would part and allow air activity by both sides to resume with undiminished ferocity. In short, it had become a horrible place to fight a war.

The only notice that the Hungarian theater of operations received in the daily *Wehrmachtsbericht* for 29 January was a short paragraph that merely stated,

"In Hungary, difficult defensive battles continued between Lake Balaton and the Danube, as well as the western portion of Budapest. Thirty-three enemy tanks were destroyed there today."[1] That same day, the *IV. SS-Pz.Korps Ic* report summarized what had become a very bloody day:

> Between the Danube and Lake Velencze, the enemy carried out constant attacks with strong infantry forces and groups of 10 to 20 tanks. In this way, he was able to achieve a penetration along the railroad line northwest of Szinatelep and was also able to eliminate our bridgehead over the Váli northeast of Aggszentpéter as well as the salient south of Baraczka. Hard fighting [there] is ongoing. Along the rest of the corps' front, little fighting of any significance was reported.[2]

Monday, 29 January marked the last day of participation by the *1. Pz.Div.* in *Unternehmen Konrad III*. Its regiments and battalions had all managed to complete their withdrawal from the Pettend–Kápolnás Nyék area during the evening of 28/29 January and assemble in the area south of Lake Velencze around Gárdony. Following its brief reorganization, the division—with its remaining 12 operational tanks and assault guns—began moving south towards Perkáta after midnight to begin its participation in the attempt by the *III. Pz.Korps* to stop the counteroffensive by the 26th Army (see below). *Generalmajor* Thünert and his veterans would rejoin the ranks of the *IV. SS-Pz.Korps* in the very near future.

Brigadeführer Becker and his *Totenkopf* Division were able to hold the line between Baraczka and Kápolnás Nyék against a series of determined attacks by the XXIII Tank Corps in what *A.Gr. Balck*'s chief of staff, *Gen.Maj.* Gaedke, later described as "quite heavy defensive fighting."[3] Although the attack by the Soviet 3rd Tank Brigade was able to create a salient in the lines between Pettend and Kápolnás Nyék, a counterattack by *Stubaf.* im Masche's *I. Btl./Danmark*, *1. Bttr./SS-Flak-Abt. 3*, and *III. Bataillon* of the *Totenkopf* Regiment managed to stop it near Ferenczmajor, despite the wounding of the *III. Btl./Totenkopf*'s commander, *Stubaf.* Kiklasch.

When the *Totenkopf* Division's commander realized that an attack to the south out of Baraczka by the 39th Tank Brigade and the 151st Rifle Division of the CIV Rifle Corps threatened to separate his division from the neighboring *Wiking* Division, cutting them both off from their lines of communication near Felsö Besnyö, Becker ordered *I. Btl./Eicke* out of its assembly area south of Lake Velencze near Gárdony. Joined by a few newly repaired tanks of *SS-Pz.Rgt. 3*, the battalion launched a counterattack in conjunction with the *Wiking* Division to force the enemy grouping to partially withdraw.[4] This left the *III. Btl./Totenkopf* in an exposed salient immediately south of Baraczka, which it was forced to evacuate during the night of 29/30 January.

The *Wiking* Division was also hard-pressed that day, having been forced to give up its bridgehead over the river held by *I. Btl./Germania* east of Aggszentpéter and compelled to begin pulling back from the Váli in order to maintain the integrity of the main defensive line. Kis Halom and Aggszentpéter were abandoned and by the evening, 20 Soviet tanks had occupied the hill 3 kilometers north of the railroad station at Szinatelep, which the division had captured the week before. On the division's far right (or southern) flank, the counterattack that day by the *1. Pz.Div.* had at least temporarily ended the threats against Perkáta. That night, the *Wiking* Division's *O1* wrote about the day's events:

> This massed enemy attack achieved a number of deep penetrations ... With the help of our reconnaissance battalion, which we had kept in reserve for the final push towards Budapest, it was possible by the evening to seal off all of these enemy breakthroughs and to "iron them out" during the night ... the division was surprised by this massed tank assault, which we attributed to insufficient intelligence about the enemy situation. Before this, we had believed that we were facing only a battered cavalry corps ... Two days later we learned that the *Ic* of the [*6. Armee*] was cooperating with the Russians [*sic*] and was supposedly convicted and shot.[5]

Though this was only a *Latrinenparole* (barracks rumor) shared by other SS officers in Gille's corps, Jahnke and other *Wikinger* could not come up with another explanation as to how the XXIII Tank Corps and CIV Rifle Corps had arrived in the front lines undetected and in such strength. That this lapse was due to a simple failure of the German intelligence services (not to mention effective Soviet operational security), and not high treason as they suspected, was beyond their imagination. Regardless, the attack of 29 January must have come as quite a rude shock.

Fortunately for *Div.Gr. Holste*, it had been a relatively uneventful day, enabling *Gen.Maj.* Rudolf Holste to put his house in order. Taking advantage of the temporary pause in the battle in his sector, he reorganized his command to begin incorporating the *356. Inf.Div.* into his order of battle and to put some of his existing units back together, such as ordering one battalion from *Reiter-Rgt. 41* of the *4. Kav.Brig.* out of the line on *Div.Gr. Holste*'s right flank inside Stuhlweissenburg and move it into a reserve position at Magyaralmás. The Hungarian *Btl. Holczer* was to remain in place at Körakás, as would *SS-Rgt. Ney* at Csala. *Panzergrenadier Regiment 126* of the *23. Pz.Div.*, holding the far right flank of *Div.Gr. Holste* in the southeastern corner of Stuhlweissenburg, had already been replaced overnight by the first-arriving unit of the *356. Inf.Div., II. Btl./Gren.Rgt. 871*, located to the right of *SS-Rgt. Ney*. The arrival of the remaining elements of the division had been delayed when the troop trains transporting them to Várpalota had to stop and clear the tracks of deep snowdrifts, and it would require nearly a week for all of it to arrive.

The *356. Inf.Div.* was not a first-rate combat unit, and in fact had spent most of its first year of existence either defending the Italian coastline or conducting anti-partisan operations in northern Italy until June 1944, when it was finally sent into action in the Gothic Line south of Florence. Activated on 1 May 1943 in Toulon as a *Gisela-Einheit*,[6] it was created by combining various reserve regiments from the *189. Res.Div.* of *Wehrkreis IX*. By January 1945, the division adhered to the same three-regiment structure of most *Kriegsetat 1944* infantry divisions, with two battalions per regiment (*Gren.Rgter. 869, 870*, and *871*), a three-battalion artillery regiment, a *Pionier-Bataillon*, and a *Divisions-Füsilier* (reconnaissance) battalion, along with logistics and administrative units that relied on horse-drawn transportation.[7] Unfortunately, its *Gren.Rgt. 869* and *Div.Füs.Btl. 356* had been stripped of all their foot soldiers to fill out the other two regiments and the remaining *Rahmen* (framework) of these units were shipped to Germany to undergo a complete reactivation. This left the division short of three battalions until the end of the war, since neither *Gren.Rgt. 869* nor *Div.Füs.Btl. 356* ever rejoined the division. Still, this late-war German division was a welcome addition.

Its acting commander was *Oberst* Claus Kühl, a 47-year-old professional soldier from Karlsberg who had been awarded the German Cross in Silver. A veteran of World War I and a year of combat on the Italian front, he had previously served as the commander of *Gren.Rgt. 145* of the *65. Inf.Div.*, where his name had been mentioned in the *Wehrmacht's* daily bulletin for leading his regiment in battle, though until 1943 he had served on a corps staff in Norway. Upon arrival, Kühl's division immediately became the strongest infantry division in *H.Gr. Süd.* It had never served on the Eastern Front before and was completely unaccustomed to conditions there. Nevertheless, it was the only fresh division that the *OKH* could spare. Arriving in snow-covered Hungary with temperatures hovering below freezing after traveling for several days in unheated boxcars must have come as quite a shock to soldiers accustomed to a sunnier climate.

Its northern neighbor was Holste's veteran *4. Kav.Brig.*, consisting of *Reiter-Regiment 5* (known as the *Feldmarschall Mackensen* regiment) and *Reiter-Regiment 41*, each with two mounted infantry battalions, *Art.Rgt. 870* (with three artillery battalions), *Pz.Jäg.Abt. 70* (with five operational assault guns), *Pz.Aufkl.Abt. 70*, and division services. Severely depleted after four weeks of uninterrupted combat, its *Kampfstärke* had sunk to 1,194 men as of 27 January, though it did have 300 men available in its field replacement battalion. The brigade had been augmented by the attachment of *s.Pz.Abt. 503 FHH*, which had no operational Tiger IIs on the last report date of 27 January, as well as by the aforementioned Hungarian *SS-Rgt. Ney* and *Btl. Holczer*, with a combined *Kampfstärke* of 305 men.

The Hungarian *2. Pz.Div.* rounded out *Div.Gr. Holste*. Relatively small compared to German *panzer* divisions, it fielded one three-battalion tank regiment and a three-battalion motorized infantry regiment, though it lacked any *SPW*s of its own. Its artillery component was rather weak, with only two battalions, though it could be augmented by *Volks-Art.Korps 403* as the situation dictated. It also possessed a good armored reconnaissance battalion, a small combat engineer battalion, and an anti-aircraft battalion, along with division services. Led by *Gen.Maj.* Zoltán Zsedényi, it had thus far acquitted itself well in fighting around Felsőmajor and Csólkakő, and reportedly had good morale, though its desertion rate was increasing. On 27 January, it reported its *Kampfstärke* as 1,350 men and its tank regiment had 14 operational *Pz. IV*s. How well it would perform under the command and control of a *Waffen-SS* corps headquarters was yet to be seen.

To the left of the *IV. SS-Pz.Korps*, *Korpsgruppe Harteneck/I. Kav.Korps* reported that Hungarian forces were in the process of eliminating a small number of enemy troops that had been encircled east of Hill 398. Other than that, the rest of the corps' front was quiet. The anticipated resumption of the Soviet X Rifle Corps' drive towards Gran failed to materialize, to the relief of the men of the *711. Inf.Div.*, whose overextended regiments had to defend not only Gran, but a significant portion of the southern bank of the Danube, a duty it shared with the neighboring Hungarian *23. Inf.Div.* Although not mentioned in the reports, *II. Btl./Pz.Gren.Rgt.* FHH was still occupying a defensive position east of Gran, where it had ended up after *K.Gr. Philipp*'s original *Husarenritt* had been canceled during *Konrad II*. At a point in the near future, it would be recalled and sent to join the newest incarnation of the *Feldherrnhalle* Division after its original namesake was destroyed in Budapest.

The focus of most of the heavy fighting, as it had the day before, took place in the *III. Pz.Korps'* area of operations. Facing the brunt of the attack by the 26th Army, *Gen.d.Pz.Tr.* Breith's corps—consisting of the *3. Pz.Div.* and *23. Pz.Div.* (minus its *Panzergruppe*), augmented later that morning by the full weight of the *1. Pz.Div.*—was busily engaged in fighting off a number of large-scale armored assaults led by the brigades of the XVIII Tank Corps. That night, the corps' *Ic* attempted to cobble together a comprehensive report, which barely touched upon the savagery of the fighting:

> The enemy was able to achieve a breakthrough in the southwestern portion of a nameless village five kilometers east-northeast of Káloz, that we were able to seal off. Two further [enemy] assaults from the area near Hill 103 towards the northeast were unsuccessful. Our troops [*23. Pz.Div.*] attacking towards the southeast from Gazdamajor against stiffening resistance, were able to throw an attacking enemy force out of Kis Hantos Puszta and Kis Venyim Puszta, despite his use of a large number of antitank guns that challenged our attack in Nagy Lók. A strong enemy force was ejected from Perkáta [by *1. Pz.Div.*] and the heights to the southwest and in Dunapentele [our troops] were able to overcome a local breakthrough, nor was the enemy able to prevent the advance of [the *3. Pz.Div.*] *Panzergruppe* from Dunapentele to the southwest.

Though all of its divisions were understrength, the counterattack launched that day by the *III. Pz.Korps* and its *1, 3,* and *23. Pz.Div.* managed to destroy 36 Soviet tanks, four assault guns, and 16 antitank guns, but the larger objective of encircling and destroying the bulk of the enemy's armor in the vicinity of Herczegfalva remained beyond Breith's reach. Fortunately, the attack on the corps' left flank towards Dunapentele by the *1. Pz.Div.* was successful, relieving the embattled troops of *K.Gr. Medicus*, who had been surrounded there for the past two days.

In the Hungarian *3. Armee* sector, things were beginning to heat up, an indication that its positions along the *Sió-Abschnitt* had now become the focus of attention of the CXXXV Rifle Corps. Along both sides of Ádánd, two enemy groups with the strength of two or three battalions each from the 236th Rifle Division crossed the

Sió River and were able to achieve a local penetration to a depth of 5 kilometers that troops of the Hungarian *25. Inf.Div.* could not seal off on their own. Later that day, with the assistance of the *Panzergruppe* from the *6. Pz.Div.* (*K.Gr. Martini*) which had been diverted from Stuhlweissenburg, the Hungarians were able to prevent this setback from becoming a catastrophe. Despite this defensive success, the lost ground could not be regained that day.

At reporting time, the Hungarian *III. Btl./Inf.Rgt. 26* was in the process of clearing out a local penetration near Ozora. In the southeast corner defended by *Div.Gr. Pape*, elements of the 233rd Rifle Division in the strength of up to two battalions attacked north of Igar, a village northwest and north of Simontornya. The Soviets also carried out an attack against the village of Örs Puszta, located on the western bank of the Sárviz Canal, which was fended off by *Pz.Aufkl.Abt. 1*. As the evening reporting deadline approached, *Gen.Lt.* Heszlényi's headquarters reported that the enemy had later returned to the same area and resumed his attack with up to two rifle regiments, a confirmation that the 57th Army had committed an entire division to this effort.

In Budapest, the situation worsened. Enemy attacks against the northern and western sections of the perimeter continued without let-up. In the north, Soviet assaults forced the German and Hungarian forces to withdraw several blocks since they no longer possessed sufficient troops to hold the formerly extended line. Hungarian troops launched a counterattack against the penetration the Soviets managed to make in the western portion of the line, and although they were unable to eliminate it completely, they were able to considerably narrow it. Shortly before noon, the entrapped garrison within the *Brückenkopf* reported that the amount of artillery, mortar, and rocket fire against the southern perimeter began to noticeably increase, perhaps an indication that the 46th Army intended to begin its final effort to eradicate the *IX. SS-Geb.Korps*.

The daily ration inside the pocket was reduced once more, with front-line troops now receiving only a slice of bread, some horsemeat, or a thin bowl of soup, while all the wounded got was the latter, if that. Despite the weather and Soviet antiaircraft fire, the *Luftwaffe* dropped 57 metric tons of supplies over the city; once again, how much of that reached the garrison is unknown. During the night, gangs of roving soldiers—both German and Hungarian—would seek out missdropped supply bundles and loot them of their contents, despite the death penalty this incurred if they were caught. In his nightly report, Pfeffer-Wildenbruch, who still did not know that *Konrad III* had been officially canceled, highlighted the plight of his troops when he wrote, "If the *IV. SS-Pz.Korps* does not arrive in the very near term future, they will come too late. We are nearing the end."[8]

In the air that day, there was a considerable amount of activity by the Red Air Force, estimated to be as many as 200 sorties by *Luftwaffe* observers (the Red Air Force reported flying 460).[9] Aircraft of the 5th and 17th Air Armies were particularly active in the sky above the *IV. SS-Pz.Korps* east of Lake Velencze, including constant attacks by fighter-bombers and ground-attack aircraft using bombs and on-board weapons directed against front-line positions and suspected command post locations. Over the *III. Pz.Korps*, enemy air activity was lively, though scattered and ineffective. *Luftflotte 4* managed to launch 100 sorties of its own, enjoying some degree of success when its fighter-bombers scored two direct hits on the bridge over the Danube at Dunaföldvar using aerial bombs, as well as destroying six Soviet locomotives pulling supply trains.[10]

In regards to the overall intelligence situation, as viewed by the *A.Gr. Balck/6. Armee Ic* staff, it was a mixed bag. While *Hptm.* von Pander and his superior, *Oberstlt.* Wüstenberg (who had been neither arrested nor executed, despite rumors to the contrary), were heartened by the news that the counterattack against the 26th Army by the *III. Pz.Korps* was beginning to display the hoped-for results, they did not feel as sanguine about the chances that the Hungarian *3. Armee* would be able to stop attacks against its forces arrayed along the *Sió-Abschnitt* or the Sárviz Canal unless it was substantially reinforced. One bit of good news was the realization that the VII Mechanized Corps had not joined the 26th Army after all; it was now being assessed that it was being kept in reserve east of the Danube for a future operation or the protection of the Soviet bridgehead at Dunaföldvar.

Hauptmann von Pander and his associates also assessed that the XXIII Tank Corps, CIV Rifle Corps, I Guards Mechanized Corps, and V Guards Cavalry Corps would continue with their defense of the Váli line, as well as persist in their attempts to push the *IV. SS-Pz.Korps* as far away as possible from Budapest, rendering any relief of the city impracticable. In regards to Budapest itself, the *Ic* mentioned that the 46th Army appeared to be reinforcing its forces on the southern portion of the perimeter, in preparation for resuming its attacks against the ever-shrinking *Festung*. The report concluded with suppositions about the future disposition of the II Guards Mechanized Corps, as well as that of Cavalry-Mechanized Corps Pliyev.

Of course, any German actions must be seen in light of Soviet reactions, and vice versa. While the counterattacks in the north by the four Soviet corps arrayed northeast and east of Lake Velencze had been unable to achieve the decisive breakthrough they had sought, on the other hand they had eliminated one of the two bridgeheads over the Váli in the *Wiking* Division's sector and had nearly reclaimed all of the river's western bank. However, Tolbukhin was dissatisfied with the performance of the 26th Army in the south; he felt that its commander, Lt.Gen. Skvirsky, had dispersed the efforts of the XVIII Tank Corps when it should have been concentrated instead. Apparently, he had ordered uncoordinated and widely dispersed attacks that led to the loss of 95 of its armored fighting vehicles in only three days (two-thirds of its original complement).

This dispersion of effort and heavy loss in tanks and other armored vehicles had rendered the 26th Army's counteroffensive vulnerable to further attacks by

A. Gr. Balck/6. Armee, whose *III. Pz. Korps* had initially achieved a considerable degree of operational surprise. The very next day, 30 January, Skvirsky was replaced by Lt.Gen. N. A. Gagen. Rather than continue moving against Perkáta, where the *1. Pz. Div.* had concentrated, Tolbukhin directed Gagen to focus on opening up the river road leading from Dunaföldvar to Adony and linking up with the approaching columns from 4th Guards Army to the north.[11] In regards to operations by the 57th Army against the Hungarian *25. Inf. Div.* and *Div. Gr. Pape* along the Sió River and Sárviz Canal, these would continue, especially since they were beginning to show promising indications of success. However, neither the commander of the Third Ukrainian Front nor that of the 26th Army were as yet aware of the movement of the *Panzergruppe* from the *6. Pz. Div.* towards Enying, where it would soon reinforce the Hungarians in their efforts to eliminate the breakthrough at Ádánd.[12]

The XXIII Tank Corps and CIV Rifle Corps, whose attacks between 27 and 29 January had not yet achieved the desired breakthrough, would continue their assaults scheduled for the following day with the intent of pushing the *IV. SS-Pz. Korps* further back from the Váli. General Zakharov's orders had been changed to the effect that these two corps were directed to seek a shallow breakthrough to the south along the Danube river highway between Adony and Dunaföldvar in order to link up with the spearheads of the approaching 26th Army, rather than a deeper attack towards Sárosd as originally planned. If the opportunity presented itself, the XXIII Tank Corps was ordered to take Puszta Szabolcs on the right flank, though this was stretching it a bit because Lt.Gen. Akhmanov's corps had not yet replaced all of the armored fighting vehicles it had lost between 27 and 28 January (see Map 9).

Meanwhile, Tolbukhin's intelligence services had detected the movement of the *23. Pz. Div.* away from the former *Korpsgruppe Breith* sector north of Stuhlweissenburg and its shift to the south. However, his headquarters did not initially detect the departure of the *III. Pz. Korps* headquarters on 27 January, though by 29 January its presence south of Lake Velencze was well-established. The resulting weakening of the German defenses between Stuhlweissenburg and Zámoly presented a momentary opportunity that Tolbukhin sought to capitalize upon by shifting the V Guards Cavalry Corps and I Mechanized Corps away from the Váli line and, in conjunction with the XX and XXI Guards Rifle Corps already positioned there, carry out a large-scale counterattack against *Div. Gr. Holste*. If successful, it would cut off the *III. Pz. Korps* counterattack towards the south at its base, as well as the Hungarian *3. Armee*. At the time he made his decision, Tolbukhin was unaware that this sector had become the responsibility of the *IV. SS-Pz. Korps* since midnight on 28 January, believing instead that Holste's motley collection of forces was all that stood in their way. The 4th Guards Army's attack was scheduled to begin on 31 January, after the two corps handed off their positions to the XXIII Tank Corps and CIV Rifle Corps along the Váli. This was followed by a 45-kilometer road march through heavy snowstorms and congested roadways to reach their new assembly

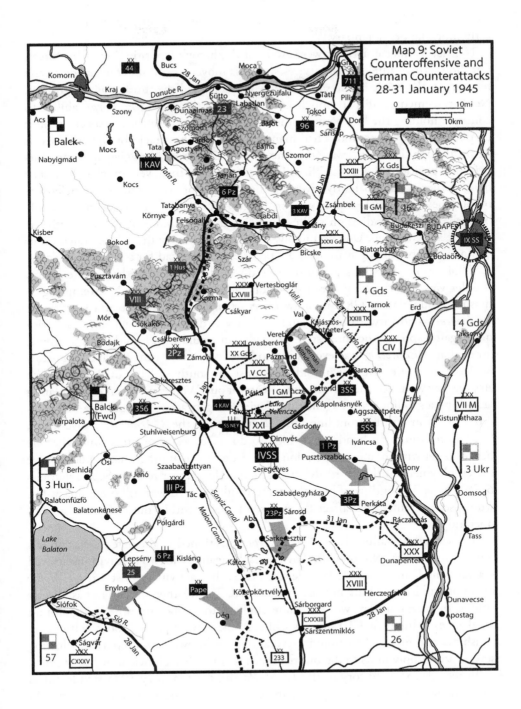

Map 9: Soviet Counteroffensive and German Counterattacks 28-31 January 1945

areas in the vicinity of Lovasberény, which was completed after great effort by the early morning of 31 January.[13]

Neither Wöhler nor Balck were aware of Zakharov's repositioning of his forces, nor did German intelligence services spot this movement. Both commanders were focused on the battle in the south, where they believed the threat was the greatest. Neither seemed to display much concern about the *IV. SS-Pz.Korps'* ability to continue holding the line between the Danube and Lake Velencze, especially since it appeared that Gille's troops had managed to blunt the attacks by the 4th Guards Army, though they were aware that the *Wiking* Division had to give up some of its defensive positions along the Váli. This did not concern them very much either, since both of them had apparently given up the thought of ever rescuing the defenders of Budapest, in which case it was no longer necessary to hang on to the single bridgehead Ullrich's division still occupied at the confluence of the Váli with the Danube at Szinatelep. Unaccountably, they failed to notify the *Wiking* Division of this new reality, forcing it to defend a pointless bridgehead for several more days.

While most of Balck's attention was directed towards Breith's counterattack, Wöhler was also thinking about other operations. He persisted in attempting to persuade Guderian at *OKH* to allow *Unternehmen Eisbrecher* (the attack by the *2. Pz.Armee*) to go forward on 31 January, but was disappointed when his superior once again expressed no interest. That Guderian would turn him down was ironic, given that if *Eisbrecher* was ever going to be effective at a time when a large-scale Soviet counteroffensive was unfolding against the southern flank of *A.Gr. Balck/6. Armee*, now would be the perfect time to carry it out. Wöhler was also contemplating launching a spoiling attack against the Soviet bridgehead west of the Gran River in order to "clean up" the front line and free up forces in the *8. Armee* defensive sector, but had no forces on hand with which to do so. It was about this time when he began to get wind of a new operation that Hitler was planning, that would involve the employment of the Third Reich's last remaining armor reserve, Sepp Dietrich's *6. Pz.Armee*. The outline of how this force would be used was still preliminary, but would soon dramatically affect the course of events within the *H.Gr. Süd* area of operations.

The second day after the *IV. SS-Pz.Korps* transitioned to the defense was no less tense than the first. Not only did Soviet attacks against the two SS divisions arrayed between the Danube and Lake Velencze persist, but activity against *Div.Gr. Holste* north of Stuhlweissenburg noticeably increased. The weather, though not as bitterly cold as the previous day, was still quite chilly, with temperatures hovering around 14 degrees Fahrenheit (-10 degrees Celsius). Skies were partly cloudy with some sunshine, and for the first time in several days no snowfall was reported, allowing service and supply units to dig out the roads that had been blocked by heavy drifts.

In regards to the history of the *IV. SS-Pz.Korps*, 30 January 1945 stands out as the only day for which a completely intact copy of one of its situation reports still exists. It was captured by Soviet troops shortly after it was written, and translated into Russian. For readers, this has been translated into English because the original German language copy is on file within the *TsAMO* (The Central Archives of the Ministry of Defense of the Russian Federation), located in Podolsk outside of Moscow, and is not yet available for researchers. The situation report, composed by Fritz Rentrop, the corps *Ia*, and Hans Velde, his *O1*, reads in its entirety as follows:

Corps Summary: With the maximum concentration of large infantry and tank forces, the enemy tried to achieve a breakthrough in the southern and southwestern directions. The attacking enemy tanks were stopped by our own weaker tank forces, while 30 enemy tanks were knocked out. We expect the continuation of enemy attacks in the area tomorrow. The attacks undertaken today against the area of *Div.Gr. Holste* are regarded as a reconnaissance in force. In this regard, with the removal of reserves from the area between the Danube and Lake Velencze which was established by air reconnaissance, one should expect major attacks in the Stuhlweissenburg area soon.

Corps mission for following day: Defend and carry out local attacks to improve the position between the Danube and Lake Velencze.

5. SS-Pz.Div. Wiking. From early morning, the enemy, having taken up its initial positions in the Aggszentpéter area, continued attacks with large infantry and tank forces, mainly in the southwestern and western directions. In many places, the enemy managed to break through the security screen of the division and penetrate in the area of Felsöbesnyö and to the north of it. Further attacks from the Felsöbesnyö area to the south were repelled. Many enemy tanks were knocked out. During the most difficult battles, which lasted all day with varying success, our formations were mainly able to stay in the defile area [the area between the Váli River and eastern edge of Lake Velencze] and, together with *3. SS-Pz.Div. Totenkopf,* gain a foothold on the lines of Göböljárás-Felsöbesnyö, Györgymajor, Gróf, Ferenczmajor, Ménesmajor, and Hill 155 1 kilometer northeast of Ménes. By the counterattack of the *Pz.Gren.Rgt. 9 Germania*, undertaken at 3 p.m. in the direction of Nagy Halom, after stubborn resistance by large infantry forces and enemy tanks, by 5 p.m. Hill 146 was occupied southwest of Nagy Halom. After an attack by a large enemy force on our screen line on the road along the Danube, our units were pressed out behind the Iváncsa area. Battles continue in the area of the enemy's penetration by a company-strong force northeast of Göböljárás. The enemy supported his attacks with strong artillery fire.

3. SS-Pz.Div. Totenkopf. Starting at dawn, uninterrupted strong attacks by the enemy with the support of tanks took place against *I. Btl./SS-Pz.Gren.Rgt. 24 Danmark.* Attacks undertaken with strong artillery support were mostly repelled by the well-organized fire of our artillery and infantry weapons. The enemy managed to penetrate to the forest southwest of Kápolnás-Nyek, but the enemy strike force was beaten back by a counterattack. Around 8 a.m., the enemy, after a strong artillery preparation, launched a southbound attack from the area east of Annamajor, supported by tanks. In this section, a series of heavy engagements were also fought all day. Our units temporarily surrounded in Annamajor made their way to Hill 155 1 kilometer south of Anna and remained there. Our forces, encircled in Jánosmajor, were able to break out before dark. Massive enemy attacks were successfully repulsed by our artillery and self-propelled antiaircraft guns, working in the direct fire role. The enemy suffered heavy losses.

Divisionsgruppe Holste. In the first half of the day, insignificant activity of enemy reconnaissance units took place in the area of the Hungarian *2. Pz.Div.* Beginning at 2:30 p.m. the enemy launched an offensive [at ten points] along the entire front of the *Divisionsgruppe* with forces ranging in strength from 100 to 200 men, partly after strong mortar and artillery preparation. The attacks, with the exception of three—located in Csala, the forest north of

Csala, and Borbála major, 2 kilometers south of Zámoly—were repelled. The enemy managed to achieve a penetration only in areas held by Hungarian units, the fighting spirit of which, including *Inf.Rgt. 3 (mot.)* of their *2. Pz.Div.*, has greatly decreased. At 6 a.m. the change-out of *I. Schw./Kav.Rgt. 41* by *II. Btl./Gren.Rgt. 871* [in Stuhlweissenburg] was successfully completed.

Air Situation. Throughout the day, continuous activity of numerous enemy attack aircraft and fighter-bombers was reported, including use of aerial bombs and firing at our troops using on-board weapons. Our own fighters displayed an insignificant level of activity.[14]

Thirty-five years after this date, Manfred Schönfelder, in his own account based on notes taken at the time, could only add, "Between the Danube and Lake Velencze, the enemy launched attacks towards the south aimed at penetrating into our operational depths. Portions of the *Wiking* and *Totenkopf* Divisions were encircled, but were able to break out. A new main defense line was constructed."[15]

This somewhat bland and unemotional statement contrasts starkly with that made by *Ostuf.* Heinrich Kerkhoff, acting commander of *5. Kp./SS-Pz.Rgt. 5*, who was in the thick of the fighting that day. He later described the fighting on the *Wiking* Division's far right flank on 30 January:

All hell broke loose around noon. Infantry attacks in battalion strength. We and the artillery were able to turn them back. Then, like a phoenix rising out of the ashes, 30 enemy tanks—T-34s and T-43s [note: T-34/85s]—appeared out of the light fog. By evening, 17 enemy tanks and two trucks were burning. Grenadiers needed to come forward for the night. Regiment attempted to help [us].[16]

On the right of Gille's embattled corps, the situation was just as fluid. That night, the *Ic* of Breith's *III. Pz. Corps* wrote that an enemy attack in regimental strength from the CXXXIII Rifle Corps took place along the railroad line running along the Sárviz Canal through Sárbogárd and Sárkeresztur, as well as a battalion-sized attack originating from Gazdamajor aimed towards the north.

Both of these were repulsed by counterattacks by the *23. Pz.Div.* Troops and tanks from the 110th Tank Brigade were able to seize the heights south of Nagy Lók and were able to ward off four attacks by the *3. Pz.Div.* Undaunted by the previous day's setback, the Soviets launched a tank-supported attack against Nagy Hantos and the area to the northwest, but failed to achieve any noteworthy results. The *1. Pz.Div.* was involved in combat with strong enemy infantry and armored forces southwest and south of Perkáta that was still ongoing when the evening report was submitted.[17]

The last action reported by the corps was another tank attack by the 170th Tank Brigade against the village of Galambos Puszta, approximately 6 kilometers northwest of Dunapentele, which was repulsed by the *1. Pz.Div.* after the loss of 16 Soviet tanks. After two solid days of counterattacks, the heretofore successful advance by the *III. Pz.Korps* had begun to lose momentum, especially once the XXX Rifle Corps, XVIII Tank Corps, and CXXXIII Rifle Corps began transitioning to a defensive posture, however temporary. The tank-led counterattacks that Breith's troops encountered that day were apparently intended to slow down the advancing

German columns and buy time for the two rifle corps of the 26th Army to begin constructing a consolidated defense line, as well as to bring up artillery and antitank regiments to protect the gains that Gagen's army had made since 27 January.

On Gille's left, *Korpsgruppe Harteneck/I. Kav.Korps* reported that its Hungarian *1. Hus.Div.* had experienced a setback near Csakvár, when it was forced to abandon the commanding height of Hill 398 after a strong Soviet attack. It also reported that an assault group from the same Hungarian division was repulsed when it attempted to push enemy forces away from the village of Kozmá, part of its plan to improve its overall position and create a more defensible line. Along the portion of the corps' main defense line between Sarisap and Körteles held by the *96. Inf. Div.*, front-line observers reported a considerable amount of movement occurring behind the Soviet front lines, including several tanks, though what this signified was unknown. Northwest of Pilisszentlélek, the *711. Inf.Div.* reported an increase in enemy sniper activity, but otherwise the situation was calm.

On the *A.Gr. Balck/6. Armee* far right flank, defended by the Hungarian *3. Armee*, the situation between Ádánd and Ozora, site of the previous day's enemy breakthrough, had improved considerably. The commitment of *K.Gr. Martini* from the *6. Pz.Div.*, combined with the Hungarian *Inf.Rgt. 25*, was enough to overpower the two understrength Soviet regiments that had managed to cross the Sió. In the aftermath of the battle, the Hungarians counted "at least" 300 enemy dead and 60 prisoners. Of far more concern to Generals Balck and Heszlényi was the continuing attack north of Simontornya by a large force of Soviet infantry from the 233rd Rifle Division backed up by several tanks, which had managed to widen the area of their breakthrough to incorporate the town of Szilas-Balhàs (modern-day Mezőszilas). Clearly, this force was aiming for the town of Dégh; if they were able to cover the 10-kilometer distance before the Germans and Hungarians could react and the town fell into their hands, it threatened to cut off the Hungarian *25. Inf.Div.* from the rest of their *3. Armee*. A counterattack by *Pz.Aufkl.Abt. 1* of *Div.Gr. Pape* was able to stop the enemy from reaching the agricultural estate of Huszár Puszta between the two towns and throw them all the way back to Szilas-Balhàs.[18]

In Budapest, the garrison continued fighting with the kind of courage born of despair; despite ammunition shortages, there was no shortage of bravery, for its troops managed to destroy three Soviet tanks and three antitank guns that day. While the men of the *13. Pz.Div.* and *Pz.Gren.Div. FHH*, along with their German comrades in the *8.* and *22. SS-Kav.Div.*, fought determinedly, the morale of the Hungarian troops began to erode with increasing speed. Pfeffer-Wildenbruch reported that "large numbers" of *Honvéd* troops, joined by Hungarian police units, defected in droves to the Soviet besiegers during the night of 29/30 January, often in complete units with their own officers leading them across the lines where they could not be observed by their German counterparts. Though airdrops continued, most of them landed behind enemy lines. The civilians trapped in the ever-shrinking

Festung, some 300,000 people in all, were completely demoralized and growing increasingly desperate; starvation was rampant. In his situation report that evening, the commander of the *IX. SS-Geb.Korps* ended with the fateful words, "Situation very critical. The last battle has begun."[19]

While *Korpsgruppe Harteneck* reported only sporadic enemy air activity, the rest of *A.Gr. Balck/6. Armee's* units reported heavy and sustained attacks by Red Air Force aircraft throughout the depths of the entire *Kampfraum*. These attacks, which included at least 460 sorties according to *Luftwaffe* estimates, targeted the German and Hungarian front line, artillery positions, villages where their troops were quartered, main supply routes, and the remaining defenses in Budapest.[20] The *Luftwaffe's* own ground-attack units were also active, seeking to counter the Red Air Force and stop the Soviet advance on the ground. The *14. Staffel* of *Schlachtgeschwader 9* managed to get five or six *Henschel Hs-129* twin-engine tank-busters into the air. Once they arrived over the battlefield at Felsö Besnyö at noon, they savaged the 135th Tank Brigade, knocking out or destroying up to 12 T-34s in repeated attacks.[21] The 12 German aerial reconnaissance missions flown that day over the entire *A.Gr. Balck* area of operations detected no abnormal activity, other than the usual amount of traffic.

In its assessment of enemy plans and intentions, the *Armeegruppe Ic* detected the arrival of the 236th Rifle Division along the *Sió-Abschnitt*, which was a sign that the Soviet CXXXV Rifle Corps was planning on continuing its attacks towards the east and north. The *Ic* also concluded that the 57th Army was no longer the headquarters controlling events between the Sárviz Canal and the Danube, which would soon lead to the identification of a new army controlling operations there (i.e., the 26th Army). German intelligence also assessed that the forces that had broken through between Dunapentele and the Sárviz Canal would resume their counteroffensive aimed towards Sárosd and Stuhlweissenburg once they had consolidated their forces and brought up their customary artillery support. The report recognized that the scale of the fighting taking place in the *IV. SS-Pz.Korps'* positions defended by the *Totenkopf* and *Wiking* Divisions between the Danube and Lake Velencze was a sign that the enemy counteroffensive there would continue as the XXIII Tank Corps and CIV Rifle Corps sought their elusive breakthrough towards the south.

More importantly though, the *Ic* staff was beginning to see indications of offensive preparations being made by the 4th Guards Army to encompass the area between Lake Velencze and the foothills of the Vértes Mountains, based on the large-scale enemy ground reconnaissance carried out that day along the front line held by *Div.Gr. Holste* of the *IV. SS-Pz.Korps*. Based on previous intelligence and aerial reconnaissance, *Hptm.* von Pander and his analysts estimated that the Soviet 4th Guards Army could commit between six and eight rifle divisions should an attack unfold in this area. However, von Pander's report concluded, these rifle divisions were considered to be *abgekämpft* (exhausted or worn out), inadvertently downplaying the considerable danger that loomed ahead.

As for the leadership of the Third Ukrainian Front, Marshal Tolbukhin's decision remained firm—three of his four armies (the 1st Bulgarian Army would remain on the defense in the west against the *2. Pz.Armee*) would continue their attacks against *A. Gr. Balck* all along the line. The 26th Army would continue with its counteroffensive to the north after a brief pause to consolidate, the 57th Army's CXXXV Rifle Corps would continue exerting pressure against the Hungarian *3. Armee* along the Sió River, and the XXIII Tank Corps and CIV Rifle Corps of the 4th Guards Army would continue attacking, not only to link up with the Soviet units approaching from the south, but to continuing tying up the two SS divisions of the *IV. SS-Pz. Korps* in defensive operations between the Danube and Lake Velencze.

While these attacks continued, the other four corps of the 4th Guards Army would crush *Div. Gr. Holste* and seize the important road hubs of Mór and Stuhlweissenburg, thus cutting off the bulk of the *IV. SS-Pz.Korps*, all of the *III. Pz.Korps*, and most of the Hungarian *3. Armee*. Soviet intelligence had already notified General Zakharov that the *356. Inf.Div.* (which was assessed as being "less combat capable") was arriving in Stuhlweissenburg to replace the *23. Pz.Div.*, so its sector was automatically seen as the weak point in the German and Hungarian defenses. With Tolbukhin having made his decision, it was now up to the commander of the 4th Guards Army to ensure that the rest of the I Guards Mechanized Corps and V Guards Cavalry Corps, along with their divisions and supporting artillery, got into position during the night of 30/31 January in order to commence their attack the following day.[22] As events were to prove, this was somewhat optimistic, and what occurred instead was that the leading elements of both corps attacked from the line-of-march during the mid-afternoon with insufficient time to orient themselves on the battlefield or to adequately prepare. But the element of surprise they achieved by doing so was near-total.

As far as can be ascertained from German records, both Balck and Wöhler remained focused on the fighting in the south, though they were becoming increasingly aware, due to the above-mentioned intelligence reports, that something was brewing north of Stuhlweissenburg. To that end, on 30 January, Balck ordered the *IV. SS-Pz.Korps* once again to ensure that the reserve force it had earlier been tasked to send southeast of the city—consisting of *SS-Pz.Pio.Btl. 3* from the *Totenkopf* Division along with four tanks—was in place by the morning of 31 January. At some point in the near future, this miniscule force, that had a *Kampfstärke* three days earlier of 375 men, was supposed to be augmented by a *Regimentsgruppe* from one of the *Panzergrenadier* regiments from either SS division as soon as one could be spared.

In addition, all of the tank and vehicle repair workshops in Stuhlweissenburg were to be evacuated beginning that same day, while the civilian population were ordered out of their homes to begin constructing defensive barriers on the city's eastern and northern outskirts. *Oberst* Kühl, the commander of the *356. Inf.Div.*, would become responsible for the city's defense, and was consequently named its *Kampfkommandant*.[23] Five *Pz. VI* Tiger IIs from *s.Pz.Abt. 509* that had been recently repaired were ordered to remain in the city to bolster its defenses, and were attached to the *IV. SS-Pz.Korps* instead of being sent south to join the rest of the battalion fighting with the *III. Pz.Korps*.[24] *Divisionsgruppe Holste* was also given control of *Volks-Werf.Brig. 17*, as well as the 12.2cm battalion from *Volks-Art.Korps 403*, which would have to move from their firing positions behind the *Wiking* Division the next morning, 31 January, to new ones northwest of Stuhlweissenburg.

Having slowed the counteroffensive in the south by the 26th Army and built up a new defensive line along the line Dunapentele–Perkáta–Káloz, Breith's corps with its three *panzer* divisions was ordered that evening to transition to the defense, beginning the next day. According to its new orders, any counterattacks that Breith's divisions needed to carry out would be strictly limited to those needed to retake any ground lost and not to extend the new main defense line any further. Any withdrawals from this line could only be carried out with the permission of the *Armeegruppe* headquarters, requested in advance, although the withdrawal of *K.Gr. Medicus* of the *3. Pz.Div.* from Dunapentele the following day had already been approved. To ensure that *III. Pz.Korps* had sufficient combat power to hold this line against further expected Soviet attacks, Breith would be given the bulk of any available close air support by *Luftflotte 4*, which of course was weather-dependent.[25]

Wednesday, 31 January was to prove the last day when *A.Gr. Balck* and the *IV. SS-Pz.Korps* could lay any possible claim to be in a position to relieve Budapest, had they any intention of ever doing so. On that day, the *Wiking* Division was finally forced to pull back from the remaining bit of ground it still held on the eastern bank of the Váli River near Szinatelep. Having given this up, there was no more possibility of a bridgehead, no more possibility of a *Husarenritt* or any other fantastical idea for that matter, even if it or any other division in the *IV. SS-Pz.Korps* still had the strength to do so. This final withdrawal from the Váli line put paid to any hopes of ever relieving the city, no matter how many exhortations to hold out that Guderian, Wöhler, and Balck sent to its defenders over the airwaves.

The weak sun rose over a cloudy, mist-shrouded landscape, covered with snow as far as the eye could see. Temperatures were still bitterly cold. Meteorologists at *H.Gr. Süd* recorded a low that morning of 23 degrees Fahrenheit, or –5 degrees Centigrade. The number of men who succumbed to the cold is not recorded. As the day progressed though, things got very hot indeed in the two widely separated sectors now held by the *IV. SS-Pz.Korps* between the Danube and the foothills of the Vértes Mountains. Two almost separate battles would take place that day, rendering any effective command and control by the corps headquarters in Seregélyes an extremely difficult proposition. The first of these two battles began on the corps' right flank, where the 133rd Rifle Division and 66th Guards Rifle Divisions of the CIV Rifle Corps, supported by tanks from the XXIII Tank Corps, attempted to punch their way through the *Wiking* Division and begin their advance along the river highway towards Dunapentele.

In the *Wiking* Division's sector, a Soviet attack in regimental strength supported by nine tanks against *I. Btl./Westland* was able to achieve a local breakthrough on both sides of the village of Szinatelep due east of the railroad station at Iváncsa, though by dint of effort the division was just able to seal it off. At the larger and more dangerous site of the Soviet penetration at Aggszentpéter, back-and-forth fighting raged throughout the day, and although in broad terms an enemy breakthrough was avoided, Soviet troops were able to reestablish firm control of the small forest 2 kilometers southwest of the town, a move that threatened the division's right flank with encirclement. This attacking force also got dangerously close to the division headquarters. Günther Jahnke, an eyewitness to the event, recorded:

> Enemy attacks are growing constantly in number and in strength. Several deep penetrations took place in the *Westland*'s area that they no longer have the strength to seal off. Once again, 10 enemy tanks appeared from the south and approached the collective farm 3 kilometers south of the division headquarters. Three of our assault guns were sent there to counter them, but had to show great respect to the two [JS-II] Stalin tanks that were with them. In the south [of our position], the situation appears to be completely unclear; there doesn't seem to be any German front at all. We can't contemplate carrying out another attack; the division has suffered heavy casualties and losses. Without reinforcements, it doesn't seem possible that we can hold our position.[26]

To the left of the *Wiking* Division, Becker's *Totenkopf* Division was also engaged in heavy fighting, especially in Kápolnás Nyék, where its defenses were under increasing pressure.

To the northeast, the *III. Btl./Totenkopf* was trying to hold on to its position south of Pettend despite the numerous company- and battalion-sized attacks it had to beat back that day. On the right, *III. Btl./Eicke* continued to stand firm at Gróf Puszta in the face of multiple enemy attacks, enabling the division to maintain contact with the *Germania* Regiment on its right, which was barely holding on to Aggszentpéter. Overall, despite the enormous pressure being exerted upon them, both SS divisions managed to hold their ground and prevent any major breakthroughs.

The biggest action fought on 31 January in the *IV. SS-Pz.Korps* sector took place north of Lake Velencze between Stuhlweissenburg and Zámoly, where the troops of *Div.Gr. Holste* fought against numerically superior enemy forces intent on breaking through and cutting off German units arrayed to the south. According to the *A.Gr. Balck/6. Armee Ic*:

> During the afternoon, the enemy, who had previously begun the day before with a reconnaissance in force between Lake Velencze and Zámoly, increased his strength and transitioned to the attack, supported by as many as 35 tanks. He was able to break through our positions between the roads linking Stuhlweissenburg and Lovasberény, as well as 2 kilometers south of Zámoly. Stubborn fighting within the 3-kilometer deep breakthrough area is ongoing.[27]

According to *H.Gr. Süd*, which had suspected that something was afoot, it was surprised that the enemy had "carried out a major repositioning at unusual speed" north of Stuhlweissenburg, especially since the I Guards Mechanized Corps and V Guards Cavalry Corps were believed to have still been fighting along the Váli River only the day before. After a brief artillery barrage, the attacking force—supported by up to 62 tanks and assault guns, as well as five rifle and airborne divisions from the XX and XXI Guards Rifle Corps—had managed to increase the size of its penetration by the late afternoon to six kilometers in width and four in depth, clear indications of a major offensive operation.

Both the *356. Inf.Div.* and *4. Kav.Brig.* of *Div.Gr. Holste* were in the path of the Soviet surprise attack. The unit most affected was *Oberst* Kühl's division, whose *II. Btl./Gren.Rgt. 871* had been occupying its new position in the front line northeast of Stuhlweissenburg for less than two days, while the rest of the division, including a few firing batteries of *Art.Rgt. 356*, had been in position for less than 24 hours. Portions of the division's other infantry regiment, *Gren.Rgt. 870*, was still underway from Várpalota. The *II. Btl./Gren.Rgt. 871*, holding the line between Borbálamajor and Mariamajor, was struck by the reinforced 12th Guards Cavalry Division in mid-afternoon.

With no experience of fighting against the Red Army, the battalion was quickly overrun and its remnants fled from the path of the relentless assault. In an assessment written that night, Gille criticized the battalion's performance, stating that "based on the experience of today, the *356. Inf.Div.* in no way corresponds to the demands of warfare on the Eastern Front, particularly in the winter. The conduct of *II. Btl./Gren.Rgt. 871* on the battlefield threatened to undermine the combat morale of the neighboring units."[28] But there was no solution for it; the *356. Inf.Div.* was too badly needed at that moment, so it would have to stay where it was because no other replacements were available. Although Gille did not mention it, the division's combat engineer battalion, *Pio.Btl. 356*, which was used that afternoon to reinforce *SS-Rgt. Ney*, had fought tolerably well.

To the right of *Gren.Rgt. 871*, the Hungarian *Btl. Holczer* and *SS-Rgt. Ney*, both tactically subordinated to the *356. Inf.Div.*, were also hit hard by the vanguard of the I Guards Mechanized Corps, whose attack was also heralded by a short but powerful artillery barrage. *Bataillon Holczer*, defending the Körakás area on the western bank of the Csäszari River, sustained heavy losses, while *SS-Rgt. Ney*, which had not yet recovered from its setback of 28 January, was quickly forced back towards Stuhlweissenburg, where *I. Schw./Kav.Rgt. 41* from *Div.Gr. Holste* had been ordered out of its reserve position to establish a thin defensive line. To reinforce Ney's regiment, four *Pz. IVs* from the Hungarian *2. Pz.Div.* and *Pio.Btl. 356* were briefly subordinated to it until the crisis passed.

On Holste's left flank between Csákberény and Zámoly, the 11th and 63rd Guards Cavalry Divisions, preceded by attacks from infantry from the XX Rifle Corps, broke through the line held by the *3. Inf.Rgt. (mot.)* of the Hungarian *2. Pz.Div.* and made a beeline towards the town of Magyaralmás, where the *II. Abt./Kav.Rgt. 41* was positioned in a rest area. South of Zámoly, *Kav.Rgt. 5* was threatened with encirclement when the left wing of the XI Guards Cavalry Corps broke through its main defense line and headed towards Borbála Puszta, where after a brief pause the Soviet cavalrymen continued towards their ultimate objective of Sárkeresztes. By the late afternoon, the situation appeared extremely serious. Not only had the German and Hungarian front line been penetrated in numerous places, but unless the Soviet assault was stopped, the road hubs of Stuhlweissenburg and Mór could easily fall into enemy hands.

As the corps commander, this attack against his newly assigned left flank placed Gille in a difficult position, because he now had the responsibility for controlling two separate battles—one involving the *Totenkopf* and *Wiking* Divisions east of Lake Velencze against the XXIII Tank Corps and CIV Rifle Corps, and another north and east of Stuhlweissenburg with *Div.Gr. Holste*. Clearly, countering the new Soviet offensive unfolding in the *Div.Gr. Holste* area was the most urgent of the two situations, but neither could he let the other one go unnoticed. To Gille's south, Breith had his hands full, while Harteneck to his north had nothing of substance to offer.

All of *A.Gr. Balck/6. Armee* had been momentarily forced on the defensive everywhere, and there was little that Balck could do except move exhausted and understrength units around the map from one hot spot to the next. As for the *IV. SS-Pz.Korps*, Gille's command and control mechanisms—radio, landline field telephone, teletype, *Fernschreiber*, and even his daily front-line visits (after all, he had no helicopter)—compelled him to remain at his forward headquarters in Seregélyes and monitor the reports flowing in. The most Gille could do at this stage of the battle, until he could move his *Gefechtstand* (his corps' *Quartiermeister* and *Adjutantur* had remained in Jenö) to a more central location, was to entrust most of the local decision-making authority north of Lake Velencze to *Gen.Maj.* Rudolf Holste and send him as many reinforcements as he could. Gille had already dispatched a rocket launcher brigade and a heavy artillery battalion in Holste's direction, but the *Divisionsgruppe* commander would soon need more than that.

By late afternoon, the German and Hungarian response to the 4th Guards Army's attack began to swing into action. Both of the reserve battalions of *Div.Gr. Holste*—*I. Abt./Kav.Rgt. 41* in Stuhlweissenburg and *Pz.Aufkl.Abt. 70* of the *4. Kav.Brig.* in Sárkeresztes—began conducting a series of counterattacks designed to slow, then seal off breaches made in the front line by the Soviet assault. From Stuhlweissenburg, *I. Abt./Kav.Rgt. 41*, bolstered by nine assault guns and four *Pz. IVs* from the Hungarian *2. Pz.Div.*, advanced to the north along the Stuhlweissenburg–Zámoly highway. To its north, *Pz.Aufkl.Abt. 70*, along with nine *Pz. VI* Tiger IIs from *s.Pz.Abt. 503 FHH*, attacked to the east out of Sárkeresztes.

While these two powerful German-Hungarian forces were unable to encircle and destroy the elements from the I Guards Mechanized Corps and V Guards Cavalry Corps that had broken through, they did blunt the force of their attack and prevent them from widening the gap, thus preventing them from advancing any further and forcing portions of them to fall back. German and Hungarian infantry fought a number of small-unit actions throughout the area, in which some units, such as the Hungarian *5. Btl./Inf.Rgt. 3 (mot.)*, particularly distinguished themselves. Though nightfall found the 233rd Rifle Division in possession of the town of Gyúlamajor, thus blocking the highway between Stuhlweissenburg and Zámoly, overall the Soviet counteroffensive had been forced to a halt far short of its intended objectives. Once again, Gille's post-battle assessment was typically brief and to the point when he reported, "The *6. Armee* has been forced onto the defense. Enemy has reinforced his front at Stuhlweissenburg. There he is attacking towards the southwest."[29]

That day also proved to be a busy one for the three *panzer* divisions in the *III. Pz.Korps*. Furthest west, the *23. Pz.Div.* reported a large enemy force moving into an assembly area southwest of Káloz on the western bank of the Sárviz Canal, a sign of yet another impending attack. It also reported that its troops had successfully rebuffed three separate battalion-sized attacks from the CXXXIII Rifle Corps south and southwest of *Pz.Gren.Rgt. 128*'s front-line positions near Szilfamajor. In the center sector, *K.Gr. Weymann* of the *3. Pz.Div.* reported that its artillery had smashed another enemy assembly area southeast of Nagy Hantos. On the corps' left flank along the Danube, the *1. Pz.Div.* reported sighting a strong enemy force occupying the rail and highway intersection 3 kilometers northwest of Ráczalmás.

Generalmajor Thünert's headquarters further reported that 10 enemy tanks from the XVIII Tank Corps had managed to infiltrate past Perkáta and into the area just northeast of the town in an attempt to block the highway paralleling the Danube. During the German counterattack that followed, *Pz.Rgt. 1* managed to knock out one Soviet tank by the reporting deadline, though additional tank kills had not yet been tallied. Adony, still held by the *Wiking* Division's *Alarmbataillon*, was almost isolated, lying in the path of two approaching Soviet spearheads—one in the north from the XXIII Tank Corps, and the other in the south from the XVIII Tank Corps. Only a small screen of troops from the *Wiking* Divison and *1. Pz.Div.* in either direction prevented the enemy from surrounding the garrison there.

Bolstered by the counterattack by the *Panzergruppe* from the *6. Pz.Div.* that defeated the attempt by the CXXXV Rifle Corps to cross the Sió River at Ádánd the previous day, the Hungarian *25. Inf.Div.* continued its efforts to mop up any remnants still holding out in the towns of Szabadi and Sio-Maros on 31 January. On the division's southern flank, its *II. Btl./Inf.Rgt. 26*, fighting as part of *Div. Gr. Pape*, was able to throw out Soviet troops that had infiltrated into the large town of Mezö Szilas. In fact, the division had fought so well during the past three days that Balck drafted a special citation praising its troops and its leadership for their performance in battle, where it had suffered heavy casualties. This message of appreciation was sent to *Gen.d.Inf.* Wöhler at *H.Gr. Süd*, who then forwarded it to the *Honvéd* ministry of defense, accompanied by a request for replacements to bring its *25. Inf.Div.* back up to strength.[30]

In comparison, action in the *Korpsgruppe Harteneck/I. Kav.Korps* sector was relatively minimal. On its right, the Hungarian *1. Hus.Div.* in the Vértes Mountains reported that its observers had spotted reinforcements being moved forward by the Soviet LXVIII Rifle Corps, though no attacks were anticipated. Its troops were also able to observe that enemy tanks were spotted in Csakvár for the first time. Northwest of Bicske, the *3. Kav.Brig.* reported that it had driven off a Soviet assault troop that had attempted to infiltrate its front lines, as well as an unsuccessful enemy attack in battalion strength with the support of four tanks that had tried to force a breach in its front line south of Mány.

In Budapest, the slow and painful death of the *IX. SS-Geb.Korps* had entered its final phase. With the Váli line and the *Wiking* Division's bridgehead at Aggszentpéter finally abandoned, there was no longer any chance the city could be relieved. The ever-shrinking perimeter of the pocket was pounded throughout the day by artillery of every caliber, ranging from light field guns to the super-heavy 30.5cm howitzers. Numerous company-sized Soviet incursions were fended off, including one on the southern front line where the attackers had achieved a temporary breakthrough before they were wiped out in heavy fighting. Hungarian civilians were conscripted into labor battalions and were used to construct defensive works around the *Burgpalast* (Budavári Palota), the large castle overlooking Buda, which served as Pfeffer-Wildenbruch's headquarters as well as the garrison's last-ditch center of resistance.

It was on this day, 31 January, when *A.Gr. Balck* informed the commander of the *IX. SS-Geb.Korps* that its forces had been forced to assume a defensive posture everywhere, implying that it would no longer be able to relieve the city. By this point, Pfeffer-Wildenbruch and his troops probably already suspected this; except for what the *Luftwaffe* could provide, he was on his own. The fate of his troops now lay in his hands. Forbidden by Hitler himself to order a breakout, it remained to be seen whether he had the moral courage to disobey this order and save his men. Certainly, Wöhler and Balck had both lacked the courage to order a breakout on their own authority. Now it was up to an SS general to do so.

Although the leadership of *H.Gr. Süd* and *A.Gr. Balck/6. Armee* had apparently written off the brave defenders of Budapest, the *Luftwaffe* had not yet, or not quite. That night, up to 152 cargo aircraft airdropped or delivered by glider 110 tons of supplies, including rations, fuel, and ammunition. The six glider pilots deserve special mention for their bravery, for not only did they have to survive the glider tow to the landing area and the landing itself, but once they had completed their mission, there was no way out, leaving them no choice but to join the garrison as infantrymen. *Luftflotte 4* also flew 215 day and night missions, focusing its efforts on the Danube River crossings, vehicular columns, and suspected troop concentrations.

Over the rest of the *H. Gr. Süd* area of operations, the only Soviet air activity of any significance reported by *Luftwaffe* ground observers were the 400 sorties flown by ground-attack aircraft against the *IV. SS-Pz. Korps* and *III. Pz. Korps*. A fleet of Allied four-engine aircraft was spotted flying overhead at great altitude from the west to east in the mid-afternoon, probably American bombers flying from Italy towards targets in Austria. One of these aircraft was forced to conduct an emergency landing somewhere in the center of the German main defense line, and its 10 crewmembers were immediately captured.[31]

That night, in his consolidated portion of the daily intelligence report, *Hptm.* von Pander commented on the appearance of the I Guards Mechanized Corps and V Guards Cavalry Corps between Lake Velencze and the southern foothills of the Vértes Mountains. Although the departure of these two corps from the front line along the Váli had already been detected as early as that morning, this was not immediately seen as a cause for alarm because the usual Soviet practice in such cases was that units would take one or two days to regroup before they would carry out any sort of an attack. That Zakharov had directed them to initiate their attacks towards Stuhlweissenburg directly from the line of march without pausing to consolidate caught the Germans and Hungarian completely off guard, leaving them unprepared when the attack by the two Soviet corps commenced in the middle of the afternoon.[32]

This unexpected event, in turn, led the *A. Gr. Balck/ 6. Armee Ic* staff to speculate whether the XXIII Tank Corps might also be committed, perhaps as a second-echelon force for this same attack, or whether it might be attached to the 26th Army instead once its spearheads linked up with the XVIII Tank Corps approaching from the south. Perhaps, von Pander and company speculated, even the II Guards Mechanized Corps—at the time still in position around Bicske—might also be regrouped and sent to the area between Zámoly and Stuhlweissenburg, or across the river to the north opposite Gran, or even sent to the south; in short, they had no idea what the future intentions of the Third Ukrainian Front were regarding this unit's future employment. Despite all of the signals intelligence, aerial reconnaissance, POW interrogations, and agent reports, the *Wehrmacht* could not yet penetrate the minds of Soviet senior field commanders or the *STAVKA*, and were left with speculation.

One thing that the intelligence organs did get right was their assessment that this new attack against Stuhlweissenburg might be joined by another one approaching from the south. The 26th Army was trying to do just that via Simontornya or along the Sárviz Canal, though its main effort was still being directed on 31 January along the Danube in a bid to link up near Adony with the approaching spearheads of the XXIII Tank Corps of the 4th Guards Army (though the employment of the VII Mechanized Corps had not yet been ruled out). One thing that the intelligence staffs did not contemplate was a Soviet advance towards Stuhlweissenburg along the southern shore of Lake Velencze. This possibility was not mentioned at all (note: this was the last daily intelligence situation report available from surviving records of *A. Gr. Balck/6. Armee Ic.* No other records beyond that date are known to exist).

With such an existential danger staring him in the face, *Gen.d.Pz.Tr.* Balck could now only react to this challenge by doing what he always did best: improvise an immediate solution based on the means at hand. Whether the II Guards Corps or VII Mechanized Corps attacked the next day or the day after that was immaterial; Balck focused on what he needed to do to combat the threat on that particular day in that particular moment. While Holste, with Gille' approval, had deftly employed the forces he had at his disposal to slow down the Soviet attack, Balck knew that much more had to be done to avert the larger danger. That afternoon, while the initial response of *Div.Gr. Holste* was still in progress, Balck ordered the *IV. SS-Pz. Korps* to carry out the following tasks:

a) Immediately regroup *Werf.Brig. 15* and the 12.2cm heavy battalion of *Volks-Art.Korps 403* and move it to the area behind the *356. Inf.Div.* [though this had already been ordered, the units had either not begun moving yet or had not yet arrived];

b) Either the *Wiking* or *Totenkopf* Division was to immediately provide a tank-reinforced *Regimentsguppe* to be at the corps' disposal in the Stuhlweissenburg area [this had also been ordered the previous evening as an "on-order" mission; on 31 January, Balck ordered its immediate implementation];

c) After this *SS Regimentsgruppe* had arrived in Stuhlweissenburg, any remaining elements of *Kav.Rgt. 41* in the city, along with any attached tanks, were to be sent immediately to the Sárkeresztes–Magyaralmás area;

d) Upon arrival, the rest of the *356. Inf.Div.* would form its two remaining *Grenadier* regiments into battle-ready *Regimentsgruppe* and place them at the disposal of the *IV. SS-Pz.Korps* in the Stuhlweissenburg–Sárkeresztes area [this would happen as a matter of course];

e) Ensure that artillery fire plans were developed to concentrate all available fire on Pákozd, Pátka, Lovasberény, and Csakvár and to report the number of available artillery pieces as well as any ammunition shortages [note: Gille's competent ARKO, the recently promoted *Brig.Fhr.* Brasack, would most likely have carried this out without being told];

f) Ensure that the outer defense line of Stuhlweissenburg was tightly integrated, including the incorporation of damaged tanks in the overall defensive fire plan for the city;

g) Maintain the emergency battalion of the *Totenkopf* Division [*SS-Pz.Pio.Btl. 3*] at a high state of readiness in the Börgönd area [located at the southwest corner of Lake Velencze];

h) Cross-level any existing shortages of artillery ammunition and ensure that all infantry heavy weapons are incorporated within the overall fire plan, including the targeting of known enemy jump-off positions and movement routes [again, Brasack would have done this as a matter of course];

i) Prepare tank destruction teams from rear-area services to be ready to defend themselves against any tanks that have broken through their local areas; and

j) Ensure that every artillery battery has prepared an antitank fire plan including the incorporation of *Flak* artillery to thicken their defenses.[33]

The most significant element of this order was the requirement for the *IV. SS-Pz. Korps* to send a *Regimentsgruppe* towards Stuhlweissenburg. As events were to prove, Gille chose the *Totenkopf* Division as the source for this task force, mainly because one of its regiments was already being "pinched out" of the line between Kápolnás Nyék and Pettend. Several days before the Soviet counteroffensive began, Balck had considered ordering Becker's division into a rest area, but events were soon to prove this to be impossible to carry out.

Shortly afterwards, Balck's headquarters issued a follow-up order that directed the *III. Pz.Korps* to also form an armored *Eingreifreserve* (emergency reserve) of its own and position it in the Sárkeresztur–Aba area, where it would be employed, depending upon the situation, either west of the Sárviz Canal or in the Stuhlweissenburg area. In this same order, Balck also instructed Breith to pull *K.Gr. Medicus* out of Dunapentele and have it rejoin the rest of the *3. Pz.Div.* that evening. As a precaution, *Korpsgruppe Harteneck* was ordered to bolster its right flank unit, the Hungarian *VIII. Armee-Korps*, with *Sturm-Art.Brig. 239* and *II. Btl./Art.Rgt. 52*.[34] Another order issued at the same time instructed the Hungarian *lei.Art.Abt. 73*, which was already fighting in the Stuhlweissenburg area, to attach itself to the *356. Inf.Div.* until all of that division's artillery battalions had arrived.

In addition to issuing these tactical orders, the *A. Gr. Balck/6. Armee* headquarters had other correspondence that it deemed just as critical, especially messages stressing the importance of maintaining the combat power of the units under its command. One of these, signed by *Gen.Maj.* Gaedke and addressed to the *H.Gr. Süd Adjutantur*, concerned the rapidly declining manpower strength of the three *panzer* divisions under Breith's command. As of 27 January, all three of them—the *1.*, *3.*, and *23. Pz.Div.*—were well below their authorized *Kampfstärke*, which had only worsened in the four days since. The *1. Pz.Div.* reported its *Kampfstärke* as 806, the *3. Pz.Div.* as 781, and the *23. Pz.Div.* as 1,390 men (the average combat strength of a *panzer* division in 1944 lay between 2,600 and 2,800 men, while a full-strength one had a *Kampfstärke* of approximately 3,700), so all three of these divisions were considerably understrength.

To remedy this situation, *A. Gr. Balck/6. Armee* urgently requested the provision of several *Marsch* or draft replacement battalions, one for each of these veteran divisions, before they were completely *ausgeblutet* (bled white), including the loss of their nearly irreplaceable junior officers and experienced NCOs. Gaedke made it plain that *A. Gr. Balck* could not wait for *H.Gr. Süd*'s field replacement unit, the *182. Res.Div.*, to provide replacements according to the usual training program (up to six weeks), but instead requested that replacements be sent immediately from the zone of the interior. It is unknown how long it took *H.Gr. Süd* to respond to this request, but it is an indication of just how dire the manpower situation had become.[35]

In a similar vein, *Gen.d.Kav.* Harteneck penned a two-page *Beurteilung der Lage* (assessment of the situation) to Balck that same day, describing the perilous position of his *Korpsgruppe*, arrayed as it was between the Vértes Mountains in the southwest and the Pilis Mountains in the northeast, a defensive sector over 95 kilometers in width, which was even longer when the actual front-line was taken into account. This did not include the length of the southern bank of the Danube, where his troops kept the opposite bank under observation. Against his five understrength divisions (two of which were Hungarian) and one cavalry brigade, with a combined *Kampfstärke* of 12,973 men, the Soviet 46th Army had positioned up to four rifle corps with 12 divisions and one mechanized corps, outnumbering Harteneck by over three-to-one, although the Soviet units were also understrength.[36]

Harteneck pointed out that most of his front line was a series of strongpoints, with the gaps in between screened by a thin line of infantry that had no chance of repelling any serious enemy attack. Against such an attempt, he wrote, his *Korpsgruppe* possessed no meaningful reserve forces whatsoever. Having painted a picture of the dire situation he and his troops found themselves in, the main point of his screed was a request for reinforcements, preferably in the form of a full-strength division. Although this appeared to be a sincere request for the help he thought *Korpsgruppe Harteneck/I. Kav.Korps* needed to carry out its mission, Harteneck may also have had an ulterior motive, in that he might have submitted this request to be included into the official record in a bid to absolve himself of any future blame should his corps collapse under an enemy attack.

How Balck responded to this assessment by one of his most senior corps commanders is unknown; at any rate, he had nothing more to offer for the next several days so *Korpsgruppe Harteneck/I. Kav.Korps* would have to fend for itself. Luckily for Harteneck, his corps did not seem to have been of any special interest to the 46th Army, which was more focused on eliminating the Budapest garrison than anything else. Once this task was completed, then Harteneck would once again find himself the object of its attention; until then, he would be able to continue holding the line, using what he had. Unknown to him, his corps would play a pivotal role 11 days later when the Budapest drama finally reached its bloody conclusion.

Harteneck's assessment was a fairly accurate portrayal of his corps group's strengths and weaknesses, but it did not paint a picture of the losses his corps had suffered, or those the other corps in *A.Gr. Balck/6. Armee* (excluding the troops trapped in Budapest) had sustained, for that matter. Those statistics were provided by the *IIa/IIb* of *6. Armee* in a memorandum prepared for Balck on 31 January that was forwarded to the personnel office of *H.Gr. Süd*. This memorandum listed the numbers of German troops killed, wounded, missing, and sick for the entire month of January 1945, covering the losses incurred during *Unternehman Konrad I, II*, and *III*. It did not differentiate between *Wehrmacht* and *Waffen-SS* casualties, and did not include any losses suffered by their Hungarian allies.

In all, during that month the *6. Armee* element of *A.Gr. Balck* lost 3,598 men killed, 16,504 wounded, and 1,520 missing in action, as well as 12,751 reported as sick, of which 12,554 were returned to duty. In all, not counting the sick, Balck's *6. Armee* lost 21,622 men, with only a fraction of those being replaced. Although not included in this particular report, during the same period of January 1945, the German divisions of *A.Gr. Balck/6. Armee* lost 164 tanks, assault guns, and tank destroyers deemed "irrecoverable." This number only refers to those that were completely burned out or left behind to the enemy because they could not be recovered in time. This number was not the same as the total "knocked out" or mechanically inoperable. In most cases, if they could be recovered, armored fighting vehicles considered "knocked out" could be repaired locally using spare parts cannibalized from other vehicles that had to be shipped back to the zone of the interior for factory repair. Holes in turrets or hulls could be plugged or welded over, engines could be replaced, as could interior fittings. Usually, blood needed to be scrubbed off the interior if crewmen had been killed or injured once their armored fighting compartment was penetrated by an antitank shell.

By way of contrast for the same period, the Third Ukrainian Front in its own after-action report stated that it had irretrievably lost 570 tanks of all types and 234 assault guns and SP guns, for a total loss of 804 armored fighting vehicles. In turn, the Germans claimed to have knocked out or captured 1,444 Soviet armored fighting vehicles during January 1945, though certainly—if both the German and Soviet numbers are correct—as many as 640 Soviet AFVs were successfully recovered and repaired or sent back to the factory for rebuild. In regards to troop losses, the 4th Guards Army, which provided the bulk of the soldiers that stopped all three German relief attempts, reported that it had lost up to 24,113 men in its rifle divisions alone, excluding losses in the armored and mechanized units, which would not have been as high.

While the German and Hungarian divisions had undoubtedly inflicted more casualties upon their opponents and destroyed more of their tanks than they had lost themselves, Balck's troops lost proportionately more of their combat power, making such comparisons ultimately irrelevant, because the Soviets could easily replace their losses, whereas the Third Reich could not. The armored strength report, compiled during the evening of 31 January/1 February and submitted to *H.Gr. Süd* the following morning, bears this out, a stark testimony to how weak *A.Gr. Balck/6. Armee* had actually become after a month of ultimately futile combat. It was this force, that had been fought to the brink of exhaustion, that Balck would have to rely upon for the next three weeks of operations.

In regards to the *IV. SS-Pz.Korps*, on 1 February its armored fighting vehicle status revealed that the *Totenkopf* Division had five operational *Pz. IV*s out of 17 on hand, three *Pz. V* Panthers out of 17, two *Pz. VI* Tiger Is out of 10, two *Jg.Pz. IV*s out of eight, and seven operational *StuG III/IV*s out of 19, a total of 19 operational AFV out of 71 on hand. The *Wiking* Division was even worse off, with two out of four *Pz. IV*s operational, eight out of 20 *Pz. V* Panthers, no operational *Jg.Pz. IV*s out of 10, and no *StuG III/IVs* out of five, giving its division commander only 10 operational AFV out of 39. Of the armor attached to *Div.Gr. Holste*, also under the command of *IV. SS-Pz.Korps*, the Hungarian *2. Pz.Div.* had only 10 operational *Pz. IVs* out of 26 assigned, the *4. Kav.Brig.* had three operational *StuG III/IVs* out of 17, and *s.Pz.Abt. 503 FHH* had eight operational *Pz. VI* Tiger IIs out of 26 assigned. Thus, Gille had at his disposal a total of 50 operational AFVs out of 162 assigned, a pitifully small force, especially when compared to what was being hurled against it.[37]

General der Panzertruppe Breith's *III. Pz.Korps* was slightly better off, with its *1., 3.,* and *23. Pz.Div.*—along with the attached *I. Abt./Pz.Rgt. 24* and *s.Pz.Abt. 509*—reporting a total of 80 operational AFVs of all types. The Hungarian *3. Armee*, the poorest of the three forces in terms of armored strength, had a total of 45 operational tanks, assault guns, and tank destroyers, including 13 reported by *K.Gr. Martini* of the *6. Pz.Div.* that was temporarily attached. Thus, counting operational armored fighting vehicles of all types, excluding *SPWs* within *A.Gr. Balck/6. Armee* as well as *Korpsgruppe Harteneck/I. Kav.Korps*, Balck had 184 vehicles at his disposal all told, including two *Pz. II Luchs* armored reconnaissance *panzers* and seven *Pz. III Flammpanzer* (flamethrower tanks), both types equally useless in a tank-on-tank fight.

Against this, on the same date the Third Ukrainian Front—with its two tanks corps, four mechanized corps, one cavalry corps, divisional units, and supporting or independent units—could immediately field 307 tanks and 245 SP guns for a total of 552, as well as a further 84 tanks and 66 SP guns under short-term repair, giving Tolbukhin's army group a three-to-one advantage in armor over *A. Gr. Balck/6. Armee* for the battles in progress as well as those about to begin. In addition, within the Front commander's reserve pool of armored vehicles, 88 more AFVs of all types were immediately available to replace losses if needed upon request through command channels.[38] This also did not include the number of vehicles within the 6th Guards Tank Army or VII Mechanized Corps, both of which were undergoing complete reconstitution east of Budapest as part of the *STAVKA* strategic reserve.

For the headquarters of *A.Gr. Balck/6. Armee*, the first day of February 1945, a Thursday, began with an urgent message from *H.Gr. Süd* that arrived at 1:20 a.m. The message, signed by the army group's chief of staff, *Gen.Lt.* von Grolman, was an order providing updated guidance to Balck for his *Armeegruppe*'s mission for that day. The first and most important task, its primary mission, was to prevent an enemy breakthrough between Stuhlweissenburg and the Vértes Mountains at all costs. Wöhler had already alluded to this two days before, but with the anticipated Soviet attack now a reality, this mission had assumed even greater importance, especially since it had drawn Hitler's personal attention.

The second updated task involved the need to seal off the breakthrough in the Hungarian *3. Armee* sector north of Simontornya and to destroy any enemy units that had broken through. The last task directed that the line between the Sárviz

Canal and the Danube, the *III. Pz.Korps'* area of operations, to be defended using *Angriffsweise Abwehr* (active defense), a tactical term that was becoming increasingly common whenever there was insufficient infantry available to hold a cohesive front line, which by this point in the war, meant nearly all of the time.[39]

The weather that morning was typically cloudy, with the temperature hovering around freezing point, an indication that a change in the weather was on the way. Light rain showers were reported in the low-lying areas of the *Puszta*, while snow fell in the Vértes and Pilis Mountains. As the day progressed, a slight thaw began to unfold, making life even more miserable for the combatants. Paying no heed to the weather, fighting continued without let-up throughout the day, as the *IV. SS-Pz. Korps*, *III. Pz.Korps*, and *Div.Gr. Pape* struggled to contain the Soviet advance. Again, Gille's corps found itself fighting on two fronts, one between the Danube and Lake Velencze and the other between Stuhlweissenburg and Zámoly.

In the corps' official morning report to *A.Gr. Balck*, Gille's chief or staff (*Ia*) wrote that overnight in the *Wiking* Division's sector, there had been an enemy breakthrough supported by tanks in the south headed towards Adony, held by a weak force of truck drivers and supply personnel from *Alarm-Btl. Wiking* augmented by the division's own small *Begleitkompanie*. On the northern flank on the eastern tip of Lake Velencze, the *Totenkopf* Division reported a quiet night. Five kilometers north of Stuhlweissenburg, attempts during the night to close the gap between Zámoly and the city had been unsuccessful, after a counterattack by *I. Abt./Kav.Rgt. 41* failed to overcome the enemy's strong defensive position held by an estimated infantry regiment. Another attack against a large farm 6 kilometers north of Stuhlweissenburg at Gyúlamajor by *II. Abt./Kav.Rgt. 41* was still ongoing when the morning report was submitted. Additionally, a battalion's worth of enemy infantry had broken through the German lines 3.5 kilometers west of Zámoly and had continued heading west, forcing *Div.Gr. Holste* to organize another counterattack. The good news was that during the night, *Div.Gr. Holste* was able to destroy six Soviet tanks.

The fighting only intensified as the day progressed. The situation in Adony worsened when the small force defending there was attacked from the northwest by a Soviet infantry battalion supported by 14 tanks from the XVIII Tank Corps. After a difficult struggle including house-to-house fighting, the *Wiking* Division's troops were able to force the enemy to withdraw after destroying five tanks and one SP gun when the few remaining tanks of *SS-Pz.Rgt. 5* came to the rescue with a well-timed counterattack. A participant in that action, a dispirited *Ostuf.* Kerckhoff of *5. Kp./SS-Pz.Rgt. 5*, wrote that evening, "It became clear to us that [our] attack on Budapest was also over. Every hour, we noticed the enemy being reinforced … the weather grew worse hour by hour. A heavy snowfall ensued. Fog surrounded our position. What would the night bring? We were still holding Adony."[40] South of the confluence of the Váli River with the Danube, another company-sized Soviet force was able to infiltrate the lines held by *I. Btl./Germania* and continue heading towards Adony in the south.

Battalion- and regiment-sized attacks south and west of Aggszentpéter, supported by 25 tanks, achieved several local penetrations, but the *Wiking* Division—with the aid of the *Totenkopf* Division—was able to seal them off by the evening. Evidently, the division's entire right flank was hanging in thin air and vulnerable to the much larger Soviet offensive approaching from the south, where the *1. Pz.Div.* was defending. Consequently, *Oberf.* Ullrich ordered his division command post to be moved to Hippolitpuszta, 7 kilometers to the west, at 10 a.m. after its previous one at Felsocikőla Puszta was threatened by Soviet tanks earlier that morning.[41] The *Totenkopf* Regiment, holding the line at Kápolnás Nyék, reported a similar situation, but it too was able to seal off the breakthrough and restore the front line by nightfall. The rest of the *Totenkopf* Division, preceded by the *Eicke* Regiment and the *panzer* regiment's few remaining tanks, were in the process of moving to their new reserve position south of Stuhlweissenburg, where portions of the Eicke Regiment had already arrived.

SS-Regiment Ney, defending east of Stuhlweissenburg along with *Pio.Btl. 356*, was thrown back to the city's eastern outskirts, but quickly launched a counterattack that forced the Soviets back to the vineyard country east of the city and retook the vitally important height of Hill 182, which it had been forced to abandon three days before. West of Pátka, where the I Guards Mechanized Corps had launched its attack the previous day, a strong armored attack with at least 30 tanks drove towards Stuhlweissenburg from the north and threw the defenders from *Gren. Rgt. 871* back into the city's northern outskirts. To avert this danger, *Gen.Maj.* Holste ordered *Oberst* Kühl to commit his division reserve, *I. Abt./Kav.Rgt. 41* and a battalion from the *Eicke* Regiment, which counterattacked and forced the enemy to retreat as far as the large agricultural estate 7 kilometers north of the city, where the German forces were able to withstand a tank-supported Soviet counterattack.

While this savage little battle was unfolding, another regiment-sized Soviet attack broke through the German *HKL* northwest of Zámoly and penetrated as far as 2 kilometers northwest of Magyaralmás, while another enemy force took Zámoly from the east and north. This attack had forced the defenders from *Kav.Rgt. 5* to withdraw and construct a hasty defense line several kilometers west of the town, though a counterattack to retake the town, consisting of a force composed of the *IV. (schwere) Abt./4. Kav.Brig.* and the attached battalion from the *356. Inf.Div.* (*I. Btl./ Gren.Rgt. 870*), was still underway when the evening report was submitted. Besides the inherent difficulty in having to fight and outmaneuver a numerically superior opponent, the *IV. SS-Pz.Korps* was experiencing additional problems.

That evening, the corps' staff highlighted certain shortages in supply when it reported, "Our defense is very difficult due to an acute shortage of ammunition for light and heavy field howitzers and heavy mortars." Dependent as the Germans were on their ability to employ heavy weapons at the small-unit level, insufficient ammunition for these critical weapons could determine defeat or victory. Despite these shortcomings, which were beyond the corps' control, overall its divisions had fought well. In his post-war manuscript, Manfred Schönfelder summed up the day's events:

> The *IV. SS-Pz.Korps* fought to hold Adony and experienced further local-level successes in the north. We were able to prevent an enemy breakthrough north of Stuhlweissenburg. In view of the threatening situation there, the *6. Armee* had been given the freedom of action to withdraw its forces in order to shorten the front and free up troops for a counterattack.[42]

The implications of Schönfelder's last comment will be discussed shortly, since this order would soon have wide-reaching ramifications for not only the *IV. SS-Pz.Korps*, but for the *III. Pz.Korps* and all of the Hungarian *3. Armee* as well.

Things were just as hot that day in Hermann Breith's corps' area of operations. Having to transition to an "active defense" did not mean that his three *panzer* divisions would have less fighting to do, but rather more. Along the boundary shared by *Gen.Lt.* Radowitz's *23. Pz.Div.* and *Div.Gr. Pape* of the neighboring Hungarian *3. Armee*, the former division had to ward off numerous battalion-sized enemy incursions south of Káloz. Southeast of Sárkeresztur, the *23. Pz.Div.* had to seal off a breakthrough after it had thrown the enemy back. Along its left flank that it shared with the *3. Pz.Div.*, Radowitz's division had to deflect a company-sized assault that had attempted to get past his defenses and reach Sárosd.

In the *3. Pz.Div.* sector, *Gen.Maj.* Söth (who had been promoted to that rank effective 30 January) learned through POW interrogation that a large Soviet assembly area, estimated to contain as many as three rifle regiments, was forming in the area of Nagy Lók, which shortly thereafter was engaged by the division's artillery. At the same time, his *Pz.Aufkl.Abt. 3* warded off company- to battalion-sized assaults in the vicinity of Tóthmajor. The most important threat that *3. Pz.Div.* faced that day was yet another large Soviet assembly area forming east of Nagy Hantos, which was caught by surprise during an armored strike by *K.Gr. Weymann*, inflicting "bloody losses" on the enemy.

The most threatened area by far was on the *III. Pz.Korps'* left flank along the Danube, where the *1. Pz.Div.* was doing its utmost to prevent the two approaching spearheads from the north and south from linking up. Although Thünert's division was unable to prevent this from happening, it was able to rescue the survivors of *K.Gr. Medicus* of the *3. Pz.Div.*, who had managed to break out from their encirclement in Dunapentele during the night of 31 January/1 February. After a Soviet infantry force had approached Perkáta, the linchpin of the division's center sector, Thünert ordered his division's *Panzergruppe*—now led by *Hptm.* Elias after the wounding of *Oberstlt.* Philipp—to carry out a counterattack.

In the brutally rapid action that followed, Elias and his remaining tanks overran the Soviet battalion, killing 50 men and capturing 50 more, as well as 10 antitank guns. Seven kilometers east of Perkáta, another strong Soviet force, including some tanks, forced the left flank of the division away from the village of Radicsa Puszta and further to the northwest along the Dunapentele–Adony road. Northeast of Perkáta, another tank-supported force managed to slip past the division's left flank and occupy the village of Also Cikolamajor, a mere 5 kilometers southeast of the *Wiking* Division's command post in Felsocikőlamajor. The attached armored reconnaissance battalion from the *23. Pz.Div.*, *Pz.Aufkl.Abt. 23*, at the time serving as the division's *Eingreifreserve*, carried out a counterattack that retook the town and destroyed three Soviet tanks in the process.

The first day of February was also an intensive one for the elements of the Hungarian *3. Armee* fighting south of Lake Balaton. A regiment-sized attack supported by five tanks launched by the 233rd Rifle Division against Szilas-Balhás was again beaten back by the Hungarian *II. Btl./Inf.Rgt. 26*, with the aid of *Pz.Aufkl. Abt. 1* and five tanks from *K.Gr. Martini* of the *6. Pz.Div.*, after destroying four Soviet tanks. A battalion-sized Soviet attack southwest of the town was also forced to withdraw after a counterattack by the *I. Btl./Inf.Rgt. 26*. North of Szilas-Balhás, the *Panzergruppe* from the *6. Pz.Div.* had to repulse another Soviet breakthrough attempt, on this occasion a far more dangerous one aimed at Dégh. After heavy fighting, the Soviet troops only got as far as a village 5 kilometers to the southeast, where they were forced to withdraw. The tanks and troops of *K.Gr. Martini* pursued them aggressively until they ran onto an extensive Soviet minefield and were forced to a halt.

On the opposite side of *A.Gr. Balck*, most of the area defended by *Korpsgruppe Harteneck* was quiet, except for that south of Felsőgalla and Mány. Near Felsőgalla, the Hungarian *1. Hus.Div.* carried out an attack to straighten out the front line 4 kilometers to the southwest of the town, and after achieving this objective had to fend off a battalion-sized enemy counterattack. The positions held south of Mány by the *3. Kav.Brig.* were attacked at 10 a.m. by a large tank-supported force from the XXXI Guards Rifle Corps, but was able to repulse it after destroying two tanks and one SP gun with its three *StuG*s.

After a lengthy artillery preparation, the eastern side of the salient was attacked an hour later by a regiment-sized enemy force supported by 20 tanks from the II Guards Mechanized Corps approaching from the direction of Zsámbék. In the heavy fighting that ensued, Soviet troops were able to achieve a 4-kilometer wide and 3-kilometer deep breakthrough that threatened to cut the salient off at its base. The *3. Kav.Brig.* carried out an immediate counterattack with all of its remaining assault guns and single tank destroyer from a patch of woods southwest of Szomor, though the outcome was still unknown when the evening report was submitted.

In regards to aerial activity, the weather situation had grown so adverse as the day progressed that few missions were carried out by either side. What few *Luftwaffe* sorties that were flown were limited to high-altitude reconnaissance flights over *A.Gr.*

Balck/6. Armee. For the same reason, no aerial resupply missions for the city were flown on the night of 31 January/1 February. (The fate of Budapest, no longer the objective of the *IV. SS-Pz.Korps'* relief attempts, will be covered in a separate section.)

Shocked at the speed of the Soviet advance, particularly along the Danube where the 4th Guards Army and 26th Army finally linked up near Adony, as well as by the size and scope of the counteroffensive taking place in the gap between Zámoly and Stuhlweissenburg, both Balck and Wöhler had to act, and quickly. Although Balck had already begun to anticipate the steps that would need to be taken should a breakthrough north of Lake Velencze occur, and had directed Gille to begin moving forces as a counterweight (for example, pulling out *SS-Pz.Gren.Rgt.6 Eicke* from the *Totenkopf* Division as an *Eingreifreserve*), it soon became apparent that this would not be enough to stop the assault by the I Guards Mechanized Corps and V Guards Cavalry Corps. While the local reserves had been able to achieve some success, they were unable to close the yawning gap between Zámoly and Stuhlweissenburg.

After conducting an initial commander's assessment, Balck concluded by 11 a.m. that morning that the only way this could be done was by taking a division away from Breith and tasking Gille to pull the entire *Totenkopf* Division out of the line on the eastern tip of Lake Velencze, sending them both towards Stuhlweissenburg, where they would conduct an attack towards Zámoly to cut off and destroy the Soviet force that had broken through. In developing this course of action, it was vintage Balck at work, doing what he did best, sacrificing ground to concentrate enough forces to strike the enemy hard and regain the ground lost after the crisis had passed.

The other crisis along the inner flanks of the *IV. SS-Pz.Korps* and *III. Pz.Korps* could not be ignored either. By removing one of his three *panzer* divisions, Breith's corps would be too weak to withstand the concerted efforts of the 26th Army to continue its drive to the north, but it still had to be stopped. The only way this could be accomplished would be by substantially withdrawing the *III. Pz.Korps* from its current front line, allowing its length to shrink sufficiently to free up a division. Such a movement would also require the Hungarian *3. Armee* to pull in its southern front before the CXXXIII Rifle Corps could achieve a penetration along the long, exposed inner flank it shared with Breith's corps. Most importantly, both moves—concentrating two *panzer* divisions in Stuhlweissenburg while pulling in the front line in the south—would have to be done simultaneously and within the next 24 hours if Balck's gambit was to work.

Due to the *Führerbefehl* of 21 January, Balck could not order such a drastic action on his own authority. It had to be approved first by Wöhler at *H.Gr. Süd*, then by Guderian at *OKH*, and finally by the ultimate authority at the *Führerhauptquartier*, Hitler himself. Thus Balck began to make a flurry of field telephone calls to *H.Gr. Süd* in order to outline his plan and then convince Wöhler as well as von Grolman, his chief of staff, of the need to act according to the concept he laid before them. Wöhler had felt Balck had at first been overly optimistic about what he believed was the improbability of a Soviet counteroffensive between Stuhlweissenburg and Zámoly, and had been somewhat miffed that Balck had moved *SS-Pz. Gren. Rgt. Eicke* the previous day without his permission. Now Wöhler was equally alarmed at the developing situation and willingly agreed to Balck's proposal.

What Balck asked for, and what the situation demanded, was freedom of action, but Wöhler—who was also bound by the same *Führerbefehl*—could not authorize this either. He did forward Balck's concept to the *OKH* at 2:15 p.m. Twenty minutes later, the *OKH Führungsabteilung* called Balck directly and authorized him to order Gille to withdraw from the salient rapidly forming east and south of Kápolnás Nyék. Three hours later, the other part of Balck's request was approved when *Gen. d. Pz. Tr.* Wenck called him directly from *OKH* headquarters to authorize the movement of the two *panzer* divisions towards Stuhlweissenburg. Finally, the freedom of action that Balck requested was granted by Hitler at 11 p.m. The movement of troops would begin during the night of 1/2 February. The only caveat was that *H. Gr. Süd* directed that the withdrawal from the south could go no further than the line Siófok–Meze Komárom–Dégh–south of Káloz–Sárosd–middle of the southern shore of Lake Velencze.[43]

Without waiting for the bulk of the *Totenkopf* Division to arrive, or requesting permission from *Gen. d. Inf.* Wöhler for that matter, Balck ordered Gille to direct the entire *Eicke* Regiment, along with the available Tiger IIs of *s. Pz. Abt. 509*, be sent out that very evening from Stuhlweissenburg towards Zámoly and conduct an attack to close the gap as far as Sárkeresztes. Once it reached this location, the regiment was to wait for the rest of the division and the *1. Pz. Div.* before the attack would continue to close the gap completely. Balck also issued Gille instructions regarding placement of the several cannon battalions of *Volks-Art. Korps 403* to support the counterattack.

In the deliberations concerning where these individual battalions should be placed, Hitler himself got involved, despite the distance between the *Führerbunker* in Berlin and the scene of the fighting. He had returned to Berlin from the *Adlerhorst* on the Western Front on 16 January after the failure of Operation *Nordwind*, and perhaps felt the need to once again demonstrate his once-vaunted *Fingerspitzengefühl* (German term for an instinctive understanding of an unfolding action, similar to the French *coup d'oeil*). Despite Hitler's meddling, which was becoming an all-too-frequent occurrence since his edict of 21 January, most of Balck's original concept of operations was approved.

The plans for the operation were sent out via teletype and *Fernschreiber* that evening from Balck's *Hauptquartier* in Martinsberg. Gille and his staff, upon receipt of this order, drafted their own version to issue to the subordinate units of the *IV. SS-Pz. Korps*. After conducting a quick mission analysis of the *Armeegruppe's* order, the corps' *Führungsabteilung* would have identified specified and implied tasks, discussed possible enemy courses of action, and drafted the concept of operations to accomplish these tasks, along with any other supporting tasks that needed to be accomplished in the course of the mission, plus logistics and signal requirements. In addition to pulling out the *Totenkopf* Division in its entirety and sending it to Stuhlweissenburg, the corps would also incorporate the *1. Pz.Div.* into its order of battle once again when it arrived in its area of operations early the next morning, so its supply requirements would need to be added to the calculations too.

The difficult part entailed the retrograde movement of the *Wiking* Division, which would have to disengage all of its units from contact with the enemy and pull them back to the new designated *HKL* along the line (from south to north) Göböljárás–Felsö Besnyö–Györgymajor–northeast corner of Lake Velencze at Kis Velencze. This would entail abandoning Adony, Aggszentpéter, and Iváncsa, localities where the men of Ullrich's division had fought for nearly the past two weeks. This was only Phase I.[44] Like it had during *Unternehmen Brückenschlag* the previous August, the *Wiking* Division could expect that it would be pursued closely by the enemy throughout the movement. The instructions for the location of the new main defense line to be taken up during Phase II were not sent out by *A.Gr. Balck* until after midnight, so it would mean a long night with no sleep for Gille's operations staff.[45]

The final line would be drawn between Hill 130, 8 kilometers east of Seregélyes, to Gárdony, a distance of approximately 12 kilometers. On the right flank of the corps would be positioned the *III. Pz.Korps' 3. Pz.Div.*; on the left would be Lake Velencze. The biggest danger during this retrograde movement would involve the disengagement of the *1. Pz.Div.* from the front line near Perkáta. If followed too closely by a pursuing enemy, the situation could become very complicated indeed, especially should Soviet mechanized units infiltrate during the rearward movement in the hours of darkness when the situation was in flux. To remind the commanders of the *IV. SS-Pz.Korps* and *III. Pz.Korps* of the importance of maintaining contact with adjacent units during the withdrawal, the final order stated, "On this point, the [two corps] have to provide strong contact groups along their inner flanks. The movement of both corps is to be carried out in close and immediate agreement with one another."[46]

Besides the movement of the rest of the *Totenkopf* Division and all of the *Wiking* Division during the next 12–24 hours, Gille's staff would have to plan for the relocation of forward ammunition, fuel, and rations dumps in coordination with *Ostubaf.* Scharf at the corps' main headquarters in Jenö and the *6. Armee Oberquartiermeister, Oberstlt.* Mitlacher. In addition, they would also have to plan for the evacuation of all the forward dressing stations and the wounded, movement of any inoperable vehicles if possible and their demolition if they could not be moved, and practically everything else if time permitted, such as communication wires and cables, barbed wire, land mines, and even the dead if they had not yet been buried, providing there was room to carry them. Prisoners of war engaged as labor battalions would also be sent back to collection points in the *A.Gr. Balck/6. Armee* rear area.

Besides all of these unstated tasks, *Brig.Fhr.* Brasack would have to ensure that *Volks-Art.Korps 403* and all of its battalions knew they would have to begin displacing incrementally to ensure constant fire support to the *Wiking* Division, as well as attached *Luftwaffe Flak* batteries, *Volks-Werfer Brig. 17*, *Bau-Pionier* and *Brückenbau* battalions, and all the other corps troops and attached *Heerestruppen*, including attached Hungarian units. Many of these units would be relying on horses to pull their artillery pieces or supply wagons. Most of this withdrawal had to be done at night, over snow-covered and ice-encrusted roads, during rain showers and snowstorms, possibly under artillery fire, and with the constant threat of the enemy breaking through looming in the background.

From the viewpoint of today, it is a wonder that the *IV. SS-Pz.Korps* could pull off such a complex movement by the deadline, but it did, without cell phones or secure Motorola radios, and none of the modern command and control systems that armies now take for granted, such as NATO's "Blue Force Tracker" system. Another unstated task was the contemporaneous displacement of the corps *Vorgeschobener Gefechtstand* (forward command post) to a new location, because the one in Seregélyes would soon find itself situated dangerously close to the front line. The new site that *A.Gr. Balck* assigned it was Falubattyán, nearly 20 kilometers west of its present location.

Quickly drafting the relevant order, Gille's *Führungsabteilung* distributed copies of it to the corps' subordinate units using motorcycle dispatch riders, radio teletype, and *Fernschreiber* systems and began to pack up for the move to its new location, planned for mid-morning the following day. Throughout the evening, harried and exhausted division and corps *Feldgendarmerie*, along with *A.Gr. Balck/6. Armee Wehrmachts-Streifendienst* (traffic patrol service), did their best to regulate traffic movement to ensure that units adhered to the movement routes designated for their divisions, regiments, and battalions, as well as to catch any deserters. With oaths, shouting, and the occasional brandishing of machine pistols, these few "traffic cops" were able to accomplish their mission in nightmarish conditions, untangling traffic jams, accidents, and interference by high-ranking officers attempting to throw their weight around.

Although this vast repositioning of two corps and five divisions was not accomplished without friction, it was carried out in the limited time allotted and with minimal casualties, ample testimony to the skill and efficiency of all of the staffs concerned, including that of the *IV. SS-Pz.Korps*, which had been accused of incompetence by none other than its *Armeegruppe* commander. An incompetent staff would never have been able to plan and supervise a maneuver as complex as this one in such a constrained timeframe, despite Balck's accusations to the contrary. The fact is that Gille's *Führungsabteilung* was very talented, and on this occasion they performed their duties very well indeed.

The third day of the Soviet counteroffensive north of Lake Velencze—Friday, 2 February—opened with temperatures slightly below freezing, but clear skies. As the day lengthened, thawing temperature set in again, warming up to 46 degrees Fahrenheit in the lowlands (8 degrees Centigrade), further accelerated by the clear, sunny weather. Roads were soon affected by mud from melting snow and black ice, hampering the movement of German forces into their new positions. Overnight in the *IV. SS-Pz.Korps* sector, the *Wiking* Division began moving out to its new positions, beginning at 2 a.m., under the cover of a strong rear guard. Meanwhile, the attack by the *Eicke* Regiment became bogged down a few kilometers north of Stuhlweissenburg after encountering numerous incursions by Soviet infantry and tanks.

Most of the fighting that occurred overnight took place in the *Div.Gr. Holste* area, with a Soviet force of up to two battalions of infantry supported by 15 tanks surrounding the small *Kampfgruppe* from *Kav.Rgt. 41* occupying Gyulamajor, 6 kilometers south of Zámoly. After heavy fighting, the battlegroup broke through the encircling ring and escaped, establishing a new defense line 3 kilometers to the west of the village. Another Soviet attack against the front lines of *Kav.Rgt. 5*, 3 kilometers southwest of Zámoly, managed to punch its way through, but a German counterattack quickly sealed off the penetration and threw the invaders back. However, the 6-kilometer gap between Zámoly and Stuhlweissenburg was still wide open, though before dawn broke neither the I Guards Mechanized Corps nor V Guards Cavalry Corps made any attempt to drive further into the rear of the German defenses.

After the fighting north of Stuhlweissenburg subsided that morning, except for minor actions, the forces of the 4th Guards Army operating north of Lake Velencze halted for the day to briefly consolidate and wait for all of its artillery and supply services to catch up. General Zakharov intended to resume his counteroffensive the following day, the same day when the *IV. SS-Pz.Korps* was to begin its own counterattack to eliminate the penetration between Zámoly and Stuhlweissenburg. Not all of the artillery designated to support the counteroffensive had finished repositioning from their previous firing positions east of the Váli defense line, nor had all of the support army-level antitank and antiaircraft regiments finished moving.

The main body of the *Totenkopf* Division, except for a few minor rear guard elements, had been able to reach its assembly area in or near Stuhlweissenburg undisturbed. Portions of the division, such as *II. Bataillon* of the *Totenkopf* Regiment, actually moved into the city itself, where it went into positions on the eastern edge. The leading columns of the *1. Pz.Div.*, which had a greater distance to travel, did not begin arriving in their assembly area located in the Stuhlweissenburg–Falubattyán–Sárszent Mihaly area until 8 p.m. after a long march over muddy roads while enduring Soviet air attacks. West of Kisfalud, a company-sized Soviet reconnaissance in force supported by two tanks, most likely from the I Guards Mechanized Corps, attempted to penetrate the German front lines southeast of Stuhlweissenburg, but *SS-Rgt. Ney* reported that it had forced it to withdraw; however, this same unit reappeared further south a short while later, with fateful consequences.

The only truly significant actions that took place that day in Gille's sector involved a Soviet tank-supported force that attempted unsuccessfully to break through the *Wiking* Division's left flank at Gárdony, and another one consisting of 30 tanks with mounted infantry, most likely from a brigade of the XXIII Tank Corps, that succeeded. This second force managed to slip in that morning between the boundary that the *Wiking* Division shared with the *3. Pz.Div.* at the same time the *1. Pz.Div.* was concluding its withdrawal. Although the *Wiking* Division itself was able to disengage from its old front line behind the Váli relatively undisturbed, Soviet forces followed up closely until the division's rear guard reached the outskirts of Puszta Szabolcs.

Here, taking advantage of the fluid situation and the heavy morning mist, the enemy tanks and mounted infantry attacked and forced the *Wiking* Division's *Nachhut* to pull back beyond the town early that morning. Meanwhile, 15 tanks along with their *Tankodesantniki* (accompanying infantry) pushed unobserved along both sides of the railroad line between Puszta Szabolcs and Seregélyes. Here, they easily broke through the *Wiking* Division's new *HKL* 8 kilometers east of the town of Seregélyes, where it had established its new division command post, before they were driven back by a counterattack launched by the *Eingreifgruppen* of the *3. Pz.Div.* and the *Wiking*. In the post-war history of the *3. Pz.Div.*, this engagement by the division's *Begleitkompanie* received a brief mention when the author wrote, "The gloom and heavy fog made the fighting difficult. Tanks, antitank guns, and machine-gun fire resounded from every direction, without anyone knowing what they were shooting at."[47]

Not all of the Soviet incursions were intercepted and driven back. Besides the aggressive pursuit carried out by the XXIII Tank Corps, a mounted reconnaissance patrol from the I Guards Mechanized Corps managed to infiltrate German lines at Kisfalud, a village at the western tip of Lake Velencze, and penetrate as far south as the northern outskirts of Seregélyes. Somehow, this small force had managed to slip past *SS-Rgt. Ney* and the *1. Kp./SS-Pz.Pio.Btl. 3* of the *Totenkopf* Division posted there to prevent such incursions. This particular group consisted of two tanks and up to 60 mounted troops from the 11th Guards Motorcycle Battalion, and would not normally have been considered a serious threat. Possibly lost or unsure of their direction of travel, the Soviet column emerged several kilometers north of Seregélyes and began driving south along the highway linking that town with Stuhlweissenburg. At the same moment, the *Führungsabteilung* of the *IV. SS-Pz.Korps* set out using the same road to begin its own movement north to its new command post location at Falubattyán. Each staff element of the headquarters was moving in increments of one to several vehicles separated by intervals of a few minutes, beginning at 10 a.m.

The lead vehicle in the column, moving several hundred meters in front of the next group of vehicles along the fog-enshrouded road, was a staff car driven by 19-year-old *Sturmmann* Gottfried Hofmann carrying *Stubaf.* Fritz Rentrop, the *Ia* of the *IV. SS-Pz.Korps*, who had been in this position for less than a month after graduating from the *Kriegsakademie*. After traveling several kilometers, their staff car nearly collided with a roadblock erected by the Soviet patrol a few kilometers northwest of Seregélyes. The commander of the motorcycle company, Senior Lieutenant I. I. Churanov, ordered his troops to fire on Rentrop's car, which came to a halt when Hofmann was killed. Rentrop himself was seriously wounded. Hardly believing his good luck, Churanov ordered his men to take Rentrop, along with all of the documents he was carrying, and quickly returned through German lines to his own unit.

A few minutes later, the next vehicle in the convoy, containing the corps Ic, *Stubaf.* Herbert Jankuhn, and most of his personnel, found the abandoned blood-soaked staff car but no bodies. Only moments before, the Soviet troops had absconded with Rentrop and what they could gather from his car. Civilian eyewitnesses came forward to tell Jankuhn and others that they had seen the Soviet troops taking a wounded German officer into captivity. The rest of the convoy made it safely to Falubattyán and immediately got to work placing the headquarters into operation, which was reported as being completed by noon that day. The exact fate of Rentrop was unknown; German radio intercepts picked up a Soviet radio message that same day stating that a German major had been captured, but whether it was Rentrop was unknown. Rentrop likely died from his wounds or was murdered soon thereafter, and was apparently buried in an unmarked grave along with the body of his driver (see figures 5 and 6).[48]

Whether he was interrogated by his captors is unknown, though due to the seriousness of his wounds he probably died before the *NKVD* could get their hands on him. What he had in his briefcase was enough. To this day, both men are still listed as missing in action by the *Deutsches Rotes Kreuz* (German Red Cross). The loss of Knight's Cross holder Rentrop and the contents of his attaché case was indeed a setback, but the war had to go on. He was immediately replaced by the *O1, Hstuf.* Hans Velde, who would act as the temporary *Ia* until Schönfelder could find a new *Kriegsakademie* general staff graduate. Rentrop's disappearance would spark an investigation by an angry Hermann Balck, which will be covered in a following paragraph. Although

Rentrop Fritz
Berufssoldat
19.11.17   X
o.A.
SS-Stuba.   B
Stuhlweißenbg.1.45

Figure 6. Missing in Action photo of *SS-Stubaf.* Fritz Rentrop from the album of the missing compiled by the *Deutsches Rotes Kreuz* (German Red Cross), depicting the date and the location where he was declared to be missing in action (the actual date he was captured was 2 February 1945). Rentrop's body has never been recovered.

tragic, the war would not stop simply because of the death of a talented staff officer and his driver. Hans Velde would fill in admirably until *Stubaf.* Friedrich Rauch was assigned a month later to fill his position.

Since it, too, was displacing, the *III. Pz.Korps* and its two divisions (*3. Pz.Div.* and *23. Pz.Div.*) were involved in very little fighting, except that which their rear guards had to do in order to fend off Soviet units closely shadowing them. For example, south of Nagy Hantos, the *3. Pz.Div. Nachhut* fought off several company- to battalion-sized enemy attacks, but it and its sister division were able to make it safely back to their new *HKL* without any serious damage. How 30 Soviet tanks had managed to slip between its left flank at Puszta Szabolcs and the *Wiking* Division's right flank and nearly seize Seregélyes was not addressed in its evening report. On the right of Breith's corps, the Hungarian *3. Armee* also withdrew to its new main defense line in an orderly manner, with *Pz.Aufkl.Abt. 1* of *Div.Gr. Pape* and *K.Gr.*

Hofmann Gottfried
Arbeiter
10.4.26   0
Zöblitz/Sachs.
SS-Strm.
Stuhlweißenb. 1.45

Figure 7. Missing in Action photo of *SS-Sturmmann* Gottfried Hofmann, Rentrop's driver, from the album of the missing compiled by the *Deutsches Rotes Kreuz.* His body has not been found either, although his unidentified remains, like Rentrop's, might lie in the German War Graves cemetery in Budaörs or Szekesfehervar, Hungary.

Martini of the *6. Pz.Div.* comprising the bulk of the rear guard, since they were the only truly mobile units under *Gen.Lt.* Heszlényi's command. On the *A.Gr. Balck/6. Armee's* far left flank, *Korpsgruppe Harteneck/I. Kav.Korps* reported little combat activity, with the exception of Mány, where once again the *3. Kav.Brig.* found itself engaged in repelling an attack by a combined infantry and armor force from the XXXI Guards Rifle Corps. The single penetration the Soviets made in its defenses was in the process of being sealed off and eliminated by a counterattack when the evening report was submitted.[49]

On account of the clear skies over Soviet airfields that day, there was a considerable amount of Red Air Force activity, including ground-attack aircraft and fighter-bombers, focused primarily against the *III. Pz.Korps*, which was forced to conduct most of its withdrawal during daylight hours. Although the number of sorties was not recorded by *Luftwaffe* observers, it must have been considerable. The *Luftwaffe's* airfields, located northwest of the Bakony Forest, once again experienced poor flying conditions overhead, although up to 80 strike sorties were flown again the bridge at Dunaföldvar and the since-repaired bridge at Dunapentele. German ground-attack aircraft also shot up four Soviet trains and a number of freight cars, while *Luftwaffe* fighter aircraft scored five kills in the skies over Budapest, which must at least have boosted the morale of the troops who observed the aerial combat.[50] During the night of 1/2 February, six transport aircraft managed to deliver 2½ tons of supplies to the city, despite the atrocious weather.

Viewing activities from the perspectives of Marshal Tolbukhin and Generals Zakharov and Gagen, the day had been a very good one. Although there was no major ground combat activity such as there had been the day before, the mechanized advance mounted by the XVIII and XXIII Tank Corps had managed to shadow the withdrawing Hungarian and German forces nearly as far as the old *Margarethestellung* between Lakes Velencze and Balaton. More importantly, by joining up their forces at Adony, the 4th Guards Army and 26th Army had wrested control of the entire western bank of the Danube away from their opponents and could now combine their efforts in a united drive towards Stuhlweissenburg from the east and south.

Following a one-day pause in combat operations, the 4th Guards Army's four corps arrayed north of Stuhlweissenburg would continue their efforts to break through towards Mór and seize Stuhlweissenburg from the east and north, an effort that would be assisted by the 26th Army's attack through Seregélyes from the south, while the 57th Army would continue pressuring the Hungarian *3. Armee* from the west. The following day, 3 February, would see a resumption of the offensive, with both armies now able to operate in close unison. Neither Soviet commander was apparently aware of the impending German counterattack, scheduled to unfold the same day.

The only limiting factor at this point was the low numbers of tanks, assault guns, and self-propelled guns, for losses had been very heavy during the fighting of the past six days. In just the XXIII Tank Corps on 1 February alone, it reported only 37 operational armored vehicles, with another 29 undergoing short-term repair. A total of 87 armored vehicles had been total write-offs since its counterattack against the *IV. SS-Pz.Korps* on 27 January.[51] The XVIII Tank Corps' losses in tanks and other armored vehicles had not been as high, reporting 88 tanks and other armored vehicles as still being operational on the same date (this does not include losses suffered on 2 February). The V Guards Cavalry Corps reported 34 armored fighting vehicles available, including 24 M4A2 Shermans, and the I Guards Mechanized Corps reported 81 operational tanks, assault guns, and self-propelled guns. Though well below their established strength, these four mechanized formations still had enough armor remaining (240 vehicles on 1 February) to continue with their offensive.

In regards to German intentions for the following day, at least pertaining to *A.Gr. Balck/6. Armee*, Balck intended to close the gap between Zámoly and Stuhlweissenburg. He apparently thought that this would be relatively easy task, after optimistically stating that "the Russians [*sic*] were at the end of their strength" in an exchange with *H.Gr. Süd* headquarters.[52] To carry out this counterattack, he intended to have the *IV. SS-Pz.Korps* employ three assaults groups, consisting of the *Totenkopf*

Division, which would attack on the right (southern) flank, the *1. Pz.Div.* in the center, and the *4. Kav.Brig.* attacking on the left (north) flank. All three formations were to commence their attack at 10 a.m. from jump-off positions in the areas on either side of Sárkeresztes, oriented in an easterly direction and advancing as far as the vineyards east of Stuhlweissenburg, the large agricultural estate 5 kilometers east of Sárkeresztes, and the other large farm 3 kilometers east of Zámoly. *Volks-Artillerie Korps 403* would complete its change of position by the evening of 2 February. Overall, conditions appeared to be promising for the following day's attack.

To this end, Balck's headquarters issued detailed guidance that afternoon, concentrating primarily on the role that the *IV. SS-Pz.Korps* would perform the following day. This four-paragraph order is worth repeating in its entirety, in that it provides a good example how Balck and Gaedke—contrary to the previous (and prevailing) *Wehrmacht* custom of issuing mission-type orders to subordinate commanders—kept a tight rein on Gille and his staff by assigning them detailed and specific orders regarding exactly what the *Armeegruppe* commander wanted his subordinate SS corps to do and how to go about it. The order approved by Balck read as follows:

1) *IV. SS-Pz.Korps* will counterattack in the area north of Stuhlweissenburg in order to restore the previous situation and crush the enemy forces that have broken through. Pursuant to this objective, the *1. Pz.Div.*, the *SS-Pz.Div. Totenkopf*, and additional forces being brought up along with the concentrated fire of the entire artillery of the corps will carry out its attack in a tightly unified and controlled manner.

   1st Attack Objective: the line running through the vineyards east of Stuhlweissenburg–Gyúlamajor–Borbála Puszta–heights 2.5 kilometers east of Csákberény.

   2nd Attack Objective: the line running through the northwest corner of Lake Velencze–Csala–Fülópmajor–Zámoly–highway intersection 3 kilometers north of Zámoly–southern edge of Gánt.

2) In the course of this attack, it is vital that the units concerned, without exception, be very tightly controlled. *Grenadier Regiment 871* must be pulled out of the front lines early in the morning on 3 February. This is an opportunity to put this unit back in order. Condition of attacking units [afterwards] must be reported no later than 8 p.m. on 3 February via telex.

3) In order to ensure the maximum effectiveness of this counterattack, the gap in the front lines between Stuhlweissenburg and Sárkeresztes must be secured by armored assault groups using mobile tactics.

4) The corps commander will immediately report the start time and initiation of the counterattack once it has begun.

   Signed,
   Gaedke, *Gen.Maj.*
   Chef des Generalstabes, *A. Gr. Balck*[53]

This astonishing order, contrary to the traditions of the Greater German General Staff, certainly left little room for interpretation or for initiative on Gille's part. Whether Gille interpreted this as a calculated insult is unknown; in the past, Balck had been accused him of interpreting orders as he saw fit and failing to submit situation reports in a timely manner. Although it remains unknown whether Gille was chagrinned by what any other commander in his position would have seen as *A. Gr. Balck*'s deliberate exceeding of the normal bounds of command, or at least its traditions, being the good soldier that he was, he most likely obeyed these orders without question. Gille certainly had little time to brood even if he had the inclination to do so, for he was far too busy ensuring that his divisions were in position and had everything they needed before they began their attack.

The *Wiking* Division was not included in any of these plans, since it was tasked with defending Seregélyes, which the division had barely reached ahead of the pursuing Soviets that morning. This tactically important town, which lay astride the southern approaches to Stuhlweissenburg, had to be held at all costs in order to secure the cohesion of the entire *HKL* along the *A. Gr. Balck/6. Armee* southern flank between Lakes Velencze and Balaton. In view of the *IV. SS-Pz. Korps'* ongoing commitment to the counterattack north of Stuhlweissenburg, Balck and Gaedke considered attaching it to Breith's *III. Pz. Korps*, though withheld their decision for the time being—perhaps persisting in their belief that Gille and his staff were not up to the challenge of fighting on two separate fronts, although the command and staff of the *IV. SS-Pz. Korps* had repeatedly demonstrated their ability to do so since the beginning of *Unternehmen Konrad I* on 1 January. The animus felt by Balck and his chief was staff was simply too great to give the *Waffen-SS* officers the benefit of the doubt.

In recognition of their performance over the past several days, Balck recommended that the *1. Pz. Div.*, *s. Pz. Abt. 509*, and *I. Abt./Pz. Rgt. 24* be mentioned in the *Wehrmachtsbericht* for their conspicuous conduct during the fighting south of Lake Velencze, including the destruction of 78 enemy tanks against the loss of only seven of their own. The *IV. SS-Pz. Korps* was not nominated for any such mention, though its troops had performed just as well, yet another example of a petty slight against both the *Waffen-SS* and Gille. Instead of praising the corps' performance, Balck singled it out for criticism in his report later that evening to *H. Gr. Süd*, where his staff brought up the issue of the capture of Fritz Rentrop and the loss of classified documents.[54]

Upon learning of Rentrop's disappearance at 9:45 p.m. that evening, Balck immediately demanded that the *IV. SS-Korps'* chief of staff provide a list of documents he was carrying at the time he was reported missing. This, of course, was a logical request because Rentrop may have been carrying documents of an extremely sensitive nature, which if they fell into enemy hands could reveal *A. Gr. Balck*'s plans and intentions. Because he was the corps' *Ia*, he might have been carrying all of the working papers that he had in his possession at the time the command post was shut down in preparation for its move to its new location in Falubattyán. Since the area between Seregélyes and Stuhlweissenburg was believed to still be under German control, neither Rentrop nor anyone else on the staff seems to have taken particular precautions for what, to them, seemed yet another administrative rather than a "tactical" move. Had the corps staff known there were Soviet patrols roaming about, the column would have been consolidated and protected by the corps' *Begleitkompanie*. In his initial report, the corps chief of staff reported that Rentrop was only carrying "a list of code names."

This later proved to be an incomplete accounting. Schönfelder ordered the acting *Ia* and the *Ic*, as well as their staff groups, to conduct a thorough search of their files to determine what actually had been lost. Shortly thereafter, *Hstuf.* Velde contacted the *A. Gr. Balck/6. Armee Ia* and notified him that Rentrop had been carrying at the time of his capture a wealth of documents, including the current list of code names, the current enemy situation map, a list of attached units, the artillery organization, the map depicting the corps' current situation, munition and fuel status reports, the most recent weekly reports submitted by the *3.* and *5. SS-Pz.Div.*, the daily report of 1 February and morning report of 2 February, tank and antitank gun readiness reports, current and past orders from the field army, and several other relevant documents. The list ended with one of the most prized of all documents, the corps *Ia Kriegstagebuch*, which recorded the entire progress of *Konrad I–III*. All of these documents apparently fell into Soviet hands and were quickly translated and analyzed. How much the capture of these documents influenced the 4th Guards Army's subsequent operations can only be surmised, though if nothing else, they did provide a window into the minds of those conducting the plans and operations of not only Gille's corps, but *A. Gr. Balck/6. Armee* too.[55]

It was a sad and regrettable incident, but a recurring example of how the "fog of war" (both literal and figurative in this case) can influence what happens on the battlefield when the shooting starts. However, in his memoirs, Balck presents this as yet another case of "all too typical" *Waffen-SS* false reporting and disobedience. Describing Rentrop's disappearance as "a classic example of the sort of imponderables senior commanders have to deal with," Balck wrote that "I had closed a certain road to all traffic because it was within the reach of the Russians [*sic*]. But ignoring that order, it goes without saying, that one of Gille's general staff officers drove down that road and the Russians captured him, complete with the operations orders he was carrying."[56] Written over thirty years after the war, Balck's memory is faulty in this particular case, in that no order had ever been issued by *A. Gr. Balck* that forbade travel along this road. In fact, the road connecting Seregélyes and Stuhlweissenburg was a *Rollbahn* (main supply route) and there was no other route that Gille's staff could have taken to reach their destination of Falubattyán. It is also noteworthy that there is nothing in the *H. Gr. Süd* war diary about this road being closed to movement.

Neither Rentrop nor anyone else could have known that a Soviet reconnaissance patrol from the area north of Lake Velencze had slipped past *SS-Rgt. Ney's* screen line guarding the southwestern tip of the lake; all eyes were focused on the approaching

Soviet tanks coming from the southeast of Seregélyes. Later, Balck also claimed that he had not approved the relocation of Gille's forward headquarters, another example, to him at least, of the *Waffen-SS* acting without proper authority.[57] While there is no evidence in the documentation to prove his claim either way, it made no sense whatsoever for a corps headquarters—the bulk of whose divisions were about to begin a counterattack at Stuhlweissenburg—to remain in Seregélyes over 20 kilometers away, and less than 8 kilometers from the front line rapidly forming east and southeast of the town that was easily within range of mortar fire.

Placing a corps headquarters so close to the front lines is never a good idea, and that Gille would have to wait for an order from his higher headquarters telling him when to move in such a fluid and highly dangerous situation is simply preposterous. Remaining where they were would have put Gille and his staff at extreme risk. Though Rentrop and the documents he was carrying were lost, that was far better than the entire corps forward command post being scooped up by the Soviets. This point seems to have eluded Balck.

The day of the scheduled counterattack by the *IV. SS-Pz.Korps* was plagued by the continuing low-level heavy fog, worsened by the below-freezing weather. At altitude, the weather was clear, with occasional patches of clouds, portending a strong reappearance by the Red Air Force. Black ice covered most of the roads, especially in places where puddles from the previous day's thaw froze overnight. In the Bakony Forest, portions of the supply routes through the hills were completely covered by virtual lakes caused by melting snow, making them nearly impassable by wheeled vehicles and causing a nearly two-day delay in the delivery of fuel and ammunition. This latter item was being consumed by the corps and divisions of *A.Gr. Balck/6. Armee* at the rate of 535 metric tons a day, while as much as 272 cubic meters (71,855 U.S. gallons) of gasoline was consumed on 2 February alone.[58]

In the *IV. SS-Pz.Korps* area of operations, the corps headquarters reported that during the night of 2/3 February, there had been a considerable amount of fighting in Seregélyes, the important crossroads town being defended "at all costs" by Ullrich's *Wiking* Division. Taking advantage of the fog, an enemy force of unknown size attacked the town from the northeast, east, and south. The *Wiking* Division immediately launched a counterattack along with the *3. Pz.Div.* that was still underway by mid-morning, a harbinger of what the day's fighting would bring. The report also mentioned that the Hungarian *2. Pz.Div.*, located on the far left flank of the *IV. SS-Pz.Korps* north of the *4. Kav.Brig.*, had its positions probed by a strong Soviet reconnaissance in force that approached 2.5 kilometers north of Csákberény, but the Hungarians managed to force it to retreat after engaging it with antitank and artillery fire.

The primary focus of the *IV. SS-Pz.Korps'* attention that day was the large-scale counterattack by the *1. Pz.Div.* and the *Totenkopf* Division north of Stuhlweissenburg to close the gap between the city and Zámoly (see Map 10). While Becker's division reported a *Kampfstärke* that day of 1,832 men (not counting its *Feld-Ersatz* battalion), it reported only six operational *Pz. IVs*, two *Pz. VI* Tiger Is, and seven assault guns and tank destroyers, for a total of 15 combat-ready armored vehicles, hardly sufficient for such an ambitious undertaking. To ease this situation, the *Totenkopf* Division was reinforced once again by the attachment of 18 Panthers from *I. Abt./Pz.Rgt. 24*. *Generalmajor* Thünert's division, which did not occupy its jump-off position until 9 a.m., reported a *Kampfstärke* of only 997 men, though it was further augmented by a battalion of 401 men from the Hungarian *1. SS-Sturmjäger Regiment*. The long and arduous road march through the mud from Perkáta to its position east of Sárkeresztes had taken a heavy toll on its armored vehicles, leaving the *1. Pz.Div.* with only two operational *Pz. V* Panthers when it arrived in its assembly area, though 14 more were made battle-ready by the time the attack began. To bolster its tank strength, 12 operational Tiger IIs of *s.Pz.Abt. 509* were attached to the division.[59]

Before the attack even began, Balck was already fuming about what he perceived as the corps' failure to position its units properly in order to begin the attack at 10 a.m. as scheduled. Apparently, one regiment from the *Totenkopf* Division was supposed to have occupied a jump-off position northwest of the city, but had instead gone into position inside its northern and eastern outskirts. Shortly before the deadline for the attack, the *I. Btl./Totenkopf* had already driven off a counterattack that began at 9 a.m., launched by the 3rd Guards Mechanized Brigade as part of the 4th Guards Army's resumption of the previous day's operation. This attack, supported by 12 M4A2 Shermans from the 9th Guards Tank Brigade, had attempted to break into the city's industrial area via the cemetery located on the northern edge of Stuhlweissenburg near Kiskecskemét. Surprised to find SS troops occupying Stuhlweissenburg instead of the "soft" soldiers of the *356. Inf.Div.*, the Soviet troops were forced to retreat, *Hstuf.* Stienen's battalion knocking out seven Shermans using hollow-charged projectiles fired from an *SPW*-mounted 7.5cm infantry howitzer. This important defensive action, which could not have been avoided, was yet another legitimate reason why the *IV. SS-Pz.Korps'* attack had been delayed past 10 a.m.

For reasons unknown, Balck does not seem to have taken this engagement into account when he excoriated Gille for the attack's delay. In anger, Balck contacted *H.Gr. Süd* at 9:45 a.m. to complain, stating, "The *3. SS-Pz.Div.* has occupied a position in the Stuhlweissenburg area different from the one they were ordered. The *IV. SS-Pz.Korps* wants to have them attack first to the northeast, then swing eastwards. This is a difficult maneuver, which the *Armeegruppe* has warned against."[60] Instead of ordering Gille to go to that location and sort it out, Balck personally intervened by telephone, ordering Becker to move the *Totenkopf* Regiment out of the city towards the northwest, where it would commence its attack. This of course caused more delay, though Becker was doing his best, especially considering that his opponent was also attempting to initiate his own attack. Finally, at 11:30 a.m., the operation commenced after the initial artillery preparatory fire began striking known and suspected Soviet positions.

After making initial progress, by midday the *Totenkopf* Division's attack began to bog down in the face of strong Soviet resistance, backed up by tanks, antitank gun *Pakfronts*, and extensive minefields, especially on the division's right flank west of Kiskecskemét, where the 3rd Guards Mechanized Brigade was now defending. The fighting there was extremely heavy. One participant in the attack, *Sturmmann* Krawadt of *II. Btl./Eicke*, later described the scene in a letter home:

> We pushed into the heights northwest of Stuhlweissenburg. To our left ran the road leading to Mór. We began to receive enemy rifle fire diagonally from our right. Mortar rounds exploded, throwing large chunks of frozen earth high in the air, which fell with a lot of racket. We stepped up the pace of our attack and continued rushing forward, occasionally throwing ourselves to the ground. The first men of our group who were killed or wounded had to be left behind. We reached our objective, the fork in the road [running from Stuhlweissenburg to Zámoly], on the left there was nothing to be seen except a water well. I rolled into a trench. A nearby mortar blast showered me with mud and filth. Someone ordered a halt. Then came a new command: We are turning to the east! A few Panthers remained behind us as a security screen.[61]

With his attack on the right brought to a halt by the enemy's stiff resistance, Becker ordered a brief pause to reorganize and to shift his *Schwerpunkt* to the division's left, where it finally began to make progress. The attached *I. Abt./Pz.Rgt. 24* knocked out two Soviet armored fighting vehicles—a Sherman and a self-propelled gun—as well as two antitank guns.[62]

To the left of the *Totenkopf* Division, the *1. Pz.Div.* attacked out of the Sárkeresztes area towards the Stuhlweissenburg–Zámoly highway. On the division's left, *K.Gr. Huppert*—consisting of *Pz.Gren.Rgt. 1* and the *panzer* regiment's 16 remaining tanks, plus six *Pz. VI* Tiger IIs—was able to push through as far as the highway along both sides of Gyúlamajor, 6 kilometers south of Zámoly, and seized the large farming estate there while it waited for *K.Gr. Bradel* to catch up on the right, as well as the *4. Kav.Brig.* on the left. The division's combat engineer battalion, *Pz.Pio. Btl. 37*, attached to Huppert's battlegroup, seized Hill 171, which commanded the approaches to Zámoly. While holding its position, *K.Gr. Huppert* was subjected to intense Soviet air attacks, especially against its supporting artillery battalion from *Pz.Art.Rgt. 73*. Attacked by a group of enemy tanks that afternoon, the battlegroup destroyed eight of them before the remainder retreated.

On the division's right flank, which it shared with the *Totenkopf* Division, the attack by *K.Gr. Bradel*, consisting of *Pz.Gren.Rgt. 113*, was stopped by 30 Soviet tanks blocking the road between Kisber and Mór. At that moment, the six Tiger IIs of *2. Kp./s.Pz.Abt. 509*, led by *Ltn.* Werner Böttger, arrived on the scene and counterattacked the enemy tanks in the flank, destroying 22 of them in a single engagement and causing the survivors to flee eastwards. *Oberst* Bradel himself was lightly wounded by a shell splinter, his fifth wound of the war, when his command

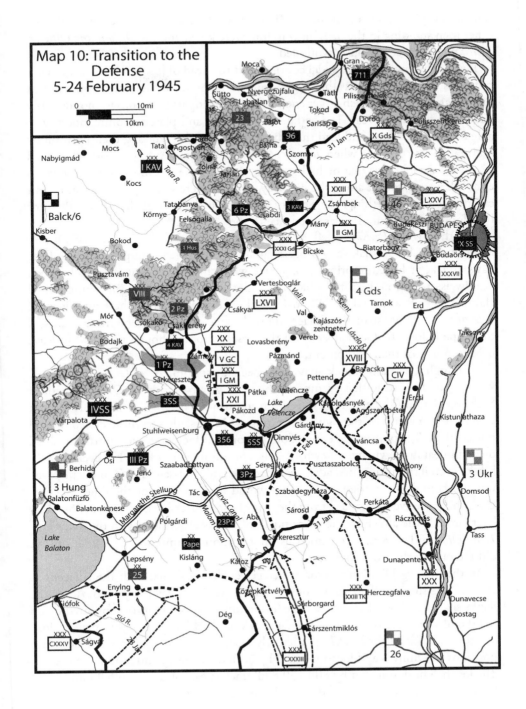

Map 10: Transition to the Defense 5-24 February 1945

0 ____ 10mi
0 ____ 10km

vehicle was pierced by a tank shell. Miraculously, he was only scratched, while two other men standing in the *SPW* next to him were killed and his *Ordonnanz Offizier*, *Leutnant* Stiebeler, seriously wounded.

Despite his own injury, Bradel continued at the head of his *Kampfgruppe*. On the right, his troops watched as the neighboring battalion from the *Eicke* Regiment was counterattacked by a much larger enemy force, causing its SS troops to momentarily panic and flee to the rear. The battalion's company and platoon commanders were able to rally their men and lead them back into the fight, retaking their position by nightfall, a rare instance when *Totenköpfler* broke and ran. At 8 p.m., Bradel recalled a forward detachment that he had sent out ahead of the rest of the *Kampfgruppe* to establish a strongpoint along the highway, because there were signs of an imminent enemy attack. If anything, the Soviets were not at the end of their strength—not by a long shot, despite Balck's assurance to the contrary.[63]

On the *IV. SS-Pz.Korps'* left flank, the attack by the *4. Kav.Brig.* of *Div.Gr. Holste* was unable to make any progress at all. Despite the incomplete results of the day's attack, at least the primary objective was achieved, in that the gap between Stuhlweissenburg and Zámoly had been closed. Additionally, Gille's troops had claimed to have knocked out 32 Soviet tanks, most of them by the King Tigers of *s.Pz.Abt. 509.*[64] Most of the Soviet troops located west of the highway managed to escape before the Germans cut off their escape route, though they had to leave behind much of their equipment.

Although Hermann Balck may have been disappointed, *H.Gr. Süd* evidently was not, its *Ia* writing that evening in the army group's report to *OKH*, "North of Stuhlweissenburg the enemy has been forced onto the defense." The report did not conceal the severity of the fighting, stating, "Our assault spearheads encountered powerful, tank-supported defenses of our opponent." However, the report concluded on an upbeat note, when the *Ia* wrote, "The continuity of our front has been reestablished, even if the anticipated advance across the Stuhlweissenburg–Zámoly highway was not completely carried out."[65] That would have to wait for the following day. Describing the events that day from the corps headquarters' perspective, Schönfelder later wrote, "The attack by the corps north of Stuhlweissenburg with the *Totenkopf, 1. Pz.Div.*, and *4. Kav.Brig.* gained us only a minimal amount of ground, but we did reestablish the front line."[66]

In the *Wiking* Division's sector at Seregélyes that it shared with the adjacent *3. Pz.Div.*, the situation had gone from bad to worse as the day progressed. Along the flanks shared by both divisions, a large formation of Soviet infantry supported by up to 60 tanks conducted a series of frontal attacks and achieved numerous penetrations of the newly established *HKL*, particularly against the *Wiking* Division's defensive positions in Dinnyés and locations held by both divisions in and around Seregélyes. The key height dominated by Hill 130 8 kilometers east of the town fell into enemy hands. Despite the severity of the attacks, both towns remained in German hands.

One particularly dangerous attack, consisting of an infantry battalion supported by 15 tanks, managed to break through and block the *Rollbahn* running through Seregélyes to Sárosd, which was used by both the *3. Pz.Div.* and the *23. Pz.Div.* The armored battlegroup of the *3. Pz.Div.* undertook a counterattack to eliminate this breakthrough, which was making slow progress when the evening report was submitted.

Overall, according to German records describing the chaotic situation, "The enemy bypassed many friendly, widely-dispersed strongpoints—in some instances, avoiding a fight—in the fog, which made command and control extremely difficult, and [they] continued advancing west."[67] When an element of the *Germania* Regiment, along with some of the division's artillery, were briefly encircled between Seregélyes and Dinnyés, a small *Kampfgruppe*—consisting of the 72 remaining combat troops of Fritz Vogt's *I. Btl./Norge* supported by a few tanks from *SS-Pz.Rgt. 5*—set out from Seregélyes to relieve it. Successfully dispersing a numerically superior enemy force with the speed and audacity of its attack, Vogt's small force continued on to Dinnyés, the village at the southernmost tip of Lake Velencze, after liberating the surrounded SS troops. Vogt and his tiny "battalion" joined the village's defenses there by evening, thus anchoring the *Wiking* Division's left flank. Because its headquarters was now practically in the front line, *Oberf.* Ullrich was forced to order his own division command post to move further to the rear, finally settling in Belsöbáránd, 5 kilometers west of Seregélyes.

In the rest of the *III. Pz.Korps* sector that day, the *23. Pz.Div.* was forced to ward off numerous Soviet company- to battalion-sized attacks, often supported by several tanks, along the front line stretching between the Sárviz Canal on its right and Sárosd on its left. An enemy breakthrough in the area of a small village 4 kilometers south-southwest of Sárkeresztur was sealed off by a counterattack from the *Panzergruppe* of the *23. Pz.Div.*, during which it suffered the loss of three of its tanks due to the action of antitank gunners from the 233rd Rifle Division.[68] By this point, the division had been reduced to a *Kampfstärke* of only 962 men, but its *Feld-Ers.Btl. 128* had recently received 670 replacements which in the coming days would help alleviate the manpower shortage, and its *Pz.Pio.Btl. 51*—currently serving with the *IV. SS-Pz.Korps*—would be returned to it the following day. It also still fielded 15 operational *panzers*, including seven *Pz. V* Panthers, three *Pz. IV*s, and four *Jg.Pz. IV*s.

That evening, Balck finally saw the logic of detaching the *Wiking* Division from the *IV. SS-Pz.Korps*, since Gille clearly needed to be able to concentrate on one battle, not two. *General der Panzertruppe* Breith had practically incorporated Ullrich's division into his corps anyway. With the *Wiking* Division now subordinated to the *III. Pz.Korps*, the boundary between it and Gille's corps was redrawn so it now ran from the southwest corner of Lake Velencze past the southern outskirts of Stuhlweissenburg. Everything below that would become the responsibility of Breith's corps. The order went out that evening, stating, "In order to guarantee the unified command and control in the Seregélyes area, the *SS-Pz.Div. Wiking* is immediately but temporarily subordinated to the command of the *III. Pz.Korps.*"[69] Although this violated Himmler's stipulation that SS divisions were only to fight under the control of SS corps or army headquarters, the tactical situation dictated nothing less; there was no time for sentimentality. This marked the first time in seven months that the *Wiking* Division was to be "temporarily" detached from the *IV. SS-Pz.Korps*, but it would soon be brought back in the fold.

By this point, the *5. SS-Pz.Div.* had been tremendously weakened after over a month of continuous combat. The weekly strength report submitted to *A.Gr. Balck/6. Armee* reveals that the division's *Kampfstärke* had been reduced to only 634 men, not including the 128 men of the attached *I. Btl./Norge* and *I. Btl./Danmark*, which increased its strength to 764. However, the division's combat power was supplemented by the addition of a battalion from the Hungarian *1. SS-Sturmjäger Regiment.* Although weak in infantry, the division still boasted a nearly full-strength artillery regiment with 10 gun batteries, though by the end of the day *SS-Pz.Rgt. 5* could only report four operational *Pz. V* Panthers. The weakest division of Breith's corps was *Gen.Maj.* Söth's *3. Pz.Div.*, which by 3 February had been reduced in strength to a *Kampfstärke* of only 760 men, with no troops in its *Feld-Ersatz* battalion. The division did, however, field seven artillery batteries and 15 tanks, assault guns and tank destroyers, so it still had a lethal punch. It was this depleted force that Breith would have to rely upon to hold back the onrushing Soviet flood.

On Breith's right flank, the Hungarian *3. Armee*, with a total *Kampfstärke* of 4,079 men south of Lake Balaton (including 925 German troops from *Div.Gr. Pape*), reported no combat activity along the *Sió-Abschnitt* or along the northern shoreline of Lake Balaton, but along its left flank—defended by *Div.Gr. Pape*—some fighting had taken place along the boundary it shared with *III. Pz.Korps*. It reported several attempts by closely following Soviet forces to feel out the new German front-line positions, but *K.Gr. Martini* of the *6. Pz.Div.*, successfully employing mobile defense tactics, was able to keep them at bay while destroying two enemy tanks that got too close. Although numerically small, *K.Gr. Martini*—along with *Pz.Aufkl.Abt. 1* of the *1. Pz.Div.*—bobbed and weaved like a skilled boxer, providing its opponent with little opportunity to strike a telling blow, while keeping him at arm's length with armored jabs and feints.

On the *A.Gr. Balck/6. Armee* far left flank, *Korpsgruppe Harteneck*'s attention was primarily focused on the small battle unfolding around Mány, where *Oberst* von der Groeben's *3. Kav.Brig.* continued the successful defense of its exposed position against yet another tank-supported Soviet attack on its eastern perimeter. Little other activity was reported throughout the rest of the *I. Kav.Korps* and Hungarian *VIII. Armee-Korps* sectors. In regards to its overall combat power, Harteneck's corps had the greatest *Kampfstärke* of all, totaling some 12,645 men, of which 8,313 were German. However, since his corps had the largest amount of ground to cover (over

110 kilometers), it was numerically weak all along the line. It was also the weakest in terms of the number of operational armored vehicles, reporting only 16 *Jg.Pz. IVs*, 15 *StuG III/IVs*, four *Pz. IVs*, and eight *Jg.Pz. 38t Hetzers*, a total of 43, with most of these concentrated in the *6. Pz.Div.* and *3. Kav.Brig.* On the northern bank of the Danube in the neighboring *8. Armee* sector, no combat activity was reported at all by the *IV. Pz.Korps FHH*, where things were eerily quiet.

In the air, the situation was the same as it was the previous day, with ground fog rendering any take-offs and landings extremely difficult. Other than the usual high-altitude reconnaissance flights, *Luftflotte 4* was only able to get one ground-attack squadron in the air, which scored hits on a Soviet supply train carrying fuel, bombing it with "good effect." During the evening of 2/3 February, several additional night missions were flown by ground-attack aircraft, concentrating on targets on the opposite side of the Danube northwest of Gran. No aerial resupply missions over Budapest were flown that night due to the bad weather. For once, the Red Air Force was completely grounded in the Budapest area that day, providing the Germans and Hungarians with a sorely needed reprieve from this dangerous and usually ever-present menace.[70]

From the Soviet perspective, the day's events were a mixed bag. In the south, things had gone very well. The troops of the 26th Army, particularly those of the XVIII Tank Corps, had successfully pressed the German rear guards further to the north along with the accompanying troops from the XXX and CXXXIII Rifle Corps. They had disrupted initial German attempts to establish a solid main defense line around Seregélyes, and had even been able to send armored units past the town to tie up German rearwards communications. On the right of the 26th Army, the forward elements of the XXIII Tank Corps had advanced along the southern shore of Lake Velencze beyond Gárdony, and had even reached Dinnyés before they were finally brought to a halt. Although the XVIII Tank Corps had lost 15 armored fighting vehicles at Seregélyes that day, this was a small price to pay in exchange for the complete disruption of the German defensive plans. Further advances were planned for the following day, particularly along the "seam" separating the *III. Pz.Korps* from *Div.Gr. Pape* along the Sárviz Canal.

In the 4th Guards Army area of operations, particularly between Zámoly and Stuhlweissenburg, things had not gone as well. The attack planned against Stuhlweissenburg from the north by the I Guards Mechanized Corps had not progressed as planned, though the troops of the XXI Guards Rifle Corps had been able to slowly work their way into city's eastern outskirts, where the weak *SS-Rgt. Ney* and *356. Inf.Div.*, as well as small elements of the *Totenkopf* Division, were holding a very thin defensive line. However, the powerful German assault that began at 11:30 a.m., shortly after the attack by the I Guards Mechanized Corps had been blocked near the city's northern cemetery, caused General Zakharov to change his plans. Deciding not to risk the outcome of a movement-to-contact against two *panzer* divisions, he ordered all four of the corps engaged in that area to temporarily assume a defensive posture and let the Germans wear themselves out in frontal attacks against Soviet minefields and antitank gun networks.

Once the drive by the *IV. SS-Pz.Korps* had reached its culmination within a day or two, the 4th Guards Army would resume its counteroffensive if there were still sufficient forces available to do so. Another logical explanation for his temporary transition to the defense is the tantalizing possibility that Zakharov had read the documents taken when *Stubaf.* Rentrop was captured, which contained a complete copy of Balck's and Gille's operations orders. Had Zakharov read the German plans as well as his superior Marshal Tolbukhin, they both would have known exactly what was headed their way in terms of the enemy's intentions and available forces, and that knowledge may have compelled Zakharov to postpone his offensive when he did. Either way, time was on the side of the Third Ukrainian Front.[71]

As previously mentioned, *Gen.d.Pz.Tr.* Balck was not happy with the outcome of the day's fighting. While Gille's corps had indeed closed the gap, it had not been able to advance very far beyond the Stuhlweissenburg–Zámoly highway, nor had it been able to trap and destroy any sizeable Soviet units. Balck was also chagrined concerning the situation unfolding around Seregélyes, where the *Wiking* Division and *3. Pz.Div.* seemed unable to establish anything resembling a cohesive *HKL.*[72] Although at first glance things seemed bad, upon closer examination, both division commanders had been working together without orders to come up with a more practical solution to the problem than the one that Balck and Gaedke dictated.

While Balck and his chief of staff viewed this as yet another example of *Waffen-SS* incompetence, both Ullrich and Söth knew that the *Armeegruppe's* concept of operations could not be carried out with the extremely weak units under their command, especially when actions were influenced by the low-lying fog that hampered visibility. Rather than attempting to wage a static defense, both division commanders had actually been following Balck's initial guidance to fight the enemy using active defense tactics. Once Soviet attempts to seize Seregélyes had been blunted, both divisions would transition to a more traditional defense. Nevertheless, Balck singled out the *Wiking* Division for particular criticism that evening, while he expressed no negative opinions regarding the performance of the *3. Pz.Div.*

The other incident that took place on 3 February also incurred Balck's wrath. This involved the movement of the *IV. SS-Pz.Korps' Generalkommmando* (corps headquarters), on the orders of *Ostubaf.* Schönfelder, from Falubattyán to the town of Inota, 3 kilometers east of Várpalota. Indeed, this does seem unusual since Gille's forward command post had been in the previous location for only one day. The reason why the move was made has never been explained, though it could possibly have been connected to the fact that the *Totenkopf* Division's command post was also located in Falubattyán, a relatively small town for two headquarters to be based.[73] A quick look at the map from the period reveals that Inota was a much more central location for Gille to command his corps. Due to the detachment of the *Wiking* Division to *III. Pz.Korps*, his focus was strictly focused on the divisions fighting north of Stuhlweissenburg. It was also much closer to the corps' *Hauptquartier*, or "rear" headquarters, operated by the *Quartiermeister* and *Adjutantur* staffs in Jenö.

Balck's primary complaint stemmed from his belief that the *IV. SS-Pz.Korps* command post had moved without his permission and that his headquarters had not been informed about it in advance, learning about the move only after the fact. He was additionally concerned that this displacement to a new location during the morning when the counterattack was about to start may have contributed to the already mentioned delay. Neither Gille nor Schönfelder mentioned this incident in any of their notes or diaries, so it can be assumed they did not believe it was worth spilling any ink about. Balck, however, did.

This "transgression" was first brought to the *A.Gr.* commander's attention on 3 February, when the required noontime report from the *IV. SS-Pz.Korps* failed to arrive. Balck probably believed that, due to this unsanctioned move, he would be unable contact anyone in the *IV. SS-Pz.Korps* headquarters at all, especially Gille, at such a critical time (Gille was probably forward visiting the troops, as was his custom). Balck felt so strongly about it, that he not only submitted a complaint in his daily commander's narrative report to *Gen.d.Inf.* Wöhler at *H.Gr. Süd*, but also penned a strongly worded hand-written letter of reprimand at 3:45 p.m. that day, the contents of which was first sent by radio, then the actual note later delivered to Gille in person. It read:

> To the Commanding General of the *IV. SS-Pz.Korps*:
>
> *SS-Obergruppenführer und General der Waffen-SS* Gille
>
> On the 3rd of February around 11 o'clock a.m. the corps command post was occupied neither by the commanding general [Gille] nor by the chief of the general staff. The only one who was available was the *O1* [Hans Velde] who was inadequately informed about the situation. The general command's headquarters was carrying out a change of position further to the rear, which was not announced in advance. In this respect, this action clearly violated the existing orders. I decree that the corps must immediately issue orders to prevent a repetition of these incidents.
>
> Signed,
> Balck[74]

It must be noted that Balck did not personally visit the command post, but simply had someone pick up the telephone and attempt to contact it. Upon examination, Balck's accusations are mainly unfounded. Hidden in the hoard of captured documents of *A.Gr. Balck/6. Armee* at the Central Archives of the Ministry of Defense of the Russian Federation are two transcribed radio messages addressed to the *Ia* of *A.Gr. Balck* from the *IV. SS-Pz.Korps*.

The first one, sent at 10:40 a.m., notified Balck's *Führungsabteilung* that the *IV. SS-Pz.Korps* command post had begun moving to Inota at 10:30 a.m. This was received by the *Ia Schreiber*, an unnamed *Unteroffizier* who worked under the supervision of Balck's newly assigned *Ia*, *Oberstlt.* Heinz Toop. The second radio message from the *IV. SS-Pz.Korps* was sent by Schönfelder himself at 1:10 p.m., notifying *A. Gr. Balck* about the battalion-sized Soviet attack supported by seven tanks against one of the *Totenkopf* Division's forward assembly areas near Kiskecskemét that began at 10:15 a.m. The note further stated that the corps' attack, scheduled to begin at 11:30 a.m., was already underway. Both of these messages were received at the times noted by Balck's very own headquarters, and Schönfelder was correct to expect that they would be given to Balck, his chief of staff, or the *A. Gr. Ia* as soon as possible.

After all, the *IV. SS-Pz.Korps* was in the middle of a fairly consequential counterattack, and it was not the corps chief of staff's responsibility to supervise the clerks in *Gen.Maj.* Gaedke's operations department.[75] It is also noteworthy that neither Balck nor Gaedke mentioned this incident in their memoirs. Upon review, while Schönfelder did not request permission in advance to move Gille's command post as he should have, he did notify his higher headquarters soon after it began that he was doing so. Additionally, he provided a subsequent message notifying the *A. Gr.* staff that the corps' attack had begun. Both messages were sent well before Balck wrote his evening report. Why no one relayed these messages to Balck in sufficient time cannot be explained, other than to suppose that his own headquarters was not very well organized either.

This incident was, in Balck's eyes, yet another black mark against Gille and Schönfelder's record, but to their credit, they remained focused on the mission at hand. Although the attack that day had only been partially successful, they would prosecute it the next day with the same amount of effort and dedication. Towards this end, the *A. Gr. Balck/6. Armee* commander had his chief of staff send out updated guidance for 4 February at 9:15 p.m. to ensure that his corps commanders knew what they were supposed to do the following day. It specified the following tasks:

Hungarian *3. Armee*: Continue delaying the enemy from closing up in the sector running along the line between Mezö-Komárom and the Sárviz Canal by carrying out a reconnaissance in force using its armored units [i.e., *Div.Gr. Pape*];

III. Pz.Korps: Hold the line that you have reached [along both sides of Seregélyes], delay any further advance by the enemy towards the west, re-establish the old *HKL* (eastern edge of Seregélyes–Hill 130–eastern edge of Agárd) in a limited attack;

IV. SS-Pz.Korps: Continue the attack north of Stuhlweissenburg towards previously designated objectives;

Korpsgruppe Harteneck/I. Kav.Korps: Straighten out the front line south of Felsőgalla and reincorporate Hill 480 into your *HKL* using the [attached] *I. Btl/Gren.Rgt. 731* [from the *711. Inf.Div.*].[76]

The following day would be an important one, especially in the *III. Pz.Korps* sector, though if the *IV. SS-Pz.Korps'* attack succeeded on 4 February, it would considerably relieve the pressure being exerted against the critically important city of Stuhlweissenburg and enable Balck to pull out one of Gille's divisions to form an armored reserve for his *A.Gr.*

To commemorate the period of fighting that had ended with the unsuccessful attempts to relieve Budapest, to boost the men's spirits and prepare them for the rigorous campaign that was to come, Wöhler issued an order of the day to recognize *A.Gr. Balck* and its performance of duty. Issued before midnight on 3 February in printed broadsheet format, as far down as to each individual *Kompanie*, it read:

Soldiers of *A.Gr. Balck*!

After weeks of hard fighting, you have eliminated the danger of enemy breakthrough to the west and reconquered vast stretches of Hungarian soil through your vigorous attacks and tough defense. Your harsh blows have inflicted very high, bloody losses on the enemy and decisive losses of war matériel, especially tanks. The *panzer* divisions outdid themselves in mobile, offensive combat.

Our situation has forced upon us a temporary regrouping, although our task remains unchanged. I demand of all of you: Hold or recover the previous main defense line. I know that all of you—Germans and Hungarians shoulder to shoulder—will meet my demand.

Hail to the Führer of the Greater German Reich!

Hail Szalási, the leader of Hungary!

Your commander in chief,
Wöhler
General der Infanterie[77]

He was not exaggerating when he referred to the hard fighting endured during January. In the *Totenkopf* Division alone, casualties for that month amounted to 4,350 men, including 813 killed in action, 3,300 wounded, and 237 missing.[78] Most of these losses occurred in the *Panzergrenadier, Pionier,* and *Aufklärungs* battalions, as was usually the case. The *Wiking* Division's losses were similarly high (2,787 in all). The number of replacements processed that month through the divisions' *Feld-Ers.Btl. 3* and *5* did not come close to replacing those lost; at that time, most of the *Waffen-SS* fresh replacements were being funneled to the *6. Pz.Armee's* four SS *panzer* divisions in order to bring them up to strength for an important future mission.

Interestingly, Budapest and its garrison were not mentioned at all in Wöhler's order of the day, a sign that they had indeed been written off for good. However, the city's defenders did get a mention in the day's *Wehrmachtsbericht*, which stated, "The brave garrison of Budapest continues to hold out, concentrated in a narrow area around the fortress, they are being supplied by air while they stand firm against the Bolshevik onslaught." For the encircled troops still within hearing distance of a radio, the airwaves had now gone silent, where once before they were filled with messages of encouragement from the approaching relief force. At least they were mentioned in the *Wehrmachtsbericht*, perhaps a sign that they had not been forgotten after all. But with Wöhler's order of the day omitting any reference to Budapest, in practical terms they already were. One veteran of the fighting from the *Wiking* Division, who remembered the moment when *Unternehmen Konrad III* was cancelled, later wrote in his diary, "We keep hearing increasingly pessimistic reports out of Budapest, but we feel no guilt."[79] Indeed, everyone in the *IV. SS-Pz.Korps* had done their utmost to save the city, but it was all in vain.

To the average *Landser* in the divisions of the *IV. SS-Pz.Korps*, as with the other corps within *A.Gr. Balck/6. Armee*, Sunday, 4 February must have seemed like any other day, no different than any other of the past five weeks. Each day seemed to consist of attacking, defending, or withdrawing to a new position, only to start all over again the next day. By this point, nearly all of the front-line soldiers were filthy, lice-ridden, unshaven, and hungry. Few men had been able to get more than a few hours of sleep or a chance to warm themselves. Hours of intense combat, often within close range of the enemy, and cold food had taken a physical and emotional toll as well. Most German and Hungarian troops in the *IV. SS-Pz.Korps* were exhausted from these combined effects, accentuated by having to perform heavy physical labor such as digging fighting positions or carrying ammunition, tasks that drained every last ounce of energy. However, while their equipment and clothing may have been in tatters, their weapons were clean and ready for action. How much longer the men could continue functioning in these conditions was a question uppermost in the minds of commanders at nearly every level, from platoon leader all the way up to the corps commander.

Once again, the soldiers fighting in the Hungarian *Puszta* along the front between Zámoly and Seregélyes awoke to temperatures hovering around freezing and partially clear skies. The awful road conditions of the previous day persisted throughout 4 February. German and Hungarian troops in the *IV. SS-Pz.Korps* area of operations, particularly those from *SS-Rgt. Ney* and *II. Btl./Totenkopf* defending the eastern outskirts of Stuhlweissenburg, were awoken by a strong Soviet attack at 4:30 a.m. At approximately the same time, troops from the *Totenkopf* Division on the city's northern outskirts were also attacked at several points, but were able to ward them off. Evidently, these attacks were conducted to throw the Germans off balance and prevent them continuing with their attack of the previous day. This did not stop the *1. Pz.Div.*, which resumed its attack that morning at the same time the Soviets attacked Stuhlweissenburg. Shortly after crossing the Zámoly–Stuhlweissenburg highway, *K.Gr. Huppert*'s troops encountered strong enemy resistance 4 kilometers to the east of the large farming estate at Gyúlamajor that featured an attack by 19 Soviet tanks, which Huppert's battlegroup was only able to defeat after several Tiger IIs of *s.Pz.Abt. 503 FHH* (on loan from the *4. Kav.Brig.*) came to their assistance, knocking out eight Soviet tanks in short order and forcing the rest to pull back. On the right flank, *K.Gr. Bradel* ensured the connection between the rest of the division and the *Totenkopf* Division on the right.[80]

After warding off several Soviet counterattacks northeast and east of Stuhlweissenburg, the *Totenkopf* Division resumed its attack, with the intent of enveloping the enemy defenses northeast of Stuhlweissenburg. However, Soviet resistance, primarily by the XX and XXI Guards Rifle Corps, backed up by tank-led counterattacks of the V Guards Cavalry Corps and I Guards Mechanized Corps, was so effective that both divisions were only able to gain ground slowly while suffering heavy losses. The *III. Bataillon* of the *Totenkopf* Regiment, part of the right wing of the *Totenkopf* Division's attack, became tied up in heavy fighting once again in the industrial area on the northern outskirts of Stuhlweissenburg, west of Kiskecskemét. After several hours of house-to-house fighting, the area was finally brought under German control.

Meanwhile, the left wing of the division, comprising the bulk of the *Eicke* Regiment, was able to advance alongside the *1. Pz.Div.* In the hills northeast of Stuhlweissenburg, portions of the regiment and *SS-Pz.Pio.Btl. 3* captured a large Soviet ammunition dump containing over 10,000 antitank and mortar rounds, which the sappers blew up to deny them to the enemy.[81] Both divisions continued moving beyond the highway, and by working together were able to seize the heights that lay a kilometer or two to the east, though they were not able to advance beyond that due to determined Soviet resistance, particularly a barrier consisting of large numbers of antitank guns that had to be taken out one by one. On this day alone, the *1. Pz.Div.* and *Totenkopf* Division claimed to have destroyed 72 of these guns, a testimony to the high number of antitank guns employed and why both divisions found their attack such tough going.[82]

For the first time, Gille's attack was amply supported by German and Hungarian ground-attack aircraft, which, taking advantage of the relatively good flying weather, strafed and bombed Soviet positions and even individual tanks. The *Königstiger* (King Tiger) from s.*Pz.Abt. 509* and *503 FHH* knocked out numerous Soviet tanks, including a number of M4 Shermans and SU-76 assault guns, greatly reducing the number of operational Soviet armored vehicles. The *IV. SS-Pz.Korps* claimed that its units had knocked out as many as 59 Soviet tanks on that day alone. Despite this, neither the *1. Pz.Div.* nor the *Totenkopf* Division could advance beyond the Stuhlweissenburg–Zámoly highway, and it soon became apparent that the attack could not do so without both divisions incurring heavy losses.

Except for sending s.*Pz.Abt. 503 FHH* to the aid of the *1. Pz.Div.*, the *4. Kav. Brig.* had been unable to make any headway at all, having to repel a number of Soviet counterattacks between Csákberény and Borbála Puszta that kept it penned into its jump-off positions. During the period 1–4 February, the brigade suffered 347 casualties, a testimony to the severity of the fighting, which helps to explain why the brigade was never able to contribute much to the counterattack.[83] With a *Kampfstärke* of only 928 men on the evening of 3 February, it had lost roughly a third of its combat strength in infantry since the counterattack began. The Hungarian *2. Pz.Div.* was not in much better shape, and the best it could do was to hold its present position.

In recognition of the situation, as well as the deteriorating situation south of Lake Velencze, Balck decided that it was time to call a halt to the operation and declare it a success; that evening in its *Tagesmeldung* sent to *H.Gr. Süd*, *A.Gr. Balck/6. Armee* claimed that between 28 January and 4 February, the *IV. SS-Pz. Korps* had destroyed 186 Soviet tanks, of which 50 were knocked out by *s.Pz. Abt. 509*, in exchange for nine of their own tanks declared irrecoverable losses. According to Soviet sources, in the area north of Lake Velencze during the same period, the I Guards Mechanized Corps lost 3,030 men killed, wounded, and missing in action, with 1,388 men lost on 4 February alone, and had been reduced in strength to only 39 operational tanks and assault guns. During the same period, the V Guards Cavalry Corps suffered 330 casualties and lost seven tanks and assault guns.[84]

As corps commander, once his two divisions had begun their assault, the most that Gille could do was to ensure that Becker and Thünert were being provided with everything they needed, including artillery and close air support, ammunition and fuel, and prompt evacuation of the wounded. In turn, Gille and his staff had to ensure that relevant tactical and intelligence information was kept flowing between the divisions and *A.Gr. Balck/6. Armee* headquarters in order to keep Balck informed of the situation. As was his habit, Gille would have visited each division at least once a day to speak with the division commanders and get as close to the front as possible in order to "feel the pulse" of the battle as it unfolded, including gaining an appreciation of the morale of his troops. In recognition of the performance of his *1. Pz.Div.*, both at Stuhlweissenburg and east of Lake Velencze, Gille had already nominated Thünert for the Knight's Cross, which certainly would have boosted his and his division's morale because it was bestowed in recognition of the division's achievements as well as his own leadership.

As dramatic as *IV. SS-Pz.Korps'* situation north of Stuhlweissenburg was on 4 February, that of *III. Pz.Korps* along its sector between the southern shore of Lake Velencze and the Sárviz Canal at Káloz was far more critical. Here, the XVIII and XXIII Tank Corps, supported by the XXXI, CIV, and CXXXIII Rifle Corps, were aiming for nothing less than an operational breakthrough between Lakes Velencze and Balaton. The fulcrum point was, as it had been the day before, the crossroads town of Seregélyes, on either side of which the *Wiking* Division and *3. Pz.Div.* were fighting desperately to delay the oncoming enemy forces long enough to form some kind of a defensible front line that could be held for more than a day. Both divisions were heavily outnumbered and reaching the end of their strength.

On Breith's right flank, the *23. Pz.Div.* was also under enormous pressure, fighting off several tank-supported infantry attacks by Soviet troops in company- to battalion-strength between Heinrichmajor and Káloz, where enemy troops were attempting to separate it from *Div.Gr. Pape* on its right and *Gen.Maj.* Söth's division on its left. In the *3. Pz.Div.* sector, Söth's troops found themselves under attack that day by three infantry regiments—in other words, a full division—backed up by as many as 30 tanks. This force, taking advantage of the persisting ground fog, was able to take the village of Jakabszállás on the boundary between the two divisions and the important town of Sárosd, defended by *4. Kp./Pz.Gren.Rgt. 3*, with a concentric tank attack from the south, east, and north. The last words of the company commander, before the radio went silent, were "Russians [*sic*] all around us!"[85] Under overwhelming pressure from the enemy, *Pz.Gren.Rgt. 394* was forced to pull back from the agricultural estate of Csillagmajor, while the rest of *Pz.Gren. Rgt. 3* had to withdraw to Belsöbáránd to avoid encirclement.

North of Seregélyes, during the night of 3/4 February, the 337-man *Germania* Regiment was forced to withdraw to the old positions of the *Margarethestellung*, where it turned around and occupied defensive positions dug the previous December. The enemy's advance guard remained focused on breaking through the gap between the town of Dinnyés on the southern shore of Lake Velencze and Seregélyes, where there were few obstacles or German forces to impede their movement except the vast swamp that stretched to the town's northwest. A Soviet armored unit with at least 25 tanks, followed by infantry, slipped past the northern outskirts of Seregélyes despite the *Wiking* Division's best efforts and continued moving to the northwest. Another 10 tanks punched through the *Germania* Regiment's position a few kilometers north of that point, reaching the Nádas Canal, where they were forced to halt due to the width and depth of the canal. Hastily organizing a response, Ullrich sent his *Eingreifreserve* to stop it with a counterattack and seal off the breach in the lines. In Dinnyés, Vogt reputed that *I. Btl./Norge* and *I. Btl./Danmark*, with a few assault guns, had beaten back a number of company- to battalion-sized enemy attacks, backed by up to 15 tanks, originating from the south and northeast. Vogt's own counterattack faltered when it encountered a *Pakfront* south of the town and was forced to pull back.

The situation north of Seregélyes had grown so dire that *H.Gr. Süd*, when informed of the breakthrough, contacted the *OKH Führungsabteilung* at 12:55 p.m. and requested freedom of action to withdraw all of *A.Gr. Balck's* forces between Dinnyés and Káloz, as well as the Hungarian *3. Armee*, all the way back to the old *Margarethestellung*. It was a tacit admission that *III. Pz.Korps'* defensive efforts had failed. A few moments later, the report arrived at *A.Gr. Balck's* headquarters that Seregélyes had fallen to the enemy. All that the *Wiking* Division and *3. Pz.Div.* could do at the moment was establish a *Riegelstellung* (bolt or switch position) to prevent the Soviet troops from penetrating the *Margarethestellung*.

This line, prepared in early December 1944 as a last-ditch defense against the initial Soviet attack towards Budapest, would serve as a suitable defense line, assuming that *III. Pz.Korps* got there before their opponents did.[86] As for how far this event influenced the *IV. SS-Pz.Korps'* ongoing operation, it had contributed to Balck's decision to deem the counterattack north of Stuhlweissenburg a success, since it seemed to be stalled anyway. This probably contributed to his decision to take the *1. Pz.Div.* away from Gille and assign it to Breith in order for him to use it to counterattack and throw back the approaching brigades of the XVIII and XXIII Tank Corps before all of the German and Hungarian forces south of the lakes were trapped.

Directly affected by the events unfolding east of the Sárviz Canal, the Hungarian chain of command in the *3. Armee* was most likely unaware of the significance of the fighting taking place on its left flank. The northern shore of Lake Balaton was quiet, as was most of the opposite bank of the Sió River, with the exception of increased Soviet reconnaissance and combat patrol activity. However, along the Sárviz Canal in the east and at the town of Dégh in the south, the Soviet front line was advancing inexorably against the Hungarian *25. Inf.Div.* and *Div. Gr. Pape*. Between Lajos-Komárom, Közép Bogárd, and near Nagyhöresök, Soviet troop formations ranging in size from individual infantry companies to entire regiments were carrying out attacks, which were only barely fended off.

Kampfgruppe Martini, the armored battlegroup from the *6. Pz.Div.*, counterattacked south of Dégh, inflicting heavy casualties upon the incautiously approaching Soviet troops. The biggest challenge that *Div.Gr. Pape* faced at that moment was to maintain physical contact with the neighboring *23. Pz.Div.*, whose right flank was slowly withdrawing to the north from the outskirts of Káloz. Should Lt.Gen. Gagen's 26th Army manage to slip a tank brigade or two behind *Div.Gr. Pape* and block any withdrawal by German and Hungarian units into the *Margarethestellung*, the situation would become dangerous indeed.

Korpsgruppe Harteneck/I. Kav.Korps had to report that the *3. Kav.Brig.* was finally forced to abandon Mány, after it was attacked from the south and east by two rifle regiments supported by 20 tanks. Withdrawing in some disorder, the defending cavalrymen were able to reestablish the front line a few kilometers northwest of Mány by nightfall under the cover of the rear guard provided by the brigade's last three operational assault guns. On the right of Harteneck's corps, the Hungarian *1. Hus.Div.*, reinforced by troops of *I. Btl./Gren.Rgt. 731* of the *711. Inf.Div.*, launched a concentrated assault to pinch out an enemy-held salient in the front line northwest of Szár and retake Hill 480. Hampered by terrain difficulties in the southern foothills of the Vértes Mountains, the attacking troops had managed to take only half of their objective by evening reporting time. In Csabdi, the *6. Pz.Div.* (minus its *Panzergruppe*) repulsed two battalion-sized attacks.

Luftflotte 4, in addition to providing much-needed close air support to the *IV. SS-Pz.Korps* north of Stuhlweissenburg, was active elsewhere, flying 460 sorties that included bombing and strafing attacks against Soviet forces operating south of Lake Velencze, as well as motor vehicle traffic across the bridges over the Danube between Dunaföldvar and Budapest. Some German and Hungarian fighter-bombers engaged in locomotive-hunting behind Soviet lines south and northeast of Budapest, and one aircraft scored a hit on the railroad bridge at Budafok. Another aerial attack against a Soviet assembly area destroyed six tanks, two antitank guns, and a number of soft-skinned vehicles. In addition, German fighter aircraft downed 12 Soviet aircraft, in exchange for nine German and Hungarian aircraft claimed by the Soviets. That evening, cargo transports managed to drop 6.9 tons of ammunition over the city to help its defenders hold out for another day.[87]

Ominously, German reconnaissance aircraft detected the movement of between 800 and 1,000 motor vehicles on the highway south and northeast of Lake Velencze. Once again, the weather prevented an accurate assessment of their direction of movement, leading German intelligence analysts to conjecture that this might signify the arrival of the ever-elusive II Guards Mechanized Corps or even the VII Mechanized Corps. Although the results of the aerial photography were inconclusive, perhaps because of intercepted Soviet radio message traffic or because it matched Balck's preconceptions, he was convinced that these reports meant that more enemy troops were being funneled into the area where his *Armeegruppe* was the most vulnerable, which in turn convinced him even more of the need to withdraw German forces south of the lakes into the *Margarethestellung* without delay before it was too late.

There is room to speculate that this might have all been part of a Soviet operational deception plan designed to induce the Germans into withdrawing even further back from the Seregélyes area. Regardless, by this point Tolbukhin and his 26th Army and 4th Guards Army commanders were convinced that their assault was on the right track. Given the exhausted state of the German forces and their rapidly declining combat power, it must have seemed to the senior Soviet commanders, as well as those of the battalions and brigades from the leading units, that they had the Germans on the run. They would continue pushing aggressively forward until they encountered a firm enemy front line; until then, the objective was the southern outskirts of Stuhlweissenburg, which must have seemed to be within reach by the evening of 4 February.

That night, Balck realized that *III. Pz.Korps* could no longer hold the line at Seregélyes and had no hope of stopping the attacking Soviet forces unless Breith's depleted corps was quickly reinforced. The only force that could be pulled out and moved to the area south of Lake Velencze in time was the *1. Pz.Div.* Balck's original intention for it to serve as the *Armeegruppe* reserve had been overcome by events; instead, it was now needed to launch an immediate counterattack once it arrived in its new assembly area at Falubattyán. To free up this division, Balck directed his chief of staff to order the *IV. SS-Pz.Korps* to suspend its attack, consolidate its gains, and instruct the *Totenkopf* Division to assume a defensive posture. In addition, Gille's corps would have to give up *I. Abt./Pz.Rgt. 24* and *s.Pz.Abt. 509*, thereby depriving it of most of its remaining armor.

Wöhler's request to the *Führerhauptquartier* to allow *A.Gr. Balck/6. Armee* to withdraw to the *Margarethestellung* was finally approved by Hitler at 00:40 a.m. on 5 February. It had come none too soon. The following day would become a race to see who would reach and occupy the *Margarethestellung* first—the *III. Pz.Korps* and Hungarian *3. Armee*, or the 26th Army and 4th Guards Army. Meanwhile, the *IV. SS-Pz.Korps* was directed to establish a defensive front line and defend Stuhlweissenburg at all costs. Gille was not given much to work with, especially given the large grouping of Soviet forces still in position after the *1. Pz.Div.* had departed, though to be fair, most of these enemy formations were as beat up as his were. Beginning on the evening of 4/5 February, the *IV. SS-Pz.Korps* and the *Totenkopf* Division, soon to be rejoined by the *Wiking* Division, would begin transitioning to the defense—something it had not done since it barred the Second Belorussian Front from the gates of Warsaw in August 1944. After 35 days of carrying out practically non-stop attacks, Gille's corps had carried out its last major offensive operation; from this point until the end of the war, it would be on the defense.

CHAPTER 11

Transition to the Defense
5–12 February 1945

With the cessation of *IV. SS-Pz. Korps'* counterattack north of Stuhlweissenburg on the evening of 4/5 February 1945, the first chapter of the history of its participation in the Hungarian theater of operations came to a close. Although relatively full-strength (except in *panzers*) and rested after two months of defending a relatively static front when it arrived in Hungary, 35 days later the corps and its two divisions bore little resemblance to their former selves. *Unternehmen Konrad I, II,* and *III* had seen to that. Beginning on 5 February, *IV. SS-Pz.Korps* would find itself on the defense for the next month; at first in a fight waged to safeguard its new main line of defense, and then along a static front defending one of the most important linchpins of the entire German effort in Hungary, the city of Stuhlweissenburg. Bound up in defensive warfare, the corps, corps troops, and its divisions would enjoy a brief opportunity to catch their breath and rebuild while the action moved elsewhere. Finally, during the first week of March, it would play a supporting role in the last great German offensive of World War II.

During this 30-day period, there would be little change in the makeup of the corps command and staff, or its order of battle. Its mission would also remain substantially the same: hold Stuhlweissenburg at all costs. Continued possession of this key city, a vital road and railway hub strategically located between Lakes Velencze and Balaton, not only vouchsafed the safety and security of the German and Hungarian units occupying the revived *Margarethestellung* that lay south of and between both lakes, but also blocked two important avenues of approach to Soviet forces seeking to break through the Bakony Forest and Vértes Mountains and thence to Vienna. These two movement corridors, located between Lake Velencze and the Vértes Mountains and Lake Balaton and Lake Velencze, offered high-speed avenues of approach to enemy mechanized forces and access into the Hungarian *Puszta* that lay north of the Bakony Forest, especially once the harsh winter of 1944/45 released its icy grip.

To carry out this important assignment on the first day it transitioned to the defense, *Ogruf.* Herbert Gille's corps had to hold a 43-kilometer *Hauptkampflinie* with three divisions and one cavalry brigade. In the southern portion of its new front line, the weak *356. Inf. Div.* held the center and eastern suburbs of Stuhlweissenburg, along with the remnants of *SS-Rgt. Ney*; to its left, the *Totenkopf* Division was positioned between the northern suburbs of the city and Gyúlamajor; from that point to the northwest lay *Div.Gr. Holste*, consisting of the *4. Kav.Brig.* and the Hungarian *2. Pz.Div.*, which held a front line that stretched westwards around the southern outskirts of Zámoly and to the northwest, ending at the southern outskirts of Mór, where it linked up with the Hungarian *VIII. Armee-Korps* of *Korpsgruppe Harteneck/I. Kav.Korps.*[1]

To hold this extended front line, the units comprising *IV. SS-Pz.Korps* (as of 3 February) had a combined *Kampfstärke* of 4,910 men, equating to a troop density of 114 men per kilometer, not including the 261 men in the *Feld-Ersatz* battalion of the *Totenkopf* Division, which was serving as a rear area security force within Stuhlweissenburg. In regards to heavy weapons and armor, the corps possessed only 18 heavy antitank guns, 30 artillery batteries with three or four guns each, nine operational *Pz. IV*s, eight *StuG III/IV*s, three *Jg.Pz. IV*s, and two *Pz. VI* Tiger Is.[2] There were at least twice that number under short- or long-term repair, including a dozen Tiger IIs from *s.Pz.Abt. 503 FHH*, a number that fluctuated daily. In the two days since the weekly summary was submitted, there were probably even fewer troops and tanks available after the partially successful counterattack of 3–4 February was called off.

In addition to these forces, the corps still had its own rocket-launcher battalion, *SS-Werf.Abt. 504*, with over 20 launchers. At some point shortly after 7 February, the corps' firepower would be augmented when its own dedicated heavy artillery battalion, *SS-s.Art.Abt. 504* with up to 15 guns, finally arrived from the SS artillery school in Beneschau after completing its training. Lastly, after nearly a year without one of its own, the corps' dedicated artillery observation battalion, *SS-Beob.Abt. 504*, would also join the corps after a lengthy detour with the *II. SS-Pz.Korps* serving on both the Eastern and Western Fronts. Besides these units, the corps most likely still had one or two battalions from *Volks-Art.Korps 403* operating under the supervision of *SS-ARKO 504*.[3]

During the next month, the *IV. SS-Pz.Korps* would be directly or indirectly involved in four key events leading up to the great March offensive. The first, which took place between 5 and 12 February, witnessed the corps' aforementioned transition to a defensive posture as well as the fighting withdrawal of the *III. Pz.Korps* and Hungarian *3. Armee* into the old *Margarethestellung* between Lakes Balaton and Velencze; the second was the death throes of the Budapest garrison and its breakout attempt; the third was the successful *Südwind* counteroffensive north of the Danube aimed at eliminating the Soviets' Gran bridgehead; and finally, there was the arrival of the *6. Pz.Armee* as it prepared to carry out an offensive aimed at completely restoring the situation in Hungary and safeguarding Germany's last significant oil production facilities.

On the evening of 4/5 February, the return of *1. Pz.Div.* to the *III. Pz.Korps* after being with the *IV. SS-Pz.Korps* for only two days came as a bit of a surprise to Gille and his staff, for evidence indicates that he fully intended to continue with what was perceived to be a slowly but successfully developing counterattack. The primary objective of closing the gap in the front line between Stuhlweissenburg and Zámoly had at least been accomplished, and though the *1. Pz.Div.* and *Totenkopf* Division had only managed to get as far as the highway linking the two localities, Gille believed that *IV. SS-Pz.Korps* could have kept going after destroying the bulk of the available Soviet armor north of Lake Velencze. The removal of the *1. Pz.Div.* and the two separate tank battalions (*s.Pz.Abt. 509* and *I. Abt./Pz.Rgt. 24*) took away most of the corps' armor, leaving the understrength *Totenkopf* Division as the only offensively capable force, which was not enough to continue the counterattack by itself (see Map 10).

The morning of 5 February witnessed a continuation of the warming trend, with temperatures overnight remaining above the freezing point, accentuated by damp, rainy weather. As the day wore on, it grew even warmer, reaching the low 40s Fahrenheit, though heavy clouds prevented much air activity by either side. Overnight, fighting activity in the *IV. SS-Pz.Korps'* area was limited to defending against numerous small-scale Soviet reconnaissance or combat patrols, especially in the *356. Inf.Div.* sector along the eastern suburbs of Stuhlweissenburg and in the *Totenkopf* Division's sector in the northern outskirts of the city as far as the southern outskirts of Gyúlamajor. This village, actually a large agricultural estate, was held by *I. Btl./Gren.Rgt. 870* from the *356. Inf.Div.* attached to *Div.Gr. Holste*, and had been sent to replace the battlegroup from the *1. Pz.Div.* that had held it until the previous evening.[4]

Evidently, the local Soviet commanders were attempting to confirm their suspicions that the *1. Pz.Div.* had disappeared and whether the German counterattack had been called off. Their suspicions having been confirmed, and finding no armor at Gyúlamajor, the XX Guards Rifle Corps sent a reinforced battalion—either from the 5th Guards Airborne Division or the V Guards Cavalry Corps—to retake it. In a short but sharp fight, the Germans were driven out of their positions and compelled to retreat westwards. Fortunately, the Soviets were merely satisfied to have retaken the estate and did not follow up or pursue the fleeing grenadiers. Though a new *HKL* was constructed west of Gyúlamajor, as a consequence of its failure to hold the former position, *Ogruf.* Gille ordered the entire *356. Inf.Div.* to be subordinated to *Brig.Fhr.* Becker's division, which at least would allow a more unified defense under a commander known for his steadfastness as well as his ruthlessness. One of Becker's first orders was to direct the division commander to move the hapless *I. Btl./ Gren.Rgt. 870* to Stuhlweissenburg, replacing it with a battalion from the *Totenkopf* Division.[5] *Oberst* Kühl's thoughts regarding the new command relationship are not recorded. The remaining portions of the corps' defensive sector were relatively quiet for the rest of that day.

To the south of the *IV. SS-Pz.Korps*, the *III. Pz.Korps* sector was anything but quiet, as the mechanized units of the XVIII and XXIII Tank Corps aggressively pushed and probed the German defenses for an opening that would lead to them to Stuhlweissenburg. The *Wiking* Division, which had been detached from Gille's corps for the past two days, was hard-pressed to maintain any kind of effective defense that day. Tasked with holding the line between the northern edge of Seregélyes and Dinnyés in front of the *Margarethestellung*, the division was subjected to a deliberate attack that began in the early hours. The *Westland* Regiment, entrenched in the town's northwestern outskirts, along with the neighboring *Pz.Gren.Rgt. 3* of the *3. Pz.Div.* on the town's southwestern outskirts, were subjected to a powerful artillery barrage, followed by a number of tank-supported infantry assaults against Seregélyes from the southeast, east, and northeast, that once again managed to penetrate to the western edge of the town.

As the sun rose, the attacks continued and the *Westland*'s defense line was pierced along the northwestern exits of the town by a battalion-sized enemy force that continued heading up the highway towards Stuhlweissenburg, while the defenses of the neighboring *Germania* Regiment were broken through at a point 4 kilometers southwest of Dinnyés, allowing the Soviets to actually get into the *Margarethestellung*. In Dinnyés itself, the battlegroup consisting of the remnants of *I. Btl./Norge, I. Btl./ Danmark*, and a battalion from the Hungarian *1. SS-Sturmjäger Regiment*—reinforced by a few of the division's remaining *Sturmgeschütze*—was assaulted in battalion strength from three separate directions.

Upon receiving the morning report describing the fighting in the *Wiking* Division's sector, the *A.Gr. Balck/6. Armee Ia, Oberstlt.* Toop, during a mid-day orientation telephone call with his counterpart at *H.Gr. Süd*, remarked, "I have the impression that the enemy forces in front of the *Wiking* Division are not especially strong, therefore the division should and must stand fast."[6] At 3 p.m., both the *Westland* and *Germania* Regiments were able to get their counterattacks going, and after hard fighting were able to seal off or destroy the Soviet troops that had broken through. The defenders of Dinnyés were also successful in repelling numerous attacks that day, though it had become obvious that there was no longer any point in holding such an isolated position.

The rest of the *III. Pz.Korps*' units were also bound up in heavy defensive fighting. Both the *3.* and *23. Pz.Div.* were able to continue their slow withdrawal towards the *Margarethestellung* in an orderly manner during the morning, though they were closely followed every step of the way by elements of the XVIII Tank Corps. In the town of Aba, nine JS-IIs appeared on the right flank of the *23. Pz.Div.*, which sparked a counterattack by the division's *Eingreifreserve*. East of the Sárkeresztur–Stuhlweissenburg highway, two Soviet infantry battalions supported by three or four tanks were reported to be advancing to the north, prompting the division to carry out yet another counterattack. It would continue like this for the next several days. Meanwhile, the *1. Pz.Div.* began arriving in its new assembly area near Falubattyán, along with the two separate tank battalions.

In the neighboring Hungarian *3. Armee* sector, the situation was similar, though the threat of a breakthrough by Soviet tank units was not as great. The Hungarian *25. Inf.Div.*, supported on the left by *Div.Gr. Pape* and *K.Gr. Martini* from the *6. Pz.Div.*, was able to withdraw from the *Sió-Abschnitt* in good order, while maintaining contact on its left with the *III. Pz.Korps* along the Sárviz-Malom Canal. In the *Korpsgruppe Harteneck/I. Kav.Korps* sector, the counterattack by the Hungarian *1. Hus.Div.* encountered difficulty in its attempt to retake Hill 480 and straighten out its line northwest of Szár when the defenders carried out numerous battalion-sized counterattacks that slowed the cavalrymen's advance to a crawl. West of Mány, Soviet troops carried out five separate battalion-sized attacks against troops of the *3. Kav.Brig.* holding a key position in the woods, where a German counterattack was still ongoing at the evening reporting time. The rest of the corps' sector was relatively quiet.

Due to terrible flying weather during the day, relatively few missions were flown by either side during the day. During the previousnight, *Luftflotte 4* performed a remarkable feat when it launched 176 cargo aircraft, including 113 *Heinkel He-111*s and 63 *Ju-52*s, of which 22 had to abort, as well as two cargo gliders, that reached Budapest and managed to drop or deliver nearly 160 short tons (144.6 metric tons) of ammunition, fuel, rations, and medical supplies to the beleaguered *IX. SS-Geb. Korps.*[7] The corps acknowledged that the bulk of the supplies were accurately delivered and recovered, testimony to the skill of both the pilots and the ground personnel who were able to successfully mark the drop zone. How the two gliders managed to land in such a tiny space can only be imagined. German high-altitude reconnaissance flights during the day confirmed continued vehicular movement over the bridges south of Budapest and along the northern bank of the Danube between Budapest and Gran. Against these Soviet troop movements, *Luftflotte 4* was able to carry out 160 night sorties that targeted bridges, ferries, railroad lines, and highways along the Danube with *Ju-88* medium bombers.

The four Soviet corps of the 4th Guards Army located between Stuhlweissenburg and the Vértes Mountains benefitted on 5 February from the cessation of *IV. SS-Pz. Korps'* attack by taking advantage of the quiet front to reorganize, rearm, and provision their forces, which had taken a beating during the past two days as well as sustaining heavy losses during their counteroffensive between 29 January and 2 February. General Zakharov would not allow them to simply rest and recuperate, but directed all four corps to maintain pressure on the enemy. While the I Guards Mechanized Corps and V Guards Cavalry Corps would pull back slightly from the front lines into reserve positions, the divisions of the XX and XXI Guards Rifle Corps would keep up the pressure on the *IV. SS-Pz.Korps* by conducting day and night foot patrol and occasional raids on vulnerable positions like Gyúlamajor, and continuing artillery missions to harass and disrupt any German movement. At this point, there was no need for Tolbukhin to intervene or issue a change of orders because the situation was developing very favorably.

South of Lake Velencze, both the XXIII Tank Corps and CIV Corps of the 4th Guards Army, supported on its left by the advancing 26th Army, would continue attempting to break through German defenses between Seregélyes and Stuhlweissenburg and get past the *Margarethestellung* as quickly as possible. The XXIII Tank Corps had nearly succeeded in doing so on 5 February, when it pierced the *Wiking* Division's lines in two separate places. Fortunately for the Germans, the advance of the XXIII Tank Corps was stymied when its lead elements encountered the steep banks of the Nádas Canal between Dinnyés and Seregélyes. Lacking bridging assets, the lead brigade's tanks were unable to cross the 6-meter wide and 2-meter deep obstacle. Since the two rifle divisions in support of the corps were lagging behind, the brigade had to secure a bridgehead by itself as well as construct a temporary bridge. Having done so, Lt.Gen. Akhmanov's tanks got as far as the southern outskirts of the village of Börgönd before they halted for the night. Once the 66th and 151st Rifle Divisions caught up with them, the XXIII Tank Corps—with its 28 remaining operational tanks and SP guns—would continue its advance the next morning once the highest point in the Nádas Swamp, Hill 130, defended by troops from the *Germania* Regiment, could be taken.[8] Stuhlweissenburg seemed nearly within their reach.

A significant amount of *Gen.d.Pz.Tr.* Balck's efforts that day, as well as those of his superior, *Gen.d.Inf.* Wöhler, were directed towards the ultimate disposition of the entrapped garrison in Budapest. Balck even raised the question of whether it was feasible to launch yet another relief attempt, this time north of Lake Velencze, but it was clear that this stood no chance whatsoever of being approved because the additional forces needed to carry it out were simply not available.

Why Balck resurfaced this idea is unknown; perhaps it was an act of bravado designed to curry Hitler's favor or to boost the spirits of the *IX. SS-Geb.Korps* when he wrote, "Relief of Budapest ... would have the greatest possible psychological effect on the forces in general and, going beyond that, on the entire nation, now and for all time."[9] In any case, his idea never got beyond the discussion stage. His long missive on this topic is noteworthy for one thing though: in it, he referred to *Ogruf.* Pfeffer-Wildenbruch as a *"hoch bewährten Führer"* (outstanding commander), a comment he would later disavow.

Once again, Wöhler made several telephone calls to the *OKH Führungsabteilung* requesting freedom of action for *H.Gr. Süd* to decide the ultimate fate of the *IX. SS-Geb.Korps*. Wöhler wanted to order Pfeffer-Wildenbruch to break out, or at least to have the latitude to decide whether to order such an action. Both German commanders knew the futility of asking, aware that Hitler would not change his mind once he had made it up. Still, if it could save the lives of 40,000 German and Hungarian troops as well as ease the fate of 300,000 civilians, it was worth a try. *General der Panzertruppe* Wenck was sympathetic and told them both that he would ask yet again, but doubted that Hitler would relent. Both Wöhler's bid and Pfeffer-Wildenbruch's earlier request for freedom of action were refused by Hitler at 2:40 a.m. on 6 February. Five minutes later, *H. Gr. Süd* notified *A. Gr. Balck/6. Armee* that it could relay the following statement to the commander of the *IX. SS-Geb. Korps*: "We have received the *Führer*'s decision. The *Führer* has ordered there be no change in the mission."[10]

This was the ultimate death sentence for *Festung Budapest*. Despite this event, and the breakout attempt it would spawn, it had little effect on *A. Gr. Balck/6. Armee*'s critical situation, which concerned how to stop the quickly developing rupture in the German front lines between Lake Velencze and Seregélyes. Should the XVIII or XXIII Tank Corps breach the *Margarethestellung* and seize Stuhlweissenburg from the south or southwest, everything that *A. Gr. Balck/6. Armee* had been trying to avoid for the past three months would finally come to pass. As tragic as the loss of the *IX. SS-Geb.Korps* would be, it would pale in comparison to the loss of most of the army's remaining corps. Thus, great hope rested on the impending counterattack by the *1. Pz.Div.* planned for the following day. If it succeeded, the front could be patched back together; if not, *A. Gr. Balck/6. Armee*, including the *IV. SS-Pz.Korps*, would be forced to abandon the front between the Vértes Mountains and Lake Balaton and retreat to the Danube.

In the *IV. SS-Pz.Korps* defensive sector, the night of 5/6 February did not pass uneventfully. The weather continued its warming trend, with temperatures once again well above freezing. Heavy fog and cloud overcast continued throughout the day. Although the situation in *Div. Gr. Holste* remained quiet, a company-sized Soviet reconnaissance in force against the northeast corner of Stuhlweissenburg, in the *Totenkopf* Division's *HKL* along the road linking it to Zámoly, was driven off without any ground being lost. As the Soviet attack against the *Wiking* Division in the neighboring sector held by the *III. Pz.Korps* began to develop momentum throughout the day, the danger arose that elements of the XXIII Tank Corps would break through the *Wiking* Division's left flank and enter the city's southern environs. The village of Dinnyés was cut off once again.

The SS troops from Vogt's *I. Btl./Norge* defending west of Dinnyés were ordered to counterattack and throw the Soviet troops out of a position they had established along the elevated highway and railroad intersection approximately 800 meters west of the village. As the attackers approached the dug-in enemy position via the wide-open swamp land, they were struck by heavy defensive fire. Without any meaningful fire support, the attack faltered, then collapsed. With his battalion shot to pieces, Vogt had no choice but to order his men to retreat, as Soviet troops shot at them with mortars and machineguns. The survivors began showing up on the northern side of the railroad line that ran from Dinnyés to Stuhlweissenburg by mid-morning.[11]

Consequently, Gille ordered Becker to quickly establish a cordon or blocking position to cover his right flank oriented towards the southeast, using one of his *Flak* batteries equipped with 8.8cm guns to serve as an antitank defense in the area south of Kisfalud. Fortunately, the anticipated advance by Soviet tanks failed to materialize. Recognizing that this situation revealed a critical vulnerability, Becker ordered the subordinated *356. Inf.Div.* to assume responsibility for defending it. To ensure that it had the combat power to carry this out (the division's *Pz.Jäg. Abt. 356* had not yet arrived in Veszprem), *Obersturmführer* Linkert's *3. Bttr./ SS-Flak Abt. 3* remained there in position. In order to get out of the city and to position his division command post in a more central location, Becker and his staff that same day moved to the village of Iszkaszentgyörgy, approximately 12 kilometers northwest of Stuhlweissenburg. Except for another unsuccessful Soviet attempt to probe the *Totenkopf* Regiment's lines northeast of Stuhlweissenburg in the vineyard area, this time by a battalion-sized infantry unit, the night of 5/6 February passed quietly.

Once again, the greatest drama occurring that day took place in the *III. Pz.Korps* sector, where Breith's three *panzer* divisions were busily fending off Soviet attempts to break through before German and Hungarian troops could get safely behind the *Margarethestellung*. As the day before, the *Wiking* Division was subjected to the most pressure, feeling the full weight of the continued assault by the XXIII Tank Corps and its two accompanying infantry divisions. A column of 12 tanks attempted to break through the *Germania* Regiment's position northwest of Seregélyes at 3 a.m. but was counterattacked in the fog by *Panzerfaust*-wielding infantrymen. Eight Soviet tanks were destroyed, five of them by *Panzerfaust*, and the rest retreated from whence they had come. A few hours later, another Soviet column with 20 tanks, advancing from the same direction, slipped past the thin screening line erected by the *Westland* Regiment and moved along both sides of the main road leading towards Stuhlweissenburg, once again taking advantage of the same kind of foggy conditions that had led to the capture of Fritz Rentrop three days before. Shortly thereafter, this column took the village of Jánosmajor 5 kilometers away against light resistance, but stalled at the foot of the commanding height of Hill 130 a kilometer to the east and momentarily halted.[12]

Three kilometers to the north, 12 more tanks from the other column that had halted along the Nádas Canal the night before were able to advance and take Börgönd and Hill 122 after the field-expedient bridge over the canal was completed earlier that morning. In addition to reaching the area where most of the firing batteries of *SS-Pz.Art.Rgt. 5* were located, this was the same attack that sent the survivors from the *Germania* Regiment fleeing back towards Stuhlweissenburg, the event that prompted the *Totenkopf* Division to send a *Flak* battery to stop it. Both tank columns halted where they were and waited while the infantry caught up with them. This later proved to be a fatal mistake.

In Dinnyés, the three battalions—one of Norwegians, one of Danes, and the other of Hungarians sprinkled with a few Germans and *Volksdeutsche*—managed to repel all of the several attempts to storm their positions by the 151st Rifle Division and were able to hold on. Why they were still defending Dinnyés was anyone's guess; the longer they remained, the greater the odds that they would be wiped out completely. The *Wiking* Division was temporarily augmented later that day by four *Pz. VI* Tiger Is from *9. Kp./SS-Pz.Rgt. 3*, which were used along with two *Pz. IV*s from *I. Abt./ SS-Pz.Rgt. 5* to form *K.Gr. Flieder* (codenamed Lilac), led by *Ostuf.* Bauer of *SS-Pz. Rgt. 5* riding in the regiment's last remaining operational Panther.[13] Their task was to close the 2-kilometer gap between Janosmajor and Börgönd, departing from a position slightly south of the Sarkereztur–Stuhlweissenburg railway line. However, after making good initial progress, the little battlegroup was brought to a halt by heavy enemy defensive fire, which knocked out *Unterscharführer* Juhr's *Pz. IV* after his crew destroyed a Soviet antitank gun.

That evening, because it had suffered such heavy losses, each of the *Wiking* Division's two *Panzergrenadier* regiments were ordered to combine their three shattered battalions into one that was *Kampffähig* (combat capable), resulting in it being referred to as "*K.Gr. Wiking*," a division no longer. This had not happened since the relief of Kovel nearly a year before, but it would remain so until it received enough replacements to re-establish all six battalions later in the month. Regardless, that evening a staff officer in the headquarters of *Armeegrupe Balck/6. Armee*, in a conversation with his counterpart at *H.Gr. Süd*, remarked that the *Wiking* Division was still considered "combat ready."[14] In contrast to this exaggerated assessment, the division's *O1* wrote in his diary that evening, "Constant enemy attacks. Division too weak to conduct counterattacks. Past few days marked by constant defensive and withdrawal fighting leading to heavy losses. Division completely exhausted … [General Gille] visited our command post today."[15]

In the rest of Breith's corps, fighting was equally as heavy. At a point between the Malom and Nador Canals on the boundary between the *III. Pz.Korps* and *Div. Gr. Pape* near Káloz, *K.Gr. Kujacinski* of the *23. Pz.Div.* was attacked by the 200th Rifle Regiment of the 68th Rifle Division, backed up by a few tanks from the 52nd Tank Regiment. Despite the enemy's numerical superiority, all three Soviet attacks were beaten back by the battlegroup, which managed to knock out four tanks and inflict heavy losses on the infantry. Between the Sárviz Canal and the railroad line running alongside, as well as a few kilometers to the east, a rifle division supported by XVIII Tank Corps, with up to eight tanks, carried out five separate attacks against German positions in company- to battalion-strength. These attacks were beaten back by the *3. Pz.Div.*, which managed to knock out seven of the tanks from the 170th Tank Brigade.

That same day, the division's *Pz.Aufkl.Abt. 3* was temporarily attached to the right flank of the *Wiking* Division to help bolster its defensive strength. As the savage fighting by all three of Breith's divisions continued throughout the day, the *1. Pz.Div.* continued arriving at Falubattyán and began preparing for its counterattack scheduled for the following day. It would not be much of a rest. For this action, Thünert's division would be once again subordinated to the *III. Pz.Korps* along with the two separate tank battalions subordinated to it. However, instead of Balck's original intention of using it to restore the *HKL* east of Seregélyes along with joint attacks by the *3. Pz.Div.* and the *Wiking* Division, the *1. Pz.Div.* would be used to close the gap between Janosmajor and Dinnyés southwest of Lake Velencze and northwest of Stuhlweissenburg, and re-establish the *Margarethestellung*, a much less ambitious (but more achievable) goal.

That evening at the headquarters of the *III. Pz.Korps*, with *Gen.d.Pz.Tr.* Breith looking on, *Ogruf.* Gille personally presented *Gen.Maj.* Thünert with the Knight's Cross that Gille had submitted in recognition of his division's role in retaking Stuhlweissenburg on 22 January. Upon learning that their commander had received this prestigious award, one member of the division later wrote, "The joy in the division about this well-deserved award was great and unanimous." Although this had happened only two weeks before, from the standpoint of the night of 6 February, it must have seemed eons to all the men observing the ceremony.[16]

The Hungarian *3. Armee* was also hard pressed that day. Along what was left of the Sió sector, a Soviet rifle battalion was able to achieve a 1-kilometer deep and 3-kilometer wide penetration, fighting its way into the town of Sió Maros. Additional battalion-sized attacks achieved penetrations in the towns of Dégh and Nagyhöresök Puszta that the Hungarian *Inf.Rgt. 26* could not iron out. A dangerous battalion-sized attack that led to a breakthrough in Káloz was counterattacked by *K.Gr. Martini*, which managed to reduce it to remnants in a few hours. North of Káloz, another company-sized Soviet attack crossed the Malom Canal and blocked the road between Káloz and Nagy Lang, and a counterattack by the *6. Pz.Div. Panzergruppe* was still underway at reporting time. The last major event reported by the German liaison team working at *Gen.Lt.* Heszlényi's headquarters was the enemy's seizure of the commanding heights 1.5 kilometers east of Sanponya along the boundary with the *III. Pz.Korps*, which *Div.Gr. Pape* was too busy to worry about. The following day promised more of the same, though the *3. Armee* was still able to maintain its front-line integrity as it continued its withdrawal.[17]

In comparison, the situation in *Korpsgruppe Harteneck*, adjacent to the *IV. SS-Pz. Korps*, was relatively uneventful, but the day still had its share of challenges. For instance, northwest of Szár, the Hungarian *1. Hus.Div.*, augmented by the battalion from the *711. Inf.Div.*, faced tough enemy resistance, but for the second day in a row was unable to straighten out its front line near the town or retake Hill 480 in the Vértes Mountains. All it managed to accomplish was the gain of a few yards of ground at the cost of heavy casualties. Otherwise, there was no other combat activity worth reporting, and even the battlefield around Mány was relatively quiet for the first time in days. In the air, very little air activity was reported again by either side due to the atrocious weather.

On the Soviet side, General Zakharov directed the commander of the XXIII Tank Corps, Lt.Gen. Akhmanov, to break out of his bridgehead near Börgönd and continue pressing forward towards Stuhlweissenburg with his remaining tanks and the two accompanying infantry divisions. On that day, Seregélyes finally fell to the 4th Guards Army and 26th Army in its entirety, with the 155th Rifle Division of the 26th Army claiming the southern portion while the 4th Guards Army's CIV Rifle Corps siezed the rest. This was considered a significant victory. By this point, Stuhlweissenburg appeared to be within easy reach and German defenses southeast of the city non-existent. Defending German forces appeared to be confused and their actions uncoordinated. The bridgehead over the Nádas Canal had been seized with hardly a fight. In addition, the *Margarethestellung* had been pierced in several locations, rendering its utility as a German main line of resistance pointless. The final goal of the counteroffensive was clearly in sight.

At least that was the Soviet assessment. In reality, Tolbukhin's two armies had overextended themselves and begun to outrun their supply lines. The low number of operational tanks in the XXIII Tank Corps made any further advance beyond the Nádas Canal questionable. The bulk of the 26th Army lay to the southwest and its tank brigades were equally weak. Gagen's army was also vulnerable to counterattacks along his extended flanks by the *23. Pz.Div.* and the *Panzergruppe* of the *6. Pz.Div.*, and would have difficulty operating in concert with the XXIII Tank Corps.

Akhamov's three brigades on the canal's western bank could have done two things on 6 February: either take the risk and continue attacking while exploiting the evident disarray of German forces, or withdraw and defend on the opposite bank, which at least could be held, and wait for the infantry and artillery to join them. The worst course of action was to remain exposed on the west bank overnight where they were. For reasons unknown, this is what Lt.Gen. Akhmanov chose to do. Perhaps it was the fog enveloping the landscape, or perhaps it was his overconfidence. At any rate, the following day would bring the reckoning.

Besides entertaining fanciful ideas such as giving the relief of Budapest another try, as if there was any remaining time to do that, Balck also busied himself with more practical concerns. One of these was his request to the *OKH Führungsabteilung* that day to withdraw the *6. Pz.Div.* out of the line and reposition it to the south, explaining that, "The situation on the north flank [was perceived to] not to be so tense at the moment that the *6. Pz.Div.* had to remain there." With this division, Balck could at least designate it as an *Armeegruppe* reserve force behind the lines, once it was reassembled and reunited with its *Panzergruppe*. To this end, he ordered Harteneck to provide a detailed inventory of the division's shortages and equipment replacement needs, which was sent to *A.Gr. Balck's* headquarters four days later.

By this time, it had become common knowledge within the *Führungsabteilung* of *H.Gr. Süd* that something big was in the works, involving the transfer of a complete *panzer* army from the Western Front to Hungary. The details were still hazy, but based on conversations with *OKH*, it appeared that the *6. Pz.Armee*—which was in *OKW* reserve—had been designated as the headquarters to lead this army, and that the two corps constituting this army, with up to four SS divisions, were undergoing the final phases of their reconstitution process and would soon be moving by rail to Hungary to carry out a mission that was of vital importance for the future of the Third Reich.[18] By this point, *Ogruf.* Gille was probably aware of these developments through the SS rumor mill (again with the *Latrinenparole*), but probably did not know the details yet.

The other operational concept being actively considered by *H.Gr. Süd* was one of its own design that involved assembling a reserve strong enough to destroy the much-feared Soviet bridgehead over the Gran River. This was the same one that Kirschner's *LVII. Pz.Korps* had tried and failed to eliminate during the second week of January. Wöhler's fears were based on recent intelligence that indicated that some sort of Soviet build-up was taking place within the bridgehead involving the repositioning of armored units; if this was the case, he wanted to act before it could grow into a threat so great that it could break through the *8. Armee* and advance towards Vienna along the relatively level and tank-friendly Viennese Plain. In fact, the *8. Armee* plan for this operation had already been in development for several days. Codenamed *Unternehmen Südwind* (not to be confused with the operation with the same name considered for the *2. Pz.Armee* the previous month), the only thing lacking to carry it out was the necessary forces. The *8. Armee* was too weak to do it on its own, but Wöhler and his chief of staff believed it was so important that they began pitching the idea to Guderian at the *OKH* to convince him and Hitler of the need to carry it out. Although Balck was undoubtedly aware of this plan, Gille probably was not at that time, simply because his corps would not be taking apart in it.

One day soon followed the next. The morning of Wednesday, 7 February marked the first time in weeks that the *IV. SS-Pz.Korps* had not experienced any overnight enemy activity. The morning report simply noted, "The night passed quietly." The thawing period continued, with temperatures rising as high as 46 degrees Fahrenheit (8 degrees Centigrade) during the day. In the morning, a bright sun chased away the weak cloud cover, further hastening the trend, though the weather markedly worsened as the day progressed: rain meant unpaved roads became ribbons of mud that challenged even tracked vehicles, and only paved roads could be traversed with relative ease.

The warmer weather initially made things difficult for some. Troops manning trenches, dugouts, and fighting positions along the front lines had to use their helmets to bail out water and mud resulting from melting snow. Unless a unit could appropriate a local house or barn behind the lines to serve as a rest area, living conditions were horrible, although this was mitigated somewhat by the fact that field kitchens could now provide hot food on a more regular basis. Troops quartered in Stuhlweissenburg could make do, although they were closer to the front line. Even a shelter in a damp, unheated basement was better than living out in the open. If they were lucky, they shared a house with one of the few Hungarian families who had remained behind, who generously shared what food they had or wine from their cellars.

During the day, the calm persisted along most of the *IV. SS-Pz.Korps'* front line. Except for an unsuccessful enemy attack by two infantry companies directed against the *356. Inf.Div.* manning the *HKL* along the railroad line in the southeast corner between Stuhlweissenburg and Dinnyés, everywhere else was relatively quiet. Taking advantage of the temporarily calm environment, *Ogruf.* Gille ordered his troops manning the main defense line northwest of the city, including the *Totenkopf* Division, to begin "straightening out" the front by carrying out slight withdrawals or adjustment to create more defensible positions that took every advantage that the terrain offered.

By doing so, *Brig.Fhr.* Becker's division was able to extract its combat engineer battalion from the front line and have it assemble inside the city to serve as his *Eingreifreserve.* From his command post's new location in Inota, Gille could travel the 21 kilometers to the city center of Stuhlweissenburg or to Becker's headquarters in half an hour, allowing him to make more frequent visits to the front line, where he felt much more at ease. Being so close to Balck's own headquarters meant that the *IV. SS-Pz.Korps* commander and his staff began receiving regular visits from their army commander, which in the case of Balck was a decidedly mixed blessing.

As with the day before, most of the fighting took place in the adjacent sector held by the three *panzer* divisions of the *III. Pz.Korps.* On the corps' far right flank, the *23. Pz.Div.* fought the enemy to a standstill between the Malom and Sárviz Canals and maintained contact with the adjacent *K.Gr. Martini* of the *6. Pz.Div.* Despite the numerous tank-supported attacks carried out against its positions, the division was able to knock out six tanks and one assault gun and drove the Soviet forces back to the southeast. The adjacent *3. Pz.Div.* attempted to withdraw as ordered into the *Margarethestellung*, but when the advance parties reached the trenches and fighting positions that had been constructed the previous December, they found them completely under water, leaving the division no choice but to remain in its current position along the heights west of Seregélyes, where it continued to defend and protect the left flank of the *23. Pz.Div.*[19]

The primary action fought that day began at 8 a.m. when the reinforced *1. Pz.Div.* initiated its counterattack against the two tank brigades of the XXIII Tank Corps that had taken Seregélyes and established bridgeheads over the Nádas Canal the previous day. Along with the *Panzergruppen* from the *3. Pz.Div.* and *K.Gr. Wiking*, the division carried out a pincer attack, from the north against Börgönd and from the south against Jánosmajor. After eliminating the Soviet concentration positioned there and reasserting German control of the *Margarethestellung*, the division continued attacking southeast towards the highway and railroad intersection 1 kilometer northwest of Seregélyes across the Dinnyés-Kajtóri Canal. Artillery support was provided by the combined firepower of the artillery regiments from all three divisions.

The assault group on the left—composed of the *Kampfbataillon* from *Pz.Gren.Rgt. 113* led by *Hauptmann* Staudte, the *Pz. V* Panthers from *I. Abt./Pz.Rgt. 1*, and 16 tanks from *s.Pz.Abt. 509*—assaulted Börgönd from the north, destroyed 12 T-34s, broke through Soviet defensive positions, and continued pushing south, leaving the mopping up in Börgönd to *K.Gr. Germania*, supported by three Panthers from the attached *I. Abt./SS-Pz.Rgt. 3* sent from Stuhlweissenburg to lend assistance.[20] The right assault group—comprising the *Kampfbataillon* from *Pz.Gren.Rgt. 1* led by *Hauptmann* Mischke, the remaining tanks from *Pz.Rgt. 1*, *Pz.Pio.Btl. 37*, and four *Pz. Vs* from *I. Abt./Pz.Rgt. 24*—assaulted Jánosmajor. After bitter fighting, Mischke's force broke through the Soviet positions, repelled a counterattack, destroyed 17 antitank guns from the 521st Antitank Artillery Regiment, and continued pushing towards Seregélyes, stopping only after ensuring that the railway bridge over the Dinnyés-Kajtóri Canal was blown up by the engineers, thus denying it to the enemy.[21]

This completed, Mischke's task force turned back to the north and, with the aid of *K.Gr. Wiking*, attempted to regain control of Hill 130, where it linked up with Staudte's *Kampfgruppe*. After re-establishing contact with the troops from *K.Gr. Wiking* defending Dinnyés, the *1. Pz.Div.* withdrew to its reserve position in Falubattyán. The seizure of Hill 130 and the neighboring Hill 122 would have to wait until the next day. Amazingly, the assault force had lost only one of their own tanks, and except for several *SPWs* damaged in the combat engineer battalion, casualties were very low.[22] After suffering heavy losses during the course of this German attack, including 18 tanks and 43 antitank guns, the forward brigades of the XXIII Tank Corps withdrew to the opposite side of the *Margarethestellung* to lick their wounds.[23]

Balck's counterattack had been a success, halting the forward momentum of the 4th Guards Army's attack at Seregélyes; the XXIII Tank Corps would have to be withdrawn and reconstituted. After suffering the loss of so many tanks and crewmen during the past week, Akhmanov's corps could report a total of only 14 operational tanks and five SP guns in its four brigades, a fraction of what it had gone into battle with on 27 January.[24] As a result, Zakharov's goal of retaking Stuhlweissenburg had to be postponed, but his forces were able to retain control of Seregélyes.

Although Zakharov's role in the counteroffensive south of Lake Velencze was temporarily at an end, this still left the ongoing advance by Gagen's 26th Army between Seregélyes and the eastern shore of Lake Balaton, where the Hungarian *3. Armee*—along with *Div.Gr. Pape*—were heavily engaged against superior Soviet forces. While the hard-fighting Hungarian *25. Inf.Div.* was withdrawing under great pressure east from the Sió River towards Enying on the Hungarian right flank, *Div. Gr. Pape* was involved in a number of small engagements between Dégh and Káloz, successfully warding off or blunting numerous battalion- to regiment-sized attacks by Soviet infantry, supported by a few tanks, that attempted to slip past its defenses. Often working in concert with one another, the *Panzergruppen* from the *6. Pz.Div.* and *23. Pz.Div.* beat back assaults along the Sárviz-Malom Canal at Káloz, Soponya, Csösz, and Nagy Lang.

To the left of Gille's corps, *Korpsgruppe Harteneck/I. Kav.Korps* continued the operation by the Hungarian *1. Hus.Div.* to seize Hill 480 and straighten out its front line, but had to shut it down after it failed to make any further progress. Accordingly, the front line was pulled back to another terrain feature and any further hopes of seizing Hill 480 were abandoned. Along the rest of Harteneck's front, little other combat activity of any significance was reported, although this overlooked a major action fought that day by the *3. Kav.Brig.*, whose assault gun battalion, reinforced by a paratroop battalion from the *Szent László* Division, fought off a Soviet attempt to penetrate its front line northwest of Mány. Six German assault guns lay in ambush, as an enemy infantry force supported by at least seven armored fighting vehicles approached to within 100 meters of the German and Hungarian positions. In the brief action that followed, two T-34/85 tanks were knocked out, as was a JS-II. No German vehicles were destroyed, though several were damaged. Caught in the combined fire of the paratroopers and assault guns, the Soviet attack force collapsed and was forced to retreat, leaving seven of their AFVs burning in their wake.[25]

In the air, due to the worsening flying weather, neither side was able to generate many sorties. Several German ground-attack aircraft strafed and bombed Soviet locomotives in a railroad yard immediately south of Budapest, damaging six and completely destroying another, as well as scoring several hits on a railroad station with their bombs. During the night of 6/7 February, at least 16 resupply sorties were conducted over Budapest, with aircrews managing to drop some 16 metric tons of supplies for the beleaguered garrison. Due to the amount of supplies needed to keep the *IX. SS-Geb.Korps* fighting, resupply missions were being launched as early as sunset in order to maximize the number of sorties flown during the night.[26]

Viewing the events from the perspective of the Third Ukrainian Front, the command was satisfied with what the 4th Guards Army had been able to accomplish between Stuhlweissenburg and Seregélyes from 29 January to 7 February. General Zakharov's army had been able, in cooperation with Lt.Gen. Gagen's 26th Army, to push *A. Gr. Balck/6. Armee* away from both the Danube and Budapest, rendering any further relief operation impractical. Furthermore, Zakharov's forces had managed to block the counterattack by the *IV. SS-Pz.Korps* between Zámoly and Stuhlweissenburg from 4–5 February without having to sacrifice any of its units.

The XXIII Tank Corps, supported by the infantry of the CIV Rifle Corps, had pushed the German defenses as far back as the *Margarethestellung* and had seized Seregélyes before they had been stung by the *III. Pz.Korps'* counterattack, but at least the positions it still held as of nightfall on 7 February would serve as a springboard for future operations. To the west, the 26th and 57th Armies' offensive against the Hungarian *3. Armee* and the *III. Pz.Korps* still had more ground to gain, leaving open the possibility that they might yet be able to achieve some sort of tactical breakthrough if the exhausted Hungarian *25. Inf.Div.* collapsed. However, after five weeks of constant fighting, nearly all of the units of Tolbukhin's front were on the verge of exhaustion themselves, and even the Soviet marshal realized that the culmination of his counteroffensive was near at hand; when that occurred at some point in the next several days, his armies would be compelled to revert to a defensive posture and wait for Hitler's next move.[27]

The next step was up to *H.Gr. Süd* and *A.Gr. Balck*. While Hermann Balck fantasized about launching yet another relief attack towards Budapest which stood no chance whatsoever of being approved (a proposal he does not even mention in his memoirs), Otto Wöhler was focused instead on three separate operations. The first, that concerned him the most, was the deteriorating situation in Budapest. By this point, all he could do for Pfeffer-Wildenbruch was to offer him encouragement and promise more air deliveries, although both men probably knew that the fate of the city's garrison was already sealed. As yet, there had been no coordination between the two concerning an attempted breakout from the city; had there been any, the results might have been different. The second concern was his belief that the Soviet Gran bridgehead had to be completely destroyed in order to secure the integrity of *H.Gr. Süd's* defenses once the anticipated Soviet spring offensive began; and the third was the still-secret news of an impending major offensive in Hungary that was to be carried out on the expressed orders of *Der Führer*.

For the latter, Hitler had summoned Wöhler to Berlin on the night of 7 February to be briefed the next day about future operations concerning "the conduct of the defense" in Hungary. The next day, "all would be revealed" when Wöhler would have an opportunity to read the order in person. The only other significant change to *H.Gr. Süd's* mission occurred that same day, when another *Führerbefehl* was received instructing Wöhler to order Balck to withdraw the headquarters of the *I. Kav.Korps*—including both the *3.* and *4. Kavallerie-Brigaden*—from the front lines. As it turned out, only the two cavalry brigades could be pulled out within the next week, but there was no other corps headquarters available to replace Harteneck's. Thus, *I. Kav.Korps* would remain as part of *A.Gr. Balck/6. Armee* for the time being.[28]

However, Balck did receive permission to pull out the *6. Pz.Div.* and reassemble it once the situation in the Hungarian *3. Armee* defensive sector was deemed stable enough to withdraw the division's *Panzergruppe*, which was still several days away. Thus ended 7 February, an eventful day for nearly every corps in *A.Gr. Balck/6.*

Armee's area of operations, except for the *IV. SS-Pz.Korps*, which for once enjoyed a day of relative peace. However, the fight for the *Margarethestellung* was not yet over, and in the Hungarian *3. Armee* sector had only just begun.

Neither had the fighting completely died down in and around Stuhlweissenburg, demonstrating that this was no time to lower one's guard. The *IV. SS-Pz.Korps* reported that the *Totenkopf* Division and *356. Inf.Div.*, during the night of 7/8 February, had been confronted by several company-sized attacks against their lines immediately east of the city. All of them, most likely strong combat patrols undertaken to bring in German prisoners, were driven off without loss to the defenders. With the rising sun, the temperature fluctuated throughout the day, hovering between freezing point and the low 40s Fahrenheit. The skies were mostly cloudy with isolated downpours, once again limiting visibility. Along the frozen Danube, ice packs had begun to break up, hastened by the accelerating thaw. This must have come as a relief to German and Hungarian troops standing guard along the southern bank of the Danube between Gran and Komorn, where the likelihood of a river-crossing operation by the enemy had begun to diminish.

Despite fears to the contrary, 8 February proved to be another relatively peaceful day for the *IV. SS-Pz.Korps*, except for the several tanks from the *Totenkopf* Division's *panzer* regiment that had been sent to assist *K.Gr. Wiking* between Dinnyés and Jánosmajor. Gille and his staff used this opportunity to make additional changes to the corps' support/supporting unit relationships. After two days under the control of the *Totenkopf* Division, the *356. Inf.Div.* once again was subordinated directly under the *IV. SS-Pz.Korps*.[29] Its scattered infantry battalions, which had yet to operate directly within the framework of their division headquarters since their arrival, were once again united and arrayed under their proper regimental commanders.

By this point, most of the trains transporting the division's equipment and personnel from Italy had arrived, except for those carrying its antitank battalion, though the division's *Gren.Rgt. 869* and *Füs.Btl. 356* would not rejoin it, having been diverted to Germany to undergo complete reconstitution. The division boundaries were once again redrawn, with the dividing line between the *356. Inf.Div.* and Becker's division now being designated as the northern edge of Stuhlweissenburg, with the regiments of the *Totenkopf* Division defending the open terrain to the north and the *356. Inf.Div.* to the south. This decision had taken into account the fact that the infantry of Kühl's division had already demonstrated their inability to stand firm in the face of enemy tank attacks; placing them along the open highway leading to Zámoly was too risky. Instead, Gille thought that they would perform better in defensive fighting within the city proper, where at least they would stand a chance against tanks with *Panzerfausts*.

The *IV. SS-Pz.Korps IIa*, *Sturmbannführer* Meyer-Schulze, did have to deal with a minor emergency that day that required *Ogruf.* Gille's intervention. On 8 February, the *SS-FHA* informed the corps through SS administrative channels that it was to withdraw the survivors from *I. Btl./Norge* and *I. Btl./Danmark* from the front lines and send them immediately to Stettin in northern Germany to be reunited with their parent *11. SS-Pz.Gren.Div. Nordland*, then preparing for its role in the upcoming *Unternehmen Sonnenwende* (Operation *Solstice*) counteroffensive in Pomerania scheduled to begin on 15 February. Of course, both battalions were still defending Dinnyés at the time and could not be spared, simply because there were no other units available to replace them. Gille notified Balck, who then contacted the *OKH Führungsabteilung*. Even though this normally would have been thought to be a purely "SS matter," in this particular case the *SS-FHA, Ogruf.* Jüttner, acceded to Balck's request, possibly because Himmler had just taken command of *H.Gr. Vistula* and had his hands full playing at being field marshal.[30]

That Friday witnessed *K.Gr. Wiking* being used to "clean up" in the wake of the previous day's counterattack by the *1. Pz.Div.* that had left some unfinished business. Hills 130 and 122, which dominated the northeastern portion of the *Margarethestellung* at the southwestern shore of Lake Velencze, were still in Soviet hands, though their defenders were now isolated from the main body of their units. These two hills, defended by the 581st Rifle Regiment and the 56th Motorized Rifle Brigade, were supported by up to 13 tanks and SP guns and had been left behind to "protect" the XXIII Tank Corps' bridgeheads, though they had no way to retreat because the *1. Pz.Div.* had destroyed the field-expedient bridges across the Nádas Canal the day before. Essentially, these troops had no choice but to die in place or surrender. They chose the first course of action.

At 9:30 a.m., *K.Gr. Wiking*, supported by several *Pz. VI* Tiger IIs from s.*Pz. Abt. 509*, began its counterattack to seize Hills 130 and 122 and restore complete control of all of the *Margarethestellung* between Dinnyés and the western outskirts of Seregélyes. The hills' occupants did not give up without a fight, and apparently most of them fought to the death; afterwards, the troops from *K.Gr. Wiking* counted the bodies of 1,000 dead Soviet troops. During the savage fighting that raged back and forth for the two hills, 10 enemy tanks, three SP guns, and 16 antitank guns were knocked out, in exchange for 50 German troops killed or injured and five Tiger IIs damaged though deemed repairable.

Soviet sources claimed that 25 German tanks and assault guns participated, though this was probably an exaggeration, as was the physical body count reported by the Germans. Their task complete, the Tigers rejoined the rest of the battalion in Falubattyán to prepare for their next mission.[31] Summing up the day's fighting, the *Wiking* Division's *O1* wrote, "Our counterattack went forward. Hills 122 and 130 were taken in hard fighting and despite enemy attempts to retake them, we held on. This gives the division a reasonably useful line of defense. Our troops started digging in."[32]

Along the rest of the *III. Pz.Korps'* front line that day, the *3.* and *23. Pz.Div.* found themselves under renewed attack. A counterattack on the corps' right flank by the *Panzergruppe* of the *23. Pz.Div.*, *K.Gr. Tiedemann*, succeeded in routing the enemy forces between the Malom and Sárviz Canals and forced them to withdraw to a point 3 kilometers west of Aba. Along the rest of the sector held by the division, augmented by the Hungarian *I. Blt./Inf.Rgt. 26*, as well as the entire front line of the *3. Pz.Div.*, both divisions were subjected throughout the day to numerous attacks by company- to battalion-sized Soviet infantry formations, each supported by several tanks. Preceded by short but very powerful artillery barrages, the Soviet troops stormed forward, heedless of casualties, but in each and every case were beaten back after suffering *hohen blutigen Verlusten* (heavy bloody losses). Help by the *A.Gr. Reserve*, the *1. Pz.Div.*, was not needed that day.

Of greater concern was the situation of the Hungarian *3. Armee*, whose *25. Inf. Div.* was being continually pressed by both the CXXXIII and CXXXV Rifle Corps, which kept jostling the Hungarians north. The command element of *Div.Gr. Pape* was replaced that day by *Div.Gr. von Roden*, led by *Gen.Maj.* Emmo von Roden and a few personnel from the *H.Gr. Süd* staff, although the fighting units remained the same—the Hungarian *Inf.Rgt. 26* of their *25. Inf.Div.* and *K.Gr. Martini* (the *Panzergruppe* from the *6. Pz.Div.*) although on that day its strength was reduced by a third when *Pz.Aufkl.Abt. 1* was ordered to rejoin the *1. Pz.Div.* that very evening.[33] Once the Hungarian *25. Inf.Div.* had reached the safety of the *Margarethestellung*, *K.Gr. Martini* would be withdrawn as well, but it still had a long way to go.

The reason for the renaming of the *Divisionsgruppe* was because *Gen.Maj.* Pape, his division staff, and signal company from the old *Pz.Gren.Div. FHH* were to be used as the headquarters for the new *Pz.Div. FHH*, which was undergoing complete *Auffrischung*. This reconstitution process had been delayed yet again when Pape and his staff were subordinated to the Hungarian *3. Armee* for the past two weeks. The exchange of Pape's headquarters with von Roden's apparently took place without mishap, and command and control was maintained throughout the day's operations. By the end of the day, most of the German and Hungarian forces had managed to pull back in relatively good order into the temporary *HKL* drawn along the line running from Enying to the southern edge of Kisláng, ending at Soponya, while *K.Gr. Martini* of the *6. Pz.Div.* formed the hard-hitting rear guard. The crisis that Balck had feared the most that day had passed without further incident.[34] On this occasion, the Hungarian *25. Inf.Div.* had merely outpaced its pursuers, thanks to the German rear guards.

The area defended by *Korpsgruppe Harteneck/I. Kav.Korps* was remarkably quiet, with no combat activity being reported at all that day. Plans for pulling out the corps headquarters and the two cavalry brigades was postponed when the intelligence staff of *H.Gr. Süd* intercepted radio message traffic indicating that the II Guards Mechanized Corps—at that moment located in the vicinity of Bicske and Zsámbék—as well as the V Guards Cavalry Corps between Stuhlweissenburg and Zámoly, were to be pulled out and redirected to the front between Gran and Szomor. According to

German intelligence analysts, this was evidence that a large-scale operation was being contemplated against the left flank of *Korpsgruppe Harteneck* in the near future.[35] Again, whether this was another case of effective Soviet operational deception cannot be ruled out, but the Germans thought it was a genuine threat. Whatever the cause, Harteneck's headquarters stayed put, and his two cavalry brigades would convert to cavalry divisions while still occupying front-line positions.

Bad weather continued to hamper air operations by both sides, except for high altitude reconnaissance aircraft. Large formations of Allied four-engine bombers approaching from the south were reported in the skies above *H. Gr. Süd*, but as on previous days they appeared to be heading towards targets in Austria or southern Germany and did not disturb German operations in Hungary. Taking advantage of a break in the weather during the night of 7/8 February, *Luftflotte 4* managed to deliver 4.5 metric tons of supplies over the castle area in Budapest. Additional airdrops were planned for the following evening, but this proved to be the last.[36]

For the Third Ukrainian Front, the time had come for an operational pause. Although the 4th Guards Army and 26th Army had failed to take Stuhlweissenburg at the end of the two-week counteroffensive, Tolbukhin was satisfied with how the operation had concluded. The Soviet General Staff Study of the operation stated:

> The defeat of the German counteroffensive against the Third Ukrainian Front's forces from the area southwest of the city of [Stuhlweissenburg] deprived the encircled German-Hungarian group of forces of aid from without ... At the same time as the Third Ukrainian Front's forces, as a result of heavy defensive fighting, halted the enemy's group of forces that had broken through towards Budapest and then, having taken up the offensive, threw it back to its starting position, the Second Ukrainian Front's forces were successfully concluding the destruction of the encircled enemy in the western part of Budapest.[37]

Except for local attacks designed to improve its defensive positions, or others to seize favorable ground for the resumption of the offensive, large-scale operations by the armies of the Third Ukrainian Front temporarily came to an end after 10 February. One notable exception was the 26th Army's aggressive pursuit of the Hungarian *3. Armee* back to the *Margarethestellung*.

As 8 February drew to a close, *Gen. d. Pz. Tr.* Balck's focus remained on building up reserves for future operations, including reassembling the *6. Pz. Div.* His grandiose plans for yet another relief attempt of Budapest having been turned down, his attention was momentarily drawn to reports of a Soviet build-up in the *Korpsgruppe Harteneck* sector (see above). He also proposed withdrawing the *3. Pz. Div.* from the front lines around Seregélyes and have it join his *Armeegruppe*'s reserve in the Polgárdi area, but conditions there were still too tense to allow that, including the weakness of *K. Gr. Wiking*, which could not assume the defense in the area by itself. As for the future, he was unsure, writing after the war, "After conclusion of the fighting around Budapest the question then became: Now what?"[38] He appeared to be out of original ideas, at least for the moment.

As for *Gen.d.Inf.* Wöhler, while in Berlin he had been completely briefed on the upcoming operation that would involve the *6. Pz.Armee.* Elements of this army had already begun arriving by rail in the staging area between Komorn and Raab, the same area where the *IV. SS-Pz.Korps* had assembled during the last week of December 1944 while it was preparing for *Konrad I.* As they arrived, these new SS units would be temporarily incorporated into *H.Gr. Süd's* defense plans until the offensive began. Because Guderian's *OKH Führungsabteilung* had prepared the concept plan for the offensive with Hitler's input, Wöhler was not given much of an opportunity to contribute his advice, much like *G.F.M.* von Rundstedt when he had been presented with the plan for the *Wacht am Rhein* counteroffensive in the Ardennes two months earlier. Wöhler and his staff would be relegated to merely fleshing out the plan's details. However, while this *panzer* army was gathering, Wöhler proposed to Hitler that *H.Gr. Süd* be allowed to use a portion of it to eliminate the Gran bridgehead. Evidently, this demonstration of aggressive intent by a general of the *Heer* at this stage of the war impressed Hitler, who remarked, "Wöhler is no National Socialist, but at least he's a man!"[39] More on this shortly.

"No combat activity of note" was the sole entry in the morning report of the *IV. SS-Pz.Korps* submitted on 9 February. *Korpsgruppe Harteneck/I. Kav.Korps* reported the same, this sector remaining remarkably quiet throughout the day. In regards to Gille's corps, the situation intensified later that day when a company-sized infantry force supported by a few tanks conducted an attack from Pákozd along the corps' far right flank between Dinnyés (which was still in the *III. Pz.Korps* defensive sector) and Kisfaludimajor, defended by a company from the *356. Inf.Div.* backed up by the 8.8cm guns of *3. Bttr./SS-Flak-Abt. 3.* After losing five tanks to the deadly accurate "88s" of the *Flak* battery, the survivors turned and fled.

As far as events concerned the *Totenkopf* Division that day, *A.Gr. Balck/6. Armee* directed *Ogruf.* Gille to order Becker to detach his division's *Begleitkompanie*, which would join that from the *Wiking* Division to establish a security line behind the Hungarian-held portion of the *Margarethestellung.* Their purpose was to serve as a backstop to the Hungarian *25. Inf.Div.*, should it completely collapse in combat or switch sides in the middle of the battle. The thought of this possibility—"*Wenn die Ungarn versagen …*" (If the Hungarians should fail …)—had remained in the back of the minds of nearly every German commander, as well as many enlisted men, since the collapse of the Hungarian government the previous October, and had haunted them ever since.[40]

Left undisturbed for the moment, the remaining companies, battalions, and regiments of the *Totenkopf* Division busied themselves with improving their positions, assisted by *Pioniere* of the division's combat engineer battalion. As far as possible, artillery-proof troop shelters were constructed, aimed as much towards comfort as for protection. Under *Brig.Fhr.* Brasack's direction, artillery fire plans were developed or modified to enable the corps and division artillery to more quickly and accurately deliver their fire in support of the troops in the front line or to disperse any Soviet troop concentrations.

New replacements began to arrive, prompting Becker to re-establish the division's *SS-Feld.Ers.Btl. 3*, which was then located in the village of Jánoscháza under the command of *Ostuf.* Alfred Atzrott. Most of the 1,058 new recruits were from the *Luftwaffe* and *Kriegsmarine*, prompting Atzrott to institute a hasty training program designed to prepare them for the rigors of ground combat. Shortages of *Unterführer* had to be addressed by establishing NCO training courses to prepare veteran junior enlisted SS men—the so-called *Reichsrottenführer* (corporals and lance corporals)—for this most demanding and critical leadership positions. The 70 NCOs assigned to the division from the air force or navy also needed further additional training if they were to be of any use whatsoever.[41]

During January and the first week of February, the division had been forced to comb through its administrative and logistics units, from which it was able to cull 1,000 men to beef up the understrength infantry battalions. This had the predictable effect of reducing the division's overall efficiency and capability, further decreasing its readiness. Slowly, these men were returned to their old positions in the *Tross*, but many of them had already fallen in battle by this point.[42] Fortunately, the division would have nearly a month to incorporate these new men into their ranks, but they were not the same as the men it had received during October and November the previous year outside of Warsaw. As events were to prove, the new intake were not as prone as their predecessors to adopting the "SS-spirit."

While the troops of the *IV. SS-Pz.Korps* took advantage of the relative calm, the *III. Pz.Korps* experienced a fair amount of combat, as did the Hungarian *3. Armee*. Despite Marshal Tolbukhin's decision to halt large-scale operations, at the tactical level his armies continued to scramble for advantageous positions while the battle between Lakes Velencze and Balaton was still in progress. Though Stuhlweissenburg was out of reach for the time being, there was still a chance that a foothold in the *Margarethestellung* could be taken and retained, especially if the Hungarian *25. Inf. Div.* was struck so hard it collapsed. Seen in this light, the continuing offensive operations against Breith's corps and Heszlényi's army by the 4th Guards Army and 26th Army, no matter how limited the gains, make eminent sense.

Along the right flank of the *III. Pz.Korps*, which it shared with the adjacent *Div. Gr. von Roden* (formerly known as *Div.Gr. Pape*), the *23. Pz.Div.* fought off an attempt by Soviet forces to advance northwards along the highway leading through Sárkeresztur towards Stuhlweissenburg. At the same time, a similar attack took place against the right flank of the *3. Pz.Div.*, which achieved a local penetration east of the highway before it too was driven back. In the area immediately west of Seregélyes, the *3. Pz.Div.* fought off another attempt by the XXIII Tank Corps to seize key ground in front of the *Margarethestellung*, with the attackers forced to withdraw after losing a T-34, an SP gun, and five antitank guns.

Overall, only 24 Soviet tanks were observed in the corps area of operations, but most of these were not committed to the fight, a sign that they were being held back.[43] Later that day, the *3. Pz.Div.* was ordered to begin withdrawing its units from the front lines and move into the area surrounding the town of Polgárdi, where it would temporarily become part of the *A.Gr. Balck/6. Armee* reserve. Its portion of the front line would be divided up by the *23. Pz.Div.* and *K.Gr. Wiking.*[44] This movement also placed it squarely in the path of the oncoming Soviet advance, less than 10 kilometers away to the south.

The bitterest fighting in Breith's area that day took place around Dinnyés, where the 180 men from the *Wiking* Division—including the survivors of *I. Btl./Norge* and *Danmark*—held out against an attack by the 16th Mechanized Brigade, which they fended off after destroying three JS-II heavy tanks. Another battalion-sized Soviet force of 300 men from the 3rd Tank Brigade, seeking to slip past *K.Gr. Wiking* along the railway line west of Dinnyés in a further attempt to cut off the garrison, was engaged by troops from the *Germania* Regiment defending the *Margarethestellung* in the vicinity of Börgönd, forcing them to retreat. On the same day, *K.Gr. Wiking's* *SS-Pz.Rgt. 5* recorded its 1,000th tank kill since its first commitment to battle during the relief of Kovel on 28 March 1944.[45] That evening, *Oberf.* Ullrich learned that his division would be rejoining the *IV. SS-Pz.Korps* the following day.

The only fighting that the commander of *A. Gr. Balck/6. Armee* was truly concerned about that day involved the situation unfolding in the Hungarian *3. Armee* sector, where its *25. Inf.Div.* was being slowly ground into bits. While *Div.Gr. von Roden* was able to hold on to its sector in the center of the Hungarian line, to its left the Hungarian regiment arrayed between the villages of Csösz and Balaton Bozsok was overrun by a large force supported by 15 tanks from the XVIII Tank Corps that quickly punched a hole 12 kilometers wide and 3 kilometers deep. Another Soviet force supported by 10 tanks carried out an attack several kilometers to the west against the town of Mezöszentgyörgy, where a Hungarian battalion from *Inf.Rgt. 25*—accompanied by 24 Hungarian-manned *Jg.Pz. 38t Hetzers* from their *Sturm-Art. Btl. 20*—conducted a counterattack that brought the Soviet force to a halt.[46]

To provide additional backing to the Hungarian *3. Armee* should the following day bring a decisive Soviet breakthrough along its front, Balck, with the permission of *H.Gr. Süd*, placed the *1. Pz.Div.*, *s.Pz.Abt. 509*, and *I. Abt./Pz.Rgt. 24* directly under Heszlényi's army. Along with the armor supporting the Hungarian *25. Inf. Div.*, this would create a nearly unstoppable force that Lt.Gen. Gagen's spearheads would be unable to withstand when Balck launched his counterattack against them the following day.[47]

Along the *Div.Gr. von Roden* left flank, the farming community of Felsöternocza fell to a Soviet two-regiment assault that managed to advance 1.5 kilometers beyond this point until it was attacked in the flank by the massed combat power of *K.Gr. Martini* of the *6. Pz.Div.*, which had just restored the situation in Csösz. The

Soviet force was thrown back, Felsöternocza reoccupied, and the link between the Hungarian *3. Armee* and *III. Pz.Korps* temporarily restored. Throughout the day, both German and Hungarian forces had fought hard, but it was becoming apparent that the Hungarian *25. Inf.Div.* was nearing the end of its strength. How much longer it could withstand such punishment was an open question, hence Balck's decision to backstop the Hungarian portion of the *Margarethestellung* with the escort companies from both the *Totenkopf* and *Wiking* Divisions.

Once again, bad flying weather rendered any effective intervention by both sides nearly impossible, allowing only high-altitude reconnaissance flights that were unable to provide much in the way of useful intelligence. Resupply of Budapest would be attempted again that evening, though the available drop zones had shrunk to a very small area around the castle and fortress, rendering any accurate delivery of supplies problematic. But the effort would be made all the same.

Soviet plans and intentions in the short term had not changed. The events of 9 February, seen in the light of the last several days, once again appeared to be last-minute jockeying for favorable positions for future operations, although the size and determination of German-led counterattacks was making these attempts difficult and costly. The continuing pressure being placed against the Hungarian *3. Armee* was beginning to pay off and there were clear signs that its disintegration was imminent. There is no indication that Gagen or his subordinate commanders were aware of the counterattack that Balck was preparing, otherwise he would have had his forward units stop and consolidate, like General Zakharov's corps had. Thus, another movement to contact between two unsuspecting enemy forces would take place, to the disadvantage of the troops of the 26th Army.

That evening, Balck's chief of staff argued with *Gen.Lt.* von Grolman about the need to withdraw the troops from *K.Gr. Wiking* holding Dinnyés, an exposed position outside of the *Margarethestellung* that would be lost sooner or later. Its 180-man garrison was needed elsewhere, an indication of how dire the German manpower situation had become. Both Gaedke and von Grolman discussed the matter several times that day, but von Grolman finally relented.[48] As for Balck, he was focused on the attack the following day by the *1. Pz.Div.* and the need to shore up the Hungarian *3. Armee* and its one division fighting south of Lake Balaton, the *25. Inf.Div.* Although it had fought well up to this point, it was clearly reaching the time when it would become combat ineffective; hence the need to buy time in order to get it behind the safety of the *Margarethestellung*. Due to the change in the orientation of its front lines from southeast to the south, he also ordered a boundary change the next day between the *IV. SS-Pz.Korps* and the *III. Pz.Korps*.

Wöhler himself was concerned with larger matters, and had already set his staff to work on developing the plan to eliminate the Gran bridgehead, using one of the SS corps from the arriving *6. Pz.Armee* along with *IV. Pz.Korps FHH* of the *8. Armee*.

Another concern of Wöhler's was the increasing scarcity of fuel and ammunition. To alleviate the shortages, *H.Gr. Süd* ordered units to "drastically reduce the use of artillery ammunition in quiet sectors of the front."[49] Fuel rationing measures had been in effect for some time, a constant headache not only for the army group commander, but to those as far down the chain of command as individual tank and *Panzergrenadier* companies. There had been instances during *Unternehmen Konrad I——III* when armored units had been stalled for hours or even as long as a day due to want of fuel; if any future efforts in Hungary were to succeed, fuel reserves had to be built up. Until then, commanders at every level would have to economize.

Dawn on 10 February was again cloudy and cold. Temperatures gradually increased from freezing point to a high of 39 degrees Fahrenheit, as the skies slowly cleared during the afternoon. The thaw continued, affecting off-road travel. That morning, the *IV. SS-Pz.Korps* began carrying out the directive it had received the previous night to shift its corps boundary further to the south, extending it as far as the western outskirts of Seregélyes, through Föveny Puszta, and to Urhida in the west. This required that the *356. Inf.Div.* shift its lines as far south as the eastern-most extension of the *Margarethestellung*, where it would take up positions to the left of *K.Gr. Wiking*. A Soviet battalion tried to interfere with the movement of the *356. Inf.Div.* into its new positions, but it was forced to withdraw by German artillery fire. To their relief, the men of *K.Gr. Wiking* finally returned to Gille's order of battle, though Ullrich's men had to continue defending the *Margarethestellung* between Börgönd and Belsöbáránd.[50]

On the corps' left flank, *Div.Gr. Holste* reported that its front line had awoken to a battalion-strong Soviet attack supported by two tanks that attempted to penetrate its defenses before it was smashed by heavy fire. Another Soviet attack that day, aimed at the seam between the Hungarian *2. Pz.Div.* and the neighboring Hungarian *VIII. Armee-Korps*, also failed. In the center of the corps' *HKL*, the *Totenkopf* Division initiated nightly combat patrols, designed to gather information from Soviet forces opposite its position regarding the enemy's future plans and intentions. In other developments, both *I. Btl./Norge* and *I. Btl./Danmark*—which had been withdrawn from Dinnyés and sent to rest facilities in the *Totenkopf* Division's rear area—were tactically subordinated to Becker's division, though both were designated part of the corps reserve. Each battalion would require a period of rest and rehabilitation before they would be ready for combat again.[51] For instance, during the fighting of the past several weeks, *Stubaf.* Vogt's battalion had been reduced to an effective strength of only 40 men.[52] Other than the extension of the corps' right flank to the south, little other combat activity took place.

To the right of the *IV. SS-Pz.Korps*, the *23. Pz.Div.* continued its active defense, driving off a Soviet battalion that once again attempted to penetrate its line between the Malom and Sárviz Canals. Southwest of Felsöszentiván, enemy troops managed to achieve a small local penetration, but this was later sealed off and wiped out by another German counterattack. During the day, the remaining units of the *3. Pz.Div.* continued withdrawing to their assembly area around Polgárdi.

As it had been the day before, most of the fighting on 10 February took place in the Hungarian *3. Armee* area of operations. To relieve the pressure against the *25. Inf.Div.*, the counterattack by the *1. Pz.Div.* began at 7 a.m., and by 10 a.m. had penetrated Soviet lines and advanced as far as Felsöternocza. *Generalmajor* Thünert's division, augmented by several Hungarian infantry battalions, had to overcome strong enemy resistance and suffered the loss of several tanks due to mines and antitank guns. Within the village of Felsöternocza, bitter close-quarters fighting broke out around its strongly built farmhouses, forcing German commanders to call forward the division's 15cm SP *Hummel* howitzers to blast their positions point-blank. By the late afternoon, the *1. Pz.Div.* had advanced as far south as Mezöszentgyörgy and broken the back of their opponents, destroying a least one rifle regiment, five tanks, 32 antitank guns, and eight artillery pieces for the loss of 115 of its own men and the temporary loss of three tanks.[53]

To the left of the *1 Pz.Div.*, the supporting attack by *K.Gr. Martini* of the *6. Pz.Div.*, supported by a battalion of Hungarian troops, attacked Soviet forces entrenched in the vineyards west of Soponya to regain the town of Csösz, which finally fell after heavy fighting. The consolidated report submitted that evening stated, "Between Lake Balaton and the Sárviz Canal, our armored assault groups struck deep into the salient made by the enemy and destroyed strong enemy forces. The fighting to complete the elimination of the enemy forces that broke through is still underway. East of the Sárviz Canal, weak enemy attacks were driven off." Thus, the danger to the right flank of *A.Gr. Balck/6. Armee* was temporarily averted and the Hungarian *25. Inf.Div.* survived to fight another day. On balance, this division had fought well but at a high price: between 20 January and 10 February 1945, the Hungarians suffered the loss of 567 men killed in action, 1,764 wounded, and 1,882 missing in action, representing over half of the division's available *Kampfstärke*.[54]

The air forces of both sides were again grounded for most of the day, which benefited the German counterattack the most. Although the skies above the battlefield were mostly clear, heavy ground fog plagued the airfields of both combatants, rendering air operations too risky to attempt. Again, only reconnaissance aircraft were able to take to the skies, though the Germans were able to launch some deep strikes with a few *Jagdflieger* (fighter aircraft) against Soviet locomotives and rail traffic in the rear area of the Third Ukrainian Front. The weather over Budapest prevented any accurate drops that evening, though in another day that problem would solve itself when the garrison began its desperate breakout attempt. Still, *Luftflotte 4* would make one last attempt to deliver supplies during the night of 10/11 February.

That evening, to simplify command and control, Balck detached *Div.Gr. von Roden*, the entire Hungarian *25. Inf.Div.*, and *K.Gr. Martini* of the *6. Pz.Div.* from the Hungarian *3. Armee* and placed them under the control of the *III. Pz.Korps*, along with the *1. Pz.Div. Generalleutnant* Heszlényi's *3. Armee* would once again be made responsible only for the defense of the northern shore of Lake Balaton, a task easily within its capabilities, especially since the ice covering the lake had begun to melt. The task for *A.Gr. Balck/6. Armee* for the following day was relatively simple: the *IV. SS-Pz.Korps* and *Korpsgruppe Harteneck* would continue defending their present positions; the *III. Pz.Korps* would finish eliminating any remaining enemy forces between the eastern shore of Lake Balaton and the Sárviz Canal.

On 10 February, the weekly unit status reports of all the brigade-sized and divisional maneuver units (infantry, cavalry, and armor) of *A.Gr. Balck/6. Armee* were submitted to the headquarters of *H.Gr. Süd*, which consolidated them with the reports from its other two armies (*2. Pz.* and *8. Armee*) for submission to the *OKH* chief of staff for the evening situation briefing for Hitler in Berlin. This document provides an illuminating view into the material condition of each unit as an expression of combat power in terms of *Kampfstärke* (infantry, engineers, and reconnaissance troops), anti-armor weapons and armored fighting vehicles (tanks, assault guns, and tank destroyers), available artillery, and percentage of mobility, whether horse-drawn or mechanized. Based on these metrics, a unit's commander then awarded his unit a subjective *Kampfwert*, ranging from *Stufung* (step/category) I (the highest) to *Stufung V* (the lowest). It also illustrates how much the strength of the units in the *IV. SS-Pz.Korps* had declined after 41 continuous days of heavy and sustained combat.

The *Totenkopf* Division on this date reported that it had one *meistens-stark* (mostly strong or nearly full-strength) infantry battalion of 300–400 men, two infantry battalions of *durchschnitt* (average) strength of 200–300 men, four *schwach* (weak) battalions of 100–200 men, as well as one average-strength combat engineer battalion and a strong *Feld-Ersatz* battalion. In addition, it fielded 12 operational heavy antitank guns, 11 operational assault guns, two operational *Jg.Pz. IV* tank destroyers, 10 *Pz. IVs*, eight operational *Pz. V* Panthers, and two *Pz. VI* Tiger Is. It also had five light and four heavy artillery batteries, with approximately 42 howitzers and field cannon. Its mobility was rated at 85 percent, because it had a high number of its wheeled vehicles still operational. Overall, this earned the division a capability rating of *Stufe II*—signifying that it was suitable for limited offensive assignments, as well as fully suited for defense. This gave Balck, as well as Wöhler, a good understanding of what the division was still capable of in terms of the kind of missions it could still be expected to carry out successfully.[55]

The report of the *Wiking* Division was not so encouraging. According to the same *Wochenmeldung*, it reported only two battalions of average strength, five *abgekämpft* ("fought -out", exhausted) battalions with a *Kampfstärke* of less than 100 men, one fought-out combat engineer battalion, and a strong *Feld-Ersatz* battalion. It also reported that it had two attachments—*I. Btl./Norge* and *I. Btl./Danmark*—both of which were also rated as fought-out. In regards to armor and antitank weapons, it had three operational antitank guns, two *Pz. IVs*, and seven operational *Pz. V* Panthers in its tank regiment. The only good news was that it still had nearly all of its artillery, reporting six light and four heavy batteries, for a total of 40 howitzers and field cannons. Its mobility was rated at only 44 percent. However, because it was temporarily designated as merely a *Kampfgruppe* instead of a fully capable division, Ullrich was allowed to assess his combat worthiness as a II, equivalent to that of a brigade, although had it been rated as a fully capable division, its *Kampfwert* would have been assessed much lower.

Oberst Kühl's evaluated his *356. Inf.Div.* as having a *Kampfwert* of III, meaning that it was fully suited for defensive combat, but nothing more than that. Two weeks of combat had not been kind to it, for it reported two average battalions, two weak ones, and one weak combat engineer battalion. Portions of its *Pz.Jag.Abt. 356* had finally arrived, reporting five operational antitank guns. It possessed nine light and two heavy batteries of artillery, a respectable number, though all of them were horse-drawn. In terms of mobility, its horse-drawn transport was rated at 85 percent ready and its small motorized component at 75 percent. It was the weakest division in Gille's corps and had not particularly distinguished itself so far.

Finally, *Div.Group Holste* was evaluated, with Holste reporting his own *4. Kav. Brig.* as having three average and two weak battalions, five heavy antitank guns, eight assault guns, one tank destroyer (*Jg.Pz. IV*), three light artillery batteries, and three heavy mortar batteries. Its mobility was assessed at 65 percent in regards to its horse-drawn equipment and 55 percent in terms of motorized equipment. It was also rated as a *II*. The addition of several more artillery batteries and its own combat engineer and reconnaissance battalions within the next week would soon elevate it to full division status.

By far the weakest unit in Gille's order of battle was the Hungarian *2. Pz.Div.* Its acting commander, *Oberst* Vitéz-Zadar, reported having one strong, one average, and two weak infantry battalions, as well as one weak combat engineer battalion. At that moment, it also reported only two operational antitank guns, but had 16 fully operational Pz. IVs. Its degree of mobility was assessed at only 43 percent, earning it the lowest *Kampfwert* of IV, indicating that it was suited only for limited defensive assignments. Combining it with the *4. Kav.Brig.* at least gave Gille something approximating the strength of a weak *Panzergrenadier* division on his left flank, though this was a paper evaluation only. So far, the Hungarian armored division had fought tolerably well.

In this report, none of the *IV. SS-Pz.Korps* corps troops or attached *Heerestruppen* were evaluated; although this would have boosted the number of artillery, rocket launcher, assault gun, and separate tank battalions. Still, with these reports, Gille, Balck, and Wöhler would have been able to obtain a good understanding of the capabilities of each of the units. Gille's assessment would have been reinforced by daily visits to the front line, as well as evening dinners with selected commanders and staff members of subordinate units, a practice that he was able to re-establish now that operations in his defensive sector had diminished to a "steady-state" level. His primary concern for the next several weeks, besides continuing the successful defense of his widely spaced corps' front line, was the rebuilding of his two SS divisions. Both had fought hard during the past month and a half but had suffered correspondingly, and he needed to get them as ready as possible before their next important assignment.

By this point Gille knew that his corps would not be playing a role in the upcoming *Südwind* offensive scheduled to take place north of the Danube. However, as a corps commander near the area of operations where it would unfold, he did have the "need to know," so he would have been briefed on the plan for what was about to take place on his far left flank and provided with some knowledge about the great offensive planned for the end of the month that would involve the *6. Pz.Armee*. His corps' role in that impending operation at this early stage was still speculative, though if it took place where he thought it would, the *IV. SS-Pz.Korps* most likely would play a role. But as 10 February came to an end, all eyes were drawn to Budapest, where the final act of the drama that began on Christmas Day 1945 was about to unfold.

Sunday, 11 February began like any other day. As far as nights go, that of 10/11 February was relatively uneventful. The *A.Gr. Balck/6. Armee* morning report was short and succinct:

> On the Lake Balaton Front and by *Div.Gr. von Roden*, the night passed quietly. Our attack to recapture Csösz is still in progress. Weak enemy probes against the eastern edge of Stuhlweissenburg were fended off. Along the entire front of the *I. Kav.Korps* numerous platoon-to company-sized attacks were fought off. Northwest of Gant one of our strongpoints was lost. Our own counterattack is in progress.[56]

The early morning weather was cloudy, with temperatures once again hovering around freezing. Ice floes were reported on the upper Danube near Gran. With daybreak, temperatures again rose to the high 30s and clouds were reported in the mid altitudes. Local downpours were reported throughout the area, as well as stationary fog. The conditions of roadways were unchanged.

For the evening input to the daily *Tagesmeldung*, both the *IV. SS-Pz.Korps* and *Korpsgruppe Harteneck/I. Kav.Korps* reported no combat activity occurring in their sectors worth mentioning. What fighting that did occur in the *A.Gr. Balck/6. Armee* area of operations took place between the eastern shores of Lake Balaton and the Sárviz Canal, where *Gen.d.Pz.Tr.* Hermann Breith's *III. Pz.Korps*, now in control of everything south of the *IV. SS-Pz.Korps*, fought throughout the day to consolidate the gains it had made the day before and ensure that Soviet forces did not make a dash for the *Margarethestellung*, despite the fact that it appeared that the Hungarian *25. Inf.Div.* would be able to reach it in time. Between the Malom and Sárviz Canals, the Hungarian *I. Btl./Inf.Rgt. 26* was pushed back several kilometers towards the northeast by a Soviet attack, but with the support of portions of *Pz.Aufkl.Abt. 23*, the battalion was able to retake its old positions and re-establish its *HKL*.

On the left flank of the corps, a battalion-sized Soviet attack, preceded by an artillery barrage, was able to carry out a series of local penetrations in the Felsöszentiván area, but these were sealed off by counterattacks. On the left flank of the *23. Pz.Div.*, Soviet forces supported by five tanks broke through one of the division's battle positions, prompting a counterattack by the division before the attack reached the *HKL*. On the right, the entire *3. Pz.Div.*—brought out of reserve for the occasion—joined the fray, along with the *1. Pz.Div.*, *K.Gr. Martini* of the *6. Pz.Div.*, and portions of the Hungarian *25. Inf.Div.* Heavy fighting took place at Balaton Bozsok, Siófok, Lepseny, Mezöszentgyörgy, and Kisláng.

Against extraordinarily tough Soviet resistance, including that given by a punishment battalion, the Germans and Hungarians inexorably fought their way forward. The *1. Pz.Div.* carried out a shallow envelopment northeast of Felsöternocza and was able to link up with the right flank of a battlegroup from the *23. Pz.Div.* that was attacking from the opposite direction. Together, both divisions re-established a solid defensive line along the entire *III. Pz.Korps* front. Finally, during the night, the tactically important town of Csösz was finally retaken. For the next day, operations by the *III. Pz.Korps* would continue until all of the Soviet forces had been destroyed or driven back a safe distance away from the *Margarethestellung* so the Hungarians could finish occupying it in peace.

On account of bad weather, daylight flight operations again were limited. The last week had been one of the worst in regards to conducting flight operations; both sides had been equally affected and most of their squadrons had been grounded. During the night of 10/11 February, *Luftflotte 4* made one last supreme effort to deliver badly needed supplies to the *IX. SS-Geb.Korps*. Of the 22 *Ju-52*s that took off, 15 made it to the target area above the city and dropped 11.6 metric tons (12.7 short tons) of supply bundles "in the blind" over Pfeffer-Wildenbruch's troops. How much of this landed within their lines will never be known.

While fighting raged between Lake Balaton and the Sárviz Canal in the *A.Gr. Balck/6. Armee* area, the fighting in Budapest was reaching its bloody climax. Although it would only affect the *IV. SS-Pz.Korps* tangentially, many of the officers on Gille's staff and in the *Totenkopf* and *Wiking* Divisions had friends in Pfeffer-Wildenbruch's *IX. SS-Geb.Korps*. Some, such as Franz Hack of the *Westland* Regiment, had served with them, such as *Brig.Fhr.* Joachim Rumohr, commander of the *8. SS-Kav.Div. Florian Geyer*. Many of Gille's troops had spoken to some of their comrades by radio during each of the three failed relief attempts, and had exhorted them to "keep holding on, we're on the way!" For many of the SS veterans, they had taken the mission of relieving Budapest very seriously, which had motivated the men to keep on going whenever the situation seemed desperate. Some SS men were distraught when they received the final news that the relief attempt had been given up and were faced with the reality that the troops trapped in the city had been left in the lurch. There was nothing more to be done, but they had done all that was humanly possible. As Günther Lange wrote, "We have no guilt!"

The initiative now lay in the hands of the commander of the *IX. SS-Geb. Korps*, *Ogruf.* Pfeffer-Wildenbruch. Despite being denied the freedom of action or permission to break out that he had repeatedly requested, he finally decided on his own initiative that he would order his troops to begin the operation at 10 p.m. on 11 February. His choices were stark: either surrender his command like *G.FM.* Friedrich von Paulus had done with his *6. Armee* at Stalingrad two years before—an unthinkable act for a dedicated senior SS officer—or fight to the last round as ordered and certainly sacrifice the lives of his men.

He cared for neither choice, opting instead for a breakout. In a dramatic radio message to the *6. Armee* commander, composed at 3:50 p.m. and sent out that afternoon, Pfeffer-Wildenbruch announced:

1) Rations are used up, the last round is in the barrel. The choice is capitulation or the defenseless massacre of the Budapest garrison. As a result, I have decided to take to the offensive with the remaining combat effective German elements, Honvéds, and Arrow Cross members … to fight to a new combat and supply position.
2) We will break out with the fall of darkness on 11 February. Request passage between Szomor–Máriahalom [i.e., Kirva]. If passage not possible there, I will advance into the Pilis Mountains. Request passage there in the area north of Pilisszentlélek.
3) Light Signals: Two Green Flares = friendly troops.
4) Unit strength:

> German 23,900 of which 9,600 wounded
> Hungarian 20,000 of which 2,000 wounded
> Civilians 80–100,000

Received by *A. Gr. Balck*: 10:40 p.m. 11 February 1945[57]

A breakout by this late stage of the siege stood little chance of success. Had it been ordered two weeks before, when the *IV. SS-Pz. Korps* was little more than 20 kilometers away along the Váli River, it might have worked, especially if the encircled garrison had been able to meet Gille's spearheads halfway.

On 26 January, the *IX. SS-Geb.Korps* still had a number of able-bodied fighting men, a few operational tanks and other armored vehicles, and several battalions of artillery as well as sufficient ammunition and fuel for a one-way trip. But all along, Hitler did not want to give the city up, even if every last man in Pfeffer-Wildenbruch's corps perished. Neither Balck nor Wöhler had the courage to disobey the *Führer*. As a corps commander, Gille did not have the authority to order it, but if either of his higher commanders had allowed him freedom of action, he probably would have taken advantage of it; his own troops would certainly have urged him to do so.

However, by 11 February, this was all but a pipe dream. The *IX. SS-Geb.Korps* had few fighting troops, no more fuel for its remaining armored fighting vehicles, and its artillery was out of ammunition. Its troops would have to fight through at least a dozen blocks of enemy-occupied urban area without heavy weapons in order to break out, at which point they would still have to march through 15–20 kilometers of open country held by powerful enemy forces to reach the nearest German unit, which happened to be the *3. Kav.Brig.* defending in the area between Mány and Szomor. How the troops breaking out would manage to bring along so many wounded was left unsaid. As it turned out, a large number of them were left behind in cellars and other buildings that had been converted into hospitals and dressing stations. A plan had been worked out to leave them under the protection of the Papal Nuncio, but Pfeffer-Wildenbruch had waited too late to carry out effective coordination. In any case, the Red Army's surrender ultimatum and its generous terms had been refused weeks before. Besides, relying upon international law and the Vatican at this point for protection was illusory.

The commander of *A.Gr. Balck/6. Armee* received Pfeffer-Wildenbruch's message at 7:45 p.m. that evening, notifying him that the Budapest garrison would break out sometime that night. No coordination had been made by Balck's staff with the encircled garrison concerning the breakout, and no preparations had been made to assist it because doing so had been forbidden by Hitler himself, who in any case had already made up his mind. The radio message from *IX. SS-Geb.Korps* announcing the breakout did not reach the hand of *Gen.d.Inf.* Wöhler until 10:30 p.m., for reasons unknown. His chief of staff, von Grolman, believed that the garrison stood little chance of making it through safely because he was certain that they would never be able to fight their way through the II Guards Mechanized Corps and V Guards Cavalry Corps, both of which stood squarely in their path. Regardless, Wöhler ensured that *OKH* was notified of the breakout 35 minutes later.[58]

Plans were hurriedly put together by the staffs of *H.Gr. Süd* and *A.Gr. Balck* to assemble some kind of armored relief force that could link up with the escaping garrison and ensure their passage through German lines. The flaw in any such plan was that it would require two or three days to assemble such a force, and by then it would be over. The only available force that could be used without weakening the front lines was the one currently assembling in the Raab–Komorn area from the *6. Pz.Armee*, but Wöhler knew that Hitler would never approve such a course of action because this army had been brought to Hungary to serve as the linchpin of his grandiose plan to reclaim the west bank of the Danube; any premature commitment might result in heavy losses for no appreciable gain.

Besides, as earlier mentioned, Hitler had already expressly forbidden a breakout, and to approve a plan now would have gone completely against his character. As previously demonstrated at Stalingrad, Hitler never cared about the fate of his men; the lives of the Budapest garrison meant nothing to him. He had already written them off. *Heeresgruppe Süd* had not, however, and its leaders still hoped for the best. The next morning, the following entry was made in the *H.Gr. Süd* war diary:

The Budapest garrison decided to break out after the western bridgehead [i.e., Buda] had been split open yesterday by an enemy attack between the citadel and the palace, in which the artillery positions and the aerial resupply field were lost. It had defended the city during seven weeks of constant, stubborn, house-to-house fighting without adequate supplies; it had tied up considerable enemy artillery, tank, and infantry forces; and it had kept the enemy from using the important supply route along the west bank through the city.[59]

By the time this report had been written, the remnants of the garrison had already initiated their breakout attack from the citadel to the northwest nearly 12 hours earlier. The *IX. SS-Geb.Korps* operational section had already shut down its radio transmitter, and now all that *H.Gr. Süd* and *A.Gr. Balck* could do was wait. It would take nearly half a day before word began to filter back to *A.Gr. Balck/6. Armee* about the breakout's progress.

The results were predictable. It was a bloodbath. Pfeffer-Wildenbruch had intended his corps to break out in three separate groups and fight their way towards the northwest, but the plan fell apart almost immediately when the spearheads encountered heavy Soviet defensive fire, barricades, and minefields. To top it off, the troops of the 46th Army had been waiting for them. To make matters worse, Pfeffer-Wildenbruch had not issued his plan for the breakout until a few hours before it began, and even then to his top commanders only; most of the remaining combat units did not get their orders until the very moment the attack was to begin. Surprised by the degree of enemy resistance, most of the assault formations broke up into smaller groups and had to fight their way through the western part of the city using only rifles, machine guns, and *Panzerfausts*. Some troops made their way initially through the city's sewer system. Some gave up after only one attempt and either returned to their cellars, or, like many of the SS troops, shot themselves.

The only units that stood much of a chance of escaping were the combat units that had borne the brunt of the fighting from the beginning—approximately 12,000–20,000 men from the *13. Pz.Div., Pz.Gren.Div. FHH, 8. SS-Kav.Div.* and to a lesser extent the *22. SS-Kav.Div.* Most of the Hungarian troops, except for fanatical Arrow Cross members, faded away or simply surrendered. Men who were wounded during the escape attempt were usually left behind. Once they reached the city's western outskirts, most of those who had fought their way out struck out towards the west, seeking to link up somewhere in the area between Zsámbék and Bicske, though a hardy few took the longer route through the Pilis Mountains towards Gran.

Having thought that getting out of the city meant that they were in the clear, the survivors were shocked when they were greeted by a virtual curtain of fire in the hills between Budaörs, Budakeszi, and Pesthidekút, where the troops of the LXXV Rifle Corps and XXXVII Guards Rifle Corps constituting the inner ring of encirclement were waiting for them. For the few groups that were able to slip past this net, they still had to fight their way through or infiltrate the lines of the outer ring of encirclement, held by the divisions of the II Guards Mechanized Corps, XXIII Rifle Corps, V Guards Cavalry Corps, and XXXI Guards Rifle Corps. Traveling in small groups of less than 100 men, the hardiest souls sought shelter in the forests, hills, and outlying buildings during the day, moving only at night. They were hunted down and killed by the hundreds, relatively few being captured during the breakout itself. Many of them, exhausted and without food, simply surrendered to the first Soviet unit they found.

The first group of survivors appeared in the area around Szomor held by the *3. Kav.Brig.* on 13 February, nearly two days after the breakout began. This group, consisting of three German officers, one Hungarian officer, and 23 enlisted men, told a harrowing tale of how they had survived the breakout and the efforts of the Soviets to hunt them down. The officers stated that command and control was almost immediately lost at the beginning of the operation, and that they had fought their way out on their own without the benefit of any sort of tactical plan, food, or ammunition. Some sought shelter with Hungarian civilians, while other men attempted to escape by themselves.

The only successful large-scale attempt to relieve the breakout was that made by the *96. Inf.Div.* on 15 February, when *Gen.d.Kav.* Harteneck authorized its commander, *Gen.Maj.* Harrendorf, to carry out a relief operation, again near Szomor, in coordination with the neighboring *3. Kav.Brig. Major* Pipo, the commander of *Füs.Btl. 96*, launched the attack with his battalion supported by nine assault guns from the *3. Kav.Brig.* After making initial progress, Pipo's attack ran into strong Soviet resistance, though his *Füsiliere* kept going, despite numerous antipersonnel mines that killed and wounded many of them. This attack was able to rescue 50 men of the *IX. SS-Geb.Korps* near Szomor, but it had cost Pipo's battalion twice that number of men killed or wounded.[60]

By 16 February, it was all over. The last 14 survivors made it to German lines that day, though it is believed that other isolated small groups kept trying to make their way out long after the fighting was over. Other than the efforts by the *3. Kav.Brig.* and *96. Inf.Div.*, no other relief attempts materialized. The *Luftwaffe* had conducted numerous reconnaissance flights over the area throughout the breakout attempt and dropped supply bundles over any groups of men that they could identify as German or Hungarian troops. Efforts by *H.Gr. Süd* and *A.Gr. Balck* in the immediate aftermath of the breakout to assemble a relief force to attack towards the city came to nothing. If anything, these "paper" efforts were most likely initiated by Wöhler and Balck to assuage their own consciences, so at least they could claim afterwards that "they had tried." Ironically, the best chances that any relief force ever had of reaching the city before it was too late had already occurred, not once, not twice, but three times—on 6, 12, and 26 January.

The final report written by *Gen.d.Inf.* Wöhler's headquarters on 16 February serves as the garrison's epitaph. Something had to be said to commemorate the sacrifices made by the troops and offer it up as some kind of inspiring or morale-boosting event. It simply stated:

> After heroic resistance, the garrison had to evacuate the section of the city east of the Danube on 18 January. Squeezed together in a very small area, the garrison continued to defy all attacks. The worries concerning a city of millions, the extraordinarily slim rations as a consequence of inadequate air supply because of foul weather, the high number and inadequate care of the wounded, and the moral burden imposed as a result of the presence of the civilian population placed the greatest possible demands on the fighting spirit and leadership of the forces. This unique achievement came from the inseparable cohesiveness of the formations of the *Heer*, the *Waffen-SS*, the Hungarian Forces and the members of the Arrow Cross Party, all under the command of *SS-Obergruppenführer und General der Waffen-SS* Pfeffer-Wildenbruch.[61]

A final tally included in an annex of the final report laid out the butcher's bill. There were 44,200 German and Hungarian troops still reported on the rolls of the *IX. SS-Geb.Korps* as of the morning of 11 February, including 11,600 wounded. Only between 600 and 800 men fought their way out, though accounts vary. The most definitive accounting by Ungváry states that the number was approximately 700, though the exact number may never be known.[62]

Marshal Malinovsky's Second Ukrainian Front claimed to have killed approximately 19,250 German and Hungarian troops during the breakout, and had captured approximately 23,350 more between 11 and 15 February. How many of the wounded survived is not known. All of the corps' equipment, including all of the armored vehicles of two mechanized divisions, was lost and the city of Budapest was left in ruins, its population shattered and destitute. Soviet casualties had been astronomical. In the 108-day period from when the encirclement of Budapest began at the end of November 1944, through the 7-week siege itself, and until its final capture on 12 February 1945, the Second and Third Ukrainian Fronts estimated that they had suffered the combined loss of 44,000 troops killed in action, 130,000 wounded, and 2,000 captured, for a total of 176,000 casualties, well over twice the number suffered by the *IX. SS-Geb.Korps*.[63] After 17 February, the words "Budapest" and "*IX. SS-Geb.Korps*" no longer appeared in any official German communiques.

As for *Ogruf.* Karl Pfeffer-Wildenbruch, whose award of the Knight's Cross had been approved by Hitler on 10 February and delivered to him by air the same day (it did not land within the citadel and hence he never received it until 1955) as an incentive to fight to the death, he and his staff attempted to escape the city via the Czertovaya Canal. They did not get very far before they were captured after taking shelter in a villa the following morning. As they were led out by their captors, he and his staff were photographed and his image immediately used for Soviet propaganda purposes. Although he had urged his men to carry out a near-suicidal escape attempt, he himself had surrendered without a fight. Pfeffer-Wildenbruch was also personally berated by Marshal Malinovsky shortly after his capture, purportedly for holding on as long as he did. An enraged Malinovsky told him, "If I weren't obliged to account for your head in Moscow, I'd have you hanged in the main square of Buda."[64] The defeated German general did not return home until he had endured 10 years of harsh captivity in the Soviet Union. He died in an automobile accident in 1971.

This is not the place for an evaluation of Pfeffer-Wildenbruch's performance of duty or his fitness as a commander. Few would ever wish to have been burdened with the responsibilities assigned to him. Like von Paulus had been at Stalingrad, Hitler ordered Pfeffer-Wildenbruch to stand fast and defend his position to the last in order to tie up enemy troops that would have been used against German forces elsewhere. Once Budapest was surrounded, the only hope for relief rested on outside forces being marshaled in time to come to the rescue. Once these efforts failed, like the obedient solder he was, he kept his corps fighting for two more weeks, despite the tremendous odds stacked against them. Only when all hope was lost did he order a breakout, long after the point when it could have enjoyed any chances of success.

After the war, he was singled out for harsh criticism by Hermann Balck, who wrote that he was a general "who at best was a politician." Although some of his criticism of the SS commander was legitimate, most of it was not. Laying most of the blame for the disaster at the feet of a man who had been dead nearly ten years before he wrote his memoirs, Balck held him up as an example of what happens when a politician—"a police general at that!"—was put in charge of a large body of troops. Balck wrote, "All of this is a warning that politicians should keep their hands off military matters and they must never be put in a position of command in the face of the enemy. The soldier pays with his blood, and he is too valuable for that."[65]

Of course, Balck did not mention that Pfeffer-Wildenbruch had been a successful division commander, having led the *SS-Polizei-Division* 1939–40. Although he had served in a succession of *Ordnungspolizei* (Order Police) positions between 1941 and 1943, he assumed command of the *VI. SS-Freiwilligen Armee-Korps* in September 1943 and successfully led it until June 1944, leading it competently if not brilliantly during heavy fighting along the Baltic coast. In November 1944, he took command of the *IX. SS-Geb.Korps*, ably serving as its leader in the battles east of Budapest and during the siege of the city itself.

Commissioned in 1908, like Balck, he was a veteran of World War I, where he had earned the Iron Cross, 1st and 2nd Classes. Pfeffer-Wildenbruch was also a graduate of the wartime *Kriegsakademie* general staff course in 1914 and had remained in the postwar *Reichswehr* until 1919, having served a total of 12 years in the German Army.[66] So labeling him as a "politician" was not only a deliberate insult, but inaccurate. While the commander of the *IX. SS-Geb.Korps* was no military genius by any stretch of the imagination, he was probably just as competent as any other general officer of the *Heer* endowed with average abilities. He merely served as a convenient target of Balck's scorn after the war. Yet when he entered a remark about Pfeffer-Wildenbruch's performance into the official record on 5 February

1945 while outlining plans for another relief attempt, Balck described him as an "outstanding commander."[67]

Once the breakout began on the night of 11/12 February, and as it unfolded over the next several days, there was never any chance that the survivors of the *IX. SS-Geb. Korps* would reach the front lines of the *IV. SS-Pz. Korps*. It was simply too far away and interspersed with too many enemy troops and tanks. Since the corridor between Budapest and Stuhlweissenburg was mostly wide-open *Puszta*, unlike the route to the northwest that many of Pfeffer-Wildenbruch's men took that was interspersed with forests and mountains, anyone attempting a breakout to Gille's lines would never have stood a chance. There is no record showing that any of them, even if they had tried, ever made it that far. All that the men of the *IV. SS-Pz. Korps* could do was mourn the loss of so many men or gnash their teeth in frustration.

And so ended the saga of the Budapest siege and relief efforts. The men of the *IV. SS-Pz. Korps* had no reason to feel shame for the failure of *Unternehmen Konrad*. They had done everything they had been asked to do, at great costs to themselves. However, no amount of self-sacrifice and valor could overcome the flawed and overly ambitious plans concocted by *H. Gr. Süd* or *A. Gr. Balck*, especially given the unfavorable force ratios, terrain, and weather conditions. The failure of Wöhler and Guderian to coordinate *Konrad* with supporting attacks by the *2. Pz. Armee* and *H. Gr. F* until the operation was well underway stand as black marks against their otherwise excellent military records. Had these attacks been a part of an integrated plan from its inception, *Unternehmen Konrad* would most likely have succeeded; in fact, that was the course of action that Marshal Tolbukhin feared the most. This idea had not been given up entirely, as shall be seen. In the meantime, *Ogruf.* Gille and the rest of his corps would take advantage of the temporary lull in the fighting to do what they could to prepare for the next battle.

IV. SS-Pz.Korps Battle and Campaign Participation Credits awarded for the period 25 November 1944 to 22 February 1945

2. Armee (*Generaloberst* Walter Weiss) 25 November–24 December 1944

IV. SS-Pz.Korps:

Defensive Battles east of Modlin, 25 November–24 December 1944
Transfer to the Tata area (Hungary), 26–31 December 1944

6. Armee (*General der Panzertruppe* Hermann Balck) 31 December 1944–8 May 1945

Battles between the *Plattensee* (Lake Balaton) and Danube River, 19 December 1944–5 March 1945

IV. SS-Pz.Korps:

First Relief Attack of Budapests (Bicske and Pilis Mountains), 1–13 January 1945
Movement to Vesprém area and 2nd Relief Attack of Budapest, 14–27 January 1945 (Advance to the Danube)
Withdrawal Battles south of Stuhlweissenburg, 28 January–22 February 1945

Selected Orders of Battle, 6 December 1944 to 15 March 1945

6 December 1944

Corps Staff and Corps Headquarters Command

Divisions

3. SS-Panzer-Division Totenkopf
5. SS-Panzer-Division Wiking
    I. Bataillon/SS-Pz.Gren.Rgt. 23 Norge
    I. Bataillon/SS-Pz.Gren.Rgt. 24 Danmark
35. Infanterie-Division
252. Infanterie-Division
542. Volks-Grenadier Division

Army Troops

SS-ARKO 504
Werfer Brigade 1
Beobachtungs-Abteilung 21
SS-Werfer-Abteilung 504
II. Abteilung/schwere Heeres Artillerie-Regiment 69 (mot.)
Luftwaffe Flak-Regiment 77
Infanterie-Bataillon z.b.V. 560
Festungs Infanterie-Bataillon 1405
Landesschutz-Bataillon 998
II. (azerbaijani) Bataillon/Sonderverband "Bergmann"
Feldstrafgefangenen-Abteilung 1

Corps Troops

SS-Korps-Nachrichten-Abteilung 104
SS-Sanitäts-Abteilung 104
Feld-Ausbildungs-Battalion IV. SS-Panzerkorps

SS-Kraftfahrzeug-Kompanie 104
SS-Bekleidung-Instandsetzungs-Zug 504
SS-Feldpostamt 104

1–17 January 1945—Operation *Konrad I* and *II* (Budapest)

Corps Staff and Corps Headquarters Command

Divisions

3. SS-Panzer-Division Totenkopf
5. SS-Panzer-Division Wiking
    I. Bataillon/SS-Pz.Gren.Rgt. 23 Norge
    I. Bataillon/SS-Pz.Gren.Rgt. 24 Danmark
    1. ung. SS-Sturmjäger Regiment
    I. Abteilung/Panzer-Artillerie Regiment 80
    II. Abteilung/Heeres-Artillerie Brigade 959
6. Panzer-Division
96. Infanterie-Division
711. Infanterie-Division
Divisionsgruppe Pape
Divisionsgruppe Bieber
23. ung.Infanterie-Division

Army Troops

SS-ARKO 504
Sturmartillerie-Brigade 239
Sturmpanzer-Abteilung 219
Volks-Artillerie Korps 403
Volks-Werfer-Brigade 17
SS-Werfer-Abteilung 504
Heeres-Pionier Bataillon 751

Corps Troops

SS-Korps-Nachrichten-Abteilung 104
SS-Sanitäts-Abteilung 104
SS-Kraftfahrzeug-Kompanie 104
SS-Bekleidung-Instandsetzungs-Zug 504
SS-Feldpostamt 104

18–30 January 1945—Operation *Konrad III* (Budapest)

Corps Staff and Corps Headquarters Command

Divisions

3. SS-Panzer-Division Totenkopf
5. SS-Panzer-Division Wiking
1. Panzer-Division
3. Panzer-Division
356. Infanterie-Division
Divisionsgruppe Pape
25. ung. Infanterie-Division

Army Troops

SS-Regiment Ney
1. ung. SS-Sturmjäger Regiment
I. Bataillon/SS-Pz.Gren.Rgt. 23 Norge
I. Bataillon/SS-Pz.Gren.Rgt. 24 Danmark
schwere Panzer-Abteilung 509
I.Abteilung/Panzer Regiment 24
SS-ARKO 504
Sturmartillerie-Brigade 303
Sturmpanzer-Abteilung 219
Volks-Artillerie Korps 403
Volks-Werfer-Brigade 17
SS-Werfer-Abteilung 504
lei.Beob.Abt. 32
lei.Flak-Abt. 77
lei.Flak-Abt. 91
Brücken-Kolonne K 4
2. Kp./Heeres-Pionier Brig. (mot.) 52
1.Kp./Heeres-Pionier Btl. 255
1. and 3. Kp./Brückenbau-Btl. 552
Brücken-Kolonne B 929

Corps Troops

SS-Korps-Nachrichten-Abteilung 104
SS-Sanitäts-Abteilung 104
SS-Kraftfahrzeug-Kompanie 104

SS-Bekleidung-Instandsetzungs-Zug 104
SS-Feldpostamt 104

5–12 February 1945—Defense of Stuhlweissenburg

Corps Staff and Corps Headquarters Command
Divisions

3. *SS-Panzer-Division Totenkopf*
5. *SS-Panzer-Division Wiking*
356. Infanterie-Division
4. Kavallerie-Brigade
2. ung.Panzer-Division

Army Troops

SS-Regiment Ney
I. Bataillon/SS-Pz.Gren.Rgt. 23 Norge
I. Bataillon/SS-Pz.Gren.Rgt. 24 Danmark
SS-ARKO 504
SS-Werfer-Abteilung 504
schwere SS-Artillerie-Abteilung 504
SS-Beobachtungs-Abteilung 504

Corps Troops

SS-Korps-Nachrichten-Abteilung 104
SS-Sanitäts-Abteilung 104
SS-Kraftfahrzeug-Kompanie 104
SS-Bekleidung-Instandsetzungs-Zug 504
SS-Feldpostamt 104

Source: *Schematische Kriegsgliederung der Wehrmacht 1944–1945*, accessed on the *Deutsch-Russisches Projekt zur Digitalisierung Deutscher Dokumente in Archiven der Russischen Föderation* (German-Russian Project for Digitalizing German Documents in Archives of the Russian Federation), Records Group 500, Inventory 12451—High Command of the Ground Forces (OKH) Case 84–85, Diagrams of the Combat Strength of the German Ground Forces for 1944–45, accessed 10 January 2020.

German Army, *Waffen-SS* and U.S. Army Rank Equivalents

Wehrmacht-Heer	*Waffen-SS*	Abbreviation	U.S. Equivalent
Generalfeldmarschall	N/A	*G.F.M.*	General of the Army
Generaloberst	*SS-Obergruppenführer und Generaloberst der Waffen-SS*	*Gen.O./Obstgruf.*	General
General der Infantrie, Kavalerie, etc.	*SS-Obergruppenführer und General der Waffen-SS*	*Gen.d.Inf./Ogruf.*	Lieutenant General
Generalleutnant	*SS-Gruppenführer und Generalleutnant der Waffen-SS*	*Gen.Lt./Gruf.*	Major General
Generalmajor	*SS-Brigadeführer und Generalmajor der Waffen-SS*	*Gen.Maj./Brig.Fhr.*	Brigadier General
Oberst	*SS-Oberführer*	*Oberf.*	Senior Colonel
Oberst	*SS-Standartenführer*	*O./Staf.*	Colonel
Oberstleutnant	*SS-Obersturmbannführer*	*Oberstlt./Ostubaf.*	Lieutenant Colonel
Major	*SS-Sturmbannführer*	*Maj./Stubaf.*	Major
Hauptmann or *Rittmeister*	*SS-Hauptsturmführer*	*Hptm./Hstuf.*	Captain
Oberleutnant	*SS-Obersturmführer*	*Oberlt./Ostuf.*	First Lieutenant
Leutnant	*SS-Untersturmführer*	*Lt./Ustuf.*	Second Lieutenant
Stabsfeldwebel	*SS-Sturmscharführer*	*Stabs Fw./*none	Sergeant Major
Oberfeldwebel	*SS-Hauptscharführer*	*Ofw./Hscha.*	Master Sergeant
Feldwebel	*SS-Oberscharführer*	*Fw./Oscha.*	Sergeant First Class
Unteroffizier	*SS-Unterscharführer*	*Uffz./Uscha.*	Staff Sergeant
Obergefreiter	*SS-Rottenführer*	*Ogefr./Rttf.*	Coporal/Specialist

Gefreiter	*SS-Sturmann*	*Gef./Strm.*	Private First Class
Obergrenadier, *Oberkannonier,* etc.	*SS-Obergrenadier,* etc.	none	Private Second Class
Grenadier, Kanonier, *Funker,* etc.	*SS-Grenadier,* etc.	none	Private

Feldpost Numbers for
IV. SS-Pz.Korps 1944–45

Feldpostnummer (FPNr.) 12278
(24.3.1944–6.11.1944) 14.4.1944 *Stab u. Kartenstelle VII. SS-Korps,*
(24.3.1944–6.11.1944) 28.7.1944 *Stab u. Kartenstelle IV. SS-Korps,*
(24.3.1944–6.11.1944) 19.9.1944 *Stab u. Einheit IV. SS-Korps.*

FPNr. 10887
(24.3.1944–6.11.1944) 14.4.1944 *Stab Artillerie-Kommandeur VII. SS-Korps,*
(24.3.1944–6.11.1944) 28.7.1944 *Stab Artillerie-Kommandeur IV. SS-Korps.*

FPNr. 57933
(8.9.1943–22.4.1944) 24.3.1944 *schwere Beobachtungs-Batterie 104 (IV. SS-Korps).*

FPNr. 07240
(7.11.1944–*Kriegsende*) *Wehrgeologen Einsatz-Zug IV. SS-Korps.*

FPNr. 41927
(23.4.1944–24.11.1944) 15.7.1944 *Stab u. Einheit Werfer-Abteilung 507*
(VII. SS-Korps),
(23.4.1944–24.11.1944) 28.7.1944 *Stab u. Einheit Werfer-Abteilung 104*
(IV. SS-Korps),
(23.4.1944–24.11.1944) 8.9.1944 *Stab u. Einheit Werfer-Abteilung 504*
(SS-Korps-Trupp).

FPNr. 22801
(6.4.1944–9.11.1944) 8.5.1944 *Stab u. Einheit schw. SS-Artillerie-Abteilung 501,*
(6.4.1944–9.11.1944) 8.9.1944 *Stab u. Einheit schw. Artillerie-Abteilung 504*
(SS-Korps-Trupp).

FPNr. 42351
(23.4.1944–24.11.1944) 21.6.1944 *Feldgendarmerie-Trupp 107* (*VII. SS-Korps*),
(23.4.1944–24.11.1944) 28.7.1944 *Feldgendarmerie-Trupp 104* (*IV. SS-Korps*).

FPNr. 43100
(23.4.1944–24.11.1944) 21.6.1944 *Feldpostamt 107* (*VII. SS-Korps*),
(23.4.1944–24.11.1944) 28.7.1944 *Feldpostamt 104* (*IV. SS-Korps*).

FPNr. 40431
(23.4.1944–24.11.1944) 6.6.1944 *Flak-Kompanie VII. SS-Panzer-Korps*,
(23.4.1944–24.11.1944) 28.7.1944 *Flak-Kompanie IV. SS-Korps*.

FPNr. 13603
(1.8.1943–23.3.1944) 8.3.1944 *Stab, 1.-3. Kompanie u. Kolonne SS-Nachrichten-Abteilung 107* (*VII. SS-Korps*),
(24.3.1944–6.11.1944) 28.7.1944 *Stab, 1.-3. Kompanie u. Kolonne SS-Nachrichten-Abteilung 107* (*IV. SS-Korps*),
(24.3.1944–6.11.1944) 8.9.1944 *Stab, 1.-3. Kompanie u. Versorgungsstaffel Korps-Nachrichten-Abteilung 104* (*IV. SS-Korps*).

FPNr. 40023
(23.4.1944–24.11.1944) 21.6.1944 *1. Kraftfahr-Kompanie Korps-Nachschubtrupp 107* (*VII. SS-Korps*),
(23.4.1944–24.11.1944) 28.7.1944 *1. Kraftfahr-Kompanie Korps-Nachschubtrupp 104* (*IV. SS-Korps*),
(23.4.1944–24.11.1944) 6.9.1944 *1. Kraftfahr-Kompanie 104* (*IV. SS-Korps*).

FPNr. 02262
(1.8.1943–23.3.1944) 4.9.1943 *2. kleine Kraftwagen-Kolonne SS-Kolonne Generalkommando* (*IV. SS-Panzer-Korps*),
6.10.1943 *2. kleine Kraftwagen-Kolonne SS-Kolonne IV. Panzer-Korps*,
3.2.1944 *2. kleine Kraftwagen-Kolonne SS-Korps-Nachschub-Trupp 104* (*IV. SS-Panzer-Korps*),
(24.3.1944–6.11.1944) 4.5.1944 *gestrichen*.

FPNr. 09064
(1.8.1943–23.3.1944) 4.9.1943 *3. kleine Kraftwagen-Kolonne Gen. Kommando* (*IV. SS-Panzer-Korps*),
(1.8.1943–23.3.1944) 6.10.1943 *3. kleine Kraftwagen-Kolonne* (*IV. SS-Korps*),
(1.8.1943–23.3.1944) 3.2.1944 *3. kleine Kraftwagen-Kolonne Korps-Nachschub-Trupp104* (*IV. SS-Korps*),
(24.3.1944–6.11.1944) 4.5.1944 *gestrichen*.

FPNr. 12425
(1.8.1943–23.3.1944) 4.9.1943 *4. große Kraftwagenkolonne für Betriebsstoff Kolonne Generalkommando* (*IV. SS-Panzer-Korps*),
(1.8.1943–23.3.1944) 6.10.1943 *4. große Kraftwagenkolonne für Betriebsstoff* (*IV. SS-Korps*),
(1.8.1943–23.3.1944) 3.2.1944 *4. große Kraftwagenkolonne für Betriebsstoff Korps-Nachschub-Trupp 104* (*IV. SS-Korps*),
(24.3.1944–6.11.1944) 4.5.1944 *gestrichen.*

FPNr. 41651
(23.4.1944–24.11.1944) 21.6.1944 *Kfz.-Instandsetzungs-Zug Korps-Nachschubtrupp 107* (*VII. SS-Korps*),
(23.4.1944–24.11.1944) 29.7.1944 *Kfz.-Instandsetzungs-Zug Korps-Nachschubtrupp 104* (*IV. SS-Korps*),
(23.4.1944–24.11.1944) 6.9.1944 *Kfz.-Instandsetzungs-Zug Nachschubtrupp 104* (*IV. SS-Korps*),
(23.4.1944–24.11.1944) 8.9.1944 *Kfz.-Instandsetzungs-Zug 104* (*IV. SS-Korps*).

FPNr. 13243
(1.8.1943–23.3.1944) 4.9.1943 *SS-Bekleidung u. Instandsetzungs-Kompanie Generalkommando* (*IV. SS-Panzer-Korps*),
(1.8.1943–23.3.1944) 6.10.1943 *Bekleidung Instandsetzungs-Kompanie104* (*IV. SS-Panzer-Korps*),
(1.8.1943–23.3.1944) 3.2.1944 *Bekleidung Instandsetzungs-Kompanie 104* (*IV. SS-Korps*),
(24.3.1944–6.11.1944) 4.5.1944 *gestrichen.*

FPNr. 16567
(24.3.1944–6.11.1944) 5.8.1944 *Feldlazarett 504* (*IV. SS-Korps*),
(24.3.1944–6.11.1944) 8.9.1944 *Feldlazarett 504* (*IV. SS-Korps-Trupp*).

FPNr. 29186
(6.4.1944–9.11.1944) 5.8.1944 *1. Kranken-Kraftwagen-Zug 504* (*IV. SS-Korps*),
(6.4.1944-9.11.1944) 8.9.1944 *1. Kranken-Kraftwagen-Zug 504* (*IV. SS-Korps Trupp*).

FPNr. 13910
(24.3.1944–6.11.1944) 14.4.1944 *Sicherungs-Kompanie VII. SS-Korps, am* 28.7.1944 *Sicherungs-Kompanie IV. SS-Korps.*

Glossary

Abteilung (Abt.): Literally, detachment. A German unit of company size or greater, though normally of battalion size. Traditionally used to designate artillery, armor, or reconnaissance battalions.

Abteilungsartzt: Unit physician or medical doctor.

Alte Hase: Old hare, German army slang for front-line veterans who have served for a significant time in a unit.

Armee: Field army. Its headquarters was designated as an *Armee Oberkommando* (*AOK*).

Armeegruppe: Field army-level task force, normally consisting of one or more armies, including those from allied nations.

Armee-Korps: German infantry corps headquarters, capable of controlling two to four tank, armored infantry, or infantry divisions as well as various corps troops, such as artillery, engineer, antiaircraft, and antitank battalions or regiments.

Armee-Oberkommando (AOK): Field army headquarters, under which several *Armee-Korps* or divisions might operate.

Auffrischung: Reconstitution, a weeks-long process wherein a unit that has been destroyed or in combat for a prolonged period of time is pulled out of the line and rebuilt in a rest area behind the front lines, including the absorption of replacement personnel, weapons, and equipment.

Aufgefrischt: Description of a unit that has recently undergone reconstitution

Aufklärungsabteilung (Aufkl.Abt.): Reconnaissance Battalion.

Ausbildung: Training, including individual and unit level. Normally carried out when not involved in direct combat.

Ausführung (Ausf.): Model, or type. Used to designate a particular version or production series of a vehicle or weapon.

Befehlshaber: Field army commander.

Befehlspanzer: Command tank, equipped with necessary radio equipment to command and control armored formations and to communicate with adjacent and higher units.

Bergepanther: Tank recovery vehicle build on the chassis of *Pz. V* Panther.

Berichtszeit: Reporting time stated for morning, midday, and daily reports.

Bewährungsbataillon: A probationary battalion, formed from troops who have committed some form of disciplinary offense, but who have been evaluated as being redeemable after a period of service in the front lines at a lesser rank. Once a certain period of rehabilitation has been completed, its members are frequently reassigned to their former units in their previous rank.

Divisionsgruppe (Div. Gr.): A temporary division-sized task force, normally created to accomplish short-term objectives or missions that may consist of companies, battalions, or regiments from different divisions or *Heerestruppen*, as in *Div. Gr. Pape.* Also may be defined as a late-1943 measure instituted by the *OKH* in which a composite regiment is formed from the remnants of other destroyed or deactivated regiments from the same division and controlled by a *Korpsgruppe* headquarters formed from the headquarters of another destroyed or deactivated division.

Einsatzbereit: Operational, especially in regards to armor vehicles, meaning that the vehicle is fully capable of shooting, driving, and communicating.

Ersatzheer: The Replacement or Home Army, responsible for training replacements and sustaining the forces of the Field Army (*Feldheer*) fighting on the various fronts.

Fahrer: Vehicle driver; implies that the soldier also maintains the vehicle.

Fahrzeug und Motorenbau GmbH (FAMO): German automobile and truck manufacturer famous for their production of the enormous halftrack prime mover, the 18-ton *Sd.Kfz. 9.*

Fallschirmjäger: Paratrooper.

Feldausbildungs: Designation of a training unit located in close proximity to the front lines established to provide advanced individual training or reclassification training for soldiers from other branches of the *Wehrmacht* being transferred to ground combat branches, such as the infantry.

Feldgendarmerie: Field police. Normally tasked with traffic regulation, also serve a disciplinary role or assist a division's intelligence staff with counterespionage work.

Feldlazarett: Field hospital.

Fernschreiben: Telex message sent via *Hellschreiber* or teletype.

Flakvierling: four-barreled 20mm *Flak*, often on a self-propelled mount.

Fliegerabwehrkanonone (FlaK): Any kind of German antiaircraft gun.

Fliegerverbindungsoffizier (Flivo): *Luftwaffe* officer, usually a qualified pilot, assigned or attached to a ground unit to coordinate the employment of air assets in support of combat operations.

Freiwilligen: Volunteer; pertains especially to the *Waffen-SS* or foreign units serving under the German banner.

Frontschwein: "Front-line pig." Slang for veterans who had survived serving in the front lines for several months or even years.

Führungsabteilung: The operations and intelligence staff of a German brigade-level unit or higher, usually consisting of the *Ia* (Operations) and *Ic* (Intelligence) officers and their assistants. Has same connotation as *Führungstaffel*.

Gebirgs-Korps (Geb.Korps): German mountain corps headquarters, capable of controlling two to four infantry, mountain, or light infantry divisions as well as various corps troops, such as artillery, engineer, antiaircraft, and antitank battalions or regiments.

Gefechtstand: Command post of the *Führungsabteilung*, usually located closer to the front than a *Hauptquartier*.

Gefechtsvorposten: Screen line, or forward line of troops who serve as an early warning to spot or delay an approaching enemy. Usually designates a thin line of troops who are required to fall back into the main defense line upon contact with the enemy.

Gruppe: Group; in an infantry company, usually denotes a rifle squad.

Hauptquartier: Headquarters; may denote the headquarters company of a division, corps, or field army.

Heer: German Army.

Heeresgruppe (H.Gr.): Army Group, consisting of two or more field armies.

Heeres-Drückvorschrift: Army regulation published and disseminated throughout the *Wehrmacht-Heer* and *Waffen-SS*.

Heeresrüstungsamt: The ordnance department of the German Army that was responsible for managing the provision of weapons and equipment, including armored vehicles, for the field forces.

Heerestruppen: Independent general headquarters (GHQ) troops organized, trained, and equipped to carry out specific functions, including supply and transportation, medical care, construction, communications, and rear area security. Also may include artillery, combat engineer, antitank, tank, antiaircraft, and specialized assault units, as well as penal or rehabilitation units, that operate in the army, corps, or division areas within a designated *Kampfraum* (area of operations).

Honvéd: Title of the Royal Hungarian Army

Hussar: Hungarian mounted infantryman

Infanterie-Division (*Inf.Div.*, or *I.D.*): German Army infantry division.

Jagdpanzer: Tank destroyer mounting a 7.5cm gun built on the chassis of a *Pz. IV* or Czech *38t* chassis.

Jäger: *Luftwaffe* designation for fighter aircraft or infantry troops in *Luftwaffe* field divisions, the *Hermann Göring* division, or paratroopers.

Kampfgruppe (*K.Gr.*): A temporary task-organized body of troops, which may range in size from a company to brigade in size plus attached troops, normally identified by its commander's name, and used to achieve a given, short-term military objective.

Kampfraum: Operational area, combat area, or combat zone.

Kampfstärke: Combat strength, used as a means to measure the combat power of an infantry, mechanized, or armored division, focusing on the number of ground troops serving in the front line, specifically infantry, combat engineer, and reconnaissance troops. Used by higher headquarters as a tool to measure a unit's combat power or to calculate the number of troops holding a given length of front line.

Kommandeur: Unit commander, designated by official orders confirming an officer in that position, as opposed to being a *Führer*, an officer acting in a temporary command capacity.

Kommandierender General (*K.G.*): Commanding general of a corps or service command.

Korpstruppen: Corps troops, consisting of those created specifically to provide the corps' *Hauptquartier* with logistical, communications, medical, traffic control, and security support. Generally remained with the corps throughout their existence, unlike *Heerestruppen*, which were moved around constantly.

Korsettenstange: Literally, "corset stays," a term used to describe small German units inserted between allied units of dubious reliability in order to insure that they are able to hold their assigned defensive line.

Korück: Abbreviation for *Kommando Rückwärtiges Gebiet*, the rear area or communications zone of a field army, normally commanded by a *Generalleutnant*.

Kraftfahrzeug (*Kfz.*): Any German motor vehicle, except armor.

Kraftrad (Krad): Motorcycle.

Kriegsberichter (KB): War correspondent.

Kriegsmarine: German Navy.

Kriegsstärkenachweisung (K.St.N): War Strength Inventory Directive, a document similar to the modern U.S. Army's table of organization that describes an organization's structure and lists the total number of personnel and major end items authorized.

Kübelwagen: "Bucket car," slang term for Volkswagen equivalent of U.S. Jeep.

Landeschützen-Bataillon (Ldsch.Btl.): German local defense battalion, formed from older reservist. Often used for local security duties in the occupied regions or during emergencies as front-line infantry.

Landser: German slang for infantryman.

Luftflotte: Air Fleet, *Luftwaffe* administrative headquarters similar in function to an army headquarters or *Armee-Oberkommando (AOK)*.

Luftwaffe: German Air Force.

Mannschaften: Enlisted men.

Marder: Self-propelled antitank gun, usually mounted on an obsolete tank chassis such as a *Pz. II* or Czech *38t*.

MP-40: *Maschinepistole 40*; German automatic 9mm machine pistol designed for use by assault troops.

MP-44: *Maschinepistole 44*: German 7.92mm assault rifle capable of semiautomatic and full automatic fire. Also known officially as *Sturmgewehr* (assault rifle) *44* or *Stg-44*.

Nachhut: Rear guard unit; usually used to cover a withdrawal or serve as a security force during a retreat.

Nationalsozialistische -Führungs Offizier (NSFO): National Socialist Leadership Officer, who acted somewhat in the capability of cheerleader and commissar responsible not only for ensuring that everyone in the command continued to display the proper Nazi attitude, but also responsible for monitoring troops morale and welfare. In the *Waffen-SS*, the NSFO was usually assigned as the VI Staff Officer. Assigned to division, corps, and field army staffs.

Nebelwerfer: "Smoke Launcher" or mobile rocket launcher firing high-explosive projectiles ranging in in size from 15cm to 32cm; had a distinctive moaning sound when fired, giving rise to the nickname "moaning minnies."

Oberbefehlshaber (O.B.): Army group commander.

Ordnungspolizei (OrPo): Order Police; paramilitary police force, frequently organized into battalions and regiments operating under the auspices of the SS, often used for rear-area security duties as well as for combating partisans. During the waning months of the war, increasingly incorporated into the front lines as ordinary infantry, a task for which they were neither trained nor equipped to carry out.

Pakfront: German term for an integrated Red Army antitank gun defense, usually consisting of multiple antitank gun units, employing everything up to and including the 12.2 cm gun.

Panzerfaust: A recoilless antitank grenade launcher designed to be used against armor at ranges from 25–100 meters. It consisted of a steel launching tube, which contained a percussion-fired propellant charge, and a hollow-charge antitank grenade mounted at the end. Could penetrate up to 6 inches of rolled steel plate.

Panzergrenadier (Pz.Gren.): Armored or mechanized infantryman.

Panzergruppe (Pz.Gr.): Armored Group, could range in size from battalion to field army.

Panzerkampfwagen (Pz.Kfw.): Armored battle vehicle, or tank, called *panzer* for short.

Panzerabwehrkanone (PaK): Antitank gun.

Panzerjäger: Antitank troops.

Panzer-Korps (Pz.Korps): Armored corps, controlling two or more divisions of various types, though primarily trained and equipped to control armored divisions or *Panzergrenadier* divisions.

Rollbahn: "Trunk road" or main supply route for divisions and higher.

Raketenpanzerbüchse: A rocket-propelled antitank launcher, better known as the *Panzerschreck* ("Tank terror"). Its 8.8cm rocket was extremely effective against all types of Allied armor.

Ritterkreuz: Knight's Cross of the Iron Cross. The *Ritterkreuz* was the highest class of the Iron Cross and the most prized of the German World War II military decorations awarded for bravery in combat or decisive leadership in critical situations.

Sanitäter: Medic or corpsman.

Schützenpanzerwagen (SPW): Armored Personnel Carrier of the *Sd.Kfz. 250* or *251* type.

Schwere Panzerabteilung (s.Pz.Abt.): Heavy tank battalion, usually equipped with *Pz. VI* Tiger I/E or *Pz. VI* King Tiger IIb tanks.

Schwerpunkt: German term of the military art that designates where the point of main effort is for any given operation, whether offensive or defensive.

Schwimmwagen: Amphibious version of the Volkswagen.

Sicherheitsdienst (*SD*): Security Service of the SS; charged with combating or carrying out espionage.

Sicherungs-Regiment (*Sich.Rgt.*): Line of communications security regiment, often consisted of older *Landes-Schüzten* personnel. Often committed to front-line combat when situations dictated.

Sonderkraftfahrzeuge (*Sd.Kfz.*): Special purpose vehicle, such as half-tracks, or recovery vehicles.

Sperrverbände: Blocking formations, established for the purpose of barring or blocking important roads or highways to prevent breakthroughs by enemy mobile formations. Normally formed using *Bau-Pionier* (construction engineers) or *Pioniere* equipped with explosives, barrier materials, and antitank weapons.

SS-Führungshauptamt (*SS-FHA*): The main leadership office of the SS, responsible for coordinating the manning, equipping, and training of SS units, including the *Waffen-SS*.

Strafbataillon: Punishment battalion, usually consisting of men who have been charged with non-capital offenses and have been sent to one of these units to serve out their term of punishment, usually near the front lines and in conditions that are considered extremely hazardous. Survivors are usually restored to their previous ranks or may be posted to a *Bewährungsbataillon* (see above) for further rehabilitation.

Stuka: Short for *Sturzkampfflugzeug*, or dive-bomber. Generally refers to the Junkers *Ju-87*.

Sturmabteilungen (*SA*): Paramilitary arm of the Nazi Party which propelled Hitler to power. Its influence was severely reduced when it attempted to compete with the SS.

Sturmgeschütz (*StuG*): Armored assault gun specifically built to provide close-in infantry support using its 7.5cm or 10.5cm howitzer. Normally built on a *Pz.Kfw. III* or *IV* chassis, they were at a disadvantage when fighting tanks in open terrain due to their lack of a rotating turret, but were formidable when employed in built-up areas or as a tank destroyer firing from hidden positions.

Totenköpfler: Informal term of endearment relating to the men of the *Totenkopf* Division.

Tross: The "Trains" where a unit's logistical and administrative units were located, from company to regimental level.

Volksgrenadier: Honorific title of an infantryman or the divisions formed during September 1944 under a new infantry division structure designed to economize on manpower by adding additional weaponry, such as more heavy weapons and the *MP-44* assault rifle.

Vorgeschobener Gefechtstand: Forward command post, usually staffed by a minimum number of personnel needed for a commanding officer to control an ongoing engagement near the front lines.

Vorübergehend unterstellt: A German military term, designating a unit (company, battalion, regiment, etc.) that has been placed under the temporary tactical control of a higher level organization other than its own. The unit concerned will normally remain the administrative and logistical responsibility of its parent organization, and usually reverts to its control once a particular mission or tactical objective has been accomplished.

Waffen-SS: Militarized SS; the combat arm of Heinrich Himmler's SS. When deployed in a combat zone, normally fell under the operational or tactical control of an appropriate field army or corps headquarters of the *Heer*.

Waffenwillig (*Wawis*): Term used to describe foreign "volunteers" who were willing to take up arms and fight alongside German forces. Frequently were integrated within individual German infantry squads.

Wehrkreis: Defense District, geographically designated areas in Germany and occupied areas of Europe that were designed to serve as the *Ersatzheer*'s (Home Army) base for the generation and constitution of forces for the *Feldheer* (Field Army), as well as to serve as the headquarters for controlling the various local security forces and POW camps in the zone of the interior.

Wehrmacht: The German Armed Forces, which included the *Heer*, *Luftwaffe*, and *Kriegsmarine*. Technically, the *Waffen-SS* was not a part of the *Wehrmacht*.

Wehrmachtbefehlshaber: Commander of the German armed forces in a geographic area; technically, had control over all three branches of the *Wehrmacht* but not the *Waffen-SS*.

Wikinger: Informal term of endearment relating to the men of the *Wiking* Division.

Zugführer: Platoon leader, usually a senior NCO but occasionally a junior grade officer, such as a *Leutnant* or *Untersturmführer*.

Zugkraftwagen (*ZgKw*): Artillery half-tracked prime mover.

Endnotes

Chapter 1: The Lost Month

1   *Abschiedsnachricht an IV. SS-Pz.Korps, Oberbefehlshaber der 9. Armee, Armee-Hauptquartier*, 25 November 1944 (source: Vopersal, 508).

2   When the *IV. SS-Pz.Korps* was placed under the control of *2. Armee* on 27 November, its corps field hospital and field dressing company, under the supervision of the corps surgeon, *Brig.Führer* Rotthardt, were both relocated in order to be integrated into the *2. Armee* medical treatment infrastructure. *SS-Feld-Laz. 504* was moved to the town of Schrötttersburg (modern-day Plonk), while *SS-San.Kp. 504* was moved to Waldrode (modern-day Gostynin). Both were located over 75 kilometers behind the front lines, but as previously discussed, their primary purpose was to serve the medical needs of corps troops and attached *Heerestruppen*, not front-line divisions unless ordered otherwise. *AOK 2, Abteilung IVc (Armee-Arzt), Lage- und Tatigkeitsbericht Monat Dezember 1944, Anlage 1*, entries dated 1, 3, 4, and 9 December 1944.

3   *Zustandberichte* for the *Gen.Insp.d.Pz.Tr.* from the *Totenkopf* (*Ia Tgb.Nr. 11/45*) and the *Wiking* Divisions (*Ia Tgb.Nr. 7.45*), both dated 1 January 1945. At this point, the *Totenkopf* Division's field hospital had been moved to Plöhnen, while that of the *Wiking* had been moved from Litzmannstadt to Thorn.

4   *Div.Gef.Stand, 542. Volks-Grenadier Division, Abt. IIa, Tätigkeitsbericht* from 1 October to 31 December 1944, *Anlage 2*, 10 January 1945.

5   According to a periodic weapons and vehicles status report submitted by the *Oberquartiermeister* (*O.Qu.*) of *2. Armee*, as of 18 December 1944, the *Totenkopf* Division was short 59 percent of its authorized number of *MG-42* machineguns, while it was missing 41 percent of its authorized machine pistols (includes both *MP-40* and *MP-44*). The *Wiking* was in similar straits; it only had on hand 39 percent of its authorized machineguns but had 78 percent of its machine pistols. Overall, the *IV. SS-Pz.Korps* was short 369 rifles throughout the corps, including corps troops. The shortfall in rifles was partially made up by taking them away from rear-echelon troops, who were issued pistols in lieu of rifles. All of this points to the continuing difficulties the German armaments industry was having with keeping up with the enormous demand for all types of weaponry. Source: *AOK 9, O.Qu./Qu.1, Nr. 9789/44 geheim, Betr: Stellungsnahme zu den Zustandberichte*, dated 18 December 1944, pp. 8–9.

6   According to German records, during the month of December 1944, divisions fighting on the Western Front, excluding Italy, were issued 957 tanks, assault guns, and tank destroyers of all types, compared to the Eastern Front, which received only 570, despite there being nearly three times as many divisions in the East as compared to the West. Source: *Generalinspekteur der Panzertruppen. Unterlagen für den Führervortrag am 28.12.1944*. Berlin: *Oberkommando des Heeres*, 1944. 14 p. *Gen. Insp. d. Pz. Tr. Org. Nr. 4730/44 g.Kdos* (courtesy of Christian Ankerstjern of Panzerworld.com).

7   *Generalinspekteur der Panzertruppen. Zuführung Jagdpanther: April 1945*, 1 (courtesy of Christian Ankerstjern) and Monograph, "Panzer Issues to *SS-Pz.Rgt. 5*" by Ian Michael Wood, undated.

8   *Stellungsnahme zu den Zustandberichte*, 8–9. Incidentally, an *SPW* was not viewed as an armored fighting vehicle.

9   The continually outstanding efforts of the maintenance sections of both divisions' *panzer* regiments were recognized by the award of the prestigious German Cross in Silver to *SS-Ostubaf.* Friedrich Schuster in March 1945 and the Knight's Cross of the War Service Cross to *SS-Hstuf.* Erich Wiese in November 1943.

10 Refer to Chapter 12 of Volume I for more detail and Klapdor, p. 439.

11 Email from Michael Ian Wood, 7 September 2019.

12 Wilhelm Tieke, *Tragedy of the Faithful: A History of the III. (germanisches) SS-Panzer-Korps.* (Winnipeg: J. J. Fedorwicz Publishing, 2001), pp. 398–400 (English translation of the original 1968 Munin Verlag version). According to eyewitness reports, both battalions—at least until their renewed destruction on 15 February 1945—were used together, as a kind of "third regimental combat group" under the command of the divisional commander. (Source: Herr Ingo Apel).

13 Both battalions, importantly, arrived with their full complement of arms and equipment, including the heavy weapons company, which had four heavy machine guns, four 8cm mortars, two light machine guns, and two 7.5cm antitank guns. (Source: Tieke, 399.)

14 *AOK 2, Ib KTB, IV. SS-Pz.Korps Ib* report dated 27 November 1944.

15 Extract from the account of former Norwegian *SS-Rottenführer* J.B., "*Pettend fest in unsere Hand,*" personal archive of Tommy Natedal, March 2017, courtesy of John Moore.

16 *I. Abteilung/SS-Pz.Rgt. 5 KTB*, entries dated 16–30 November 1944, pp. 62–63.

17 *AOK 2, Ib KTB, IV. SS-Pz.Korps Ib* reports 26 November–6 December 1944.

18 *542. Volks-Grenadier Division, Abt. Ia Nr. 967/44 geheim, Divisionsbefehl Nr. 60 fuer die Befehlsuebername bis zum Bug, Div.Gef.Stand*, 1 December 1944; and *542. V.G.D. Abt. Ia/Op. 3 Nr. 987/geheim, Divisionsbefehl Nr. 62 fuer den Einsatz des Füsilier-Btl. 542, Div.Gef.Stand*, 5 December 1944.

19 Strassner, p. 191.

20 Vopersal, p. 510.

21 Vopersal, pp. 505, 515 and Angolia, p. 99.

22 *Weisung Nr. 68 für die Kriegführung, Führerhauptquartier, den 28. 11. 44*, "*Führerbefehl über die Befehlsführung bei auf sich selbst gestellten Truppenteilen,*" *Der Chef des Oberkommandos der Wehrmacht WFSt/Qu. 2 Nr. 1409/44*, and Vopersal, p. 512.

23 Vopersal, p. 511

24 *Korpsgefechtstand, Gen.Kdo. IV. SS-Pz.Korps, Ia Tagebuch nr. 1109/44 geheim*, 3 December 1944; and *Abschrift, Gefechtsbericht, 6. Kp./SS-Pz.Gren.Rgt. 9 "Germania,"* 3 December 1944.

25 *Korpsgefechtstand, Gen.Kdo. IV. SS-Pz.Korps, Ia Tagebuch nr. 1131/44 geheim, Betr: Alarmübung in rückwärtiger Stellungen*, 5 December 1944.

26 Bernau, p. 139.

27 *Div.Gef.Stand, 542. Volks-Grenadier Division, Abt. Ia Nr. 1074/44 geheim, Betr: Ausbau Fort Debe*, 18 December 1944.

28 *Verleihungslist für Verleihung des Eisernes Kreuz un Kriegsverdienst Kreuz, Generalkommando IV. SS-Panzerkorps, Adjutantur IIa*, October–December 1944 (*Bundesarchiv Zentralnachweisstelle, Heerespersonalamt, RH 7A, 1338, Folie 1–19*. Awards were also parceled out for deserving members of *Heeres-Art.Abt. 154, Beob.Abt. 21, Gren.Btl.z.b.V. 560, Heeres-Pz.Jäg.Abt. 743, Bau-Pio.Btle. 9* and *421, Stab./Art.Rgt. 69*, and *Stellungs-Werf.Rgt. 103.*

29 *Wiking Ruf: Mitteilungsblatt der europäischen Soldaten der ehemaligen Waffen-SS für Vermissten-Such und Hilfsdient*, "Tapfere Söhne Europas—Treue Kameraden," Vol. 4, February 1952. (Hannover: J. F. Wiese & Ahlert, 1952), p. 4.

30 Vopersal, p. 515.

31 Interview with Günther Lange, Handeloh, Germany, 7 October 2017.

32 Vopersal, p.514.

33 *Div.Gef.Stand, 542. Volks-Grenadier Division, Abt. Ia/Op. 3 Nr. 1108/44 geheim; Divisionsbefehl Nr. 72 für verstärkte Sicherung in der Nacht vom 24./25.12.44*, 23 December 1944.

34 *SS-Stubaf.* Fritz Messerle, commander of *IV. Abt./SS-Pz.Art.Rgt. 3 "Totenkopf,"* provides an excellent description of the last Christmas on the Eastern Front and the efforts his men made to celebrate the occasion (Ullrich, p. 248).

35 *542. V.G.D., Ia KTB*, 24 December 1944, and Bernau, p. 140.

36 Strassner, p. 191.

37 *Ibid.*

38 Julius Heinrich Dorpmüller (24 July 1869–5 July 1945) was general manager of Deutsche Reichsbahn-Gesellschaft from 1926–45 and the Reich Minister for Transport from 1937–45. Source: Wikipedia, https://en.wikipedia.org/wiki/Julius_Dorpm%C3%BCller, accessed 12 September 2019.

39 Messerle, in Vopersal, p. 516. Julischka is an apéritif popular in southeastern Europe, a combination of plum slivovitz and pear liqueur.

Chapter 2: The Hungarian Theater of Operations

1 As related in the previous chapter, no troops from the *Heer* were involved in this transfer, since all of them had been removed from Gille's control and attached to other corps or field armies before the *IV. SS-Pz.Korps* departed. This meant that only the two SS divisions, the corps headquarters, and corps troops were shipped to Hungary, which accounts for this relatively low number of troops serving with the corps. That would soon change upon arrival in their new area of operations when additional *Heerestruppen* and divisions would be attached.

2 Perry Pierek, *Hungary 1944–1945: The Forgotten Tragedy* (Nieuwegein, The Netherlands. Aspekt 1995), p. 153.

3 Earl F. Ziemke, *Stalingrad to Berlin: The German Defeat in the East* (Washington, D.C.: U.S. Army Center of Military History, 2002), pp. 369–70.

4 *Ibid*, pp. 356–58.

5 A fascinating account of *Unternehmen Panzerfaust* is found in Eric Kern's postwar book, *Dance of Death*, published in 1948 as *Der Grosse Rauch* (The Great Frenzy). The pen name of former *SS-Ustuf.* Eric Kernmayr, who was serving under Otto Skorzeny's command for this operation, he was responsible for psychological operations, including the seizure of the radio station and preventing renegade Arrow Cross members from using the station for their own nefarious ends.

6 Frieser *et al*, *Germany and the Second World War*, Volume 8, p. 876.

7 Ziemke, pp. 363–64.

8 This account from Friessner is from his history of the campaign, *Verratene Schlachten, die Tragödie der deutschen Wehrmacht in Rumänien* (Hamburg: Holsten Verlag, 1956) and quoted in *Campaign: Fortress Budapest* by Warlord Games (Oxford, U.K.: Bloomsbury Publishing PLC, 2019).

9 Ziemke, pp. 378–82.

10 *Ibid*, pp. 382–83.

11 Johannes Friessner, *Verratene Schlachten, die Tragödie der deutschen Wehrmacht in Rumänien* (Hamburg: Holsten Verlag, 1956), p. 193.

12 Krisztián Ungváry, *The Siege of Budapest: 100 Days in World War II* (New Haven: Yale University Press, 2002), p. 36.

13 Peter Gosztony, *Endkampf an der Donau 1944/45* (Vienna: Verlag Fritz Molden, 1969), pp. 97–98; Ungváry, pp. 35–36.

14 Ziemke, pp. 383–84.

15 *Ibid*, pp. 394–85.

16 When writing his memoirs after the war, Friessner noted that he believed that both he and Fretter-Pico were relieved of command "Because they needed a scapegoat." Friessner's calls to Guderian and his chief of staff that day to enquire the reasoning behind his dismissal was finally explained as a "spontaneous decision on the part of the Führer" (Pierek, p. 116).

17 *Ibid*, pp. 385–86.

18 The details were spelled out in an order from Hitler dated 1 December 1944, *Führerbefehl zur Verteidigung von Budapest*, sent through the headquarters of *H.Gr. Süd* under Friessner's signature. The order, citing *Führerbefehl Nr. 11* dated 8 March 1944, *Kommandanten der festen Plätze und Kampfkommandanten*, enunciated specific duties and expectations of the fortress commander and its troops, including fighting "to the last man" if necessary.

19 Pierek, p. 125. Interestingly, Albert Speer, Hitler's Minister of Armaments, stated that same year (1944) that the war had "already been lost in production-technical terms" (*ibid*, p. 119). Therefore, whether there was sufficient fuel may very well have been a moot point. In a geopolitical-strategic sense, Germany had already lost the war by 1942.

20 Guderian, p. 312.

21 Frieser *et al*, p. 904.

22 *Ibid*, pp. 309–11.

23 *Ibid*, pp. 311–12.

24 Frieser *et al*, p. 904.

25 Georg Maier, *Drama Between Budapest and Vienna: The Final Battles of the 6. Panzer-Armee in the East 1945*. (Winnipeg, Canada: J. J. Fedorowicz Publishing, 2004), p. 13. (Note: this is the English translation of the original book published by Munin-Verlag, which appeared in 1985 under the original title *Drama zwischen Budapest und Wien; Der Endkampf der 6. Panzerarmee 1945*. Hereafter referred to as Maier).

26 Maier, p. 13, quoting Steiner from his book *Die Freiwilligen—Idee und Opfergang* (Gottingen: Plesse Verlag, 1958), p. 294.

27 Vopersal, Vol. 5b, p. 517.

28 Source: ULTRA Special Intelligence History of the Eastern Front, Chapter IV, p. 106. Thanks to David O'Keefe for providing the report.

Chapter 3: Arrival in Hungary

1 Strassner, p. 191; Ullrich, p. 251; Klapdor, p. 382.

2 *AOK 9 Führungsabteilung KTB*, entry dated 25 December 1944, and *AOK 2, Ib Quartiermeister KTB*, entry dated 25 December 1944.

3 *Zustandberichte* for the *Gen.Insp.d.Pz.Tr.* from the *Totenkopf* (*Ia Tgb.Nr. 11/45*) and *Wiking* (*Ia Tgb.Nr. 7.45*) Divisions, both dated 1 January 1945.

4 *IV. SS-Pz.Korps Ib/Quartiermeister* daily status reports to *AOK 2, Ib Quartiermeister KTB*, entries dated 24–27 December 1944, and Pierek, p. 151.

5 ULTRA Special Intelligence History of the Eastern Front, p. 109.

6 *AOK 9 O.Qu. Ib 1 KTB*, entry dated 25 December 1944.

7 *AOK 9 Führungsabteilung KTB*, entry dated 25 December 1944, p. 303.

8 *Ibid*, p. 303.

9 *Ibid*.

10 *Ibid*, p. 304.

11 Vopersal, p. 518.

12 Maier, p. 17.

13 Strassner, p. 191, and Klapdor, p. 386.

14 Klapdor, p. 386.

15 *AOK 9 Ia KTB, Tagesmeldung* entry dated 6:40 p.m., 26 December 1944.

16 *AOK 2, Ib Quartiermeister KTB*, entry dated 27 December 1944.

17 Ullrich, p. 251.

18 Maier, p. 16.

19 Vopersal, p. 521.

20 *AOK 9 O.Qu. 1 KTB*, entry dated 27 December 1944.

21 *AOK 9, Ia KTB, Tagesmeldung*, 9:15 p.m., 27 December 1944.

22 *AOK 9, Ia KTB, Tagesmeldung*, 9:15 p.m., 28 December 1944.

23 *AOK 9, Ia KTB, Tagesmeldung*, 8:30 p.m., 29 December, and 8 p.m., 30 December 1944.

24 Hermann Balck, *Order in Chaos: The Memoirs of General of Panzer Troops Hermann Balck*, edited by Maj.Gen. David T. Zabecki and Lt.Col. Dieter J. Biedekarken (Lexington, KY: The University Press of Kentucky, 2015), p. ix.

25 *Ibid*, p. 405.

26 Maier quoting entry in *OKW Kriegstagebuch IV/1, 30*. (Private letter from Balck to Jodl) in Drama Between Budapest and Vienna, p. 16.

27 Friedrich W. von Mellenthin, *Panzer Battles: A Study of the Employment of Armor in the Second World War*, 2nd edition (New York: Ballantine Books Inc., 1973), p. 404.

28 Balck, p. 405. In his memoir, Balck states that Guderian told him after the war (though not in his own memoir *Panzer Leader*) that he too thought his relief of command of *H.Gr. G* was also due to Himmler's intrigues.

29 Balck was certainly not enamored of the SS; much of this can be laid at the door of his personal dislike of Himmler. However, in his memoirs, he praised the performance of the *1. SS-Pz.Div. Leibstandarte Adolf Hitler* and considered it an elite force on par with *Wehrmacht panzer* divisions. Balck, p. 335.

30 *Ibid*, p. 405.

31 An *Armeegruppe* (field army group) is larger than an army, but smaller than an army group. In this particular case, Balck, like Fretter-Pico before him, would also command one and occasionally two Hungarian armies (the 2nd and 3rd) of dubious reliability; so although on paper it appeared to be a much larger and powerful organization, in reality only the German elements could be considered reliable and combat effective, so it still had the combat power of a German field army. The only exception that Balck noted was the Hungarian Saint Lazlo infantry division, which he thought was well led and equipped.

32 *Stabsbefehl, Der Oberbefehlshaber der 6. Armee, Armee-Hauptquartier*, 23 December 1944.

33 The separation of the armored elements from the main body of these divisions, in conformance to the *Führerbefehl*, had been ordered by *6. Armee* on 19 December 1944 (Source: Fernschreiben, *A.Gr. Fretter-Pico* 1a Nr. 6459/44 geheim, 19 December 1944).

34 Balck, p. 406. There is no satisfactory explanation for why Guderian did this. His autobiography remains mute on the topic. Perhaps an impatient Hitler had ordered the separation of the armored elements from the rest of the *panzer* divisions, which in reality were only partially equipped with armored vehicles. As a result, this partial solution doomed *Unternehmen Spätlese* before it had even begun.

35 Heinz Gaedke, *Wege eines Soldaten* (Norderstedt: Books on Demand, 2005), p. 237.

36 Balck, p. 406.

37 Pierek, p. 160.

38 Balck, p. 406.

39 *Ibid*, p. 408.
40 Gaedke, p. 201.
41 Gaedke, p. 236; Balck, p. 408; and Pierek, p. 160.
42 Hack *et al*, *Panzergrenadier der Panzerdivision Wiking im Bild*, p. 197.
43 Pierek, p. 160.
44 Gaedke, p. 199.
45 In his own autobiography, Gaedke frankly admits his own doubts at the time as to whether any breakout attempt from Korsun was even possible under the adverse conditions both encircled corps faced. He felt that it would be an extremely risky endeavor, and that if it failed, both corps and their encircled divisions would be cut up and wiped out (Gaedke, p. 193). Were any such pessimistic thoughts expressed in the presence of Gille or any other SS commander, it may well have been interpreted as defeatism, though in reality it was merely an expression of their actual situation.
46 Balck, p. 408.
47 Pierek, p. 160.
48 *Ibid*, p. 133.
49 Balck, p. 407. His assessment accords nearly word for word with the preface from the actual *Lagebeurteilung* he submitted to *H.Gr. Süd* three days later, which went into considerably more detail in regards to how he expected to accomplish his objective. The only unit that he was able to get out of Budapest was the division headquarters of the *Feldherrnhalle Panzergrenadier Division* (*Pz.Gren.Div. FHH*), part of its signal battalion, one *Panzergrenadier* battalion, and various smaller elements of the division. This was used to form the basis of *Divisionsgruppe Pape* on 21 December 1944.

Chapter 4: Preparations for the Relief of Budapest—*Unternehmen Konrad*

1 Számvéber, p. 19.
2 *H.Gr. Süd Ia Nr. 5000/44 g.Kdos., Fernschreiben: Befehl für die Kampfführung*, 28 December 1944.
3 Számvéber, p. 19.
4 Maier, pp. 14–15.
5 Számvéber, p. 39.
6 Pierek, p. 154.
7 Maier, p. 14.
8 Számvéber, p. 19.
9 *Ibid*, p. 20.
10 *Ibid*, p. 19, quoting from the *H.Gr. Süd 1a KTB* entry for 28 December 1944.
11 Manfred Schönfelder, Manuscript, "Einsatz der Verbände der Waffen-SS auf dem Kriegsschauplatz in Ungarn in der Zeit vom 1.1.–31.3.1945," 1 December 1981, p. 4.
12 *Armeegruppe Balck Ia Nr. 1967/44 g.Kdos., Fernschreiben—Konrad Einsatz*, 30 December 1944, and Maier, p. 15.
13 Maier, p. 15.
14 Guderian, p. 313. Interestingly, his statement about the lack of "agressiveness" was viewed as an affront by the veterans of the *Waffen-SS*, leading former SS officers to state that the fault lay not with the troops, and that the senior leadership at *OKH* seemed to lack the same "drive" as the old days as well.
15 Balck, p. 408.

16 *Ibid*, p. 408. In his postwar account, Balck claims, with the benefit of hindsight, that the attacking troops would have to contend with 54 rifle divisions, five mechanized corps, three tank corps, and two cavalry corps, but this exceeds contemporary estimates of the number of Soviet formations available. While Balck's figures are technically correct, it includes all of the forces available to both the 4th Guards Army and 46th Army, including those investing Budapest. This clashes with his own estimate his headquarters issued on 27 December 1944 (*Armeegruppe Balck, Ia Nummer 1949/44 g.Kdos., Betr: Lagebeurteilung*, 27 December 1944).

17 Maier, p. 17.

18 Számvéber, p. 20.

19 *H.Gr. Süd Ia KTB, Nummer 211/44 g.Kdos, Chefsachen vom* 31 December 1944, as quoted verbatim in Számvéber, p. 21.

20 A temporary organization, *Korpsgruppe Breith* consisted of both German and Hungarian units, commanded by *Gen.d.Pz.Tr.* Hermann Breith of *III Pz.Korps*. Similar to the logic behind the designation of an *Armeegruppe*, it would control two or more corps for a limited period and would revert to its normal status as a *panzer* corps once the operation was completed.

21 *Divisionsgruppe Pape* was established on 21 December 1944 using the headquarters and one signal company of *Pz.Gren.Div. Feldherrenhalle*, which unlike the rest of the division, was not trapped inside Budapest. It was used instead to control the armored elements of the *3., 6.,* and *8. Pz.Div.* which had been earmarked to participate in *Unternehmen Spätlese*, while the rest of these divisions went north of the Danube to defend along the Gran River against the attack by the Second Ukrainian Front. Its composition shifted constantly; by 1 January 1945, it consisted of *K.Gr. Bieber*, including one battalion-sized *Alarmeinheit* consisting of remnants of the *271 V.G.D.* and *Pz.Abt. 208*, *K.Gr. Knoop* of the *8. Pz.Div.*, *K.Gr. Philipp* from the *6. Pz.Div.*, *Pz.Jäg.Abt. 13*, and *Sturmgeschütz-Brigade 239*. Major Ernst Philipp was the actual commander of *Pz.Rgt. 1* of the *1. Pz.Div.*, but had been hand-picked as the acting commander of *Pz.Rgt. 11* from the *6. Pz.Div.* to lead the *Kampfgruppe* of the same name. Upon the conclusion of *Unternehmen Konrad* at the end of January 1945 he returned to his old division and resumed command of his *panzer* regiment. As of 31 December 1944, *Div.Gr. Pape* fielded 81 operational tanks, 18 assault guns, and 20 tank destroyers, for a total of 119 of all types (source: *Armeegruppe Balck/6. Armee Ia KTB, Anlage, Panzer-, Pak- und Sturmgeschützlage*, 31 December 1944).

22 Oddly, *Gen.d.Kav.* Hartenek's *I. Kav.Korps* was sandwiched between the left and right flanks of *Gen.d.Pz.Tr.* Breith's *III. Pz.Korps*, rather than assigning the entire right flank effort to Hartenek. The reasoning behind this somewhat unconventional tactical disposition cannot be explained satisfactorily, especially since Hartenek's corps was not subordinate to Breith's corps administratively, only tactically.

23 Számvéber, p. 30. Soviet sources estimated that the Germans and Hungarians had 775 aircraft, though they did not specify how many of this number were operational.

24 Számvéber, p. 21, from *H.Gr. Süd, Ia KTB, Beurteilung der Angriffsmöglichkeiten bei der Armeegruppe Balck am* 30 December 1944.

25 *Armeegruppe Balck*, Supplement to *Ia Nr. 1967/44 g.Kdos., Fernschreiben: Konrad Einsatz*, 30 December 1944.

26 Maier, Appendix 9, "Overview of Attachments to the *IV. SS-Pz.Korps* During the Period of 1 to 8 January 1945," p. 405.

27 Számvéber, p. 31.

28 Its four infantry battalions were from various units. On 30 December, these consisted of *Maschinegewehr (M.G.) Btl. Mark (Heerestruppen)*, *Divisions-Btl. 271* (formed from remnants of the *271. V.G.D.*), a *Marsch-Btl.* originally slated to provide replacements for *Pz.Gren.Div. FHH*, and *II. Btl./Pz.Gren.Rgt. 114* of the *6. Pz.Div.* All told, the division possessed only 918 men in its

infantry *Kampfstärke* and no artillery to call its own (source: *Armeegruppe Balck, Ia KTB, Anlage Kampfstärken*, 30 December 1944).

29 Tessin, Vol. 6, pp. 142–43.

30 Maier, p. 407, and *Armeegruppe Balck, Ia KTB, Anlage Kampfstärken* 6 January 1945 and *Panzer und Panzerabwehrwaffen Zustandbericht*, 15 January 1945.

31 Tessin, Vol. 12, pp. 169–70.

32 Pierek, p. 169, Maier, p. 407, *Armeegruppe Balck, Ia KTB, Anlage Kampfstärken* 6 January 1945 and *Panzer und Panzerabwehrwaffen Zustandbericht*, 15 January 1945.

33 David Glantz, in *1986 Art of War Symposium*, "From the Vistula to the Oder: Soviet Offensive Operations—October 1944 to March 1945" (Carlisle, PA: U.S. Army War College Center for Land Warfare, 1986), p. 670.

34 Gosztony, p. 118.

35 Számvéber, p. 38, and report from *Fremde Heeres Ost concerning Ist-, Gefechts- und Graben-Stärke der sow. Russ. Schützen Verbände bei verschiedenen Kampfräume, 1944*.

36 Herbert Schmeisser, *Die Panzer-Nachrichten-Abteilung Wiking: Manner mit Mikrofon und Morsetaste*. (Welzheim, Germany: Eigenverlag, 1985), p. 42.

37 Számvéber, p. 31. He relates an account by Hungarian Captain Janos Barczy, who watched as troops from *SS-Pz.Rgt. 3* jumped on the railway cars carrying a company's worth of their tanks, started them up, and drove all of them off onto the waiting platform "in not more than three to four minutes."

38 Vopersal, p. 520.

39 Strassner, p. 194.

40 Some of the units had to work in a hurry. The *Wiking* Division's signal battalion, *SS-Nachr.Abt. 5*, which only arrived on 31 December, had to immediately begin laying wire to forward positions, mere hours before the attack began, as described in Georg Dornisch, "Drei Entsatzangriffe auf Budapest," in *Unser Wiking Ruf*, 10/2005 (Handeloh, Germany: Truppenkameradschaft Wiking, 2005), p. 93.

41 *AOK 6, Ic KTB, Tätigkeitsbericht für Dezember 1944*.

42 *Der Oberbefehlshaber der Heeresgruppe Süd, Tagesbefehl*, 31 December 1944.

43 *Armeegruppe Balck/6. Armee, Armee-Hauptquartier*, 1 January 1945.

44 *Der Oberbefehlshaber der Heeresgruppe Süd Führungsabteilung KTB*, 1 January 1945.

45 Maier, p. 17.

46 *AOK 6, Ia KTB Nr. 6692/44 geh., Fernschreiben, Konrad Einsatz*, 29 December 1944, and *Nr. 6827/44 geh.*, 31 December 1944. *Gneisenau* battalions were emergency units activated under the codeword *"Gneisenau,"* which involved the mobilization of *Ersatz* and *Ausbildungs* units stationed in Germany or occupied countries. They were makeshift organizations of limited capability, and generally given security duties in the absence of actual combat units. Once their mission was completed, they were either incorporated into existing units as replacements or returned to their home station to carry on with their normal mission.

47 *AOK 6, Ia KTB, Fernschreiben, Betr: Konrad, Nr. 6720/44 geh.*, 29 December 1944. At first, *Oberstlt.* Marcks, the *Ia of 6. Armee*, mistook Ney's regiment for *Pz.Gren.Rgt. 5 "Totenkopf,"* but this error was soon corrected. Károly Ney, born in 1906, was a very controversial figure, both during and after the war. He was convicted and sentenced to death among several others of his regiment for war crimes involving the murder of five American aviators who had bailed out of a stricken B-24. Ney's death sentence was commuted to life imprisonment before it was carried out, and he was pardoned and released in 1948. Two of his men who were also found guilty were hanged in 1946. After the war, Ney worked in Austria and Hungary as an informant for the CIA and died in 1989.

48 Vopersal, p. 522.
49 Klapdor, p. 387.
50 Vopersal, p. 522.
51 Klapdor, p. 387.
52 Balck, p. 408.
53 *AOK 6, Ia KTB Funkspruch from IX. SS-Geb.Korps, Ia Nummer 312/44 g.Kdos*, 8:45 a.m., 30 December 1944.

Chapter 5: The First Relief Attempt of Budapest—*Konrad I*

1   Számvéber, pp. 47–48.
2   *Ibid*, p. 48, and Rolf Stoves, *1. Panzer-Division 1935–1945: Chronik einer der drei Stamm-Divisionen der deutschen Panzerwaffe* (Bad Nauheim: Verlag Hans-Henning Podzun, 1961), pp. 705–06.
3   Stoves, p. 705. Sparwasser commanded a mounted company from *SS-Kav.Rg. 18* of the *8. SS-Kav. Div. Florian Geyer*, the bulk of which had been encircled in Budapest along with the rest of the *IX. SS-Geb.Korps*. How his *Schwadron* managed to avoid being trapped in the city is unknown.
4   Számvéber, p. 49.
5   Soviet General Staff, *The Budapest Operation 1945: An Operational–Strategic Study* (Solihull, U.K.: Helion and Company Ltd, 2017), pp. 278–79. Hereafter referred to as "Soviet General Staff." Also, see *Korpsgruppe Breith/III. Pz.Korps, Ia KTB, Tagesmeldung*, 31 December 1944, 9 p.m.
6   Aleksei Isaev and Maksim Kolomiets, *Tomb of the Panzerwaffe: The Defeat of the Sixth SS Panzer Army in Hungary 1945* (Solihull, U.K.: Helion and Company Ltd, 2014), p. 23, and Soviet General Staff, p. 279.
7   Isaev and Kolomiets, p. 30. The Soviet intelligence summary for 1 January 1945 stated, "The enemy is striving to hold its present positions with all it forces; on separate sectors of the front, the adversary is undertaking attacks for reconnaissance purposed and with the aim of improving local positions."
8   Isaev and Kolomiets, p. 30.
9   *Armeegruppe Balck/AOK 6 Ic KTB*, entry dated 1 January 1945.
10 *Ibid*.
11 Hartwig Pohlman, *Geschichte der 96. Infanterie Division* (Bad Nauheim, Germany: Podzun-Verlag, 1959), p. 355.
12 Számvéber, p. 51, and Maier, p. 19.
13 Számvéber, p. 51, Gosztony, p. 118, and Vopersal, p. 525.
14 Interestingly, in his own account, Balck states that the landing was proceeding well until the engines of the assault craft stopped working because "of carbon build-up" (Balck, p. 410). None of the records from the time mention this as being any sort of problem; the biggest obstacle the troops faced during the crossing were the large floes of ice in the river that threatened to smash or overturn their assault craft, which consisted chiefly of rubber rafts and small boats.
15 Pohlman, p. 355.
16 *H.Gr. Süd KTB*, entry dated 1 January 1945, p. 9, as quoted in Maier, p. 97.
17 Gaedke, p. 237.
18 Vopersal, p. 525.
19 Günther Jahnke, Personal diary, entry for 1 January 1945, p. 2.
20 Vopersal, p. 524.
21 The badly wounded Pleiner died in a military hospital in Vienna on 9 January 1945 (source: John Moore's *SS Fuhrerliste, Wiking Officer Casualties*).
22 Strassner, p. 195.

23 John Toland, *The Last 100 Days* (New York: Random House, 1966), p. 140. In contrast, a more deeply researched and nuanced account can be found in Ungvary, pp. 348–57, which portrays sexual abuse as prevalent and widespread.

24 The Budapest Operation, p. 280.

25 *Ibid.*

26 Számvéber, p. 52.

27 Vopersal, p. 526.

28 *Ibid*, p. 527.

29 *Ibid.*

30 *Ibid*, pp. 527, 530.

31 Számvéber, p. 56.

32 Jahnke diary, entry for 2 January 1945, p. 2.

33 Számvéber, p. 56, Maier, p.19, and *AOK 6, Ia KTB, Fernschreiben Ia Nr. 39/45*, 2 January 1945. More detailed instructions were sent the following day to both *LVII. Pz.Korps* and *6. Pz.Div.*, providing the details of the division's new assignment with the *IV. SS-Pz.Korps* (*AOK 6, Ia KTB, Fernschreiben Ia Nr. 84/45*, dated 3 January 1945).

34 Számvéber, pp. 54–55, and Vopersal, p. 532.

35 *Uscha.* Marienfeld from *SS-Pz.Aufkl.Abt. 3*, quoted in Vopersal, p. 532.

36 *Pz.Funker* Edelmann, *5. Kp./SS-Pz.Rgt. 3*, quoted in Vopersal, pp. 531–32.

37 Vopersal, p. 532, and Számvéber, p. 54.

38 Günter Bernau, *SS-Panzer Artillerie-Regiment 5 in der Panzer-Division Wiking* (Wuppertal, Germany: Eigenverlag Kameradschaft ehem. Pz.Art.Rgt. 5, 1990), p. 141.

39 Klapdor, pp. 387–88, and Számvéber, p. 55.

40 *Armeegruppe Balck/AOK 6 Ic KTB, Tagesmeldung* from *IV. SS-Pz.Korps* dated 2 January 1945.

41 Herbert O. Gille, "Angriff zum Entsatz der Stadt Budapest, December 1944–8 May 1945" In *Truppenkameradschaft Wiking* Archives (Stemmen, Germany: undated private manuscript), p. 2.

42 *Ibid, Tagesmeldung* from *Korpsgruppe Breith/III. Pz.Korps* dated 2 January 1945.

43 *Ibid, Tagesmeldung* from *Korpsgruppe Kirschner/LVII. Pz.Korps* dated 2 January 1945. The order to Kirschner to transfer the bulk of *6. Pz.Div.* did not apply to the division's reconnaissance battalion, combat engineer battalion, and the antitank battalion, which were to remain in support of *Div. Gr. Rintelen* for the time being.

44 Maier, p. 20.

45 *Armeegruppe Balck/AOK 6 Ic KTB*, entry dated 2 January 1945.

46 *Ibid, Tagesmeldung* from *AOK 6 Ic*, dated 2 January 1945.

47 Számvéber, p. 58.

48 *H.Gr. Süd, Chef des Generalstabes, Abt. Ia Nr. 1/45/g.K. Chefs. Befehl: Endziel der Operation "Konrad"*, 2 January 1945. Reproduced in the original in Maier (Munin Verlag Edition), p. 495.

49 Maier, p. 18.

50 *Ibid*, quoting from *H.Gr. Süd* KTB, entry dated 11:40 p.m., 2 January 1945.

51 Gaedke, p. 237.

52 Pohlman, p. 356.

53 Vopersal, p. 536. Incidentally, the aircraft were most likely twin-engine *Henschel He-129* tank-busters, equipped with 3.7cm or 5cm antitank guns, flown by *Schlachtgeschwader 9* (Számvéber, p. 59), since there were no *Ju-88* equipped with that type of weapon in the *Luftflotte 4* order of battle.

54 Vopersal, p. 537.

55 Klapdor, p. 388.

56 *Ibid.*

57   Számvéber, p. 64.
58   Soviet General Staff, p. 281. The poor performance of the 93rd Rifle Division, including the poor coordination between division and regimental headquarters, was specifically commented on in this study, accusing the division and regimental staffs of poor planning and the "absence of organized cooperation with the artillery" (p. 283). The Soviet General Staff study reported that the Germans were provided with close air support for this attack, though eyewitness statements from the *Wiking* Division remarked on the total lack of any close air support that day.
59   Günther Jahnke, Diary December 1944–4 August 1945. *Truppenkameradschaft Wiking* Archives (Munich: Undated private manuscript), p. 3.
60   Gille, p. 2, and Jahnke, p. 3.
61   Maier, p. 23.
62   Számvéber, p. 66.
63   Jahnke Diary, entry 3 January 1945.
64   *Anlage H.Gr. Süd KTB*, entry dated 3 January 1945, quoted in Maier, p. 22.
65   Számvéber, p. 67.
66   Maier, p. 21.
67   Számvéber, p. 65. Incidentally, this attack was supported by three *Pz.Kfw. VIb* King Tigers from *schw.Pz.Abt. Feldherrenhalle* (formerly *schw.Pz.Abt. 503*).
68   Soviet General Staff, p. 282.
69   *Armeegruppe Balck/AOK 6 Ic KTB*, entry dated 3 January 1945.
70   Maier, p. 21, quoting from the *H.Gr. Süd Ia KTB Tagesmeldung* for 3 January 1945.
71   Maier, p. 22.
72   *AOK 6, Ia Anlage, Fernschreiben Ia 22/45 geheime Kommandosache*, 3:15 p.m., 3 January 1945.
73   Számvéber, p. 74, and Pohlman, p. 356.
74   Számvéber, p. 74.
75   *Ibid*, pp. 74–75.
76   *Ibid*, pp. 68–69.
77   Vopersal, p. 543, and Számvéber, p. 70.
78   Maier, p. 23.
79   Számvéber, pp. 72–73.
80   *Ibid*, p. 73.
81   Maier, p. 23.
82   The division's *O1*, Günther Jahnke, wrote in his diary that day that there was "Major action by the supply units, which were able to bring fuel and ammunition all the way to Tarjan." Up to that point, delivery of supplies had been sporadic and insufficient to meet the unit's needs. Jahnke Diary, entry 4 January 1945.
83   Számvéber, pp. 73–74.
84   *H.Gr. Süd Ia KTB, Tagesmeldung* dated 4 January 1945.
85   Számvéber, p. 75.
86   *AOK 6, Ia KTB, Anlage*, message dated 11:30 p.m., 4 January 1945.
87   Maier, p. 23.
88   *Ibid*.
89   By 4 January, within the *Konrad* operational area, the *Armeegruppe*'s *Ic* had identified the XVIII Tank Corps with the 110th, 170th, and 181st Tank Brigades and the 32nd Mechanized Brigade; the VII Mechanized Corps with a tank brigade; the II Guards Mechanized Corps with a tank brigade; and the V Guards Cavalry Corps with portions of a tank brigade. In addition, the *Ic* also identified three rifle corps (X and XXXI Guards and LXVIII Rifle Corps) with the 4th, 34th, 49th, 80th, and 86th Guards Rifle Divisions, and the 93rd and 223rd Rifle Divisions.

90 Maier, p. 23, quoting from *AOK 6 Ia KTB, Tagesmeldung*, 4 January 1945.

91 *AOK 6 Ia KTB Anlage, Fernschreiben Ia Nr. 95/45* and *96/45*, both dated 4 January 1945.

92 Maier, p. 24.

93 *AOK 6 Ia KTB Anlage, Fernschreiben Nr. 104/45* and *109/45*, dated 4 January 1945.

94 Számvéber, p. 82.

95 *Ibid.*

96 Pohlman, p. 357, and Maier, p. 25. According to Soviet records, three of the giant JS-IIs were knocked out later that day, though it does not state whether they were destroyed by air attack or antitank guns (Számvéber, p. 82).

97 Vopersal, p. 544.

98 *Oscha.* Zährl in Vopersal, p. 544.

99 Ullrich, p. 252, and Számvéber, p. 78.

100 Vopersal, p. 546.

101 *Ibid.*

102 Franz Hack and Fritz Hahl, *Panzergrenadier der Panzer-Division Wiking in Bild* (Osnabruck: Munin Verlag GmbH, 1984), p. 226.

103 Hack *et al,* p. 226.

104 Számvéber, p. 79.

105 Manfred Renz, "Kämpfe um Ungarn 1945," p. 3, Számvéber, p. 81, and Klapdor, p. 390.

106 Renz, p. 4.

107 Willi, Fey, *Armor Battles of the Waffen-SS 1943–1945* (Mechanicsburg, PA: Stackpole Books, 2003), p. 229. (Note: this book was originally published in 1987 by Munin-Verlag as *Panzerkampf im Bild*.) A brief radio message sent by the *Wiking* Division to Gille's headquarters was monitored by the *6. Armee* signal battalion, *Armee-Nachr.Btl. 549*, at 1 p.m., several hours after Darges's tanks had gone to ground at Hegyks Castle.

108 Strassner, p. 197. This article, titled "Schloss Hegyiks: Das Fort der Unbeugsamen" (The Fort of the Undefeated), was penned by the unnamed *SS-Kriegsberichter* on 1 February 1945 and featured in the 1945/5 issue of *Das Schwarze Korps*.

109 Gille Diary, p. 2.

110 Soviet General Staff, pp. 287–88.

111 The *I. Abt./Pz.Rgt. 26*, originally part of the *26. Pz.Div.*, was a *Heerestruppen* asset and was attached to several units, including the *6. Pz.Div.* during the prosecution of the first two *Konrad* attempts before finally being shipped back to Germany for reconstitution on 18 January 1945. After leaving behind its 29 remaining tanks, only 13 of which were operational, it was re-equipped and later assigned to *Pz.Div. Brandenburg*.

112 Számvéber, p. 82. The *I. Abt./Pz.Lehr-Rgt. 130* would be shipped home to Germany to be re-equipped with new tanks, leaving behind as many as 46 *Pz. V* Panthers, of which only nine were combat-ready on 7 January.

113 Számvéber, pp. 82–83.

114 *Armeegruppe Balck/AOK 6 Ic KTB*, entry dated 5 January 1945.

115 Maier, p. 25.

116 *Armeegruppe Balck/AOK 6 Ic KTB*, entry dated 5 January 1945.

117 *Armeegruppe Balck/AOK 6 Ic KTB Anlage, Verlust seit Beginn der Angriffes 1. bis 5. Januar 1945.*

118 Guderian, p. 314.

119 *Ibid* and Hans Fischer, *Standartenführer Johannes Mühlenkamp und seine Männer*, Vol. 2 (Erpe, The Netherlands: The Warrior Publishing, 2005), p. 383.

120 Maier, p. 25.

121 *AOK 6, Ia KTB Anlage, Fernschreiben 122/45*, dated 5 January 1945.

122 *AOK 6, Ia KTB Anlage, Fernschreiben 135/45*, dated 5 January 1945.

123 *AOK 6, Ia KTB Anlage, Fernschreiben 137/45*, dated 5 January 1945.

124 Glantz *et al, Art of War Symposium*, p. 680.

125 Glantz *et al*, pp. 680, 682.

126 Számvéber, p. 88, and Maier, p. 26.

127 Számvéber, p. 87.

128 Klapdor, p. 391.

129 Számvéber, p. 85.

130 Wood, *Tigers of the Totenkopf*, p. 229.

131 Maier, p. 26. Post actually was awarded the medal on 28 February 1945 (Számvéber, p. 88).

132 Schönfelder, p. 2, and Gille Diary, p. 2.

133 Maier, p. 26.

134 *H.Gr. Süd Ia KTB*, entry dated 6 January 1945, pp. 70–88, quoted in Maier, p. 27.

135 Manfred Schönfelder, Commentary dated 1 December 1981, "Concerning the operations of formations of the *Waffen-SS* in the Hungarian theater of operations during the time from 1 January 1945 to 3 March 1945," as quoted in Maier, p. 99.

136 *Ibid*, p. 99.

137 *Armeegruppe Balck/AOK 6 Ia KTB Anlage, Personelle und material Verluste des IV. SS-Pz.Korps in der Zeit vom 1.–7.01.1945*, dated 2:45 p.m., 9 January 1945.

138 *Armeegruppe Balck/AOK 6 Ia KTB Anlage, Kampfstärken, Stand 6.01.1945*, entry dated 6 January 1945.

139 Pohlman, p. 359.

140 Jahnke Diary, p. 5.

141 Vopersal, p. 550.

142 *Ibid*, p. 551.

143 Pohlman, p. 357.

144 Számvéber, pp. 189–90.

145 Gille Diary, p. 2.

146 *H.Gr. Süd Ia KTB* for 7 January 1945, pp. 89–108, quoted in Maier, pp. 29–30.

147 These discussions, available in the *H.Gr. Süd* war diary for 7 January, are related in detail by Maier, pp. 30–31.

148 Klapdor, p. 391, and Jahnke Diary, p. 5.

149 Számvéber, pp. 109–10.

150 *Armeegruppe Balck/AOK 6 Ic KTB*, entry dated 8 January 1945.

151 *Ibid*.

152 *H.Gr. Süd Ia KTB*, entry for 8 January 1945, quoted in Maier, p. 32, and Számvéber, p. 110.

153 Számvéber, p. 110.

154 *Aus dem Führerhauptquartier: Das Oberkommando gibt Bekannt, Die Berichte des Oberkommandos der Wehrmacht*, Volume V: 1.1.1944–9.5.1945 (Munich: Verlag für Wehrwissenschaften, 2004), entry dated 8 January 1945.

Chapter 6: The Second Relief Attempt of Budapest—*Konrad II*

1 Gille Diary, 9 January 1945, p. 2.

2 Maier, p. 30.

3 Maier, pp. 41–43; Schönfelder Manuscript, pp. 4–5. Although unremarked upon at the time, Gille was probably the only commander on the scene who knew what was possible and what was not; Balck's typical over-optimism may have blinded the *6. Armee* commander to the reality that

there were only sufficient forces to rescue the garrison, not to reincorporate Budapest into the old defense line. And even then, any rescue mission would only have succeeded if the encircled garrison had been allowed to conduct an attack towards the rescue force, while abandoning the city to its fate. Hitler had already ruled this out as an option, a decision that condemned the garrison to its inevitable destruction. Gille was apparently operating under the belief that Hitler would allow a breakout at the last moment, like von Manstein had done at Cherkassy. Or perhaps that Pfeffer-Wildenbruch would disobey the *Führer* and lead a breakout on his own authority, unlike what *G.F.M.* von Paulus had failed to do at Stalingrad when issued identical orders to stand fast. In his own book, Balck does not even broach the topic of authorizing a breakout from Budapest until it was too late. He may have also misled or encouraged Gille into believing that he would do whatever was needed to be done to rescue the garrison, but there is no evidence for this except Gille's own actions. The fact that Balck failed to challenge Hitler about this, despite his purported good relationship with the dictator, must stand as a black mark on his record.

4   Vopersal, p. 554.
5   Maier, pp. 35–37, Vopersal, p. 556. It remains unclear whether Gaedke was the originator of the idea, though evidence seems to indicate so. Balck was also a strong proponent, but when the *Husarenritt* later failed, Balck claimed that it was Hitler's idea all along. Gaedke does not mention *Kampfgruppe Philipp* at all in his memoir.
6   Maier, p. 34.
7   Philipp's *Kampfgruppe* consisted of *II. Btl./Pz.Gren.Rgt. FHH* with two infantry companies mounted in Volkswagen *Kübelwagen* and *Kettenkräder* (half-tracked motorcycles), *Maj.* Hillermann's *II. Btl./ Gren.Rgt. 284* from the *96. Inf.Div.*, *II. Abt./Art.Rgt. 96*, one Sapper platoon, 6 *SPW*s (from the *Wiking* Division), two *Pz. IV*s and three *StuG*s from the *Totenkopf* Division, and three eight-wheeled armored cars from *SS-Pz.Aufkl.Abt. 3 Totenkopf* (source: Pohlmann, pp. 360–61, and Számvéber, pp. 118–19).
8   The *1. Ung. Hussar-Division* was a unit already familiar to Gille and his staff, for it had been previously been titled the *1. Ung.Kavallerie-Division* when it was under the corps' control between August and October 1944, when it had performed very well.
9   Balck, p. 411.
10 Vopersal, p. 555, quoting an account by *SS-Junker* (Officer Candidate) Renold from *II. Btl./Eicke*.
11 Jahnke Diary, p. 5.
12 Vopersal, pp. 555–56.
13 Schmeisser, p. 43.
14 Maier, p. 37.
15 Soviet General Staff Study, p. 294.
16 *Ibid.*
17 Isaev and Kolomiets, p. 40.
18 *Ibid.*
19 Maier, p. 35.
20 *AOK 6, Ic KTB Tagesmeldung*, entry dated 9 January 1945.
21 Maier, p. 34.
22 *Ibid.*, p. 36, quoting the *AOK 6 Ia KTB, Anlage* entry dated 9 January 1945.
23 Jahnke Diary, p. 5.
24 *Ibid.*
25 Maier, p. 101 n. 147.
26 The story of *K.Gr. Philipp* and its *Husarenritt* is worthy of a book of its own. Whether it ever stood any chance of success can be debated; certainly the delay between 9 and 10 January 1945, and false reporting by the *96. Inf.Div.*, contributed to its failure. Several sources describe the course of

this failed mission, including the *KTB* of *H.Gr. Süd* (entries dated 9–12 January), Maier, p. 38, Számvéber, p. 131, Vopersal, in particular the story as related by *Uscha.* Marienfeld, pp. 557–58, and Pohlmann, pp. 360–61.

27 Jahnke Diary, p. 5.

28 Vopersal, p. 557.

29 *AOK 6 Ic Tagesmeldung*, 10 January 1945.

30 Számvéber, pp. 119–20, Soviet General Staff Study, pp. 294–95. According to former Soviet studies, 6,000 antitank mines were laid from 10–11 January alone.

31 *AOK 6 Ic Tagesmeldung*, 10 January 1945.

32 Maier, quoting *H.Gr. Süd Ia KTB* for 10 January 1945, p. 38.

33 Maier, p. 38, summarizing *Beurteilung der Lage bei Armeegruppe Balck am 10.1.45 Abends, nach Rücksprache des Oberbefehlshaber (H.Gr. Süd) mit General Balck.*

34 Maier, quoting *H.Gr. Süd Führungsabteilung KTB*, entry dated 10 January 1945.

35 Hack, quoted in *Panzergreandiere der Panzer-Division Wiking im Bild*, p. 226. What he saw was not evidence of the advance of *K.Gr. Philipp*, which at any rate was occurring at the same time several mountain ridges to the east; rather, this was most likely debris from the fighting left over from the last week of December when German and Hungarian forces were fleeing ahead of the Soviet advance after the encirclement of Budapest, as described in Ungváry, pp. 68–69. Many of the rear-echelon or *Tross* elements of the German and Hungarian divisions located outside Budapest chose this escape route through the mountains to make their way to Gran, which was still in German hands at this point.

36 Számvéber, p. 126, Maier, p. 39, and Andris J. Kursietis and Antonio M. Munoz, *The Hungarian Army and its Military Leadership in World War II* (Bayside, NY: Axis Europa Books, 1999), p. 58.

37 Gille Diary, entry dated 11 January 1945, p. 2. In his memoirs, Balck claims that "over a thousand" wounded troops and the medical staff was rescued, but this is an exaggeration.

38 Klapdor, p. 387, and Maier, n. 97–98.

39 Fey, p. 229. This order directing Lichte's battalion to withdraw depicts how orders for redirecting the relief attempt to the south began to contradict the ongoing operation in the north. Instead of being completely pulled out, however, Lichte's few remaining tanks were used to establish a new outpost line linking the remaining *Panzergruppe* under Darges at the Hegyks Castle Estate with the regiment's main command post in the vicinity of Vasztely (conversation with Mirko Bayerl, 30 January 2020).

40 *AOK 6 Ic KTB Tagesmeldung*, 11 January 1945.

41 Számvéber, pp. 122–24.

42 Számvéber, pp.125–26, Soviet General Staff Study, p. 295, and Maier, p. 39.

43 Maier, p. 39, and *AOK 6 Ic KTB Tagesmeldung*, 11 January 1945.

44 Ungváry, pp. 195–96.

45 Maier, p. 39, and *AOK 6 Ic KTB Tagesmeldung*, 11 January 1945.

46 Schönfelder Manuscript, entries covering period from 11–12 January 1945, pp. 3–4.

47 Jahnke Diary, p. 6. At least *I. Btl./Germania* was still in position near Csabdi.

48 Hack, in *Panzergrenadiere der Panzer-Division Wiking im Bild*, pp. 226–27. Incidentally, Rumohr only commanded his division; the actual *Kampfkommandant* of Budapest was *Ogruf. Pfeffer-Wildenbruch.*

49 One historian asserts that *K.Gr. Westland*'s advance units had reached as far as the Csobánka fork on the road to Pomáz, only 17 kilometers from Budapest, but this is disputed by Soviet records (Ungvary, p. 195). Unbeknownst to anyone at the time, the 99th Rifle Division was rallying its regiments beyond the next hill and the V Guards Cavalry Corps had been ordered to the area as well.

50 Pohlman, p. 362.
51 Vopersal, pp. 562–63.
52 *AOK 6 Ic KTB Tagesmeldung*, 12 January 1945.
53 Maier, quoting the *H.Gr. Süd Ia KTB* entry for 12 January 1945.
54 Hack, in *Panzergrenadiere der Panzer-Division Wiking im Bild*, p. 232.
55 Maier, pp. 41–43, *H.Gr. Sud Ia KTB* dated 12 January 1945, and message exchanges in *AOK 6 Chefsache*.
56 Maier, p. 41.
57 Vopersal, pp. 563–64.
58 Gille Diary, entry dated 12 January 1945, p. 2.
59 Jahnke Diary, entry dated 12 January 1945, p. 6.
60 Schönfelder Manuscript, pp. 4–5.
61 Balck, p. 410.
62 Jahnke Diary, entry dated 13 January 1945, p. 6. Incidentally, what they saw to the south was most likely not Budapest, but the church spires in the large town of Pilisvörösvár, 11 kilometers away. Budapest lay 10 kilometers beyond that point. Nevertheless, the alleged sighting of Budapest from Dobogókó has become a commonly accepted *Wiking* Division legend.

Chapter 7: Change of Mission

1 Balck, p. 436.
2 Schönfelder manuscript, pp. 4–5, and Maier, pp. 42–43. After the war, the former *O1* of the *Wiking* Division, Günther Jahnke, wrote that Generals Wöhler and Balck could have disobeyed Hitler and allowed Gille's attack through the Pilis Mountains to continue. Jahnke, Schönfelder, and Ullrich, the division's commander, staunchly held firm in their belief that Budapest could have been relieved through this route. Whether Gille would have disobeyed orders and continued the attack on his own was disavowed by Jahnke, who stated that this was not in Gille's character (Letter from Günther Jahnke to Mirko Bayerl, 20 June 1988, courtesy of Mirko Bayerl).
3 *Führerbefehl für den Neuansatz der Operation (durch OKH/Gen.Std.H./Op.Abt.) mit Zusätzen der H.Gr. Süd Ia Nr. 3/45 g.Kdos.Chefsache*, reproduced verbatim in Maier, p. 410.
4 *Zusätze der H.Gr. Süd, Ia Nr. 3/45 g.Kdo. Chefsache vom 12.1.1945*, as reproduced verbatim in Maier, p. 411.
5 Guderian, p. 321.
6 Balck, pp. 411–12.
7 Gosztony, p. 128, quoting letter to the author from Herbert Otto Gille dated 1962.
8 *Zeitberechnung, Bewegungen, Befehlsgliederung, und Angriffsbegin zu "Konrad 3," Armeegruppe Balck, Ia Nr. 5/45*, 12 January 1945. Original copy reproduced in Munin Verlag edition of Maier, pp. 503–04.
9 *Armeegruppe Balck/AOK 6 Oberquartiermeister O.Qu.1/Qu.1 Chefsachen Nr. 290/45 g.Kdos., Unterlagen für die Versorgungsführung*, 11 January 1945, pp. 1–5.
10 War Department Technical Manual TM 30-506, *German Military Dictionary* (Washington, D.C.: War Department, 7 May 1944), p. 195.
11 For example, *Armeegruppe Balck/AOK 6* issued an order on 16 January 1945 that stated, "The extremely tense fuel situation forces all vehicles not needed for *Konrad III* to be parked. If this order is not obeyed, there is a danger that *Konrad III* operations will come to a standstill after a short time due to a lack of fuel." *Armeegruppe Balck/AOK 6 Ia Anlage, Fernschreiben Ia Nr. 91/45 g.Kdos.*, 16 January 1945.
12 *Armeegruppe Balck/AOK 6, Oberquartiermeister/Qu. I, Nr. 290/45, Unterlagen für die Versorgungsführung*, 11 January 1945, pp. 1–5.

13 Klose would depart the corps on 16 January to become the *Ia* of the *Wiking* Division; he in turn was replaced as the corps *Ia* by *Stubaf.* Fritz Rentrop, also a recent graduate of the *Kriegschule Generalstabslehrgang.*

14 *H.Gr. Süd, Ia Nr. 5/45, g.Kdos. Chefsache, Unternehmen "Konrad 3,"* reproduced in Maier, Munin Edition, p. 505.

15 Glantz, pp. 507–12, 516, and Ziemke, pp. 416–17.

16 Guderian, p. 315.

17 *Armeegruppe Balck/AOK 6 Ia KTB, Fernspruch von Ia IV. SS-Pz.Korps für Ia. Armeegruppe Balck,* 1:45 p.m., 13 January 1945.

18 *Zeitberechnung, Bewegungen, Befehlsgliederung, und Angriffsbegin zu "Konrad 3," Armeegruppe Balck, Ia Nr. 5/45,* 12 January 1945.

19 Vopersal, p. 564.

20 Maier, p. 43.

21 How much of the *Germania* Regiment had arrived in the Gran area by 12 January 1945 is still a matter of dispute, since original division records did not survive the war and existing records and postwar reminiscences are contradictory. Based on this, the most likely situation is that at least one battalion remained behind at Csabdi under the control of the *6. Pz.Div.*, a portion, perhaps a battalion, had already arrived in the Gran area, while the remainder of the regiment was strung out along the roads between those two locations. *Ostubaf.* Dorr's regimental command post was located in Vasztely, where the *panzer* regiment's headquarters was also located, since Dorr himself was still there on 12 January. The Division *O1*, Günther Jahnke, wrote at the time that the *Germania* Regiment was "approaching" Pilisszentkereszt and that a portion of the regiment was already operating on the right flank of the *Westland* Regiment, though this may have been the result of a garbled radio message. A cursory examination of existing maps indicates that there were no roads paralleling the one between Pilisszentlélek and the previously mentioned town, so Jahnke's belief may have been mistaken.

22 Letter from Willi Hein to Mirko Bayerl, 1997.

23 Vopersal, p. 564. Incidentally, Vogt's battalion had suffered the loss of over 50 men, half of them being killed in action, while the commanders of every one of his four line companies were killed or wounded.

24 Maier, p. 43.

25 *SS-Sturmmann* Hochreuter, *3. Kp./SS-Pz.Jäg.Abt. 3,* quoted in Vopersal, pp. 564–65.

26 Vopersal, pp. 565–66.

27 Számvéber, p. 133 (source: *H.Gr. Süd, Ia KTB, Nr. 156/45 g.Kdos.*, dated 15 January 1945).

28 *H.Gr. Süd, Ia KTB Chefsachen, Fernschreiben Ia KTB Nr. 91/45 g.Kdos.*, issued 2:35 p.m., 15 January 1945.

29 According to German records, 930 of *Armeegruppe Balck's* men voluntarily deserted to the Red Army between 1 and 17 January, the overwhelming majority of whom were Hungarian troops (source: *H.Gr. Süd Ia KTB, Ia Nr. 234/45 g.Kdos.*, report dated 22 January 1945).

30 Soviet General Staff Study, pp. 79, 297–98; Isaev and Kolomiets, p. 42, and Számvéber, pp. 132–33. In his own memoir, Balck also refers to the success of this deception operation, p. 412.

31 *H.Gr. Süd Ia KTB*, entry dated 13 January 1945, pp. 198–211, and entry dated 14 January 1945, pp. 212–25, referred to in Maier, pp. 45, 102.

32 Maier, p. 45.

33 The movement of *IV. SS-Pz.Korps* was closely monitored by both *Armeegruppe Balck/6. Armee* and *H.Gr. Süd.* Two documents, one dated 15 January and the other dated two days later, still exist that portray the arrival of its constituent elements as well as that of its two SS divisions. An armored fighting vehicle status report was also drafted on 15 January by *Armeegruppe Balck,* depicting both the total numbers of each type of vehicle on hand as well as the number that

were deemed operational. It shows that both SS divisions combined on that date had a total of 55 operational tanks, assault guns, and tank destroyers out of 158 on hand, the remaining 103 being in various stages of repair. While the total number of available vehicles would improve slightly before 18 January, the *Totenkopf* and *Wiking* Divisions would go into battle that day with roughly a third of their remaining 158 vehicles (source: *Armeegruppe Balck/AOK 6 Ia KTB Anlagen, Aktennotiz,* dated 15 January and 17 January 1945, and *Ia KTB Anlage, Nachmeldung, Stand der einsatzbereiten Panzer und Panzerabwehrwaffen am 15 Januar 1945*).

34 *Armeegruppe Balck/AOK 6 Ia KTB Anlage, Anruf von IV. SS-Pz.Korps,* 18 January 1945.

35 Számvéber, pp. 149–50; Soviet General Staff Study, p. 303, and Isaev and Kolomiets, pp. 43–44. Also refer to *Armeegruppe Balck/AOK 6 Ia KTB Anlage, Nachmeldung, Stand der einsatzbereiten Panzer und Panzerabwehrwaffen am 15 Januar 1945.*

36 Isaev and Kolomiets, p. 45. For example, the Soviet 1st Guards Fortified Region alone reported on average that 10 Hungarian deserters reached their lines each day until 15 January (a total of 205 since 1 January 1945), when German troops replaced Hungarians in the front lines.

37 Balck, p. 412.

38 *H.Gr. Süd Ia KTB Anlage, Fernschreiben Ia Nr. 481/45 Betr: Zur Hebung des Selbstvertrauens der Kampfwilligen Ung. Verbände,* 2:17 a.m., 11 January 1945.

39 Incidentally, by 18 January, *SS-Regiment Ney* would be placed under the operational control of the *23. Pz.Div.* of *III. Pz.Korps* and would not operate under the *IV. SS-Pz.Korps* until 28 January 1945.

40 Söth would be promoted to *Gen.Maj.* 12 days later.

41 Szamveber, p. 150. This number conflicts somewhat with that provided by the 4th Guards Army after the war, which was somewhat less (see note 42).

42 Számvéber, p. 150. Soviet sources claim that the Germans had 521 guns, though this probably includes those howitzers and other field pieces of the Hungarian Army. The Red Army also grouped antitank guns under the artillery category (Soviet General Staff Study, p. 303).

43 Számvéber, p. 148, and Fernschreiben, *IV. SS-Pz.Korps Chef des Stabes an AOK 6 Ia,* 12:35 a.m., 16 January 1945.

44 *Hauptquartier IV. SS-Pz.Korps, Führungsabteilung: Planung und Kräfteberechnung für die Operation Konrad III,* 15 January 1945, p. 11.

45 Számvéber, p. 151.

46 Soviet General Staff Study, pp. 299–300.

47 *Ibid,* p. 302, and Isaev and Kolomiets, p. 45.

48 Soviet General Staff Study, p. 297.

49 *Ibid,* p. 302.

50 Isaev and Kolomiets, p. 43.

51 *Ibid,* p. 45. The 1st Guards Fortified Region also had 38 7.6cm guns, 31 4.5cm guns, 7 12cm mortars, 32 8.2cm mortars, and 253 heavy and light machine guns.

52 Soviet General Staff Study, pp. 302–03. The Red Army calculated combat strengths differently than the *Wehrmacht,* including nearly every soldier in any category comprising the attacking or defending force. Therefore, while the German method of calculating *Kampfstärke* resulted in an initial number of approximately 13,000 fighting troops in both the *III.* and *IV. SS-Pz.Korps,* the Red Army counted 49,850 German and Hungarian troops arrayed against them for *Konrad III* in the *IV. SS-Pz.Korps* area of operations alone. This was probably much closer to the actual *Sollstärke* (authorized strength) of the units concerned, though not an accurate indicator of actual German combat power.

53 Soviet General Staff Study, p. 302.

54 Isaev and Kolomiets, p. 49.
55 Számvéber, pp. 435–37.
56 *Ibid*, p. 438, Soviet General Staff Study, pp. 303–04, and Isaev and Kolomiets, pp. 44–45.
57 Gille manuscript, p. 3.
58 *Der Oberbefehlshaber der Armeegruppe Balck, Armee Gefechtstand, Armee Tagesbefehl*, issued 16 January 1945.
59 This prevailing attitude of the *Waffen-SS* troops about to take part in *Konrad III* is summed up in Erich Kern's *Die Letzte Schlacht*, p. 159. A similar attitude was displayed by troops from *Heeres-Divisionen*, such as the *1. Pz.Div.* (Stoves, pp. 712–13).
60 Számvéber, p. 135.
61 Maier, p. 45.
62 *Ibid*, p. 46.
63 *Armeegruppe Balck/6. Armee Ia KTB Anlage, Fernschreiben—KR Einsatz, Ia Nr. 450/45*, dated 17 January 1945.
64 Balck, p. 412.
65 *Führungsabteilung, IV. SS-Pz.Korps, Ia Nr. 37/45 g.Kdos.*, 7 p.m., 17 January 1945.
66 Jahnke Diary, entry dated 16 January 1945, p. 7.
67 Isaev and Kolomiets, p. 45.

Chapter 8: The Third Relief Attempt of Budapest—*Konrad III*, Part I

1   Maier, p. 46, quoting *H.Gr. Süd Ia KTB* for 18 January 1945, pp. 22–32.
2   *Armeegruppe Balck/AOK 6 Ic KTB*, entry for 18 January 1945, p. 1.
3   *Ibid*.
4   Maier, p. 64 (Munin Verlag German language edition).
5   Gille manuscript, entry dated 18 January 1945, p. 3, and Jahnke Diary, entry dated 18 January, p. 7.
6   Strassner, p. 200.
7   Maier, p. 64–65 (Munin Verlag German language edition).
8   Számvéber, pp. 157–58. Additionally, *SS-Pz.Rgt. 3* reported the loss of two *Pz. V* Panthers and one *Pz. IV*.
9   Maier, p. 65 (Munin Verlag German language edition), and Számvéber, pp. 159–60.
10 *Armeegruppe Balck/AOK 6 Ia KTB, Anlage, O.Qu. Fernschreiben Nr. 479/45 geheim*, dated 2 a.m., 19 January 1945.
11 Soviet General Staff Study, pp. 79–80, 301.
12 *Armeegruppe Balck/AOK 6 Ic KTB*, entry for 18 January 1945, p. 2.
13 Vopersal, p. 579. This report appeared in the 22 February 1945 issue of *Das Schwarze Korps*.
14 *Armeegruppe Balck/AOK 6 Ic KTB*, entry for 19 January 1945, p. 1.
15 Gille manuscript, p. 3.
16 Maier, p. 48, quoting *H.Gr. Süd Führungsabteilung KTB*, entry dated 5:15 p.m., 19 January 1945.
17 Maier, p. 48, quoting *H.Gr. Süd Führungsabteilung KTB*, entry dated 9 p.m., 19 January 1945.
18 Maier, p. 67 (Munin Verlag German language edition).
19 Maier, p. 66 (Munin Verlag German language edition).
20 *Ibid*.
21 *Armeegruppe Balck/AOK 6 Ic KTB*, entry for 19 January 1945, p. 1.
22 *Ibid*.

23 Ungváry, p. 164,
24 Isaev and Kolomiets, p. 49.
25 *AOK 6, Ia KTB Anlage, Mitgehörte Funksprüche*, 3:20 p.m., 19 January 1945.
26 *Armeegruppe Balck/AOK 6 Ic*, entry for 19 January 1945, p. 1.
27 Számvéber, pp. 174, 178.
28 Balck, p. 412.
29 Maier, p. 48, quoting a report sent from *H.Gr. Süd* at 5:45 p.m., 19 January 1945, to the *Führungsabteilung* of *OKH*.
30 *Ibid.*
31 Isaev and Kolomiets, pp. 48–49.
32 Maier, p. 49.
33 *Armeegruppe Balck/AOK 6, Ia KTB Anlage, Ia Nr. 529/44 geh., Fernschreiben an Oberkommando H.Gr. Süd, Betr: Absicht für 20.1.45*, dated 19 January 1945.
34 *Armeegruppe Balck/AOK 6 Ic KTB*, entry dated 20 January 1945.
35 Maier, p. 68 (Munin Verlag German language edition).
36 *Ibid.* Additionally, on 20 January, the Hungarian *25. Inf.Div.* reported a *Kampfstärke* of 5,330 men, a very large amount for this period of the war. It also reported having 49 artillery pieces and 12 antitank guns (source: *AOK 6, Ia KTB Anlage, Kampfstärke der Armeegruppe, Stand 20.1.1945*).
37 *Armeegruppe Balck/AOK 6, Ia KTB Anlage, Funkspruche von 5. SS-Pz.Div. Wiking an IV. SS-Pz. Korps*, dated 9:02 a.m., 20 January 1945. Incidentally, Balck claimed in his memoir that this report was a lie, stating that when he had someone go to that very spot several days later to substantiate this claim, no destroyed or captured Soviets trucks and antitank guns were to be found (Balck, p. 412). This accusation was based on the flimsiest of evidence; any captured material would have been incorporated into Dorr's *Panzergruppe* as a matter of course, while destroyed matériel would not necessarily have been concentrated into one spot where it could easily be counted, assuming that Balck's liaison officer went to the correct location. Balck also claimed that his account was supported by a *Luftwaffe* general officer, *Gen.Maj.* Hans-Detlef Herhudt von Roden, who Balck claimed was the *Flivo* for *IV. SS-Pz.Korps*. This is patently false; von Roden became chief of the 8th Department (War Science Department) of the General Staff of the *Luftwaffe* in 1943, a position which he still held in January 1945. Additionally, the duty position of a *panzer* corps *Flivo* was filled by either a *Major* or *Oberstleutnant*, but not a *Generalmajor*, according to Günther Lange, Gille's former *O5 Begleitoffizier*. Additionally, there are no records or recollections that mention any *Luftwaffe Generalmajor* accompanying Dorr's *Panzergruppe* on 20 January 1945.
38 Klapdor, pp. 394–95, Fey, pp. 230–31, and Jahnke Manuscript, entry dated 20 January 1945, p. 9.
39 Letter, Gunter Bernau, Bad Worishofen, Germany, to John P. Moore, 12 March 1996. Copy of letter in author's possession.
40 Számvéber, pp. 186–87, Vopersal, pp. 584–85.
41 Maier, pp. 68–69 (Munin Verlag German language edition).
42 Isaev and Kolomiets, p. 54.
43 Vopersal, p. 586.
44 Maier, p. 69 (Munin Verlag German language edition).
45 *Armeegruppe Balck/AOK 6 Ia KTB Anlage, Fernschreiben*, dated 12:40 p.m., 20 January 1945, and Schönfelder manuscript, entry dated 20 January 1945, p. 6.
46 Vopersal, p. 587.
47 Stoves, pp. 718–19, Számvéber, pp. 190–91.
48 Gille Manuscript, p. 3.
49 *Armeegruppe Balck/AOK 6 Ic KTB, entry dated 20 January 1945.*
50 *Ibid.*

51 *Ibid*, Számvéber, p. 194.

52 Percy E. Schramm (ed.), *Kriegstagebuch des Oberkommando Der Wehrmacht, 1944–45, Teilband II*, entry dated 20 January 1945, p. 1025.

53 Tessin, Vol. 3, p. 110. The purpose of a *Kommandeur der Nachrichtenaufklärung* (*KONA*) regiment was to supply intelligence to the staff of the *Armee-Korps*, *Armeen* and *Heeresgruppen*. Each *KONA* unit consisted of a regimental evaluation center and possibly five or six intercept and intelligence companies. The *KONA* regiment operated with the signal intelligence platoons operating close to the front line, with its companies situated close to the *Armee* HQ and the main evaluation unit situated in the rear at *H.Gr.* headquarters (source: Signal Intelligence Regiment (KONA), accessed on Wikipedia 26 May 2020).

54 M. M. Malakhov, *The Liberation of Hungary and Eastern Austria (October1944—April 1945)* (Moscow: Voenizdat, 1965), p. 123, quoted in Isaev and Kolomiets, p. 50.

55 Maier, pp. 48–49; Isaev and Kolomiets, p. 50, and the Soviet General Staff Study, pp. 81–82.

56 Balck, pp. 417–19. Information about the Hungarian *25. Inf.Div.* can be found in Leo W. G. Niehorster's *The Royal Hungarian Army, 1920–1945. Volume I: Organization and History* (Privately published manuscript, copyright © 1998 and 2010 by Leo W. G. Niehorster), p. 250.

57 Meier, p. 50.

58 *Armeegruppe Balck/AOK 6 Ia KTB, Anlage. Fernschreiben—KR Einsatz, Ia Nr. 438/45 geh.*, dated 20 January 1945.

59 *Armeegruppe Balck/AOK 6 Ia KTB, Anlage. Fernschreiben—KR Einsatz, Ia Nr. 556/45 geh.*, dated 20 January 1945.

60 Maier, p. 51, citing the *H.Gr. Süd KTB* entry for 20 January 1945.

61 *Armeegruppe Balck/AOK 6 Ic KTB*, entry dated 21 January 1945.

62 Gille manuscript, entry dated 21 January 1945, p. 3.

63 Számvéber, pp. 203, 208, quoting the *H.Gr. Süd Ia KTB* for 24 January 1945.

64 So much Soviet war matériel had fallen into German hands but not yet been recovered, that Balck became concerned that it might be recaptured during a Soviet counterattack. Consequently, he issued an order on 21 January 1945 that directed all units to destroy with demolition charges any captured Soviet combat vehicles and weapons that could not be recovered in time. Each division was to form special demolition teams under the control of a responsible officer that would comb the rear area of the battlefield and destroy tanks, guns, and other weaponry with special explosives and to report the results to *Armeegruppe Balck/6. Armee* (source: *Armeegruppe Balck Ia KTB Anlage, Ia Nr. 561/45 geheime Fernschreiben*, dated 21 January 1945).

65 Maier (Munin Verlag German language edition), pp. 70–71.

66 Vopersal, p. 589, Számvéber, p. 200.

67 Soviet General Staff Study, p. 309.

68 Számvéber, pp. 199–200, quoting the *H.Gr. Süd Ia KTB Morgen- and Tagesmeldung* for 21 January 1945.

69 *Armeegruppe Balck/AOK 6 Ia KTB Anlage, Mitgehörter Funkspruch von Wiking an IV. SS-Pz.Korps, Betr: Wöchentlicher Zustands-Kurzbericht ohne Gren.Rgt. Germania und Feldausb.Btl.*, dated 5 a.m., 21 January 1945, and *Kampfstärken IV. SS-Pz.Korps, Stand* 21 January 1945 (note: both of these reports were due to *AOK 6* headquarters the previous day, but due to communications difficulties were delayed approximately 24 hours).

70 Jahnke Diary, p. 9.

71 *Ibid.*

72 Gille manuscript, p. 3

73 Yerger, Vol. 7, pp. 175–77. After initial treatment for his wounds in Veszprém, Dorr was evacuated to a base hospital at Silvana in Boden, a small town near Judenburg, Austria, where he died on 21 March 1945 from an infection (some sources incorrectly state his date of death as 17 April

1945). On 28 March 1945, Dorr was given a State funeral in the town of Judenburg, one of the last of many conducted by the Third Reich. Heinrich Himmler was represented by *Brigadeführer* Fritz Freitag, the commander of the *14. Waffen-Gren.Div. der SS (Ukrainische Nr. 1)*, who escorted Dorr's widow during the ceremony. Source: Peter Stockert, "Hans Dorr: 'Verteidiger des Dnepr'" in *Schwerterträger* magazine, Nr. 2 (Bad Soden, Germany: Deutsche Militärzeitschrift Verlag, 2017), pp. 20–21.

74 Vopersal, p. 590.

75 Számvéber, p. 196.

76 Vopersal, p. 588.

77 *Armeegruppe Balck/AOK 6 Ia KTB Anlage, Kampfstärken IV. SS-Pz.Korps, Stand* 21 January 1945.

78 Számvéber, pp. 201–02.

79 Számvéber, pp. 201, 204.

80 Stoves, pp. 719–20.

81 Incidentally, *Panzerkorps Feldherrnhalle* was created on 27 November 1944 by re-designating the newly activated *IV. Pz.Korps*. Originally intended to control both the *13. Pz.Div.* and *Pz.Gren. Div. Feldherrnhalle*, its activation plans were disrupted when both divisions were encircled in Budapest and was sent to *8. Armee* instead to control several infantry divisions.

82 *Armeegruppe Balck/AOK 6 Ic KTB*, entry dated 21 January 1945, and Maier, p. 52.

83 Számvéber, p. 205.

84 *Armeegruppe Balck/AOK 6 Ic KTB*, entry dated 21 January 1945.

85 Számvéber, p. 205, and Ungváry, p. 199.

86 Wöhler had singled out the SS units for special criticism on 21 January, since he believed that they had better communications equipment than a *panzer* corps of the *Heer* and should therefore have been able to maintain continuous radio contact with Balck's headquarters. This is nonsense, especially when one considers that Gille's corps headquarters was organized according to the same *Kriegsstärkenachweisung* as an army one, with the same number and type of radios, field telephones, teletype, and *Fernschreiber* equipment (source: *H.Gr. Süd Ia KTB, Aktennotiz des OB der H.Gr. Süd*, dated 23 January 1945).

87 Maier, p. 52.

88 *H.Gr. Süd Ia KTB, Anlage, Fernschreiben, Ia Nr. 238/45 geheim*, dated 11:40 p.m., 21 January 1945.

89 Maier, p. 53.

90 *Armeegruppe Balck/AOK 6 Ic KTB*, entry dated 22 January 1945.

91 Schönfelder manuscript, p. 6.

92 Maier (Munin Verlag German language edition), p. 73.

93 Jahnke Diary, p. 9.

94 *KTB, schwere-Panzerabteilung 509*, entry dated 23 January 1945, pp. 20–21.

95 Kraas' older brother, Hugo, at the time was an *Obersturmbannführer* and commander of *SS-Pz. Gren.Rgt. 2 LSSAH*, surviving the war after eventually attaining the rank of *Brigadeführer* and command of the *12. SS-Pz.Div. Hitlerjugend*.

96 Stoves, pp. 719–22, and Mirko Bayerl, "Husarenstreich: The Attack on Stuhlweissenburg January 22 1945" *Nordic Edge Model Gallery*, Vol. 2 (Stockholm: Canfora Grafisk Form & Förlag, 2007), pp. 94–98.

97 *SS-Rgt. Ney* suffered heavy losses during the recapture of Stuhlweissenburg. According to two sources, out of 1,500–2,000 men engaged, the regiment lost five officers and 166 enlisted men killed, and two officers and 47 enlisted men missing in action. It also reported 300 men as being wounded in the fighting, an overall total of 520 men killed, wounded, and missing—up to one-third of the regiment's strength. Ney's troops also destroyed 17 Soviet tanks and recaptured 12 damaged German tanks in repair shops that had been previously captured by Soviet troops

when they first took the town (source: *RF-SS Brigade "Ney"* (*Kampfgruppe Ney*) at www.hunyadi. co.uk, and Antonio Munoz, "Teutonic Magyars," p. 57).

98 Gille manuscript, p. 4.

99 *Armeegruppe Balck/AOK 6 Ia KTB Anlage, Fernschreiben*, dated 1:20 p.m., 22 January 1945.

100 *Armeegruppe Balck/AOK 6 Ib KTB Anlage, Fernschreiben, Tagesmeldung für den 22.1.1945, O.Qu. Nr. 542/45 geheim*, dated 2 a.m., 23 January 1945.

101 *Armeegruppe Balck/AOK 6 Ic KTB*, entry dated 22 January 1945.

102 Soviet General Staff Study, p. 82.

103 Isaev and Kolomiets, p. 56.

104 Soviet General Staff Study, p. 311.

105 *Ibid.*

106 *Armeegruppe Balck/AOK 6 Ia KTB Anlage, Fernschreiben Ia Nr. 282/45 geheim*, dated 7:50, 22 January 1945.

107 Maier, p. 53, quoting *H.Gr. Süd Ia KTB* entry for 22 January 1945.

108 Maier, p. 54.

109 Isaev and Kolomiets, p. 56.

110 Maier, p. 53.

111 Maier, p. 55, quoting Balck's *Beurteilung der Lage*, found in the *H.Gr. Süd Ia KTB Anlage* for 22 January 1945.

112 Maier, p. 54.

113 Schönfelder manuscript, p. 6.

114 Maier, p. 55.

115 Kern, p. 168.

116 *Armeegruppe Balck/AOK 6 Ia KTB Anlage, Fernschreiben, Betr: Absicht für 23.01.45, Ia Nr. 606/45 geheim*, dated 11 p.m., 22 January 1945.

117 On 25 March 1945, *H.Gr. F* was redesignated *H.Gr. E.*

118 Maier, p. 55.

119 Guderian, p. 329.

120 Számvéber, quoting *H.Gr. Süd Ia KTB, Zustand der Divisionen, Stand vom* 22 January 1945.

121 *Armeegruppe Balck/AOK 6 Ia KTB Anlage, Fernschreiben, Ia Nr. 608/45 geheim*, dated 22 January 1945.

122 *Armeegruppe Balck/AOK 6 Ic KTB*, entry dated 23 January 1945.

123 *Armeegruppe Balck/AOK 6 Ib KTB Anlage, Fernschreiben, Tagesmeldung für den 22.1.1945, O.Qu. Nr. 542/45 geheim*, dated 2 a.m., 23 January 1945.

124 *Armeegruppe Balck/AOK 6 Ib KTB Anlage, Truppenbestand*, 22 January 1945.

125 Klapdor, p. 396.

126 Maier, p. 77 (Munin Verlag German language edition).

127 Vopersal, p. 602.

128 Gosztony, p. 139. Incidentally, during a briefing that Gille gave to the staff of the *3. Pz.Div.* between 15 and 17 January, one of the participants, *Major* Arnold Freiherr von Rotberg, who was then serving as the *Division Ia*, recalled that Gille had told them that "a small success, the relief of Budapest, was not enough for Hitler; and that was why we had to discontinue the operation [*Konrad II*]. Therefore, we had to prepare for the larger-scale blow ... the 'southern solution' [i.e., *Konrad III*] designed to destroy more Russians but also to be able to be [hold] firm in Budapest" (source: Glantz, *1986 Art of War Symposium*, p. 758).

129 *Armeegruppe Balck/AOK 6 Ic KTB*, entry dated 23 January 1945.

130 Percy E. Schramm, *Kriegstagebuch des Oberkommando der Wehrmacht: Eine Dokumentation, Band 4, Teilband 2, 1944–1945* (Bonn: Bernard & Graefe Verlag, GmbH und Co. KG, 2005), p. 1033, and Maier, p. 56.

131 Schramm, p. 1033, and Számvéber, p. 235.
132 Isaev and Kolomiets, p. 57, and Glantz, p. 703. The *STAVKA*'s intent to transition to a coun-teroffensive was expressed in Special Directive 11013 dated 22 January 1945, and explained in detail on pages 83–84 of the Soviet General Staff Study's *The Budapest Operation, 1945: an Operational-Strategic Study.*
133 Maier, pp. 57, 415. This tendency was seconded in a note in the *H.Gr. Süd* war diary on 23 January 1945.
134 *Armeegruppe Balck/AOK 6 Ia KTB Anlage, Ergebnis der Erkundung im Raum Sárosd und Aba nach abgeschossenen Panzer,* dated 23 January 1945.
135 *Armeegruppe Balck/AOK 6 Ia KTB Anlage, Fernschreiben Ia Nr. 625/45 geheim,* dated 23 January 1945.
136 *Rechtzeitige Meldung der Absichten, Erstattung wahrer Meldungen und Halten der Verbindungen unter drakonischer Strafandrohung, OKW/WFSt/Op (H) Nr. 00688/45 g.Kdos,* 21 January 1945, and *H.Gr. Sud, Ia KTB Anlage, Fernschreiben Ia Nr. 239/45 g.Kdos,* 8:30 p.m. 23 January 1945.
137 Maier, p. 57.
138 Stoves, pp. 722–23.

Chapter 9: The Third Relief Attempt of Budapest—*Konrad III,* Part II

1 Schönfelder manuscript, entry dated 23 January 1945, p. 6.
2 Earl F. Ziemke, *Stalingrad to Berlin: The German Defeat in the East,* p. 436.
3 Vopersal, p. 604.
4 Maier, p. 79 (Munin Verlag German language edition), and *Armeegruppe Balck/AOK 6 Ic KTB,* entry dated 24 January 1945.
5 Jahnke Diary, entry dated 24 January 1945, p. 9.
6 Vopersal, p. 605.
7 *Ibid* and *s.Pz.Abt. 509 KTB,* entry dated 24 January 1945, p. 21.
8 Vopersal, p. 606.
9 Wood, pp. 233–34.
10 Gille manuscript, entry dated 24 January 1945, p. 3. Gille is referring to the heights on the eastern bank of the Váli River.
11 On 10 February, Jürgens was made acting commander of the *14. Pz.Div.,* a post he held for only a month before being place in the *Führerreserve,* never serving actively in field again in a leadership position.
12 *AOK 6 Ic KTB,* entry dated 24 January 1945, and Maier, p. 58.
13 Soviet General Staff Study, p. 312.
14 Ibid, p. 315.
15 Ibid, p. 315.
16 Maier, p. 58, quoting *H.Gr. Süd KTB* entry dated 24 January 1945.
17 Describing his new orders, Gille simply wrote, "New orders from the [*Armeegruppe*]: Cease the current attack and immediately attack in a northward, then northwestward, and finally in a westerly direction in order to attack the enemy from the rear in conjunction with [an attack by] our left-hand neighbor." Gille manuscript, entry dated 26 January 1945, p. 3.
18 Schönfelder manuscript, entry covering the period 23–27 January 1945, p. 6.
19 Balck, pp. 412–13.
20 Maier, p. 59.
21 *Armeegruppe Balck/AOK 6 Ia KTB Anlage, Fernspruch von 1. Pz.Div.,* 1:45 p.m., 24 January 1945.

22 Interestingly, a copy of the entire concept plan for *Unternehmen Eisbrecher* has survived in the archives of the *Totenkopf* Division's veterans association, an indication that a draft of this plan was distributed throughout the *Armeegruppe Balck* chain of command.

23 Vopersal, p. 608.

24 Soviet General Staff Study, p. 315.

25 *AOK 6 Ic KTB*, entry dated 25 January 1945.

26 Klapdor, p. 397.

27 Vopersal, p. 610, and Maier (Munin Verlag German language version), p. 82.

28 Stoves, p. 725.

29 Tommy Natedal, "Norwegische Freiwillige im Kampf in Ungarn 1945," and "Pettend fest in unserer Hand" in *Der Freiwillige*, 2/2000 and 3/2000 (Osnabrück: Munin Verlag GmbH, 2000), p. 24 and p. 10.

30 Stoves, p. 726.

31 *Ibid.*

32 *Armeegruppe Balck/AOK 6 Ia KTB Anlage, Fernschreiben Ia Nr. 140/45 g.Kdos*, dated 24 January 1945.

33 *AOK 6 Ic KTB*, entry dated 25 January 1945, and Maier, p. 104.

34 Soviet General Staff Study, pp. 83–84.

35 *Ibid.*

36 Balck knew all too well how weak Gille's corps was. In a commander's assessment written on the night of 25/26 January, he wrote that "the external situation in the East is very depressing, particularly the arriving reinforcements. Major difficulties: the uninterrupted employment of the *panzer* divisions has severely worn out not only the tanks and [*SPWs*], but the remainder of the vehicles as well. The situation with fuel, tires, and spare parts is dire. The shortage of infantry divisions and the related losses in men and material have led to a situation in which the *panzer* divisions, being employed along a broad front, have lost a significant share of their combat capability, which could not be rectified by the arrival of reinforcements from the reserve … the high level of ammunition expenditure has caused serious problems, particularly in the provisioning of antitank artillery shells. The fuel situation is even worse." (Soviet General Staff Study, p. 315)

37 Soviet General Staff Study, p. 314.

38 For example, on 29 August 1943, in a telegram to its division commander, Wöhler expressed his "deepest gratitude" towards the *Totenkopf* Division for its "tremendous combat performance" during the retreat to the Dnieper River line from 23–28 August. On another occasion, Wöhler wrote, "The 8. Armee is proud to be able to count on the *Totenkopf*, whose unshakable steadfastness in combat and exemplary readiness for action has risen to every occasion, whether as an unshakeable cliff in the sea in the defense, or in the attack as a flashing sword of vengeance." (Karl Ullrich, *Wie Ein Fels in Meer: 3. SS-Panzerdivision "Totenkopf" im Bild*, p. 7)

39 Maier, p. 61, quoting verbatim the entry from the *H.Gr. Sud KTB* for 25 January 1945.

40 Gille even submitted Thünert for the Knight's Cross and presented it himself on 6 February 1945, an indication how highly he thought of the *1. Pz.Div.* commander (Stoves, p. 739).

41 Maier, pp. 61–62.

42 *Ibid*, p. 62.

43 *Ibid.*

44 *Armeegruppe Balck/AOK 6 Ia KTB Anlage, Fernschreiben Ia Nr. 684/45 geheim*, dated 25 January 1945.

45 *Armeegruppe Balck/AOK 6 Ia KTB Anlage, Fernschreiben Ia Nr. 687/45 geheim*, dated 11:10 p.m., 25 January 1945.

46 Letter from Günther Lange, Handeloh, Germany, to the author on 15 April 2020.

47 Wood, p. 234.
48 *Armeegruppe Balck/AOK 6 Ia KTB Anlage, Panzerlage Meldung,* dated 5:50 p.m., 25 January 1945, quoted in Vopersal, p. 612.
49 *AOK 6 Ic KTB,* entry dated 26 January 1945.
50 Maier, p. 63, quoting the *H.Gr. Süd Ia KTB* for that day.
51 *Armeegruppe Balck/AOK 6, Ia KTB Anlage, Mitgehörte Funkspruche,* 26 January 1945.
52 Vopersal, p. 614.
53 Soviet General Staff Study, p. 316.
54 *Ibid,* p. 614.
55 Vopersal, p. 615.
56 Maier, p. 64.
57 Soviet General Staff Study, p. 316.
58 Számvéber, p. 272.
59 *Ibid.*
60 Wood, p. 235, and Vopersal, pp. 616–17. Vopersal states that Pittschellis was temporarily replaced by a *Stubaf.* Meier as the acting commander, but there is no one in the *SS-Führungsliste* who matches that description.
61 Vopersal, p. 618.
62 *Ibid,* p. 620.
63 *Ibid,* p. 620. The substance of these conversations are found in the *H.Gr. Süd Ia KTB* for 26 January 1945.
64 Ziemke, p. 436. Ziemke drew on the memorandum of Wöhler's for his evaluation, which as we know today was heavily influenced by Balck's negative comments.
65 Vopersal, p. 619. Incidentally, Zährl had been awarded the Honor Roll Clasp of the *Heer* for the citing of his performance in combat during the three battles of Warsaw on 5 December 1944.
66 Maier, p. 64.
67 Stoves, p. 729.
68 *Ibid,* p. 730.
69 Gosztony, p. 141.
70 Stoves, p. 731.
71 *Ibid.*
72 Maier, p. 63.
73 Kern, p. 202.
74 Számvéber, pp. 270–71.
75 *AOK 6 Ic KTB,* entry dated 26 January 1945.
76 Maier, p. 65.
77 *AOK 6 Ic KTB,* entry dated 26 January 1945.
78 Számvéber, p. 260, referencing an entry in the *H.Gr. Süd Ia KTB* for 25 January 1945.
79 Soviet General Staff Study, p. 316.
80 Maier, p. 64, quoting the transcript of the conversation between *H.Gr. Süd* and the Chief of Staff, *OKH,* as found in the *Ia KTB Anlage* for 26 January 1945.
81 Maier, p. 64.
82 Schönfelder manuscript, entry dated 27 January 1945, p. 7. In his memoirs, Balck expressed his frustration with what he perceived as the lack of professionalism of the *Waffen-SS.* At one point, he asserted that "each major *Waffen-SS* unit had a direct telephone line to Himmler, who routinely interfered in everything and who probably wanted to make Gille the savior of Budapest" (Balck, p. 416).

83 Trophy documents of the *IV. SS-Pz.Korps* held in the Central Archive of the Russian Ministry of Defense, *TsAMO* Podolsk, Fund: 243, Inventory No. 2900, Case: 2011, pp. 281–85, folio. Original translation by Lieutenant Glushkin on 2 February 1945, translated into English in 2019 by Olivia J. Allison, Kiev.

84 Balck, p. 413.

85 *IV. SS-Pz.Korps* Trophy Document.

86 Balck, p. 434.

87 Maier, p. 65.

88 *AOK 6 Ic KTB*, entry dated 27 January 1945.

89 Schönfelder manuscript, p. 6.

90 In a preliminary strength report compiled on 27 January, Vogt's battalion had been reduced to a *Kampfstärke* of less than 100 effectives, rendering it suitable for only limited defensive assignment (Számvéber, p. 457, and Maier, Appendix 25, p. 417).

91 Vopersal, pp. 623–24, Jahnke Diary, entry dated 29 January 1945, p. 9.

92 *Armeegruppe Balck/6. Armee Ia KTB, Fernspruch vom Meldekopf A.Gr. Balck, Stuhlweissenburg (Maj. Müller-Gülich)*, dated 10 a.m., 27 January 1945.

93 Vopersal, p. 624.

94 *Ibid.*

95 *Ibid*, p. 625.

96 *Ibid*, pp. 625–26.

97 *Ibid*, p. 627.

98 Knight's Cross with Oak Leaves award citation for Fritz Vogt dated 10 February 1945, and Számvéber, pp. 280–81.

99 Számvéber, p. 283, referring to Combat Report of the XXIII Tank Corps, 22 January–28 February 1945, p. 7.

100 In addition to what he expressed in the order, Gille also marked the occasion that evening in a radio message he had his *Ia* send to *Armeegruppe Balck* that simply stated, "After previously incomplete reports, today between midnight [26 January] and 8 p.m., 122 enemy tanks were destroyed" (*Armeegruppe Balck/6. Armee, Ia KTB Anlage, Funkspruch von IV. SS-Pz.Korps*, dated 9:35 p.m., 27 January 1945).

101 Soviet General Staff Study, p. 316.

102 *Ibid.*

103 Vopersal, p. 620.

104 *Ibid.*

105 Számvéber, Appendix XII, "Weekly Strength Report of the Units of the *IV. SS-Panzerkorps* according to data as of 27 January 1945," quoting directly from *H.Gr. Süd Ia KTB, Wochenmeldung vom 27 Januar 1945, Zustand der Div., Stand* 27 January 1945.

106 Maier, p. 67, quoting an entry in the *H.Gr. Süd Ia KTB Anlage*, 27 January 1945.

107 *AOK 6 Ic KTB*, entry dated 27 January 1945.

108 *Ibid.*

109 *Ibid*, Maier, p. 66, and Számvéber, p. 287.

110 *Wehrmachtsbericht*, 27 January 1945, p. 1.

111 Maier, p. 66.

112 *AOK 6 Ic KTB*, entry dated 27 January 1945.

113 *H.Gr. Süd, Ia KTB Anlage Ia Nr. 117/45, Hitlers Tagebefehl an die Besatzung von Budapest*, dated 7:20 p.m., 27 January 1945. Reproduced in full in Maier, p. 418.

114 Számvéber, p. 286.

115 Stoves, p. 732.

116 *AOK 6 Ic KTB*, entry dated 27 January 1945.

117 The Pliyev Cavalry-Mechanized Group, commanded by Lt.Gen. Issa A. Pliyev, consisted of the IV Guards Cavalry Corps and I Mechanized Corps. On 26 January 1945, it was renamed the I Guards-Cavalry Mechanized Group.

118 Maier, p. 67.

119 Soviet General Staff Study, p. 320, and Számvéber, p. 297.

120 Maier, pp. 67–68.

121 *Ibid*, p. 68.

122 *Armeegruppe Balck/6. Armee Ia KTB Anlage*, handwritten note of telephone call from *Gen.Maj.* Gaedke to Headquarters, *IV. SS-Pz.Korps*, dated 7:50 p.m., 27 January 1945.

123 The written order and the two subsequent additional orders are found in *Armeegruppe Balck/6. Armee Ia KTB Anlage, Ia KTB Nr. 719/45, 727/45*, and *728/45*, all dated 27 January 1945.

124 *Armeegruppe Balck/6. Armee Ia KTB Anlage, Ia KTB Nr. 727/45*, dated 27 January 1945.

125 *IV. SS-Pz.Korps Führungsabteilung, Befehl Nr. 199/45 geheim, Korpsbefehl für 1.28.45*, dated 27 January 1945.

126 Maier, p. 68.

127 *Armeegruppe Balck/6. Armee Ia KTB Anlage, Ia Fernschreiben Nr. 697/45 geheim*, dated 26 January 1945.

128 *AOK 6 Ic KTB*, entry dated 27 January 1945.

129 Zährl, in Vopersal, p. 630.

130 Messerle, in Vopersal, p. 635.

131 Maier, p. 73, and endnote, p. 107.

132 Stoves, pp. 733–34.

133 Jahnke Diary, entry dated 30 January 1945, p. 11.

134 Gille Diary, entry dated 27/28 January, p. 3. (Note: There were actually only 40 Norwegians remaining in the battalion. The rest of its members were a mixture of native German SS veterans, involuntary transfers from the *Kriegsmarine*, and *Volksdeutsche* (ethnic Germans) from the Ukraine and the Balkans. Tieke, p. 399, and Barstein, p. 1.)

135 *Kriegstagebuch des OKW, 1944–1945*, Vol. 2, pp. 1047–48, and Maier, p. 73.

136 *AOK 6 Ic KTB*, entry dated 28 January 1945, and *Kriegstagebuch des OKW, 1944–1945*, Vol. 2, p. 1048.

137 The VII Mechanized Corps had been completely withdrawn to the eastern side of the Danube, with the exception of its 16th Mechanized Brigade, where it went into *STAVKA* reserve and would not be committed into battle again until a month later.

138 *AOK 6 Ic KTB*, entry dated 28 January 1945.

139 In fact, General Pliyev's I Guards Cavalry-Mechanized Corps was in Slovakia as part of the Second Ukrainian Front's operational reserve.

140 Számvéber, Appendix XIII, "Armored Replenishment of the Third Ukrainian Front in January 1945," p. 458 (source: Central Archive of the Russian Ministry of Defense [*TsAMO*], Podolsk, f. 243, op. 2928, gy. 340, 1, 129).

141 Balck, p. 414.

Chapter 10: Battling to a Stalemate

1 *Der Bericht des Oberkommandos der Wehrmacht*, Monday, 29 January 1945, p. 1.

2 *Armeegruppe Balck/6. Armee Ic KTB*, entry dated 29 January 1945.

3 Vopersal, p. 637.

4 *Ibid*.

5   Jahnke Diary, entry for 29 January 1934, p. 9. Interestingly, the *Ic* of *H.Gr. Süd, Oberstlt.* Karl-Heinrich Graf von Rittberg, *was* arrested for treason and shot in Haidholz, Austria, on 12 April 1945 by a Flying Courts-Martial. What act of treason he actually or allegedly committed is unknown.

6   A Gisela-Einheit (Gisela Unit) was the designated codename given to three reserve infantry divisions serving as occupation troops in France that were mobilized for front-line service on 1 May 1943. All three divisions (the 148., 159., and 189. Reserve-Division) were reorganized along the lines of a standard three-regiment infantry division and renumbered as the 282., 355., and 356. Inf. Div., respectively (Tessin, Vol. I, pp. 66–67, and IX, p. 275).

7   Tessin, Vol. 9, pp. 275–77.

8   Maier, p. 74.

9   Számvéber, p. 309.

10 *Kriegstagebuch des OKW, 1944–1945, Teilband 2*, entry dated 29 January 1945, p. 1050.

11 Isaev and Kolomiets, pp. 65–66.

12 *Armeegruppe Balck/6. Armee Ia KTB Anlage, Fernschreiben Ia Nr. 777/45 geheim*, dated 29 January 1945.

13 Isaev and Kolomiets, p. 66.

14 *Hauptquartier IV. SS-Pz.Korps, Führungsabteilung: Tagesmeldung an Armeegruppe Balck*, dated 30 January 1945.

15 Schönfelder manuscript, entry dated 30 January 1945, p. 8.

16 Klapdor, p. 399.

17 *Armeegruppe Balck/6. Armee Ic KTB*, entry dated 30 January 1945.

18 *Ibid.*

19 Maier, p. 75.

20 *Kriegstagebuch des OKW, 1944–1945, Teilband 2*, entry dated 30 January 1945, p. 1056

21 Számvéber, p. 318.

22 Soviet General Staff Study, pp. 322–23.

23 *Fernschreiben, IV. SS-Pz.Korps an Armeegruppe Balck/AOK 6 Ia*, dated 6:35 p.m., 30 January 1945.

24 *Armeegruppe Balck/6. Armee Ia KTB, Anlage, Fernschreiben Ia Nr. 800/45 geheim*, dated 30 January 1945.

25 *Armeegruppe Balck/6. Armee Ia KTB, Anlage, Fernschreiben Ia Nr. 802/45 geheim*, dated 30 January 1945.

26 Jahnke Diary, entry dated 31 January 1945, p. 10.

27 *Armeegruppe Balck/6. Armee Ic KTB*, entry dated 31 January 1945.

28 Isaev and Kolomiets, p. 70, quoting Gille after-action report written 31 January 1945, found in TsAMO reference files, Captured German Records, f. 243, op. 2900, d. 2011, 1313.

29 Gille manuscript, entry dated 31 January 1945, p. 8.

30 *Armeegruppe Balck/6. Armee Ia KTB Anlage, Fernschreiben Ia Nr. 801/45 geheim*, dated 31 January 1945.

31 Maier, p. 76, and *Kriegstagebuch des OKW, 1944–1945*, p. 1059.

32 *Armeegruppe Balck/6. Armee Ic KTB*, entry dated 31 January 1945.

33 *Armeegruppe Balck/6. Armee Ia KTB Anlage, Fernschreiben Ia Nr. 822/45 geheim*, dated 31 January 1945.

34 *Armeegruppe Balck/6. Armee Ia KTB Anlage, Fernschreiben Ia Nr. 835/45 geheim*, dated 31 January 1945.

35 *Armeegruppe Balck/6. Armee Ia/Id Fernschreiben Nr. 836/45 geheim*, dated 9:50 p.m., 31 January 1945. In fact, several days later, the *23. Pz.Div.* did receive an influx of new replacements, which were initially assigned to its *Feld-Ersatz* battalion.

36 *Gen.Kdo. I. Kav.Korps Ia Nr. 299/45 geheim, Betr: Beurteilung der Lage, Korps Gefechtstand*, 31 January 1945.

37 Számvéber, p. 463, referencing armored vehicle strength report submitted by *Armeegruppe Balck/6. Armee* to *H.Gr. Süd* during the evening of 1 February 1945.

38 Számvéber, p. 465, quoting tank and self-propelled gun strength of the Third Ukrainian Front on 1 February 1945, stored in *TsAMO* Podolsk, f. 243, op. 2928, gy. 340, 123–128, available at https://pamyat-naroda.ru/.

39 *Armeegruppe Balck/6. Armee Ia KTB Anlage, Fernschreiben H.Gr. Süd Ia Nr. 348/45 Gen.Kdos.*, dated 1:20 a.m., 1 February 1945.

40 Klapdor, p. 400.

41 Jahnke Diary, entry dated 1 February 1945, p. 10.

42 Schönfelder manuscript, entry dated 1 February 1945, p. 8.

43 *Armeegruppe Balck/6. Armee Ia KTB Anlage, Fernschreiben H.Gr. Süd Ia Nr. 367/45 Gen.Kdos.*, dated 11:15 p.m., 1 February 1945.

44 *Armeegruppe Balck/6. Armee Ia KTB Anlage, Fernschreiben Ia Nr. 853/45 geheim*, dated 1 February 1945.

45 *Armeegruppe Balck/6. Armee Ia KTB Chefsachen, Fernschreiben Ia Nr. 185/45 geheim*, dated 1 February 1945.

46 *Ibid*, para. 2.

47 Traditionsverband der Division, *Geschichte der 3. Panzer-Division Berlin-Brandenburg 1935–1945* (Berlin: Günter Richter, 1967), p. 462, and Vopersal, p. 648.

48 Isaev and Kolomiets, p. 71, Maier, p. 77, Vopersal, p. 648, Számvéber, p. 347, *H.Gr. Süd Ia KTB*, entry dated 2 February 1945, p. 8, and Schönfelder manuscript, entry dated 2 February 1945, pp. 8, 10.

49 *H.Gr. Süd Ia KTB*, entry dated 2 February 1945, p. 5.

50 *H.Gr. Süd Ia KTB, Luftlage*, entry dated 2 February 1945, p. 6.

51 Isaev and Kolomiets, p. 71, and Számvéber, p. 465.

52 Maier, p. 79.

53 *Armeegruppe Balck/6. Armee Ia KTB Chefsachen, Fernschreiben, Ia Nr. 191/45 g.Kdos.*, dated 2 February 1945.

54 *H.Gr. Süd Ia KTB*, entry dated 2 February 1945, p. 8.

55 *Armeegruppe Balck/6. Armee Ia KTB Anlage, Aktennotiz: Meldung IV. SS-Pz.Korps O1 Hstuf. Velde*, dated 2 February 1945. Incidentally, a number of Rentrop's documents are still stored somewhere in the *TsAMO* archive in Podolsk; translated copies of them can be viewed here (in Russian) at https://pamyat-naroda.ru/documents/view/ ?id=130017567&backurl=q%5C%D1%82%D1%80%D0%BE%D1%84%D0%B5%D0%B9%D0%BD%D1%8B%D0%B5%20%D0%B1%D1%83%D0%B4%D0%B0%D0%BF%D0%B5%D1%88%D1%82::use_main_string%5Ctrue::group%5Call::types%5Copersvodki:rasporyajeniya:otcheti:peregovori:-jbd:direktivi:prikazi:posnatovleniya:dokladi:raporti:doneseniya:svedeniya:plani:plani_operaci-y:karti:shemi:spravki:drugie::page%5C13. The current status of the *IV. SS-Pz.Korps Ia KTB*, which has not yet been translated or available online, is unknown.

56 Balck, p. 421.

57 Maier, p. 77.

58 *Armeegruppe Balck/6. Armee Ib KTB Tagesmeldung für 2 Februar 1945, Fernschreiben, O.Qu. Nr. 792/45 g.Kdos.*, dated 1:30 a.m., 3 February 1945.

59 *Armeegruppe Balck/6. Armee Ia KTB Anlage, Kampfstärken Stand 3.2.1945, 1; H.Gr. Süd Ia KTB, Betr: Wochenmeldung*, dated 3 February 1945; Vopersal, pp. 654–55, and *Ia KTB s.Pz.Abt. 509*, entry dated 3 February 1945, p. 22.

60 Maier, p. 78.

61 Vopersal, p. 654.

62 *Ibid*, p. 655.

63 Stoves, p. 738

64 Vopersal, p. 655, quoting *H.Gr. Süd Ia KTB* entry for 3 February 1945.

65 *H.Gr. Süd Ia KTB, Tagesmeldung*, 3 February 1945, p. 1.

66 Schönfelder manuscript, entry dated 3 February, p. 9.

67 Klapdor, p. 401.

68 Számvéber, p. 352.

69 *Armeegruppe Balck/6. Armee Ia KTB Anlage, Fernschreiben Ia Nr. 890/45 geheim*, dated 3 February 1945.

70 *H.Gr. Süd Ia KTB, Tagesmeldung*, 3 February 1945, p. 3, and Számvéber, p. 356.

71 Interestingly, the portion of the Soviet General Staff study concerning the activities of the Third Ukrainian Front does not mention the capture of Rentrop or the possible exploitation of the documents he was carrying, though the after-action report of the 4th Guards Army does. How much the captured documents influenced Soviet decision-making during the next several days can only be surmised.

72 Számvéber, p. 357, describing commander's comments accompanying the *H.Gr. Süd Ia KTB* Tagesmeldung for 3 February 1945.

73 Shortly afterwards, *Brig.Fhr.* Becker moved his forward command post to Stuhlweissenburg, while that of the *Wiking* Division shortly thereafter moved into Falubattyán in its place.

74 *Armeegruppe Balck/6. Armee Führungsabteilung, Fernschreiben von Oberkommando, Armeegruppe Balck an Kommandiernen General IV. SS-Pz.Korps*, dated 3:45 p.m., 3 February 1945.

75 *Armeegruppe Balck/6. Armee Ia KTB Anlage, Fernschreiben IV. SS-Pz.Korps*, dated 10:40 a.m. and 1:10 p.m., 3 February 1945.

76 *Armeegruppe Balck/6. Armee Ia KTB Anlage, Chef des Generalstabes Fernschreiben Ia Nr. 908/45 geheim*, dated 9:15 p.m., 3 February 1945.

77 *Der Oberbefehlshaber der Heeresgruppe Süd, Tagesbefehl*, 3 February 1945. (Note: This was the one of the last documents in the hoard of *Armeegruppe Balck/6. Armee* captured by the Red Army at the war's end. Nothing beyond this date is known to remain, though the *TsAMO* office in Podolsk is continually adding to the documents available online.)

78 Vopersal, p. 645.

79 Jahnke Diary, entry dated 1 February 1945, p. 10.

80 Számvéber, p. 362.

81 Vopersal, pp. 659–61.

82 *H.Gr. Süd Ia KTB, Tagesmeldung*, 4 February 1945, p. 7.

83 Számvéber, p. 363.

84 *H.Gr. Süd Ia KTB, Tagesmeldung*, 4 February 1945, p. 7, and Számvéber, p. 363, according to Soviet records.

85 Vopersal, p. 657.

86 *Ibid.*

87 *H.Gr. Süd Ia KTB, Tagesmeldung*, 4 February 1945, pp. 8–9, and Számvéber, p. 364.

Chapter 11: Transition to the Defense

1 *Armeegruppe Balck/6. Armee Ia KTB Anlage Kampfstärken Stand 3.2.45*, dated 3 February 1945, p. 1. According to this document, *SS-Rgt. Ney* had been reduced to an effective strength of only 25 men, but this only includes a portion of the regiment still in the front lines because most of Ney's surviving troops had been withdrawn to the town of Súr, 16 kilometers west of Mór, to undergo a period of rest and reconstitution, where it was intended to be upgraded to brigade status.

2   *H.Gr. Süd Ia KTB, Betr: Wochenmeldung, Stand 3.2.45*, dated 3 February 1945, pp. 4–5.

3   *SS-Führungshauptamt Org.Abt. Ia/Org.Abt. II Fernschreiben Nr. II/2568/45 geheim an SS-Art.Schule II Beneschau und Kommandantur SS-Truppenübungsplatz Böhmen*, dated 10:05 p.m., 7 February 1945.

4   Vopersal, p. 663.

5   *H.Gr. Süd Ia KTB, Tagesmeldung*, 5 February 1945, pp. 2, 4.

6   Vopersal, p. 662.

7   *H.Gr. Süd Ia KTB, Tagesmeldung*, 6 February 1945, p. 3.

8   Isaev and Kolomiets, pp. 71–72. Not the same Hill 130 that was 8 kilometers east of Seregélyes.

9   Maier, p. 80.

10 *Ibid*, p. 81.

11 Vopersal, p. 664, and Letter, Horst Meyer to Tommy Natedal, Erfurt, Germany, dated 2 August 1994, p. 16, courtesy of Tommy Natedal Archive, pp. 15–16.

12 *H.Gr. Süd Ia KTB, Tagesmeldung*, 6 February 1945, p. 2, Vopersal pp. 663–64, and Számvéber, pp. 373–74.

13 Klapdor, p. 403, and Wood, pp. 237–38.

14 Maier, p. 81.

15 Jahnke Diary, entry dated 6 February 1945, p. 11.

16 Stoves, p. 739.

17 *H.Gr. Süd Ia KTB, Tagesmeldung*, 6 February 1945, p. 2.

18 Although Dietrich's *panzer* army has been frequently referred to as the "*6. SS-Pz.Armee*," this was not its officially designated title. Although its headquarters was composed predominately of SS personnel, as much as a third of its staff and headquarters battalion was filled with soldiers detailed from the *Heer*. It was officially activated on 24 September 1944 by renaming the surviving staff of the *Wehrmachts-Befehlshaber Belgien–Nordfrankreich*, as well as from the staff of the *XII. Armee-Korps*. In addition to the two *SS-Panzerkorps* and its four SS divisions subordinated to it, between November 1944 and May 1945 it frequently had divisions and brigades of the *Heer*, as well as Hungarian units, also fighting under Dietrich's command. (Source: Tessin, Vol. 2, p.8, and 3, pp. 230–231)

19 Vopersal, p. 665.

20 Wood, p. 238.

21 Wood, p. 238, Vopersal, p. 665, and Isaev and Kolomiets, p. 72.

22 According to *H.Gr. Süd*'s own *Tagesmeldung*, an additional 22 German armored vehicles were disabled during the fighting, though deemed repairable. Some had fallen out due to mechanical troubles, while others were damaged in combat (*H.Gr. Sud Ia KTB, Tagesmeldung*, 7 February 1945, p. 6).

23 Vopersal, p. 665.

24 Isaev and Kolomiets, p. 73.

25 Számvéber, p. 378.

26 *H.Gr. Süd Ia KTB, Tagesmeldung*, 7 February 1945, p. 4, and *Kriegstagebuch des OKW*, Vol. 8 Part II, p. 1075.

27 Soviet General Staff Study, p. 324, and Isaev and Kolomiets, pp. 72–73.

28 Maier, p. 82. Hitler had decided to upgrade both cavalry brigades to division status; though this would entail no significant changes to their organizational structure, both needed to undergo a rest and refitting period before they could be deemed ready for offensive assignments (Tessin, Vol. 2, pp. 179, 247–48).

29 *H.Gr. Süd Ia KTB, Tagesmeldung*, 8 February 1945, pp. 4, 5.

30 Klapdor, p. 404.

31 Számvéber and *s.Pz.Abt. 509 Ia KTB*, entries dated 6–10 February 1945, p. 22.
32 Jahnke Diary, entry dated 8 February 1945, p.11.
33 *H.Gr. Süd Ia KTB, Tagesmeldung*, 8 February 1945, p. 4.
34 Számvéber, pp. 386–87, and *H.Gr. Süd Ia KTB, Tagesmeldung*, 8 February 1945, p. 4.
35 Maier, p. 82, and Vopersal, p. 667.
36 *H.Gr. Süd Ia KTB, Tagesmeldung*, 8 February 1945, p. 3.
37 Soviet General Staff Study, p. 86.
38 Balck, p. 419.
39 Guderian, p. 346.
40 Vopersal, p. 667.
41 *Ibid*, pp. 667–68.
42 *Zustandsbericht, 3. SS-Pz.Div. Totenkopf,* dated 1 March 1945.
43 *H.Gr. Süd Ia KTB, Tagesmeldung*, 12 February 1945, p. 2.
44 Vopersal, p. 667.
45 *H.Gr. Süd Ia KTB, Tagesmeldung*, 12 February 1945, p. 6.
46 *H.Gr. Süd Ia KTB, Tagesmeldung*, 12 February 1945, p. 2, Számvéber, pp. 392–93, and Vopersal, p. 667.
47 *H.Gr. Süd Ia KTB, Tagesmeldung*, 9 February 1945, p. 4.
48 Számvéber, pp. 394–95, Maier, pp. 83–84.
49 Maier, p. 84.
50 *H.Gr. Süd Ia KTB, Morgenmeldung*, 10 February 1945, p. 1.
51 Vopersal, p. 669.
52 Letter, Horst Meyer to Tommy Natedal, Erfurt, Germany, dated 2 August 1994, p. 16, courtesy of Tommy Natedal Archive.
53 Számvéber, pp. 397–98.
54 Szamveber, p. 397, and *H.Gr. Süd Ia KTB, Morgenmeldung*, 10 February 1945, pp. 1–2.
55 *H.Gr. Süd, Ia Wochenmeldung*, dated 10 February 1945, p. 4.
56 *H.G. Süd, Ia Morgenmeldung*, dated 11 February 1945.
57 *IX. SS-Geb.Korps, Funkspruch*, 3:45 p.m. (tactical time 5:50 p.m.), 11 February 1945 (source: Munin Verlag German text version, p. 518).
58 Maier, p. 85.
59 *Ibid*, pp. 84–85.
60 Pohlman, p. 370, and Maier, p. 89.
61 *H.Gr. Süd, Ia KTB Anlage, Abschlussmeldung Budapest, Ia Nr. 2191/45 geheim,* dated 11:20 p.m., 16 February 1945, reprinted in Maier (Munin Verlag German language edition), pp. 520–21.
62 Ungváry, p. 427.
63 *Ibid*, p. 430.
64 *Ibid*, p. 376.
65 Balck, p. 416–17.
66 Yerger, *Waffen-SS Commanders*, pp. 146–48.
67 Maier, p. 80.

Bibliography

Books and Journal Articles

Anonymous. "SS-Werfer-Abteilung 504—Solche Kerle!" in *Der Freiwillige*, Vol. 9, 1965 (Osnabrück, Germany: Verlag der Freiwillige GmbH, 1965).

Bacyk, Norbert. *Warsaw II: The Tank Battle at Praga July—September 1944: The 4th SS Panzer Corps vs. the 1st Belorussian Front* (Stockholm: Leandoer & Eckholm Publishing, 2006).

Balck, Hermann. *Order in Chaos: The Memoirs of General of Panzer Troops Hermann Balck* (Lexington, KY: The University Press of Kentucky, 2015).

Barstein, Jan. "Norwegische Freiwillige im Kampf in Ungarn 1945" and "Pettend fest in unserer Hand" in *Der Freiwillige*, 2/2000 and 3/2000, respectively (Osnabrück: Munin Verlag GmbH, 2000), 24, 10.

Batov, Pavel I. *Campaigns and Battles* (Moscow: Progress Publishing, 1965).

Bayerl, Mirko. "Husarenstreich: The Attack on Stuhlweissenburg January 22nd 1945" in *Nordic Edge Model Gallery*, Volume 2 (Stockholm: Canfora Grafisk Form & Förlag, 2007), pp. 94–98.

Bender, Roger J. and Taylor, Hugh-Page. *Uniforms, Organization and History of the Waffen-SS* Vol. 2 (San Jose: R. James Bender Publishing, 1971).

Bernau, Gunter. *SS-Panzer Artillerie-Regiment 5 in der Panzer-Division Wiking* (Wuppertal, Germany: Eigenverlag Kameradschaft ehem. Pz.Art.Rgt. 5, 1990).

Brenden, Geir, Kjellander, Petter and Westberg, Lennart. *III. Germanic SS Panzer-Korps: The History of Himmler's Favorite SS-Panzer-Korps, 1943–1945, Vol. 1: Creation—September 1944* (Warwick, U.K.: Helion & Company Ltd, 2019).

Condell, Bruce and Zabecki, David T. (eds). *On the German Art of War: Truppenführung: German Army Manual for Unit Command in World War II* (Mechanicsburg, PA: Stackpole Books, 2008).

Davies, Norman. *Rising '44: The Battle for Warsaw* (New York: Viking Press, 2003).

Erlings, Ron, Fischer, Hans and Oosterling, Paul. *Standartenführer Johannes Mühlenkamp und seine Männer* (Erpe, The Netherlands: Uitgeverij De Krijger, 2003).

Fey, Willi. *Armor Battles of the Waffen-SS, 1943–45* (Winnipeg, Canada: J. J. Fedorowicz, 1990).

Fraschka, Günter. *Mit Schwerten und Brillanten: Die Träger der höchsten deutschen Tapferkeits-auszeichnung* (Munich: Limes Verlag Niedermayer & Schlüter GmbH, 1977).

Frieser, Karl-Heinz (ed. and contributing author), Schmider, Klaus, Schönherr, Klaus, Schreiber, Gerhard, Ungvary, Krisztian and Wegner, Bernd. *Germany and the Second World War, Vol. VIII: The Eastern Front 1943–1944—The War in the East and on Neighboring Fronts* (Oxford: Clarendon Press, 2017).

Fürbringer, Herbert. *9. SS-Panzer-Division 1944: Normandie–Tarnopol–Arnhem* (Paris: Editions Heimdahl, 1984).

Gaedke, Heinz and Brugmann, Gerhard. *Wege eines Soldaten* (Norderstedt: Books on Demand, 2005).

Glantz, David M. "The Red Army's Lublin–Brest Offensive and Advance on Warsaw (18 July–30 September 1944): An Overview and Documentary Survey" in *Journal of Slavic Military Studies*, 19 (London: Taylor & Francis Group, LLC. 2006), pp. 401–41.

Glantz, David M. *Atlas of the Lublin–Brest Operation and the Advance on Warsaw* (Carlisle, PA: Privately published, 2005).

Gosztony, Peter. *Endkampf an der Donau, 1944/45* (Vienna: Verlag Fritz Molden, 1969).

Guderian, Heinz. *Panzer Leader* (New York: Ballantyne Books, 1957).

Hack, Franz. "Kämpfe in Ungarn" in *Unsere Wiking Ruf*, 7/2002 (Ziegenhain, Germany: Truppenkameradschaft 5. SS-Panzer Division Wiking, Geschichtlicher Verein Treysa, 2002).

Hahl, Fritz. *Mit "Westland" im Osten* (Osnabrück, Germany: Munin Verlag, 2000).

Haupt, Werner. *Army Group Center: The Wehrmacht in Russia 1941–1945* (Atglen, PA: Schiffer Military History, 1997).

Haupt, Werner. *Die Schlachten der Heeresgruppe Mitte aus der Sicht der Divisionen* (Friedberg, Germany: Podzun-Pallas Verlag, 1983).

Heder, Eberhard. "Der Kampf des IV. SS-Panzerkorps um Budapest" in *Unsere Wiking Ruf* 7/2002 (Ziegenhain, Germany: Truppenkameradschaft 5. SS-Panzer Division Wiking, Geschichtlicher Verein Treysa, 2002).

Heiber, Helmut and Glantz, David M. (eds). *Hitler and His Generals: Military Conferences 1942–1945* (New York: Enigma Books, 2003).

Hinze, Rolf. *East Front Drama—1944* (Winnipeg, Canada: J. J. Fedorowicz Publishing, Inc., 1996).

Husemann, Franz. *Die guten Glaubens waren*, Band II (Osnabrück: Munin Verlag GmbH, 1977).

Isaev, Aleksei and Kolomiets, Maksim. *Tomb of the Panzerwaffe: The Defeat of the Sixth SS Panzer Army in Hungary 1945* (Solihull, U.K.: Helion & Company Ltd, 2014).

Jauss, Karl. *Glück Allein Kann Es Nicht Gewesen Sein* (Göppingen, Germany: Privately published, 1984).

Kathagen, Friedhelm and Lechtenböhmer, Heinz. *Chronik der 2./SS Pz.Nachr.Abt. 5, 1940/45* (Witten, Germany: Selbstverlag, 1991).

Kern, Erich. *Die Letzte Schlacht, Ungarn 1944–45* (Göttingen: Verlag K. W. Schütz, 1960).

Kern, Erich. *Dance of Death* (London: Collins, 1951).

Klapdor, Erich. *Viking Panzers: The German 5th SS Tank Regiment in the East in World War II* (Mechanicsburg, PA: Stackpole Books, 2011; translation of 1981 edition).

Knobelsdorff, Otto von. *Geschichte der niedersächsichen 19. Panzer-Division 1939–1945* (Friedberg, Germany: Podzun-Pallas Verlag GmbH, 1985).

Kurowski, Franz. *Panzer Aces II: Battle Stories of German Tank Commanders of WWII* (Mechanicsburg, PA: Stackpole Books, 2004).

Kursietis, Andris J. *The Hungarian Army and its Military Leadership in World War II* (New York: Axis Europa Books & Magazines, 1999).

Lange, Günther (ed.). "Der Mai 1945" and "Ein Flucht durch Deutschland—Glück Gehabt!" in *Unser Wiking Ruf*, Nr. 11/2006 (Handeloh, Germany: Truppenkameradschaft 5. SS-Panzer Division Wiking, 2006).

Maier, Georg. *Drama Between Budapest and Vienna: The Final Battles of the 6. Pz.Armee in the East—1945* (Winnipeg, Canada: J. J. Fedorowicz Publishing, 2004), p. 509.

Maier, Georg. *Drama Zwischen Budapest und Wien: Der 6. Panzerarmee, 1945* (Osnabrück: Munin Verlag, 1985), p. 672.

Mehner, Kurt. *Die Deutsche Wehrmacht 1939–1945: Führung und Truppe* (Norderstedt, Germany: Militair-Verlag Klaus D. Patzwall, 1993).

Model, Hans-Georg. *Der deutsche Generalstabsoffizier* (Frankfurt am Main: Bernard Graefe Verlag für Wehrwesen, 1968).

Moore, John P. *Führerliste der Waffen-SS: Personalakten*, Vols 1–6 (Portland: Self-published, 2003).

Munoz, Antonio J. *Forgotten Legions: Obscure Combat Formations of the Waffen-SS* (New York: Axis Europa Book, 1991).

Munoz, Antonio J. "Teutonic Magyars: Hungarian Volunteers in the Waffen-SS 1944–1945" in Kursietis, Andris J. *The Hungarian Army and its Military Leadership in World War II* (New York: Axis Europa Books, 1999).

Nebolsin, Igor. *Stalin's Favorite: The Combat History of the 2nd Guards Tank Army from Kursk to Berlin* (Solihull, U.K: Helion & Company, 2016).

Nevenkin, Kamen. *Fire Brigades: The Panzer Divisions 1943–1945* (Winnipeg, Canada: J. J. Fedorowicz, 2008).

Niehorster, Leo W. *The Royal Hungarian Army 1920–1945* (New York: Axis Europa Books, 1998).

Pierek, Perry. *Hungary 1944–1945: The Forgotten Tragedy* (Nieuwegein, The Netherlands: Aspekt Publishing, 1996).

Pohlmann, Hartwig. *Geschichte der 96. Infanterie Division* (Bad Nauheim, Germany: Podzun-Verlag, 1959).

Rauchensteiner, Manfred. *Der Krieg in Österreich 1945* (Vienna: Österreicher Bundesverlag, 1984).

Regiments-Kameradschaft des ehemaligen SS-Panzergrenadier Regiment 10 "Westland," *Panzergrenadiere der Panzerdivision "Wiking" im Bild* (Osnabrück, Germany: Munin Verlag GmBH, 1984).

Regiments-Kameradschaft Panzerregiment 5 "Wiking." *Verweht sind die Spuren: Bilddokumentation 5. SS-Panzerregiment "Wiking"* (Osnabrück, Germany: Munin Verlag GmBH, 1979).

Reitlinger, Gerald. *The SS: Alibi of a Nation 1922–1945* (New York: The Viking Press, 1957).

Rikmenspoel, Marc. *Soldiers of the Waffen-SS: Many Nations, One Motto* (Winnipeg, Canada: J. J. Fedorowicz Publishing, Inc., 1999).

Rokossovsky, Konstantin. *A Soldier's Duty* (Moscow: Progress Publishers, 1985).

Sanchez, Alfonso E. *Feldherrnhalle: Forgotten Elite: The Panzerkorps Feldherrnhalle and Antecedent Formations, Eastern and Other Fronts, 1942–1945* (Bradford, West Yorkshire, U.K.: Shelf Books, 1996).

Schmeisser, Herbert. *Panzer-Nachrichten-Abteilung Wiking: Männer mit Mikrofon + Morsetaste* (Welzheim, Germany: Eigenverlag, 1985).

Schneider, Jost W. *Their Honor Was Loyalty! An Illustrated and Documentary History of the Knight's Cross Holders of the Waffen-SS and Police 1940–1945* (San Jose: R. James Bender Publishing, 1977).

Schulze-Kossens, Richard. *Militärischer Führernachwuchs der Waffen-SS* (Osnabrück: Munin Verlag, 1982).

Smelser, Ronald and Syring, Enrico. *Die SS: Elite unter dem Totenkopf–30 Lebensläufe* (Paderborn, Germany: Ferdinand Schöningh, 2000).

Stein, George H. *The Waffen SS: Hitler's Elite Guard at War, 1939–45* (NY: Cornell University Press, 1984).

Stöber, Hans. *Die lettischen Divisionen im VI. SS-Armeekorps* (Osnabrück: Munin Verlag GmBH, 1981).

Stocker, Peter. "Mit Kopfverband un Armschlinge: SS-Obersturmbannführer Hans Dorr" in *Schwerterträger*, 2, October—December 2017 (Selent, Germany: Verlag Deutsche Militärzeitschrift, 2017), pp. 3–21.

Stoves, Rolf. *1. Panzer-Division 1935–1945: Chronik einer der drei Stamm-Divisionen der deutschen Panzerwaffe* (Bad Nauheim: Verlag Hans-Henning Podzun, 1961).

Strassner, Peter. *European Volunteers: 5 SS Panzer Division Wiking* (Winnipeg, Canada: J. J. Fedorowicz Publishing, 1988).

Számvéber, Norbert. *The Sword Behind the Shield: a Combat History of the German Efforts to Relieve Budapest 1945—Operation "Konrad" I, II, III* (Solihull, U.K.: Helion & Company Ltd, 2015).

Tessin, Georg. *Verbände und Truppen der deutschen Wehrmacht und Waffen-SS im Zweiten Weltkrieg 1939–1945*, Vol. I–XVI (Osnabrück: Biblio-Verlag, 1979).

Tieke, Wilhelm. *Tragedy of the Faithful: A History of the III. (germanisches) SS-Panzer-Korps* (Winnipeg, Canada: J. J. Fedorowicz Publishing, Inc., 2001).

Tiemann, Ralf. *The Leibstandarte*, Volume IV/2 (Winnipeg, Canada: J. J. Fedorowicz Publishing, Inc., 1998).

Traditionsverband der 3. Pz.Div.: *Geschichte der 3. Panzer-Division Berlin-Brandenburg 1935 – 1945.* (Berlin: Gunter Richter Verlag, 1967).

Trevor-Roper, H. R. *Hitler's Secret Conversations, 1941–1944* (New York: Farrar, Straus and Young, Inc., 1953).

Ulrich, Karl. *Wie ein Fels im Meer: 3. SS-Panzerdivision "Totenkopf,"* Vol. 2 (Osnabrück: Munin-Verlag, 1984).

Ungváry, Krisztián. *The Siege of Budapest: 100 Days in World War II* (New Haven: Yale University Press, 2002).

Vopersal, Wolfgang. *Soldaten, Kämpfer, Kameraden, Marsch und Kämpfe der SS-Totenkopf Division*, Vols Va and Vb (Bielefeld, Germany: Selbstverlag der Truppenkameradschaft der 3. SS-Pz.Div. e.V., 1991).

Vuksic, Velimir. *SS Armor on the Eastern Front 1943–1945* (Winnipeg, Canada: J. J. Fedorowicz Publishing, Inc., 2005).

Wegner, Bernd. *The Waffen-SS: Organization, Ideology and Function* (Oxford: Basil Blackwell Ltd, 1990).

Westerlund, Lars. *The Finnish SS-Volunteers and Atrocities, 1941–1943* (Helsinki: The National Archives of Finland, 2019).

Wood, Ian M. *Tigers of the Death's Head: SS Totenkopf Division's Tiger Company* (Mechanicsburg, VA: Stackpole Books, 2013).

Yerger, Mark. *German Cross in Gold Holders of the SS and Police*, Vols 8 & 9 (San Jose, CA: R. James Bender Publishing, 2015.)

Yerger, Mark. *Waffen-SS Commanders: The Army, Corps and Divisional Leaders of a Legend*, Vols. I and II (Atglen, PA: Schiffer Military History, 1997).

Ziemke, Earl F. *Stalingrad to Berlin: The German Defeat in the East* (Washington, D.C: U.S. Army Center of Military History, 2002).

Diaries, Notes and Manuscripts

Barstein, Jan. "Bericht Jan Barstein" (Unpublished private manuscript, courtesy of Tommy Natedal), four pages.

Gille, Herbert O. "Angriff zum Entsatz der Stadt Budapest, Dezember 1944–8 Mai 1945" in *Truppenkameradschaft Wiking* Archives (Stemmen, Germany: undated private manuscript), four pages.

Jahnke, Günther. "Diary December 1944–4 August 1945" in *Truppenkameradschaft Wiking* Archives (Munich: Undated private manuscript), 18 pages.

Kovács, Zoltán András and Számvéber, Norbert. "The 1st Hungarian Sturmjäger Regiment" (Budapest, 2001), http://www.hunyadi.co.uk/; accessed 20 November 2015.

Kovács, Zoltán András and Számvéber, Norbert. "RF-SS Brigade 'Ney' (Kampfgruppe Ney)" (Budapest, 2001), http://www.hunyadi.co.uk/; accessed 20 November 2015.

Mallis, Herbert. "Chronik 1. SS-Pz.Gren.Btl. Norge 1944–1945" (Lalling, Germany: Unpublished manuscript, 1981), 51 pages.

Martini, Karl. "Die Apokalypse: Der Untergang des Bataillons 'Norge' SS-Pz.Gren.Reg. 23" (Helmstedt, Germany: Unpublished undated manuscript), 20 pages.

Nash, Douglas. "73. Infanterie-Division at Warsaw, September 1944" (Dumfries, VA: September 2017).

Pfeiffer, Roland. "Das Generalkommando IV. SS-Panzer-Korps" (Unpublished timeline, May 2015).

Pfeiffer, Roland. "Zur Geschichte der schweren Artillerie-Einheiten der Waffen-SS" (Unpublished outline, 5 December 2012) from *Forum der Wehrmacht* at https://www.forum-der-wehrmacht.de/

index.php?thread/32759-zur-geschichte-der-schweren-artillerie-einheiten-der-waffen-ss/; accessed 27 January 2017.

Renz, Manfred. "Battles in Hungary 1945" (Heilbronn, Germany: Unpublished private manuscript), four pages.

Schönfelder, Manfred. "Einsatz der Verbänder der Waffen-SS auf dem Kriegsschauplatz in Ungarn in der Zeit vom 1 January–31 März 1945" (Hamburg: Unpublished manuscript in author's possession, 1 December 1981).

Skarlo, I. Ivar. "Tarjan–5 Januar 1945" (Unpublished private manuscript, courtesy of Tommy Natedal), eight pages.

Wood, Ian M. "Short History of I./SS-Pz.Rgt. 3 (Panther), 1942 to 1945."

Published Official Government Records, Manuals and Internal Publications

Foreign Military Studies

Berlin, Wilhelm. *Comments on the Study "Russian Artillery in the Battle for Modlin and German Countermeasures,"* MS C-030, undated manuscript (Heidelberg: Historical Division, U.S. European Command).

Brasack, Kurt. *Russian Artillery in the Battle for Modlin and German Countermeasures*, MS D-228 (Heidelberg: Historical Division, U.S. European Command, 29 July 1952).

Center for Land Warfare, U.S. Army War College. *1986 Art of War Symposium*, "From the Vistula to the Oder: Soviet Offensive Operations—October 1944 to March 1945" (Carlisle, PA: U.S. Army War College, May 1986).

Dörffler-Schuband, Werner. *Officer Procurement in the Waffen-SS: Reception, Processing and Training*, Military Study D-178 (Heidelberg: Office of the Chief Historian, Headquarters, U.S. European Command, Ref. Draft published 13 July 1945).

Förtsch, Hermann. *Training and Development of German General Staff Officers*, MS P-031b, Project # 6, Vol. VIII (Heidelberg: Historical Division, U.S. European Command, 22 June 1951).

Gille, Herbert Otto. *The 4th SS Panzer Corps May 1945*, Military Study #B-166 (Heidelberg: History Division, U.S. Army Europe, 27 April 1946).

Krause, Walther. *Fighting in West Hungary and East Steiermark in the Area of the Sixth Army from March 25 to May 8, 1945*, MS B-139 (Heidelberg: Historical Division, US Army Europe, 13 June 1952).

Reinhardt, Helmuth. *Size and Composition of Divisional and Higher Staffs in the German Army*, Military Study P-139 (Karlsruhe, Germany: Historical Division, Headquarters, U.S. Army Europe, 1954).

Rendulic, Lothar Dr. *Report of the Commander: Stabilization of Eastern Front*, MS #B-328 (Frankfurt: US Army Europe Historical Division, 1 April 1947).

Reuther, Karl and Ulms, Ulrich. *XII SS Corps: Reflections and Experiences* (Heidelberg: Historical Division, U.S. European Command, 8 December 1947).

Westphal, Siegfried. *German General Staff Training and Development of German General Staff Officers*, MS P-031b, Project # 6, Vol. XXI (Heidelberg: Historical Division, U.S. European Command, August 1948).

Contemporary German Operational and Doctrinal Sources

Deutscher Rotes Kreuz—Suchdienst Munchen. Vermisstenbildliste, Hauptquartier IV. SS-Pz.Korps, Band WA Seite 60, 1944–1945. This finding aid, located at http://193.159.223.62:8081/vbl/

Truppenanschrift-Polizei/TA_P.aspx, identifies 54 members of the headquarters and headquarters troops of the *IV. SS-Pz.Korps* who were still declared as missing in action as late as 1958.

Gen.Kdo. IV. SS-Pz.Korps Adjutantur IIa, Verleihungsliste Nr. 5, Korpsgefechtstand, 16 February 1945. Bundesarhiv: Zentralnachweisstelle Heerespersonalampt, Verleihungsliste für Verleihung des Eisernes Kreuzes, RH 7A/1338 Folio 1.

Gen.Kdo. IV. SS-Pz.Korps Führungsabteilung, various reports, orders, and records of conversations, 12 January to 2 February 1945, from captured documents held in the Central Archive of the Russian Ministry of Defense, TsAMO Podolsk, Fund: 243, Inventory No. 2900, Case: 2011, pages 281–285, folio. Originals translated into Russian by Lieutenant Glushkin on 2 February 1945, translated into English 2020 by Viktor Ukhov, Rostov-on-Don, Russia.

Gen.Kdo. IV. SS-Pz.Korps Adjutantur IIa, Korps Gefechtstand, Führerbefehl, 5 March 1945. *"Im Auftrage Hitlers vom Chef des Oberkommandos der Wehrmacht, Generalfeldmarschall Wilhelm Keitel, unterzeichneter Befehl über Sippenhaft,"* issued 9 March 1945.

Kriegsarchiv der Waffen-SS, IIb. an Gen.Kdo. IV. SS-Pz.Korps, Betr: Kriegstagebücher, Gefechts- und Tätigkeitsberichte sowie im V.Bl.d.W.-SS verlautbare Schlacht- und Gefechtsbezeichnungen, dated 5 January 1945.

Kriegstagebuch (Ia), SS-Pz.Rgt. 5, 26 March–30 November 1944.

Kriegstagebuch (Ia), I. Abteilung, SS-Pz.Rgt. 5, 9 February–30 November 1944.

Kriegstagebuch (Ia), schwere-Pz.Abt. 509, 12 January–9 May 1945, pp. 18–27.

Kriegstagebuch (Ib) und Anlagen, Armeeoberkommando (AOK) 2, 1 October–31 December 1944. (This includes daily reports, including ammunition, fuel, and food expenditures, tank and other armored vehicles losses, and daily supply status for the *IV. SS-Pz.Korps* compiled by the *Quartiermeister*.)

Kreigstagebuch (Ia) Anlage: Meldungen und Befehle, Armeegruppe Balck/6. Armee, 16 December 1944–3 February 1945. (This includes daily orders, armor and infantry strengths, transcripts of radio and/or telephone message traffic, reports from subordinate units, rail and highway movement status, and orders/instructions from higher headquarters, including *Heeresgruppe Süd*, located in Documents Inventory Number 12472, Case Folders 408–410. Accessed on the "German Documents in Russia" website at http://wwii.germandocsinrussia.org.

Kriegstagebuch (Ia), Armeeoberkommando (AOK) 9, 1 August–31 December 1944.

Kriegstagebuch (Ia) Anlagen, Armeeoberkommando (AOK) 9, 1 August–31 December 1944. This includes morning, midday, evening, and daily reports, as well as armor and infantry strengths, radio and/ or telephone message transcripts, reports from subordinate units, commanders' daily summaries, rail and highway movement status, and orders/instructions from higher headquarters, including *Heeresgruppe Mitte*.

Kriegstagebuch (Ia), Heeresgruppe Süd, 1 February–31 March 1945.

Kriegstagebuch (Ia), Anlagen, Heeresgruppe Süd, 1 February–31 March 1945. This includes morning, midday, evening, and daily reports, as well as armor and infantry strengths, radio and/or telephone message transcripts, reports from subordinate units, commanders' daily summaries, and orders/ instructions from higher headquarters, including message traffic with the *Oberkommando des Heeres* (*OKH*) *Führungsabteilung*.

Kriegstagebuch (Ic), Armeegruppe Balck/6. Armee, Documents of the Ic department of *AOK 6*: KTB, File H, Volume 21, January 1945. Activity reports of the *Ic/AO* of *AOK 6* and the departments and units subordinated to it for January 1945, *Ic* reports, enemy order of battle updates for *AOK 6*, located in Documents Inventory Number 12472, Case Folder 411. Accessed on the "German Documents in Russia" website at http://wwii.germandocsinrussia.org.

Kriegstagebuch (Ia), Armeegruppe Balck/6. Armee, Documents of the Ia department of *AOK 6*: KTB, 1 December 1944–3 February 1945, including daily orders and reports, combat strengths, *Heeresgruppe Süd* messages, and other related items located in Documents Inventory Number 12472, Case Folders

382, 387–388, 408–410, and 447. Accessed on the "German Documents in Russia" website at http://wwii.germandocsinrussia.org.

Kriegstagebuch (Ia), Armeegruppe Balck/6. Armee, Documents of the *Ia* department of *AOK 6*: KTB, 1 December 1944–3 February 1945 daily situation maps, located in Documents Inventory Number 12472, Case Folders 396–404, 412, and 415–445. Accessed on the "German Documents in Russia" website at http://wwii.germandocsinrussia.org.

Oberbefehlshaber der 8. Armee, Armee Gefechtstand, Massnahmen in der nationalsozialistischen Führung der Truppe für die jetzige Lage, 8 April 1945.

Personnel and Materiel Strength Reports, including monthly *Kriegsgliederung*, for *3. SS-Pz.Div. "Totenkopf"* July 1944–April 1945.

Personnel and Materiel Strength Reports, including monthly *Kriegsgliederung*, for *5. SS-Pz.Div. "Wiking"* July 1944–April 1945.

SS-Führungshauptamt, Amt II, Org. Abt. Ia/II SS-Führungshauptampt. Kriegsgliederungen der Panzer Divisionen der Waffen-SS. (Berlin: SS-Führungshauptampt, 24 October 1944).

SS-Personalamt, Org.Abt. IIb, Verlustmeldungen der Waffen-SS, Band Ws 664–666, Gen.Kdo. IV. SS-Pz. Korps, schw.SS-Beob.Bttr. 104, und SS-Nachr.Abt. 104, March–August 1944, Band Ws 703, *SS-Werfer Abt. 504* September—November 1944. Documents now stored at the *Deutsche Dienststelle* (Wehrmachtauskunftstelle, WASt), Berlin and administered by the *Bundesarchiv*.

Wehrmachtführungsstab (Percy Schramm et al). *Kriegstagebuch des Oberkommando der Wehrmacht 1944–1945: Eine Dokumentation*, Band 8, Teilband 2 (Augsburg, Germany: Verlagsgruppe Weltbild GmbH, 2005).

Contemporary Allied Intelligence Sources

Joint Intelligence Staff, JIC, Chiefs of Staff Committee, Joint Intelligence Sub-Committee: *Germany's War Effort and its Failure, The Eastern Front 1944–1945*, 1945 (aka "The ULTRA History of the Russian Front"), 273 pages.

War Department, Military Intelligence Division. Special Series No. 12, *German Military Abbreviations*, 12 April 1943 (Washington, D.C.: U.S. War Department, 1943).

War Department, Military Intelligence Division. *German Military Symbols*, Vols I and II, 1 April 1944 (Washington, D.C.: U.S. War Department), 1944.

War Department, War Department Technical Manual TM 30-506, *German Military Dictionary, German–English, English–German*, 20 May 1944 (Washington, D.C.: U.S. War Department, 1944).

War Department, Military Intelligence Division. *Order of Battle and Handbook of the Hungarian Armed Forces* (Washington, D.C.: U.S. War Department, February 1944).

Contemporary Red Army Operational and Doctrinal Sources

Central Archive of the Russian Ministry of Defense [*TsAMO*], Podolsk "Armored Replenishment of the Third Ukrainian Front in January 1945," f. 243, op. 2928, gy. 340, l.129, available at https://pamyat-naroda.ru/.

Central Archive of the Russian Ministry of Defense [*TsAMO*], Podolsk. "Tank and self-propelled gun strength of the Third Ukrainian Front on 1 February 1945," f. 243, op. 2928, gy. 340, l.23–128, available at https://pamyat-naroda.ru/.

Soviet General Staff. *The Budapest Operation 1945: An Operational–Strategic Study* (Solihull, U.K.: Helion & Company Ltd, 2017). This publication, translated by Richard W. Harrison, consists of two separate documents. The first one is Volume 21 of the *Sbornik Materialov po Izucheniyu Opyta Voiny* series (Collection of Materials on the Study of War Experience) titled "The Budapest Operation (28 October 1944–13 February 1945)," and was originally published by the *STAVKA* in 1945. The second document, "The Third Ukrainian Front's Activities in the Budapest Operation

(An Operational-Tactical Sketch)," was written by Major General S. P. Tarasov and issued to students at the Red Army's General Staff Academy in 1957.

Trophy documents of the *IV. SS-Pz.Korps* held in the Central Archive of the Russian Ministry of Defense, *TsAMO* Podolsk, Fund: 243, Inventory No. 2900, Case: 2011, pp. 281–323, folio. Original translation by Lieutenant Glushkin on 2 February 1945, translated into English in 2019 by Olivia J. Allison, Kiev, and in 2020 by Viktor Ukhov, Rostov.

Interviews

Interview with *Oberstleutnant der Bundeswehr a.D.* Günther Lange, Handeloh, Germany, 7 October 2017, and continuing correspondence 2005–2020.

Index

References to notes are indicated by n; references to images are in *italics*.